An Introduction to the New Testament and the Origins of Christianity

First published in 2002, this book offers an authoritative and accessible introduction to the New Testament and early Christian literature for all students of the Bible and the origins of Christianity. Delbert Burkett focuses on the New Testament, but also looks at a number of non-biblical texts to examine the history, religion, and literature of Christianity in the years from 30 CE to 150 CE. The book is organized systematically with questions for in-class discussion and written assignments, step-by-step reading guides on individual works, special box features, charts, maps, and numerous illustrations designed to facilitate student use. An appendix containing translations of primary texts allows instant access to the writings outside the canon.

For this new edition, Burkett has reorganized and rewritten many chapters, and has also incorporated revisions throughout the text, bringing it up to date with current scholarship. This volume is designed for use as the primary textbook for one- and two-semester courses on the New Testament and early Christianity.

DELBERT BURKETT is Seynaeve Professor of Christian Origins at Louisiana State University. He has written or edited a number of books and articles on Jesus, the New Testament title "Son of Man," and the Synoptic Gospels. He has received several teaching awards and a major research grant. He is a member of the Society of Biblical Literature and was elected to the Society for New Testament Studies.

An Introduction to the New Testament and the Origins of Christianity

Delbert Burkett
Louisiana State University

CAMBRIDGE
UNIVERSITY PRESS

University Printing House, Cambridge CB2 8BS, United Kingdom

One Liberty Plaza, 20th Floor, New York, NY 10006, USA

477 Williamstown Road, Port Melbourne, VIC 3207, Australia

314–321, 3rd Floor, Plot 3, Splendor Forum, Jasola District Centre, New Delhi – 110025, India

79 Anson Road, #06-04/06, Singapore 079906

Cambridge University Press is part of the University of Cambridge.

It furthers the University's mission by disseminating knowledge in the pursuit of education, learning, and research at the highest international levels of excellence.

www.cambridge.org
Information on this title: www.cambridge.org/9781107172784
DOI: 10.1017/9781316779361

First published 2019

Printed in the United Kingdom by TJ International Ltd. Padstow Cornwall

A catalogue record for this publication is available from the British Library.

Library of Congress Cataloging-in-Publication Data
Names: Burkett, Delbert Royce, author.
Title: An introduction to the New Testament and the origins of Christianity /
Delbert Burkett, Louisiana State University.
Description: New York: Cambridge University Press, 2018. |
Series: Introduction to religion | Originally published: Cambridge, UK;
New York: Cambridge University Press, 2002. | Includes index.
Identifiers: LCCN 2018038853 | ISBN 9781107172784 (hardback) |
ISBN 9781316624944 (pbk.)
Subjects: LCSH: Bible. New Testament–Introductions. | Christianity–Origin.
Classification: LCC BS2330.3.B87 2018 | DDC 225.6/1–dc23
LC record available at https://lccn.loc.gov/2018038853

ISBN 978-1-107-17278-4 Hardback
ISBN 978-1-316-62494-4 Paperback

Contents

List of Illustrations   *page* vii
Preface to the Second Edition   xi
Preface to the First Edition   xiii

PART I   **HISTORICAL AND RELIGIOUS BACKGROUND**   I

  1 Introduction   3
  2 Jews among Greeks and Romans   15
  3 Basic Second-Temple Judaism   32
  4 Varieties of Second-Temple Judaism   46
  5 Jewish Hopes for the Future   62
  6 Hellenistic Religion, Philosophy, and World-View   75
  7 An Overview of Early Christian History   93
  8 The Making of the New Testament   108

PART II   **JESUS AND THE GOSPELS**   123

  9 Introduction to the Gospels   125
  10 The Synoptic Problem   144
  11 The Gospel of Mark   156
  12 The Gospel of Matthew   177
  13 The Gospel of Luke   199
  14 The Gospel of John   218
  15 The Apocryphal Jesus   241
  16 The Quest for the Historical Jesus   247

PART III   **ACTS**   265

  17 The Book of Acts   267

PART IV   **PAULINE CHRISTIANITY**   291

  18 Paul, His Letters, and His Churches   293
  19 Gentiles and the Law (1): Galatians   307
  20 Gentiles and the Law (2): Romans   319
  21 Problems of Church Life (1): 1 Corinthians   334

22   Problems of Church Life (2): 2 Corinthians   345

23   The Imminent Parousia: 1 and 2 Thessalonians   351

24   Prison Epistles (1): Philippians and Philemon   360

25   Prison Epistles (2): Colossians and Ephesians   371

PART V   **JUDAIC CHRISTIANITY**   387

26   Judaic Christianity   389

27   The Letter of James   399

28   The Didache   407

PART VI   **GNOSTIC CHRISTIANITY**   417

29   Gnostic Christianity   419

30   The Gospel of Thomas   428

PART VII   **PROTO-ORTHODOX CHRISTIANITY**   435

31   Proto-Orthodox Christianity   437

32   Conflict in the Church (1): Pastoral Epistles   446

33   Conflict in the Church (2): Jude and 2 Peter   461

34   Conflict in the Church (3): Johannine Epistles   470

35   Conflict in the Church (4): Letters of Ignatius   481

36   Conflict in the Church (5): 1 Clement   487

37   Relation of Christianity to Judaism (1): Hebrews   492

38   Relation of Christianity to Judaism (2): Epistle of Barnabas   503

39   Conflict with the Roman World (1): 1 Peter   508

40   Conflict with the Roman World (2): Revelation   521

           APPENDIXES   543

APPENDIX   1 Lucian on Sacrifices   545

APPENDIX   2 The Essenes   546

APPENDIX   3 Jewish Messianic Hopes   550

APPENDIX   4 Divine Humans and Their Births   555

APPENDIX   5 Apotheoses   562

APPENDIX   6 Miracle Stories in the Ancient World   565

APPENDIX   7 The Infancy Gospel of Thomas   575

APPENDIX   8 The Gospel of Peter   579

APPENDIX   9 The Didache   583

APPENDIX   10 Selections from the Gospel of Thomas   591

APPENDIX   11 Ignatius to the Smyrnaeans 1–9   599

APPENDIX   12 Selections from 1 Clement   602

APPENDIX   13 Selections from the Epistle of Barnabas   606

APPENDIX   14 Conflict with Rome   611

           Index   615

Illustrations

2.1	Bust of Alexander the Great	*page* 17
2.2	Alexander's empire at his death in 323 BCE (map)	18
2.3	The Roman Empire in the first century CE (map)	21
2.4	Marble statue of Augustus Caesar in military dress	22
2.5	Palestine in the time of Jesus (map)	24
2.6	Timeline of political events in Palestine from Alexander to Hadrian	26
3.1	Depiction of the scribe Ezra reading from a scroll	37
3.2	Scale model of the temple in Jerusalem during the time of Herod the Great	39
3.3	Ground plan of Herod's temple and its courts	40
3.4	Ruins of the ancient synagogue at Capernaum	42
4.1	Aerial view of the ruins at Qumran	50
4.2	Fragments of 1 Samuel from Cave 4 near Qumran	51
4.3	The Temple Scroll from Qumran	52
4.4	Aerial view of Masada	54
6.1	Bronze statue of Zeus, king of the Greek gods	77
6.2	Statue of Isis, an Egyptian goddess	78
6.3	Fresco of a worshipper offering sacrifice before a statue of Dionysus	79
6.4	The infant Heracles strangles snakes sent against him by Hera	83
6.5	Fresco depicting a philosopher leaning on a walking stick	86
7.1	Scale model of Jerusalem in the time of Jesus	95
7.2	A fifth- or sixth-century mosaic of the apostle Paul	100
7.3	Marble head from a colossal statue of Constantine	105
8.1	Greek Papyrus 52, the oldest surviving text of the New Testament	116
8.2	End of 2 Thessalonians and beginning of Hebrews in Codex Vaticanus	118
8.3	Portrait of James I of England and VI of Scotland	120
9.1	Christ as judge surrounded by the four living beings	129
11.1	Fourth-century fresco of a woman healed by touching Jesus' garment	160
11.2	Jesus sleeps as the storm threatens	167
11.3	Transfiguration of Jesus	172
12.1	An angel dictates the gospel to the apostle Matthew	178

12.2	Wise men from the East bring gifts to the infant Jesus	190
12.3	Jesus sits on a throne to exercise judgment	196
13.1	Scene from the parable of the prodigal son	204
13.2	Early Christian engraving of the shepherd who seeks the lost sheep	209
13.3	The penitent criminal crucified with Jesus	215
14.1	Fourth-century fresco of Jesus speaking to the Samaritan woman at the well	229
14.2	Jesus washing the disciples' feet	232
14.3	Jesus raises Lazarus	236
15.1	A twelfth-century mosaic of Jesus Christ	243
15.2	Jesus frees souls imprisoned in Hades	245
16.1	A fishing boat returning to Capernaum	249
16.2	Inscription from ancient Caesarea	252
16.3	An ancient ossuary, a container for holding the bones of a deceased person	259
17.1	A view of modern Antioch	271
17.2	The acropolis in Athens seen from the Areopagus (Mars' Hill)	274
17.3	The ancient amphitheater at Ephesus	277
17.4	Missionary journey of Barnabas and Paul (map)	284
17.5	Paul's second missionary journey (map)	285
17.6	Paul's third missionary journey and journey to Rome (map)	287
18.1	Imaginative portrait of the apostle Paul	294
18.2	Old road between Israel and Damascus	301
18.3	Street in ancient Ephesus	302
19.1	The Roman province of Galatia in Asia Minor (map)	309
20.1	Scale model of ancient Rome at the time of Constantine	320
21.1	The bema (raised platform) in the forum at Corinth	336
21.2	Third-century fresco depicting the Christian communal meal	342
22.1	A page from Papyrus 46	347
24.1	St. Paul in Prison	362
24.2	The possible sites of Paul's imprisonment (map)	365
25.1	Greek inscription on a stone from the outer wall of Herod's temple	381
26.1	A detail from the Arch of Titus	391
28.1	Third-century depiction of Christian baptism	408
28.2	Third-century fresco of a Christian praying	413
29.1	Manuscript covers of the Nag Hammadi Coptic library	421
30.1	Last page of the Gospel of Thomas	430
31.1	Sixth-century mosaic of a basket of bread between two fish	443
32.1	Fresco of a young woman with writing utensils	452
33.1	A sixth- or seventh-century icon portraying Peter	464
35.1	Sites on Ignatius' journey from Antioch to Rome (map)	482
35.2	The Via Egnatia near Philippi	483
35.3	A tenth-century illustration of the martyrdom of Ignatius	484

36.1   Fourth-century bas-relief of the apostles Peter and Paul   489
37.1   A Jewish high priest in ceremonial garb   497
39.1   The Christian Martyrs' Last Prayer   511
39.2   Provinces of Asia Minor to which First Peter is addressed (map)   514
39.3   Marble bust of the Roman emperor Trajan   515
40.1   The seven churches of the Roman province of Asia (map)   525
40.2   John and his vision of one like a son of man   530
40.3   Twelfth-century illustration of visions from Revelation 12–13   535
40.4   Michael the archangel thrusting down Satan in chains   540

Preface to the Second Edition

The second edition of this textbook takes into account new publications that have appeared since the first edition. I have revised the bibliographies at the end of each chapter, incorporating some of the newer works and keeping older ones that have retained their significance. In addition, my own understanding of the subject matter has grown since the first edition, enabling me to see that parts of the text could be improved. I have revised a few chapters extensively, while others have undergone minor changes. The original structure of the work remains the same.

Preface to the First Edition

This book introduces the history, literature, and religion of early Christianity in the years from about 30 to 150 CE. In this book, I have two aims:

- to provide a textbook for a one-semester course in the New Testament and the origins of Christianity;
- to provide a selection of primary sources from outside the New Testament that are relevant for the origins of Christianity.

With this textbook and a Bible, the student should have the basic texts necessary for an introductory study of Christian origins.

This book has developed as I have taught undergraduate courses in the New Testament at several state universities. The students for whom I write are therefore undergraduate students in a liberal arts or humanities program. The book presupposes no prior knowledge of the New Testament or early Christianity.

Significant features of this textbook include the following.

1. As an introduction to Christian origins, the book takes a primarily historical approach to the literature. Chapter 1 explains more fully than most comparable textbooks the differences between the historical-critical method and the confessional method of studying the New Testament. At the same time, the book introduces students to various other current methods of interpretation and gives specific examples of each. The bibliographies also suggest books that employ these methods or explain them further. Some of the discussion questions allow the students to consider the contemporary relevance of the material.

2. In keeping with a recent trend, this textbook discusses not only the New Testament but other early Christian literature as well. To study the history and religion of early Christianity, we must examine all the literature relevant for that purpose, whether canonized or not. At the same time, we must impose some limit on the material to accommodate it within a single semester. I have discussed all the books of the New Testament, as well as most other Christian literature written before 150. Instructors may need to limit the material further by selecting what they wish to emphasize.

3. No comparable textbook on this subject includes a selection of primary texts in the same volume. In a series of appendixes, I include three types of primary texts: selections relevant to the cultural and religious context; selections from the Apostolic Fathers; and several apocryphal or Gnostic Gospels. Some available sourcebooks contain one or two of these types of texts, but no sourcebook that I am aware of contains all three.

4. Chapters in this book that focus on a particular text usually include two main parts: (1) an introductory section that discusses critical issues, themes, and other features of the literature; (2) a reading guide designed to be read concurrently with the primary text. Previous students have found the reading guides particularly valuable in directing them step by step through the primary text with explanatory comments. Chapters also include discussion questions that the instructor can use for written assignments or in-class discussions, review questions that focus the student's attention on the central ideas of the chapter, and suggestions for further study.

5. Discussion questions in each chapter suggest how to integrate primary sources with that chapter. For example, in Chapter 4 (Varieties of Second-Temple Judaism), the discussion question suggests reading Josephus' discussion of Essenes (Appendix 2) along with controversy stories from the New Testament. Whereas some textbooks do not relate the introductory section to the primary sources, this approach correlates the "background" material with relevant selections from the New Testament and other literature. Following this approach, students will start reading from the New Testament beginning with Chapter 2. They will become

familiar with controversy stories, miracle stories, birth narratives, parables, and example stories before they read a whole gospel.

6. A basic consideration in presenting the New Testament is whether to start with the earliest literature (Paul) or the literature relating to the earliest period (the gospels). It is difficult to understand Paul without knowing the gospels, yet it is difficult to understand the gospels without knowing Paul. To resolve this problem, I have provided an initial overview of early Christian history (Chapter 7). This chapter provides a framework for the study of literature that follows. It gives students the basic information about early Christianity that they need for an informed reading of the gospels, after which they read Paul.

7. After sections on the gospels and Acts, I classify the remaining literature according to the type of Christianity that it represents: Pauline, Judaic, Gnostic, or Proto-Orthodox. Each type of Christianity receives treatment in a separate section, with an initial chapter that describes its distinctive features. Subsequent chapters in each section discuss particular texts representative of that type. This approach allows the student to see the literature not merely as a series of documents but as illustrations of particular perspectives within early Christianity.

8. In discussing each type of Christianity, I pay attention not only to its history and literature, but also to the distinctive features of its religion. By religion I mean not merely theology, but the various dimensions that the phenomenology of religion has used to describe religion, particularly the conceptual, social, ritual, and ethical dimensions.

9. In discussing Proto-Orthodox Christianity, I focus on three central concerns that appear in the literature: conflict within the church, the relation of Christianity to Judaism, and conflict with the Roman world.

Thanks go to Kevin Taylor, my editor at Cambridge University Press, for his keen interest in this project; to Jenny Landor for soliciting reviews; to Laura Hemming for assisting with the illustrations; to Lucy Carolan for copyediting; to the numerous scholars who read the manuscript and offered suggestions for improvement; and to all my former students, who taught me how to teach.

PART I

Historical and Religious Background

1   Introduction

Billions of people throughout the world today practice the religion of Christianity. It consists of three primary divisions: Eastern Orthodoxy, Roman Catholicism, and Protestantism. It can be further subdivided into thousands of distinct denominations and sects, each differing to some degree in belief and practice. Though none of these Christian groups existed in the beginning of Christianity, all look back to that time as having fundamental significance for their own tradition. It is this foundational period of Christianity that we will study in this book. We will examine the history, literature, and religion of Christianity in its earliest stages.

Our study will focus on the years from about 30 to 150 of the present era, from the beginning of Christianity through the first half of the second century. Occasionally, we will take a look beyond those years. At the beginning of that period, a Jewish man named Jesus of Nazareth went about Palestine preaching and attracting followers. After his crucifixion by the Roman governor, his Jewish followers continued to preach in his name, proclaiming him as the Jewish Messiah or Christ. Christianity thus emerged as a sect of Judaism in Roman Palestine. It quickly developed into various competing factions. Some of these factions remained primarily Jewish, while others opened the door to Gentiles (non-Jews). Some of these factions disappeared from history, while others survived and developed into forms of Christianity that still exist today.

In studying the origins of Christianity, we will examine numerous writings relating to the foundational period, some Christian and some non-Christian. Much of the Christian literature from this period has been preserved in various collections: the New Testament, the Apostolic Fathers, the New Testament Apocrypha, and the Nag Hammadi Library. Since much of our study will focus on the writings in these collections, we will begin by discussing the nature of this literature and our method of studying it.

THE NEW TESTAMENT

Some of the earliest Christian writings, dating from the first and second centuries, have been preserved in a collection called the **New Testament**.

The New Testament as Christian Scripture

The New Testament has special significance for the Christian religion. Like many other religions – such as Hinduism, Buddhism, Judaism, and Islam – Christianity has **scriptures**, sacred writings that members of the religion consider especially authoritative or important. The Christian scriptures have two main divisions. (1) Like Judaism, Christianity has traditionally viewed the **Hebrew Scriptures** as sacred writings. These are a collection of documents pertaining to the history and religion of ancient Israel and Judaism. Because Christianity developed out of the Jewish religion, early Christians took over the Jewish scriptures as their own. Christians generally call the Hebrew Scriptures the **Old Testament**. (2) In addition, Christian scriptures include the New Testament, a collection of twenty-seven writings pertaining to Jesus and the early Christian church. The story of how these writings came to be considered scripture is told in Chapter 8. Together the Old Testament and the New Testament make up the Christian **Bible**, a word that literally means "books."

The New Testament as Testament

The term "testament" in the title of these two collections could be translated more accurately as "covenant," an agreement between two parties. In the Christian religion, the terms "old covenant" and "new covenant" express the idea that God entered into two covenants or agreements. According to this idea, in the old covenant he entered into an agreement with the nation of Israel: "I will be your God and you will be my people" (Leviticus 26:12). In the new covenant, he entered into a similar agreement with people from all nations. According to this view, the Old Testament contains the writings that relate to the old covenant, while the New Testament contains those that relate to the new.

From the Jewish perspective, God made only one covenant, a covenant with the people of Israel. For Judaism, therefore, there is neither an "old covenant" nor a "new covenant," but simply the covenant. There is no "Old" Testament, but simply the Hebrew Scriptures.

Contents of the New Testament

The New Testament contains the following books in the order given. Frequently the names of these books are abbreviated, as indicated.

BOOKS	ABBREVIATIONS
Gospels	
Matthew	Matt
Mark	Mark
Luke	Luke
John	John
Acts	
Acts of the Apostles	Acts
Letters ascribed to Paul	
Romans	Rom
First Corinthians	1 Cor
Second Corinthians	2 Cor
Galatians	Gal
Ephesians	Eph
Philippians	Phil
Colossians	Col
First Thessalonians	1 Thes
Second Thessalonians	2 Thes
First Timothy	1 Tim
Second Timothy	2 Tim
Titus	Titus
Philemon	Philem
Non-Pauline letters	
Hebrews	Heb
James	James
First Peter	1 Pet
Second Peter	2 Pet
First John	1 John
Second John	2 John
Third John	3 John
Jude	Jude
Apocalypse	
Revelation	Rev

Types of Literature

The New Testament contains twenty-seven different writings or "books." Four types of literature are represented: gospels (4), a book of Acts (1), letters (21), and an apocalypse (1).

The term "**gospel**" ("good news") refers to a type of writing that contains stories about Jesus and/or sayings that are attributed to him. Early Christians wrote many works called gospels, but only four made their way into the New Testament. These are traditionally called the Gospels of Matthew, Mark, Luke, and John, after their supposed authors.

The term "**Acts**" refers to a type of literature that relates the deeds of some particular person or group. The one book of Acts in the New Testament is called the Acts of the Apostles, a work that describes the beginning of the Christian church and its spread in the Roman world.

The twenty-one **letters** in the New Testament, also called epistles, were written by early Christian leaders to various churches and individuals to give instruction and exhortation. Thirteen of these letters claim to be written by one man, the apostle or missionary known as Paul.

An "**apocalypse**" ("revelation") is a type of literature that claims to give secret information from God, often about the end of history. Many apocalyptic writings survive from the centuries before and after Jesus, but only one apocalypse, the book of Revelation, is included in the New Testament.

Chapters and Verses

The books of the Bible are divided into chapters, and the chapters are divided into verses. When we wish to refer to a particular passage in the Bible, we give the book, the chapter, and the verse (or verses) in a conventional form. For example, Matthew (or Matt) 5:3–10 refers to the book of Matthew, the fifth chapter, verses 3 through 10 of that chapter.

THE APOSTOLIC FATHERS

Early Christians wrote numerous works besides those that eventually became the New Testament. Before the New Testament came to be considered the only scripture, some of these other works were read in churches and esteemed just as highly as those in the New Testament. Gradually, as church leaders limited the contents of the New Testament to twenty-seven books, these other writings declined in importance. New copies were seldom made and the old copies wore out or were destroyed. As a result, some of the works have disappeared while others are preserved in only a few copies.

In the modern period, as some of these writings were rediscovered, a new interest arose in the early literature that did not make it into the New Testament. In 1672 an editor named J. B. Cotelier assembled a collection of early Christian writings that he called "Works of the holy Fathers who flourished in apostolic times." In 1699 the next editor renamed the collection a library of **Apostolic Fathers**, a title that it has borne since that time.

Most of these writings are letters from church leaders to various churches instructing them in what the author considers to be true faith and practice. The Didache or "Teaching of the Twelve Apostles" is a church manual that gives directions for the rituals and organization of the church. The Shepherd of Hermas, an apocalypse, consists of a series of visions and revelations that a Christian prophet claimed to receive.

Contents of the Apostolic Fathers

Letters of Ignatius
Ephesians
Magnesians
Trallians
Romans
Philadelphians
Smyrnaeans
To Polycarp

Other letters
First Clement
Epistle of Barnabas
Polycarp to the Philippians

Manual of church order
The Didache

Apocalypse
The Shepherd of Hermas

Three other writings in this collection are later than the period we are studying and will not be considered here: Second Clement, Martyrdom of Polycarp, and Epistle to Diognetus.

OTHER RELEVANT LITERATURE

New Testament Apocrypha

The writings of the New Testament and the Apostolic Fathers do not exhaust the literary output of early Christianity. In the second century and afterward, Christian writers turned out other letters, gospels, books of acts, and apocalypses. Some of these disappeared. We know they existed either because later writers quoted from them or because small fragments of them survived. Other works survived in more complete form. Such quotations, fragments, and more complete works have been collected and published under the title **New Testament Apocrypha** or "The Apocryphal New Testament." Originally the term "apocrypha" meant "hidden writings," but it has come to refer to the writings that belong to neither the New Testament, nor the Apostolic Fathers, nor the collection of later authors known as the "Church Fathers."

Some of these apocryphal writings develop the portrayal of Jesus found in the New Testament. For example, the Infancy Gospel of James and the Infancy Gospel of Thomas provide further stories about Jesus' birth and childhood. The Gospel of Peter has an account of Jesus' trial, death, and resurrection that differs somewhat from those in the New Testament. Other apocryphal writings preserve legends about Jesus' earliest followers, the apostles. The Acts of John, the Acts of Paul, and the Acts of Thomas, for example, tell various stories about these apostles. Still other apocryphal writings claim to be revelations of heaven or the afterlife. In the Apocalypse of Peter, for instance, Jesus describes to the apostles the rewards and punishments of the final judgment.

The Nag Hammadi Library

Christianity in the second century came in several varieties, one of which has come to be called "Gnostic." In 1945 an Egyptian digging in the sand at a place called Nag Hammadi discovered a large sealed jar that contained forty-five different writings in the Coptic (ancient Egyptian) language, the contents of a Gnostic Christian library. Though in their present form these texts date from the fourth century, some are translations of earlier Greek texts from the second century or at least reflect ideas that were current at that time. These texts have now been translated and published in English as **The Nag Hammadi Library** or "The Nag Hammadi Scriptures."

Many different types of literature are found among these texts. For instance, the Gospel of Thomas is a collection of sayings attributed to Jesus. The Apocryphon (secret book) of John purports to be a revelation given by Jesus to John concerning the origin of the world from a Gnostic perspective. The library also includes other such revelatory discourses, sermons or treatises on religious subjects, and accounts of otherworld journeys. To examine all of this literature would require a separate book, but I have included a discussion of one such work, the Gospel of Thomas.

THE HISTORICAL-CRITICAL METHOD

In our study of early Christianity, some of the writings we will examine belong to the Christian Bible and are thus considered scripture by Christians. Since most Christians are accustomed to studying these writings from a religious perspective, as scripture, it is important to stress from the beginning that we will be taking a different approach.

The New Testament can be studied either confessionally (i.e. religiously, theologically, devotionally) or academically. In the confessional approach, the reader is a Christian who takes these writings as scripture, as a norm or standard for Christian belief and practice. The reader seeks guidance for life, edification, and instruction in the Christian faith. This is how most Christians read the New Testament, either in private devotion or as part of a believing community.

In an academic setting, we approach the New Testament in such a way that both Christians and interested non-Christians can participate. We seek to understand the New Testament without necessarily ascribing normative status to it. This approach is like that of a Christian student who wishes to study the scripture and religion of Islam or Hinduism. The student may want to have a description of these religions without necessarily adopting them. In an academic setting, then, we treat Christianity, Islam, Hinduism, and all other religions in the same way: we seek to understand them, not necessarily to adopt or practice them.

Since the period of Christianity that we are studying belongs to the ancient past, the primary method that scholars use to understand it is the same as that used to understand any period of ancient history. The method used to understand the documents from that period, including the New Testament, is the same as that used to understand any other documents from the past. This method, called the historical-critical method or historical criticism, has been the primary method by which scholars have studied the New Testament academically since the eighteenth century. Today this method is employed not only in secular colleges and universities, but also in many religious institutions – seminaries, divinity schools, and schools of religion. It is a method of studying the New Testament that can be employed by Jews, Christians, and people of another or no religious persuasion. It is the primary method that will be employed in the present textbook.

Differences from the Confessional Approach

As the two parts of its name suggest, the historical-critical method has two aspects. First, the scholar who uses this method is concerned with history; and second, the scholar exercises his or her critical faculties, the faculties of reason and judgment. This historical-critical method differs from the confessional approach in several ways.

1. The confessional approach transports a text out of the past into the present. The reader is concerned not so much with what it meant then but with what it means now – what guidance or encouragement it gives to the reader in the present. In contrast, the historical method transports the reader out of the present into the past. It is concerned with what the text meant then, to the person who wrote it and the people to whom it was originally written. The goal of historical study is to understand and explain the past, to find out what happened and why. This involves locating events in time and space and understanding them in the context of the culture and beliefs of that time and place. The scholar of early Christianity working with the historical method therefore seeks to understand the political, cultural, and religious climate of the lands where Christianity originated and spread: first-century Palestine and the Greco-Roman world. The scholar then uses this background knowledge to interpret particular texts from that time, to help understand the events, ideas, and customs expressed in these texts. In this approach, one seeks to understand how the New Testament came about, who wrote it, why it was written, when it was written, what historical circumstances led to its writing, what the original writers intended to say, and what literary forms they used to express themselves.

2. The confessional approach is a theological approach. That is, a person who takes it often speaks about the activities of God: what God thinks, says, does, or intends. By contrast, the historical approach is non-theological. The historian speaks only about history, and since God would be outside of history, the historian cannot speak about the activities of God. History, as historians understand it, consists of the events in the world that could be observed by anyone, whether religious or not, who stood in the right place at the right time. What historians are able to observe in history is not divine activity but human activity. For example, a person speaking from the confessional perspective might make a statement of faith about what God did: "God came to earth in the person of Jesus." The historian, however, can only observe and state what human beings did or said: "Many early Christians claimed that God came to earth in the person of Jesus."

A historian who is also a Christian might make a statement of faith such as "God came to earth in the person of Jesus"; but if so, he or she would be speaking as a Christian, not as a historian.

3. This non-theological character of the historical method affects the way the historian deals with the New Testament. From the confessional point of view, many Christians regard the New Testament as the inspired word of God. This perspective is equivalent to making a theological statement about the activity of God: "God inspired the authors of the New Testament to write the word of God." But as we have seen, the historian cannot make statements about what God said or did, only about what human beings in history said or did. The historian therefore focuses on the human character of the documents in the New Testament, asking who wrote them, when, where, and why. The historian does not work with any theory of inspiration, since this is a theological claim, a claim of religious faith, rather than a historical claim.

4. The Christian who regards the New Testament as the inspired word of God gives it a privileged status over all other literature. Often such a person has the view that the New Testament contains no error or inconsistency and should not be questioned but simply accepted at face value. The historian, working with no theory of inspiration, but focusing on the human character of the documents, cannot operate by these theological principles. The historian does not take any text from the past at face value but questions it and evaluates it to determine whether it is authentic, whether it is accurate and reliable, whether it has been altered from what the author originally wrote. The text is like a witness in a court of law, and historical criticism is the method by which the witness is questioned and evaluated. In this respect, the historian gives no special status to the New Testament writings, but treats them like every other document from the ancient past. The critical scholar does not come to the documents with the assumption that they are necessarily authentic, reliable, or free from error. The scholar makes judgments about these matters not beforehand, but only after investigation. Nor does the scholar assume that all the New Testament documents agree with one another. The historian is open to the possibility that different authors of the New Testament may present different perspectives.

5. Since the purpose of the confessional approach is to benefit the believer's religious life, and since it regards New Testament scripture as the primary source of such benefit, it makes the New Testament its primary focus of attention. Other early Christian literature is disregarded because it is not scripture. Since the historian, however, has a different purpose,

to study history, he or she cannot focus only on the New Testament but must examine all the literature that sheds light on the history of early Christianity. Christian writings that did not become scripture may be as valuable or more valuable for the historian than writings that did. Non-Christian writings may be equally valuable.

Christian Responses to Historical Criticism

The critical examination of the Bible may disturb some Christian students. Such disturbance may stem from a feeling that the Bible should not be questioned, but simply believed. Frequently it stems from the belief that every writing in the Bible is inspired by God verbally (word for word) and contains no possible error. From this viewpoint, it is not acceptable to find inaccuracies, contradictions, or inconsistencies in the Bible. Those students who have doubts about examining the Bible critically should keep one thing in mind: this textbook does not intend simply to substitute one set of authorities (critical scholars) for another (parents and church leaders). Rather, in keeping with the goal of a liberal arts education, it aims to help you think for yourself. It provides you with the information you need to make an informed evaluation of one method of reading the Bible. What you appropriate or do not appropriate from it ultimately remains your own decision to make.

Other Christian students have less trouble with the historical-critical method, since they recognize the human element in the Bible. While most Christians acknowledge a human element in the writing and formation of the Bible, some acknowledge it more fully than others. From this viewpoint, the Bible was written and collected by people who had religious experiences, but who nevertheless remained limited and fallible. For these Christians, Christian faith depends not upon a perfect, error-free Bible, but only upon the validity of its central message, whatever that is understood to be. From this perspective, it is important to question and examine the Bible critically and historically: critically, since what is true should stand up to scrutiny; historically, lest ideas and practices that simply reflected a particular situation or culture be exalted to the status of eternally valid truth.

One Value of a Historical Perspective

The problem just mentioned, that of elevating a particular historical situation to the status of eternal truth, is illustrated by the role the New

Testament has played in promoting anti-Jewish sentiment. The New Testament was produced during a time of strife between the followers of Jesus and the Jewish establishment. The New Testament writings reflect that strife. They include some rather severe denunciations and criticisms of the Jewish people and religion. In times past, Christians who take the New Testament as scripture have been influenced to adopt a similar negative attitude toward Judaism. During the Inquisition of the Middle Ages, for example, Christians persecuted Jews, forcibly converting them or expelling them from Christian countries. Less severe forms of anti-Jewish sentiment have been more frequent.

Many contemporary Christian leaders, aware of the problem, have sought ways of establishing more positive Jewish–Christian relations. Part of the solution lies in recognizing the historically limited nature of the New Testament. A historical perspective helps make us aware that the conflicts between early Christians and Judaism belong to a particular historical time and situation. They should not serve as a model for Jewish–Christian relations today.

Abbreviations for Dates

In the present textbook, the abbreviation CE ("common era") is used instead of AD ("in the year of our Lord") to refer to dates after the birth of Jesus. The abbreviation BCE ("before the common era") appears instead of BC ("before Christ") to refer to dates prior to the birth of Jesus. Most scholarly writing has abandoned the abbreviations AD and BC out of deference for non-Christians, who do not consider Jesus as "Lord" or "Christ."

REVIEW QUESTIONS

1. Define or identify: New Testament, scriptures, Hebrew Scriptures, Old Testament, Bible, CE, BCE.
2. Describe the four types of literature that the New Testament contains.
3. Distinguish between the New Testament, the Apostolic Fathers, the New Testament Apocrypha, and the Nag Hammadi Library.
4. Explain the two aspects of historical criticism.
5. Explain how the historical-critical method differs from the confessional approach to studying the Bible.

SUGGESTIONS FOR FURTHER STUDY

Primary Sources

Elliott, J. K., ed. *The Apocryphal New Testament: A Collection of Apocryphal Christian Literature in an English Translation* (Clarendon, 1993). One-volume collection of apocryphal writings in English translation, with brief introductions.

Holmes, Michael W., ed. *The Apostolic Fathers* (3rd ed.; Baker Academic, 2007). Lightfoot's edition of the Apostolic Fathers, revised by Holmes. Greek and English on facing pages, with introductions and bibliography.

Meyer, Marvin, ed. *The Nag Hammadi Scriptures: The International Edition* (HarperOne, 2007). Standard English translation of the writings discovered at Nag Hammadi.

Schneemelcher, Wilhelm, ed. *New Testament Apocrypha* (rev. ed.; 2 vols.; Westminster John Knox, 1991, 1992). Substantial collection of apocryphal writings in English translation, with extended introductions.

Other Suggestions

Koester, Helmut. *Introduction to the New Testament* (2nd ed.; 2 vols.; De Gruyter, 1995, 2000). Volume 2 surveys the history and literature of early Christianity.

Krentz, Edgar. *The Historical-Critical Method* (Fortress, 1975). A brief introduction to the rise of historical criticism, its goals, techniques, presuppositions, and achievements.

Law, David R. "A Brief History of Historical Criticism," in David R. Law, *The Historical-Critical Method: A Guide for the Perplexed* (Bloomsbury T&T Clark, 2012). Traces the development of historical criticism from the early church to the twenty-first century.

Young, Frances, Lewis Ayres, and Andrew Louth, eds. *The Cambridge History of Early Christian Literature* (Cambridge University Press, 2004). A reference work that surveys the literature of early Christianity in the first five centuries and explores the context in which it emerged.

2 Jews among Greeks and Romans

Christianity arose in **Palestine**, the homeland of the Jewish people. This region touches the Mediterranean Sea on the west, the Arabian desert on the east, Syria on the north, and Egypt on the south. In the first century CE, Palestine belonged to the **Greco-Roman world**, a world governed by the Roman Empire but united by Greek language and culture. This government and culture prevailed in the lands surrounding the Mediterranean. To understand the emergence of Christianity, therefore, we must have some knowledge of the history of Palestine and the culture of the Greco-Roman world to which it belonged.

PALESTINE UNDER ANCIENT ISRAEL

According to the Hebrew Scriptures, a man named Moses led a group of Hebrew slaves out of Egypt into the wilderness. After Moses' death, his assistant Joshua led the people into the land of Canaan, or Palestine, which they began to take over from its former inhabitants. These Hebrew people, traditionally divided into twelve tribes, called themselves and their land "Israel." Eventually the Israelites established a monarchy, and the second king, David, subjugated the entire land. The people of Israel believed that their God, Yahweh, had promised this land to their ancestors – Abraham, Isaac, and Jacob – and that Yahweh had brought them out of Egypt to possess it. The kingdom of Israel reached its peak under David's son Solomon. During this period of peace and prosperity, Solomon built a temple for Yahweh in the capital city, Jerusalem.

After the reign of Solomon, in the tenth century BCE the kingdom split in two. The northern kingdom retained the name "Israel." It continued in existence until about 722 BCE, when the Assyrian Empire conquered it and deported much of its population. The northern kingdom never again existed as an independent state. The southern kingdom consisted primarily of the tribe of Judah and had its capital in Jerusalem. The land of Judah or "Judea" gave its inhabitants the name "Judeans," from which comes the term "Jews."

PALESTINE UNDER BABYLON AND PERSIA

After the fall of Israel, the southern state of Judea maintained its independence until 587 BCE, when Nebuchadnezzar, king of the Babylonian Empire, brought it to an end. He captured Jerusalem, destroyed Solomon's temple, and exiled many of the Jews to Babylon.

Under Cyrus the Great, the Persian Empire took control away from Babylon. In 539 BCE, Cyrus allowed the Jewish exiles to return to Judea. Many did not return, but those who did built a new temple in 520–516 BCE. The period of Judaism during which this temple existed is designated Second-Temple Judaism (516 BCE–70 CE).

PALESTINE UNDER GREEK RULE

Alexander the Great

In the fourth century BCE, the kingdom of Macedonia gained mastery over Greece through the military organization and diplomacy of Philip II. Upon his death in 336 BCE, his son **Alexander the Great** took the throne. Using the military tactics developed by his father, Alexander led his army against the Persians to the east. In 333 BCE he established the supremacy of the Greek Empire by defeating the Persians at Issus in Asia Minor. Palestine thus became subject to the Greeks.

Alexander then turned south, conquering Egypt and establishing the city of Alexandria. Turning from there to the northeast, he defeated the Persian king Darius III in 331 BCE. After taking Babylon, he continued east, ultimately conquering all the territory between Greece and modern Pakistan before his soldiers forced him to stop. Returning to Babylon, he died in 323 BCE at the age of thirty-two.

Alexander not only conquered most of the known world, but also sought to unite it by spreading Greek culture to other lands. He introduced Greek as the common language ("koine") throughout his empire. Since the Greeks called themselves "Hellenes," such Greek influence on oriental civilizations is called **Hellenization** and produced a culture known as "Hellenistic." The Hellenistic period lasted from Alexander into the third or fourth century CE.

The Hellenistic Kingdoms

After Alexander's death, his goal of a politically unified empire collapsed, as his generals strove for power and divided the territory. Ptolemy gained Egypt and established the Ptolemaic dynasty there. Seleucus established the Seleucid dynasty over a vast area that included Syria. Other leaders battled for Macedonia and Greece.

During the period of these Hellenistic kingdoms, the cultures of western Asia underwent further Hellenization as they adopted Greek language and commodities, and eventually Greek customs, ideas, art, and

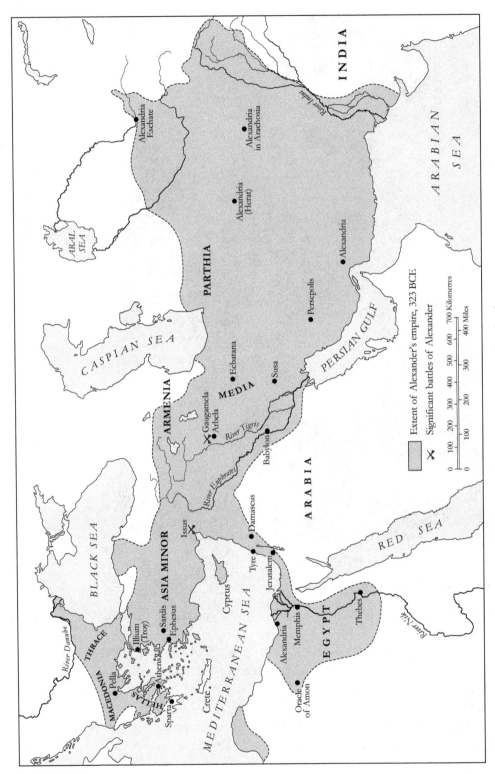

Figure 2.2 Alexander's empire at his death in 323 BCE.

literature. The degree to which Hellenization progressed varied from one country to the next and affected the cities more than the countryside.

From 320 BCE, Ptolemy's dynasty in Egypt ruled Palestine, but in 198 BCE the Seleucid dynasty in Syria took it away from them. In 175 BCE the Seleucid ruler **Antiochus IV** came to power. Antiochus called himself "**Epiphanes**" ("the manifest god"), but the Jews soon had reason to rename him "Epimanes" ("the Insane"). In 169 and again in 168, he looted the temple in Jerusalem to finance his military campaigns. At the same time, he instituted a policy of enforced Hellenization in order to unite his empire. He outlawed Jewish religious practices, such as circumcision and abstinence from pork, and rededicated Yahweh's temple to the Greek god Zeus, using the altar to sacrifice a sow, an animal considered unclean by the Jews.

PALESTINE UNDER THE HASMONEANS

The outrage of the Jews surfaced in 167 BCE in a revolt begun by an elderly man named Mattathias and his five sons. Mattathias died soon after, but his son **Judas "Maccabeus"** ("the Hammerer") led the Jews in guerrilla warfare against the Syrians. By 164 BCE, Judas had gained control of Jerusalem so that the Jews were able to purify the temple from its foreign worship and rededicate it. The Jewish feast of Hanukkah ("dedication"), celebrated at the same time of year as Christmas, commemorates this event.

After Judas' death, leadership passed to his brother Jonathan and subsequently to a third brother, Simon. Under Simon's leadership, the Jews won complete independence in 142 BCE. For about eighty years, until 63 BCE, the Jews maintained their independence under the rule of Mattathias' descendants, known as the **Hasmoneans**. The events of the Maccabean Revolt and Hasmonean rule are recorded by the first-century Jewish historian **Josephus** in his *Antiquities of the Jews* and in the Jewish books of First and Second Maccabees.

PALESTINE UNDER ROMAN RULE

Two factors led to the end of Hasmonean rule: a constant struggle for power among various factions and the rise of the Roman Empire.

The Rise of Rome

The city of Rome, built on seven hills in central Italy, became the center of a power that would extend throughout the Mediterranean world. By the middle of the third century BCE, Rome had gained sovereignty over most of Italy. After defeating Carthage in North Africa in the Punic Wars, the Romans expanded eastward. In 148 BCE, they made Macedonia a Roman province and in 146 added most of Greece to it.

The consul Pompey completed the conquest of the Seleucid Empire in 64 BCE, making Syria a Roman province. The following year, two rivals for power in Jerusalem both appealed to Pompey for support. Pompey entered Jerusalem and made Judea subject to the Roman province of Syria. Later, in 30 BCE, Egypt became a Roman province. Rome thus took control of all the Hellenistic kingdoms.

Beginning of the Empire

Traditionally Rome had been a republic, governed by a Senate composed of wealthy men of the highest social class. The transition to an empire, ruled by an emperor, began with a civil war, in which Pompey was slain, and from which Julius Caesar emerged victorious. He was made dictator in 46 BCE, but was assassinated in 44 BCE. Another period of struggle ended in 27 BCE, when Caesar's adopted son Octavian became the first emperor of the Roman Empire. Octavian took the name Augustus Caesar, and the name **Caesar** became a title adopted by all subsequent emperors. The Senate continued to play a role, though diminished, in governing the empire.

The first Roman emperors

Augustus reigned from 27 BCE to 14 CE. After him, Roman emperors who ruled during the formative period of Christianity were the following:

14–37	Tiberius
37–41	Caligula
41–54	Claudius
54–68	Nero
68–69	Galba, Otho, Vitellius
69–79	Vespasian
79–81	Titus
81–96	Domitian
96–98	Nerva
98–117	Trajan
117–38	Hadrian

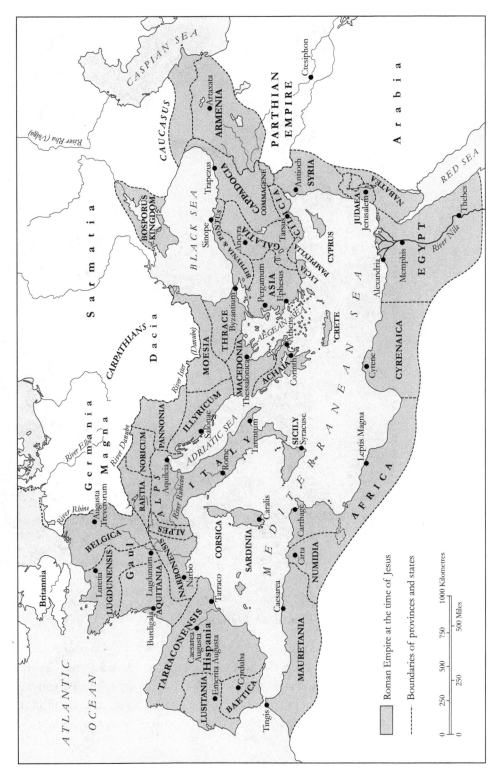

Figure 2.3 The Roman Empire in the first century CE.

Roman Empire at the time of Jesus

------- Boundaries of provinces and states

Figure 2.4
Marble statue of
Augustus Caesar
in military dress.
Vatican Museums
(Erich Lessing/Art
Resource, NY).

The Herodian Dynasty

In Judea at the beginning of Roman rule, political instability continued until 40 BCE, when the Romans appointed **Herod ("the Great")**, the governor of Idumea, as king of Judea. Backed by a Roman army, Herod gained control of Judea in 37 BCE, establishing a new dynasty and bringing Hasmonean power to an end. Herod ruthlessly destroyed any possible rival, including his own wives and children. Among his numerous building projects was the renovation of the temple in Jerusalem.

At the death of Herod the Great in 4 BCE, Rome divided his kingdom among three of his sons. (1) Archelaus received southern Palestine, including Judea. Subsequently the Romans deposed him for cruelty and placed Judea under Roman governors. One of these, **Pontius Pilate**, governed Judea from 26 to 36 CE, during which time Jesus was crucified. (2) Galilee and Perea went to Herod Antipas. (3) Philip received northern and northeastern Palestine. The city he built, Caesarea Philippi, bore his name.

The entire area ruled by these three Herodians subsequently passed to Herod Agrippa I, a grandson of Herod the Great by another son. From 41 to 44 CE his territory included all of Palestine. At his death, Palestine reverted to Roman governors until his son, Herod Agrippa II, came of age. This Herod ruled Galilee and the north, while Judea continued under Roman governors.

Was Jesus Born "before Christ"?

The Gospel of Matthew places the birth of Jesus shortly before the death of Herod the Great, which scholars date to 4 BC (or BCE). On this reckoning, Jesus was born four years "before Christ." But how could Jesus be born before himself? This peculiar state of affairs originated in the sixth century, when Dionysius Exiguus, a Scythian monk living in Rome, introduced a calendar that counted years from the birth of Jesus. Dionysius apparently determined the year of Jesus' birth from two statements in the Gospel of Luke. First, Luke dates the ministry of John the Baptist to the fifteenth year of the Roman emperor Tiberius (Luke 3:1). If John preached for a year before Jesus came along, then Jesus would have begun his own ministry in the sixteenth year of Tiberius. At that time, according to a second statement in Luke, Jesus was "about thirty years old" (Luke 3:23). Dionysius apparently took that number as an exact figure, counted back thirty years from the sixteenth year of Tiberius, and designated that year as Jesus' first year, i.e. 1 AD (or CE). Dionysius probably had no way of knowing that Herod had died four years earlier than that and so was unaware that his dating conflicted with Matthew's account, which put Jesus' birth in the time of Herod. Dionysius' calendar soon caught on and eventually became the basis for the calendar we use today.

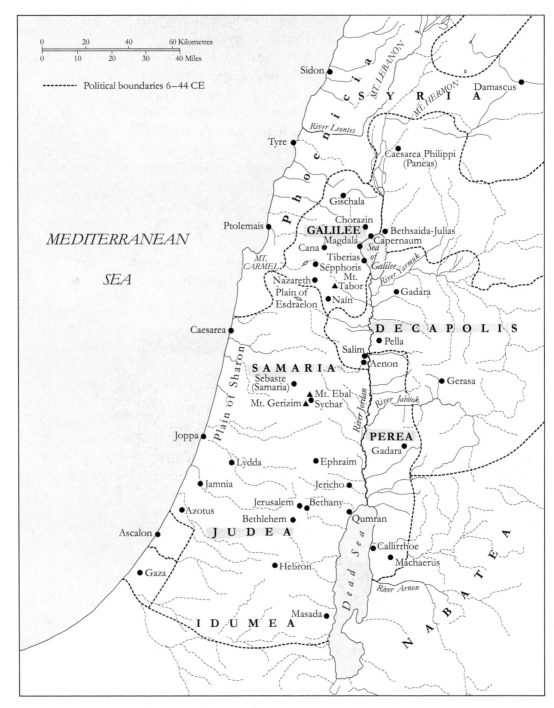

Figure 2.5 Palestine in the time of Jesus.

Divisions of Palestine

In the first century CE, Palestine included the following political divisions.

Judea in a narrow sense was the southern area of Palestine west of the Dead Sea with its capital in Jerusalem. In a broader sense, the term referred to all of Palestine, since the whole area was subjugated by the Hasmoneans and ruled from Jerusalem.

Galilee was the northern region of Palestine west of the Jordan River. In the Old Testament it is called "Galilee of the Gentiles" (Isaiah 9:1), indicating the presence of a large non-Israelite population. The Assyrians captured it from the northern kingdom of Israel and deported some of its inhabitants (2 Kings 15:29). Later the Hasmoneans conquered it and made it a part of Jewish territory. Afterward the population became more Jewish. At the birth of Jesus it was ruled by Herod the Great and subsequently by his son Herod Antipas. Jesus spent most of his life there, including most of his public ministry.

Samaria was the central area of Palestine between Galilee and Judea, named after the former capital city of Israel. Samaritans and Jews did not usually associate with each other.

Decapolis was the area southeast of the Sea of Galilee. A short time before the birth of Jesus, a protective alliance of ten Greek cities was established in this area, hence the name "Decapolis" ("ten cities").

Perea was the area east of Samaria across the Jordan. This area was strongly Hellenistic.

Jewish Wars against the Romans

Many Jews resented Roman rule. Such resentment came to a head in 66 CE in the **first Jewish war against the Romans**. When Florus, the Roman governor of Judea, demanded money from the temple treasury, fighting broke out in various parts of Palestine. The Roman general Vespasian responded. He had subdued Galilee and most of Judea by 69 CE, when he received news that the Roman emperor Nero had died. Vespasian quickly returned to Rome, where he became emperor. Meanwhile, the war was suspended.

A year later in 70 CE, Vespasian's son Titus resumed the war by besieging Jerusalem. When the Romans took the city, they looted the temple and destroyed it. Thousands of Jews perished or were sold into slavery. These events repeated the destruction of Jerusalem and the temple by the Babylonians in 587 BCE. The Jewish historian Josephus, who participated in many of these events, described them in his work *History of the Jewish War against the Romans*. After the fall of Jerusalem, a band of rebels held out for three more years in the fortress of Masada.

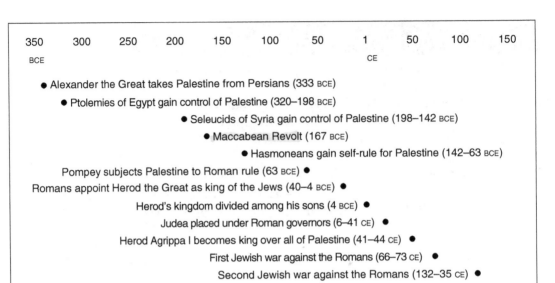

350	300	250	200	150	100	50	1	50	100	150
BCE							CE			

● Alexander the Great takes Palestine from Persians (333 BCE)

● Ptolemies of Egypt gain control of Palestine (320–198 BCE)

● Seleucids of Syria gain control of Palestine (198–142 BCE)

● Maccabean Revolt (167 BCE)

● Hasmoneans gain self-rule for Palestine (142–63 BCE)

Pompey subjects Palestine to Roman rule (63 BCE) ●

Romans appoint Herod the Great as king of the Jews (40–4 BCE) ●

Herod's kingdom divided among his sons (4 BCE) ●

Judea placed under Roman governors (6–41 CE) ●

Herod Agrippa I becomes king over all of Palestine (41–44 CE) ●

First Jewish war against the Romans (66–73 CE) ●

Second Jewish war against the Romans (132–35 CE) ●

Figure 2.6
Timeline of
political events
in Palestine from
Alexander to
Hadrian.

A **second Jewish war against the Romans** broke out in 132 CE. In that year, the Roman emperor Hadrian decreed that Jerusalem should become a Roman colony. This decree provoked the remaining Jews into a desperate revolt led by Simon bar Coseba, nicknamed Bar Cochba ("Son of the Star"). When this revolt too was crushed in 135 CE, the Romans completely rebuilt Jerusalem as a Roman city and renamed it Aelia Capitolina in honor of the Roman god Jupiter Capitolinus. Hadrian erected a temple to Jupiter on the site of the former Jewish temple and forbade all Jews to enter the city on pain of death. From that time, no Jewish state existed in Palestine until the United Nations created the present state of Israel in 1948.

GRECO-ROMAN CULTURE AND SOCIETY

As part of the Greco-Roman world, Jews participated in and interacted with the surrounding culture. Features of that culture included Roman government, an agrarian society, marked social and economic inequality, and traditional values.

Roman Government

The emperor and the Senate in Rome governed the provinces of the empire. The emperor oversaw imperial provinces, over which he appointed governors (prefects or procurators). The Senate oversaw senatorial provinces, over which they appointed proconsuls. Rome ruled other territories indirectly through subject kings such as Herod the Great.

Governors of provinces collected a tax on agricultural produce and a head tax. For other taxes, such as tolls on the trade routes, cities and districts contracted with local men of wealth and influence to collect what was due to Rome.

Military units of various sizes were stationed in the imperial provinces. The smallest unit of the Roman army was the century, consisting of a hundred men commanded by a centurion. Six centuries (600 men) made up a cohort, and ten cohorts (6,000 men) made up a legion.

Agrarian Society

In an agrarian society such as the Greco-Roman world, most people depended on agriculture for their livelihood. In some cases, families owned and worked their own land. In other cases, wealthy landholders with large estates leased the land to tenant farmers, who paid them with part of the produce.

The use of plows and draft animals improved the productivity of the land, creating a surplus capable of supporting large settlements. Large cities in the Greco-Roman world included Rome in Italy, Alexandria in Egypt, Athens in Greece, Ephesus in Asia Minor, and Damascus in Syria. The majority of the population, however, lived in small towns and villages.

Social and Economic Inequality

Greco-Roman society exhibited marked social and economic inequality. At the top of society stood the ruler and a small governing class. It has been estimated that this 1–2 percent of the population accounted for 50 percent of the wealth.

Beneath the ruling elite stood a few classes that had a measure of wealth and influence: retainers (scribes, bureaucrats, and generals who served the ruling elite), as well as merchants and priests. However, the bulk of the population, the common people, had little access to wealth or power. These consisted primarily of peasant farmers, but also included artisans (weavers, builders, and potters) and even less reputable classes (prostitutes, outlaws, beggars, and underemployed itinerant workers).

What Language Did Jesus Speak?

Several different languages were spoken in Palestine in the first century.

Ancient Israelites spoke **Hebrew** until the Babylonian captivity. Most of the Jewish scriptures were written in Hebrew. In the time of the New Testament, Hebrew continued in use, primarily among rabbis and scholars of the Law.

During their exile in Babylon, the Jews began to speak **Aramaic**, a language closely related to Hebrew. Aramaic became the primary language for most of the common people. When the Hebrew Scriptures were read in the synagogues, an interpreter would make an Aramaic paraphrase called a Targum for the people who did not know Hebrew.

The conquests of Alexander ultimately made **Greek** the common language of the entire Greco-Roman world. Jews who had business dealings with non-Jews would necessarily speak Greek. All of the books of the New Testament and the Apostolic Fathers were written in Greek.

Latin was the official language of the Roman Empire. Though the Roman soldiers and governors in Palestine used it, most Palestinians knew little more than a few common words. In later centuries, Latin became the common tongue of the West, while the East continued to speak Greek.

Jesus undoubtedly grew up using Aramaic as his native language. Possibly he spoke Greek as well. In the synagogue he may also have learned Hebrew.

Slaves composed about a third of the population. Slaves came from conquered peoples, criminals, debtors sold to pay their debts, infants sold or found abandoned, and children of slaves. Some slaves experienced a hard life, working in the fields. Others with education were relatively well off, serving in households as administrators or tutors. They could be freed if they were set free by their masters or bought their freedom.

Relations between classes took the form of a patron/client system. Lower-class "clients" provided loyalty and services for a higher-class "patron." In return, the patron looked out for their interests and acted as intermediary on their behalf with other higher-class individuals.

Traditional Values

The Roman virtue of *pietas*, piety or dutiful conduct, played a key role in every aspect of Roman life. Piety meant duty and devotion toward one's family, friends, country, and gods. The precise requirements of duty depended on one's place in society.

In the family, piety consisted of adhering to patriarchal values. The father or oldest brother headed the family and looked out for its interests. The household usually consisted of the extended family. Several generations of relatives might live together, along with slaves and domestic employees.

The position of women varied according to geography and socio-economic status. Wealthy, aristocratic women had more opportunities to participate in the cultural life of society than poor women, whose lives revolved around the household.

DIASPORA JUDAISM

In the Hellenistic period, most Jews lived outside of Palestine. At the Babylonian exile, the upper classes of Jews had been deported to Babylon. Even after the exile, many Jews did not return to Judea but remained in Babylon. Migrations during the Hellenistic period increased the Jewish population outside Palestine. Large populations of Jews lived in Babylon, Egypt, and Asia Minor as well as other parts of the empire. The term **Diaspora** ("dispersion") referred to those Jews living outside of Palestine as well as to the place to which they had been dispersed.

Jews of the Diaspora more readily adopted Greek language, thought, and customs than those in Palestine. While Jews in Babylon spoke Aramaic, like Palestinian Jews, those in the rest of the Diaspora spoke Greek. The influence of Greek thought can be seen in the work of the first-century Jewish philosopher **Philo of Alexandria**, who interpreted the Jewish scriptures in a manner compatible with Greco-Roman philosophy.

DISCUSSION QUESTION

Read the following passages from the New Testament. Describe the contrasts of wealth and poverty, economic class, and social status that these passages illustrate.

1. Landowners and workers: Matthew 13:24–30; 20:1–16; 21:33–41; Luke 17:7–10; James 5:1–6
2. Rich and poor: Luke 16:19–31; 21:1–4; James 2:1–4

1. Identify or define: Palestine, Greco-Roman world, Alexander the Great, Hellenization, Antiochus IV Epiphanes, Judas Maccabeus, the Hasmoneans, Josephus, Caesar, Herod the Great, Pontius Pilate, Diaspora, Philo of Alexandria.

2. Identify the various nations or governments that ruled over Judea. Which empire ruled over Judea at the time of Jesus? Which two empires destroyed the Jewish temple in Jerusalem?

3. Locate on a map: Galilee, Samaria, Decapolis, Perea, Judea. In what part of Palestine did Jesus spend most of his life?

4. What was the outcome of the first Jewish war against the Romans? The second Jewish war?

5. Describe the following features of Greco-Roman culture and society: Roman government, agrarian society, social and economic inequality, and traditional values.

6. What was the common language of the Greco-Roman world? What language was probably Jesus' native language?

SUGGESTIONS FOR FURTHER STUDY

Primary Sources

Feldman, Louis H., and Meyer Reinhold, eds. *Jewish Life and Thought among Greeks and Romans: Primary Readings* (Fortress, 1996). A collection of primary sources illustrating Jewish life and thought from Alexander to rabbinic Judaism.

Josephus, Flavius. *The Jewish War* (rev. ed.; Penguin, 1981). An account of conditions in Palestine at the time of the first Jewish war against Rome, by the first-century Jewish historian Flavius Josephus. English translation by E. Mary Smallwood.

Shelton, Jo-Ann. *As the Romans Did: A Source Book in Roman Social History* (2nd ed.; Oxford University Press, 1997). A compilation of sources from the Roman period illustrating all aspects of Roman society.

Other Suggestions

Adams, Samuel L. *Social and Economic Life in Second Temple Judea* (Westminster John Knox, 2014). Surveys family life and marriage, the status of women and children, work and financial exchanges, taxation and the role of the state, and the ethics of wealth and poverty.

Ferguson, Everett. *Backgrounds of Early Christianity* (3rd ed.; Eerdmans, 2003). Chapters on Greco-Roman political history, society, and culture.

Koester, Helmut. *Introduction to the New Testament* (2nd ed.; 2 vols.; De Gruyter, 1995, 2000). Volume 1 surveys the history, culture, and religion of the Hellenistic age.

Pomeroy, Sarah. *Goddesses, Whores, Wives, and Slaves: Women in Classical Antiquity* (Schocken, 1975, 1995). Examines the history of women in ancient Greece and Rome, utilizing the insights of modern feminism.

Schürer, Emil. *The History of the Jewish People in the Age of Jesus Christ (175 BC–AD 135)* (rev. English ed.; 3 vols. in 4; ed. Geza Vermes, Fergus Millar, Matthew Black, and Martin Goodman; T&T Clark, 1973–87). Reference work on the Jewish context of the birth of Christianity from the Maccabean period to the second Jewish war against Rome.

3   Basic Second-Temple Judaism

Christianity arose among the followers of Jesus of Nazareth. Yet neither Jesus nor his disciples were "Christians" in the sense that we use that term today. They were Palestinian Jews who practiced the religion of Judaism. Even after Jesus' death, the earliest community of his followers also consisted of practicing Jews and was at first considered merely a branch of Judaism. To understand the rise of Christianity, therefore, we must first consider the religious context out of which it grew, the religion of first-century Judaism.

The time of early Christianity actually overlaps two distinct periods of Jewish religion. In the former period, religion revolved around the temple, and the leading religious figures were priests. This period, called **Second-Temple Judaism**, extended from the completion of Jerusalem's second temple in 516 BCE to its destruction in 70 CE. After the destruction of the temple came the period of **rabbinic Judaism**. In this period, religion focused on study of Jewish Law (the Torah), and the leading religious figures were rabbis (scholars of the Law).

Here we will focus primarily on Second-Temple Judaism. The religion of this period included certain basic beliefs, practices, and institutions that nearly all Jews shared. Among these we will consider the God of Judaism, Jewish religious writings, the covenant and the Law, the temple and the priests, the national festivals, synagogues, and eschatology.

THE GOD OF JUDAISM

Central to the Jewish faith is the confession of one God expressed in Deuteronomy 6:4: "Hear, O Israel: Yahweh is our God, Yahweh alone [or 'Yahweh is one']. This confession of faith begins a traditional Jewish prayer, known as the **shema** ("hear") from its first word in Hebrew. Originally this confession meant simply that Jews were to worship only the one God Yahweh (though other gods might exist). By the time of Jesus, however, Jews understood it to mean that only one God existed, a belief known as **monotheism.**

The Jewish people believed that their God had revealed his name to Moses as "YHWH." These four consonants, called the Tetragrammaton ("four-letter word"), formed a name so sacred to the Jews that only the high priest on certain special occasions was permitted to pronounce it. The original pronunciation of the name is uncertain, but many scholars vocalize it as "**Yahweh.**" When reading the biblical text or speaking, Jews did not pronounce the name but substituted a circumlocution such as "the Lord" or "the Holy One." Many translations of the Hebrew Scriptures even today follow this practice.

THE JEWISH SCRIPTURES

By the time of Jesus, the Jewish community accepted twenty-four books as inspired scripture. Today we count these as thirty-nine books by dividing some books in two or more parts (such as 1 and 2 Kings, 1 and 2 Chronicles). These books, the Hebrew Scriptures, were divided into three sections: the Law (Torah), the Prophets (Neviim), and the Writings (Khetuvim).

The first five books of the Hebrew Bible (**the Torah**) contain narratives about Israel's beginnings combined with collections of laws that regulated the life of ancient Israel. Modern scholars recognize that these laws were collected over a long period of time. The Jewish people, however, believed that Yahweh had revealed them to Moses on Mount Sinai. They referred to this legal material as the Torah, a Hebrew term literally meaning "instruction" or "teaching," but translated into Greek as "law." This term was also used to refer to the five books which contained the Torah. These five books probably assumed their final form around 500–400 BCE.

The second section of the Hebrew Scriptures (**the Prophets**) includes (1) stories about ancient Israel, which the Jews believed were written by prophets (the Former Prophets), and (2) collections of messages delivered by prophets (the Latter Prophets).

The third section of the Hebrew Scriptures (**the Writings**) includes whatever did not fit in either of the first two sections. The last book to be added was the Book of Daniel, written about 164 BCE.

This threefold canon of scripture was generally accepted by the Jewish community by around 150 BCE, though some doubt persisted into the first century CE about certain books (Ezekiel, Proverbs, Ecclesiastes, Song of Songs, Esther). Already by about 132 BCE, the grandson of Jesus ben Sirach referred to the three sections of the canon as "the Law and the prophets and the other books of our fathers" (Preface to Ecclesiasticus). Jews today call the Hebrew Scriptures by the acronym TaNaKh, formed from the first letters of Torah (Law), Neviim (prophets), and Khetuvim (writings).

Since many Jews did not know Hebrew or Aramaic, the languages in which the Jewish scriptures were written, they used a Greek translation known as the **Septuagint** ("the seventy," abbreviated as LXX). It received its name from the tradition that seventy or seventy-two scholars had translated it. This translation was made in the third and second centuries BCE for Greek-speaking Jews in Alexandria Egypt.

THE COVENANT AND THE LAW

For the Jews, Yahweh was a God who had revealed himself to various people in their history. Above all he revealed himself by delivering the Israelites from slavery in Egypt and establishing a **covenant** with them at Mount Sinai. On his part, God agreed to take the Israelites as his special people. On their part, Israel agreed to take Yahweh as their God, to worship him alone, and to obey his commandments. These commandments were contained in the **Torah**, the Law that, according to Jewish tradition, Yahweh gave to Moses on Mount Sinai.

For the Jews, the way to serve Yahweh, the way to keep the covenant, was to observe the Torah. Two basic types of material occur in the five books of the Torah: ethical and cultic. Commandments such as "Do not kill" and "Do not steal" set forth ethical requirements regulating the conduct of one person toward another. Most of the commandments, however, deal with the cultic aspects of Israel's religion, that is, the rituals and ceremonies of the religion. For example, the Torah provides specific regulations concerning sacrifices, festivals, and the consecration of priests.

Other important regulations include the command not to work on the **Sabbath** (the seventh day of the week). Since the Jewish day began at sundown, the Sabbath lasted from sundown on Friday to sundown on Saturday.

The Torah also commanded Jewish parents to circumcise their male children on the eighth day after birth. It presents such **circumcision** as a sign of God's covenant with Israel.

Apocrypha and Pseudepigrapha

In the first century CE, certain circles of Judaism highly esteemed many other writings in addition to the Hebrew Scriptures. The book of 4 Ezra, written about 100 CE, alleges that God dictated two sets of writings to the scribe Ezra. God then said to Ezra,

> Make public the twenty-four books that you wrote first and let the worthy and the unworthy read them; but keep the seventy that were written last, in order to give them to the wise among your people. For in them is the spring of understanding, the fountain of wisdom, and the river of knowledge. (4 Ezra 14:45–47)

The first twenty-four books are the Hebrew Scriptures; the seventy books reserved for "the wise" are the apocryphal ("hidden") writings that circulated in some circles. Though this story does not give an accurate account of the writing of these works, it does show that the author, and presumably others, esteemed these apocryphal works as highly as, or even more highly than, the Hebrew Scriptures. Many of these apocryphal works still exist today and can be found in two collections of writings: the Old Testament Apocrypha and the Pseudepigrapha.

The Old Testament **Apocrypha** are to be distinguished from the New Testament Apocrypha that we discussed in Chapter 1. Most of the former are regarded as scripture by Catholics and/or Orthodox Christians and are thus called "deuterocanonical." These include the books of Tobit, Judith, the Wisdom of Solomon, Ecclesiasticus (or the Wisdom of Jesus the Son of Sirach), Baruch, 1 and 2 Maccabees, as well as certain additions to the books of Daniel and Esther. These can be found mixed with the other Old Testament books in Catholic Bibles or as an appendix in some ecumenical Bibles.

The **Pseudepigrapha** (writings "falsely attributed") are so called because they claim to have been written by famous people in Israel's history who actually did not write them. Scores of such writings, both Jewish and Jewish-Christian, circulated during the period from about 200 BCE to 200 CE and even later. Many of these works have survived, including, to name only a few, the Psalms of Solomon, 1 Enoch, and 4 Ezra.

Jews also observed other traditional religious practices, such as **ritual prayer**, **fasting**, and **charitable giving** to the poor (Matt 6:1–6, 16–18). Jewish men prayed a standard set of prayers either two or three times a day, depending on the tradition that they followed. The Jewish Law commanded fasting only on the Day of Atonement (Lev 16:29, 31; 23:26–29). However, in Second-Temple Judaism, fasting became a more important aspect of Jewish piety. The Pharisees fasted twice a week (Luke 18:12; Did 8:1). According to the Book of Tobit, "Prayer with fasting is good, but better than both is charitable giving with righteousness" (Tob 12:8).

According to the **purity rules** of the Law, certain actions or occurrences made one ritually "unclean" or impure. Ritual impurity in this sense was not to be dirty, but to be unholy or unfit to be in God's presence. Persons could be rendered unclean by such occurrences as touching a corpse or having a bodily discharge (semen or menstrual fluid). Objects could also be unclean, such as items touched by a ritually unclean person. A person who was not unclean would become unclean by coming into contact with unclean persons or objects. Purifying oneself from uncleanness involved bathing oneself or washing one's clothes. Washing the hands and feet was prescribed for priests before they could perform rituals in the temple.

Among such purity rules were **dietary regulations**. Certain animals were considered clean and therefore permitted as food, while animals considered unclean were not to be eaten. Cows, for example, were clean, while pigs were unclean. The basis for these distinctions is set out in Leviticus 11. Even clean animals had to be slaughtered in a certain way, since it was not permitted to consume the blood of the animal.

Another significant regulation was the **prohibition against images**. The second of the ten commandments prohibited Jews from making or worshipping any "graven image," a representation of any being or creature in heaven, on the earth, or in the sea (Exod 20:4–6; Deut 4:16–18; 5:8–10). This commandment originally prohibited the worship of idols. Whereas most Greco-Roman temples contained a statue of the deity, the Jewish temple in Jerusalem contained no such representation of Yahweh. In the Second-Temple period, some Jews interpreted this commandment more broadly as a prohibition against images of any kind.

Jews who kept these regulations of the Law were considered "righteous," while those who did not were considered "sinners." By definition, all Gentiles were sinners, because they did not keep the Jewish Law. If a Jew transgressed the Law, he or she could be restored to a proper

Figure 3.1
Depiction of the
scribe Ezra reading
from a scroll,
probably the Torah.
The Torah contains
the Law that has
traditionally guided
the life of the Jewish
people. Detail
from a mural in
the third-century
CE synagogue of
Dura-Europus
in Syria. www.
BibleLandPictures.
com (Zev Radovan).

relationship with Yahweh by repentance and offering the appropriate sacrifice at the temple.

THE TEMPLE AND THE PRIESTS

The official state religion of Judea had its seat in the temple at Jerusalem. Destroyed by the Babylonians in 587 BCE, it was rebuilt in less splendid form by the exiles returning from Babylon. When Herod the Great came to power in Judea, he began to enlarge and adorn this second temple, a process completed only a few years before the Romans burned it in 70 CE.

While the temple (*naos*) was a single building, it was part of a larger sacred area, the **temple complex** (*hieros*). The temple sat within a huge square court, the Court of the Gentiles, so named because it was open to Gentiles as well as Jews. Surrounding this court were rows of pillars forming colonnades or porticos. Within the court, a stone wall separated off a rectangular area, within which no Gentiles were permitted. Jews who entered the eastern end of this rectangle would come first into the Women's Court, beyond which women were not allowed to pass except for sacrificial purposes, then into the Court of Israel (Israelite men), and finally into the Court of the Priests, in which sat the temple proper. This rectangular building consisted of an outer chamber, the Holy Place, and an inner chamber, the Most Holy Place or Holy of Holies, where the Jews believed God was enthroned. The priests entered the Holy Place daily to offer incense to God, but only the high priest could enter the Holy of Holies. He entered it once a year on the Day of Atonement and performed a ritual to atone for the sins of the people.

Thus the structure of the temple complex represented a hierarchy of holiness that determined how close one could approach to God. Moving outward from the center of holiness, the Holy of Holies where Yahweh dwelt, holiness decreased as one moved from the high priest to the priests, to the Jewish men, to the Jewish women, and finally to the Gentiles.

The temple ritual was performed by the **priests**, who were divided into twenty-four "courses," each of which served in the temple for a week at a time. Most of the priests lived outside of Jerusalem, but the chief priests came from the leading priestly families in Jerusalem. Over the chief priests was the high priest. The high priest was also head of the Sanhedrin ("council"), the Jewish supreme court, which tradition says

Figure 3.2
Scale model of the temple in Jerusalem during the time of Herod the Great. Holy Land Hotel, Jerusalem (Erich Lessing/Art Resource, NY).

was composed of seventy-one members. As such, he held the highest rank in the Jewish community.

As the principal act of **worship**, the priests sacrificed an unblemished lamb on the altar of burnt offering in front of the temple proper. This occurred twice daily at about 9:00 a.m. and 3:00 p.m., at which times Jews gathered within the Women's Court and the Court of Israel for worship and prayer. After the public worship, individuals offered sacrifices of various sorts. For worshippers who came from a distance, unblemished sacrificial animals were sold in the Court of the Gentiles.

The ritual of animal sacrifice, in which an animal was slain and completely or partly burned on the altar, was an ancient practice that the Jews shared with all other peoples of the Greco-Roman world. It arose from the idea that the gods had the same sorts of appetites as humans. The worshipper usually ate part of the animal, while the part burned on the altar was thought to be consumed by the god. Criticism of this idea can be found in both Jewish and non-Jewish texts of antiquity.

NATIONAL FESTIVALS AND FASTS

The Torah required all Jewish men to travel to Jerusalem for the three **pilgrim festivals** of the year: Tabernacles, Passover, and Weeks. That

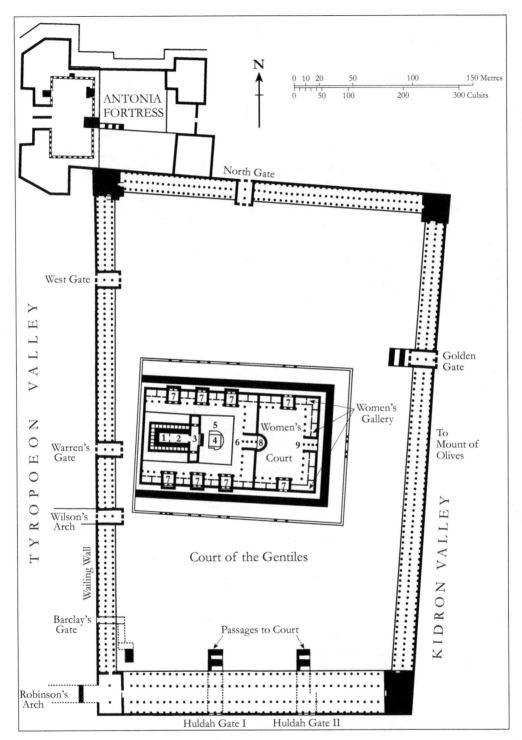

Figure 3.3 Ground plan of Herod's temple and its courts: (1) most holy place; (2) holy place; (3) porch; (4) altar of burnt offering; (5) court of the priests; (6) court of Israel; (7) sanctuary gates; (8) Nicanor Gate; (9) Beautiful Gate (?).
W. E. Stinespring, "Temple, Jerusalem," in *Interpreter's Dictionary of the Bible* (Abingdon, 1962), vol. IV, p. 556. Based on L.-H. Vincent and A.-M. Steve, *Jerusalem de l'Ancien Testament* (Gabalda & Cie, 1954–56).

requirement was made when all Jews lived fairly close to the city. Later, as Jews spread all over the world, it became impractical for many. Nevertheless large numbers of pilgrims came to Jerusalem at these times. Other festivals and one major fast also occurred throughout the year.

Jewish festivals and fasts

FESTIVAL/FAST	TIME	SIGNIFICANCE	RITUAL
New Year (Rosh Hashanah)	Autumn	Beginning of Jewish year	Blowing of shophar (ram's horn)
Day of Atonement (Yom Kippur)	Autumn	Atonement for sins of the people	People fast. High priest takes blood of sacrifice into Holy of Holies
Tabernacles or Booths	Autumn	Ingathering of fall harvest. Commemorates Israel's wilderness wanderings	People live outside in booths or tents for a week
Hanukkah	Winter	Commemorates rededication of temple by Judas Maccabeus	Lights kindled in temple and Jerusalem
Purim	Spring	Commemorates preservation of Jews in Persia by Queen Esther	Book of Esther read and reenacted
Passover and Unleavened Bread	Spring	Commemorates Israel's exodus from Egypt	Families go to Jerusalem, slaughter a lamb in the temple for an evening meal
Weeks or Pentecost ("fiftieth")	Fiftieth day after Passover	First fruits of harvest. Commemorates giving of Law on Mount Sinai	People bring first part of harvest to temple as offering of thanks

SYNAGOGUES

Jews living at a distance from Jerusalem could not participate in the temple worship on a regular basis. For most Jews, therefore, religious life centered around the local **synagogue**. Literally meaning a "gathering" or "assembly," the term refers either to the community assembled for worship or to the building in which the worshippers met. The synagogue served as a meeting place for the Jewish community as well as a house for prayer

Figure 3.4
Ruins of the
ancient synagogue
at Capernaum,
dating from
the late second
or early third
century CE. It
was built over an
earlier synagogue
where Jesus may
have taught.
Albatross Aerial
Photography.

and study of scripture. While meetings occurred throughout the week, the major service was held on the morning of the Sabbath. Worship included prayers, the reading and exposition of scripture, and a closing blessing. The synagogue had no special minister, though an official called "the ruler of the synagogue" oversaw the building and preparation for worship. All members of the community were free to participate, including visitors, who might be asked to address the congregation. Jesus spread his message in the synagogues of Galilee, while later Jewish-Christian missionaries preached in synagogues throughout the Roman world.

ESCHATOLOGY

Jewish authors of the Second-Temple period often expressed the hope for an ideal future, far superior to the present. They believed that the present age or world would be replaced with a superior age to come. Such beliefs about the end of the present age are called "**eschatology**" (from the Greek "eschaton," meaning "end"). In some forms of Jewish hope, God himself would overthrow the enemies of Israel and establish a new age in which the Jews were no longer subject to foreign powers. In other forms, an agent of God called the **Messiah** would do this. The term Messiah translated into Greek becomes "Christ." Early Jewish followers of Jesus believed that he was the Messiah, the Christ.

Rabbinic Judaism after 70 CE

After the destruction of the temple in 70 CE, the focus of Judaism shifted from the temple cult to study of the Torah. The leadership shifted from the priests to the rabbis, scholars of the Law.

The task of reorganizing Judaism after the destruction of the temple fell to Yohanan ben Zakkai (d. 80 CE). One of the leaders in the school at Jerusalem, he left in 68 CE in opposition to the war faction among the Jews. Obtaining permission from the Romans, he settled in the coastal city of Jamnia to establish a new school. After the war, he and others who followed him there led in the restructuring of Jewish religion. They formed a rabbinic legal court (Beth-Din) at Jamnia to make decisions previously left to the priests, such as calculating the Jewish calendar and setting the dates of festivals. The festivals themselves had to be revised, since they could no longer be celebrated at the temple. Passover, for example, came to be celebrated in the home. Since sacrifices to atone for sin could no longer be offered at the temple, the rabbis stressed atonement through good deeds, prayer, and study of Torah.

Originally, the rabbis did not write down their teachings. They gathered students about themselves and repeated the teachings until the students had them memorized. This tradition was passed down orally until about 200 CE, when Rabbi Yehuda committed it to writing in what is called the **Mishnah** ("repetition"). As time passed, later rabbis interpreted and commented on the Mishnah. These comments were collected and added to the Mishnah to make up the **Talmud** ("instruction"). Two editions were made of the Talmud, one in Palestine in the fourth century and a longer and more authoritative version in Babylon in the fifth. For rabbinic Judaism the Talmud was Torah and just as authoritative as the Hebrew Scriptures.

DISCUSSION QUESTION

The book of Leviticus in the Hebrew Bible includes instructions to the priests for offering various sorts of sacrifices at the temple in Jerusalem. Read the instructions for the peace offering (Leviticus 3:1–17; 7:11–36) and the sin offering for the common person (Leviticus 4:27–35). Identify the main features and purpose of these sacrifices. Contrast the attitude toward sacrifice in these passages with that of Lucian in Appendix 1 (p. 545).

REVIEW QUESTIONS

1. Distinguish between Second-Temple and rabbinic Judaism.
2. Identify or define: shema, monotheism, Yahweh.
3. What are the three divisions of the Hebrew Scriptures?
4. Identify or define: Septuagint, Apocrypha, Pseudepigrapha.
5. Explain the following features of Second-Temple Jewish religion: covenant, Torah, Sabbath, circumcision, ritual prayer, fasting, charitable giving, purity rules, dietary regulations, prohibition against images.
6. Describe Jewish worship at the temple in Jerusalem, including the function of priests and the status of women.
7. Identify or define: pilgrim festivals, Day of Atonement, Passover, synagogue, eschatology, Messiah.
8. Identify or define: Mishnah, Talmud.

SUGGESTIONS FOR FURTHER STUDY

Primary Sources

Charlesworth, James H. *The Old Testament Pseudepigrapha* (2 vols.; Doubleday, 1983, 1985). A substantial collection of non-canonical Jewish writings from the centuries immediately before and after the rise of Christianity. English translations with introductions.

Danby, Herbert. *The Mishnah: Translated from the Hebrew with Introduction and Brief Explanatory Notes* (Oxford University Press, 1933; reprinted, Hendrickson, 2011). Standard English translation of the Mishnah.

Other Suggestions

Cohen, Shaye J. D. *From the Maccabees to the Mishnah* (3rd ed.; Westminster John Knox, 2014). Includes chapters on Jewish religion and literature in the Second-Temple period.

Grabbe, Lester L. *Judaic Religion in the Second Temple Period: Belief and Practice from the Exile to Yavneh* (Routledge, 2000). Surveys the sources for our knowledge of Second-Temple Judaism and discusses various aspects of Jewish religion in this period.

Nickelsburg, George W. E. *Jewish Literature between the Bible and the Mishnah: A Historical and Literary Introduction* (2nd ed.; Fortress, 2005). An introduction to Jewish literature in the Second-Temple period.

Sanders, E. P. *Judaism: Practice and Belief 63 BCE–66 CE* (Trinity, 1992). A comprehensive survey of Jewish practice and belief at the end of the Second-Temple period.

4   Varieties of Second-Temple Judaism

While all Jews believed in one God and followed the Torah, great diversity existed with respect to other beliefs and practices. Such differences led to the formation of different religious groups, parties, or sects. Josephus described three main Jewish groups – the Pharisees, the Sadducees, and the Essenes – calling them "philosophies" with an eye to the Greek culture of his day. He also mentioned a "fourth philosophy" without giving it a name. In addition to the groups mentioned by Josephus were the Samaritans, who, though not Jews, practiced a form of the same religion. Also in the first century, at least two other branches of Judaism appeared: the followers of John the Baptist and the followers of Jesus. Most of the population belonged to none of these groups.

PHARISEES

Because of our limited information, it is difficult to describe the Pharisees precisely. Scholars have conceived of them variously as a religious sect, a political party, a group of legal scholars, or an association of laymen who ate together. According to Josephus, there were Pharisees as early as the time of the Hasmonean ruler John Hyrcanus (135–105 BCE). They numbered about 6,000. Some Pharisees were priests, though apparently most were not. Some served as members of the Sanhedrin, the highest political and religious body in Judaism. Some were scribes, learned scholars of the Law. We do not know what other roles they may have filled in society, though Paul, a Pharisee who adopted Christianity, worked as a tentmaker. Josephus mentions three outstanding features of the Pharisees.

1. They followed a tradition of oral law in addition to the written law of the Torah. According to Josephus,

the Pharisees had passed on to the people certain regulations that they had received from the succession of fathers, regulations that were not written in the laws of Moses. For that reason, the Sadducean party rejects them, saying that one must regard the written regulations as binding, but that one need not keep the tradition of the fathers. (*Antiquities* 13.297)

Apparently, the scribes of the Pharisees took the general laws of the Torah and made specific applications. For example, the Law forbade working on the Sabbath; the scribes went a step further and defined what should be considered "work." Their students passed on these interpretations and judgments by word of mouth. In this way, they developed a complex tradition of oral law that interpreted and explained the written law. In the New Testament, this oral law is called "the tradition of the elders" (Mark 7:3).

We cannot fully reconstruct the Pharisees' particular perspectives on the Law, but according to the gospels, they washed their hands before eating and bathed after coming home from the marketplace, where they might come into contact with unclean persons or objects (Mark 7:1–4). They also thought that it was improper to associate with "tax collectors and (other) sinners" (Mark 2:15–17). In defining what constituted working on the Sabbath, they seem to have been less strict than the Essenes, but stricter than the early Jewish Christians.

The interpretations of the Pharisees were apparently well received by the populace. Josephus states in one place that they were "thought to interpret the laws with accuracy" (*Jewish War* 2.162). In another place he says, "they are very persuasive in the popular assemblies, and all religious rites pertaining to prayers and production of sacred objects are performed according to their interpretation" (*Antiquities* 18.15).

2. Like the early Christians, the Pharisees believed in resurrection of the dead, though only for the just. As Josephus said,

> It is their belief that souls have the power of immortality; and that under the ground there are penalties and rewards for those who have practiced virtue or vice in this life; and that eternal imprisonment is appointed for the latter, but the relief of living again for the former. (*Antiquities* 18.14)

3. The Pharisees took a middle position between the Essenes and the Sadducees on the role of fate or predestination in human life: they thought that human actions result from a combination of fate and free will.

Because the gospels of the New Testament frequently refer to the Pharisees as "hypocrites," most readers have this impression about them. But Pharisees as a group were no more hypocritical than any other group. Most were undoubtedly quite sincere in following the Law as they believed God wanted them to. The charges of hypocrisy arose out of a disagreement between the Pharisees and early Christians. In such conflicts, it is not uncommon to find each side denouncing the other. What has been preserved in the New Testament is the Christian side of the argument, in which the Pharisees get denounced.

SADDUCEES

We know even less about the Sadducees than about the Pharisees. Josephus puts them in a higher social class than the Pharisees: "This doctrine has reached only a few men, those, however, who are first in the places of honor" (*Antiquities* 18.17). Scholars sometimes associate them with the priests, because the name Sadducee (Zadokite) is the same as that of a class of Jewish priests who held the priesthood before the Hasmoneans took power.

Josephus attributes to them three beliefs. They did not believe in an afterlife, either resurrection of the body or immortality of the soul. They gave no role to fate or predestination but thought that humans have free will to choose good or evil. And they believed that no regulation outside of the Torah was binding, thus rejecting the oral tradition of the elders followed by the Pharisees.

Josephus goes on to say that in disputes over interpretation, the Sadducees had persuaded the wealthy but had no following among the populace, whereas the Pharisees had the masses on their side. Whenever the Sadducees took some office, they had to follow the Pharisees' rules or the masses would not tolerate them (*Antiquities* 18.17).

ESSENES

Jewish sources also speak of a sect of Jews known as "Essenes." This name may come from an Aramaic word meaning "pious ones." Josephus and Philo, Jewish authors of the first century, both set their number at 4,000. Josephus mentions two divisions of the sect, one of celibate men and one of families. They lived in various towns and elected officers to oversee the affairs of the community. Their most distinctive feature lay in their sharing of property. New members who joined surrendered all their possessions to the order, so that each shared equally in the common resources. When they traveled, they took no baggage, since sect members in the place where they were going would supply their food and clothing. They met before dawn for prayer, then full members would assemble again for a midmorning meal and an evening meal. New members had to undergo a three-year period of initiation before they could participate in the communal meals. Josephus mentions their devotion to study of ancient writings and their strict observance of the Sabbath. They were divided into four grades, based on the length of their training, and a senior member could not be touched by a junior member without becoming unclean. They believed that fate (or God) determined everything that happened. They also believed in the immortality of the soul, which would receive reward or punishment after death, but apparently not in resurrection of the body.

THE QUMRAN COMMUNITY

One sect of Jews, whose identity has been debated, lived in an isolated community near the Dead Sea. Evidence concerning this group came to light between the years 1947 and 1956, when ancient manuscripts were discovered in eleven caves along the northwest shore of the Dead Sea. These "Dead Sea Scrolls," as they came to be called, included scrolls and fragments of about 800 manuscripts, written in Hebrew, Aramaic, and Greek. The manuscripts have been dated to the last three or four centuries BCE and the first century CE.

The caves that held these manuscripts were located near the ruins of some ancient buildings at a place called Qumran. When archaeologists excavated the site in the 1950s, they concluded that the ruins at Qumran were communal buildings used by members of a Jewish sect who lived there between about 140 BCE and 68 CE. The manuscripts appeared to be their library. This view, though not unchallenged, is still accepted by most scholars. For two reasons, scholars came to believe that the inhabitants of Qumran were Essenes. First, the Roman geographer Pliny (23–79 CE) stated that a community of Essenes lived in that area in his day. Second, some of the scrolls describe the beliefs and practices of a Jewish sect, and these correspond to what is known about the Essenes from other sources.

A letter found among the manuscripts suggests that the founders of the sect were Zadokite priests who separated themselves from the Jerusalem temple when the Hasmonean ruler Jonathan took over the

Figure 4.1 Aerial view of the ruins at Qumran with the Dead Sea in the distance and the cliff holding Cave 4 across a ravine to the right. Albatross Aerial Photography.

high priesthood for himself and his descendants (152 BCE). The scrolls speak of the leader of the group as "the Teacher of Righteousness" and of his opponent as "the Wicked Priest," probably referring to Jonathan. Led by the Teacher of Righteousness, the group went into the Judean wilderness and established the community at Qumran about 140 BCE.

The manuscripts found in the caves include three main types of writings. (1) About one-fourth of the manuscripts are books of the Hebrew Bible. These are the oldest known copies of the Hebrew Scriptures, dating around a thousand years earlier than the oldest manuscripts previously known. They provide invaluable new information about the history of the text and canon of the Hebrew Bible. (2) Other manuscripts are copies of Jewish apocryphal and pseudepigraphal works. (3) Still other manuscripts are documents that relate specifically to the life and thought of the sect.

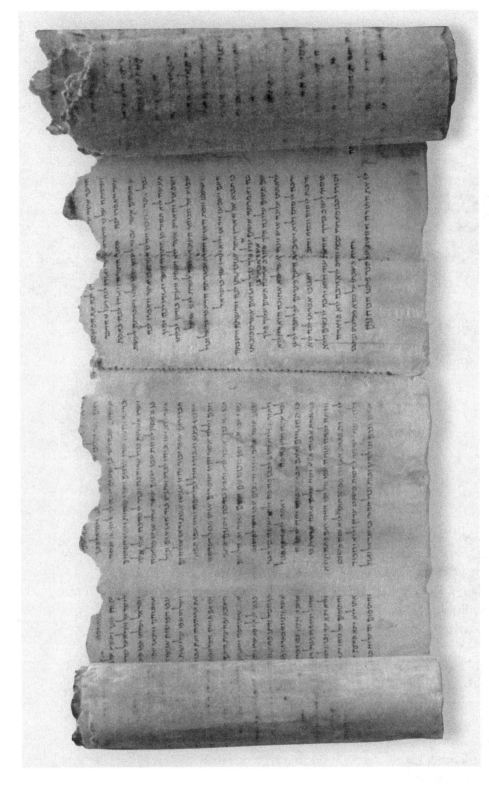

Figure 4.3 The Temple Scroll from Qumran, a previously unknown manuscript, which describes plans for building an ideal temple. www.BibleLandPictures.com/Alamy Stock Photo.

Those who joined the community led a very strict and simple communal life, studying the Law and waiting for the new age. They contributed all their possessions to the community and took their meals together. They considered themselves the people of the new covenant that God had promised to make with Israel (Jeremiah 31:31–34). As such they regarded themselves as the true people of God in contrast to all other groups. They were "the sons of light" in contrast to "the sons of darkness." The sons of light followed a spirit called "the prince of lights" or "the spirit of truth," while the sons of darkness were motivated by "the angel of darkness," "the spirit of error," or "Belial." They gave a central role to predestination, believing that God decided whether each individual would be a son of light or a son of darkness.

The sect expected two Messiahs – one a priest and one a king. In the new age, since the old temple had been desecrated, God would build a new temple. The old age would end with a great war against Rome, in which the forces of light would defeat the forces of darkness. Since they expected to play a role in this war, they kept themselves ready by following the regulations set out in the Hebrew Scriptures for soldiers of ancient Israel engaged in holy war. This readiness involved maintaining ritual purity, including abstaining from sex. Hence only celibate men could be full members of the community, although associate members who lived outside the community could marry. When the war came, it did not turn out as the community expected. The Romans destroyed the community in 68 CE.

FREEDOM FIGHTERS

Josephus speaks of a fourth "philosophy" among the Jews, whose members generally agreed with the Pharisees but differed in one respect: "they have an unconquerable love of freedom, supposing that God alone is ruler and master" (*Antiquities* 18.23). In fact, more than one band of Jews advocated the use of military force to drive out the Romans and reestablish Jewish independence. In 6 CE, when the Romans imposed a tax on Judea, a Galilean man named Judas, supported by a Pharisee named Zadok, declared that "the taxation imposed nothing other than outright slavery" (*Antiquities* 18.4). Judas called the people cowards "if they endured paying tribute to the Romans and tolerated mortal masters" after having God as lord (*Jewish War* 2.118). When he persuaded others to join him in a revolt against Rome, the Romans killed Judas and scattered his followers (Acts 5:37).

Figure 4.4 Aerial view of Masada, a cliff-top fortress and palace built by Herod the Great. Here Jewish freedom fighters held out against the Romans for several years after Jerusalem fell in 70 CE. Richard Nowitz Photography.

At a later period, a revolutionary group called Sicarii ("dagger men" or "assassins") concealed daggers under their cloaks and mingled with the crowds in Jerusalem, assassinating fellow Jews who collaborated with the Romans. When the first war with Rome started, another group that Josephus called "Zealots" fled from Galilee to Jerusalem and fought not only against the Romans but also against other rebels.

SAMARITANS

Though not Jews, the Samaritans practiced and still practice a religion related to Judaism. The origin of the Samaritans is uncertain. According to one tradition, they were descendants of Israelites from the ancient northern kingdom of Israel. According to another, they were non-Israelites whom the Assyrians settled in the region of Samaria after they conquered the northern kingdom in 722 BCE. In any case, they practiced a form of Israelite religion, worshipping Yahweh as their God.

Samaritan practice differed from that of the Jews in two primary respects. First, they accepted as scripture only the first five books of the Hebrew Bible, the Torah that they believed Yahweh gave Moses. Second, whereas the Jews sacrificed to God only at the temple on Mount Zion in Jerusalem, the Samaritans sacrificed at their own temple on Mount Gerizim near Shechem (cf. John 4:20). This temple stood until 129 BCE, when John Hyrcanus, one of the Hasmonean rulers, destroyed it.

Since the Samaritans did not accept two divisions of the Jewish canon, the prophets and the writings, they did not expect a Messiah of the type that Jews found predicted in those works. They did, however, await the coming of another eschatological figure, a prophet like Moses, whose coming they found predicted in Deuteronomy 18:15–19. Their eschatology also included the belief that God would restore their temple on Mount Gerizim.

Samaritans and Jews, because of differences in religious practice and historical tensions between them, generally did not have the most cordial relations.

DISCIPLES OF JOHN THE BAPTIST

Another Jewish sect arose shortly before the year 30 CE, when a Jewish preacher called John the Baptist began to warn the people to repent of their sins. According to the gospels, John proclaimed that God was about

Conceptions of the Afterlife

The question of what happens after death has troubled human beings ever since our first ancestors began to reflect on their own mortality. Before the Babylonian captivity, ancient Israelites expected to experience a bleak existence after death in a gloomy, underground pit called "Sheol." This was not a place of punishment but simply a grave for all mortals. When the body entered the grave, whatever remained of human awareness went underground with it. The ancient Greeks had a similar underworld called "Hades." For both cultures, any good that a person hoped to experience had to come before death – there would be none afterward.

After the Babylonian captivity, the Jews absorbed new ideas from the Persian religion Zoroastrianism. According to this religion, a god of good and a god of evil waged a cosmic battle in which humans took part by following one or the other. At some time in the future, the forces of good would defeat the forces of evil. Humans who had died would be resurrected – raised from the dead with their bodies restored. The good god would hold a final judgment, rewarding some in paradise and punishing others in hell. Afterwards all would be purified in fire and ultimately saved. God would create a new world without death in which all would live happily ever after. Many Jews in the Persian period adopted some form of this new conception.

When the Jews came under the dominion of the Greeks, their ideas underwent further developments. In one such development, Sheol came to be identified with Hades, which had become a place of reward and punishment for the soul. Souls would now undergo judgment immediately upon death, separated in different compartments of the underworld. This preliminary judgment did not necessarily rule out a later resurrection and final judgment.

A second idea borrowed from the Greeks was not simply a refinement of earlier ideas but a total reversal. The Hebrew tradition had always thought of the body as necessary for a truly human life. Under the influence of Greek thought, especially the philosophy of Plato, some Jews began to regard the soul as better off without the body. For Plato, the soul, especially the rational aspect, represented the divine element in human nature, whereas the body, composed of the baser elements of the physical world, weighed it down and enslaved it to base passions of human nature. Salvation for the soul, then, consisted of its being released from the body at death and allowed to ascend upward to the heavenly world of divine beings. Jews with this perspective sought not resurrection of the body, but immortality of the soul.

A third Greek influence came from the Epicureans. The philosophers of this school held that both soul and body consisted of atoms. When the atoms broke up at death, neither soul nor body survived.

According to Josephus, each of the major Jewish groups of his day had a different conception of the afterlife. While the Essenes looked for immortality of the soul in a paradise beyond the sea, the Pharisees hoped for bodily resurrection of the righteous dead. The Sadducees expected dissolution of both body and soul.

Early Christianity also divided over the issue of the afterlife. As long as it remained a Jewish sect, it primarily followed the Pharisaic perspective in hoping for resurrection of the dead. Once it became a movement that included Gentiles, however, some Christians, especially those known as "Gnostics," took the Platonic view, denying the resurrection and looking for immortality of the soul.

to judge between the righteous and the sinners. Those who heeded John's warning he baptized (immersed) in the Jordan River. Crowds flocked to him to hear his preaching and to be baptized. Jesus of Nazareth was one of those people. From John, apparently through Jesus, the practice of baptism passed into early Christianity.

Josephus also mentions John (*Antiquities* 18.116–19), but does not portray him as predicting an imminent judgment. According to Josephus, John baptized in order to purify the body, not to cleanse the soul from sins. Some scholars think, however, that John intended his baptism to replace the sacrifices at the temple. If one's sins could be forgiven by baptism, then sacrifices of atonement would become unnecessary.

John's popularity alarmed Herod Antipas, who was at that time the ruler of Galilee and Perea. According to Josephus, Antipas feared that John would incite the people to some form of rebellion. The gospels say that John criticized Antipas for marrying Herodias, the wife of Antipas' brother (Mark 6:17–29). In any case, Antipas had John arrested and beheaded.

John started a movement that continued after his death. The New Testament occasionally mentions the disciples of John (Mark 2:18; Luke 7:18; 11:1; John 3:25; 4:1; Acts 19:1–7). Some of these apparently believed that John was the Messiah (Luke 3:15; Pseudo-Clementine, *Recognitions* 1.60.1–2). The disciples of Jesus, on the other hand, claimed that Jesus, not John, was the Messiah, and that John had only been his forerunner. In some localities the two movements competed for disciples (John 4:1).

Similarities between Essenes and Christians

ESSENES	JEWISH CHRISTIANS
The sharing among them is amazing, and you will not find anyone among them who possesses more than another. For they have a law that those entering the sect must surrender their property to the order, so that neither inferiority of poverty nor superiority of wealth is seen among any of them, but they all, like brothers, have a single fund in which the possessions of each are combined. (Josephus, *Jewish War* 2.122)	All the believers were together and held all things in common. They sold their possessions and belongings and distributed them to all as anyone had need. (Acts 2:44; cf. 4:32–35)
Every word spoken by them is more binding than an oath, while they avoid swearing, considering it worse than perjury. For they say that a person who is not believed without swearing by God is already found guilty. (Josephus, *Jewish War* 2.135)	Above all, my brothers, do not swear, either by heaven or by earth or by any other oath. But let your "yes" be "yes" and your "no" be "no," lest you fall under condemnation. (James 5:12; cf. Matt 5:33–37)

THE JESUS MOVEMENT

Most people today do not think of Christianity as a sect of Judaism, but in the beginning that is precisely how it was regarded by both those inside and those outside. Jesus of Nazareth was a Jew and practiced the Jewish religion his entire life. Likewise his earliest followers were Jews and continued to practice the Jewish religion after his death. They apparently had no intention of starting a new religion. They differed from other Jews primarily in their belief that Jesus was the Jewish Messiah. Many Jews expected some type of Messiah. The early Jewish Christians simply believed they knew who that was.

Eventually this movement did become a new religion distinct from Judaism. This happened after Gentiles began to join the movement and became more numerous than the Jews. A movement that consisted primarily of Gentiles could no longer be considered a sect of Judaism. According to Acts, it was not until Gentiles entered the movement that its members received the name "Christians" (Acts 11:26). Prior to that time it may have been called "the sect of the Nazoreans" (Acts 24:5; cf. 24:14; 28:22). Scholars sometimes use the term "Jesus movement" to refer to those who followed Jesus when the movement was still Jewish, before it became a religion distinct from Judaism.

Controversy Dialogues

Jewish Christians sometimes felt a need to define themselves over against other groups or to defend their practices against criticism from other groups. One form that this self-definition or self-justification took was the **controversy dialogue**. A number of these occur in the gospels (e.g. Mark 2:1–3:6; 7:1–23; 12:13–34). The main characters in these stories are Jesus, his disciples, and representatives of some competing group: usually the Pharisees and scribes, but sometimes the disciples of John or the Sadducees. Many of the stories defend a particular practice and have the same form: (1) Some action is performed by Jesus and/or his disciples; (2) the opposing group criticizes them for this action; (3) Jesus utters a short saying that justifies the practice. Other stories have another form: (1) representatives of some group ask Jesus a question about some issue of Jewish belief or practice; (2) Jesus gives an answer that silences his opponents. Jewish Christians probably used such stories in disputes with other Jewish groups or other Jewish Christians. The answer given by Jesus states the point that the Jesus movement wanted to make in order to defend its practice or express its point of view.

As a new sect of Judaism in the first century, the Jesus movement showed many similarities to other Jewish groups. With the Pharisees they shared a belief in resurrection of the body. Also like the Pharisees they believed that the Law had a central core. A story about the Pharisaic Rabbi Hillel (c. 50 BCE–20 CE) illustrates this point. When Hillel was asked to explain the Law while standing on one foot, he replied, "What you yourself hate, do not do to your neighbors. This is the whole Law, and the rest is commentary." The same basic saying appears also in the "golden rule" of the New Testament: "So whatever you want people to do for you, do the same for them. For this is the Law and the prophets" (Matthew 7:12).

Jewish Christians also shared a number of features with the Qumran community. Both groups believed that they were living in the last days before the new age. Both thought of themselves as the people of the new covenant, the true people of God, the sons of light as opposed to the sons of darkness. Other parallels appear between the early Christians and the Essenes described by Josephus: namely, sharing of goods and avoidance of oaths. At the same time, Jewish Christians differed from such groups over specifically Jewish issues. For example, a saying in the New Testament assumes that a person whose sheep falls into a pit should lift it out, even on the Sabbath (Matt 12:11). While the Pharisees would have agreed, this ruling contrasts with that found in the Qumran community, which prohibited helping an animal out of a pit on the Sabbath (*Damascus Document* 11:13–14). Both the similarities and the differences show that Jewish Christians were concerned with the same issues as other Jewish religious groups of the time.

DISCUSSION QUESTION

Read the following selections. How did the beliefs and practices of the early Jewish Christians agree with or differ from those of other Jewish groups?
1. Controversy dialogues: Mark 2:15–17; 2:23–28; 3:1–5; 12:13–17; 12:18–27; 12:28–34
2. Appendix 2: The Essenes (pp. 546–549)

REVIEW QUESTIONS

1. Describe the distinctive features of the Pharisees, the Sadducees, and the Essenes.
2. Describe the community at Qumran, its literature, beliefs, and practices. Why do most scholars identify the members of the community as Essenes?
3. What distinctive features characterized Jewish revolutionaries, Samaritans, and the movement of John the Baptist?
4. In what ways can the Jesus movement be considered a sect of Judaism?
5. Describe the conceptions of afterlife held by the various branches of Second-Temple Judaism.
6. Describe the form and purpose of the controversy dialogue.

SUGGESTIONS FOR FURTHER STUDY

Varieties of Second-Temple Judaism
Anchor Bible Dictionary (6 vols.; Doubleday, 1992). Includes articles on Pharisees, Sadducees, Essenes, Samaritans, etc.
Neusner, Jacob, and Bruce D. Chilton, eds. *In Quest of the Historical Pharisees* (Baylor University Press, 2007). A collection of essays on the portrayals of Pharisees in first-century accounts, rabbinic sources, and modern theology.

Stemberger, Gunter. *Jewish Contemporaries of Jesus: Pharisees, Sadducees, Essenes* (Fortress, 1995). A survey of what is known concerning the teaching and history of the three main varieties of Second-Temple Judaism.

Dead Sea Scrolls

VanderKam, James C. *The Dead Sea Scrolls Today* (2nd ed.; Eerdmans, 2010). An excellent introduction to the scrolls, including their discovery, contents, background, and significance. Contains further bibliography.

Vermes, Geza. *The Complete Dead Sea Scrolls in English* (7th ed.; Penguin Classics, 2012). The non-biblical scrolls in English translation with an overview of scholarly research, a sketch of the Qumran community, and a bibliography.

The Jesus Movement

Horsley, Richard A. *Sociology and the Jesus* Movement (2nd ed.; Continuum, 1994). Portrays the Jesus movement as a response to the poverty, hunger, and sickness of peasants burdened by the taxes and tribute required by an oppressive ruling class.

Theissen, Gerd. *Sociology of Early Palestinian Christianity* (Fortress, 1978). Portrays the Jesus movement as a band of "wandering charismatics" supported by settled communities of sympathizers, and sees the movement as the "peace party" among Jewish groups.

5   Jewish Hopes for the Future

During the Roman period, some Jews reconciled themselves to living under foreign domination. Others chafed under the yoke of Roman rule and hoped for independence. Different Jews envisioned this hope in different ways. Some advocated armed revolt against the Romans. Others waited for God to end the rule of foreign oppressors and establish his own rule over Israel. Still others looked for the coming of a human liberator, a king or some figure from Israel's past. While some expected life to continue as before, others expected a new age, far superior to the age in which they lived. In this chapter, we will examine some of the traditional Jewish hopes for the future and see how early Christianity adapted those traditions.

ESCHATOLOGY IN THE HEBREW PROPHETS

The Hebrew Bible, especially the prophetic writings, provided the source from which Jews derived hope for the appearance of various figures at the end of the age. These included Yahweh on his Day, the Davidic Messiah, the prophet like Moses, and Elijah the prophet.

The Day of Yahweh

In some forms of Jewish hope, God himself would overthrow the enemies of Israel. The Hebrew prophets spoke of "the day of Yahweh" or "the day of the Lord." Originally this concept referred not to the end of the age, but to a time in history when God would punish a specific enemy of Israel. For example, Isaiah 13 presents the day of Yahweh as a time when Yahweh would destroy the Babylonian Empire. Later prophets saw the day more as an eschatological event. Yahweh would cause the nations to gather against Jerusalem, at which time he would descend from heaven, destroy the nations that oppressed Israel, bring judgment on the wicked (even those who were Israelites), and establish his rule in Jerusalem over the righteous who survived his coming (Joel; Zephaniah; Zechariah 14). Descriptions of the day of the Lord depict it as a day of divine wrath and human anguish; a day of darkness and gloom, when the stars, the sun, and the moon would fail to give their light (Isaiah 13:10; Joel 2:10). Early Christians took over such imagery to describe the day on which Jesus would return from heaven (Mark 13:24–26).

The Davidic Messiah

Other Jews looked for a Messiah. The Hebrew word "Messiah" and its Greek equivalent "Christ" mean "anointed one." Anointing involved pouring olive oil over a person's head to install that person in office. The oil symbolized the Holy Spirit that God was pouring out on such individuals to set them apart as holy or to give them wisdom and power to accomplish their tasks. Certain leading figures in ancient Israel, such as kings and priests, were regularly consecrated by anointing. The Hebrew Scriptures speak of the king as "the Lord's anointed" and the high priest as "the anointed priest."

In the Hebrew Scriptures, when the term "anointed one" referred to kings, it meant the historical kings who ruled over Israel. Later the term came to refer to one ideal king of the future. This application developed in the southern kingdom from the idea that God had promised King David an everlasting dynasty, a line of kings that would always rule (2 Samuel 7:12–16). A problem with this expectation arose when the southern kingdom came to an end. After the Babylonians conquered Jerusalem, no Davidic king ever ruled again. Rather than believe that the idea of an everlasting Davidic dynasty had been a mistake, certain Hebrew prophets picked up this idea and made it the basis of their hope that God would raise up an ideal king from David's line to rule over Israel in the future.

The Prophet like Moses

Both Jews and Samaritans expected the coming of a prophet like Moses. In Hebrew tradition, Moses was the great leader who performed signs and wonders in Egypt, brought the people out of slavery, and received the Law from God on Mount Sinai. According to Deuteronomy 18:15–19, God promised to raise up a prophet like Moses to guide the people. In its historical context, this probably referred to the various prophets who spoke to Israel after Moses. Later interpreters, however, took it to mean that God would send one particular prophet who would perform the same signs as Moses. Certain groups in early Christianity assigned this role to Jesus (e.g. Acts 3:22–24).

The Davidic Messiah in Isaiah 11

Isaiah 11 became a primary expression of the hope that a Davidic king would once again rule. It pictures a branch or shoot that springs up from "the stump of Jesse," David's father (11:1). The line of kings descended from Jesse is here depicted as a "family tree" that has been cut down, leaving only a stump. Though the tree has been cut down, the stump remains; and from that stump springs fresh growth, representing a new king from the line of David. Upon that king rests "the Spirit of Yahweh" (11:2). In other words, he has been anointed and has received the Spirit of God. He is an anointed Davidic king, a Messiah.

This king performs several functions. He serves as a judge, dispensing justice for the poor and oppressed and putting to death the wicked "with the breath of his mouth," i.e. with the judgments that he pronounces (11:3b–5). He brings peace among the animals, perhaps representing different nations (11:6–9). He rules the Gentile nations (11:10). He gathers the Israelites and Jews that have been scattered to other nations and reunites the northern kingdom (Ephraim) with the southern kingdom of Judah (11:11–13). He conquers the surrounding nations so that the kingdom has the same boundaries it did during the time of David (11:14).

This Jewish conception of the Messiah is very different from the Christian conception that developed later. Here the Messiah is not superhuman, does not perform miracles, and does not die for the sins of the world. He is a human king from the line of David, ruling an earthly kingdom of limited extent with its capital in Jerusalem.

Elijah the Prophet

Elijah was a prophet who urged Israel to worship Yahweh alone during a time when they were worshipping other gods (1 Kings 18:17–40). According to the prophet Malachi, God promised to send Elijah once again to prepare the people for his coming:

> Behold, I am sending you Elijah the prophet before the great and terrible day of Yahweh comes. He will restore the hearts of the fathers to the children and the hearts of the children to their fathers, lest when I come I strike the land with extermination. (Malachi 4:5–6)

Later Jewish tradition took up this idea and developed it: Elijah would precede and anoint the Messiah, restore families to purity, settle disputes, perform miracles, and bring about the resurrection of the dead. In early Christianity, some circles identified John the Baptist as Elijah (Matt 11:14; 17:10–13) while others did not (John 1:19–21).

THE APOCALYPTIC TRADITION: DANIEL

Apocalyptic Literature

Subsequent to the Hebrew prophets, "apocalyptic literature" became popular in Judaism. This literature revolved around an "apocalypse," a revelation or unveiling of heavenly secrets. The author of the apocalypse wrote a story in which the main character was some famous figure from Israel's past. This character would tell how he received a revelation in a dream or vision, received a message from God or an angel, or was caught up into the heavenly world. In this way, the author expressed his views about divine matters.

Often the revelation concerned eschatology, what would happen at "the end." Sometimes this involved personal eschatology: what would happen to the soul after death, at the end of the individual's life. At other times it involved cosmic eschatology, what would happen to the world at the end of the age. Cosmic apocalyptic eschatology looked for the end of the present world order and the establishment of a new and better world brought about by divine intervention in the near future. The new world or new age would be established either by God himself or by some messianic representative of God.

This literature became common in the Persian period and afterward when Israel was influenced by the ideas of Zoroastrianism. Some of the apocalypses therefore expect a future resurrection from the dead and a final judgment. The author generally believed that the end of the age would soon arrive.

One Like a Son of Man in Daniel

One of the oldest examples of apocalyptic literature, the book of Daniel, was written in the period of the Maccabees and was among the last books to be accepted into the canon of Jewish scripture. The main character is Daniel, a Jew taken into exile by the Babylonian king Nebuchadnezzar. Part of the book consists of various visions which Daniel either sees or interprets. These visions claim to give a preview of history from the time of the Babylonian exile until the establishment of the kingdom of God.

In the symbolic vision described in Daniel 7, Daniel sees four beasts representing four world empires that have held dominion over Israel. He also sees "one that was ancient of days," representing God. The Ancient of Days takes his place on his throne and passes judgment on these beast-nations, bringing their dominion to an end. Another symbolic figure then appears: "one like a son of man," who comes to God "with the clouds of the sky" (7:13–14). The term "son of man" is a Semitic idiom for "man"; hence the figure is one who appears as a man in the vision. In the interpretation of the vision given later, this figure represents "the saints of the Most High" (7:18, 21–22) or "the people of the saints of the Most High" (7:27), probably meaning the people of Israel. Whereas Israel's oppressors are represented as beasts, Israel is represented as human. This vision expressed the hope that God would take the kingdom and authority away from the beast-like empires and give it to the human-like Israel. Thus in the original meaning of the vision, the one like a son of man probably did not represent the Messiah. However, later Jewish interpreters consistently interpreted this figure as the Messiah. Such a messianic interpretation appears in the Similitudes of Enoch, 4 Ezra, and the New Testament.

MESSIANIC CONCEPTIONS IN THE ROMAN PERIOD

Later Jewish interpreters drew on traditions from the Hebrew prophets and Daniel to create a variety of conceptions concerning the Messiah.

Messiahs at Qumran

The Essenes at Qumran drew on the original meaning of "messiah" as an anointed leader, whether priest or king. The writings of the community express the expectation that two Messiahs would come: "the Messiah of Aaron" (the anointed high priest) and "the Messiah of Israel" (the anointed king or political leader).

Messiah in Psalm of Solomon 17

Another perspective appears in the Psalms of Solomon, a collection of Jewish psalms probably dating from the first century BCE. The seventeenth psalm of this collection draws on traditions concerning the Davidic Messiah, including Isaiah 11. The author looks for a single Messiah, an ideal king ("the Lord's Anointed"). The function of the Messiah here is to drive Gentiles and sinners (those who do not keep the Jewish Law) out of Jerusalem and to reign as a just king. He is pure from sin (i.e. he keeps the Law) but nothing suggests that he is more than human.

Messiah in the Similitudes of Enoch

The Similitudes of Enoch (chapters 37–71 in 1 Enoch) is an apocalyptic work generally dated to the first century CE. The author writes in the name of Enoch, a legendary wise man from the ancient past. His portrait of the Messiah combines various traditions from the Hebrew Bible, including Isaiah 11 and the one like a son of man in Daniel 7:13. In several respects his conception is new. (1) Here for the first time appears the idea of a hidden Messiah. This idea would take various forms, but in the Similitudes God hides the Messiah in heaven before the creation of the world. The Messiah is thus preexistent. (2) In the Similitudes all saved humans are eventually transformed into angels. The Messiah has apparently already undergone this process: he is described as both a man and an angel. (3) In previous tradition, the Davidic Messiah functioned as a just judge, but his judgment was ongoing: he judged cases brought before him in Jerusalem on a day-by-day basis. It was Yahweh who would hold a more comprehensive judgment at the end of the age (e.g. Isaiah 24:21–23). In the Similitudes, however, this function of Yahweh has been transferred to the Messiah. He holds a single comprehensive judgment, a final judgment at the end of the age in which the wicked are punished and the righteous rewarded.

Messiah in 4 Ezra

The Jewish apocalypse of 4 Ezra is generally dated to around 100 CE. The author writes in the name of Ezra, a famous scribe from the period after the Babylonian exile. Several passages in the work depict the Messiah, but these may not all represent the same conception. In one passage (7:26–44)

God reveals the events of the end-time to Ezra. The author combines two traditions that were originally distinct: a messianic kingdom and a final judgment by God. Here the messianic kingdom comes first, lasting 400 years. The role of the Messiah is not specified. He is a mortal human, although he lives for 400 years. After the Messiah dies comes the final judgment. Unlike the Similitudes of Enoch, 4 Ezra has God conduct it, not the Messiah. In another passage (ch. 13), the Messiah is portrayed in terms drawn from Daniel 7:13 and passages depicting Yahweh as a warrior. The Messiah appears as a man who rises from the sea and flies through the air with the clouds. Breathing fire, he destroys the enemies of Jerusalem, and regathers the scattered tribes of Israel.

THE MESSIAH IN EARLY CHRISTIANITY

Jewish Christians drew on traditions about the Davidic Messiah, the one like a son of man, the day of Yahweh, and on other traditions to create their own conceptions of the Messiah or Christ. They regarded Jesus of Nazareth as this Messiah. They referred to him with several messianic titles, including Christ, Lord, Son of Man, and son of God.

Messiah/Christ

Jewish Christians differed from other Jews primarily in their belief that Jesus was the Messiah or Christ. Yet what kind of Messiah was he? The Davidic Messiah was a king from the line of David who would defeat Israel's enemies and reign in Jerusalem over an earthly, political kingdom. Jesus hardly fit this picture, since he had not driven out the Romans but had been crucified by them. The Messiah in the Similitudes of Enoch remained hidden in heaven from before the creation of the world until the final judgment, over which he presided. Jesus did not fit this picture either, since he appeared on earth yet did not conduct the final judgment. Even though Judaism had not a single conception of the Messiah but a variety, Jesus seemed to fit none of them.

As we have seen, the idea of the Messiah was fluid enough to be shaped into a variety of portraits. Jewish Christians adapted the conception to the circumstances of Jesus' life in two primary respects. First, they incorporated the death of Jesus into their conception of the Messiah. Since they believed that Jesus was the Messiah, they regarded his death not as a defeat but as part of a divine plan. They concluded that Jesus died to fulfill various scriptures about an innocent man who suffered (e.g. Psalm 22; Isaiah 53). Though these passages do not identify the sufferer as the Messiah, nor did prior Jews understand them to do so, Jewish Christians took them to refer to the Messiah. In this way they introduced a new, specifically Christian conception of the Messiah: the suffering Messiah. Second, since Jesus in his lifetime did not fulfill the expectations associated with the Messiah, such as driving out the Romans, they looked for him to do so in the future. They concluded that Jesus had been raised from the dead and caught up to heaven, from where he would return to reign as the Messiah (Acts 3:19–21). In this way, they introduced another specifically Christian conception of the Messiah: the returning Messiah.

Lord

Related to the Christian conception of the Messiah is their conception of Jesus as Lord. The New Testament refers to Jesus as "Lord" (*kyrios*) in two primary senses: (1) often the term is simply a title of respect, used in much the same way that English idiom uses "sir"; (2) at other times it has a much more exalted sense, used of someone who has lordship or dominion. In the latter sense, gods, emperors, and kings were called "Lord." The Jewish people used the term to refer to their God, Yahweh.

In early Christianity, the confession "Jesus is Lord" (in the second sense) became a central tenet of faith. Especially important for understanding this development is Psalm 110:1:

> The Lord [Yahweh] said to my Lord [Adonai],
> "Sit at my right hand,
> until I make your enemies a stool for your feet."

In this passage, the Hebrew words "Yahweh" and "Adonai" are both translated in the Septuagint by the Greek word *kyrios* ("lord"). Originally, the passage concerned an oracle spoken by Yahweh to Israel's king. The early Christians interpreted it as a word spoken to Jesus. They believed that God had exalted Jesus to sit at his right hand until his enemies were vanquished, when he would return. Jesus would return, they thought, in their own generation to reign as Messianic king. In the meantime, Jesus ruled in heaven as the exalted Lord (Acts 2:33–36). Because Jesus now shared the name "Lord" with Yahweh, early Christians transferred to him certain functions of Yahweh, such as coming on the day of Yahweh or the day of the Lord.

[handwritten margin note: Hebrew Yahweh LORD]

Son of Man

In the gospels, Jesus frequently calls himself "the Son of Man." This phrase appears elsewhere in the New Testament only in Acts 7:56. The Greek form of the expression represents an earlier Aramaic expression *bar enash* or its Hebrew equivalent *ben adam*, an idiom meaning simply "man" in general or "a man." However, in the gospels, this phrase has become a title for Jesus. This title apparently identifies Jesus as the "one like a son of man" in Daniel 7:13. Like earlier Jewish interpreters, such as the authors of the Similitudes of Enoch and 4 Ezra 13, Jewish Christians interpreted the "one like a son of man" in Daniel 7:13 as the Messiah. From that passage they developed the expression "the Son of Man" as a messianic title referring to Jesus.

In the gospels and Acts 7:56, the designation "the Son of Man" expresses the new Christian conception of the Messiah, as this was applied to Jesus. In Daniel 7:13, the "one like a son of man" went before God to receive an everlasting kingdom. Early Christian interpreters identified Jesus as the "son of man" in this passage. This identification helped to explain why Jesus did not rule as the Messiah during his lifetime: as the Son of Man, he first had to ascend to heaven to receive the kingdom from God. Only then would he return to reign as its king.

Son of God

Like other nations in the ancient world, the ancient Israelites thought of their king as the "son" of their god (2 Samuel 7:14; Psalm 2:7; 89:26–27). This meant not that he was more than human, but that he represented the god on earth. Later Jewish traditions also occasionally referred to the Messiah as God's son, without meaning that he was a divine being (4 Ezra 7:28–29). Early Christians agreed that, as the Messiah, Jesus was the son of God. However, the New Testament presents at least four different conceptions of what the title "son of God" actually means. These different conceptions place the beginning of Jesus' sonship at different times in his career: his resurrection, his baptism, his birth, and his pre-incarnate existence.

1. A letter written by Paul (Rom 1:3–4) and a sermon attributed to him (Acts 13:33) express the view that Jesus became God's son at his resurrection. This idea stems from Psalm 2:7, where God says to Israel's king, "You are my son; this day I have begotten you." Early Christians

identified Jesus as the son and interpreted the phrase "this day" as a reference to the day of his resurrection (Acts 13:33). God thus "begot" Jesus to
a new life as his son by raising him from the dead.

2. In Mark, Jesus is proclaimed "son of God" at his baptism, when he
receives the Holy Spirit (Mark 1:9–11). The coming of the Holy Spirit
identifies Jesus as the Messiah, the one who would receive the Spirit of
God. It is only when Jesus becomes the Messiah that God speaks from
heaven and calls him "my beloved son." This acknowledgment fulfills
God's promise concerning David's heir that "I will be his father and he
will be my son" (2 Sam 7:14). Mark's account, then, leaves the impression that it is the reception of God's Spirit which makes Jesus both the
Messiah and the son of God. The term "Messiah" refers to the reception
of God's Spirit, while "son of God" refers to the relationship established
with God through receiving God's Spirit.

3. Matthew and Luke present the conception of Jesus as a miraculous
act of God not requiring a human father. Because God takes the place
of a human father, Jesus is called "the son of God" from his birth (Luke
1:32, 35).

4. The Gospel of John presents the view that the being who became
flesh as Jesus was already the son of God before coming to earth: God
sent his son into the world (John 3:17; cf. 1 John 4:9). The idea of the
preexistent son of God also appears in the writings of Paul (Gal 4:4; Col
1:13–20; cf. Phil 2:5–7).

EARLY CHRISTIAN ESCHATOLOGY

In Judaism, the idea of the Messiah was an eschatological concept. The
Messiah would appear at the end of the age to usher in a political system
more favorable to the Jews than the one under which they lived. When
early Christians identified Jesus as the Messiah, they were making a
statement not only about who Jesus was, but also about the time in which
they lived. They believed that they were living in the last days before the
coming of a new age. That new age would begin when Jesus returned
from heaven on "the day of the Lord." In the Hebrew Scriptures, the
day of Yahweh or the day of the Lord referred to a time when Yahweh
would come from heaven to punish Israel's enemies. The early Christians
transferred that coming from Yahweh to Jesus (Mark 13:24–26; 1 Thes
5:1–5; 2 Thes 1:5–10; 2:1–12). They looked forward expectantly to Jesus'
coming, which was also called the "**parousia**" ("arrival"). They prayed for

his coming with the Aramaic phrase "maranatha," meaning "Lord, come" (1 Cor 16:22; Didache 10:6).

Several writings or passages in early Christian literature describe the events associated with the coming of Jesus. These include various parables, the eschatological discourse in the Synoptic Gospels (Mark 13; Matt 24–25; Luke 21), parts of 1 and 2 Thessalonians, 1 Corinthians 15, the book of Revelation, and Didache 16. Though these different depictions do not always agree on the exact order and nature of the events of the end-time, they do have certain themes in common. The coming of Jesus would be preceded by various events: the coming of false prophets and false Christs, persecution of Christians, and signs in the heavens. When the day arrived, Jesus would descend from heaven, bring the wrath of God on the wicked, and gather the Christians into the kingdom of God.

The early Christians believed that Jesus would come from heaven very soon, in their own lifetime. The gospels attribute this idea to Jesus himself (Mark 9:1; 13:30). Outside the gospels, we see the idea in Paul, who warns the Romans to stay alert because "the day has drawn near" (Rom 13:11–12). He tells the Philippians that "the Lord is at hand" (Phil 4:5). The author of Hebrews too advises his readers that they can see "the day drawing near" (Heb 10:25). James likewise exhorts his readers to be patient, because "the parousia of the Lord has drawn near" so that "the judge is standing at the doors" (James 5:7–9). John warned that the hour was late (1 John 2:18). The book of Revelation especially emphasized that Jesus was coming soon (Rev 1:1, 3; 22:6–7, 10, 12, 20).

When Jesus did not come within a generation, the early Christians had to revise their thinking. Some acknowledged that Jesus' parousia had been delayed longer than anticipated, but still expected him to come. Matthew and Luke, for example, include traditions with this perspective (Matt 24:48; 25:19; Luke 12:45; 18:7–8; 19:11). Others began to focus on the present rather than the future. The Gospel of John, for example, speaks of "eternal life" as something that one can have now in the present. Still others eventually concluded that Jesus would not return at all. The book of 2 Peter argues against people who held this view (2 Pet 3:1–13).

DISCUSSION QUESTION

Read the following passages concerning Jewish and Jewish-Christian hopes for the future. Explain these different perspectives.

1. Hebrew Bible
   a. Day of Yahweh: Isaiah 13:6–16
   b. Davidic Messiah: Isaiah 11
   c. One like a son of man: Daniel 7
2. Appendix 3: Jewish Messianic Hopes (pp. 550–554)
3. New Testament: Mark 13; Matt 25:31–46

REVIEW QUESTIONS

1. Explain these concepts as they appear in the Hebrew Bible: day of Yahweh, Davidic Messiah, prophet like Moses, the prophet Elijah, and one like a son of man. In what way is each significant for early Christian eschatology?
2. What are the chief features of apocalyptic literature?
3. Describe the various portraits of the Messiah found in the literature of Qumran, Psalm of Solomon 17, Similitudes of Enoch, and 4 Ezra.
4. Explain early Christian conceptions of Jesus as Messiah/Christ, Lord, Son of Man, and son of God.
5. Identify: parousia. Summarize early Christian ideas about the coming of Jesus.

SUGGESTIONS FOR FURTHER STUDY

Primary Sources

Charlesworth, James H., ed. *The Old Testament Pseudepigrapha*, Vol. 1: *Apocalyptic Literature and Testaments* (Doubleday, 1983; reprinted, Hendrickson, 2010). A substantial collection of apocalyptic literature from the centuries immediately before and after the rise of Christianity. English translations with introductions.

Reddish, Mitchell G., ed. *Apocalyptic Literature: A Reader* (Hendrickson, 1995; reprinted, 2015). A collection of early Jewish and Christian apocalyptic literature in English translation.

Eschatology and Messianic Traditions

Bockmuehl, Markus, and James Carleton Paget. *Redemption and Resistance: The Messianic Hopes of Jews and Christians in Antiquity* (T&T Clark, 2007). A collection of essays on Messianic hopes in Judaism and Christianity from the Persian period to the rise of Islam.

Burkett, Delbert. *The Son of Man Debate: A History and Evaluation* (Cambridge University Press, 1999). Surveys scholarly interpretations of the expression "Son of Man" in the gospels from early Christianity to the end of the twentieth century.

Juel, Donald. *Messianic Exegesis: Christological Interpretation of the Old Testament in Early Christianity* (Fortress, 1988; reprinted, Baylor University Press, 2017). Describes how the early Christian understanding of Jesus as Messiah developed through interpretation of the Hebrew Scriptures.

Apocalyptic Thought and Literature

Collins, John. J. *The Apocalyptic Imagination: An Introduction to the Jewish Matrix of Christianity* (2nd ed.; Eerdmans, 1998). An introduction to apocalyptic thought and the apocalypses most relevant for the origins of Christianity.

Collins, John J., ed. *The Encyclopedia of Apocalypticism*, Vol. 1: *The Origins of Apocalypticism in Judaism and Christianity* (Continuum, 1998). Chapters by various scholars on aspects of apocalypticism in early Judaism and Christianity.

6 Hellenistic Religion, Philosophy, and World-View

Christianity arose at the juncture of two primary cultures: Jewish and Hellenistic. We have seen how Judaism provided the soil out of which Christianity grew. Now we must consider the Hellenistic world-view that shaped that growth.

TRADITIONAL GREEK AND ROMAN RELIGION

Orthodox Jews worshipped only one God. By contrast, the traditional religions of Greece and Rome involved the worship of many gods, a practice known as **polytheism**. They associated various deities (gods and goddesses) with the home, the world of nature, and particular locations.

Some deities were gods of the home. The Greek home centered around the hearth (*hestia*), an area of floor in front of the fireplace. A goddess of the same name (Hestia, Latin Vestia) presided over it. Before meals, the family would place food on the hearth as an offering to Hestia and pour wine on the floor as an offering to the guardian of the house. In Roman religion too, household gods were thought to protect the family. The male head of the household functioned as family priest in performing the appropriate rituals to the gods.

Other deities dwelt in the world of nature. The chief Greek gods dwelt on Mount Olympus. Like other ancient peoples, the Greeks located the gods on a particular mountain, since the top of the mountain reached into the sky where the gods were thought to dwell. Other deities dwelt on the earth, in the sea, and in the underworld. Still others were associated with a particular location, city, or nation.

Worshippers sought the gods in temples and sacred groves, where the deity was often represented by a statue or other symbol, such as a unique rock. Worshippers brought them gifts and offered animal sacrifices burnt on altars. Later the practice of sacrifice declined, and worship consisted of prayer, hymns, burning of incense, and offering of lamps.

Greek poets such as Homer and Hesiod recounted stories or "myths" about the gods, their origins, and their exploits. In the myths, the deities appear simply as superior humans with human characters and weaknesses. Stories are told of the gods' amorous encounters, thievery, and childishness. Such portrayals led certain Greek philosophers to criticize the poets' representations of the gods.

Both in Greece and Rome, the state supported the worship of the gods. If the gods were not honored, it was believed, calamity might fall on the community. Honoring the gods ensured the well-being of the state. Because Christians did not worship the state gods, the non-Christians accused them of "atheism" and blamed them for catastrophes that occurred in the empire.

The Hellenistic age was characterized by **syncretism**, the merging of features from different religions. Deities originally associated with a particular location or nation became more universal when they were identified with similar deities of other locations or nations. Early on, the Romans identified their deities with the deities of the Greeks. During the Hellenistic age, such identifications increased as the Greeks took their gods east and Oriental deities came west. As a result, Greek deities took on Oriental characteristics that they had not possessed before, and vice versa.

Roman equivalents of Greek gods

GREEK NAME	ROMAN NAME	FUNCTION
Zeus	Jupiter	storm god, father of the gods
Hera	Juno	mother goddess
Apollo	Apollo	sun god
Ares	Mars	god of war
Hermes	Mercury	messenger god
Artemis	Diana	goddess of hunting
Aphrodite	Venus	goddess of love
Athena	Minerva	goddess of wisdom

MYSTERY CULTS

Worship of a particular deity centered on the cult of that deity, a system of worship that included myth, ritual, and symbol. The cultic myth told

Figure 6.1
Bronze statue of
Zeus, king of the
Greek gods (fifth
century BCE).
As a storm god,
Zeus prepares to
cast a lightning
bolt (which has
not survived).
National
Archaeological
Museum, Athens,
Greece (Foto
Marburg/Art
Resource, NY).

the story of the deity. Through ritual, the worshipper participated in the life of the deity. Sacred objects symbolized the central characteristics of the deity or the cult.

Some cults were entered through an initiation ceremony that involved "mysteries" or secrets to be kept from the uninitiated. Since the secrets were well kept, we know little about them today. Such cults had the goal of bettering the worshipper in the present life as well as the afterlife. In the Hellenistic age, the native Greek cults were joined by Oriental cults.

Several popular cults centered around mother goddesses, symbols of the earth and fertility. These included the Greek goddess Demeter (goddess of the grain), whose mysteries were celebrated at Eleusis near Athens; the Phrygian mother goddess Cybele; and the Egyptian goddess

Figure 6.2
Statue of Isis, an
Egyptian goddess
whose worship
spread throughout
the Roman
Empire. Museo
Archeologico
Nazionale, Naples,
Italy (Alinari/Art
Resource, NY).

Isis. The mysteries of Demeter involved a joyful procession from Athens
to Eleusis, where the initiates entered the sacred precincts of Demeter for
a night of initiation. It was the common belief in Athens that those who
were initiated would have a glorious afterlife in the underworld abode of
Hades, while all others would have a miserable existence there. The mysteries of Isis were thought to have the same results.

Figure 6.3
Roman fresco from
Pompeii, depicting
a worshipper
offering sacrifice
on an altar before
a statue of the god
Dionysus. Museo
Archeologico
Nazionale, Naples,
Italy (Scala/Art
Resource, NY).

Another mystery cult centered around Dionysus, also known as Bacchus, who was god of fertility and vegetation, especially the grape-vine. As the essence of life, he was associated with blood, symbolized by wine, and bore the title "the Abundance of Life." His worshippers celebrated both a midwinter festival, which may have involved eating a sacred meal, and a spring festival, celebrated with the drinking of wine. Originally only women took part in his cult, though men were later allowed to participate.

Certain Christian rituals show similarities to those of the mystery cults. The initiation ceremonies of the mysteries generally included a ritual purification by washing in water, just as Christianity had an initiation ceremony (baptism) that involved immersion in water. Also like the mysteries, Christian ritual included a sacred meal shared by the worshippers.

ORACULAR CULTS

Early Christianity, like the larger Greco-Roman world, believed in prophecy, the idea that God or the gods could speak directly through some "inspired" individual. Such an individual was called a prophet or oracle. The term "oracle" also referred to the revelation uttered by the individual or the place where the utterance was given.

The primary oracles were sanctuaries of Apollo, especially the one at Delphi. To these sanctuaries came political leaders requesting guidance for cities and states, worshippers inquiring about the proper procedures for religious rituals, and individuals seeking guidance for personal concerns. The replies often had an enigmatic or ambiguous character.

Another type of oracle featured the Sibyls, prophetic women in various places, generally accepted as ten in number. The Sibyls uttered prophecies without being requested, usually predictions of doom. In the Hellenistic period, Sibylline oracles referred to books of prophecies published in the name of one of the ancient Sibyls. The prophecies generally predicted a turn for the worse in human affairs. Jews and Christians adopted this literary genre to disseminate some of their own views.

ANCIENT COSMOLOGY

In the classical conception of the world (*cosmos* in Greek), the universe consisted of three levels: the sky, the earth, and the underworld. The main gods and goddesses lived in the sky above, responsible for such natural phenomena as wind and rain. The earth was a flat disk floating on water. The underworld could be entered through a cave in the ground. Like the sky, the earth and underworld were filled with divine powers or spirits.

At the beginning of the Hellenistic age, a new cosmology replaced the classical conception. Later this cosmology received its name from Ptolemy (100–78 CE), who systematized it. In the Ptolemaic cosmology, the earth was a sphere at the center of the universe. Surrounding it at a distance were seven concentric spheres, in which orbited the moon (closest to the earth), Mercury, Venus, the sun, Mars, Jupiter, and Saturn. The eighth and outermost sphere held the stars. Except for the earth, these spheres rotated at different speeds, accounting for the apparent motion of the heavenly bodies around the earth. These heavenly bodies were conceived as living beings, gods of fire. In the sublunar realm between the moon and the earth dwelt elemental spirits and demons who exercised control over the earth.

FORTUNE, FATE, ASTROLOGY, AND MAGIC

The belief that divine powers influenced human life came to expression in popular thought concerning Fortune, Fate, astrology, and magic.

The events that overtook human beings often appeared arbitrary and capricious. The Greeks and Romans personified and worshipped such chance or luck, both good and bad, as the goddess **Fortune**. Fortune was both praised and blamed for what happened.

From another perspective, events were not arbitrary but strictly determined by **Fate**. As originally conceived, Fate was the principle of order immanent in the universe. It was described as a principle of cause and effect that determined every event in the cosmos inevitably. Even the gods were subject to it. Fate could be perceived as a welcome escape from the caprices of Fortune; it might also be perceived as itself oppressive.

The notion of Fate agreed with the perspective of **astrology**. Imported into the West from Babylon, astrology saw the heavenly bodies as deities that controlled the course of earthly events. It presumed an inner harmony between all parts of the cosmos, so that the order of the heavenly spheres could serve as a guide to events in the sublunar realm. From the regular order of the stars, astrologers sought to discern the future. They cast horoscopes to determine the course of action that would best accord with the motions of the stars.

Like astrology, **magic** presumed an inner connection between all things in the cosmos. By a spell or ritual action in one part of the cosmos, the practitioner of magic sought to produce a similar effect in another part. While astrology and Fate subjected human life to the control of higher powers, magic did the reverse. The magician sought to control the powers of the universe, which might be personified as demons, to make them serve human interests. By incantations naming the powers of the universe, one tried to manipulate them in order to gain love, protection, revenge, power, or health. Some of the Jewish and Greek opponents of

Christianity did not deny that Jesus and his followers performed healings and exorcisms, but they attributed them to demonic powers controlled by magic.

HUMANS AS DIVINE

People in the Greco-Roman world did not make as sharp a distinction between gods and humans as we might imagine. On the one hand, the gods, though immortal and possessed of superior powers, had human forms and human emotions. On the other hand, human beings with superior abilities were often considered divine. People frequently regarded emperors, great philosophers, and superior athletes or poets as gods or sons of gods.

Types of Divine Humans

These divine humans consisted of three types.

One type was the **avatar or incarnation**. Ancient peoples believed that an immortal, heavenly god might temporarily come to earth in human form. For example, the poet Horace wondered whether the highly acclaimed emperor Augustus might be a god in human form – perhaps Apollo or Venus or Mars or Mercury. Similar ideas appear in Hinduism and Christianity. Hinduism uses the term "avatar" to refer to the earthly manifestation (not always human) of an eternal god. Traditional Christianity has used the term "incarnation" ("becoming flesh") to express the idea that God became flesh in the person of Jesus.

A second type was the **demigod**. Ancient peoples also believed that divine beings could mate with human beings and produce offspring. These offspring would be "demigods" (half-gods) or "heroes." Such individuals were thought to be endowed with remarkable attributes, such as extraordinary strength, athletic ability, or wisdom. In Greco-Roman legend, Heracles (Hercules) was the son of Zeus and a human mother, while Aeneas was the son of Venus and a human father. Occasionally we encounter a female demigod: Helen of Troy inherited exceptional beauty as the daughter of Zeus. Such divine–human parentage was also attributed to historical figures, such as Plato and Alexander the Great. Ancient Judaism shared this belief in demigods.

Figure 6.4
The infant Heracles, demigod son of Zeus and the mortal Alkmene, strangles snakes sent against him by Zeus' jealous wife Hera. Painting by Pompeo Batoni (1708–87). Galleria d'Arte Moderna (Scala/Art Resource, NY).

Genesis 6:1–4 preserves a Jewish story about an occasion when "the sons of God" (angels) mated with "the daughters of men" and had superior offspring: "These were the mighty men that were of old, the men of renown" (Gen 6:4). Later Jewish writings retold this story with added details (e.g. 1 Enoch 6–16).

A third type of divine human was the **deified human**. Mortal humans through "apotheosis" (deification) might be caught up into the sky not only to live with the gods, but to become immortal gods themselves. An emperor might be considered divine during his life and then be officially enrolled among the gods at his death. A legendary figure like Heracles might be considered divine both through his birth as a demigod and through his ascent to heaven at death. Even a historical person who was not considered divine during his lifetime might be enrolled among the gods at death. Such was the case with Antinous, a slave of the emperor Hadrian.

The Cult of the Emperor

In both the Hellenistic kingdoms and the Roman Empire, the ruler often received worship as a god. Worshippers erected altars and temples to the deified ruler, just as to the traditional gods. According to official Roman policy, only emperors deified by the Senate after their death received a place among the gods of the state. In actual practice, however, worshippers frequently honored the emperor as divine while he lived. The emperors Caligula and Domitian demanded such worship, Domitian asking to be called "Lord and God." The emperor cult became a source of conflict between the Roman government and Christians. The government saw the practice as a profession of loyalty to the state, while Christians felt it violated their exclusive loyalty to Jesus.

GRECO-ROMAN PHILOSOPHIES

Ancient Greece provided the soil from which grew the discipline of philosophy ("love of wisdom"). Roman philosophers drew many of their own ideas from the Greeks. The philosophers considered basic questions of human existence in the world: what is the nature of the universe, how did it originate, what is the place of humanity in the world, and what manner of life is appropriate for human beings? Several important philosophical schools thrived in the Hellenistic period.

Platonism

Plato (427–347 BCE), a student of Socrates, established an important school of philosophy at a sacred grove outside of Athens called the Academy. Though Platonism was not the chief school of Hellenistic times, it continued to have an important influence. Some of Plato's ideas include the following.

Central to Plato's philosophy is a distinction between **being and becoming**. He distinguished between the physical world of becoming and a superior invisible world of being. The physical world is a place of constant change: as people and things grow old and decay, they are in a state of continually becoming other than they were. In contrast, the superior world is eternal and unchanging; it exists in a state of being. While the world of becoming is perceived by the senses, the world of being is perceived only by the rational mind.

To the realm of being belong the **forms**, patterns of particular objects or concepts. For example, the form of a chair would be the idea behind a chair, the essential qualities that any chair would have to have to be a chair. For Plato there are forms of things as well as forms of qualities such as goodness, truth, and beauty.

Plato's philosophy did not dispense with **gods**. He speaks of a god, the Demiurge ("craftsman"), who created the physical world or cosmos. Looking to the eternal forms as a pattern, the Demiurge fashioned the cosmos out of preexistent elements. He made the cosmos a sphere and placed a soul within it. This world-soul makes the cosmos itself a living rational being, a god. The stars are also fiery gods, who helped the Demiurge create human beings.

Related to the gods is the **human soul**. In Plato's thought, the Demiurge created the eternal part of the human soul out of the same substance as the world-soul. Human souls are thus divine and existed before the world was created. They dwelt among the stars before they were joined to human bodies, and they continue to exist after the death of the body. The body has a negative effect on the soul, making it forget its former existence and enslaving it to bodily passions.

The **goal of life** is for the soul to resist the downward pull of the body and live in harmony with the world-soul. If it succeeds, it will return to the stars and live a life of celestial bliss. If not, it will be reincarnated as some lower form of life.

Plato's idea about the conflict between soul and body, or spirit and flesh, greatly influenced Judaism and Christianity. This and his ideas about the Demiurge, the preexistence of the soul, and the return of the soul to heaven influenced a branch of early Christianity known as "Gnostic" Christianity.

The Stoics

Zeno of Citium in Cyprus (c. 336–263 BCE) established a school of philosophy at Athens in the Painted Porch ("Stoa"), from which his followers

Figure 6.5
Roman fresco
depicting a
philosopher leaning
on a walking
stick. Museo
Archeologico
Nazionale, Naples,
Italy (Scala/Art
Resource, NY).

received the name "Stoics." Stoicism was the dominant philosophy in
the Hellenistic period. Important aspects of Stoic philosophy include the
following.

For the Stoics, God was not outside the world but was the same as the
world. This view, that God is everything, is called **pantheism**. In Stoic
thought, God existed originally as an eternal fire in a void. God then
transformed himself into a cosmos, an ordered world. In the resultant
cosmos are two principles, the active principle (logos or reason) and the
passive principle (matter). The active principle, reason, is immanent in
matter like soul in a body. Hence, as in Plato's thought, the cosmos is a
living being with a soul.

Stoics had different names for the active principle that animated the cosmos, including world-soul, god, and nature. Especially important for later thought was the term "**Logos**," meaning "word" or "reason." In the New Testament, the Fourth Gospel calls Jesus "the Logos" who existed "in the beginning."

The Stoics believed in **determinism**. All things that happen are determined by the world-soul, which directs all things for the best result. Nothing that happens, therefore, is really evil if viewed from the perspective of the whole cosmos.

Stoics had a **cyclical view of history**. After a certain length of time the world would return to its original fiery state in a great conflagration that would consume all things. After another length of time, the fiery God would again transform itself into a cosmos exactly like the one destroyed and history would repeat itself exactly. This cycle of cosmic birth and fiery destruction would continue forever.

As in Plato's thought, the human soul is part of the world-soul or Logos. The **goal of life** therefore is to live in agreement with the Logos, that is, according to reason or nature. For the Stoics, this involved ridding oneself of all passions of the soul, such as desire, fear, regret, and even compassion in order to reach a state of imperturbability.

The Epicureans

Epicurus (342–270 BCE) taught in a garden that he purchased in Athens. Important aspects of Epicurean philosophy include the following.

Epicurus believed that **the gods** existed, but that they played no role in human affairs. It was therefore useless to worship them or pray for their intervention. Both Christians and pagans frequently stigmatized Epicureans as "atheists."

Epicurus followed the Greek philosopher Democritus (born c. 460 BCE) in maintaining that all things are composed of **atoms**. Since both the body and the soul are combinations of atoms, no human personality survives death, when the atoms separate. As we have seen, the Sadducees adopted this view.

Since there is no existence beyond death, the purpose of existence must be sought in this life. The **goal of life** should be "pleasure." By "pleasure" is meant not sensual indulgence, but happiness or the avoidance of pain. The happiest life can be achieved by withdrawing from society and living with others of like mind. Friendship therefore became an ideal for Epicureans.

The Cynics

The Cynics were a movement of wandering preachers who rejected the conventions of society. This movement began with Diogenes of Sinope (fourth century BCE), who was called "the dog" (*kyon*) because of his shameless behavior, such as masturbating in public.

Cynics presented a distinctive appearance, wearing a rough cloak, letting their hair grow long and uncombed, carrying a staff and knapsack. They preached to people in the marketplace or wherever else they could find an audience.

Cynics extolled the simple life, claiming that the way to happiness lay in learning to have few desires. They abandoned their possessions, making their living by begging. They slept on the ground with only their cloak for cover. By dispensing with the amenities of life, they believed that they attained freedom or self-sufficiency.

By provocative words and actions, Cynics sought to shock people into recognizing the folly of social conventions and accepted values, such as wealth and fame. In their preaching they told anecdotes, usually about Diogenes, just as early Christians told stories about Jesus. They also developed a style of argument called the diatribe, which involves arguing with an imaginary opponent. In the New Testament, the apostle Paul sometimes uses this technique.

Some modern scholars have seen a resemblance between Cynics and early Christian missionaries. Others have portrayed Jesus himself as a type of Cynic.

MIRACLE STORIES IN THE ANCIENT WORLD

Early Christians believed that Jesus and those who followed him could heal diseases, cast out demons, and perform other signs and wonders. The New Testament generally refers to such deeds as *dynameis* ("mighty deeds" or "deeds of power"). Today we normally refer to them as "miracles" ("marvelous events"), by which we mean extraordinary events that are attributed to the intervention of a divine being or supernatural power. In the ancient world we find different types of miracle stories and different types of miracle workers, not only among Christians, but in the Jewish and Greco-Roman traditions as well.

Types of Miracle Stories

The same types of miracle stories occur in Jewish, Greco-Roman, and Christian tradition. These include **exorcisms**, in which the exorcist casts a demon out of someone; **healings**, in which the healer cures a sick or diseased person; **resuscitations**, in which someone is brought back to life; **nature miracles**, which show the miracle worker's power over nature; and **miracles of knowledge**, in which the miracle worker shows knowledge that could not be obtained by normal channels.

Types of Miracle Workers

The ancient world attributed such miracles to various types of miracle workers, especially deities and their representatives.

In Jewish, Greco-Roman, and Christian tradition, the power for miracles generally came from **a god or goddess**, who sometimes intervened directly. In the Greco-Roman world, Isis and Asclepius were particularly known for their healing powers.

Early Jewish tradition attributed miracles to certain famous **prophets and holy men**. The prophets included Moses, Elijah, and Elisha, whose deeds are recounted in the Hebrew Bible. Later Jewish tradition recounted the miracles of certain holy men who were thought to have a close relationship with God, primarily Hanina ben Dosa and Honi the Circle-Drawer.

The Greco-Roman tradition sometimes associated miracles with **divine humans**, such as the philosopher Pythagoras, the Roman emperor Vespasian, and the religious teacher Apollonius of Tyana.

In popular opinion, especially among the Jews, demonic spirits sometimes possessed people, causing certain types of physical and psychological symptoms. Certain individuals made their living as **professional exorcists** by casting out such spirits.

Miracles could also be performed by **professional magicians**. In general, the magician sought to coerce a supernatural being into serving the magician. Magicians in the Greco-Roman world used certain techniques, such as special words, rituals, and potions, to bring about the desired results for their customers.

In the Christian tradition, **Christian charismatics** performed miracles. Not only Jesus but also many of his followers, such as Paul the apostle and Philip the evangelist, were credited with miracles. Christians generally identified the source of their power as the Holy Spirit, the "breath" or power of Yahweh.

Do Miracles Happen?

Did Elijah actually raise the dead? Did Jesus really walk on water? Did Pythagoras in fact teleport from one place to another? Such questions become unavoidable when we consider the number of miraculous deeds attributed to ancient heroes. Three primary explanations have been invoked to explain such miracle stories.

The **supernatural explanation** takes miracle stories at face value as factual accounts of divine intervention. Most people in the Greco-Roman world had this perspective. Yet among the educated classes we do find skeptics, such as Cicero and Lucian of Samosata. In Western Europe, the supernatural explanation of Christian miracle stories prevailed until the eighteenth-century Enlightenment, when developments in science, philosophy, and historical criticism called it into question.

The **rationalist explanation** finds the origin of miracle stories in some non-miraculous event that has been embellished or interpreted supernaturally. For example, one of the nature miracles in the gospels tells how Jesus fed a crowd of 5,000 people with only a few loaves of bread. From the rationalist perspective, Jesus actually did feed 5,000 people, but in a non-miraculous way. According to one rationalist explanation, when Jesus told his disciples to start sharing the little food that they had, others in the crowd who had brought food began to do the same until everyone was fed. From this point of view, Jesus and others actually did perform healings and exorcisms, but without miraculous results. In some cases, people with psychosomatic illnesses got better because they believed they were healed.

The **mythological explanation** regards miracle stories not as accounts of actual events, but as fictional stories invented by the faith of those who admired the alleged miracle worker. People who admired Elijah or Pythagoras or Jesus attributed miracles to them to glorify them, to confirm their authority, or to serve a need in the community. For example, one of the nature miracles in the gospels tells how Jesus calmed a storm that threatened to sink the boat carrying him and his disciples. A mythological explanation would find the origin of this story in the situation of the early church. They found themselves in a "storm" of persecution that threatened to overwhelm them. Someone in the community created the story about Jesus calming the storm in order to give them hope that Jesus would save them from their present circumstances.

DISCUSSION QUESTIONS

1. *Divine humans and their births.* Read Appendix 4 (pp. 555–561), which contains Greco-Roman stories about the births of divine humans. Compare and contrast these stories with New Testament stories about the birth of Jesus (Matthew 1:18–2:18; Luke 1:26–38; 2:1–7, 41–52) and about the incarnation of Jesus (John 1:1–5, 14–18).

2. *Apotheoses.* Read Appendix 5 (pp. 562–564) on Greco-Roman stories of apotheosis. Compare these with Luke's story about Jesus' ascension (Acts 1:9–11).

3. *Miracle stories.* Read Appendix 6 (pp. 565–574) on miracle stories in the ancient world. Compare and contrast the miracle stories in the Jewish, Greco-Roman, and early Christian traditions. What purposes would these stories have served? What approach should historians take toward miracle stories?

REVIEW QUESTIONS

1. Briefly describe the chief features of traditional Greek and Roman religion. Identify or define: polytheism.

2. Identify the major mystery cults and oracular cults and their chief concerns.

3. Distinguish Ptolemaic cosmology from classical cosmology.

4. Describe the three types of Hellenistic divine humans.

5. Compare and contrast the views of Plato, the Stoics, and the Epicureans concerning the gods, the world, the human soul, and the goal of life.

6. Identify the main types of miracle stories and the main types of miracle workers in the ancient world. What are the three main explanations of miracle stories?

SUGGESTIONS FOR FURTHER STUDY

Primary Sources

Beard, Mary, John North, and Simon Price. *Religions of Rome*, Vol. 2: *A Sourcebook* (Cambridge University Press, 1998). A collection of primary sources illustrating religious life in the Roman world.

Cotter, Wendy. *Miracles in Greco-Roman Antiquity: A Sourcebook for the Study of New Testament Miracle Stories* (Routledge, 1999). Selection of miracle stories from Jewish and Greco-Roman sources and the New Testament.

Hellenistic Religion and Philosophy

Klauck, Hans Joseph. *The Religious Context of Early Christianity: A Guide to Graeco-Roman Religions* (Fortress, 2003). Surveys domestic and civic religion, popular belief, mystery cults, ruler and emperor cults, the religious dimensions of philosophy, and Gnosticism.

Kraemer, Ross Shepard. *Her Share of the Blessings: Women's Religions among Pagans, Jews, and Christians in the Greco-Roman World* (Oxford University Press, 1992). Surveys the religious life of women in Greco-Roman paganism, Judaism, and Christianity.

Long, A. A. *Hellenistic Philosophy: Stoics, Epicureans, Sceptics* (2nd ed.; University of California Press, 1986). Traces the main developments in Greek philosophy from the death of Alexander the Great to the end of the Roman Republic.

Miller, Robert J. *Born Divine: The Births of Jesus and Other Sons of God* (Polebridge, 2003). Discusses the narratives of Jesus' birth in the context of Jewish legends, Hellenistic birth stories of divine humans, and later Christian infancy gospels.

Rives, James B. *Religion in the Roman Empire* (Blackwell, 2007). An overview of religion in the Roman Empire, primarily from Augustus to Constantine.

Miracle Stories in the Ancient World

Labahn, Michael, and Bert Jan Lietaert Peerbolte, eds. *Wonders Never Cease: The Purpose of Narrating Miracle Stories in the New Testament and Its Religious Environment* (Bloomsbury T&T Clark, 2006). A collection of essays that discuss why miracle stories were told in different religious, political, and historical circumstances.

7   An Overview of Early Christian History

To study early Christian writings historically, we need to set them within three distinct contexts: first-century Judaism, the Greco-Roman world, and early Christianity. Previous chapters have focused on the first two of these contexts. Here we focus on the third, giving an overview of early Christianity from its beginning in about 30 CE to the rise of the state church under the Roman emperor Constantine in 313 CE.

JOHN THE BAPTIST AND JESUS

Christianity had its roots in the movement begun by John the Baptist. Around the year 29 CE John began to preach, urging the Jewish people to repent of their sins and "flee from the wrath to come" (Luke 3:7). Those who received his message were baptized in the Jordan River. John began to attract followers, and because of his influence with the people, Herod Antipas, the ruler of Galilee and Perea, had him killed.

One of the people whom John baptized was a man named Jesus. The New Testament calls him "Jesus the Nazarene" or "Jesus the Nazorean." The former expression probably indicates that he came from the village of Nazareth in Galilee. Whether the latter expression means the same thing or not is uncertain.

After being baptized by John, Jesus branched out on his own. He began to preach in Galilee and to attract his own followers. What Jesus preached and what he thought of himself are questions that scholars still debate. The problem is that the New Testament was written decades after Jesus lived, by various people who had differing views of him. He is variously depicted as a preacher like John, a prophet, a rabbi, a miracle worker, a suffering servant, a Messiah, and even as God. Cutting through these differing portrayals to find the real man, the "historical Jesus," is a task that still occupies New Testament scholars. We will return to this question in Chapter 16.

What we can say for sure about Jesus is that he met a fate similar to that of John the Baptist. When he went to Jerusalem for the Jewish Passover celebration, he was arrested and crucified by the Roman governor Pontius Pilate. Pilate apparently thought that Jesus' popularity posed a threat to the peace imposed by Roman rule.

JUDAIC CHRISTIANITY (C. 30–70 CE)

After Jesus' death, some of his followers claimed that God had raised him from the dead, that he had ascended to heaven, and that he would soon return to reign as Messiah. Since these earliest disciples of Jesus were Jews, we could call them **Jewish Christians**. We will use the term "Jewish Christian" in a broad sense to refer to any Jew who believed in Jesus as some sort of savior figure.

Jewish Christianity came in a variety of flavors. Not all had the same attitude toward their Jewish heritage. For example, the apostle Paul was a Jewish Christian who rejected the Jewish Law as the way to God. Some Jewish Christians agreed with Paul, others took a Gnostic perspective, and still others continued to practice Judaism as the way to God. If we think of these Jewish Christians as strawberry, chocolate, and vanilla, still others may have been Neapolitan.

Here we will focus on one particular type of Jewish Christians: those who continued to practice the Jewish Law as the path to life with God. Unfortunately, scholars have not come up with a generally accepted name for these people. Some call them "Judaizers" when they appear in Paul's letters and Acts, but that term has a somewhat negative connotation, since it came out of Paul's polemic against them. We will use the more neutral term **Judaic Christians**, meaning Jews who acknowledged Jesus as the Messiah but continued to practice the religion of Judaism as the way to God.

These Judaic Christians continued to follow the Jewish Law, circumcising their male children, observing the Jewish dietary restrictions, keeping the Sabbath, and offering sacrifices at the temple. They differed from other Jews primarily in the fact that they regarded Jesus as the Jewish Messiah. At first they continued to worship in the Jewish synagogues. When other Jews began to oppose the new movement, they withdrew to form their own synagogues or congregations in private homes. Jews

Figure 7.1
Scale model of Jerusalem in the time of Jesus, with the temple mount at the top right. Judaic Christianity had its center here after the death of Jesus. Holy Land Hotel, Jerusalem (Erich Lessing/Art Resource, NY).

outside this movement called it the sect of "the Nazoreans" (Acts 24:5). The members of the movement referred to themselves as "disciples" ("students") of Jesus. They may also have called themselves the "congregation" or "church."

Our knowledge of this early Judaic Christianity comes primarily from the gospels, the book of Acts, the letter of James, the Didache, and some scattered references in the letters of Paul. Our information is very incomplete. Only Acts describes the rise of the movement, and its information must be used with caution. The early chapters of Acts focus on Judaic

Christianity in Jerusalem, though it must also have existed elsewhere, especially in Palestine.

Leading Figures

Some of the leading figures among the Judaic Christians in Jerusalem included the twelve apostles, the members of Jesus' family, and the "pillars."

Paul says that Jesus first appeared to Peter, who was one of **the twelve**, and then to the twelve (1 Cor 15:5). Elsewhere these twelve are called "apostles," a term meaning "emissaries" or "missionaries," i.e. those who are sent. According to traditions in the gospels, the twelve followed Jesus during his lifetime and assisted him in his preaching and healing activities. The book of Acts says they were witnesses to the resurrection of Jesus (Acts 1:22). The number twelve corresponds to the traditional number of tribes in ancient Israel, most of which had disappeared centuries before Jesus. The early Judaic church saw itself as a new Israel and believed that the twelve tribes would be restored. In the new age that they expected to arrive soon, they believed that the twelve apostles would rule the twelve tribes of Israel (Matt 19:28).

Paul also says that Jesus later appeared to James and the rest of the apostles (1 Cor 15:7). Apparently, then, there were other apostles besides the twelve, one of whom was James. This James was a brother of Jesus (Gal 1:19). In the later chapters of Acts, he appears as the head of the Jerusalem church (Acts 12:17; 15:13; 21:18). Other **members of Jesus' family** also played a leading role in the Jerusalem community. Acts 1:14 mentions Mary, the mother of Jesus, as well as the brothers of Jesus.

Three apostles occupied a place of pre-eminence in the Jerusalem community. In the earliest period, these three were apparently Simon (also known as Cephas or Peter) and the two sons of Zebedee, James and John. Several stories in the gospels depict these three as an inner circle who stood closest to Jesus (Mark 9:2; 14:33; cf. 10:35–37). One of these, James the son of Zebedee, was executed as a Christian between 41 and 44 CE, when Herod Agrippa I, a grandson of Herod the Great, was king of part of Palestine (Acts 12:1–2). It may have been at this time that the position of James the son of Zebedee was taken by James the brother of Jesus. When Paul visited the Jerusalem church about 49 CE, he found three apostles who were considered the "**pillars**" of the community: James the brother of Jesus, Cephas (the Aramaic word for "Peter"), and John the son of Zebedee (Gal 2:9). Some scholars have seen in this trio, in connection with the twelve, a resemblance to the structure of leadership at Qumran. There the council of the community consisted of twelve men and three priests (Manual of Discipline 8:1).

The Mission to Jews

Itinerant Judaic-Christian missionaries went from place to place, establishing churches throughout Palestine (Gal 1:22; Acts 9:31). They prayed for the sick and proclaimed that the kingdom of God was at hand. Lists of instructions were drawn up for the missionaries (Matt 10; Luke 10:1–12). In the gospels, these mission instructions are presented as instructions from Jesus to his disciples, but they also reflect the practices of the Judaic-Christian missionaries after Jesus' death.

Missionaries preached in Galilee, apparently without great success. One passage in the gospels denounces Galilean villages that had not repented at the preaching (Luke 10:13–15). Nevertheless, churches were established in Galilee (Acts 9:31). Some of the stories and sayings preserved in the gospels probably originated there.

Some of the early converts may have been pilgrims who had come to Jerusalem for the festivals. These would have taken the Christian message back to their homes, not only in Palestine but also in the Diaspora. Acts 9:1 indicates that there were Jewish Christians in the synagogues of Damascus (Syria). The letter of James is addressed to "the twelve tribes that are in the Diaspora," i.e. to Jewish Christians outside of Palestine.

EARLY NON-JUDAIC FORMS OF CHRISTIANITY

Developing alongside Judaic Christianity, we see another type of Christianity that was Jewish but non-Judaic, in the sense that these Jews began to regard the practice of Judaism as unnecessary. This type of Christianity apparently had its roots among Hellenistic Jewish Christians in Jerusalem and came to fuller expression in Johannine Christianity.

The Hellenists

Acts speaks of two distinct groups in the church at Jerusalem: the Hebrews and the Hellenists (Acts 6:1). Apparently, the Hebrews were Jews whose primary language was Aramaic, while the Hellenists were Jews whose primary language was Greek. Some members of each group would have been bilingual. Most of the Hebrews would have been native Palestinians, while the Hellenists were mainly Jews from the Diaspora who had moved to Jerusalem. The Hellenists met in their own synagogues. Acts, for example, mentions a synagogue composed of people from Cyrene, Alexandria, Cilicia, and Asia (Acts 6:9).

A certain amount of tension apparently existed between the Hebrews and the Hellenists in the Jerusalem church. As a result, the Hellenists appointed their own council of seven men. According to Acts, this council oversaw the daily distribution of food to Hellenistic widows (Acts 6:1–6). Most scholars believe, however, that the council did more than distribute food. It apparently served as the primary body of leadership for the Hellenists, comparable to the council of twelve for the Hebrews. At least two of those named to the council, Stephen and Philip, also played important roles as preachers and missionaries.

The Hellenistic Christians at Jerusalem seem to have had a more liberal attitude toward the temple and the Law than the more traditional Hebrews. They may have felt that Christianity necessitated changes to the Jewish religion. This progressive character brought them into conflict with fellow Jews in the Hellenistic synagogue at Jerusalem. Some of these Jews brought Stephen before the Sanhedrin, accusing him of saying that Jesus would destroy the temple and change the Law of Moses. According to Acts, Stephen never denies these charges. In any case, he was put to death. Stephen's death was followed by a general persecution of Christians in Jerusalem, and many Christians fled the city. This persecution seems to have been directed primarily against Hellenistic Christians, since the apostles, representing the Hebrews, did not flee (Acts 8:1).

Johannine Christianity

The liberal attitude toward the temple and the Law that seems to have characterized some of the Hellenists finds expression in the Gospel of John. The community among which this gospel arose consisted initially of Jewish Christians who worshipped in the same synagogues as other Jews. They were expelled from the synagogues because they adopted ideas that were diametrically opposed to those of traditional Judaism (John 9:22, 34; 12:42; 16:2). They found "grace and truth" (i.e. true salvation) in Jesus rather than in the Law of Moses (John 1:17). They saw sacrifice at the temple as unnecessary, since they viewed Jesus as "the Lamb of God" whose death atoned for sins (John 1:29). To traditional Jews, they seemed to compromise the very heart of Judaism, belief in one God, since they worshipped not only the God of Judaism, but also Jesus as God (John 1:1).

GENTILE CHRISTIANITY AND PAUL

It was apparently the Hellenists who began to preach to non-Jews. After Stephen's death, Philip, another council member of the Hellenists, preached in Samaria and converted many there (Acts 8:4–25). Since Jews were generally hostile to Samaritans, Jewish church members probably needed some convincing to accept Samaritans as fellow Christians. A number of stories in the gospels perform this function. They generally portray Samaritans in a positive light or show Samaritans responding positively to Jesus (Luke 10:25–37; 17:11–19; John 4:1–42). Only one story depicts Samaritans rejecting the message (Luke 9:51–55).

Another form of non-Jewish Christianity arose when Hellenists began to preach to Gentiles. Hellenists from Jerusalem went to Antioch in Syria and preached to Greeks as well as Jews (Acts 11:20). Antioch thus became the home of the first church to include Gentiles. Once the church accepted Gentiles into its ranks, it was only a matter of time before it would no longer be considered a Jewish sect. It would become recognizably distinct from Judaism. Appropriately, therefore, tradition records that it was at Antioch that the church received a new name: members of the movement were first called "Christians" there (Acts 11:26). Eventually Christianity would include more Gentiles than Jews and become a basically Gentile movement.

The Apostle Paul

In recounting the progress of the Gentile mission, Acts focuses primarily on one individual, Saul of Tarsus, later known as the apostle Paul. Paul was a Jew who had moved from the Diaspora (the city of Tarsus in Cilicia) to Jerusalem. At first he opposed the sect of the Nazoreans, assisting those who put Stephen to death (Acts 7:58; 8:1). Going to the house churches, he hauled off Jewish Christians to prison and voted that they be condemned to death (Acts 8:3; 22:4–5; 26:9–11; Gal 1:13–14; 1 Cor 15:9; Phil 3:6).

Later he had an experience in which he believed that Jesus appeared to him (Acts 9:1–19). Accepting Jesus as the Christ, he began to preach, first in Damascus, then in Tarsus, and eventually in Antioch, there joining

Figure 7.2
A fifth- or sixth-century mosaic gives an imaginative depiction of the apostle Paul. Archbishop's Palace, Ravenna, Italy (Scala/Art Resource, NY).

a man named Barnabas. With Barnabas, and later with others, he traveled through Asia Minor and Greece, establishing churches. Though he preached to both Jews and Gentiles, he had his greatest success with Gentiles. Many of the letters included in the New Testament were written by Paul to churches or individuals to whom he ministered.

Gentile Christians and the Law

The inclusion of Gentiles in the church was not accomplished without controversy. Judaic Christians in Judea maintained that Gentile converts should be made to follow the Jewish Law: Gentile males should be circumcised, and all Gentiles should follow the dietary restrictions prescribed by the Law (Acts 15:1, 5). In effect, they argued that Gentiles must become Jewish converts in order to become Christians. Paul argued vehemently against this perspective, and even the pillars at Jerusalem (James, Peter, and John) agreed with Paul that Gentile converts did not have to be circumcised (Gal 2:1–10). Other Judaic Christians, however, maintained that they did. Missionaries with this perspective visited the churches that Paul had established and convinced some of his Gentile converts that they should be circumcised. In some of his letters, Paul argued against such teaching (Gal 5:2–12; Phil 3:2–11). The question of dietary restrictions also continued to be an issue in some churches (Rom 14–5; Col 2:16, 21; cf. Didache 6:3).

In the conflict over the application of the Law to Gentiles, Paul expressed a perspective similar to that in the Gospel of John: salvation for both Jew and Gentile came through Jesus, not through the Law; sacrifice at the temple was no longer necessary, since Jesus' sacrificial death atoned for sins; and Jesus himself was a preexistent divine being.

The Growth of Gentile Christianity

Under the influence of Paul and others like him, early Christianity underwent two significant transitions. From its beginning among Palestinian Jews, it became a primarily Gentile movement; at the same time, its character changed from primarily rural to primarily urban.

According to Acts, when Paul evangelized a city in the Roman world, he began by preaching in the local Jewish synagogue. The synagogue gave him a point of contact with the Jewish community and with Gentile "God-fearers," i.e. Gentiles who attended the synagogue but did not become full Jewish converts. Paul's preaching, however, often provoked opposition from the Jewish community, and he was forced to continue his work in private homes or a rented building. While Christian missionaries like Paul had little success among the Jews, they had greater success among the Gentiles. Thus outside of Palestine, Christianity grew and thrived as a primarily Gentile movement.

Christian missionaries such as Paul traveled the main Roman roads that connected the cities of the empire. They did most of their evangelizing in the cities. While Christianity grew in the urban centers, the rural areas of the empire continued to practice the ancient polytheistic religions. Later, when Christianity had conquered the cities, the term "pagan," originally meaning simply an inhabitant of the countryside, came to mean a non-Christian, an adherent of the ancient religions.

FORMS OF POST-APOSTOLIC CHRISTIANITY

The first phase of Christianity, sometimes called the apostolic period, extended from about 30 to 70 CE. Near the end of this period, tradition records that several of the leading apostolic figures met their deaths: James the brother of Jesus, Peter, and Paul. Little is known about the fate of the other apostles. At the same time (70 CE), the Romans sacked Jerusalem, and the preeminence of Jerusalem in Christianity came to an end.

After the apostolic period, early Christianity developed along three major paths: (1) Judaic Christianity continued in the East until it eventually died out around the beginning of the fifth century; (2) a type of Christianity called "Gnostic" became widespread; (3) Pauline, Johannine, and related forms of Christianity developed into "Proto-Orthodox" or "early Catholic" Christianity.

The Demise of Judaic Christianity

Around the year 62 CE, James, the brother of Jesus, met his death in Jerusalem. The Jewish high priest had him tried before the Sanhedrin, condemned to death, and stoned (Josephus, *Antiquities* 20.200; cf. Eusebius, *Ecclesiastical History* 2.23.4–18). A few years after the death of James, the Jewish war against Rome broke out (66 CE). The Romans took Jerusalem in 70 CE, slaughtering many and destroying the temple. With the defeat of Jerusalem, the Jewish church would fade out of the picture. After the war, Christian authors mention Judaic Christians living east of the Jordan, calling them either Nazoreans or Ebionites ("the poor"). These Judaic Christians relied on the Jewish Law as the way to God, but otherwise our knowledge about them is scanty.

Judaic Christians were repudiated by the larger Jewish community. They were also repudiated by Gentile Christians, who came to doubt that anyone who relied on the Law could be saved. By the beginning of the fifth century we cease hearing about Judaic Christians at all.

The Rise of Gnostic Christianity

Scholars use the term "Gnosticism," from the Greek *gnosis* ("knowledge"), to describe a set of religious beliefs and practices that flourished during the second century CE and later. Some Gnostics considered themselves Christians, while others did not. Gnostic Christianity, as we use the term here, arose when Christian traditions were incorporated into a basically Greek world-view.

Gnostic Christians generally thought of salvation as immortality of the soul rather than resurrection of the body. The soul originally existed in a divine realm of light and was itself part of that light. Below this realm of light was the material world, a place of darkness, ignorance, and evil. When the soul descended to the material world, it became trapped in a physical body. The physical body had a negative impact on the soul, enslaving it to various passions and making it forget its true origin and divine nature. Salvation for the soul consisted of recalling its true origin and nature, a knowledge that would allow the soul at death to return to the divine realm. The progress of the soul was impeded by various evil powers that ruled the material world. In some branches of Gnosticism, it was aided by a divine being who descended from the realm of light to reveal the saving knowledge to the soul. Gnostic Christians identified this figure as Jesus or Christ. Some regarded him as a purely spiritual being with no physical body.

Some of the teaching combated in certain books of the New Testament appears very similar to Gnostic beliefs and may reflect early stages of Gnostic Christianity. The Pastoral Epistles, for example, condemn a type of "knowledge, falsely so called," while the letters of John oppose the view that Christ had no physical body.

The Response of Proto-Orthodox Christianity

The type of Christianity that ultimately prevailed was neither Judaic-Christian nor Gnostic, but developed from churches with a Pauline, Johannine, or similar orientation. Christians of this type called their own perspective orthodoxy ("correct opinion"), while other perspectives were rejected as heresy (false doctrine). They also called their church "catholic," meaning "universal." Scholars call this type of Christianity "Proto-Orthodoxy" or "early Catholicism," because it was the forerunner of the types of Christianity that developed later, known as Orthodoxy and Catholicism. The Proto-Orthodox considered both Judaic Christianity and Gnostic Christianity as heresy and ultimately prevailed against both. In their efforts to stifle diversity and to promote a unified form of Christianity, they raised certain safeguards against divergent beliefs and practices. These included a professional clergy, entrusted with preserving the Proto-Orthodox traditions; creeds or statements of faith that defined orthodox belief; and a canon of scripture that distinguished between acceptable and unacceptable writings.

PERSECUTION OF EARLY CHRISTIANITY

A major development in post-apostolic Christianity took place when the Roman Empire began to persecute Christians.

Initial Persecution

Even from its beginning, Christianity suffered persecution. Jesus himself suffered death at the hands of the Jewish and Roman authorities. The New Testament contains numerous warnings to Jesus' followers that they too must be prepared to experience persecution and even death on his account. As the message about Jesus spread into the larger world, the new movement experienced opposition not only from the Jewish community but from Gentiles as well. For example, Acts relates that opposition arose in Ephesus from idol-makers whose trade was jeopardized by the numerous conversions away from idolatry to Christianity (Acts 19:23–41). Pagan critics called the Christians "atheists," because they did not believe in the official gods of the Roman state, and blamed them for disasters thought to result from the gods' anger. Rumors were spread, charging the Christians with cannibalism, wildly immoral behavior, and strange rituals, such as worshipping a donkey's head.

State Persecution in the First Century

At first the persecutions were local affairs. In 64 CE, Nero was suspected of having caused a great fire that ravaged Rome. To protect himself, he shifted the blame to the unpopular Christians. Nero had a large number of Christians in Rome crucified, burned, or tortured to death (Tacitus, *Annals* 15.44). According to tradition, Nero executed both Peter and Paul at this time. The letter of 1 Clement, written from Rome near the end of the first century, speaks of their martyrdoms without specifying where they died. According to a tradition preserved by Eusebius (*Ecclesiastical*

Figure 7.3
Marble head from a colossal statue of Constantine. Constantine helped change Christianity from a persecuted cult into the official religion of the Roman state. Musei Capitolini, Rome (Erich Lessing/Art Resource, NY).

History 2.25.5), they died under Nero in Rome, where Paul was beheaded and Peter crucified.

Persecution in the Second Century

Persecution of Christians occurred sporadically throughout the second century, primarily because of hostility from the pagan and Jewish populace, supported by the local authorities. Under the emperor Trajan (98–117 CE), Christians were required to worship the Roman gods and to curse Christ. If they refused, they were executed. Those who suffered death for their faith came to be known as martyrs ("witnesses"). Faced with this situation, Christian intellectuals began writing "apologies," that is, defenses of the Christian faith. These apologists sought to show that the popular antagonism toward Christianity was unfounded.

The Final Phase of Persecution

In the first half of the third century, Roman emperors began to issue edicts against the Christians, forbidding them to make converts, ordering them to sacrifice to the gods, and forbidding Christian worship. Such edicts resulted in new waves of martyrdom. After a brief respite in the second half of the third century, the persecution climaxed under the emperor Diocletian and his successors, during the years 303–13. Roman officials executed Christian leaders, seized church property, and destroyed Christian books.

A dramatic turnabout came in 313. After a battle for control of the Roman Empire, Constantine emerged as the victor. Constantine's father had been a Christian, and he himself apparently attributed his victory to the Christian God. Upon becoming emperor, he issued the Edict of Milan granting Christians complete freedom of worship. With Constantine's support Christianity became the favored religion of the state, and a whole new era of Christianity began.

DISCUSSION QUESTION

Identify and briefly describe the major stages in the development of early Christianity.

REVIEW QUESTIONS

1. Identify: John the Baptist, Jesus.
2. Distinguish between "Jewish Christians" and "Judaic Christians."
3. Identify the leading figures in the Judaic-Christian church in Jerusalem.
4. Distinguish between Judaic and non-Judaic forms of early Christianity. Distinguish between Hebrews and Hellenists. How does the Gospel of John exemplify non-Judaic Christianity?

5. Describe the controversy that arose over preaching to Gentiles, including the role of the apostle Paul.
6. Describe the three major forms of post-apostolic Christianity.
7. Describe the roles of Nero and Constantine with respect to Roman persecution of Christianity.

SUGGESTIONS FOR FURTHER STUDY

Primary Sources

Eusebius. *The Church History: A New Translation with Commentary.* Translated by Paul L. Maier (Kregel, 1999). English translation of the first history of Christianity (commonly known as the *Ecclesiastical History*), written by Eusebius, bishop of Caesarea (c. 260–340 CE).

Lane, Eugene N., and Ramsay MacMullen, eds. *Paganism and Christianity 100–425 C.E.: A Sourcebook* (Augsburg Fortress, 1992). A collection of primary texts illustrating Christian and non-Christian religion, and their interaction, in the early centuries of Christianity.

Other Suggestions

Brent, Allen. *A Political History of Early Christianity* (Bloomsbury T&T Clark, 2009). Traces the history of early Christianity as a political movement from Jesus to Constantine.

Brox, Norbert. *A Concise History of the Early Church* (Continuum, 1995). A brief survey of Christian history up to the Council of Chalcedon (451).

Grant, Robert M. *Augustus to Constantine: The Rise and Triumph of Christianity in the Roman World* (Harper & Row, 1970; reprinted Westminster John Knox, 2004). Surveys Christian history up to Constantine.

Mitchell, Margaret M., and Frances M. Young, eds. *The Cambridge History of Christianity*, Vol. 1: *Origins to Constantine* (Cambridge University Press, 2014). A collection of essays covering the first three centuries of Christian history.

Rowland, Christopher. *Christian Origins* (2nd ed.; SPCK, 2002). Traces the development of Christianity from a Jewish messianic sect into the Christian religion.

8   The Making of the New Testament

Of all the literature of early Christianity, the collection known as the New Testament is today the most widely known, being considered scripture by the vast majority of Christians. However, before the New Testament could become available to modern English readers, three events had to occur. (1) Someone had to decide what writings would be included in it. (2) The texts of these writings had to be passed down from ancient times to our day. (3) The texts had to be translated out of the original language into English. These three processes will be described in the present chapter.

FORMATION OF THE NEW TESTAMENT CANON

The process of deciding what writings should be included in the Bible is called the formation of the **canon**. The term "canon" comes from a Greek word meaning a ruler, a standard of measurement. In early Christianity it referred to "the rule of faith" or traditional teaching in the church, the standard by which ideas and teachings were evaluated. Later it was applied to the writings that conformed to this standard. In this sense, the term "canon" refers to the collection of writings accepted by the church as scripture.

At first, the early church had no scriptures except the Hebrew Scriptures or Old Testament. Since the earliest Christians were Jewish, they continued to esteem the scriptures of Judaism. Since many of them could not read Hebrew or Aramaic, the languages in which the Jewish scriptures were written, they used the Greek translation known as the Septuagint.

> ## Canons of the Old Testament
>
> By the first century CE, the Jewish community accepted thirty-nine books as the canon of the Hebrew Scriptures. The early church, however, made its own judgments about what books to include in its canon of the Old Testament. Eventually the three main branches of Christianity (Orthodox, Catholic, and Protestant) adopted different canons of the Old Testament.
>
> The Protestant canon of the Old Testament includes only the thirty-nine books of the Hebrew Scriptures, the same canon accepted by Jews. The Catholic canon of the Old Testament includes not only these thirty-nine books, but also seven other books (Tobit, Judith, Wisdom of Solomon, Ecclesiasticus, Baruch, 1 Maccabees, and 2 Maccabees) as well as additions to Esther, additions to Daniel, and the Letter of Jeremiah (= Baruch ch. 6). Protestants consider these works "apocryphal," but Catholics consider them "deuterocanonical."
>
> Orthodox canons of the Old Testament includes all the works in the Catholic canon plus five others: Prayer of Manasseh, Psalm 151, 1 Esdras (= 2 Esdras in the Slavonic Orthodox Bible), 3 Maccabees, and either 4 Maccabees (Greek Orthodox) or 3 Esdras (Slavonic Orthodox).
>
> While the three main branches of Christianity have different canons of the Old Testament, they all accept the same canon of the New Testament.

As Christianity developed, new Christian writings appeared, which the churches read and studied. Gradually, as these works were read in church along with the Hebrew Scriptures, some of them acquired the same level of authority. The Hebrew Scriptures became known as the Old Testament, while the Christian writings became the New Testament. At first there was no fixed collection of New Testament writings that was acknowledged everywhere by everyone: each locality had its own collection of approved writings. Only gradually and over a long period of time did agreement develop concerning the books that make up the New Testament as we know it today.

Writings of the First Century

Among the earliest Christian writings were collections of sayings and stories about Jesus. These did not come directly from Jesus, since Jesus himself left no written records. After Jesus' death, his followers related stories about him and passed on teachings attributed to him. These sayings and stories circulated by word of mouth as oral tradition and were also assembled in written collections. Eventually, some of these were incorporated into the gospels.

Another form of early Christian literature consisted of letters. These were written as Christian missionaries traveled throughout the world establishing churches. One such missionary was the apostle Paul. As Paul established churches, he kept in touch with them by writing letters, giving advice and instruction. The churches that received these letters regarded them highly and sent copies to other churches as well. The churches collected these letters and read them in public services of worship. Some churches also collected letters from other Christian teachers besides Paul.

By the end of the first century, most of the books that now make up the New Testament had been written and were being collected and read in the churches. Except for the book of Revelation, these writings make no explicit claims to be revelations from God. Paul writes with a sense of authority, but sometimes distinguishes his own opinions from what he considers commands of Jesus (1 Cor 7:10, 12, 25, 40). None of these authors seem to have a sense that they are writing "scripture."

Apostolic Fathers

Christian writings continued to appear after the first century. A group of writings dating primarily to the period from 95 to 150 CE have been collected under the title **Apostolic Fathers**. These include 1 and 2 Clement, the letters of Ignatius, the Didache, the Epistle of Barnabas, and the Shepherd of Hermas, among others. Some early churches regarded one or more of these writings as highly as the writings that became the New Testament.

The Apostolic Fathers provide valuable information about early Christianity and about the formation of the canon. They refer to many of the writings now found in the New Testament. They show that at this period these writings were known and valued. These authors regarded the words of Jesus as authoritative, but it did not seem to matter whether these words were written in any particular gospel or simply known from oral tradition. They also valued the letters of Paul as authoritative writings.

Proto-Orthodoxy and Divergence

In the second and third centuries, the church consisted of a variety of competing groups with different conceptions of Christianity. The group responsible for the canon of the New Testament considered its own position "orthodoxy" ("correct opinion") and its churches as "catholic" ("universal"). Scholars generally call this tradition "Proto-Orthodoxy" or "early Catholicism." Many of the groups that diverged from this perspective were Gnostic in character. Since the Gnostic Christians supported their positions by appealing to various writings, they forced the Proto-Orthodox to carefully define which writings they believed contained orthodox truth. Gnostic groups thus played an important role in stimulating the development of a fixed Proto-Orthodox canon of New Testament writings.

The movement begun by **Marcion** adopted a canon that the Proto-Orthodox felt was too restricted. Marcion, who was excommunicated by the church in Rome in 144 CE for his views, rejected the Old Testament and its God. He distinguished between an inferior God of the Old Testament and a superior Supreme God. He also taught that Christ only appeared to be human. To support these views, he limited his canon of scripture to ten letters of Paul and the Gospel of Luke, from which writings he deleted anything favorable to the Old Testament or the God of the Old Testament. In combating Marcion, the Proto-Orthodox church maintained a more inclusive canon of scripture.

The Proto-Orthodox took a more restrictive view toward **Gnostic pseudepigrapha**, eliminating from their canon any writings with a Gnostic perspective. Gnostic Christians wrote numerous gospels, acts, letters, and apocalypses which contained their special teachings and which they often attributed to the apostles of Jesus. Until 1945, these writings were known primarily by references to them in the writings of the Proto-Orthodox church leaders. In that year, however, an ancient Gnostic library was discovered in Nag Hammadi, Egypt. This library contained manuscripts from the fourth century that included forty-five different works. Among these are writings attributed to the apostles of Jesus, such as the Gospel of Thomas, the Gospel of Philip, the Acts of Peter and the Twelve Apostles, and the Apocryphon of John. In combating Gnosticism, the Proto-Orthodox church had to evaluate such writings to determine which writings supported their views and which did not.

The Proto-Orthodox also had to evaluate **Proto-Orthodox pseudepigrapha**. The Gnostics were not the only ones to put out writings under a false name. The Proto-Orthodox, too, wrote gospels and other literature in the names of the apostles. For example, about 170

CE, a Proto-Orthodox church leader wrote the Acts of Paul, supposedly giving previously unknown information about the apostle Paul. In one story, Paul preached to a lion, which confessed its faith and was baptized. Later, when Paul was arrested and put in an arena to be eaten by a lion, he was saved, because the lion turned out to be the one he had previously baptized. When the author of this forgery was discovered, he was tried and deposed from his office by his associates, but his book continued to be popular among people in the church. Another such example is the Epistle of the Apostles, which claims to have been written by eleven of the apostles after Jesus' resurrection. Actually it was written in the second century by a Proto-Orthodox Christian. The author attributed secret teachings to Jesus in order to discredit the views of his Gnostic opponents.

Sifting the Documents

As the number of religious writings proliferated in the second and third centuries, church leaders began to issue lists of writings that could be read by the church. These lists sometimes distinguished between books that could be read in public worship services and those that could be read privately.

The list called the **Muratorian Canon** is the earliest such list known, if, as many scholars believe, it dates from the end of the second century. This canon discusses the writings accepted in or near Rome at that time. These include all of the books now in the New Testament except Hebrews, James, 1 and 2 Peter, and possibly one letter of John. Of works outside the present New Testament, the author accepts the Apocalypse of Peter, though he adds that some believe it should not be read in church. The Shepherd of Hermas can be read, but is not on the same level as the other writings.

The **canon of Eusebius** came about a century later, when the church historian Eusebius in his *Ecclesiastical History* (3.25.1–7) gave a list of books of the New Testament. He first named the books that were accepted by everyone: the gospels, Acts, the letters of Paul (probably including Hebrews), 1 John, and 1 Peter. He then listed the "disputed" books, those about which there were differences of opinion. He gave two classes of these. First were the disputed books which nevertheless were acknowledged by most (and presumably should be accepted): James, Jude, 2 Peter, 2 and 3 John. Next were the disputed books which Eusebius deemed spurious: the Acts of Paul, the Shepherd of Hermas, the Apocalypse of

Peter, the Epistle of Barnabas, the Teachings of the Apostles, and the Gospel of the Hebrews. Eusebius added that some would put the book of Revelation among the acknowledged books; others, among the spurious books. Eusebius' canon shows that at the beginning of the fourth century the core of the New Testament was fixed but that a good deal of variety still existed in the precise limits of the canon.

Closing the Canon

Various other church leaders also issued canonical lists. In 367 CE, **Athanasius**, bishop of Alexandria in Egypt, first listed the twenty-seven books that we know today as the New Testament. Athanasius' list did not immediately settle the question, however. Other listings continued, and the churches continued to read works not on his list.

A few decades later, Athanasius' canon received support from Augustine, bishop of Hippo in Africa. Under Augustine's influence, three church councils in northern Africa (393, 397, and 419 CE) declared these twenty-seven books the only canonical scriptures.

Further support for Athanasius' canon came from Jerome, a fourth-century scholar who translated the Bible into Latin. In his translation of the New Testament, Jerome included the twenty-seven books of Athanasius' canon and these alone. Jerome's translation exercised great influence during the Middle Ages, since it formed the primary basis for the Latin Bible in common use, known as the **Vulgate** ("common edition"). Common use of the Vulgate reinforced acceptance of Athanasius' canon, though many copies of the Vulgate also included the Epistle to the Laodiceans, a writing forged in the name of the apostle Paul. At the end of the Middle Ages, at the Council of Florence in 1439–43, the church in Rome made its first decree concerning the canon, affirming Athanasius' list.

At the time of the Renaissance and Reformation, scholars and Protestant church leaders renewed the discussion of the disputed books. Many scholars expressed doubts about the traditional authorship of Hebrews, James, 2 Peter, 2 and 3 John, Jude, and Revelation. The German Reformer **Martin Luther**, in his German translation of the New Testament (1522), expressed doubts about the theological value and canonical status of Hebrews, James, Jude, and Revelation. He left these four books in his translation, but relegated them to the end of the collection. In later editions of Luther's translation, these books were labeled "apocryphal" or "non-canonical."

Despite these continuing questions about the canon, various church councils in the sixteenth and seventeenth centuries – both Catholic and Protestant – reaffirmed the twenty-seven books of Athanasius' canon. Today, every edition of the New Testament contains these books and these alone. Yet questions about the canon remain. Some theologians see the need for "a canon within the canon," that is, the need to recognize that some books within the canon have greater importance and authority than others.

Criteria of Canonicity

In the history of the canonizing process, three factors were especially important in determining whether a book was accepted or rejected: conformity to the rule of faith, apostolic origin, and widespread use.

The content of the writing had to conform to "**the rule of faith**," the traditional teaching of the Proto-Orthodox church on matters of belief and practice. On the basis of this standard, Christian leaders determined whether or not a writing expressed orthodox views.

Writings with an **apostolic origin** were more likely to be accepted than those that did not. These included writings that originated with an apostle or the associate of an apostle. The letters of the apostle Paul, for example, were among the earliest and most universally accepted writings of the canon.

Applying this principle required making judgments about authorship, since many writings of the second and third centuries were falsely attributed to apostles. While some of these writings were recognized as inauthentic by the church and rejected, others found their way into Athanasius' canon. For instance, many ancient scholars and the great majority of modern scholars agree that the apostle Peter did not actually write 2 Peter. Though the letter remained among the disputed writings throughout the canonizing process, as part of Athanasius' canon it is now included in the New Testament. Similarly, the Pastoral Epistles (1 and 2 Timothy and Titus) entered the canon as letters of the apostle Paul, yet most modern scholars agree that Paul did not write them.

The third factor affecting the selection of a writing was **the extent of its use**. Those writings which were found most edifying and useful would be read more widely in the churches and hence be more universally accepted.

It does not appear that **inspiration** by God was a criterion for determining canonicity. The ancient church saw divine inspiration not only in the scriptures, but also in other writings as well as in unwritten, oral communications. Clement of Alexandria, for example, deemed all religious truth inspired, whether from pagans or Christians. He thus quotes non-Christian philosophers, canonical Christian authors, and non-canonical Christian authors as equally inspired. The basis for including a work in the canon, then, was not so much its inspiration as its relation to the apostolic period, its orthodoxy, and the extent of its use.

TRANSMISSION OF THE GREEK TEXT

All the writings of the New Testament were originally written by hand in the Greek language. Since the printing press had not been invented, copies of these writings also had to be made by hand. Such a hand-written composition is called a **manuscript**, while the original manuscript is called the **autograph**. As Christianity grew, the need for more copies of its scriptures also grew. Copies were made from the autographs, other copies from the copies, and so forth. Today, no autograph of any New Testament writing has survived. Fragments and copies of individual books have survived from the second and third centuries. The earliest copies of the complete New Testament come from the fourth century. Most of the manuscripts date from the Middle Ages. In all, we have about 5,700 manuscripts of part or all of the New Testament.

Scribes and Variant Readings

The ancient world knew two ways to make copies of manuscripts. A single **scribe**, a person trained in writing, might look at a manuscript and copy what he read. Alternatively, a group of scribes might sit together in a room called a "scriptorium" and write what they heard as one person read the manuscript aloud. In the latter case, more than one copy could be made at a time.

Scribes using either of these methods could easily make errors in copying. A scribe copying from a manuscript might make an error of sight, such as overlooking a word or a line. He might also make an error of mind, reading one thing but absent-mindedly writing something else. A scribe in a scriptorium, not hearing the reader clearly, might introduce an error of hearing into his copy. Through such errors, differences arose between the autographs and the copies made later.

Differences also arose when the scribes intentionally changed the original reading. They did this for various reasons: sometimes to bring the wording of one gospel into line with the wording in a similar passage in

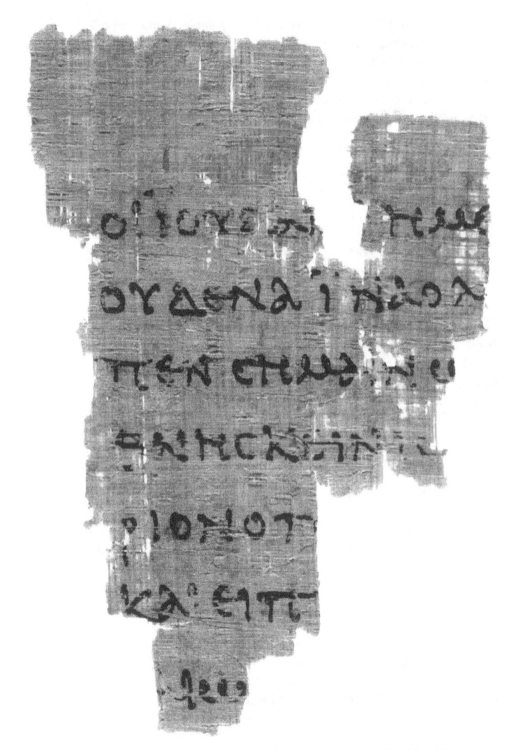

Figure 8.1 Greek Papyrus 52, the oldest surviving text of the New Testament (c. 125–150 CE), a fragment with John 18:31–33 on the front and 18:37–38 on the back. www.BibleLandsPictures.com (Zev Radovan).

another gospel, sometimes to correct what they believed was a mistake, sometimes even to change something with which they disagreed.

As a result of such scribal activity, the manuscripts of the New Testament show many differences in wording, or **variant readings**. Of the 5,700 extant manuscripts, no two have exactly the same wording. These manuscripts exhibit hundreds of thousands of variant readings. Fortunately, most of these variations, such as differences in spelling or word order, do not affect the sense of the passage. Others do affect the sense. For instance, in Romans 5:1 some manuscripts have the Greek word ἔχομεν ("we have"), while others have ἔχωμεν ("let us have"). The difference involves only one letter, a difference that probably arose in a scriptorium as some scribes heard a short "o" (o), while others heard a long "o" (ω). This variation raises the question of whether Paul said "we have peace with God" or "let us have peace with God."

Another significant variant occurs in the last chapter of the Gospel of Mark. Most manuscripts include the description of Jesus' resurrection appearances in Mark 16:9–20. However, two of the most important manuscripts leave these verses out. Did Mark, then, originally tell of these appearances or not? Yet another important example involves the story in which Jesus forgives a woman caught in adultery. Some manuscripts include this story in John 7:53–8:11; a few others include it after Luke 21:38, or after John 7:36, or after John 21:25; most of the earliest manuscripts do not include it at all. Did this story, then, originally form part of the New Testament or not?

Textual Criticism

Before the Greek text can be translated into English, someone has to examine the variant readings in the manuscripts and try to determine what the author originally wrote. This process of restoring the original reading is called **textual criticism**. Over the years, scholars engaged in this endeavor have developed certain guidelines for determining the original reading. The process is therefore not completely subjective. On the other hand, the process is more of an art than a science, and in many cases leaves room for differences of opinion.

Since the invention of the printing press, textual critics have produced various printed editions of the Greek New Testament. Today, two such texts have achieved general use: the *Novum Testamentum Graece*, edited by Nestle and Aland, and *The Greek New Testament*, published by the United Bible Society. Both editions print the Greek text adopted by the editors and give variant readings in the footnotes. In earlier editions,

Figure 8.2
End of 2
Thessalonians
and beginning
of Hebrews in
the important
fourth-century
manuscript Codex
Vaticanus. www.
BibleLandsPictures.
com/Alamy Stock
Photo.

these two Greek texts differed somewhat, but in the latest editions the editors have agreed on a common text. This standardization, however, does not necessarily mean that this Greek text exactly matches that of the autograph manuscripts.

ENGLISH TRANSLATIONS OF THE NEW TESTAMENT

As Christianity spread among people who spoke no Greek, the need arose for translations of the scriptures into other languages. In the ancient period, translations were made into Latin, Syriac, Coptic, and several other languages. The Latin Vulgate became the standard Bible in Europe throughout the Middle Ages. Eventually the Bible was translated into English.

Early English Versions

The first complete English Bible was translated from the Vulgate by disciples of John Wyclif around 1382–96. At first, such translation into English was opposed by leaders of the Catholic Church, who felt that allowing the common people to read the Bible in their own language without the interpretation of a priest would lead to heresy.

As knowledge grew concerning the original text and languages of the Bible, so grew the desire for an English translation from the original languages. The first such translation was made by the Reformer William Tyndale in 1522–25. Tyndale was subsequently arrested, strangled, and burnt at the stake by Catholic authorities in Belgium in 1536. After Tyndale, several English translations appeared, including the Douai–Rheims Bible (1582–1610). Based on the Vulgate rather than the original languages, this was the first English translation sanctioned by Catholic authorities.

King James Version

In 1611, King James I of England and VI of Scotland appointed fifty-four scholars to make a new translation of the Bible. The completed version, called the Authorized Version or (in America) the **King James Version** (KJV), soon replaced all previous versions and for several hundred years remained the only version in common use among English-speaking Protestants.

By the end of the nineteenth century, the King James Version had become obsolete in two respects. First, the English language had changed since 1611. The Shakespearean language of the King James Version was no longer completely intelligible to many people. Second, in the centuries since 1611 many early manuscripts of the Bible had been discovered, older than those available to the translators of the King James Version. Advances had also been made in the study of biblical Greek and Hebrew. These advances in understanding made possible a translation that would be closer to the original meaning of the texts. For these reasons, a committee of scholars in England produced the Revised Version in 1881–85, with an Americanized version, the American Standard Version, appearing in 1901.

Figure 8.3 Portrait of James I of England and VI of Scotland by John De Critz (1555–1641). James authorized the production of the King James Bible (1611), once the most widely used English translation. By courtesy of the National Portrait Gallery, London.

Contemporary Versions

Since the beginning of the twentieth century, the number of new translations of the whole Bible or the New Testament has multiplied. Over seventy different translations or editions have appeared. Only a few of these can be mentioned here.

The King James Version (1611) was revised in 1901 as the American Standard Version. This in turn was revised as the Revised Standard Version or RSV (1946–57). This was produced by a committee composed primarily of Protestant scholars, but including Catholic, Greek Orthodox, and Jewish members as well. It soon became the most widely used version among biblical scholars. A thorough revision of the entire translation appeared in 1989 as the **New Revised Standard Version** (NRSV). Among other new features, it uses gender-inclusive language.

The New English Bible (1961–70) was commissioned by British churches. A major revision of the text appeared in 1989 under the title the **Revised English Bible**. It is a fluent, contemporary translation that uses gender-inclusive language.

The **New American Bible** (1970) is a contemporary translation produced by Roman Catholic scholars in America. Unlike most earlier English versions made by Catholics, which were translations of the Vulgate, this version was translated from the original languages. A revision, called the New American Bible Revised Edition, came out in 2011.

The **New International Version** (1973–78), produced by a team of evangelical Protestant scholars, tends to be less literal than the RSV in seeking to attain a more idiomatic English style. It has become widely popular in churches and for personal devotional use. It was revised in 1984 and again in 2011.

REVIEW QUESTIONS

1. What three events had to occur before the New Testament could become available to modern English readers?
2. Identify or define: canon.
3. How do the Protestant, Catholic, and Orthodox canons of the Old Testament differ?
4. Explain the significance of the following for the development of the New Testament canon: Apostolic Fathers, Marcion, Gnostic and Proto-Orthodox pseudepigrapha, Muratorian Canon, Eusebius, Athanasius, Vulgate, Martin Luther.

5. What three factors determined whether or not a writing was accepted into the New Testament canon?
6. Define: manuscript, autograph, scribe, variant readings, textual criticism.
7. Explain the significance of the following for the translation of the Bible into English: King James Version, New Revised Standard Version, Revised English Bible, New American Bible, New International Version.

SUGGESTIONS FOR FURTHER STUDY

Formation of the Canon

Ehrman, Bart D. *Lost Christianities: The Battles for Scripture and the Faiths We Never Knew* (Oxford University Press, 2003). Describes the origin of the New Testament canon as the outcome of a battle between Proto-Orthodoxy and competing forms of Christianity (Ebionite, Marcionite, and Gnostic).

McDonald, Lee Martin. *The Formation of the Christian Biblical Canon* (3rd ed.; Hendrickson; Baker Academic, 2007). An account of the formation of the Christian Old Testament and New Testament.

Metzger, Bruce M. *The Canon of the New Testament: Its Origin, Development and Significance* (Clarendon, 1987). A classic work on the formation of the New Testament canon.

Textual Criticism

Aland, Kurt, and Barbara Aland. *The Text of the New Testament: An Introduction to the Critical Editions and to the Theory and Practice of Modern Textual Criticism* (2nd ed.; Eerdmans, 1989). Best used as a supplement to Metzger's more balanced treatment.

Metzger, Bruce M., and Bart D. Ehrman. *The Text of the New Testament: Its Transmission, Corruption, and Restoration* (4th ed.; Oxford University Press, 2005). A classic introduction to textual criticism by Metzger, updated by Ehrman.

English Versions of the Bible

Lewis, Jack P. *The English Bible from KJV to NIV: A History and Evaluation* (2nd ed.; Baker, 1991). Detailed evaluation of the major English translations from the King James Version to the New International Version.

Metzger, Bruce M. *The Bible in Translation: Ancient and English Versions* (Baker Academic, 2001). Discusses ancient versions and a selection of English translations, giving attention to problems faced by translators.

PART II

Jesus and the Gospels

9 Introduction to the Gospels

The term **gospel** literally means a message of good news. In early Christianity, it had three different senses. First, it referred to the message that Jesus preached: that the kingdom of God was at hand (Mark 1:14–15). Second, it referred to the message that early Christians preached about Jesus: that Jesus died for sins and rose from the dead (1 Cor 15:1–8). Third, it referred to a type of literature: a writing concerning Jesus.

From the same Greek root as "gospel" (Greek *evangelion*) comes the term **evangelist**. This term can refer either to a preacher of the gospel message or to the author of a written gospel.

TYPES OF GOSPELS

When we speak of "the gospels" we normally mean the four found in the canon of the New Testament. The term "gospel," however, has also been used to refer to a variety of other early Christian texts. Among the gospels that survive, we find passion gospels, infancy gospels, collections of sayings, dialogues, and collections of meditations.

The canon of the New Testament contains four **passion gospels** bearing the titles "According to Matthew," "According to Mark," "According to Luke," and "According to John," respectively. We cannot be sure that these titles give the true names of the authors since these headings were probably added to the gospels years after they were written. The gospels themselves tell us nothing about who wrote them or when they were composed. Scholars, however, generally date them to the years between 70 and 100 CE. These four works contain stories about Jesus and sayings attributed to him. All culminate in a passion narrative. In this context, the term "passion" means "suffering." A passion narrative is an account of the events surrounding Jesus' death.

Another gospel, called the Gospel of Peter, also contained a passion narrative. Unfortunately only a fragment of this gospel has survived. It recounts the end of Jesus' trial, his crucifixion, his burial, and his resurrection, breaking off in the middle of what appears to be a post-resurrection appearance of Jesus in Galilee. Because of the fragmentary nature of the text, we do not know whether this passion and resurrection narrative stood alone or was preceded by sayings and stories like those in the canonical gospels.

Certain works called **infancy gospels** tell stories about Jesus' birth or childhood. The Infancy Gospel of James begins with the birth and childhood of Jesus' mother Mary and continues the story down to the birth of Jesus. The Infancy Gospel of Thomas contains stories of Jesus' miraculous abilities as a child between the ages of five and twelve.

Another work called a gospel is a collection of sayings. This is the Gospel of Thomas (to be distinguished from the Infancy Gospel of Thomas). It contains various sayings attributed to Jesus. Some of these also appear in the canonical gospels, while others do not. Since many of the sayings have a Gnostic flavor, we can infer that this collection apparently circulated among Gnostic Christians.

The Gospel of Judas and the Gospel of Mary both present Jesus' teachings in the form of a dialogue or conversation between Jesus and one of his disciples. Both present a Gnostic Christian perspective.

Yet other works called gospels consist primarily of a series of meditations on religious themes. These include the Gospel of Philip and the Gospel of Truth, both written from a Gnostic Christian perspective. These are the furthest removed from the form of a canonical gospel.

A number of gospels are no longer extant. These include the Gospel of the Hebrews and the Gospel of the Ebionites, both used by Jewish-Christian groups. A few quotations of these works survive in the writings of other early Christian authors. A scrap of manuscript known as Papyrus Egerton 2 records four stories about Jesus, one of which does not occur in the canonical gospels. A manuscript whose authenticity has not been verified includes two excerpts purported to come from an expanded version of Mark called the "Secret Gospel of Mark."

THE GENRE OF A GOSPEL

Since the term "gospel" has been applied to writings of various kinds, it is difficult to formulate a single definition that fits all of them. If we limit ourselves to the canonical gospels, these do not fit neatly into any single well-defined genre of literature but have affinities with several precursors: the oral gospel, ancient biographies, and sacred history.

First, they have affinities with the **oral gospel** (kerygma), the message preached by early Christians about Jesus. One summary of this early Christian preaching includes the following elements: Jesus is the Christ; the gospel began with John the Baptist; God anointed Jesus with holy spirit and power; Jesus began preaching in Galilee; he went about doing good and curing all who were oppressed by the Devil; witnesses saw all that he did; he was crucified in Jerusalem; God raised him on the third day; he appeared to his students after he rose from the dead, and he commanded them to preach about him (Acts 10:36–42). This summary of early Christian preaching could just as easily be a summary of Mark's gospel. Mark follows the same basic outline but expands it with additional stories and sayings.

Second, the canonical gospels have affinities with **ancient biographies** in the Greco-Roman world. Matthew and Luke preserve the basic structure of Mark but add stories about Jesus' birth and childhood at the beginning. By doing so, they perhaps show more of a biographical interest than Mark. Some scholars, in fact, have seen the gospels as a form of ancient biography. Ancient biographies, unlike their modern counterparts, did not relate the entire life of an individual in chronological order. Nor did they show the psychological development of the individual. Generally they began by mentioning the hero's ancestry and family, his birth, and a few incidents in his childhood. They then moved on to the hero's public life, stringing together a series of anecdotes and sayings to illustrate the subject's character. Some devoted a good deal of space to the subject's death. In all these respects, the gospels resemble ancient biographies in form and content. Some ancient biographies defended the subject or praised his virtues. Like these works, the gospels have nothing negative to say about their hero but extol his greatness.

Third, the canonical gospels have affinities with **sacred history**, works of religious piety based loosely on a historical figure or historical events. This type of literature includes most of the narratives in the Hebrew Bible. Especially relevant are the stories about individuals, such as Abraham, Joseph, Moses, David, Elijah, Elisha, and Jonah. While some of these stories are based on historical events, they are not history in the sense that modern historians understand this term. They differ from modern historical accounts in several respects. First, they have a thoroughly theological perspective. They present events in relation to the Hebrew God, and they claim to know what this God thinks, wills, plans, says, and does. Second, they exhibit a pre-scientific perspective. Miraculous, supernatural events have just as much a place in these stories as do events produced by natural causes. Third, they do not distinguish between history and legend. They present traditional, legendary stories as if these were accounts of actual events. And fourth, they do not have the same purpose as modern historical accounts. While history aims to report what happened as accurately as possible, the aim of these stories is to promote religious belief and behavior. The gospels have more affinities with this type of literature than with historical writing in the modern sense.

FORMATION OF THE GOSPELS

To study the gospels historically, we must take into account the manner in which the gospels developed. Here we will consider the stages through which the gospel material went and the ways in which this material underwent change and development.

Stages of the Material

Modern scholarship has concluded that the material in the canonical gospels went through three main stages as it took the form of a gospel.

The first stage consisted of **traditions**. Before the gospels were written, early Christians passed on traditions about Jesus, either by word of mouth or in writing. These traditions included various types of stories about Jesus: for example, stories about Jesus healing the sick or debating with his opponents. These traditions also included various types of sayings attributed to Jesus, such as parables and teachings on various subjects. In most cases, a story or saying was passed on as a separate, self-contained unit. Most of the traditions were not connected in any kind of chronological order. The early Christians, while transmitting these traditions orally, also wrote some of them down. They made written collections of the traditions, such as collections of miracle stories and collections of Jesus' sayings.

The second stage consisted of **gospel sources**. At some point, early Christians began to combine the collections and other traditions into larger compositions. Even before the canonical gospels came into existence, there were probably other, earlier gospels that have now been lost. Luke says that he knew "many" earlier narratives about Jesus (Luke 1:1). Some of these may have been proto-gospels. Scholars have also determined that Matthew and Luke knew a lost document that

Figure 9.1
Christ as judge surrounded by the four living beings described in Revelation 4:6–8. In early Christianity, these beings came to symbolize the four evangelists: Matthew (human), Mark (lion), Luke (ox), and John (eagle). From the tympanon over the central portal on the west façade of the French cathedral at Chartres. © Guillaume Piolle.

scholars call "Q." These early compositions served as sources for the canonical gospels.

The third stage consisted of the **gospels**. The individual evangelists combined some of the earlier sources and traditions in order to create their own gospels. The evangelists played an important editorial role in shaping the final form of the gospels. (1) They decided what material to include. Each gospel shares some material with the others but also includes some material unique to that gospel. (2) They decided in what order to put the material. For example, the first three gospels put the story about Jesus cleansing the temple at the end of his ministry, but the Gospel of John puts it at the beginning. The order of events in the gospels, therefore, often reflects the choices of the evangelists, not necessarily the actual order of events in Jesus' ministry. (3) They connected the originally independent sources and traditions, linking them together with editorial comments. This practice explains the episodic character of the gospels, which present a series of loosely connected episodes. (4) They "redacted" (edited or revised) the sources and traditions that they inherited. They often rewrote the material in their own words and in their own style, shaping the material to express their own interests. Sometimes the evangelists conflated (combined) different versions of the same story. At other times, they abridged or expanded the material from their sources.

Transformation and Growth of the Tradition

As the early Christians passed down their traditions about Jesus and incorporated them into gospels, these traditions changed and developed. We can discern three major ways in which the tradition changed and developed: (1) existing traditions were adapted to the needs and beliefs of the church; (2) sayings from Christian and non-Christian sources were incorrectly attributed to Jesus; (3) new traditions about Jesus were created.

1. The evangelists frequently modified the traditions that they inherited. We can see such modification by comparing the same saying as it appears in two different gospels. Both Matthew and Luke include the same teaching about prayer (Matt 7:7–11; Luke 11:9–13). However, in the final sentence, where Matthew says that God will give "good things" to those who ask him, Luke says that he will give "the Holy Spirit" to those who ask him. Since Luke elsewhere shows a special interest in the Holy Spirit, we can assume that Matthew's version is more original and that Luke changed "good things" to "Holy Spirit" in order to emphasize one of his special themes. Interestingly, Luke displays no sense that the words in his source were inspired. Rather he felt free to alter and adapt them to bring out the point that he wished to emphasize.

The evangelist Matthew sometimes modified a tradition in order to bring it into closer agreement with a scripture that he considered prophetic. We can see an example by comparing Matthew's version of Jesus' entry into Jerusalem with the same story in Mark and Luke. Mark and Luke relate that Jesus rode into Jerusalem on a "colt," that is, a young donkey (Mark 11:1–7; Luke 19:29–35). Matthew, however, has two donkeys where the other evangelists have only one (Matt 21:1–7). Why would Matthew introduce a second donkey into the story? Probably because he wanted to make Jesus' entry into Jerusalem correspond more closely to Zechariah 9:9 in the Old Testament:

> Rejoice greatly, daughter of Zion;
> shout for joy, daughter of Jerusalem.
> Behold, your king will come to you,
> righteous and victorious is he,
> Humble and riding on a donkey,
> and on a young donkey, the foal of a she-ass.

Matthew quoted this scripture in his account (Matt 21:5) and claimed that Jesus' entry into Jerusalem "fulfilled" it. In the process, however, he apparently misunderstood it. In the last line of the passage, the terms "donkey" and "young donkey" refer to the same animal. The latter term is simply a poetic variation of the first, a practice known as "synonymous parallelism," which is common in Hebrew writing of an exalted style. Matthew, however, apparently interpreted the passage literally, assuming that it referred to two different animals. To make Jesus' entry match his interpretation of Zechariah, he introduced a second donkey into the account.

2. The tradition also developed as early Christians attributed to Jesus sayings that he did not originally speak. The early church preserved the words not only of Jesus, but of other Christian teachers and prophets as well. Sometimes they passed these sayings on without identifying who spoke them. When the evangelists came across such unidentified sayings, they could easily mistake the words of Christian teachers and prophets for the words of Jesus. Sayings that originated in the church could thus be incorrectly attributed to Jesus. Matthew 18:15–17 is probably an example:

> If your brother sins against you, go correct him between you and him alone. If he listens to you, you have gained back your brother. If he does not listen, take one or two others along with you, so that every word may be established by the mouth of two or three witnesses. If he will not listen to them, tell it to the church. But if he will not listen even to the church, let him be to you like the Gentile and the tax collector.

Matthew attributes this saying to Jesus, but two facts indicate that it did not originate with Jesus. First, the attitude toward tax collectors expressed here is inconsistent with the attitude of Jesus in other passages in the gospels. This saying advises that contentious members of the community should be shunned just as one shuns tax collectors. It thus assumes that the proper attitude toward tax collectors is to have nothing to do with them. Elsewhere, however, Jesus accepts tax collectors and sinners, even eating with them (Mark 2:15–17). In such passages, it is not Jesus, but the scribes and Pharisees who express a negative attitude toward tax collectors. Second, this passage presupposes the existence of the church, an institution that did not exist in Jesus' lifetime. Here the church appears as an organized body of people with rules governing relations between the members. This picture would fit the time of the early church, but not the time of Jesus. For these two reasons, it appears that this saying originated in the early church, serving as a rule for resolving conflicts between members of the community. Only later did Matthew attribute it to Jesus.

In some cases, sayings may have originated when Christian prophets spoke in the name of Jesus. It was believed that Jesus, who had risen and ascended to heaven, was speaking directly through the prophet in the first person (as in Revelation 2–3). In time, such sayings spoken by Christian prophets in the name of the risen Jesus might be mistaken for sayings uttered by Jesus during his earthly ministry. One such saying may be Luke 12:8:

> Everyone who confesses me before other people, the Son of Man will confess him before the angels of God. He, though, who denies me before other people will be denied before the angels of God.

This saying presupposes a situation in which Christians were being pressured to deny their faith in Jesus. Such a situation did not exist during Jesus' lifetime, but did exist after Jesus' death, when Christians were expelled from the synagogue, imprisoned, or killed if they did not renounce their faith in Jesus. This saying was therefore probably spoken not by Jesus, but by a Christian prophet speaking in his name, urging the believers to consider the consequences of denying their faith.

3. The early church not only adapted and modified existing traditions about Jesus, but also created new traditions. Certain stories in the gospels may have come into existence as sermon illustrations, stories about Jesus created by the preacher to illustrate a point, but without any basis in the life of Jesus. As these were passed on by word of mouth, the distinction between them and authentic stories about Jesus would have been lost. Other traditions in the gospels may have come into existence in the same way that legends grow up around other famous people. A good example is the legend about George Washington as a child: when asked if he cut down his father's favorite cherry tree, he confessed, saying, "I cannot tell a lie." This and other stories glorifying Washington were created by one of his early biographers, Mason Weems, and soon became fixed in the popular imagination as authentic history. The same type of legends grew up around famous men in antiquity, as the various stories about divine humans illustrate.

Such legends tend especially to grow up around founders of a religion. In nearly every religion a discrepancy exists between what the founder said of himself and what his disciples claimed for him. For example,

Mani, the founder of the Manichean religion, identified himself simply as "an apostle of Jesus Christ," while his followers identified him as a "son of the gods" or even as "God." It would be surprising if some such development had not taken place with respect to Jesus.

METHODS OF INTERPRETATION

Studying the gospels, as well as other early Christian writings, may involve a number of different methods of interpretation or criticism. The term "criticism" here means "critical study," that is, careful, analytical evaluation. Different types of criticism focus on different aspects of the communication process: the author "behind" the text, the text itself, or the contemporary reader "in front of" the text. Following Paul Ricoeur, we can think of these three aspects of communication as constituting three "worlds":

- **the world behind the text:** the cultural and historical setting of the author and the intended audience;
- **the world within the text:** the text itself, its rhetoric or its story world viewed independently of the real world outside the text;
- **the world in front of the text:** the meaning of the text for contemporary readers.

Methods of interpretation differ according to which of these worlds they focus on.

The World behind the Text

Several different methods focus on the world behind the text. These include source criticism, redaction criticism, form criticism, genre criticism, socio-historical criticism, and historical criticism.

Source criticism seeks to determine what written sources were used by the evangelists in composing their gospels. Since these sources have not survived, we can only infer what they were by comparing the gospels that we do have. On the basis of such comparison, scholars have theorized that each of the four evangelists used earlier written sources – proto-gospels and written collections of traditions – in composing their gospels. The first three gospels, called the Synoptic Gospels, probably used some of the same sources, since they have many of the same stories and sayings in the same order. We will discuss the sources of the Synoptic Gospels in the next chapter.

Redaction criticism studies the manner in which authors have "redacted" (revised, edited) the material from their sources. This method presupposes that we know what those sources were. Redaction criticism can therefore come only after source criticism. If we can identify the sources of a gospel and compare that gospel with its sources, then we can see how the evangelist has changed and modified those sources. Noticing such changes should tell us something about the evangelist's purpose. For example, we saw above that Luke probably changed "good things" to "Holy Spirit" in a teaching about prayer. When we see that Luke apparently added similar references to the Holy Spirit more than once, we can infer that one of his purposes in writing his gospel was to emphasize the role of the Holy Spirit.

Form criticism focuses not on a gospel as a whole but on the individual units of tradition within the gospels, the individual stories and sayings that make up the gospel. Such a unit is called a **pericope** (something "cut out"), because the critic separates it from its present context in the gospels and studies it apart from the gospel. For example, Luke 11:1–13 is devoted to the theme of prayer. Yet if we look carefully, we see that it actually includes three separate teachings on prayer: the "Lord's Prayer" (11:1–4), a parable encouraging persistent prayer (11:5–8), and a saying about asking and receiving (11:9–13). Each is a separate pericope. In studying these pericopes, form criticism does not limit itself to a single method but actually employs three distinct methods: genre criticism, socio-historical criticism, and historical criticism.

Genre criticism may apply to either a whole gospel or to an individual pericope within the gospel. As used in form criticism, it applies to the latter. Genre criticism seeks to classify the different types of stories and sayings in the gospel. For example, a story in which Jesus performed a miracle would be classified as a miracle story, while a saying that used a comparison or analogy would be classified as a parable. We will consider such classifications more fully below.

Socio-historical criticism, as used in form criticism, seeks to understand how an individual pericope functioned within the early Christian community where it circulated. Socio-historical criticism assumes that each type of story or saying originated in a particular "life setting" (German *Sitz im Leben*). This setting was not a specific historical event but a typical activity in the life of the early Christian community, such as preaching, teaching, worship, debate, or evangelism. The early church told these stories and passed on these sayings because they met particular needs in the life of the community. By studying the gospel traditions from this perspective, we gain insight into the beliefs, practices, needs, and controversies of the earliest Christian communities. For example, a saying which encourages people who are suffering persecution gives us insight into the types of persecution that were experienced by the Christian community that preserved this saying. Socio-historical criticism often focuses on a specific community. This may be one of the communities for which the evangelists wrote, such as Matthew's community or John's community.

When socio-historical criticism uses insights from the social sciences (sociology, cultural anthropology), it is called "social-scientific criticism." This employs models taken from the study of modern Mediterranean societies and cultures to illuminate the cultural values and attitudes of early Christians as part of the Mediterranean world.

Historical criticism, in a general sense, includes all of the methods that focus on the world behind the text, because all share the presuppositions of the historical-critical method (see Chapter 1). In a more restricted sense, however, historical criticism is the attempt to determine which gospel traditions give authentic information about the historical Jesus. As we saw above in discussing the transformation and growth of the gospel tradition, not every story about Jesus gives historically accurate information. Historical criticism seeks to determine which events relating to Jesus actually happened and which sayings attributed to Jesus he actually spoke. In Chapter 16, we will discuss some of the criteria that scholars use to make these judgments and summarize some of their results.

The World within the Text

Other methods of interpretation focus on the world within the text. These methods focus not on how the text originated, but on the text in its present form as it presents itself to the reader.

Historical-theological criticism seeks to describe as accurately as possible the theological beliefs of particular groups or writings in the past. The term "theology," which literally means "discourse about God," is generally used in a broader sense to mean the study of Christian beliefs in general. In this broader sense, theology includes a number of topics: christology (beliefs about Jesus), pneumatology (beliefs about the Holy Spirit), soteriology (beliefs about salvation), ecclesiology (beliefs about the church), eschatology (beliefs about final destiny), and so forth. The task of historical theology is descriptive rather than normative. Historical theologians may or may not hold the beliefs that they describe. As applied to the New Testament, this type of criticism seeks to describe the different religious or theological views presented within the different documents of the New Testament.

Literary criticism studies a gospel not as history or theology, but as literature, as a story. To understand this concept, think of a work of fiction, such as a novel. In such a literary work, the author creates a world of characters, events, and settings. Though this world may not refer to real people or events outside the text, it has its own independent form of existence within the text or, more accurately, within the imagination of the reader. The literary critic takes this imaginative world of the text as the focus of study, without making any judgment as to whether the events actually happened or not. The literary critic has no interest in the history behind the text, its author or its sources, but in the text as it now presents itself to a reader.

One of the main literary approaches to the gospels is narrative criticism. This type of literary criticism studies narratives or stories, such as the four gospels and the book of Acts. A narrative critic analyzes the various aspects of the story, such as the narrator, the characters, the settings, the events or plot, and the literary techniques that the author employs.

Rhetorical criticism analyzes the techniques of argumentation used by authors to persuade their listeners or readers. Rhetorical critics may study the types of ancient Greek rhetoric and notice how an author used these to affect the audience. This type of criticism can be used as an aspect of narrative criticism or as an independent method.

The World in Front of the Text

Still other methods focus on the world in front of the text, i.e. its significance for the reader. Christians have traditionally used the confessional method, reading the Bible not simply as history or literature but as a text with religious significance for the present. This interest in the meaning of the text for the contemporary reader also characterizes several methods of interpretation, which have been designated **ideological criticism**. The practitioner of this type of criticism approaches the text with an explicitly acknowledged set of interests and personal commitments. This approach recognizes that all interpreters bring their own presuppositions to the text, whether they acknowledge them or not. In the past, most interpreters have been white males from the industrialized West. Now women, people of color, and inhabitants of the developing nations are interpreting the text with new sets of interests and personal commitments. Feminist criticism, for example, seeks to expose the androcentric character of the biblical text or to emphasize the role of women in early Christianity, all in the service of promoting greater equality for women in contemporary religious communities. Liberation theology has a similar commitment to interpretation that promotes liberation from other types of oppression.

The Approach of this Textbook

Since the present textbook is a study of the origins of Christianity, those methods that focus on the world behind the text or the text itself have the greatest relevance. The present chapter discusses genre criticism and socio-historical criticism. The next chapter discusses source criticism of the Synoptic Gospels. Chapters on individual gospels address redaction criticism. Chapter 16 addresses historical criticism with respect to the quest for the historical Jesus. Socio-historical criticism appears throughout, as does historical-theological criticism. Chapter 11 illustrates narrative criticism as applied to the Gospel of Mark. Chapter 19 applies rhetorical criticism to Galatians. With respect to the world in front of the text, Chapter 16 gives an example of feminist criticism as applied to the quest for the historical Jesus. Ideological criticism also appears in my concern to sensitize students to anti-Jewish and patriarchal attitudes in early Christianity. Some of the discussion questions also raise the issue of the contemporary relevance of these texts. Readers who wish to pursue particular methods in greater depth will find bibliographical references in the suggestions for further study.

FORMS OF THE TRADITION

The gospel traditions were passed down in certain typical forms. These forms consist of two broad types: **narratives** (stories, usually about Jesus) and **sayings** (words attributed to Jesus). Genre criticism attempts to classify or categorize these recurring forms.

Narratives

Most of the narratives in the gospels are stories about Jesus, though a few are about John the Baptist. Genre critics have tried to classify the stories in the gospels on the basis of their form, that is, to identify particular types of stories that have a similar form. Not all stories are easily classified in this way. The most recognizable types are pronouncement stories, controversy dialogues, scholastic dialogues, and miracle stories.

A **pronouncement story** is a brief anecdote that focuses on a statement (a pronouncement) that Jesus makes about some issue. It takes the form of a saying within a brief narrative setting. For instance, Mark 10:13–14 relates that Jesus' disciples tried to keep parents from bringing their children to him. This brief narrative provides the setting for Jesus' pronouncement: "Let the children come to me and do not prevent them; for of such is the kingdom of God."

One important type of pronouncement story is the **controversy dialogue**, which relates a dispute between Jesus (or his students) and other Jews. Some of these stories have a three-part form: Jesus or his entourage engages in some practice, their opponents question the practice, and Jesus makes a pronouncement that justifies the practice. For example, in Mark 2:15–17, Jesus eats with sinners, the Pharisees question this practice, and Jesus makes a pronouncement that justifies it: "It is the sick, not the healthy, who need a physician. I came to call sinners, not the righteous." Other controversy dialogues have a two-part form, including only the question and Jesus' response.

Another type of pronouncement story is the **scholastic dialogue**. Most of these have a two-part form: Jesus' students or other interested persons ask Jesus a question, and he provides the answer to the question. For example, in Mark 4:10–12, Jesus' students ask him why he teaches in parables, and he gives the reason.

A **miracle story** is identified not so much by its form as by its content. As its name suggests, it relates a miracle performed by Jesus. In such stories, Jesus performs various types of miracles: exorcisms, healings, resuscitations, and nature miracles.

Two types of narratives probably originated not as individual pericopes but as connected written narratives: the **passion narrative**, an account of the events surrounding Jesus' death, and the **birth narrative**, an account of the events surrounding Jesus' birth.

Sayings

Many of the traditions in the gospels are sayings: words attributed to Jesus with little or no narrative context. Such sayings may be as short as a sentence or as long as a paragraph. They include teaching on a variety of subjects, from how Christians should behave to what will happen at the end of the age. Some typical forms include the following.

In Greek usage, the term **parable** refers to a comparison or analogy. A parable clarifies one concept or situation by comparing it with a parallel concept or situation. For example, in Mark 2:17, Jesus says, "Not those who are healthy but those who are sick need a physician. I came to call not the righteous, but sinners." Just as a physician ministers not to the healthy but to the sick (the parallel), so Jesus ministers not to the righteous but to sinners (the application).

The gospel parables often compare the kingdom of God with some familiar aspect of life, such as fishing or farming, e.g. "The kingdom of heaven is like leaven which a woman took and hid in three measures of flour until it was completely leavened" (Matt 13:33). In this instance, the parable is a brief simile and gives no explanation of how the kingdom is like leaven. This lack of an explanation leaves room for interpretation.

Sometimes the parable is expanded from a single sentence into a brief story. For example, the parable of the sower presents the activity of sowing as analogous to the activity of preaching the gospel (Mark 4:3–9, 13–20). It describes how seed is sown on four different types of soil, resulting in four different outcomes. This brief story is then followed by an interpretation, which explains that each outcome represents a different response to the preaching of the gospel.

Some sayings that the gospels call parables would be better classified as example stories. An **example story** gives an example of how one should or should not act. For instance, the story of the rich fool (Luke 12:16–21) tells about a man who spent his time collecting wealth but died before he could enjoy it. The point of the story is that one should not act like this man but devote one's wealth to God.

Some sayings take the form of a **declaration**, a sentence that makes a statement. These are best classified on the basis of their content. One type of declaration could be described as a legal opinion because it expresses a judgment about some issue relating to Jewish Law or piety, eg. "The Sabbath was made for humans and not humans for the Sabbath" (Mark 2:27). Another type could be designated as a maxim (a proverb, wisdom saying, principle, or aphorism) because it expresses a generalization about the way things operate in the world or in the kingdom of God: "What you dish out will be dished out to you in the same dish" (Matt 7:2). Yet another type of declaration may be termed a prediction because it predicts what will happen in the future: "There are some of those standing here who will not taste death until they see the kingdom of God" (Luke 9:27).

Other sayings take the form of a **command**, a sentence in which the verb stands in the imperative or jussive mood. These too may be classified on the basis of their content. The command may be an instruction ("Going into all the world, preach the gospel to all the creation," Mark 16:15), an exhortation ("love your enemies," Matt 5:44), a prohibition ("do not judge, lest you be judged," Matt 7:1), or a warning ("watch out for false prophets," Matt 7:15).

Still other sayings of Jesus take the form of a conditional sentence or a rhetorical question. These too are best classified on the basis of their content.

FUNCTIONS OF THE TRADITION

The traditions about Jesus were preserved because they met certain needs in the life of the church. Christians used these traditions in their various activities, such as teaching, evangelism, debate, scriptural interpretation, and worship. Within these settings, the gospel traditions served various purposes or functions, such as instruction, moral exhortation, apologetic, worship, and faith-building. Socio-historical criticism seeks to understand how an individual pericope functioned within the early Christian community where it circulated.

Some of the tradition functioned as **instruction**. It served to instruct the community or certain segments of the community. For example, Matthew 18:15–17 told community members how to resolve conflicts with other members. Mission instructions gave directions to Christian missionaries on how to go about preaching the gospel (Matt 10:1–42; Luke 9:1–6).

Much of the tradition, especially the sayings, functioned as **moral exhortation** (parenesis). It had the purpose of exhorting Christians to live according to the standards of the Christian community. It served to motivate the audience to think and behave in a certain way, to encourage and comfort those who conformed to this expectation, to condemn and rebuke those who did not, to inform the audience of the consequences of acting in one way or another, and to warn against those who taught another way.

The basic sentence in moral exhortation is a command or prohibition, telling what to do or not to do: e.g. "love your enemies" (Matt 5:44); "do not judge, lest you be judged" (Matt 7:1); "watch out for false prophets" (Matt 7:15). Other sentences support the exhortation with arguments, threats, or promises. Such threats and promises included descriptions of the judgment that would occur when Jesus returned.

Other traditions functioned as **apologetic**. That is, they justified the beliefs and practices of the community against criticisms from within or without. The controversy dialogues, for example, justified practices and beliefs that some other groups of Jews questioned, such as healing on the Sabbath (Mark 3:1–6) or the belief in resurrection (Mark 12:18–27). The passion narrative justified the Christian belief that Jesus, even though he had been executed, was nevertheless the Messiah: it claimed that his death had been a part of God's plan, foretold in the scriptures. Stories about Jesus ministering to Samaritans or Gentiles justified the community's mission to non-Jews.

The early Christian prayer called "the Lord's Prayer" (Matt 6:9–13; Luke 11:2–4) was used in Christian **worship**, whether individual or communal.

The miracle stories served the purpose of **faith-building**. They functioned to build faith, either among community members or among outsiders. Stories about Jesus' healings and exorcisms helped to create faith that the risen Jesus could continue to perform the same miracles through members of the community. Stories about Jesus' feeding miracles built faith in Jesus' ability to continue to provide the community's needs.

DISCUSSION QUESTION

Distinguish the individual units of tradition (pericopes) in the following gospel passages and identify their form or genre. Imagine their probable setting and function in the early church, that is, in what setting they might have been used and for what purpose. Mark 2:23–28; Mark 4:35–5:43; Matt 13:44–50; Luke 18:9–14; Matt 5:43–48; Matt 6:5–15.

REVIEW QUESTIONS

1. Identify or define: gospel, evangelist.
2. Describe the various types of early Christian writings that have been called "gospels." Identify or define: passion gospels, infancy gospels.
3. What affinities do the canonical gospels have with the oral gospel? With ancient biographies? With works of "sacred history"?
4. The material in the gospels went through what three stages in the process of becoming a gospel? In what ways did the evangelists shape the final form of the gospels?

5. Describe three major ways in which the gospel traditions changed and developed.
6. What methods of interpretation focus on the world behind the text? The world within the text? The world in front of the text?
7. Identify or define: source criticism, redaction criticism, form criticism, pericope, genre criticism, socio-historical criticism, historical criticism, historical-theological criticism, literary criticism, rhetorical criticism, ideological criticism.
8. The gospel traditions consist of what two broad types?
9. Identify or define: pronouncement story, controversy dialogue, scholastic dialogue, miracle story, passion narrative, birth narrative, parable, example story, declaration, command.
10. What functions did the gospel traditions serve in the life of the early church?

SUGGESTIONS FOR FURTHER STUDY

Canonical gospels

Burridge, Richard. *What Are the Gospels? A Comparison with Graeco-Roman Biography* (2nd rev. ed.; Eerdmans, 2004). Argues that the canonical gospels have the characteristics of ancient biographies.

Koester, Helmut. *Ancient Christian Gospels: Their History and Development* (Trinity, 1990). Traces the development of the gospel tradition from isolated sayings to complete gospels, both canonical and non-canonical.

Forms of the Tradition

Hultgren, Arland J. *Jesus and His Adversaries: The Form and Function of the Conflict Stories in the Synoptic Tradition* (Augsburg, 1979). Analysis of the controversy dialogues in the gospels.

Snodgrass, Klyne R. *Stories with Intent: A Comprehensive Guide to the Parables of Jesus* (Eerdmans, 2008). A comprehensive introduction to the parables of the gospels.

Theissen, Gerd. *The Miracle Stories of the Early Christian Tradition* (Fortress, 1983). Analyzes early Christian miracle stories: their motifs and themes, development in literary settings, and functions in primitive Christianity.

Methods of Interpretation

Law, David R. *The Historical-Critical Method: A Guide for the Perplexed* (Bloomsbury T&T Clark, 2012). After a history of historical criticism, discusses textual criticism, source criticism, form criticism, and redaction criticism.

Resseguie, James L. *Narrative Criticism of the New Testament: An Introduction* (Baker Academic, 2005). Discusses rhetoric, setting, character, point of view, and plot, with a focus on the narratives of the New Testament.

10   The Synoptic Problem

The first three gospels in the New Testament (Matthew, Mark, and Luke) share many of the same sayings and stories about Jesus. For instance, nearly every story and saying in Mark's gospel also occurs in one or both of the other gospels. In the material that they share, they also tend to say the same things about Jesus. They relate the same stories and sayings in the same order with much the same wording. Because of these similarities, scholars began to place all three texts on the same page in parallel columns in order to more easily compare them. Such a comparative view is called a **synopsis**, literally a "viewing together." Because these three gospels could be viewed together in this way, they acquired the designation **Synoptic Gospels**.

The similarities among the Synoptic Gospels give rise to the **Synoptic Problem**. That is, why are these gospels so much alike? What is the relationship between them? Most scholars believe that the Synoptic Gospels have similarities because they shared some of the same written sources. The attempt to determine the sources of the gospels is called "source criticism."

At first sight, the similar content and order of the Synoptic Gospels does not seem surprising. If three of Jesus' disciples traveled with him and each independently related the events of his life, would they not relate many of the same events in the same order? Three observations show that this explanation does not suffice. First, the order of material in the Synoptics does not always reflect the order of events in Jesus' life. The gospels include collections of controversy dialogues, collections of sayings, collections of parables, and collections of miracle stories. It is not likely that Jesus divided his life so neatly into different activities, as if one day he did nothing except have controversies with opponents and the next day did nothing except perform miracles. The order of the gospels is often based not on the order of events in Jesus' life but on the practice of grouping similar kinds of material together. Therefore, if the Synoptics exhibit the same order, which is not the order of events in Jesus' life, then they are not independent accounts but dependent on the same source or sources.

A second observation confirms the first. In individual stories, the Synoptics often use similar wording. They use the same sentences in the same order with much the same wording (see Table 10.2 below). If three individuals gave independent accounts of the same event, they would not use the same sentences in the same order with the same words. This close relationship in wording shows that in such instances the Synoptics give not three independent accounts but a single account that has been modified in three different ways.

A third observation helps to explain the first two: the authors of the Synoptic Gospels were not eyewitnesses of the events that they relate. Whereas a disciple who traveled with Jesus would write in the first person ("We got into the boat"), the Synoptic evangelists write in the third person ("Jesus and his students got into the boat"). In this way, they distinguish themselves from the characters in the story. Since the evangelists were not eyewitnesses, they had to rely on sources for their information. And the similarities in their accounts show that they must have used some of the same sources. The Synoptic Problem is the question of what those sources were.

FEATURES OF THE SYNOPTIC PROBLEM

To better understand the Synoptic Problem, we must consider what material each gospel includes and in what order each gospel includes that material. To help with this process, Table 10.1 lists selected passages of the Synoptic Gospels in parallel columns to facilitate a comparison.

We can identify the following types of material in Table 10.1.

The **Markan material** is material that occurs in the Gospel of Mark. This includes the **triple tradition**, which is the material that occurs in all three gospels. For example, the passage "To Galilee" occurs in all three gospels, in Mark 1:14b and its parallels. Some of the Markan material, however, occurs only in Mark and Matthew, while some of it occurs only in Mark and Luke. Both Matthew and Luke usually include the Markan material in the same order as Mark.

Table 10.1: *Order of selected passages of the Synoptic Gospels*

	MATTHEW	MARK	LUKE
John arrested	4:12a	1:14a	
To Galilee	4:12b	1:14b	4:14a
Kingdom at hand	4:17	1:14c–15	
Fishermen called	4:18–22	1:16–20	
To Capernaum		1:21a	4:31a
Jesus teaches	5:2	1:21b	4:31b
	Q sermon		
People astonished	7:28b-29	1:22	4:32
Skin disease healed	8:2–4		
	Centurion's boy		
Demon in synagogue		1:23–28	4:33–37
At Peter's house	8:14–15	1:29–31	4:38–39
Healing the ill	8:16	1:32–34	4:40–41
Preaching tour		1:35–39	4:42–44
Skin disease healed		1:40–45	5:12–16
	On following		
Lame man healed	9:1b–8	2:1–12	5:18–26
Eating with sinners	9:9–13	2:13–17	5:27–32
About fasting	9:14–15	2:18–20	5:33–35
New and old	9:16–17	2:21–22	5:36–38
	Pray for workers		
	Mission discourse		
	Woes on cities		
	Jesus confesses		
Come unto me	11:28–30		
Plucking grain	12:1–8	2:23–28	6:1–5
Withered hand	12:9–14	3:1–6	6:6–11
Ministry to crowd	12:15–16	3:7–12	6:17–19
			Q sermon
			Centurion's boy
Widow's son			7:11–17
Jesus feeds 5,000	14:13–21	6:32–44	9:10b–17
Walk on water	14:22–33	6:45–52	
At Gennesaret	14:34–36	6:53–56	
			On following
			Pray for workers
			Mission discourse
			Woes on cities
			Jesus confesses

The **double tradition** is material that occurs in Matthew and Luke but not Mark. Some examples are listed in bold italics in Table 10.1. Matthew and Luke do not always include this material in the same order, but the table shows several passages that they do have in the same order. That is, in both Matthew and Luke, "Q sermon" is followed by "Centurion's boy," which is followed by "On following," and so forth. While Matthew and Luke have these passages in the same order, they do not include them in the same position in the order of the Markan material. For example, Matthew includes "Q sermon" early in the order of the Markan material (after Matthew's parallel to Mark 1:21b), while Luke has "Q sermon" later (after Luke's parallel to Mark 3:7–12).

Special material is material that occurs in only one gospel. Matthew and Luke both include a good deal of special material, while Mark has only a small amount. Because Matthew and Luke include not only the Markan material but also the double tradition and a good deal of special material, their gospels are both considerably longer than Mark's.

To account for these features of the Synoptic Problem, scholars have proposed various theories. The simplest type of solution theorizes that the first Synoptic written served as a source for the other two. But which Synoptic came first? On the basis of how scholars answer this question, we can classify their theories as theories of Matthean priority, Markan priority, or Lukan priority. Few scholars have proposed theories of Lukan priority since Luke himself says that he knew earlier written accounts of Jesus' story (Luke 1:1). Most theories therefore propose either Matthean priority or Markan priority.

THEORIES OF MATTHEAN PRIORITY

According to theories of Matthean priority, Matthew wrote the first gospel and the other two evangelists used it as a source. This theory appears already in the work of Augustine, bishop of Hippo, in the fifth century. He assumed that the gospels were written in the order that they occur in the New Testament. Matthew wrote the first gospel, which was abridged by Mark; Luke then came last, using both Matthew and Mark.

More frequently, scholars have advocated another theory of Matthean priority, the **Griesbach hypothesis**. Named for the eighteenth-century scholar who first proposed it, the Griesbach hypothesis was revived in the twentieth century as "the two-gospel hypothesis." This theory is illustrated by the following diagram, where the arrows are drawn from the source to the gospel that used the source.

This theory views Matthew as the original gospel. Luke came next, using Matthew as a source. Mark came last of all, combining and abridging both of these gospels.

Most critics think that theories of Matthean priority do not adequately account for the existence of Mark's gospel. Matthew's gospel contains much more material than Mark's, including such significant items as the Lord's Prayer and the Sermon on the Mount. Luke's gospel also contains much more material than Mark's, including such significant items as the parable of the good Samaritan and the parable of the prodigal son. If one or both of these gospels already existed in the church, then what purpose would be served by creating Mark's less complete gospel? It is more plausible to suppose that Mark came first and that Matthew and Luke created their gospels to include the material that Mark lacked.

THEORIES OF MARKAN PRIORITY

Most scholars think that Mark was the first gospel and was used as a source by Matthew and Luke. One of the simpler forms of this theory is **Farrer's hypothesis.** The following diagram illustrates this theory.

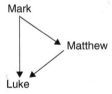

This theory assumes that Mark wrote the first gospel. Matthew came next, expanding Mark with additional material. Luke came last, using both of the other gospels.

The main problem with this theory is the lack of evidence that Luke used Matthew as a source. Such evidence is lacking in three respects. First, if Luke used Matthew as a source, we would expect Luke to include at least some of the distinctive features of Matthew's style and theme. However, such features are absent from Luke.

Second, Luke does not have the same birth narrative as Matthew or the same resurrection narrative. This fact suggests that Luke did not use

Matthew's gospel but shared a source with Matthew that did not include birth or resurrection narratives.

Third, if Luke used Matthew as a source, we would expect Luke to show knowledge of Matthew's order. However, Luke shows no such knowledge. As Table 10.1 above shows, both Matthew and Luke usually follow the same order as Mark for the triple tradition. They also sometimes follow the same order in the double tradition. However, Luke does not follow the order in which Matthew combined the double tradition with the Markan material. For example, Matthew placed the double tradition "Q sermon" (Matt 5:3–7:27) after the Markan passage "Jesus teaches" (Mark 1:21b), while Luke placed his version of "Q sermon" (Luke 6:20–49) much later, after the Markan passage "Ministry to crowd" (Mark 3:7–12). Thus Luke follows the order of the Markan material and the order of the double tradition, but he does not follow the order in which Matthew combined these two types of material. This difference suggests that Luke did not use Matthew (or vice versa) but that Matthew and Luke independently combined two different sources: one for the Markan material and another for the double tradition. This observation leads to the theory that we will describe next.

Since the beginning of the twentieth century, the most widely accepted theory of Synoptic relations has been the **two-document hypothesis**, also known as the two-source hypothesis. This theory can be represented schematically as follows.

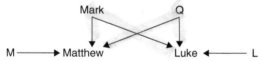

This theory proposes that the earliest gospel sources were two documents: the Gospel of Mark and a lost source designated "Q" (from German *Quelle*, "source"). According to this theory, Matthew and Luke independently copied from both Mark and Q. In addition, Matthew and Luke each had a special source or tradition, designated "M" and "L," respectively.

In this theory, Mark was the source of the triple tradition, the material shared by all three gospels. Both Matthew and Luke copied this material from Mark, revising it. Sometimes Matthew included material from Mark that Luke omitted, while at other times Luke included material from Mark that Matthew omitted. The Q document was the source of the double tradition. The material unique to Matthew is either Q material omitted by Luke, material from a special source or tradition (M), or Matthew's own composition. The material unique to Luke is either Q material omitted by Matthew, material from a special source or tradition (L), or Luke's own composition. The material unique to Mark was material that both Matthew and Luke omitted when they were copying Mark.

A PROBLEM WITH MARKAN PRIORITY

Certain aspects of the two-document hypothesis are probably correct. The Q hypothesis, though it has been challenged, still remains the most probable explanation for the material common to Matthew and Luke. More problematic, however, is **the standard theory of Markan priority,** the view that Matthew and Luke independently used the Gospel of Mark as a source for the material that they share with Mark. While most scholars still accept this theory, it has at least one serious problem, known as the **minor agreements of Matthew and Luke against Mark in the triple tradition**. These are the numerous places in the triple tradition where Matthew and Luke agree in wording with each other but not with Mark. For example, in Mark 14:65 (Matt 26:68; Luke 22:24), Matthew and Luke agree on including the question "Who is it that struck you?" Here Matthew and Luke are supposed to be copying from Mark, but Mark does not have this question. Matthew and Luke agree against Mark where, according to the theory of Markan priority, they should be following Mark. Table 10.2 below shows other agreements of this type. There are around a thousand such agreements. If Matthew and Luke were both following Mark for this material, then why do they so often agree with each other instead of with Mark?

Some of the minor agreements can be explained by recognizing that Mark and Q sometimes preserved the same story or saying and that Matthew and Luke sometimes followed Q instead of Mark. This explanation is supported by the fact that Matthew and Luke occasionally include "doublets": two forms of the same story or saying, one shared with Mark and one absent from Mark. In these cases, Mark and Q apparently preserved the same tradition. Sometimes Matthew and Luke preserved both versions; at other times, they conflated (combined) the two versions into a single new version. In the latter case, Matthew and Luke may agree against Mark because they followed Q instead of Mark at certain places.

Most of the minor agreements, however, cannot be explained by an appeal to Q, since most of the triple tradition does not have a parallel in Q. More often, all three gospels have the same version of the story from the Markan material, and no parallel version from Q appears. Yet even in these cases, Matthew and Luke still often agree against Mark in much of their wording.

Proponents of the standard theory of Markan priority have given two further explanations for these minor agreements. 1) They argue that scribes copying the manuscripts sometimes changed the original wording to make Luke agree with Matthew. This explanation, however, could account for only a small number of the agreements. 2) For most of the agreements, they argue that Matthew and Luke by coincidence made the same editorial changes to Mark independently. However, it would require a great deal of coincidence for Matthew and Luke to make so many of the same changes independently.

Despite these efforts to explain the minor agreements against Mark, one observation shows that they pose a serious problem for the standard theory of Markan priority. These agreements are so numerous that in many pericopes of the triple tradition, Matthew and Luke agree with each other more often than either agrees with Mark. The pericope shown in Table 10.2 below is one example. In this pericope, the agreements of two Synoptics against the third are as follows:

agreements of Matthew and Mark against Luke: 4
agreements of Luke and Mark against Matthew: 8
agreements of Matthew and Luke against Mark: 12

If Matthew copied Mark but did not use Luke, then Matthew should agree more often with Mark than with Luke. However, just the opposite is true. Matthew agrees more often with Luke (twelve times) than with Mark (four times). Likewise, if Luke copied Mark but did not use Matthew, then Luke should agree more often with Mark than with Matthew. Again, however, just the opposite is true. Luke agrees more often with Matthew (twelve times) than with Mark (eight times). This distribution of agreements cannot be explained by the influence of Q on Matthew and Luke, since no parallel version of this pericope occurs in the Q material. Thus this distribution of agreements is not consistent with the standard theory of Markan priority.

This pericope is not an isolated example. In the majority of pericopes in the triple tradition, Matthew and Luke agree with each other more often than, as often as, or nearly as often as, either agrees with Mark (Burkett 2017). This distribution of agreements is inconsistent with the standard theory of Markan priority. Thus the minor agreements against Mark pose a major problem for this theory.

ALTERNATIVES TO MARKAN PRIORITY

Critics who take the minor agreements seriously have proposed two main alternatives to the standard theory of Markan priority.

The **Proto-Mark hypothesis** is a variation of the two-document hypothesis. It differs from the classic two-document hypothesis in its explanation of the Markan material. It affirms that all three Synoptic evangelists took the Markan material from an earlier written source now lost. Since this source stood closest to Mark in contents and order, it has been called "Proto-Mark" ("first Mark") or in German "Urmarcus" ("original Mark"). In this theory, as in the two-document hypothesis, Matthew and Luke also used Q and their own special material. It can be represented schematically as follows.

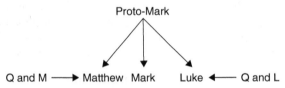

The minor agreements against Mark pose no problem for this theory. As the three Synoptic evangelists used Proto-Mark as a source, each independently revised it. Where Mark revised the source but the others did not, the result was an agreement of Matthew and Luke against Mark.

The **Deutero-Mark hypothesis** is also a variation of the two-document hypothesis. It supposes that Mark wrote first; subsequently Mark was revised into a second edition of Mark, a "Deutero-Mark" ("second Mark") which has now been lost; then Matthew and Luke both used Deutero-Mark along with Q and their own special material. The minor agreements against Mark pose no problem for this theory either. As the editor of Deutero-Mark copied Mark he made revisions to Mark's wording. Matthew and Luke agree against Mark in the triple tradition because they followed the revised wording of Deutero-Mark instead of the original language of Mark.

DISCUSSION QUESTION

The line synopsis in Table 10.2 uses parallel lines to show all three versions of the triple tradition pericope "Why parables." This synopsis uses an

Table 10.2: *Line synopsis of Mark 4:10–12 and parallels*

MATT: *And* approaching,   **the** *students*
MARK: *And* when he was alone, <u>asked him</u>   **the** ones around him
LUKE: <u>Asked him</u>, then, **the** *students* of his

MATT: <u>said to him</u>, "Why in parables speak to them?"
MARK: *with the twelve*   about the parables
LUKE: what this parable might be.

MATT: *Himself, then,* <u>replying</u> *said*   *to them* <u>that</u>, **To you**
MARK: And   he was saying *to them*,   **"To you**
LUKE: *Himself, then,*   <u>said</u>,   **"To you**

MATT: **has been given** <u>*to know*</u> <u>*the secrets*</u> **of the kingdom**
MARK: <u>*the secret*</u> **has been given**   **of the kingdom**
LUKE: **has been given** <u>*to know*</u> <u>*the secrets*</u> **of the kingdom**

MATT: of heaven. *To those,*   **though,**
MARK: <u>of God</u>. *To those,*   **though,**   <u>*to those outside*</u>
LUKE: <u>of God</u>. To the ones, **though,** remaining

MATT: <u>it has not been given. ... For this reason,</u>

MATT: **in parables** I speak to them, because **seeing**
MARK: **in parables** all things come, <u>so that</u> **seeing** <u>*they may see and*</u>
LUKE: **in parables**,   <u>so that</u> **seeing**

MATT: they do   not <u>*see*</u>   **and hearing**
MARK: <u>they may not</u> perceive **and hearing** <u>*they may hear and*</u>
LUKE: <u>they may not</u> <u>*see*</u>   **and hearing**

MATT: <u>they do not hear</u> nor do they understand.
MARK: <u>they may not understand</u>
LUKE: <u>they may not understand</u>

MATT: *... lest ... they turn back and I heal them.*
MARK: *lest   they turn back and are forgiven.*
LUKE:

overly literal English translation in order to reflect both the similarities and the differences in the underlying Greek. In the synopsis, four types of agreements are marked in different fonts: agreements of all three Synoptics (in bold font), agreements of Matthew and Mark against Luke (italicized), agreements of Luke and Mark against Matthew (underlined), and agreements of Matthew and Luke against Mark (italicized and underlined twice). Explain how each type of agreement would be explained by the Griesbach hypothesis, by the standard theory of Markan priority, and by the Proto-Mark hypothesis.

REVIEW QUESTIONS

1. Identify or define: synopsis, Synoptic Gospels, Synoptic Problem.
2. What three observations show that the Synoptic Gospels were not written by three of Jesus' disciples who traveled with him and independently related the events of his life?
3. Identify or define: triple tradition, double tradition, special material.
4. Explain the Griesbach hypothesis. Why do most critics think that this and other theories of Matthean priority do not adequately account for the Gospel of Mark?
5. Explain Farrer's hypothesis. What is the main problem with this theory?
6. Explain the two-document hypothesis, including the standard theory of Markan priority and the Q hypothesis. Explain the problem that is posed for the standard theory of Markan priority by the minor agreements of Matthew and Luke against Mark in the triple tradition.
7. Explain the Proto-Mark hypothesis and the Deutero-Mark hypothesis. What advantage do these theories have over the standard theory of Markan priority?

SUGGESTIONS FOR FURTHER STUDY

Synopses

Aland, Kurt. *Synopsis Quattuor Evangeliorum* (15th ed.; Deutsche Bibelgesellschaft, 1996). Prints the Greek text of the Synoptic Gospels and the Gospel of John in parallel columns using the 26th edition of the Nestle-Aland Greek text. A version with English text is available.

Crook, Zeba A. *Parallel Gospels: A Synopsis of Early Christian Writing* (Oxford University Press, 2011). Synopsis in English of the four canonical gospels, the Gospel of Thomas, and the reconstructed text of Q, using the editor's own literal translation.

Synoptic Problem

Burkett, Delbert. *The Case for Proto-Mark: A Study in the Synoptic Problem* (Mohr Siebeck, 2017). Presents evidence in favor of the Proto-Mark hypothesis and against other theories, including new evidence against the standard theory of Markan priority.

Farmer, William R. *The Synoptic Problem: A Critical Analysis* (Macmillan, 1964; reprinted, Mercer University Press, 1976). An influential modern defense of the Griesbach or two-gospel hypothesis.

Goodacre, Mark. *The Synoptic Problem: A Way through the Maze* (Sheffield Academic Press, 2001). Argues for Farrer's hypothesis.

Stein, Robert H. *Studying the Synoptic Gospels: Origin and Interpretation* (2nd ed.; Baker Academic, 2001). Sets out the arguments for the two-document hypothesis.

Studies of Q

Burkett, Delbert. *Rethinking the Gospel Sources*, Vol. 2: *The Unity and Plurality of Q* (Society of Biblical Literature, 2009). Addresses two disputed questions in the study of Q, arguing that the Q hypothesis is necessary and that the Q material came from a single source.

Kloppenborg Verbin, John S. *Excavating Q: The History and Setting of the Sayings Gospel* (Fortress, 2000). A discussion of issues in the study of Q.

11   The Gospel of Mark

Through most of Christian history, the Gospel of Mark lay neglected in the shadow of its more substantial companions, Matthew, Luke, and John. As the shortest of the four gospels, it contains few sayings of Jesus, certainly nothing as memorable as the Sermon on the Mount (Matt 5–7), the parable of the Good Samaritan (Luke 10:25–37), or Jesus' discourse on the bread of life (John 6). Yet in the modern period, Mark's star rose as scholars began to perceive it as the earliest gospel and to mine it for information about the historical Jesus. More recently, scholars have seen it as a window not so much onto Jesus as onto the concerns of early Christianity. As a work of Christian apologetic, it makes the claim that Jesus was the Messiah and defends this claim against the objection that no true Messiah would be crucified by the Romans.

THE ORIGIN OF MARK'S GOSPEL

The Gospel of Mark does not indicate who wrote it, how it originated, or what sources it drew upon. Three primary theories have been proposed concerning the origin of this gospel.

1. The earliest tradition about this gospel comes from Papias, bishop of Hierapolis, in the first half of the second century, quoted by the church historian Eusebius about 324–25 CE (*Ecclesiastical History* 3.39.15). Papias is allegedly repeating what he heard from someone called "the Elder John." According to this tradition, someone named Mark served as an interpreter for Peter, one of Jesus' closest students, and wrote the gospel based on what he remembered of Peter's preaching. This Mark would probably be the "John Mark" who is mentioned several times in the New Testament as a co-worker of the apostle Paul (Acts 12:12; 13:5, 13; 15:37; Col 4:10; Phil

24; 2 Tim 4:11). He is also mentioned once in connection with Peter (1 Pet 5:13).

Most critical scholars do not accept Papias' claim that this gospel was based on Peter's preaching. Such a claim probably arose out of the church's desire to link their writings to some authoritative figure close to Jesus. In the early church, both the Proto-Orthodox and the Gnostics attributed their writings to apostles and other authority figures in order to justify their claim that they had the true teaching.

2. In the early twentieth century, form critics theorized that the Gospel of Mark was formed from various oral and written traditions that were handed down in the early church. An unknown evangelist (whom we will continue to call Mark) was the first to gather the various independent units of tradition and connect them in a chronological framework. Most scholars today hold this theory.

3. In a variation of this form-critical theory, the first connected narrative of traditions was not Mark but Proto-Mark (see Chapter 10). After Proto-Mark was composed, it underwent revision, which resulted in the Gospel of Mark as we know it today.

INTENDED AUDIENCE AND DATE

The author of Mark's gospel wrote for Gentile Christians. This conclusion is based on the fact that Mark explains Jewish customs (7:2–4; 15:42), a courtesy that Jewish readers would not have needed. Since Mark did not expect his non-Jewish audience to know Aramaic, he translated Aramaic terms into Greek (3:17; 5:41; 7:11, 34; 14:36; 15:22, 34).

While Mark's gospel in its final form has Gentile Christians in view, some of the traditions that Mark used were intended for Jewish Christians in or near Palestine. The controversy dialogues, for example, deal with issues that would have been of interest primarily to Jewish Christians.

Where did Mark and his community live? Suggestions include Galilee, Antioch, and southern Syria, with Rome as the most frequent answer. Those who argue for a Roman audience point out that Mark uses a number of Latin words and sometimes explains a Greek word by giving its Latin equivalent (12:42; 15:16).

Most scholars date the Gospel of Mark to the period shortly after the destruction of Jerusalem in 70 CE. This dating is based on Mark 13, which describes events connected with the Roman siege of Jerusalem and the destruction of the temple. It is likely that Mark wrote fairly soon after these events, since he still expects Jesus to return within a generation from the time that Jesus died (9:1; 13:30).

READING THE GOSPELS INDIVIDUALLY

As we study each gospel, we will examine that particular gospel's portrait of Jesus. We must therefore distinguish between a harmonistic and an individual reading of the gospels.

In the harmonistic approach, the reader combines ideas from all four gospels. From John comes the idea that Jesus was a preexistent divine being, from Matthew and Luke comes the idea that he was born of a virgin, and so on. All of these ideas are mixed together to form a single composite image of Jesus. The reader then assumes that all four gospels share this whole image, even when a gospel does not mention some particular aspect of it.

In the historical-critical approach and in the literary approach, we read each gospel separately. We do not assume that all four gospels present the same image of Jesus but find that each has its own distinctive portrait. If one gospel lacks certain ideas, we do not add these ideas from some other gospel. One way of understanding this perspective is to imagine that you belong to an early Christian community that had only one gospel. For example, what would you know about Jesus if you had only the Gospel of Mark to tell you about him?

From this perspective it is important to realize not only what Mark says, but also what he does not say. (1) Unlike John, Mark does not present Jesus as a preexistent divine being. He never calls Jesus "God" or claims that he existed before his life on earth. (2) Unlike Matthew and Luke, Mark does not present Jesus as the offspring of a virgin mother and a divine Father. As far as we know from Mark, Jesus was a normal human being with a birth like that of everyone else. (3) Unlike Matthew and Luke, Mark does not give a genealogy of Jesus, tracing his ancestry back to King David. When we clear our minds of ideas such as these, derived from other gospels, we may be able to see Mark's own distinctive portrait of Jesus more clearly.

MARK'S PORTRAIT OF JESUS

Mark presents Jesus as a Spirit-filled human being who becomes a divine being. During his adult life, the Spirit of God empowers Jesus to become the Messiah or Christ, the son of God, the prophet like Moses, a miracle worker, and a Jewish religious teacher. At the end of his life, Jesus ascends to heaven to become a deified human.

Mark begins his gospel by identifying Jesus as both **Christ** (or Messiah) and **son of God** (1:1). Shortly afterward, he describes how Jesus became both. At his baptism (1:9–11), two events occur. First, the Spirit of God comes upon Jesus. In Jewish tradition, the Spirit would rest on the anointed king or messiah (Isa 11:2; Ps Sol 17:37). The coming of the Spirit thus anoints Jesus as the Messiah or Christ. Second, the voice of God proclaims Jesus as his son. In Jewish tradition, God adopted the Davidic king as his son (2 Sam 7:14; Psalm 2:7; 89:26–27). At his baptism, therefore, Mark's Jesus becomes both the Christ or Messiah and the son of God. Mark uses the term "Christ" in its traditional sense as referring to an expected king. It is equivalent to "the king of Israel" (15:32) or "the king of the Jews" (15:2, 9, 12, 18, 26). In Mark's presentation, though Jesus was the Christ, he would reign as king only after he ascended to heaven and returned.

The Spirit also makes Jesus a prophet. In ancient Israel, people believed that a prophet spoke under the influence of God's Spirit. A prophet did not necessarily predict the future but spoke a message from God to the people, often a message that they should repent. Like a prophet, Mark's Jesus receives the Spirit of God (1:10) and he speaks God's message to the people, calling them to repent because the kingdom of God is at hand (1:15). Since this is an eschatological message, he is an eschatological prophet. Jesus refers to himself as a prophet (6:4), and the people consider him a prophet (6:14–15). In Jewish tradition, God would send the people of Israel a **prophet like Moses** (Deut 18:15–19), and Mark presents Jesus as this prophet. Just as Moses fed the people of Israel with manna in the wilderness, so Jesus miraculously feeds first 5000 and then 4000 with bread in the wilderness (Mark 6:35–44; 8:1–9). And just as scripture told the Israelites to "listen" to the prophet like Moses (Deut 18:15), so God tells Jesus' students to listen to Jesus (Mark 9:7).

Some of the prophets, such as Moses, Elijah, and Elisha, were empowered by the Spirit to perform miracles. In the same way, the Spirit empowers Jesus to be a **miracle worker**. For Mark's Jesus, this power did not come naturally. When he returns to his home town, the people there express amazement that he teaches with wisdom and performs miracles (6:1–6a). This response shows that he demonstrated no special wisdom or miraculous ability as he grew up. Only after he received the Holy Spirit did he begin to exhibit extraordinary abilities. In particular, he began to cast out demons and perform miraculous healings. Ancient peoples believed that invisible spirits caused various sorts of physical and mental

Figure 11.1
Fourth-century
fresco of a
woman healed
by touching
Jesus' garment
(Mark 5:24–34).
Catacomb of
Santi Marcellino
e Pietro, Rome
(Scala/Art
Resource, NY).

afflictions. In Jewish thought, these demons were ruled by Beelzebul or Satan. Jews believed that Satan was the spiritual power behind the political power of the Romans. Therefore when God established his kingdom on the earth, it would replace not only the rule of Rome, but also the rule of Satan. Jesus' exorcisms and healings thus demonstrate the power of God's kingdom over the power of Satan's kingdom.

Mark's Jesus also functions as a **Jewish religious teacher**. In this capacity, he teaches students or "disciples" but also the people in general. His students and others address him as "Teacher" or "Rabbi." In his teaching, Jesus upholds the Jewish Law as the path to eternal life (10:17–20;

12:28–34). His interpretation of the Law is usually more lenient than that of the scribes and Pharisees (2:1–3:6) but stricter on the issue of divorce (10:2–12).

At the end of his life, Mark's Jesus becomes a **deified human**. In Hellenistic tradition, special individuals ascended to heaven not only to live with the gods but to become gods themselves (see Chapter 6). Though Mark does not use the term "apotheosis" or "deification," his Jesus undergoes essentially the same transformation. He ascends to heaven to sit at the right hand of God (12:35–37; 14:62; cf. 16:19).

THE PURPOSE OF MARK'S GOSPEL

Mark's gospel was written to answer the question, "How can a crucified man be the Messiah?" Most Jews expected the Messiah to be a victorious king who would drive out the Romans and establish the kingdom of God. Jesus did not fulfill this expectation. Instead of driving out the Romans, he was crucified by them. This fact posed a major problem for the church's proclamation that Jesus was the Messiah. The idea of a crucified Christ, as Paul put it, was "a scandal to the Jews and foolishness to the Gentiles" (1 Cor 1:23). How then could Jesus be the Messiah? Mark answered this question by presenting **a new Christian conception of the Messiah**, one in which the Messiah would come twice: the first time to die and the second time to establish the kingdom of God.

Jesus' earliest followers believed that he would establish the kingdom of God and set them free from Roman domination (Mark 11:10; Luke 19:11; 24:21). When Jesus was killed, some of his followers refused to give up this hope. They reinterpreted the concept of the Messiah in order to incorporate the fact of Jesus' death. They searched the Jewish scriptures for passages that would support this new conception. Applying these scriptures to Jesus, they created a new Christian conception of the Messiah. In this reinterpretation, Jesus had been the Messiah, but before he could rule as the Messiah he first had to suffer and die. Though the Romans crucified him, he could still reign as Messiah because in this conception he was raised from the dead, caught up to heaven, and enthroned at the right hand of God, thus receiving an eternal kingdom from God. In a short time, he would return from heaven to establish the kingdom of God on the earth.

Mark's purpose was to present this new Christian conception of the Messiah. He presented it not merely as a claim about Jesus, but in the form of a narrative, a story about Jesus. Several key elements of his story help to present this new conception. These include the messianic secret, references to fulfillment of scripture, Jesus' foreknowledge, the title "Son of Man," and the obtuseness of Jesus' students.

The Messianic Secret

Mark informs the reader from the beginning that Jesus is the Christ, the son of God (1:1). However, this identity remains a secret from most of the characters in the first half of the gospel. Only the demons recognize that Jesus is the Christ, and he forbids them to tell anyone (1:23–25; 1:34; 3:11–12). The people do not realize that Jesus is the Messiah but identify him as a prophet (6:14–16; 8:27–28). At first, even his students wonder who he is (4:41). Halfway through the story, they realize that he is the Christ, but he likewise forbids them to tell anyone else (8:29–30; 9:9). Only when he is on trial before the Jewish Sanhedrin does he publicly reveal his identity as the Christ, the son of God (14:61–62).

Such aspects of the story make up what is known as the **messianic secret**. Though scholars have given different explanations of this secret, it is most likely that it forms part of Mark's presentation of Jesus as the Christian Messiah. As readers, we can imagine what would happen in the story if Jesus announced his identity as the Messiah. Those who believed him would expect him to go to Jerusalem, drive out the Romans, and establish the kingdom of God. But in the new Christian conception of the Messiah, such an action would be premature because Jesus must first die before he can rule as the messianic king. If Jesus announced publicly that he was the Christ, it would encourage people to see him in the traditional role of the Messiah as a victorious and reigning king, a role that he was not yet ready to assume. The messianic secret thus forms part of the narrative presentation of the new conception of the Messiah.

Fulfillment of Scripture

Mark's allusions to the **fulfillment of scripture** also contribute to his presentation of Jesus as the Christian Messiah. This new conception originated as early Christians took passages from the Jewish scriptures and reinterpreted them as prophetic references to Jesus. In doing so, they defended the death of Jesus as part of a plan of God that was predicted long in advance. This origin of the concept has left its impression on Mark's narrative. Especially in the passion narrative, the events surrounding Jesus' death are presented as fulfillments of various scriptures (e.g. 9:12, 13; 14:21, 49).

Jesus' Foreknowledge

The motif of **Jesus' foreknowledge** also contributes to Mark's portrait of Jesus as the Christian Messiah. In Mark's presentation, Jesus understands the scriptures that predict his passion and therefore knows in advance what will happen to him. In three "passion predictions," he predicts his approaching death and resurrection (8:31; 9:31; 10:33–34). In this way, he sets out the new conception of the Messiah privately to his students. Later in Jerusalem, he even knows who will betray him and that his disciples will abandon him and deny him (14:18–21, 27–31). At his trial, he predicts to the Sanhedrin that they will see him sitting at the right hand of God and returning on the clouds of the sky (14:61–62). In this way, he reveals the new conception of the Messiah publicly.

By depicting Jesus' foreknowledge, Mark attempts to take the tragedy out of his death. Death is not an unexpected end to his messianic hopes but an anticipated part of God's plan to achieve those hopes. By consciously embracing death as part of God's plan, Jesus appears not as a helpless victim of the Romans but as the master of his fate.

The Title "Son of Man"

The title "**Son of Man**" is another element that contributes to Mark's portrayal of Jesus as the new Christian Messiah. In Mark's presentation, Jesus refers to himself not as the Christ or son of God, but as the Son of Man. This expression is based on the Hebrew or Aramaic idiom "son of man," which means "a human being." In two passages in Mark, it probably retains this original idiomatic sense and refers to human beings in general (2:10; 2:28). In the rest of its occurrences, it is a title for Jesus. It alludes to one specific use of this idiom in Daniel 7:13. There "one like a son of man" (i.e. a human-like figure) comes with the clouds of the sky before God to receive an everlasting kingdom. This passage of scripture played a key role in the new Christian conception of the Messiah. Early Christian interpreters identified Jesus as the "son of man" in this passage. This identification helped to explain why Jesus did not rule as the Messiah during his lifetime: he first had to ascend to heaven to receive the kingdom from God. Only then would he return to reign as its king.

Mark presents the title "Son of Man" as Jesus' preferred self-designation. If we leave aside the two passages that use the expression in its original idiomatic sense (2:10; 2:28), the first reference to Jesus as the Son of Man occurs after the students realize that Jesus is the Christ. Jesus acknowledges that he is the Christ but then speaks of himself instead as the Son of Man (8:29–31). Likewise, when the high priest asks Jesus if he is the Christ, the son of God, Jesus replies that he is but again changes the terminology to refer to himself as the Son of Man (14:61–62). This preference indicates that the title "Son of Man" better expresses the new conception of the Messiah than the traditional title "Christ." Though Mark identifies Jesus with the traditional title, he wishes to avoid the implication associated with that title, that Jesus would immediately establish the kingdom of God on earth. He prefers the title "Son of Man" because it implies that Jesus must first ascend to heaven to receive the kingdom from God before he can return to establish it on earth and reign as its king. As the best designation for this new conception of the Messiah, the title "Son of Man" becomes Jesus' regular self-designation in Mark (8:31, 38; 9:9, 12, 31; 10:33, 45; 13:26; 14:21, 41, 62).

The Obtuseness of the Students

A final element that contributes to Mark's presentation of the new Christian conception of the Messiah is **the obtuseness of Jesus' students**. In Mark's presentation, they initially fail to perceive Jesus' identity as the Messiah (4:41; 6:52; 8:16–21). This lack of perception shows that they have the traditional conception of the Messiah that was held by the majority of the Jewish people. The students expect the Messiah to be a victorious figure who would come, not twice, but once to drive out the Romans. Since Jesus shows no inclination to be such a figure, they initially fail to recognize him as the Messiah. In this respect, they do not differ from the other characters in the story, who also see nothing in Jesus to identify him as a traditional messianic figure (6:14–16; 8:27–28). Once the students do realize that Jesus is the Messiah, they continue to hold the same traditional understanding of what the Messiah would do. Consequently, when Jesus begins to explain the new Christian conception, that he must first die and be resurrected, they have difficulty reconciling this teaching with the traditional point of view (8:32–33; 9:10, 32). The reaction of the students thus represents the typical reaction of Jews when the early Christians preached to them that Jesus was the Messiah. By depicting the students as uncomprehending, Mark criticizes the Jewish people who held the same view of the Messiah.

COMMUNITY CONCERNS IN MARK

Though Mark's gospel is a story about Jesus, it reflects the concerns of the Christian community that arose after Jesus' death. Socio-historical criticism focuses on such concerns. We have already examined one such concern, their concern to defend the idea of a crucified Messiah. Other community concerns that come to expression in Mark include controversies with other Jews, the mission to evangelize Jews and Gentiles, and the problem of persecution.

Controversies with Other Jews

Though Mark's gospel in its final form is addressed to a Gentile Christian audience, it contains earlier material that reflects disputes relevant to Jewish Christians. These disputes arose between Jewish Christians and other Jews or between different groups within Jewish Christianity. The disputes are presented in a number of controversy dialogues, in which someone raises an issue by asking Jesus (or his disciples) a question. Jesus' reply expresses the position taken on that issue by the Christian community that preserved the story.

The controversy dialogues in the earlier chapters of Mark raise the following issues. Who can forgive sins except God alone? (2:7). Why does Jesus eat with the tax collectors and sinners? (2:16). Why do the students of John and the students of the Pharisees fast, but Jesus' students do not fast? (2:18). Why do Jesus' students do what is not permitted on the Sabbath? (2:24). Is it permissible to heal on the Sabbath? (3:4). Why do Jesus' students not walk according to the tradition of the elders, but eat bread with unclean hands? (7:5) These questions indicate that Jesus and/or later Jewish Christians were criticized for certain of their practices, such as claiming to forgive sins, eating with social outcasts, and doing "work" on the Sabbath. They were also criticized for omitting certain practices, such as fasting and ritually washing their hands.

Another group of questions appears later in the gospel. Is a man permitted to divorce his wife? (10:2). What must I do to inherit eternal life?

(10:17). Is it permitted to pay taxes to Caesar or not? (12:14). Concerning a woman who had seven consecutive husbands: In the resurrection, whose wife will she be? (12:23). What is the first commandment of all? (12:28). These questions represent issues that were being discussed in Judaism of the first century. The questioner provides the opportunity for Jesus to give an answer, which represents the perspective of early Jewish Christianity.

Mission to Jews and Gentiles

Mark's gospel also contains material that shows a concern for the Christian mission to evangelize Jews and Gentiles. In one story, Jesus' own home town rejects him (6:1–6). This rejection symbolizes the fact that Jesus' own people, the Jewish nation, generally rejected the message about Jesus that the early church preached.

Mark justifies the church's mission to Gentiles by finding support for it in the life of Jesus. Mark's Jesus initially exhibits a traditional Jewish prejudice against Gentiles. He regards the Jews as God's "children" but compares the Gentiles to "dogs." When a Gentile woman asks him to cast a demon out of her daughter, he replies, "Let the children [the Jews] be satisfied first, because it is not good to take the children's bread and give it to the dogs [the Gentiles]" (7:27). Despite his reluctance, he does heal the woman's daughter, thus giving "the children's bread" to the Gentiles. In this story, Jesus' attitude represents the perspective of Judaic Christians who did not minister to Gentiles. This attitude, however, is overcome in the story just as it was overcome in early Christianity.

Furthermore Jesus' reply indicates that a time would come when his ministry would extend to Gentiles. He says that the Jews must receive his ministry "first," implying that the Gentiles will receive it later. This remark appears to be Mark's version of Paul's principle that the gospel should go "to the Jew first, and then to the Greek" (Rom 1:16).

Later in Mark's gospel, the mission to the Gentiles is taken for granted. In the eschatological discourse, Jesus predicts that the gospel must be preached to all the nations before the end (13:10). And after his resurrection, in the longer ending of Mark, he instructs his students to go into the whole world and preach the gospel to all of creation (16:15).

Persecution

Other material in Mark's gospel focuses on the Christian community's response to persecution. The community experienced persecution because

Figure 11.2
Jesus sleeps as the storm threatens (Mark 4:35–41). Painting by Giorgio de Chirico (1888–1978). Vatican Museums (Scala/Art Resource, NY).

they confessed that Jesus was the Christ, the son of God. Some of the sayings in Mark's gospel encouraged Christians to maintain their confession of faith steadfastly, even if it meant following Jesus to death (8:34–38; 13:9–13). Other sayings teach the consequences of falling away from Jesus or causing others to fall away (9:42–50). One story, in which Peter denies knowing Jesus, served as a lesson for others in the community who were tempted to deny their faith (14:29–31, 54, 66–72). Two other stories, in which Jesus calms a storm threatening the students' boat, probably reflect the community's hope that Jesus would deliver them from the "storm" of persecution (4:35–41; 6:45–52).

READING GUIDE: MARK

Read the Gospel of Mark with the help of the following guide.

Part 1: John and Jesus (1:1–13)

The first main part of the gospel reveals Jesus' identity to the reader. Three witnesses testify that Jesus is the Christ, the son of God. First, the narrator states this explicitly (1:1). Second, John the Baptist implies this

Mark as Story

Narrative criticism studies Mark as literature rather than as history. Narrative critics do not look through the gospel as a window onto the historical Jesus or the concerns of the early church. Instead they look at the story itself, focusing on the elements common to all stories: a narrator, characters, settings, and a plot.

The **narrator** is the voice that tells a story. In a written text, the narrator is not the author, but a voice created by the author within the narrative. In some cases, the narrator is a character within the narrative, speaks in the first person ("I"), and has knowledge limited to those events at which he or she is present. In other instances, the narrator is not a character but simply a voice, speaks in the third person, and has unlimited knowledge (omniscience). The narrator in Mark belongs to the latter category. Mark's narrator knows what happens in public as well as what happens in private, even when Jesus is alone. The narrator knows not only what happens, but also what people are thinking or feeling. Mark's narrator tells the story not from a neutral perspective but from a particular point of view. The narrator portrays Jesus as a hero on the side of God, but his adversaries as villains who oppose God.

Characters are the actors in the narrative. In Mark, the characters include Jesus (the main character or protagonist), the demons, the Jewish authorities as a group, the crowds as a group, the students as a group, and various minor characters. The narrator does little to give these characters distinctive personalities, so that they appear somewhat underdeveloped by modern standards. The narrator characterizes Jesus in a positive way as powerful, authoritative, enigmatic, and self-sacrificing. The Jewish authorities come across as hostile, while the students appear obtuse and uncomprehending.

Settings are aspects of the world where the events of the story take place. Mark's narrative is set in Jewish Palestine under Roman domination. The story takes place in Galilean towns and villages, the mountains, and the sea, and culminates in a journey from Galilee to Jerusalem.

The **plot** is the pattern of events that make up the story. The plot of Mark's story does not merely seek to entertain but has a rhetorical purpose. It aims to persuade the reader that Jesus is the Messiah, that is, the Christ, the son of God. This plot develops in four main sections. 1) The opening scene (1:1–13) identifies Jesus as the Messiah and describes how he became the Christ and the son of God. 2) The second section (1:14–8:30) develops the theme of Jesus' identity, focusing on the question, Who is Jesus? Jesus keeps his identity as the Messiah a secret, but, at the conclusion of this section, his students realize who he is. 3) The third section (8:31–13:37) further develops the theme of Jesus' identity, focusing on the question, What type of Messiah is Jesus? Jesus reveals to his students a new conception of the Messiah. He predicts that instead of taking power at once, he must first suffer, be killed, rise from the dead, and ascend to heaven to receive the kingdom from God. Only then will he return to establish the kingdom of God and reign over it as the Messiah. 4) The final section (14:1–16:20) describes the fulfillment of Jesus' predictions: he suffers, is crucified, rises from the dead, and ascends to heaven to sit at the right hand of God. Only his prediction that he will return to establish the kingdom remains unfulfilled within the narrative.

by announcing the coming of one more powerful than himself (1:2–8). Third, when Jesus is baptized and the Holy Spirit anoints him as the Messiah, God himself speaks to Jesus from heaven, acknowledging him as his son (1:9–11). Afterward Jesus heads into the wilderness to be tested as God's son (1:12–13), just as God's earlier son, the people of Israel, was tested in the wilderness (cf. Deut 8:2–5).

Part 2: The Secret Messiah (1:14–8:30)

The second main part of the gospel (1:14–8:30) focuses on the question, Who is Jesus? It develops the theme of Jesus' identity by presenting him as the secret Messiah. Though the reader knows Jesus' identity, it remains a secret to most of the characters in the story. Beginning in Galilee, Jesus announces that the kingdom of God is at hand. He demonstrates the power of this kingdom by casting out demons, healing people, and exercising authority over nature. He does not reveal who he is, but speaks of the kingdom in veiled parables. The plot develops around the responses that various groups have toward Jesus. The demons recognize who he is, but he forbids them to speak. The Pharisees and scribes take offense at his interpretation of the Law and plot to kill him. The people follow him in droves but fail to recognize him as the Messiah. His students too see his wonders but initially fail to realize who he is. Finally, halfway through the gospel, Peter and the other students realize that Jesus is the Christ.

The **beginning of Jesus' ministry (1:14–45)** takes place in Galilee. He preaches that the kingdom of God is at hand (1:14–15) and calls four fishermen as helpers (1:16–20). His power and authority are illustrated in five narratives relating exorcisms or healings (1:23–28; 1:29–31; 1:32–34; 1:35–39; 1:40–45). The demons recognize him as the Messiah, but he forbids them to tell who he is (1:24–25; 1:34).

Jesus' interpretation of the Law and his claim to authority bring him into conflict with the scribes and Pharisees. A series of five **controversy dialogues (2:1–3:6)** concludes with the Pharisees and Herodians planning to kill him (3:6).

Jesus then withdraws to the Sea of Galilee, where he ministers to a crowd and again forbids the demons to reveal his secret identity (3:7–12). He chooses twelve of his followers as "apostles" to help him in his ministry of exorcism and healing (3:13–19). His family thinks that he is out of his mind (3:20–21), and the scribes think that he is in league with the ruler of the demons (3:22–30). He tells his followers that they are his true family (3:31–35).

In a **parable discourse (4:1–34)**, Jesus teaches the people about the kingdom of God, but he speaks in veiled parables whose meaning he explains only to his students. Jesus reveals to his students "the secret of the kingdom of God," but he keeps the people from understanding so that they will not repent and be forgiven (4:10–12, 34). This explanation of Jesus' parables conflicts with other passages in Mark, where Jesus does want the people to repent (1:15).

Mark then gives outstanding examples of Jesus' power in a series of four **miracle stories (4:35–5:43)**: a nature miracle (4:35–41), an exorcism (5:1–20), a healing (5:21–34), and a resuscitation (5:35–43). After the nature miracle, his students wonder who he is, showing that they have not yet understood his secret identity (4:41).

After Jesus is rejected at his home town (6:1–6), he sends out the twelve apostles on a preaching tour (6:7–13). His abilities raise the **question of Jesus' identity (6:14–52)**. The people consider him a prophet, failing to realize that he is the Messiah (6:14–16). After an account of John's death (6:17–29), Jesus miraculously feeds 5,000 people (6:30–44) and walks on water (6:45–52). His students are supposed to understand something from the feeding miracle, probably the secret of his identity, but they fail to understand (6:52).

The theme of Jesus' identity disappears for a while as Jesus performs miracles and has dialogues with the Pharisees (6:53–8:13).

The **revelation of Jesus' identity (8:14–30)** begins as Jesus discusses the feeding of the 5,000 and the feeding of the 4,000 with his students (8:14–21). He expects them to understand something from these miracles, probably the secret of his identity. When they show a decided lack of comprehension, Jesus berates them for their blindness (8:18). This section of the gospel comes to a climax after Jesus heals a blind man (8:22–26). This man's physical blindness parallels the mental blindness of Jesus' students. Just as it takes Jesus two attempts to remove his blindness, so Jesus performed two miraculous feedings in order to enlighten his students concerning his identity. Immediately after this symbolic episode, Jesus again raises the question of his identity, this time asking his students who they think he is (8:27–30). Peter confesses that he is the Christ, becoming the first human character in the story to realize who Jesus is. After this breakthrough, Jesus prohibits his students from telling anyone else about him.

Part 3: A New Conception of the Messiah (8:31–13:37)

The second part of the gospel asked "Who is Jesus?" and culminated in Peter's confession that he was the Christ or Messiah. Now the third main part answers the question, "What kind of Messiah is he?" In traditional Jewish understanding, the Messiah came only once, to reign in the kingdom of God. Jesus presents a new conception in which the Messiah comes twice: first to die and ascend to heaven, then to return and reign. In this section of the story, Jesus continues to teach and perform miracles. However, much of the material now focuses on Jesus' approaching death. Three times Jesus predicts his death and resurrection in Jerusalem (8:31; 9:30–32; 10:32–34). Each of these "passion predictions" is followed by a teaching that draws out the implications of this new conception for his followers (8:34–9:1; 9:33–35; 10:35–45).

After the students realize that Jesus is the Messiah, he gives his **first passion prediction (8:31)**. He predicts that he must suffer, be rejected, be killed, and be raised from the dead. In this prediction, he reveals a new conception of the Messiah and begins to call himself "the Son of Man" as the best designation for this Messiah. Peter, representing the students, has a difficult time accepting this concept (8:32–33). Jesus warns his followers that they must be willing to die as well if they follow him (8:34–9:1). Jesus then goes up on a mountain with three students and is transformed before them (9:2–10). Going up the mountain probably symbolizes going up to heaven. This story foreshadows another aspect of the new conception of the Messiah: Jesus will ascend to heaven after his resurrection and be glorified. This section also includes a teaching on Elijah (9:11–13) and an exorcism (9:14–29).

Subsequently Jesus gives his **second passion prediction (9:30–32)**. Again he predicts his death and resurrection, and again the students fail to understand. They see their relationship to the Christ as an opportunity for personal greatness, but Jesus teaches them that greatness involves humility (9:33–35). He then presents them with a series of other teachings (9:36–50). Afterward he leaves Galilee and relocates to Judea on his way to Jerusalem (10:1). There he teaches on various subjects (10:2–31).

On the way to Jerusalem, Jesus gives his **third passion prediction (10:32–34)**. James and John see their relation to him as an opportunity for personal greatness (10:35–41), but Jesus again teaches his students that greatness involves humility and service (10:42–45). Ironically a blind man is the first person besides the students to recognize Jesus as the Christ or "son of David" (10:46–52). From that point on, everyone in the story

Figure 11.3
Transfiguration of
Jesus (Mark 9:2–
8). Peter, James,
and John see Jesus
transformed,
with Moses and
Elijah. Painting
by Mario Balassi
(1604–67). S. Maria
della Concezione,
Rome (Scala/Art
Resource, NY).

either recognizes Jesus as the Messiah or suspects that he thinks of himself as such.

Jesus' time in Jerusalem centers around his **teaching in the temple
(11:1–12:44)**. Jesus moves to fulfill his destiny as he enters Jerusalem for
the feast of Passover. In a "triumphal entry" he rides in on a donkey (11:1–
11), an act which recalls a Hebrew scripture that spoke of a victorious

yet humble king riding into Jerusalem on a donkey (Zech 9:9). The people who follow Jesus expect him to restore the kingdom of David (11:10). The next day Jesus curses a fig tree that has no fruit (11:12–14) and uses this event as an object lesson in faith (11:20–25). His conflict with the Jewish leaders comes to a head in three episodes, in which Jesus disrupts activity in the temple (11:15–19), responds to a question about his authority (11:27–33), and tells the parable of the wicked tenants (12:1–12). Jesus then continues to teach in the temple on a variety of subjects (12:13–44).

Jesus concludes his teaching with an **eschatological discourse (13:1–37)**. In this, he predicts the destruction of the temple, an event that occurred in 70 CE when the Romans overthrew Jerusalem. This discourse connects the destruction of the temple with a period of tribulation (distress and suffering) immediately before the end of the age, when Jesus would come as "the Son of Man" to gather the elect. In the new conception of the Messiah, Jesus would thus come a second time in order to establish the kingdom of God on earth.

Part 4: Passion and Resurrection (14:1–16:8, 9–20)

The last main part of the gospel relates the fulfillment of Jesus' predictions. Those events associated with the new conception of the Messiah come to pass: he is rejected and crucified, but raised from the dead and seated at the right hand of God.

The first section in this part of the gospel relates Jesus' **betrayal and arrest (14:1–52)**. As the Passover approaches, the high priests and scribes plot to kill Jesus. They find an ally in Judas, one of the twelve (14:1–2, 10–11). In the middle of this narrative, a woman anoints Jesus for his coming burial (14:3–9). Jesus prepares to celebrate the Passover with his students (14:12–16). When it arrives, he predicts that one of the twelve will betray him (14:17–21). As they eat, he institutes the Lord's Supper, a rite performed by the early church (14:22–25). Afterward, on the Mount of Olives, he predicts that his students will abandon him but that he will see them in Galilee after his resurrection (14:26–28). He also predicts that Peter will deny him three times (14:29–31). At Gethsemane, he prays that God will spare him from his approaching death (14:32–42). His prediction of betrayal is fulfilled as Judas arrives with an armed crowd to arrest him (14:43–49). His prediction of abandonment is fulfilled as all his students flee (14:50–52).

The next section relates Jesus' **trial and mocking (14:53–15:20a)**. Jesus is taken that same night to stand trial before the Jewish Sanhedrin (14:53–65). For the first time, he reveals publicly that he is the Christ, the son of God (14:61–62), thus revealing the messianic secret. He predicts that they will see him as the Son of Man sitting at the right hand of God and coming with the clouds, two events that form part of the new conception of the Messiah. The passion predictions are fulfilled as he is rejected and condemned to death by the Sanhedrin. His prediction about Peter is fulfilled as Peter denies him three times (14:66–72). The next morning, the Sanhedrin takes him to the Roman governor Pilate, thus fulfilling a passion prediction that he would be turned over to the Gentiles (15:1–5). Pilate wants to release him, but the crowd urges him to release an insurrectionist named Barabbas instead (15:6–15). Pilate has Jesus flogged, fulfilling one of the passion predictions (15:15). The Roman soldiers mock Jesus as "the king of the Jews" (15:16–20).

The next section relates Jesus' **crucifixion and burial (15:20b–47)**. The Romans take Jesus to be crucified and mocked (15:21–32). He dies, fulfilling the passion prediction that he would be killed (15:33–41). A Roman centurion confesses that Jesus must have been the son of a god (15:39). A man named Joseph of Arimathaea buries Jesus in a tomb and rolls a stone over the door (15:42–47).

The final section of the gospel relates Jesus' **resurrection and ascension (16:1–8, 9–20)**. On the first day of the week, women who go to Jesus' tomb find it empty except for a young man. He instructs them to tell Jesus' students that Jesus has been raised from the dead, thus fulfilling the passion predictions. They will see Jesus in Galilee, as he told them before. The women, however, flee from the tomb in fear and say nothing to anyone.

Two important manuscripts end the story here (16:1–8). The resurrected Jesus never appears. The women simply leave the tomb and tell no one what they have seen. Most other manuscripts include a longer ending (16:9–20), which tells of Jesus appearing to his students in Jerusalem. One manuscript has a shorter ending, while others include both the longer and the shorter ending. Some scholars believe that Mark intended to end the story at 16:8 with the empty tomb. Others suggest that he never finished the gospel, or that the original ending was lost, because both 14:28 and 16:7 suggest that Mark intended to tell how the resurrected Jesus appeared to the disciples in Galilee. According to these theories, both the longer and shorter endings were added later by Christian scribes who felt that Mark's account was incomplete as it stood.

In the Proto-Mark hypothesis, Proto-Mark originally ended with a resurrection appearance in Galilee like that of Matthew (Matt 28:9–10, 16–20). The evangelist Mark removed this ending and substituted the longer ending, in which Jesus appeared in Jerusalem. In this account, Jesus appeared to Mary Magdalene (16:9–11), two unnamed students (16:12–13), and the eleven students (16:14–18). He then ascended to heaven (16:19–20) thus fulfilling his prediction that he would sit at the right hand of God.

DISCUSSION QUESTIONS

1. The motif of "secrecy" in Mark includes several different aspects. Especially significant are Jesus' prohibitions against revealing his identity (1:24–25, 34; 3:10–12; 8:30; 9:9). Explain the significance of this "messianic secret" in Mark's story.
2. Using literary criticism, consider Jesus as a literary character in Mark's story. What are some aspects of his personality or character?
3. A theological explanation for Jesus' death gives an answer in terms of God's will. What different theological explanations for Jesus' death does Mark give in the following passages: Mark 8:31; 9:12; 10:45; 12:1–12; 14:21; 14:24? A historical explanation for Jesus' death gives an answer in terms of human will, asking who wanted Jesus dead and why. What clues does Mark provide for a possible historical explanation of Jesus' death?

REVIEW QUESTIONS

1. What are three main theories concerning the origin of the Gospel of Mark?
2. What can we infer about the intended audience and date of Mark?
3. Distinguish between reading the gospels harmonistically and reading them individually.
4. How does Mark portray Jesus as the Messiah or Christ? the son of God? the prophet like Moses? a miracle worker? a Jewish religious teacher? a deified human?
5. What is the purpose of Mark's gospel? How do each of the following contribute to this purpose: a new conception of the Messiah, the

messianic secret, fulfillment of scriptures, Jesus' foreknowledge, the title "Son of Man," the obtuseness of Jesus' students?

6. How do the following concerns of early Christianity come to expression in Mark: controversies with other Jews, mission to Jews and Gentiles, persecution?

7. Describe the following aspects of narrative criticism in Mark: narrator, characters, settings, and plot.

SUGGESTIONS FOR FURTHER STUDY

Anderson, Janice Capel, and Stephen D. Moore, eds. *Mark and Method* (2nd ed.; Fortress, 2008). A guide to various contemporary methods of interpreting the gospels, using Mark to illustrate. Methods discussed are narrative, reader-response, deconstructive, feminist, and social criticism.

Collins, Adela Yarbro. *Mark: A Commentary* (Hermeneia; Fortress, 2007). A major commentary on the Gospel of Mark.

Harrington, Daniel J. *What Are They Saying about Mark?* (Paulist, 2004). Surveys scholarship on the Gospel of Mark since 1985.

Marcus, Joel. *Mark 1–8* and *Mark 8–16: A New Translation with Introduction and Commentary* (2 vols.; Anchor Bible, Doubleday, 2000; Anchor Yale Bible, Yale University Press, 2009). A major commentary on the Gospel of Mark.

Rhoads, David, Joanna Dewey, and Donald Michie. *Mark as Story: An Introduction to the Narrative of a Gospel* (3rd ed.; Fortress, 2012). An introduction to reading Mark as a story, discussing such literary features as the narrator, the settings, the plot, the characters, and the reader.

Telford, William R. *Mark* (Sheffield Academic Press, 1995; reprinted, Bloomsbury T&T Clark, 2004). A student's guide to Mark as history, literature, and theology.

Telford, William R. *The Theology of the Gospel of Mark* (Cambridge University Press, 1999). Discusses Mark's setting, major themes, theological purpose, place in the New Testament, place in history, and contemporary significance.

12   The Gospel of Matthew

The Gospel of Matthew presents a portrait of Jesus derived from both Jewish and Hellenistic categories. On the one hand, it is the most Jewish of all the gospels. The author combines traditions from several Jewish-Christian communities to present a portrait of Jesus as the fulfillment of Jewish hopes and scriptures. Here Jesus is not only the son of David (the Davidic Messiah) but also a lawgiver like Moses, confirming the Jewish Law but going beyond it. On the other hand, the author also presents Jesus in non-Jewish categories. Here Jesus is a Greco-Roman demigod, one in whom the Gentiles place their hope.

AUTHOR OF THE GOSPEL

Early in the history of the church, the tradition arose that the first gospel in the canon was written by Matthew, one of the twelve apostles of Jesus and an eyewitness of his ministry. This tradition is reflected in the title "According to Matthew" that appears in Greek manuscripts of this gospel. Modern scholars doubt this tradition for several reasons. First, the author of the gospel does not write in the first person ("we") as an eyewitness but in the third person ("they") as someone who did not participate in the events described. Second, it seems likely that the author relied on a number of earlier sources. An eyewitness would not need to rely on others for information. Third, the titles of the gospels were probably added years after the gospels were composed and do not necessarily provide accurate information. And fourth, early Christians tended to attribute their writings to apostles in order to impart greater authority to these writings.

Another tradition also mentions Matthew as an author but does not seem to refer to the Gospel of Matthew as we know it. The church historian Eusebius (*Ecclesiastical History* 3.39.16) quoted Papias, bishop of Hierapolis (c. 140 CE), as saying, "Matthew compiled the oracles in the

Figure 12.1
An angel dictates the gospel to the apostle Matthew. Painting by Rembrandt (1661). Modern scholars have a different view of the gospel's origin, seeing it as a combination of various sources by an anonymous Christian. Louvre (Erich Lessing/Art Resource, NY).

Hebrew dialect, and each person translated them as he was able." Here Papias describes a work written in Hebrew or Aramaic, while Matthew's gospel is written in Greek and does not appear to be a translation of a Semitic original. Thus if Matthew did compile such a work, it was not the gospel that now carries his name.

The gospel itself makes no claim concerning who wrote it. For modern scholarship therefore, the author is anonymous. For the sake of convenience, however, we continue to call the author "Matthew."

DATE, AUDIENCE, AND PLACE OF ORIGIN

Scholars generally place the **date** of Matthew's gospel at 80 to 100 CE. Some of the material in Matthew's sources probably circulated before the destruction of the temple in 70 CE. However, we can infer that the gospel itself did not take its final shape until after that time, since it refers to the destruction of Jerusalem (Matt 22:7; 24:2, 15–22).

Matthew's **intended audience** consisted primarily of Christians with a Jewish background, as the following facts indicate. 1) Matthew includes sayings from Q and M that stress the continuing validity of the Law (Matt 5:17–48). His readers, then, were probably Jewish Christians for whom the Jewish Law was still relevant. 2) Matthew does not explain Jewish customs that are explained in Mark's gospel (Matt 15:2; contrast Mark 7:2–3). His Jewish-Christian readers would be familiar with such customs. 3) Whereas Luke traces Jesus' ancestry back to Adam, father of the human race, Matthew traces it back to Abraham, father of the Jewish race (Matt 1:1; contrast Luke 4:23–38). While Matthew wrote to Jewish Christians, at least some of them preached to Gentiles. Several passages in Matthew's gospel presuppose a mission to Gentiles (10:18; 24:14; 28:19), including two passages in Matthew's redaction (4:13–16; 12:17–21).

Scholars have suggested several locations for the **place of origin** of Matthew's gospel. Since Matthew wrote in Greek for a church consisting of both Jews and Gentiles, this gospel must have originated in a location that had a population of Greek-speaking Jewish Christians engaged in mission to the Gentiles. Many scholars favor Antioch in Syria, north of Palestine. The fact that a bishop of Antioch (Ignatius, c. 115 CE) made the earliest allusion to the gospel supports this view. Also, the fact that Matthew's community evangelized Gentiles corresponds with what we know about Christianity at Antioch, since tradition records that Jewish Christians first preached to Gentiles there (Acts 11:19–20).

MATTHEW'S SOURCES

In composing his gospel, Matthew drew on three primary sources: the Markan material, the Q material, and Matthew's special material. 1) Matthew includes most of the material that occurs in Mark's gospel. In the theory of Markan priority, this material came from the Gospel of Mark, while in the Proto-Mark hypothesis it came from Proto-Mark. 2) Matthew shares a substantial amount of material with Luke alone. In the Q hypothesis, most of this material came from Q. 3) Matthew also includes a good deal of material that is unique to his gospel. Matthew probably composed some of this. Some of it may be Q material that Luke omitted. Other such material probably came from a different source or tradition that scholars have designated as "M."

MATTHEW AS REDACTOR

Matthew did not simply combine his sources but redacted (revised) them in order to create a new composition. Two features of his redaction call for special mention: his method of organization and his quotation of scriptures.

Method of Organization

With respect to the events in Jesus' ministry, Matthew usually follows the order of the Markan material. In addition to this primarily narrative material, however, Matthew also had two collections (Q and M) that consisted primarily of sayings that gave no clue as to when Jesus might have spoken them. He chose to group most of this material by theme, organizing it into **five major discourses** (speeches or sermons):

1. Sermon on the Mount (chs. 5–7)
2. Missionary Discourse (ch. 10)
3. Parable Discourse (ch. 13:1–53)
4. Community Relations Discourse (ch. 18)
5. Eschatological Discourse (chs. 24–25)

Each of these discourses has a central theme, and each ends with a similar transitional phrase: "And when Jesus finished these words …" (7:28; 11:1; 13:53; 19:1; 26:1). Each is preceded and followed by a section of narrative, so that narrative alternates with discourse throughout the gospel.

In the first discourse, Jesus goes up onto a mountain and gives new teaching about the Law. One can infer that Matthew is portraying Jesus as a new Moses, who also went up onto a mountain and taught the people the Law that he received. The fact that Matthew has five discourses may be related to this portrayal, since the Law consisted of five books.

Quotation of Scripture

Matthew's redaction emphasizes that events in Jesus' life fulfilled the Jewish scriptures. After describing certain events, he quotes a scripture, introducing it with a special formula, such as "This took place to fulfill what was spoken by the prophet." Such fulfillment quotations occur in 1:22–23; 2:15; 2:17–18; 2:23; 4:14–16; 8:17; 12:17–21; 13:14–15; 13:35; 21:4–5; and 27:9–10 (see also 2:5–6; 26:56).

Both Matthew and Luke portray Jesus giving a sermon on or near a mountain. Both probably got the sermon from Q, but Matthew's version is much longer than Luke's. Why? Probably because Matthew added other material to it from Q and M. Luke also knew the extra Q material, but he put it in different places in his gospel. The following table lists all the material in Matthew's version of the sermon. The last two columns show what part of this material Luke has in his version of the sermon and what part he puts elsewhere in his gospel.

	Sermon in Matt 5–7	Sermon in Luke 6	Elsewhere in Luke
Introduction	5:1–2	6:20a	
The Beatitudes	5:3–12	6:20b–26	
Salt	5:13		14:34–35
Light	5:14–16		11:33
Validity of the Law	5:17–20		
Murder and anger	5:21–24		
An accuser	5:25–26		12:58–59
Adultery and lust	5:27–30		
Divorce	5:31–32		16:18
Oaths	5:33–37		
Retaliation	5:38–42	6:29–30	
Love for enemies	5:43–48	6:27–28, 32–36	
Almsgiving	6:1–4		
Prayer	6:5–6		
Model prayer	6:7–13		11:1–4
Forgiveness	6:14–15		
Fasting	6:16–18		
Treasure	6:19–21		12:33–34
Good or evil eye	6:22–23		11:34–36
God or mammon	6:24		16:13
Trust or anxiety	6:25–34		12:22–31
On judging	7:1–5	6:37–42	
Dogs and swine	7:6		
Ask, seek, knock	7:7–11		11:9–13
The golden rule	7:12	6:31	
The two ways	7:13–14		13:23–24
False prophets	7:15–20	6:43–45	
Doing his will	7:21–23	6:46	13:25–27
Doing his word	7:24–27	6:47–49	
Conclusion	7:28–29	7:1	

What Matthew regarded as a fulfillment of scripture may not appear so to modern readers. Matthew followed a method of interpretation similar to that practiced at Qumran. The interpreter did not seek to determine the meaning of the scriptural text in its original historical setting but applied it directly to the situation of the interpreter's community. For instance, Matthew quotes Hosea 11:1 ("Out of Egypt I have called my son"). In the original context of Hosea, the verse referred to God bringing the nation of Israel out of Egypt. Matthew, however, interprets it to mean that God brought Jesus out of Egypt (Matt 2:15).

Matthew also quotes Isaiah 7:14, which in the original Hebrew says "the young woman is pregnant and bearing a son." In that context, it probably referred to the wife of the prophet Isaiah. Matthew, however, did not quote the original Hebrew but used the Greek translation known as the Septuagint. There the term "young woman" was translated as *parthenos*, a term that could mean either "young woman" or "virgin." Matthew took it in the latter sense and regarded the passage as a prediction of Jesus' birth from a virgin (Matt 1:23).

MATTHEW'S PORTRAIT OF JESUS

Matthew presented an eclectic portrait of Jesus. That is, he selected material from various sources to create his portrait. In some cases, these sources did not agree. Consequently Matthew's Jesus occasionally appears to vacillate between different points of view and to lack consistency. Here we will consider Jesus' identity; attitude toward the Law; teaching; preaching of judgment; attitude toward Gentiles; and death, resurrection, and parousia.

Jesus' Identity

Matthew exhibits several special emphases in presenting Jesus' identity.

Like Mark, Matthew presents Jesus as the **Christ** or Messiah. However, while Mark emphasized the messianic secret, Matthew significantly altered this theme. In Matthew's revision, Jesus still prohibits his students from revealing his identity (Matt 16:20; 17:9; cf. Mark 8:30; 9:9). Likewise, the students still wonder who Jesus is (Matt 8:27; cf. Mark 4:41), and the people still fail to identify him as the Messiah (Matt 16:13–14; cf. Mark 8:27–28). However, Matthew has omitted those scenes in which the demons recognize Jesus and he prohibits them from revealing his identity (Mark 1:24–25; 1:34; 3:11–12; cf. Matt 8:16; 12:15–16). He also has the students recognize Jesus' identity earlier in the narrative, after Jesus walks on water (Matt 14:33; cf. Mark 6:51–52). As a result of this redaction, the messianic secret is less conspicuous in Matthew than in Mark, and Peter's confession (Matt 16:16; cf. Mark 8:29) comes as an anti-climax since the students already know who Jesus is.

Matthew refers to Jesus as the **son of David** more frequently than any other evangelist (1:1, 20; 2:1–6; 9:27; 12:23; 15:22; 20:30, 31; 21:9, 15). This title identifies Jesus as the Jewish Messiah, whom many Jews expected to be a descendant of the famous Israelite king David. Matthew includes a genealogy that traces Jesus' lineage to David through Joseph, Jesus' reputed father (1:1–16, 20).

Matthew's sources designated Jesus as the **son of God**, though for the most part nothing suggests that they thought of him as more than human. Matthew's birth narrative, however, presents a different view (1:18–25). In this, Jesus is the son of God in a literal sense, because he is the offspring of one human parent (Mary) and one divine parent (God through the Holy Spirit). A Greco-Roman audience would recognize here the familiar idea of the **demigod**, adapted to Israel's understanding of God. This perspective, that Jesus was not actually the son of Joseph, stands in tension with the claim that Jesus was a descendant of David through Joseph (1:1–16, 20).

Three passages unique to Matthew express the idea that Jesus is spiritually present with his people. In the birth narrative, Matthew gives Jesus a name from the Jewish scriptures: "Emmanuel," meaning "**God (is) with us**" (1:23). In another passage, Jesus says, "where two or three are gathered in my name, there am I in the midst of them" (18:20). And in the final verse of the book, Jesus assures his disciples, "I am with you always, to the end of the age" (28:20).

Like the Jesus of Mark's gospel, Matthew's Jesus refers to himself as the **Son of Man**, the title most appropriate for the new Christian conception of the Messiah. This title appears not only in the material that Matthew shares with Mark, but also in Q and M.

Jesus' Attitude toward the Law

Matthew's Jesus emphasizes the necessity of keeping the Jewish Law. In the Markan material, he upholds the Jewish Law as the path to eternal life (19:16–19; 22:34–40). In the Q material, he declares that the Law would remain in force as long as heaven and earth endured (5:18). In Matthew's special material, Jesus says that he did not come to abolish the Law, but to fulfill it (5:17). Therefore even the least commandment of the Law had to be kept (5:19).

While Matthew's Jesus consistently upholds the Law, he vacillates on how strictly it must be kept. In Matthew's special material in the Sermon on the Mount, Jesus is a **strict rabbi**. He exhibits an attitude to the Law that is stricter than that of other Jewish teachers. He declares that one's righteousness (adherence to the Law) must exceed that of the scribes and Pharisees (5:20). While some teachers permitted a man to divorce his wife for almost any reason, Jesus permitted a man to divorce his wife only if she was unfaithful (5:31–32). While some teachers permitted oaths, Jesus prohibited them (5:33–37). Jesus extended the commandment against murder to include anger (5:21–22) and the commandment against adultery to include lustful thoughts (5:27–30). This very strict interpretation of the Law has been called "ethical perfectionism." It required Jesus' followers to be "perfect" like God (5:48) and set out a path that few could follow (7:13–14).

In other passages, Jesus is a **lenient rabbi**. He exhibits a more lenient attitude toward the Law than other Jewish teachers. In the controversy dialogues in the Markan material, Jesus' interpretation of the Law is less strict than that of the scribes and Pharisees (9:1–17; 12:1–14). In Q, he accuses the scribes and Pharisees of binding "heavy burdens" on the shoulders of the people (23:4), implying that he preferred a less burdensome application of the Law. Likewise, in Matthew's special material, Jesus claims that his yoke (interpretation of the Law) is easy and his burden light (11:28–30).

Jesus' Teaching

Matthew includes much more of Jesus' teaching than Mark does. In Q, much of this teaching consists of moral exhortation. In Matthew's special material, Jesus also gives a variety of teachings that regulate relations within the community. Among the gospels, only Matthew refers to the community as the **church** (16:18; 18:17). These passages show the church as an organized community with rules for maintaining order. One saying provides instructions for disciplining members who cause trouble (18:15–17). Another gives authority to the decisions made by the assembled congregation (18:18–20).

Jesus as a Preacher of Judgment

Matthew's Jesus spends much of his time issuing criticisms and threats of judgment, especially in the Q material. John the Baptist sets an example for him by calling the Pharisees and Sadducees a "brood of vipers," threatening them with the wrath to come, and warning that every tree without fruit would be cut down and burned (3:7–10). John predicts that the one who comes after him "will burn the chaff with unquenchable fire" (3:11–12). Jesus then takes up John's mantle, uttering similar threats of judgment. He retains the epithet "brood of vipers" (12:34; 23:33) and makes the same threat about trees without fruit (7:15–20; 12:33–37).

Jesus predicts that many Jews will be cast out of the kingdom of the heavens (8:12). He threatens woes on the cities of Galilee because they did not repent (11:20–24). He predicts abandonment and desolation for Jerusalem for killing the prophets (23:37–39).

Jesus often refers to his contemporaries as "this generation" in a pejorative sense as a generation that will be condemned at the judgment because they failed to repent (11:16–19; 12:38–42; 12:43–45; 16:1–4; 23:36). He frequently threatens that the sinners and unrepentant will be cast into "outer darkness" or into a fire, where they will weep and gnash their teeth (8:12; 13:41–42; 13:49–50; 22:13; 24:48–51; 25:30). He often refers to "Gehenna" as a place of fire reserved for sinners (5:22, 29, 30; 10:28; 18:9; 23:15, 33).

Matthew's Jesus reserves his greatest scorn for the scribes and Pharisees. He devotes an entire discourse to uttering woes against them (23:1–36). In the Sermon on the Mount, Jesus warned that anyone who called his brother a "fool" would go into the fire of Gehenna (5:22). However, he seems to make an exception for himself when he castigates the Pharisees as "blind fools" (23:17). He further denounces them as "blind guides" (15:14; 23:16, 19, 24, 26) and as "hypocrites" (6:2, 5, 16; 7:5; 15:7; 22:18; 23:13, 14, 15, 23, 25, 27, 29; 24:51).

Jesus' Attitude toward Gentiles

Matthew's material appears somewhat inconsistent in its attitude toward Gentiles. We can infer that Matthew himself had a positive view of Gentiles and the Gentile mission, since in his redaction two fulfillment quotations exhibit such a positive view (4:13–16; 12:17–21). However, Matthew's sources did not all share this view. Consequently Matthew's Jesus often exhibits a strong **anti-Gentile bias**. In the Markan material, Jesus refers to Gentiles as "dogs" (15:26), and he charges that the rulers of the Gentiles lord it over them (20:25). In Q, he criticizes the Gentiles for worrying about what they would eat and drink and what they would wear (6:31–32). In Matthew's special material, Jesus thinks that Gentiles lack the proper standard of love (5:47) and pray with too much repetition

(6:7). The proper way to treat Gentiles was to have nothing to do with them (18:17).

Matthew's Jesus vacillates on the question of whether Gentiles should be evangelized. In the special material, he excludes a **mission to Gentiles** completely. Jesus explains that he was sent only to the lost sheep of the house of Israel (15:24). Likewise, in his mission instructions to his apostles, he orders them specifically to stay away from Gentiles and Samaritans, limiting their mission to the lost sheep of the house of Israel (10:5–6). He tells them that they will not finish evangelizing the cities of Israel before he returns as the Son of Man (10:23). In other words, they would never evangelize Gentiles because they would never finish the job of evangelizing Jews. Later he assumes that the community of his followers would include no Gentiles and would have nothing to do with them (18:17). When Jesus returned, he would judge the Gentiles on the basis of how they had treated his "brothers," the Jewish members of the community (25:31–46).

In the material from Q, Matthew's Jesus has a more positive attitude toward a Gentile mission. When a Roman centurion asks him to heal his boy, Jesus readily agrees, praising the centurion's faith, and predicting that many Gentiles would enter the kingdom of the heavens (8:5–13). In the Markan material, Jesus is initially reluctant to heal a Gentile woman's daughter, but does so anyway (15:25–28). In the mission instructions, he assumes that his students will bear testimony to the Gentiles (10:18). This assumption makes Jesus appear somewhat absent-minded, since he has just prohibited them from evangelizing Gentiles (10:5–6). In the eschatological discourse, he predicts that his followers will preach the gospel in the whole world as a testimony to all the Gentiles before the end (24:14). Here too he appears to have forgotten that he previously predicted that his followers would not even finish evangelizing Jews before the end (10:23). After his resurrection, Jesus instructs his apostles to make disciples of all the Gentiles (28:19).

Jesus' Death, Resurrection, and Parousia

Matthew preserves two main views of **Jesus' death**. In some of the material, Jesus dies not because God intended him to die, but because his message as a prophet was rejected (21:33–46; 23:34, 37). In other material, Jesus' death is intended. Jesus gives his life as a "ransom" for others (20:28). His blood is poured out "for many" (26:28).

Matthew's presentation of **Jesus' resurrection** is distinctive. Only Matthew among the Synoptic Gospels has a resurrection narrative in which the risen Jesus appears to his students in Galilee (28:9–10, 16–20).

Only in Matthew among the gospels does Jesus refer to his second coming as the **parousia** or "arrival" (24:3, 27, 37, 39). In the material that Matthew shared with Mark, Jesus predicts that he will return within the lifetime of his contemporaries (16:28; 24:34; 26:64). In the Q material, however, Jesus seems to postpone his parousia. In a parable, he warns his followers not to fall into misbehavior when they begin to think "My Lord delays" (24:48). The delay of the parousia also appears in another parable unique to Matthew (25:5), and Matthew's redaction indicates that Jesus would return "after a long time" (25:19).

THE COMMUNITIES OF MATTHEW'S SOURCES

Socio-historical criticism seeks to better understand the community represented by Matthew's gospel. But since this gospel is a combination of different sources, we must first distinguish the communities of Matthew's sources: the community of the Markan material, the community of Q, and the community of Matthew's special material.

1. The **community of the Markan material** preserved Jewish-Christian traditions from Jerusalem along with traditions from another Jewish-Christian group engaged in preaching the gospel to Gentiles.

2. The **community of Q** was probably a Judaic-Christian community, i.e. a Jewish-Christian community that continued to follow the Jewish Law as the path to eternal life (Matt 5:18/Luke 16:17). Q presents a positive attitude toward the prospect of Gentiles entering the kingdom (Matt 8:5–13/Luke 7:1–10; 13:28–29), but it is not clear whether the Q community actively evangelized Gentiles. Some scholars think that this community resided in Galilee, since Q refers to missionary activity in Galilean cities (Matt 11:20–24/Luke 10:13–15). Some of the Q material may date from before the Jewish War, but it is likely that Q did not achieve its final form until after 70 CE since it refers to the delay of the parousia (Matt 24:48/Luke 12:45).

3. The **community of Matthew's special material** was also a Judaic-Christian community, one that emphasized that the Jewish Law remained binding (5:17–19). This community continued to practice Jewish rites, such as sacrificing at the temple (5:23–24) and performing the basic acts of Jewish piety: giving alms, praying, and fasting (6:1–18).

They followed a stricter interpretation of the Law than the scribes and Pharisees (5:20, 21–48), requiring ethical perfection (5:48) that few could attain (7:13–14).

The special material contains two important clues to the historical setting of this community. First, this community exhibited an anti-Gentile bias (5:47; 6:7; 18:17). They did not evangelize Samaritans or Gentiles (10:5) and never expected to do so (10:23). Probably they knew of others who had done so (else why bother to forbid it?), but they limited their mission to Jewish cities in Palestine and expected Jesus to return before they finished this work. Gentiles were not "brothers" of Jesus but would be judged on the basis of how they treated those brothers (25:31–46).

The second clue is the pre-eminence given to Peter in this material. Matthew's gospel includes material about Peter that appears nowhere else, and Peter is the only named disciple who plays a role in it (14:28–32; 16:17–19; 17:24–27). In one passage, Jesus calls Peter the foundation stone of the church and gives him the keys of the kingdom of heaven (16:17–19). The community represented here apparently viewed Peter as the pre-eminent authority in the church.

This high view of Peter is consistent with the role attributed to Peter in Paul's letter to the Galatians. Here Paul relates a meeting with the "pillars" of the church in Jerusalem, at which it was agreed that Paul had been entrusted with the gospel for non-Jews, while Peter had been entrusted with the gospel for Jews (Gal 2:6–10). Paul would preach to Gentiles, while Peter would preach to Jews. We can see then that Matthew's special material represents the type of community that would arise out of Peter's missionary activity: a Jewish-Christian church that looked to Peter as its pre-eminent authority and followed Peter's agreement with Paul by limiting its mission to Jews.

Since Matthew's special material limits evangelism to "the cities of Israel," it apparently came from a community somewhere in Palestine. Its date can be inferred from two considerations: 1) since it seems to presuppose the agreement between Paul and Peter in Jerusalem, it must date after 49, the approximate date of that event; 2) since community members continued to sacrifice at the temple in Jerusalem (5:23–24), it must date before 70, when the temple was destroyed.

This community did not evangelize Gentiles, but they would have been familiar with other groups that did. In particular, they would have known of Paul and his churches. They may have known that Paul and their own apostle, Peter, came into conflict over the Law at Antioch (Gal

2:11–14). In any case, they would know that Paul evangelized Gentiles and that in doing so he taught that faith in Jesus made the Law unnecessary for salvation. Probably in reaction against this teaching, they emphasized the necessity of keeping the Law.

THE COMMUNITY OF MATTHEW'S GOSPEL

As we have seen, the material in Matthew's sources came from different Jewish-Christian communities in Palestine. But what about Matthew himself? Did he belong to one of these communities, or did he belong to a different community altogether? It is possible that he belonged to a community that had no gospel traditions of its own. **Matthew's purpose** in writing the gospel, then, would have been to collect material from other communities in order to create a gospel that could be read in his own church. The Gospel of Matthew represents the end product of his work. His redaction of his sources shows that his purpose included presenting Jesus as the fulfillment of Jewish scripture and as the hope for Gentiles.

Scholarly study of Matthew's community often focuses on its **relation to Judaism.** All of Matthew's sources indicate conflict between the Jewish-Christian communities and other Jewish groups. The final stage of Matthew, the evangelist's redaction, also shows continued alienation and hostility between the evangelist's community and other Jews. The evangelist typically refers to Jewish synagogues as "their" synagogues (4:23; 9:35; 10:17; 12:9; 13:54) or "your" synagogues (23:34), showing that members of his community did not belong to the same synagogues as their opponents. The evangelist also draws together various material from his sources to create a catalogue of virulent polemic against the scribes and Pharisees (23:1–36). He also blames the Jewish people as a whole for the crucifixion of Jesus (27:24–25). Paradoxically it is Matthew, coming from a Jewish-Christian setting, which has the unfortunate distinction of making some of the strongest anti-Jewish statements in the New Testament.

READING GUIDE: MATTHEW

Read the Gospel of Matthew with the help of the following guide.

Birth Narrative (chs. 1–2)

Whereas Mark begins with the preaching of John the Baptist, Matthew begins his gospel with stories about Jesus' birth and infancy. These stories occur only in Matthew.

Matthew begins with a **genealogy** that traces Jesus' ancestry from Abraham, father of the Jewish race (1:1–17). Another significant ancestor is David, the king of Israel from whose lineage the Messiah would come, according to many Jewish interpreters. Thus Matthew introduces Jesus as the hope of Judaism: "Jesus Christ, the son of David, the son of Abraham" (1:1).

Matthew then relates the **birth of Jesus** (1:18–25). Though he tells this story from the perspective of Joseph, the husband of Mary, he depicts Jesus as the offspring of the Holy Spirit and Mary, with no human father.

Figure 12.2
Wise men from the East bring gifts to the infant Jesus, a story unique to Matthew. Painting by Vittorio Bigari (1692–1776). Pinacoteca Nazionale, Bologna, Italy (Scala/Art Resource, NY).

The child is given the name "Jesus" ("the Lord is salvation"), because "he will save his people from their sins" (1:21). Matthew quotes Isaiah 7:14, a passage which he believes predicts the birth of a child from a virgin (1:23). He takes the name of the child in that passage, "Emmanuel" ("God with us"), to mean that Jesus represents the presence of God with his people.

Matthew continues with a **three-part story** in which Herod the Great attempts to kill the infant Jesus. This story begins as wise men visit Jesus' family at their house in Bethlehem (2:1–12); it continues with the flight of Joseph, Mary, and the child to Egypt (2:13–18); and it concludes as they move to Nazareth after Herod's death (2:19–23).

First Narrative Section (chs. 3–4)

After the birth narrative, Matthew alternates a section of narrative with each of his five major discourses. In the first narrative section (chs. 3–4), Matthew takes up where Mark begins: the ministry of John the Baptist. He then relates the beginning of Jesus' ministry. Most of this material has a parallel in Mark's gospel. The following material does not occur in Mark: John's preaching (3:7–12), an apology for Jesus' baptism by John (3:14–15), and a fuller account of Jesus' temptation (4:1–11; cf. Mark 1:12–13).

First Discourse: Sermon on the Mount (chs. 5–7)

At this point, Matthew inserts a collection of teachings from various sources. This discourse is known as "the Sermon on the Mount," because Jesus is portrayed seated on a mountain teaching his students. This was not originally a single sermon of Jesus. Some of the sayings come from the Q sermon that Matthew and Luke have in common (see box above). Other sayings come from other Q material that Luke has placed elsewhere in his gospel. Still other sayings come from Matthew's special material and are absent from Luke altogether. Matthew has organized all these sayings into a single discourse.

The central theme of this discourse is true **righteousness** (5:6, 10, 20; 6:1, 33). Matthew has assembled sayings concerning right attitudes, character, and actions in order to give ethical guidance to the church for which he writes.

The sermon begins with the **Beatitudes**, a series of blessings which delineate the character required of Jesus' disciples (5:3–12). Blessing even falls on those in present difficulties (grief, persecution) because of the hope that they will fare better in the coming kingdom. Following the Beatitudes are sayings on **salt and light**, which focus on the influence for good that disciples are to have in the world (5:13–16).

In 5:17–20 Jesus affirms the continuing **validity of the Law**, even calling for a righteousness that exceeds that of the scribes and Pharisees. This introduction is followed by a series of **antitheses**, in which Jesus contrasts contemporary interpretations of the Law with his own stricter teaching (5:21–48).

The following section condemns **showing off one's righteousness** (6:1–18). Jesus warns against practicing religion in order to draw attention to oneself, specifically in three important areas of Jewish piety: alms (charitable giving), prayer, and fasting. Matthew has inserted into this section some other **teaching on prayer** (6:7–15), including the model prayer generally called "the Lord's Prayer."

Several sayings that follow promote a proper **attitude toward possessions** (6:19–34). An "evil eye" (6:22–23) may stand for covetousness. "Mammon" (6:24) is an Aramaic term for wealth.

The **miscellaneous sayings** in the next section (7:1–20) include sayings on judging others (7:1–5), brutish people (7:6), prayer (7:7–11), and the "golden rule" (7:12). The idea of two paths (7:13–14), one leading to life and one to destruction, occurs frequently in the Hebrew Scriptures and other Jewish literature (e.g. Proverbs 4:10–19; 12:28; 14:12; 15:24). A warning against false prophets (7:15–20) ends this section.

The sermon concludes with sayings on **doing the word**, two admonitions to "do" what the sermon says (7:21–23; 7:24–27).

Second Narrative Section (8:1–9:34)

Most of the second narrative section parallels material also found in Mark's gospel, although several stories occur in a different order than in Mark. The following material is not found in Mark: healing of the centurion's boy (8:5–13), a fulfillment quotation (8:17), impulsive and reluctant followers (8:18–22), and healing of the blind and mute (9:27–34).

Second Discourse: Missionary Discourse (9:35–11:1)

For his second discourse, Matthew has drawn together material from various sources on the subject of missionary activity. This discourse provided instructions and encouragement for those in Matthew's community who were engaged in preaching the community's message. Much of this material implies that Christian evangelists faced rejection and opposition as they sought to spread their message.

Matthew introduces the **mission of the twelve** (9:35–10:14) with a passage in which Jesus recognizes the need for helpers in his ministry (9:35–38). He then shows how Jesus' twelve apostles met this need. He draws together two passages about the twelve that are separated in Mark: the names of the twelve (10:1–4) and the sending of the twelve (10:7–14). From his special material he includes a restriction on the mission: the apostles are to go to Israelites only, not to Gentiles or Samaritans (10:5–6).

Matthew then adds various other **missionary instructions** (10:15–11:1). The material in 10:17–22 parallels material that occurs in Mark in the eschatological discourse (Mark 13:9–13/Matt 24:9–14). Since this material contemplates a mission to the Gentiles (10:18), it stands in tension with the previous injunction against preaching to the Gentiles.

Third Narrative Section (11:2–12:50)

The third narrative section also speaks to the situation of the early church in its missionary activity. It focuses on two related themes: the failure of the Jewish mission and the resultant expansion of the mission to include Gentiles. It reflects the fact that as the Jewish people tended to reject the gospel, the church turned increasingly to Gentiles.

The **failure of the Jewish mission** is illustrated by stories which show other Jews opposing Jesus and by sayings which condemn those who have rejected him. Several controversy dialogues show the Pharisees opposing Jesus (12:1–8, 9–14) and accusing him of being empowered by Satan (12:22–32). Jews who have criticized both John the Baptist and Jesus are compared to children who cannot be satisfied (11:16–19). The Jewish cities in Galilee that have not repented at the preaching are condemned (11:20–24). One saying attributes the failure of the mission to the divine will: God has hidden the truth from the wise and intelligent and revealed it to childlike people (11:25–27). Other sayings blame the failure on the people themselves. Those who reject the message are a generation of vipers whose hearts are not right (12:33–37). The scribes and Pharisees want to see a sign to confirm the message, but such sign-seeking is evil; they will be condemned at the judgment (12:38–42). The present generation is compared to a man who got rid of one evil spirit only to get back seven more (12:43–45).

Alongside condemnations of Jewish unbelief stand two passages which promote the **mission to the Gentiles**. In the first, Matthew applies to Jesus a passage from Isaiah 42:1–4 that speaks of God's servant who will "announce justice to the Gentiles" and in whose name "the Gentiles will have hope" (12:15–21). In the second (12:46–50), Jesus defines his family not as those who are physically related to him (i.e. the Jews), but as all who are willing to become his disciples (thus including Gentiles).

Third Discourse: Parable Discourse (13:1–53)

Matthew's third discourse is a collection of parables. It includes most of the parables that occur in Mark 4 as well as several others. Many of the parables in Matthew explicitly mention the kingdom of God, which Matthew usually calls "the kingdom of the heavens." Such parables often begin, "The kingdom of the heavens is like ..." or "To what shall I compare the kingdom of the heavens?" Matthew's explanation of why Jesus spoke in parables differs from Mark's. According to Mark, Jesus spoke in parables "so that" the people would not understand (Mark 4:12). In Matthew's redaction, Jesus spoke in parables "because" the people did not understand (Matt 13:13).

Fourth Narrative Section (13:54–17:27)

The fourth narrative section contains much material that is common to Matthew and Mark but absent from Luke (13:53–58; 14:3–12; 14:22–16:12). From his special material, Matthew added Peter's walk on the sea (14:28–33), signs of the times (16:2–3), a blessing on Peter (16:17–19), and the question about paying the temple tax (17:24–27).

Fourth Discourse: Community Relations (ch. 18)

Matthew pulls together teaching material from various sources to form his fourth discourse (18:1–5, 6–9, 10–14, 15–17, 18–20, 21–35). This discourse concerns the church, especially relations between members and how to discipline erring members. Believers are likened to children, to sheep, and to different parts of a single body.

Fifth Narrative Section (chs. 19–22)

Most of the fifth narrative section has a parallel in Mark 10:1–12:40. The following are distinctive features of Matthew.

Matthew adds **three parables** that do not occur in Mark: those of the householder (20:1–16), the two sons (21:28–32), and the marriage feast (22:1–14).

Matthew has **two blind men** who are healed (20:29–34), whereas Mark and Luke have only one. Such doubling is characteristic of Matthew (cf. the two demoniacs in Matt 8:28–34, the two blind men in 9:27–31, the two donkeys in 21:1–7).

Unlike the other Synoptics, Matthew has two donkeys in the **triumphal entry** instead of one (21:1–11). In this account, the disciples place their garments on both donkeys and then put Jesus on "them" – either the garments or the donkeys (Matt 21:7). Whether Matthew pictures Jesus somehow riding on both donkeys or riding on one with the other trailing along riderless (but why put garments on it in that case?), the portrayal is decidedly peculiar compared to the other Synoptics. Apparently the two donkeys come from Zechariah 9:9, which Matthew took to be a prophecy about Jesus, and which refers to a donkey twice. Matthew misunderstood Zechariah to mean two different animals and modified the story of Jesus' entry to make it match his interpretation of that passage.

Fifth Discourse: Eschatological Discourse (chs. 23, 24–25)

Before the eschatological discourse, Matthew includes a series of prophetic denunciations or **woes against the scribes and Pharisees** (23:1–36), including a prediction of their punishment in the present generation (23:35–36).

A **lament over Jerusalem** asserts that Jerusalem is to be abandoned by God (23:37–39). It thus serves as a transition to the eschatological discourse, which predicts Jerusalem's coming destruction. The forsaken "house" referred to in 23:38 is the Jerusalem temple, the house of God.

Matthew's **eschatological discourse** (chs. 24–25) includes quite a bit more material than the parallels in Mark and Luke. As in Mark and Luke, the discourse deals with the destruction of Jerusalem (destroyed by the Romans in 70 CE). It predicts that Jesus would return at that time to sit on a glorious throne and exercise judgment.

Figure 12.3
Jesus sits on a
throne to exercise
judgment (Matt
25:31–46). Detail
from the golden
antependium of
Emperor Otto
II, c. 1020. Dom
zu Aachen,
Schatzkammer,
Aachen (Erich
Lessing/Art
Resource, NY).

Passion and Resurrection Narratives (chs. 26–28)

Matthew's passion and resurrection narratives parallel Mark's but include
the following special material.

Matthew describes the death of Judas Iscariot (27:3–10), the resurrection of certain saints (27:51b–53), and Jesus' appearance to certain women
(28:9–10).

Some of the Jews charged that Jesus' students came at night, stole his
corpse from the tomb, and falsely proclaimed that he had been raised from
the dead. To defend against this charge, Matthew claims that the tomb

had been guarded by soldiers precisely to prevent such a fraud (27:62–66) and that the soldiers had been bribed to spread the accusation (28:11–15).

Matthew preserves a Galilean version of the resurrection story, in which the resurrected Jesus appears to the disciples in Galilee rather than Jerusalem (26:32, 28:7, 28:10, 28:16–17).

Whereas Jesus previously restricted his activity to Israel (Matt 10:5–6), the risen Jesus now commissions his disciples to evangelize and teach all nations (28:18–20). He promises to be with them "until the end of the age," which Matthew believed would come soon.

DISCUSSION QUESTIONS

1. *The Sermon on the Mount.* Read the Sermon on the Mount (Matt 5–7). The teachings collected in this discourse give us an idea of what Matthew's community would consider true righteousness. Consider in particular the "antitheses" in 5:17–48. In what ways does the righteousness required in this passage exceed that required by the scribes and Pharisees? Is such righteousness attainable?

2. *The community of Mathew's special material.* The teaching and instruction preserved in the gospels addresses various problems and concerns in the Christian communities. By examining this teaching using socio-historical criticism, we can infer what those problems and concerns were. Discuss what the following passages from Matthew's special material tell us about the community from which it came: Matt 5:17–20; 10:5–6, 23; 13:24–30; 16:17–19; 17:24–27; 18:15–17.

REVIEW QUESTIONS

1. Why do scholars doubt that the apostle Matthew wrote the Gospel of Matthew?

2. What can we infer about the date, intended audience, and place of origin of Matthew's gospel?

3. Identify Matthew's three primary sources.

4. Describe Matthew's method of organization and his quotation of scriptures.

5. How and why does Matthew's Sermon on the Mount differ from the parallel sermon in Luke?

6. Discuss Matthew's special emphases in presenting the following aspects of Jesus' identity: Christ, son of David, son of God (or demigod), God with us, and Son of Man.

7. Describe Jesus' attitude toward the Jewish Law in Matthew's gospel. In what ways does he appear as a strict rabbi? In what ways as a lenient rabbi?

8. What teaching does Matthew's Jesus include about the church?

9. In what ways does Matthew portray Jesus as a preacher of judgment?

10. In what ways does Matthew's Jesus exhibit an anti-Gentile bias? What different attitudes does he display toward a mission to Gentiles?

11. Discuss Matthew's special emphases in presenting Jesus' death, resurrection, and parousia.

12. What can we infer about the community represented by Matthew's special material?

13. What was Matthew's apparent purpose in writing his gospel? What was the relation of Matthew's community to Judaism?

SUGGESTIONS FOR FURTHER STUDY

Betz, Hans Dieter. *The Sermon on the Mount* (Hermeneia; Fortress, 1995). A commentary on Matthew's Sermon on the Mount and Luke's Sermon on the Plain.

Carter, Warren. *Matthew: Storyteller, Interpreter, Evangelist* (rev. ed.; Hendrickson, 2004). Examines the world behind the text (author, genre, sources, socio-historical setting, narrative conventions), the world of the text (point of view, plot, settings, characters), and the world in front of the text (contemporary significance).

Davies, W. D., and Dale C. Allison, Jr. *A Critical and Exegetical Commentary on the Gospel According to Saint Matthew* (3 vols.; ICC; T&T Clark, 1988–97). This major commentary written by Dale Allison is most useful for students who know Greek.

Luz, Ulrich. *Matthew 1–7, Matthew 8–20, and Matthew 21–28* (3 vols.; Hermeneia; Fortress, 2000, 2005, 2007). A major German commentary on Matthew in English translation. Adopts the Deutero-Mark hypothesis.

Saldarini, Anthony J. *Matthew's Christian-Jewish Community* (University of Chicago Press, 1994). Employs sociological categories to locate Matthew's community as a Christian form of Judaism.

Senior, Donald. *The Gospel of Matthew* (Abingdon, 1997). A survey of scholarship on important aspects of Matthew's gospel and a guide to the major sections of the gospel.

Wainwright, Elaine Mary. *Shall We Look for Another? A Feminist Rereading of the Matthean Jesus* (Orbis, 1998). Applies a feminist interpretation to four passages in Matthew as part of the search for a meaningful contemporary image of Jesus.

13　The Gospel of Luke

The Gospel of Luke must be studied both as a Synoptic Gospel and as the first volume of a two-volume work called "Luke–Acts." Unlike Matthew, Luke wrote for a Gentile audience, trying to explain how Christianity became a primarily Gentile movement. More than any other gospel, it shows a concern for the underprivileged members of society.

AUTHOR OF LUKE–ACTS

The same person wrote the Gospel of Luke and the book called "Acts." Each book begins with a preface addressed to someone named "Theophilus," and the preface in Acts refers back to the former volume (Luke 1:1–4; Acts 1:1–2). The first volume relates the story of Jesus from his birth to his ascension to heaven; the second volume picks up with the ascension and chronicles the beginnings of the early Christian church. In the present order of the canon, the first volume has been separated from its sequel in order to place it with the other Synoptic Gospels. Together Luke–Acts makes up about 28 percent of the New Testament, the largest contribution by a single author.

Since Luke–Acts nowhere explicitly identifies its author, we are dependent on internal evidence from the literature itself and on church tradition for clues to his identity.

Internal evidence provides two clues. First, the author was probably well educated, since his Greek style and vocabulary are the most literary in the New Testament. Second, the author makes an implicit claim to have traveled with the apostle Paul. In certain sections of Acts which relate Paul's journeys, the narrative shifts from third person "they" to first person "we" (Acts 16:9–18; 20:5–21:18; 27:1–28:16). These "we" sections seem to imply that the author participated in the events described. Some scholars, however, suggest that the author was using the diary of some other person as a source in these sections.

According to church tradition, dating from the end of the second century, the author was "Luke," who is mentioned three times in letters attributed to Paul (Philem 24; Col 4:14; 2 Tim 4:11). Colossians 4:10–14 suggests that Luke was a Gentile, and in verse 14 he is called "Luke the beloved physician." Nothing in Luke–Acts, however, indicates that the author had any specialized knowledge of medicine.

Many scholars reject the tradition that the author was Luke or that he was Paul's traveling companion, because the information in Luke–Acts does not always agree with what we find in Paul's letters. If the author were close to Paul, we would expect the information to agree. Other scholars, however, still accept the traditional identification of the author as Luke. We will use the name "Luke" to refer to the author of Luke–Acts, without implying that this traditional identification is correct.

SOURCES AND SETTING

Luke drew on three primary sources in composing his gospel: the Markan material, the Q material, and Luke's special material. We can infer that the gospel itself was written sometime after the fall of Jerusalem in 70 CE, since Luke 19:41–44 and 21:20–24 show knowledge of that event. Scholars generally date the two volumes of Luke–Acts to sometime between 80 and 100 CE, though many date Acts to the early second century. The emphasis on Paul in Acts suggests that Luke's two-volume work may have been written for Gentile churches established by Paul.

LUKE'S PORTRAIT OF JESUS

Luke's portrayal of Jesus' identity resembles the portraits of Mark and Matthew in many respects. Other aspects of Luke's portrayal are distinctive. Luke's Jesus is the Christ, the Davidic Messiah, a national savior; he is the son of God, a Jewish demigod; he is a prophet, the Son of Man, a deified human, Lord, and master.

From a Jewish perspective, Luke's birth narrative identifies Jesus as the **Christ** (2:11, 26). This term in Luke's usage clearly means the **Davidic Messiah**. Luke's genealogy indicates that Jesus descended from David (3:23, 31) as does Jesus' birth in Bethlehem, the city of David (2:4, 11). As the Davidic Messiah, Jesus would sit on the throne of David and reign over Israel (1:32–33). He would bring "redemption" (1:68; 2:38) and "salvation" (1:69, 71; 2:30; cf. 2:11) to Israel and Jerusalem. Only Luke among the evangelists refers to Jesus as a "**savior**" and to his work as "salvation." However, in the birth narrative, this salvation is national and political. As the Davidic Messiah, Jesus would save the Jewish people not from sin or sickness, but from their oppressors (1:71, 74), i.e., the Romans.

In Luke's presentation, Jesus' identity as the Christ is openly known in the birth narrative, where it is revealed to numerous individuals (1:32–33, 43, 46–55, 69; 2:11, 26, 30–32, 38). It is a well-kept secret in his ministry in Galilee (4:34–35, 41; 8:25, 28; 9:7–8, 18–21, 36) but once again openly known in Jerusalem (18:38, 39; 19:38; 22:67, 70; 23:2–3). Luke has done nothing to harmonize or explain this inconsistency in the messianic secret.

Luke presents two different conceptions of what it means for Jesus to be the **son of God**. First, like Mark, he relates the story of Jesus' baptism, in which the Spirit of God makes Jesus both Messiah and son of God (3:21–22). Second, like Matthew, he prefaces this account with a birth narrative, which describes Jesus as the offspring of a human mother and a divine father. Because he is literally begotten by God through the Spirit, he is called "God's son" (1:34–35). Hellenistic readers would recognize here the idea of the **demigod**, adapted to the Jewish concept of God.

Luke's Jesus identifies himself as a **prophet** (4:16), and other characters also identify him as such (7:16; 24:19). Jesus considers it the normal fate of a prophet to be rejected and killed, specifically in Jerusalem (11:47–51; 13:31–35).

Luke's Jesus identifies himself most often as **the Son of Man**. This expression serves as the most suitable designation for the new Christian conception of Jesus as the Messiah, since it implies that Jesus had to ascend to heaven to receive the kingdom before he could return and reign on earth (19:11, 12, 15). As in Mark's gospel, Jesus ascends to heaven at the end of his career (24:51). Hellenistic readers would recognize here the idea of the **deified human**, an individual who is caught up to heaven not only to live with the gods, but also to become a god himself.

In Luke–Acts, the title "**Lord**" (*kyrios*) occurs more often than any other title. It refers sometimes to God, sometimes to Jesus. When it refers to Jesus, it usually has its normal meaning as the equivalent of "master." Luke alone refers to Jesus with the synonym *epistates*, i.e. "**master**" (Luke 5:5; 8:24, 45; 9:33, 49; 17:13).

COMMUNITY CONCERNS IN LUKE

In telling his version of Jesus' story, Luke emphasizes certain characteristic themes. These give us insight into the major concerns of the communities from which he obtained his traditions, the community for which he wrote, and Luke himself. Luke emphasizes salvation for non-Jews, salvation for the underdog, the Holy Spirit, discipleship, and the coming of the kingdom.

Salvation for Non-Jews

Jesus apparently limited his ministry to Jews. After his death, however, the early church began to proclaim his resurrection to non-Jews as well. This missionary concern of the early church appears in the material Luke included in his gospel.

Luke was particularly concerned with **salvation for Gentiles**. By the time Luke wrote his gospel, the church consisted primarily of Gentiles. Most Jews had rejected the Christian message, while many Gentiles had accepted it. This situation created a theological problem, since the Messiah had been promised to the Jews. How could Jesus be the Jewish Messiah if his church consisted primarily of Gentiles? Luke's primary purpose in Luke–Acts was to answer the question, How did a Jewish Messiah wind up with a Gentile church? His answer was that God granted the Jewish heritage to the Gentiles because the Jews rejected it.

In his gospel, Luke foreshadows the shift of missionary activity from Jews to Gentiles that he will later recount in Acts. Already in the birth narrative, Simeon's prophecy hails the infant Jesus as "a light of revelation for Gentiles" (2:32). Later, Luke begins his account of Jesus' ministry by relating a story in which Jesus is rejected by the people of his home town (4:16–30). In Luke's version of this story, Jesus gives examples of prophets who were rejected by the Jews but accepted by Gentiles. The whole story serves to foreshadow what was happening in Luke's day, as missionary activity failed among Jews but succeeded among Gentiles. It justifies preaching to the Gentiles.

Other stories in Luke serve the same purpose. In 7:9, Jesus praises a Gentile's faith and contrasts it with the lack of faith among Israelites. In 8:19–21, Jesus proclaims that his true family consists not of those who are physically related to him (i.e. the Jews), but of all who hear and do his word. Another foreshadowing of the Gentile mission occurs when he sends out seventy missionaries, a story related only in Luke (10:1–24).

Just as the twelve apostles represented the twelve tribes of Israel, the seventy represent the seventy Gentile nations of Jewish tradition. Other sayings specifically predict the acceptance of Gentiles and exclusion of Jews from the kingdom. These indicate that many foreigners would enter the kingdom, while those to whom Jesus preached would be excluded (13:22–30; cf. 11:27–28). Not the invited guests, but others, would partake of the banquet of the kingdom (14:15–24). At the conclusion of the gospel, Luke includes a tradition that the risen Jesus gave his disciples a specific commission to preach to all the Gentile nations (24:46–47).

Luke was also concerned with **salvation for Samaritans**, a group more closely related to Jews than were other non-Jews. Luke's concern with the Samaritan mission is expressed in stories about Jesus coming into contact with Samaritans. Such stories occur in Luke's travel narrative, a section of the gospel in which Jesus travels through Samaria on his way to Jerusalem (17:11). At Jesus' first encounter with the Samaritans, they refuse to receive him, but he forbids his disciples to vent their anger against them (9:51–56). This story would have been used in the church to promote the proper attitude toward Samaritans who did not accept the Christian messengers. More often, Luke's stories show the Samaritans in a favorable light in comparison with the Jews. For example, the parable of "the good Samaritan" shows a Samaritan overcoming ethnic hostilities to help a Jew, after other Jews had refused to help (10:25–37). In another story, when Jesus heals ten lepers, only a Samaritan returns to thank him (17:11–19).

Salvation for the Underdog

Luke focuses on certain social groups as those who will inherit the kingdom of God. These consist primarily of those with low standing in the society of the time. Luke's material emphasizes God's choice of the underdog, including the sinful and lost, the poor and oppressed, and women. It is likely that he focused on these groups because they constituted the majority of the church for which he wrote.

First, Luke emphasizes salvation for **the sinful and lost**. Luke's Jesus brings his message of repentance to those who need it most by associating with "sinners." Chief among the sinners are tax collectors, whom people in the Greco-Roman world regarded as dishonest and held in low esteem. Luke, however, presents tax collectors in a positive light as people who repented at the preaching of John the Baptist (3:12–13; 7:29).

Figure 13.1
Scene from the
parable of the
prodigal son
(Luke 15:11–32):
a wayward son
repents and
returns to his
father. Painting by
Bartolomé Esteban
Murillo (1618–
82). National
Gallery of Art,
Washington, D.C.

A parable portrays a repentant tax collector as more acceptable to God than a righteous Pharisee (18:9–14). In one story, Jesus calls a tax collector to be one of his students (5:27–28). In another story, he visits the home of a tax collector (19:1–10), because he "came to seek and save the lost" (19:10). Because of Jesus' association with such people, he is criticized for being "a friend of tax collectors and (other) sinners" (7:34). Once when the Pharisees criticize Jesus' students for eating with tax collectors and other sinners (5:29–32), Jesus justifies this behavior by saying, "I have not come to call the righteous but sinners to repentance" (5:32). On another occasion, when the Pharisees raise the same criticism (15:1–2), Jesus responds by telling three parables about the lost – a lost sheep, a lost coin, and a lost son – all of which illustrate God's joy at the repentance of a sinner (15:3–32). Two other stories unique to Luke also portray sinners who repent and turn to Jesus: the story of a sinful woman (7:36–50) and the story of a criminal who is crucified with Jesus (23:39–43).

Second, Luke emphasizes salvation for **the poor and oppressed**. In his "inaugural address" at the synagogue in Nazareth, Jesus declares that God has anointed him "to preach good news to the poor" (4:18). The good news, as it is expressed by Mary in the birth narrative, is that in the coming kingdom there will be a reversal of status in society: God will bring down the rich and powerful and raise up the poor and lowly (1:51–53). He will bless the poor, the hungry, and those that weep but bring woe on the rich, the full, and those that laugh (6:20–26). The parable of the rich man and Lazarus illustrates this reversal of fortune in the afterlife, as the rich man receives torment, while Lazarus the poor man receives comfort in paradise (16:19–31). It is "the poor and maimed and blind and lame" who will receive a place at the great banquet of the kingdom of God (14:15–24). Therefore even now, those holding a banquet should invite "the poor, the maimed, the lame, the blind" (14:12–14).

Third, Luke emphasizes salvation for **women**. His gospel includes more material about women than the other Synoptic Gospels. While Matthew tells the story of Jesus' birth from Joseph's perspective, Luke tells it from Mary's. He also tells of numerous women disciples who play a significant role in Jesus' ministry: Anna the prophetess, who recognizes the special nature of the infant Jesus (2:36–38); the woman who overcomes a sinful past through love for Jesus (7:36–50); women who provide financial support for Jesus' ministry (8:2–3); the sisters Martha and Mary, who represent two different priorities (10:38–42); and the women who follow Jesus from Galilee to Jerusalem and become witnesses of Jesus' empty tomb (23:49, 55–56; 24:1–11). Women appear as the main characters in the parable of the lost coin (15:8–10), the parable of the persistent widow (18:1–8), and the story of the generous widow (21:1–4). Other women appear as recipients of Jesus' healing ministry (7:11–17; 13:10–17). Yet Luke's Jesus remains patriarchal. When he chooses twelve apostles to exercise positions of authority, they are all men (6:12–16).

The Holy Spirit

In the Hebrew Scriptures, God's spirit (literally "breath") is a power by which God carries out his will on earth. In the New Testament, the Spirit has become somewhat more individualized, a development that in later centuries culminated in the identification of the Spirit as one of the three "persons" of the Christian Trinity (God the Father, Jesus the Son, and the Holy Spirit).

Throughout his two-volume work, Luke places a special emphasis on the role of the Holy Spirit in the events of salvation. In his gospel, he stresses the role of the Spirit more than any other evangelist. The Spirit plays an active role in the birth narrative as well as in the account of Jesus' ministry. John the Baptist is filled with the Spirit from birth (1:15, 17, 80). The conception of Jesus takes place through the Spirit (1:35). Elizabeth, Mary, Zechariah, and Simeon all prophesy under the inspiration of the Spirit (1:41, 47, 67; 2:25, 26, 27). After relating how Jesus himself received the Spirit (3:22), Luke reminds the reader several times that Jesus' power comes from the Spirit (4:1, 14, 18).

In one Q passage where Matthew says simply "Jesus declared" (Matt 11:25), Luke has "he rejoiced in the Holy Spirit" (Luke 10:21). In another where Matthew's version states that God will give "good things" to those who ask him (Matt 7:11), Luke has that he will give "the Holy Spirit" (Luke 11:13). Luke includes both the passage concerning the blasphemy against the Holy Spirit and the promise that the Holy Spirit would teach the disciples how to answer accusations (Luke 12:10, 11–12).

In all the Synoptics, John the Baptist promises that Jesus will baptize people in the Holy Spirit (Mark 1:8; Matt 3:11; Luke 3:16), but only Luke repeats this promise at the end of his gospel (Luke 24:49), pointing forward to its fulfillment in Acts. In Acts, he portrays the early church as a community filled with the Spirit. He interprets the presence of the Spirit as a sign that "the last days" before the day of the Lord had arrived (Acts 2:17–20).

Discipleship

Luke also emphasizes what Jesus requires of his students or disciples. Disciples must follow Jesus, renounce possessions, humble themselves, and pray. Luke finds the highest expression of these virtues in Jesus.

First, disciples must **follow Jesus** wherever he leads. Following Luke's Jesus is no easy matter. He requires his disciples to adopt his own lifestyle. A disciple must abandon home, family, and possessions to follow him (9:57–58; 14:33; 18:22, 28–30). A disciple must even take up his cross and follow Jesus to death (14:27). Jesus especially emphasizes the need to put following him ahead of family ties and obligations (8:19–21; 11:27–28; 12:51–53). He does not permit his followers time to bury their parents or say goodbye to their families (9:59–62). They must hate their father, mother, wife, children, and sisters, and even their own lives (14:26).

Second, disciples of Jesus must also **renounce their possessions**. In the book of Acts, Luke portrays the Jerusalem church as a community in which the members had all things in common. They sold their possessions and brought the proceeds to the apostles, who distributed the funds to anyone who had need (Acts 2:44–45; 4:32–5:11). In Luke's gospel, many sayings, parables, and stories appear that would have been used in the church to encourage such a lifestyle. Sayings in Luke exhort disciples to share with others (3:10–11), to sell their possessions and give to the poor in order to obtain treasure in heaven (12:32–34; 18:22, 28–30). Models of generosity are given in the tax collector who gives half of his possessions to the poor (19:1–10) and the poor widow who gives all she has (21:1–4). Disciples are encouraged not to worry about obtaining food and clothes, since they can trust God to provide (12:22–31).

Certain sayings imply that money belongs to God, while the person with money is merely a steward who must make the best use of the master's money. The parable of the dishonest steward, who uses his master's wealth to win friends, provides an example for the wealthy, who should use the wealth God has entrusted to them in order to make friends of Jesus' disciples (16:1–9). Those who are faithful in using material wealth entrusted by God will be entrusted with the true wealth (16:10–12).

The wrong attitude toward wealth is illustrated in the parable of the rich fool who cannot take his riches with him at death (12:13–21) and the story of the rich young ruler who loves wealth more than the kingdom of God (18:18–30). Other sayings emphasize that no one can serve both God and mammon (money) (16:13). Though money is esteemed by humans, love of money is an abomination to God (16:14–15).

Third, disciples of Jesus must **humble themselves**. Several sayings, stories, and parables in Luke focus on the key virtue of humility. In these teachings, the path to exaltation lies in humbling oneself. Those who exalt themselves will be humbled, while those who humble themselves will be exalted (14:7–11; 18:9–14). To be the greatest, one must become the least (9:46–48; 22:24–27). The kingdom can only be entered and understood by those who humble themselves like children (9:46–48; 10:21; 18:15–17). Jesus himself serves as a model of humility through his lowly birth in a stable (2:7, 8–20) and his service to others (22:27).

Finally, disciples of Jesus must **pray**. Luke shares various teachings on prayer with Mark and/or Matthew (6:28; 11:1–4, 9–13; 20:47). To these, Luke adds two parables that emphasize the need to ask boldly and to persist in prayer (11:5–8; 18:1–8). He pictures the Jerusalem temple as a place of prayer (1:10, 13; 2:37; 19:46) and Jesus as a man of prayer, a model for disciples to follow. In Luke, Jesus prays at all the important turning points in his ministry (3:21; 6:12; 9:18; 9:28–29; 22:39–46; cf. 5:16).

The Coming of the Kingdom

Like the other evangelists, Luke includes material concerning the return of Jesus to establish the kingdom of God. These traditions came from various times and places in the early church and sometimes do not agree. Luke has not always brought the differing traditions into harmony. Some sayings predict that Jesus or the kingdom will come soon (9:27; 10:9, 11; 21:31–32, 36). Other sayings imply that Jesus' coming has been delayed longer than expected (12:45; 18:7–8; 19:11). Still another saying suggests that the kingdom will not come in a physical way, but is already present, either in the person of Jesus or within the individual (17:20–21).

These differences allow us to see the development in thought that occurred in the early church. At first, the church expected Jesus to come soon. When that did not occur, they revised their thinking in various ways, either moving his coming further into the future or reinterpreting the idea of the kingdom to mean a spiritual reality already present.

Outline of Luke

The Gospel of Luke can be divided into seven major sections:

1. Preface (1:1–4)
2. Birth narrative (1:5–2:52)
3. Preparation for ministry (3:1–4:13)
4. Ministry in Galilee (4:14–9:50)
5. Travel narrative (9:51–19:27)
6. In the temple (19:28–21:38)
7. Passion and resurrection (22:1–24:53)

The first two sections consist of material that is unique to Luke. Beginning with the third section, Luke follows the same order as Mark with the addition of material from Q and his special material. Most of this additional material is grouped together in two clusters, Luke 6:17–8:3 and 9:51–18:14. The second cluster forms the first part of Luke's "travel narrative," a section in which Jesus is portrayed as gradually journeying toward his death in Jerusalem, teaching as he goes.

READING GUIDE: LUKE

Read the Gospel of Luke with the help of the following guide. The comments will focus on Luke's special material.

Preface (1:1–4)

Luke is the only evangelist who begins with a formal preface in the style of Hellenistic literature. Like other Hellenistic authors, Luke dedicates his work to an individual. This Theophilus ("friend of God") has been instructed concerning the Christian faith and apparently represents the Christian audience for whom Luke writes. He may have been Luke's patron, paying the expenses for having Luke's work copied for publication. Luke writes so that his readers may "know the certainty" of what they have been taught. He wishes to reassure them that their faith in Jesus as the Messiah rests on a reliable foundation.

Luke indicates that "many" before him had already written about Jesus. Some of these previous accounts undoubtedly served as sources for Luke's own account.

Figure 13.2 Early Christian engraving of the shepherd who seeks the lost sheep, a parable found in both Matthew 18:12–14 and Luke 15:1–7. National Museum of Carthage, Carthage, Tunisia (Erich Lessing/Art Resource, NY).

Birth Narrative (1:5–2:52)

Luke has woven together several different types of material in composing his birth narrative: a story about the birth of John the Baptist, a story about the birth of Jesus, a story about Jesus' mother visiting John's mother, two Jewish-Christian hymns, and a story about Jesus as a boy.

Only Luke gives traditions about the **birth of John the Baptist (1:5–25, 57–67, 76–80)**. The story of John's birth parallels stories in the Hebrew Scriptures about the births of other significant characters, such as Isaac (Genesis 18:9–15; 21:1–7), Samson (Judges 13:2–24), and Samuel (1 Samuel 1). Like Abraham and Sarah before the birth of Isaac, John's parents Zechariah and Elizabeth are past the age of having children. Elizabeth, like the mothers of Isaac, Samson, and Samuel, is unable to conceive. John's birth is thus an act of God. As in the stories of Isaac and Samson, God announces John's birth beforehand. Like Samson and Samuel, John is dedicated to God by his parents and must not drink wine or strong drink. Like Samson, he is filled with the Spirit of God. These traditional motifs, associated with the births of special characters, are used in the story to show that John is not an ordinary child but has a special role to play. He will fulfill the role of Elijah, the prophet whose coming was promised in scripture (Malachi 4:5–6) and who would prepare Israel for the coming of God (Luke 1:16–17, 76–79).

As in the story of John's birth, an angel announces the **birth of Jesus (1:26–35, 38)**, giving his name in advance. But Jesus' birth is portrayed as even more miraculous than John's, in that Jesus is born of a virgin. Likewise, he fulfills a higher role than John: he is to be the Messiah, the king from David's line, who would rule over Israel forever (1:32–33). Other stories continue to emphasize the special character of the child Jesus. After Jesus is born in Bethlehem (2:1–7), angels announce his birth to shepherds (2:8–20). When Jesus' parents take him to the temple in Jerusalem, two prophets, Simeon and Anna, recognize him as the fulfillment of Israel's hopes (2:21–40).

Only Luke connects John and Jesus as relatives, by including a story in which Mary, the mother of Jesus, is related to Elizabeth, the mother of John. When **Mary visits Elizabeth (1:36–37, 39–45, 56)**, the infant John leaps for joy in his mother's womb, and Elizabeth declares that she is honored to receive a visit from "the mother of my Lord" (1:43). This story, which shows John and his mother acknowledging Jesus as their Lord, is probably directed against the disciples of John the Baptist. Just as Jesus' disciples continued to follow Jesus after his death, the disciples of

John continued to follow John. Since these two groups stood in competition with each other, the church emphasized the superiority of their own leader, as in the story considered here.

Just as Hannah exulted at the birth of Samuel with a song of praise (1 Samuel 2:1–10), so Mary and Zechariah exult at the births of Jesus and John, respectively. Luke took **two Jewish-Christian hymns (1:47, 49–55; 1:68–75)**, probably used in the worship of early Jewish Christianity, and adapted them to his narrative. The first he adapted by adding verse 48, the only verse that pertains to Mary. The second he inserted in Zechariah's prophecy about John (1:67, 76–79), though the hymn itself refers to Jesus.

Only Luke among New Testament authors relates a story about **Jesus as a boy (2:41–52)**. The point of the story is that the young Jesus recognizes God as his father (2:49). Luke describes Jesus' growth (2:52) in terms originally applied to Samuel (1 Sam 2:26).

Preparation for Ministry (3:1–4:13)

At this point, Luke picks up the story where the Markan material begins, with the preaching of **John the Baptist (3:1–20)**. Only Luke dates John's ministry in relation to world history (3:1–2), showing his desire to write for the broader world of Gentiles as well as Jews. Like Matthew, Luke gives an example of John's preaching, including some material not found elsewhere (3:10–14).

After **Jesus' baptism (3:21–22)**, he prays, thus demonstrating a typical Lukan theme.

Luke gives a **genealogy of Jesus (3:23–38)**, but one quite different from Matthew's. First, though both list the ancestors of Joseph, Mary's husband, each gives a different set of names between David and Joseph. Second, while Matthew traces Jesus' line forward from Abraham, father of the Jewish people, Luke traces it backward to Adam, seen as the father of both Jews and Gentiles.

Like Matthew, Luke includes the Q version of Jesus' **testing in the wilderness (4:1–13)**.

Ministry in Galilee (4:14–9:50)

Jesus begins his ministry in Galilee. Much of the material in this section has a parallel in the Markan material. The material from Q or Luke's special material includes the following.

The story of Jesus' **rejection in his home town (4:16–30)** plays a significant role in Luke's composition, functioning as an "inaugural address" for Jesus' ministry. In Mark and Matthew, this story occurs much later in Jesus' ministry and has much less detail. In Luke, it occurs at the beginning of his ministry and thus serves as an introduction to it. This story draws together several of Luke's central themes: the Holy Spirit (4:18), salvation for the poor and oppressed (4:18), Jesus as the fulfillment of promise (4:21), and especially salvation for the Gentiles.

In Luke, this story foreshadows Jewish rejection of the Christian message, thus justifying the transition from a Jewish to a Gentile mission. In Luke's version of the story, the people of Nazareth cannot accept Jesus as the Messiah, because they are familiar with him as a local resident (4:22b). Jesus describes this reaction in the proverb, "No prophet is acceptable in his own country" (4:24). He then illustrates this principle with examples of Israelite prophets who were received not by Israelites but by Gentiles. In the days of the prophet Elijah, when God sent a drought on the land, only a Gentile widow was blessed with Elijah's presence, even though there were many Jewish widows in the land (4:25–26; cf. 1 Kings 17:1–24). In the days of Elisha the prophet, only a Gentile leper had the faith to be healed, even though there were many Jewish lepers in the land (4:27; cf. 2 Kings 5:1–19). At these words of Jesus, the people in the synagogue are so provoked that they attempt to kill him.

This entire episode foreshadows what would happen later when the early church proclaimed Jesus as the Messiah: the Jews would reject the message while the Gentiles would accept it. Luke's point seems to be that in rejecting Jesus, the Jews were conforming to a pattern seen previously in their rejection of earlier prophets. And just as on those earlier occasions God allowed Gentiles to receive the benefits rejected by Israel, so too, in Luke's view, it was God's will that Gentiles should become the people of the Messiah, since the Jews had refused that role for themselves. Presenting this point of view is one of Luke's primary purposes in writing Luke–Acts.

A story unique to Luke is Jesus' **call of Peter and other fishermen (5:1–11)**. Compared to the corresponding story in Matthew and Mark (Matt 4:18–22; Mark 1:16–20), Luke's version gives a more dramatic account of their call.

Near the end of this section is a collection of **other non-Markan material (6:17–8:3)**. This subsection is the first large cluster of Q and special material in Luke. It includes the Sermon on the Plain (6:17–49), which is Luke's shorter parallel to Matthew's Sermon on the Mount (Matt

5–7). It also includes several stories unique to Luke in which women figure prominently: Jesus raises a widow's son (7:11–17), Jesus forgives a sinful woman (7:36–50), and women support Jesus' ministry (8:1–3).

Travel Narrative (9:51–19:27)

The next section, called the travel narrative, is a literary creation of Luke. At this point in Luke's narrative, Jesus "sets his face" to go to Jerusalem, because the time has come for him to be "taken up" into heaven (9:51). We would not expect such a journey to take long, but in fact Jesus does not arrive in Jerusalem for about ten more chapters (at 19:28). From the Markan material, Luke has taken a much briefer account of Jesus' ministry in Judea (Luke 18:15–43 = Mark 10:13–52) and expanded it with material from Q and his special material (Luke 9:51–18:14; 19:1–27). He has thus turned it into a long narrative in which Jesus journeys gradually toward Jerusalem. Luke keeps the idea of a journey alive in this section by remarking occasionally that Jesus is making his way toward Jerusalem (9:51, 57; 13:22; 17:11; 18:31; 19:11).

The travel narrative serves **three major purposes** in Luke's composition. First, it gives Luke a place to put a lot of material that does not fit elsewhere in his story. Much of the material collected by Luke consisted of isolated sayings and stories which gave no clue to their place in the life of Jesus. While Matthew grouped together material with a common theme (as in his discourses), Luke simply took several groups of unrelated material and interpolated them in the outline provided by the Markan material.

Second, Luke uses the travel narrative to symbolize Jesus' life. It pictures the life of Jesus as a journey in which he "sets his face" or resolves to follow a path that he knows will lead to his death.

Third, Luke uses the travel narrative to symbolize the path that each disciple of Jesus must also follow. Shortly after the travel narrative begins, Luke includes several sayings on following Jesus (9:57–62). The disciple must be willing to follow Jesus wherever he goes, even to the cross, leaving behind home and family, never looking back.

The following parables and teachings are some of the **highlights of the travel narrative**, drawn primarily from Luke's special material. These illustrate major concerns of Luke and his community. The theme of salvation for non-Jews, specifically Samaritans, appears in the story of a Samaritan village (9:51–56), the parable of the good Samaritan (10:25–37), and the story of a grateful Samaritan (17:11–19). The theme of salvation for the sinful and the lost appears in three parables of the lost (15:1–32). Concern for the poor is shown in teaching at a banquet (14:12–14) and the story of the rich man and Lazarus (16:19–31). Renunciation of possessions is encouraged in the parable of the rich fool (12:13–21), the exhortation to sell one's possessions (12:33–34), teaching on counting the cost (14:28–33), the parable of the unrighteous steward (16:1–9), and the story of Zacchaeus (19:1–10). The virtue of humility is promoted in teaching at a banquet (14:7–11) and the story of the Pharisee and the tax collector (18:9–14). The importance of prayer is taught in the parable of the friend at midnight (11:5–8) and the parable of the persistent widow (18:1–8).

In the Temple (19:28–21:38)

At the end of the travel narrative, Luke picks up the story of the Markan material as Jesus approaches Jerusalem. After the account of Jesus entering Jerusalem (19:28–40), Luke adds a lament over the city predicting that it will be destroyed for not recognizing Jesus' arrival as a divine visitation (19:41–44). After driving the merchants out of the temple (19:45–48), Jesus teaches there, engaging in discussion and controversy with other Jewish teachers (20:1–21:4). The temple is also the setting for Luke's version of the eschatological discourse, which predicts the destruction of Jerusalem and the return of Jesus, exhorting the reader to stay ready for these events (21:5–38).

Passion and Resurrection (chs. 22–24)

The final section of Luke's gospel consists of the passion narrative and the resurrection narrative.

At the beginning of the **passion narrative (chs. 22–23)**, Judas agrees to lead the high priests and scribes to Jesus (22:1–6). Jesus then celebrates the Passover meal with his students (22:7–18) and institutes the Lord's Supper (22:19–20). Luke includes here two items from his special material: a dispute among the disciples over which is the greatest (22:24–27) and a saying reversing the previous mission instructions not to take money or sandals (22:35–38). After the supper, Jesus is arrested and stands trial (22:39–23:25). Only Luke relates that Pilate sent Jesus to Herod Antipas, ruler of Galilee, who was in Jerusalem at the time (23:6–12). Though Jesus is convicted, crucified, and buried (23:26–56), Luke emphasizes that he is innocent of all wrongdoing (23:4, 14–15, 24, 47). To this part of the

Figure 13.3 The penitent criminal crucified with Jesus (Luke 23:39–43), a story that illustrates Luke's emphasis on accepting repentant sinners. Painting by Titian (c. 1488–1576). Pinacoteca Nazionale, Bologna, Italy (Scala/Art Resource, NY).

narrative Luke adds two further items from his special material: a saying of Jesus that predicts woe for Jerusalem (23:27–31) and the story of the penitent criminal who is crucified with Jesus (23:39–43).

Luke begins his **resurrection narrative** (ch. 24) with the discovery of the empty tomb (24:1–12). He then relates Jesus' appearance to two disciples (24:13–35) and his appearance to the eleven (24:36–43). While in Matthew the appearances of the resurrected Jesus occur in Galilee, in Luke they occur in or near Jerusalem.

Jesus then gives his students some post-resurrection instruction (24:44–49). He instructs them to remain in Jerusalem until they receive "the promise of the Father" (the Holy Spirit), after which they will preach repentance "to all the Gentiles" and testify to Jesus' resurrection. These instructions set the stage for the events that Luke will relate in Acts, the second volume of his work.

Luke concludes his gospel with an account of Jesus' ascension (24:50–53). In Matthew's story, Jesus in some sense remains with his disciples after the resurrection (Matt 28:20). In Luke, however, Jesus is taken up into heaven (cf. Mark 16:19; Acts 1:9). Such an ascension has parallels in

Greco-Roman tradition in the apotheoses of certain deified humans (see Appendix 5). It has parallels in Hebrew tradition in the ascensions of Enoch and Elijah.

DISCUSSION QUESTIONS

1. *Narratives of Jesus' birth and childhood.* Compare and contrast Luke's birth narrative (Luke 1–2) with that of Matthew (Matt 1–2).
2. *Community concerns in Luke.* Discuss how Luke's central concerns (identified above under "Community Concerns in Luke") are shown in the following passages from Luke's special material: Luke 4:16–30; 6:20–26; 10:25–37; 12:13–21; 14:7–14; 15:3–32; 16:1–9; 16:19–31; 18:1–8; 18:9–14; 19:1–10.

REVIEW QUESTIONS

1. What do internal evidence and church tradition suggest about the author of Luke-Acts? Why do many scholars reject the view that it was written by Luke the physician, a companion of Paul?
2. What are the primary sources of the Gospel of Luke? What are its probable date and intended audience?
3. Describe the following aspects of Jesus' identity in Luke's birth narrative: Christ (Davidic Messiah, national savior) and son of God (demigod). What inconsistency appears in Luke's presentation of the messianic secret? Describe the following aspects of Jesus' identity outside the birth narrative: prophet, Son of Man (deified human), and Lord or master.
4. What are some of the characteristic themes (community concerns) of Luke?
5. Luke's primary purpose in writing Luke-Acts was to answer what question concerning salvation for Gentiles? What was his answer to that question? What features of his story illustrate that answer? What features of Luke's story show that he was concerned with salvation for Samaritans?
6. On what social groups does Luke focus? Why?
7. What does Luke's Jesus require of his disciples?
8. From the reading guide: What significance does the story of Jesus' rejection in his home town have in Luke's gospel?
9. From the reading guide: What three major purposes does the travel narrative serve in Luke's composition?

SUGGESTIONS FOR FURTHER STUDY

Bovon, François. *Luke 1, Luke 2, and Luke 3: A Commentary on the Gospel of Luke* (3 vols.; Hermeneia; Fortress, 2002, 2012, 2013). A major French commentary on Luke in English translation.

Burkett, Delbert. "Jesus in Luke–Acts," in Delbert Burkett, ed., *The Blackwell Companion to Jesus*, 47–63 (Wiley-Blackwell, 2010). Examines Luke's portrayal of Jesus in the gospel and in Acts.

Fitzmyer, Joseph A. *The Gospel According to Luke* (Anchor Bible; 2 vols.; Doubleday; Yale University Press, 1981, 1985). A standard commentary on Luke.

Kingsbury, Jack Dean. *Conflict in Luke: Jesus, Authorities, Disciples* (Fortress, 1991). Discusses the narrative of Luke (settings, characters, plot) with students in mind.

Levine, Amy-Jill, and Marianne Blickenstaff, eds. *A Feminist Companion to Luke* (Sheffield Academic Press; Bloomsbury T&T Clark, 2002). Essays by various authors exploring the issue of whether Luke presents a positive or negative portrayal of women.

Pervo, Richard I. *The Gospel of Luke* (Scholars Bible; Polebridge, 2014). A commentary on the Gospel of Luke.

Tuckett, Christopher M. *Luke* (Sheffield Academic Press, 1996; reprinted, Bloomsbury T&T Clark, 2004). A student's guide to critical issues and major themes in Luke (eschatology, Jews and Gentiles, christology, poverty and possessions).

14   The Gospel of John

The Fourth Gospel presents a portrait of Jesus that differs radically from that of the Synoptics. It is the only gospel in the New Testament that calls Jesus "God" and regards him as a preexistent being. Instead of concealing his identity as in Mark, Jesus openly proclaims it. Behind this portrait of Jesus stands a community that is intriguing for both its similarities to, and differences from, other Christian groups.

AUTHOR

The traditional ascription of the Fourth Gospel to "John" comes not from the gospel but from church tradition. The gospel itself speaks of an unnamed disciple called "the disciple whom Jesus loved." This **Beloved Disciple** appears at least four times in this gospel: at the Last Supper (13:21–26), the crucifixion (19:26–27, 34–35), the empty tomb (20:1–10), and in the Epilogue (21:1–8, 18–24).

The Epilogue connects the Beloved Disciple with the composition of the gospel: "This is the disciple who is bearing witness to these things and who has written these things; and we know that his testimony is true" (21:24). Here an unidentified "we" speaks of the Beloved Disciple in the third person. The third-person references to this disciple here and elsewhere show that he did not write the gospel himself. He may have been the founder of the community in which the gospel appeared, the source of the traditions that were ultimately incorporated into the gospel.

While the gospel itself gives no name to the Beloved Disciple, church tradition names him "John." The most important witness is Irenaeus, bishop of Lyons, writing about 180 CE. According to Irenaeus, the Beloved Disciple was John "the disciple of the Lord" (presumably John the son of Zebedee, one of Jesus' twelve apostles). This John supposedly lived in Ephesus until the time of the Roman emperor Trajan (98–117 CE). Irenaeus claims that his information came from an older man, Polycarp bishop of Smyrna, who heard it from the apostles.

For several reasons, most contemporary scholars doubt that the gospel originated with John the apostle. (1) There is no evidence that John the apostle lived in Ephesus and some evidence that he did not. When Ignatius, bishop of Antioch, wrote to the church in Ephesus in the time of Trajan, he made no mention of John, though he did mention the apostle Paul's much earlier stay in Ephesus. This omission suggests that John did not live there. (2) Other traditions suggest that John the apostle suffered martyrdom prior to the composition of Mark's gospel around 70 CE (Mark 10:39). (3) The thought of the Fourth Gospel has undergone a greater degree of theological development than that of the other three gospels, making it unlikely that an eyewitness of Jesus' ministry wrote it. If the Beloved Disciple was an actual disciple of Jesus, traditions begun by him must have undergone development before being included in the gospel.

Most scholars, therefore, treat this gospel as an anonymous work, retaining the name "John" out of convenience or simply calling the author "the Fourth Evangelist" and the gospel "the Fourth Gospel." The adjective "Johannine" comes from the German form of "John."

SETTING AND DATE

John once appeared to be a Hellenistic gospel, full of non-Jewish ideas. Now, however, scholars have come to recognize that it arose among a community of Jewish Christians. This change in perspective came about for two primary reasons.

First, the discovery of the Dead Sea Scrolls demonstrated the Jewish character of John. Some of the ideas once thought to be non-Jewish have now been found in the scrolls, writings from a Palestinian Jewish sect. For instance, both John and the scrolls emphasize an ethical dualism, expressed as a contrast between light and darkness or truth and falsehood. In both sets of writings, those in the community possess light and truth, while those outside the community walk in darkness and falsehood. In making this contrast, John even employs some of the same terms as the scrolls, such as "sons of light" (12:36) and "the Spirit of Truth" (14:17; 15:26; 16:13).

Second, several passages in the gospel indicate that it arose among Jewish Christians who were being expelled from the synagogue (see below). These Jewish Christians came into conflict with the larger Jewish community because of their high esteem for Jesus and their rejection of the traditional institutions of Judaism.

Scholars generally date the gospel to the end of the first century or beginning of the second, anywhere from 80 to 110.

APORIAS AND SOURCES

The Fourth Gospel presents a major literary problem. It contains a large number of **aporias** – inconsistencies in the sequence of the narrative. For example, 2:23 refers to signs that Jesus had performed in Jerusalem, yet the gospel has related no such signs at that point. A discourse of John the Baptist (3:27–30) is continued with no new introduction by words more appropriate to Jesus (3:31–35). At the end of chapter 5, Jesus is in Jerusalem; then with no mention of a journey, chapter 6 opens with Jesus in Galilee. Jesus concludes his Farewell Discourse in 14:31, yet three more chapters of discourse follow. In the discourse, Peter asks Jesus where he is going (13:36), yet later Jesus says that no one has asked where he is going (16:5). The gospel concludes in 20:30–31, yet an entire chapter follows with a second conclusion in 21:25. Other examples could be given.

Johannine scholars generally explain these aporias by theorizing that the evangelist used one or more written sources. He may have created aporias by revising a single source or by combining more than one source. Many scholars accept the existence of at least a **signs source**, a document which emphasized Jesus' miracles as "signs" that were meant to produce faith in him (cf. John 2:11, 18, 23; 3:2; 4:54; 6:2, 14, 26; 7:31; 9:16; 10:41; 11:47; 12:18, 37). The signs source originally concluded in John 20:30–31 with a statement of purpose: "Jesus did many other *signs* in the presence of his disciples that are not written in this book. But these are written so that you may believe that Jesus is the Christ, the son of God, and that by believing you may have eternal life."

JOHN AND THE SYNOPTICS

The first three gospels show such similarities that some literary relationship must exist among them, a relationship that produces the Synoptic Problem. The Fourth Gospel, on the other hand, shows several points of contact with the Synoptics but in general presents a completely different picture of Jesus' career. Some scholars focus on the similarities to the

Synoptics and affirm that John must have been dependent on them. Other scholars emphasize the differences and argue that John preserves a tradition that is independent of the Synoptics. A balanced assessment would be that while the gospel may show knowledge of the Synoptics, they were not its sole or even primary source. The following summary indicates both the similarities and the differences between John and the Synoptics.

Similarities

Like the Synoptics, John relates the basic gospel story from John the Baptist to the resurrection of Jesus. It includes a few of the same stories as the Synoptics: the "cleansing" of the temple (2:13–22), the healing of an official's son (4:46–54), the feeding of 5,000 followed by Jesus' walking on water (6:1–21), the anointing of Jesus at Bethany (12:1–8), the final meal (13:1–38), and much of the passion narrative (chs. 18–19). In addition there are several cases of close agreement in wording between John and Mark, as in the story of Jesus' anointing at Bethany (see the box below).

Agreements in wording between Mark and John

MARK 14:3, 5	JOHN 12:3, 5
very costly ointment of pure nard	very expensive ointment of pure nard
For this ointment could have been sold for more than three hundred denarii and given to the poor.	Why was this ointment not sold for three hundred denarii and given to the poor?

Differences

John and the Synoptics differ in their presentations of Jesus' ministry, miracles, and message.

First, John differs in the presentation of **Jesus' ministry**. On the one hand, John omits many significant events that are related in the Synoptics: Jesus' baptism, temptation, transfiguration, institution of the Lord's Supper, and prayer in Gethsemane. Unlike Matthew and Luke (but like Mark), John has no stories about Jesus' birth. On the other hand, John includes material not found in the Synoptics. John relates a period of Jesus' ministry in Judea before the Galilean period (1:19–4:42).

Instead of only one trip to Jerusalem, as in the Synoptics, Jesus makes several trips to Jerusalem to attend the Jewish festivals there. As a result, most of the events in John occur in Jerusalem rather than Galilee. Since John mentions three Passovers instead of just one (2:13; 6:4; 11:55), Jesus' ministry lasts over two years instead of the single year suggested by the Synoptics.

John's dating of certain events in Jesus' ministry also differs from that of the Synoptics. While Mark dates the anointing of Jesus at Bethany two days before the Passover (Mark 14:1, 3), John dates it six days before the Passover (John 12:1). While Jesus' crucifixion occurs on the day of the Passover in the Synoptics, in John it occurs one day before the Passover (18:28; 19:14, 31). In the Synoptics, Jesus cleanses the temple at the end of his ministry; in John, at the beginning (2:13–22).

Second, John differs in the presentation of **Jesus' miracles**. John relates fewer miracles than the Synoptics, a total of seven. These miracles include healings, nature miracles, and a resuscitation, but no exorcisms. In John the miracles are "signs" which point to a deeper meaning (2:11; 4:54) or "works" which testify to Jesus' identity (5:36; 10:25). In some cases, a sign or work becomes the starting point for a discourse which clarifies its significance (chs. 5, 6, 9, 11). In other cases, the significance of the miracle is not explained (2:1–11).

Third, John differs in the presentation of **Jesus' message**. Jesus' teaching in John differs from that in the Synoptics in both form and content. In John, Jesus tells no parables, except perhaps for 10:1–6, which is called a *paroimia* (figurative saying). The short sayings and parables of the Synoptics are replaced by long discourses or dialogues.

The Johannine Jesus teaches primarily about two subjects: himself and eternal life. (1) Whereas in Mark, Jesus keeps his messianic identity a secret, in John he speaks openly about who he is. He gives long sermons or discourses about himself, proclaiming his identity, where he has come from, where he is going, his relation to the Father, and his relation to his disciples. (2) Whereas the Synoptic Jesus announces the kingdom of God, the Johannine Jesus mentions the kingdom only in 3:3, 5 and 18:36. While the Synoptics focus on the future coming of the kingdom and Jesus' return, John has only a few references to the future end of the age (5:27–29). John has no eschatological discourse or other teaching about Jesus' parousia. Instead of emphasizing a future kingdom, the Johannine Jesus emphasizes that one can possess eternal life already in the present.

JOHN'S PORTRAIT OF JESUS

In some respects, John's portrait of Jesus corresponds to that of the Synoptics. John uses the familiar titles "Christ," "son of God," and "Son of Man." Jesus is crucified, buried, and resurrected. In several respects, however, John's portrait of Jesus differs significantly from that of the Synoptics. John introduces several distinctive ideas about Jesus: his preexistence, his identity as "the Word," his identity as "God," his use of the phrase "I am," and his glory.

Jesus' Preexistence

Only John depicts Jesus as a preexistent being. The Synoptics never suggest that Jesus in any sense existed before his birth, but John explicitly states this in the first verse of his gospel. For John, Jesus existed in some form "in the beginning" before he appeared on earth as a human being. In terms of Greco-Roman ideas about divine men, John's Jesus is an incarnation of a god. While Matthew and Luke present Jesus as a Jewish demigod, who comes into existence at his birth, John presents him as an incarnation, an already existing spirit that takes on a human body.

The preexistence of Jesus gives rise to a difference in the "vertical" dimension of John's christology. In the Synoptics, Jesus originates on earth, ascends to heaven to be enthroned beside God, then promises to descend back to earth at the parousia. In John, this order is reversed. Jesus originates in heaven, descends to earth to become a human being, then ascends back to heaven at the crucifixion. Jesus is "from above" and returns there when his work on earth is done.

This difference is reflected in the special sense in which John uses traditional titles of Jesus. In John as in the Synoptics, Jesus is the son of God and Son of Man. In John, however, these titles refer to a preexistent being. God "sends" his Son from heaven to earth in order to save the world (3:16–17). Likewise, the Son of Man descends from heaven and then ascends back to heaven (3:13; 6:62).

Jesus as the Word

The Prologue of the Fourth Gospel (1:1–18) identifies Jesus as "the Logos" ("Word" or "Reason"), who existed alongside God "in the beginning" and through whom God created the world. The Logos subsequently came to earth and became incarnate (took on human flesh) as Jesus (1:14). He is a preexistent being become human. Scholars have proposed several different backgrounds as the source for John's concept of the Logos.

First, John's use of the term "Logos" has some affinities with the concept of **Logos in Greek philosophy**. The term "Logos" was used among philosophers, particularly Heraclitus, the Stoics, and the Jewish philosopher Philo of Alexandria. In the Stoic conception, the Logos was the life and mind of the universe. It resided in all matter, especially in the human soul, imparting life and thought. John may have this conception in view when he says that the Logos was "the true light that enlightens every person coming into the world" (1:9).

Second, many scholars see **personified Wisdom in Jewish tradition** behind John's Logos. As she appears in Proverbs 8:22–36 and other Jewish wisdom literature, Wisdom existed in the beginning before the creation of the earth. Like John's Logos, she is compared to light, and like Jesus in John, she speaks in long discourses.

Third, other evidence indicates that John had in mind **the word of Yahweh**, God's spoken word, mentioned in the Hebrew Scriptures. In certain passages, the word of Yahweh seems to function almost as an independent agent alongside God. John's description of "the Word" recalls this word of Yahweh. For example, in Psalm 33:6, Yahweh's word is the agent of creation:

> By the word of Yahweh the heavens were made,
> and by the breath of his mouth, all their host.

Similarly, John says of the Word, "All things came into being through him" (1:3).

Even more important for John's picture of Jesus is the word of Yahweh in Isaiah 55:10–11:

> For just as the rain descends,
> and the snow, from heaven,
> and does not return there
> until it has watered the earth,
> causing it to bear and put forth
> and giving seed to sow and bread to eat,
> so is my *word* which goes forth from my mouth:
> it does not return to me empty-handed,
> without doing what I willed
> and accomplishing that for which I sent it.

This passage likens the word of Yahweh to rain or snow, portraying it as the agent sent to carry out God's purposes in the earth. Especially significant are the following characteristics of the word in Isaiah's description: the word goes forth from God's mouth, is sent by God to the earth, descends from heaven, does the will of God, accomplishes that for which God sent it, waters the earth, gives bread to eat, and returns to God.

These same characteristics are important elements in John's description of Jesus:

- Jesus goes forth from God: "I came forth from God. I came forth from the Father and have come into the world" (16:27–28; cf. 8:42; 13:3; 16:30; 17:8).
- Jesus is sent by God into the world: "For God sent the Son into the world" (3:17; etc.).
- Jesus descends from heaven: "I have descended from heaven" (6:38; cf. 6:41, etc.).
- Jesus does the will of God: "I have descended from heaven not to do my own will, but the will of the one who sent me" (6:38; cf. 5:30).
- Jesus accomplishes that for which God sent him: "My food is to do the will of the one who sent me and to accomplish his work" (4:34; cf. 5:36; 17:3–4).
- Jesus gives living water: "Everyone who drinks of the water which I will give him will never thirst" (4:14).
- Jesus gives the bread of life to eat: "The bread which I will give is my flesh for the life of the world" (6:51).
- Jesus returns to God: "I am with you a short while longer, then I go back to the one who sent me" (7:33; cf. 16:27–28, etc.).

These parallels suggest that the Fourth Gospel portrays Jesus as the word of Yahweh in many places, even when the term "Word" does not appear.

Jesus as God

The Prologue of John asserts that the Word was not only "*with*" God in the beginning, but also "*was*" God (1:1). Jesus is thus not only preexistent, but divine. No other gospel makes this claim for Jesus. In some sense not explained, John describes the Word as both one with God and distinct from God. This paradox served as the basis for the church's discussion of the "Trinity" carried on in the fourth and fifth centuries.

The idea that Jesus is in some sense "God" is a central theme in the Fourth Gospel, expressed in several ways. (1) Jesus is called "God" in John 1:1, in 20:28, and, according to some important manuscripts, in 1:18. (2) On several occasions, the Jews become angry with Jesus because they understand that he is making himself God or equal to God (5:18; 8:58–59; 10:33). (3) Jesus explains his relation to God with the statement "I and the Father are one" (10:30). This sentence seems to be modeled on Deuteronomy 6:4, the Jewish confession of faith in the oneness of God: "Yahweh, our God Yahweh, is one." (4) In several passages, Jesus defines his oneness with the Father in terms of "mutual indwelling": "I am in the Father and the Father is in me" (14:10, 11; cf. 10:38). (5) The gospel claims that whoever has seen the Son has seen the Father (12:44–45; cf. 1:18; 14:9). When the scripture speaks of Isaiah seeing God (Isa 6:1), the Fourth Evangelist understands this to mean that Isaiah saw the preexistent son of God (John 12:41).

The "I Am" Sayings

In John's portrait of Jesus, Jesus frequently uses the phrase "I am," either by itself or with a predicate indicating what he is.

In several passages, Jesus makes the claim "I Am" (4:26; 6:20; 8:24, 28, 58; 13:19; 18:5, 6, 8). This is the same claim that God makes in several passages of the Hebrew Scriptures (Deut 32:39; Isa 41:4; 43:10, 13; 46:4; 48:12; 52:6; cf. 43:25, 51:12). The phrase ultimately refers back to Exodus 3:13–14, where God tells Moses that his name is "I Am who I Am" or simply "I Am." The Fourth Gospel's use of this phrase is thus part of its portrayal of Jesus as God.

In addition to the absolute "I Am" sayings, Jesus also uses "I am ..." with a predicate. There are seven such "I am" sayings in John:

- "I am the bread of life" or "living bread" (6:35, 51)
- "I am the light of the world" (8:12, 9:5)
- "I am the door" (10:7, 9)
- "I am the good shepherd" (10:11, 14)
- "I am the resurrection and the life" (11:25)
- "I am the way, the truth, and the life" (14:6)
- "I am the true vine" (15:1, 5)

These sayings provide a metaphorical description of Jesus' role, function, or work. Three of the sayings are illustrated by signs which Jesus performs:

- "I am the bread of life" (or "living bread") (6:35, 51).

    Sign: Jesus feeds 5,000 with a few loaves of bread (6:1–14)
- "I am the light of the world" (8:12, 9:5)

    Sign: Jesus "enlightens" a man born blind (ch. 9)
- "I am the resurrection and the life" (11:25)

    Sign: Jesus raises Lazarus from the dead (11:1–44)

Jesus' Glory

In the Synoptics, Jesus shares God's glory (honor or splendor) only after his death and resurrection. He is exalted to sit at the right hand of God and returns with the glory of God (Mark 8:38; 10:37; 13:26). In John, too, Jesus is "glorified" at his death (John 12:23, 27–28; 13:31–32; 17:1, 4–5). But in John, Jesus shares God's glory already in his ministry (1:14; 2:11; 11:4, 40) and even before the creation of the world (17:5, 24).

This comparison of Jesus' glory in John and the Synoptics may help to explain how John's unique christology arose. John's portrait of Jesus as a glorious heavenly being may have developed from the earlier conception in which Jesus was exalted to heaven and glorified after his resurrection. In this state of exaltation, he was "Lord," a name previously reserved for God. As such he shared the authority, attributes, and glory of God. It was this exalted Lord that the church worshipped. It is quite plausible that as the church focused on this glorified Jesus in their present, they began to think of Jesus in the past in the same way. They retrojected the glory of the exalted Lord into Jesus' ministry and even further into the past. The Johannine community represents a type of Christianity in which this process had come to completion.

COMMUNITY RELATIONS

The themes that receive emphasis in the Fourth Gospel allow us to form a picture of the Johannine community, including its relation to other groups. In John's gospel, we get a picture of a Jewish community that at one time had been part of the synagogue but which had been expelled for its exalted view of Jesus. The community carried on an evangelistic mission to Samaritans and Gentiles, competing for members with followers of John the Baptist and a form of Christianity that took Peter as its hero.

Expulsion from the Synagogue

A central concern of the Johannine community was the fact that its members had been or were being expelled from the Jewish synagogue. In one story in John's gospel, the Jewish leaders throw a man healed by Jesus out of the synagogue because of his positive attitude toward Jesus (9:22, 34). Others fear to confess Jesus lest they too be expelled (12:42). And in his farewell to the disciples, Jesus predicts that they will be expelled (16:1–4). John's emphasis on such expulsions suggests that the Fourth Gospel arose among Jewish Christians who were expelled from the synagogue because of their faith in Jesus.

This conflict between the Johannine community and the synagogue centered around their differing estimates of Jesus. First, they differed on whether or not Jesus was the Messiah. This difference is shown in John 9:22, which indicates that those who were put out of the synagogue were those who confessed that Jesus was the Christ. Second, the Jewish synagogue rejected the Johannine community's claim that Jesus was God. On several occasions in John's gospel, the Jews become angry with Jesus because they understand that he is making himself God or equal to God (5:18, 8:58–59, and 10:33). As the community expressed its belief that Jesus was the son of God, in some sense one with God, orthodox Jews saw this claim as blasphemy.

Mission to Samaritans and Gentiles

While the community had broken with the Jewish synagogue, they forged new relations with non-Jews, i.e. Samaritans and Gentiles. In John 4, as Jesus passes through Samaria, he identifies himself as the Messiah to a Samaritan woman. He then conducts missionary work among the Samaritans of her village. Such a story would have been most meaningful to a community engaged in such a mission. Other passages which show a concern for missionary work among non-Jews include Jesus' statement "I have other sheep which are not of this fold" (10:16) and the mention of some Greeks seeking Jesus at a festival in Jerusalem (12:20–22).

Figure 14.1
Fourth-century
fresco of Jesus
speaking to the
Samaritan woman
at the well, a story
unique to the
Fourth Gospel.
Hypogeum
of Via Latina,
Rome (Scala/Art
Resource, NY).

Apparently the community at some point began to accept Gentiles into its fellowship.

Competition with Followers of the Baptist

In their efforts to evangelize Jews and Gentiles, the community found itself in competition with other renewal movements, such as the followers of John the Baptist. Just as disciples of Jesus continued as a group after his death, so did disciples of the Baptist. The disciples of the Baptist apparently claimed that he, not Jesus, was the Messiah (Pseudo-Clementine, *Recognitions* 1.60.1–2). Such competing claims probably explain why the Fourth Gospel emphasizes the superiority of Jesus to the Baptist. In this gospel, the Baptist never baptizes Jesus but merely testifies that he saw the Spirit descending upon him (1:29–34). The author did not want Jesus to seem inferior to the Baptist by submitting to his baptism. To the contrary, he wished to emphasize the Baptist's inferiority to Jesus. While Jesus is the true light, the Baptist comes only to testify about the light (1:8). The Baptist himself admits that he is not the Christ (1:20, 28), that Jesus existed before him (1:15, 30), and that Jesus is superior to him (1:27). The Baptist tells his disciples that he (i.e. the number of his followers) must decrease, while Jesus must increase (3:30; cf. 4:1). The Baptist, unlike Jesus, never performs a sign (10:41). These unfavorable comparisons of the Baptist with Jesus can best be understood as the author's polemic against the competing views of the Baptist's disciples.

Competition with Petrine Christianity

The Johannine community also came into competition with other forms of Christianity. John repeatedly contrasts the **Beloved Disciple** with Peter in such a way as to emphasize the superiority of the former. At the Last Supper, the Beloved Disciple has the place of honor next to Jesus, while Peter can speak to Jesus only through the Beloved Disciple (13:23–25). Unlike Peter (18:17–18, 25–27), the Beloved Disciple does not deny Jesus. Of the male disciples, he alone is present at the crucifixion, and Jesus entrusts his mother to him (19:26–27). After Jesus' resurrection, the Beloved Disciple wins a race to the tomb with Peter, and only he is said to believe (20:1–10). When Jesus appears in Galilee, it is the Beloved Disciple who recognizes him and tells Peter (21:7).

By making the community's hero superior in faith and spiritual perception, the Fourth Evangelist symbolically maintains the superiority of Johannine Christianity over some form of Christianity that took Peter as its hero. This Petrine Christianity may have been that of Rome, which looked to Peter as the source of its authority. Or it may have been the Judaic Christianity represented by Matthew's special material, which also exalted Peter (Matt 16:15–19). In any case, the Fourth Evangelist saw Johannine Christianity as related but superior to this Petrine form of Christianity.

COMMUNITY BELIEFS AND PRACTICES

Unlike Q and M, John represents a non-Judaic (though Jewish) form of Christianity. That is, it represents Jewish Christians who did not feel bound to the practice of Judaism or the Jewish Law. At the heart of the community's religious understanding stood a belief in Jesus as the source of eternal life. The presence of the Holy Spirit served as a source of comfort and new revelation. Having experienced rejection from others, the community turned inward and emphasized love for other members of the community. Ritual practices included baptism, the Lord's Supper, and foot-washing.

Central to the community's concept of salvation was its belief that they received **eternal life** not through the Law, but through Jesus. As the

Johannine community broke from the Jewish synagogue, they also broke away from the Jewish Law. John contrasts the Law, which came through Moses, with "grace and truth," which came through Jesus (1:17). He also has Jesus refer to the Law as "your Law" when speaking to the Jews (8:17; 10:34). These references indicate that the community no longer saw the Law as binding upon themselves. Instead, they regarded faith in Jesus as the way to God. John has Jesus say, "I am the way, the truth, and the life. No one comes to the Father except through me" (14:6). Jesus' role as the way to God involved his death. This death was interpreted by John as a sacrifice for sin, as when he has John the Baptist say, "Behold the Lamb of God who takes away the sin of the world" (1:29). The community appropriated the saving power of this death through faith in Jesus, the result of which was "eternal life." The conclusion of the signs source states this idea: "These have been written so that you may believe that Jesus is the Christ, the son of God, and that by believing you may have life in his name" (20:31). For John, eternal life had both present and future aspects. A few passages refer to a future resurrection and judgment (5:28–29). For the most part, however, John emphasizes eternal life as a present possession, a new life that the believer has now (3:36; 5:24; 6:47, 54).

The Johannine community also believed in the **presence of the Paraclete**. Only John refers to the Holy Spirit as the "Paraclete," a term meaning "comforter," "helper," or "intercessor" (14:16, 26; 15:26; 16:7). The Johannine community regarded it as the presence of God or Jesus in their midst. The presence of the Comforter was a source of encouragement to the community. It helped to make up for the absence of Jesus after his departure (14:16–20, 25–26; 15:26–27; 16:4b–15). The community also saw the Paraclete as a source of new revelation about Jesus, presumably through Christian prophets who spoke as they felt inspired by the Spirit (14:25–26; 16:12–15). Given this perspective, the Johannine community felt no need to limit their ideas about Jesus to what the earthly Jesus might have said. They could justify a new portrait of Jesus by regarding it as a new revelation from the Paraclete.

The **central ethical principle** of the Johannine community comes to expression in the command to "Love one another." Whereas the Synoptic Jesus emphasizes the need to love one's enemies, the Johannine Jesus emphasizes loving other members of the Christian fellowship (13:34–35; 15:9–15, 17). This turning inward may have resulted from the trauma of the community's conflict with Judaism. Feeling rejected and persecuted by outsiders, community members saw the need to encourage and support one another.

Rituals of the Johannine community probably included baptism. Only John among the gospels portrays Jesus himself as baptizing followers (3:22). They also apparently took the Lord's Supper. In the discourse on the bread of life, John has Jesus make such statements as, "unless you eat the flesh of the Son of Man and drink his blood, you have no life in you" (6:53). Such language most likely presupposes the community's understanding of the Lord's Supper, in which the bread represented the body of Jesus and the wine, his blood. The community may also have practiced a rite of foot-washing. Only John records that at the Last Supper Jesus washed his disciples' feet as an example for them to follow (13:4–15).

Figure 14.2
Jesus washing the disciples' feet, a ritual that the Johannine community probably practiced. Sixteenth-century woodcut by Albrecht Dürer. © The Metropolitan Museum of Art (Art Resource, NY).

> ## Outline of the Fourth Gospel
>
> The Gospel of John has five major sections:
> 1. *Prologue* (1:1–18): introduces Jesus as a preexistent divine being, the Logos or "Word," who comes to earth and becomes flesh.
> 2. *Jesus' public ministry* (1:19–12:50): consists of signs or works performed by Jesus, accompanied by discourses in which Jesus speaks primarily of who he is and the life that he offers.
> 3. *Farewell Discourses* (chs. 13–17): set in the context of a last meal, at which Jesus bids farewell to his disciples as he prepares to return to heaven.
> 4. *Passion and resurrection narrative* (chs. 18–20): as in the Synoptics, recounts Jesus' death, burial, and resurrection.
> 5. *Epilogue* (ch. 21): foreshadows the death of Peter and the Beloved Disciple.

READING GUIDE: JOHN

Read the Gospel of John with the help of the following guide.

Prologue (1:1–18)

The Prologue traces Jesus' origin from eternity past, introducing ideas that will be important in the rest of the gospel. It presents Jesus as the Word, a preexistent divine being who was incarnated on earth.

Jesus' Public Ministry (1:19–12:50)

The gospel proper begins with a **series of days (1:19–2:12)** covering somewhat over a week. On the first day, John the Baptist testifies about himself as the forerunner of Christ (1:19–28). On the next, he testifies about Jesus as the Lamb of God and the son of God (1:29–34). On the following day, two of John's disciples, Andrew and Peter, become disciples of Jesus (1:35–42). On the next, Philip and Nathaniel become his disciples (1:43–51). Going to Galilee, Jesus turns water to wine at a marriage celebration in Cana, thus performing the first of his signs (2:1–11). Afterward, he spends "not many days" in Capernaum (2:12).

Unlike the Synoptics, John's gospel relates a **Passover in Jerusalem (2:13–3:21)** at the beginning of Jesus' ministry. At this feast, Jesus drives the merchants and moneychangers out of the temple (2:13–22). This "cleansing" of the temple occurs at the end of Jesus' ministry in the

Synoptics. The story in John reveals that it too originally belonged in the passion narrative, since Jesus' cryptic reply to the Jews anticipates his death and resurrection (2:18–22).

John refers to people who believed in Jesus at the feast because of the signs he performed (2:23–25). This reference creates an aporia, since the narrative has not related any such public signs and the next sign mentioned is only the second (4:54).

In a dialogue with a Pharisee named Nicodemus (3:1–21), Jesus emphasizes the need to be reborn spiritually, to be begotten "from above" or "again" (the Greek word can mean either). Nicodemus misunderstands, thinking that Jesus means a second physical birth. Such misunderstanding is a typical feature of John's account: while Jesus speaks on a spiritual or metaphorical level, those around him take him literally. The rest of the dialogue focuses on Jewish unbelief and the tendency of people to love "the darkness" rather than "the light."

After the Passover, Jesus progresses **from Judea to Galilee (3:22–4:54)**. In Judea (3:22–36), his activity of baptizing puts him into competition with John the Baptist for disciples. The evangelist's viewpoint is put in the mouth of the Baptist himself: he must decrease while Jesus must increase. As Jesus passes through Samaria (4:1–42), an encounter with a Samaritan woman at a well gives him an opportunity to speak about the "living water," a metaphor for the gift of eternal life that he provides. In Galilee, Jesus receives a warm reception (4:43–45) in contrast to his reception in Jerusalem. The proverb quoted here, "A prophet has no honor in his own country," implies that John regards Jesus as a Judean, unlike the Synoptics, who consider him a Galilean. In Galilee Jesus performs his second sign: healing an official's son at a distance (4:46–54).

Jesus then leaves Galilee for an **unnamed feast in Jerusalem (ch. 5)**. Here he heals a lame man (5:1–18). In John's gospel, Jesus' miracles are either "signs" or "works." The healing of the lame man is a work: Jesus has been working along with his Father. As in the Synoptics, Jesus' practice of healing on the Sabbath gets him in trouble with his more conservative brethren. An added twist in the Johannine story is that the Jews seek to kill Jesus not only for working on the Sabbath, but also for making himself equal to God (5:18).

This healing leads into a discourse by Jesus (5:19–30). Though healing is a great work, Jesus claims that he will do "greater works": giving life to the spiritually dead (5:21, 24–26) and judging those who have been physically resurrected from the dead (5:22, 27–30). In the second part of the discourse (5:31–47), Jesus lists the witnesses who testify to the fact that he has been sent by God: John the Baptist, Jesus' works, the Father, and the scriptures.

With no mention of a trip from Jerusalem, the narrative has Jesus spend **Passover in Galilee (ch. 6)**. Here he feeds 5,000 people, the only miracle that appears in all four gospels. In John's gospel, Jesus miraculously feeds the multitude with bread and fish (6:1–15). Then, as in the Markan material, he walks on the sea (6:16–21). John interprets the feeding by adding a related discourse in which Jesus claims to be "the bread of life," the bread from heaven that gives life to the world (6:22–65). Once again, while Jesus speaks on a metaphorical or spiritual level, his hearers misunderstand him, because they think on a literal level. The discourse concludes with John's version of Peter's confession (6:66–71).

The next section is set in Jerusalem primarily at the **Feast of Tabernacles (chs. 7–8)**. The individual units, however, clearly belong to more than one occasion. For example, 7:19–24 speaks of the healing of the lame man as if it had just occurred, indicating that it belongs with the story told in chapter 5 relating to another feast. Such combination of various unrelated units makes chapters 7–8 disconnected and hard to follow. The material includes various claims made by Jesus about himself and his teaching, mutual recriminations between Jesus and the Jews, speculation by the crowd concerning Jesus' identity, an abortive attempt to arrest Jesus, and veiled sayings of Jesus about his return to God.

The story of the **woman taken in adultery (7:53–8:11)** does not occur here in the best manuscripts. In some manuscripts it appears elsewhere in John or in Luke. It is probably a story about Jesus that circulated independently and only later was added at various places in the gospels.

While in Jerusalem, Jesus heals **a man born blind (ch. 9)**. The restoration of sight to this blind man illustrates Jesus' claim to be the light of the world (9:5). This healing depicts on a physical level Jesus' power to bring enlightenment to the spiritually blind. The healing brings the formerly blind man to faith in Jesus, so that he receives both physical and spiritual illumination. As a result, however, he is cast out of the synagogue, a symbol for those of the Johannine community who were experiencing the same treatment.

In both episodes of **chapter 10**, Jesus speaks metaphorically of himself as the shepherd of a flock of sheep (his followers). In the first discourse, Jesus describes himself as **the good shepherd (10:1–21)**, who lays down his life for the sheep. In the story of Jesus at **the Feast of Dedication (10:22–39)**, Jesus comes into conflict with Jews who are not his "sheep." At the end of this episode, Jesus goes **across the Jordan (10:40–42)**.

Jesus returns to Bethany to perform the **resurrection of Lazarus (ch. 11)**, a sign that illustrates Jesus' claim, "I am the resurrection and the life" (11:25). This story plays a significant role in John's narrative. In the Synoptics, the Jewish leaders' motivation for arresting Jesus is his "cleansing" of the temple. John, however, has moved that story to the front of his gospel, eliminating it as the immediate motive for killing Jesus. That motivation is supplied in the Gospel of John by Lazarus' resurrection, which the Jewish leaders fear will cause too many to believe in Jesus (11:45–57; 12:9–11).

Jesus' final **Passover in Jerusalem (ch. 12)** begins after he is anointed at Bethany (12:1–11). He then enters Jerusalem in triumphal procession (12:12–19). In the Synoptics, Jesus spends a great deal of time at the final

Figure 14.3
Jesus raises
Lazarus, a story
found only in
John. Painting
by Pasquale
Ottini, 1580–1650.
Galleria Borghese,
Rome (Scala/Art
Resource, NY).

Passover debating with the Jews. In John's gospel this does not occur. After a brief discourse on the arrival of his "hour" (12:20–36), Jesus goes into hiding (12:36). The evangelist concludes with a summary emphasizing the failure of the Jews to believe in Jesus (12:37–43). Tacked on to the end is a passage in which Jesus makes another proclamation about himself (12:44–50). Since Jesus has already gone into hiding, it strangely has no audience or setting (another aporia).

Farewell Discourses (chs. 13–17)

In the context of a final meal, Jesus bids farewell to his disciples, knowing that his "hour" has come to return to the Father. Unlike Jesus' final meal in the Synoptics, this meal in John's account is not a Passover meal but takes place before the Passover (13:1).

In John's version, Jesus does not institute a memorial meal, the Lord's Supper, but institutes the practice of **foot-washing (13:1–17)**. In Palestinian society, where the roads were dusty and people wore sandals, a host commonly provided water for guests to wash their feet or had a slave do it for them. Here Jesus takes the place of the slave and instructs his disciples to do likewise. The Johannine community apparently observed this practice as a sacred rite, symbolizing both humility and purification.

A **prediction of betrayal (13:18–30)** follows the foot-washing. As in the Synoptic accounts of the Last Supper, Jesus predicts that one of his students will betray him.

This prediction is followed by a **dialogue on Jesus' departure (13:31–14:31)**. Jesus' announcement that he is going away initiates a dialogue with the disciples, in which Jesus gives a "new commandment" to love one another (13:34–35). He then responds to the questions of Peter (13:36), Thomas (14:5), Philip (14:8), and another Judas besides the betrayer (14:22).

The dialogue ends in 14:31 as Jesus and his disciples get up to leave, yet this is followed by a further **discourse on Jesus' departure (chs. 15–16)** and Jesus' **prayer for unity (ch. 17)**.

Passion and Resurrection (chs. 18–20)

In John's account of Jesus' **betrayal and arrest (18:1–12)**, the evangelist contributes to the story by having Jesus use the phrase "I am (he)" (18:4–6).

In his account of Jesus **before the high priest (18:13–27)**, John gives no specific charge brought against Jesus at his interrogation.

In Jesus' **trial before Pilate (18:28–19:16)**, Pilate says three times, "I find no guilt in him" (18:38; 19:4, 6). John thus seeks to shift the blame for Jesus' death from Pilate to the Jews.

Unlike the Synoptics, John dates Jesus' **crucifixion and burial (19:17–42)** not to the day of Passover but to the day before the Passover (18:28; 19:14, 31), so that Jesus is crucified on the same day the Passover lambs were sacrificed in the temple. John draws attention to the symbolism of Jesus as a sacrificial lamb by noting that his legs were not broken by the Roman soldiers, just as the bones of the Passover lamb were not broken (19:36; cf. Exodus 12:46, Numbers 9:12).

John's **resurrection narrative (20:1–29)** includes a version of the empty tomb story (20:1–10) as well as appearances of Jesus to Mary Magdalene (20:1–18), ten disciples (20:11–18), and Thomas (20:26–29). Thomas' skepticism serves as a contrast to the faith required of subsequent members of the community, who must believe without seeing.

The **conclusion of the signs source (20:30–31)** is a statement telling why the author wrote it.

In a **final resurrection appearance in Galilee (ch. 21)**, Jesus predicts Peter's death by martyrdom (21:18–19), while the author denies that Jesus predicted that the Beloved Disciple would live until Jesus returned (21:20–23). In these comments, we can see the Johannine community grappling with the problem of the delay of Jesus' coming. The community originally believed that Jesus would come in the lifetime of the Beloved Disciple. When the Beloved Disciple died, the community had to revise its understanding.

DISCUSSION QUESTIONS

1. *John and the Synoptics.* Choose one or more of the following passages and explain how the portrait of Jesus found there is similar to or different from that in the Synoptics: John 1:1–18; 2:1–11; 3:1–21; 5:1–30; 6:1–59; 9:1–49; 11:1–44.

2. *The Farewell Discourses.* What are the central themes of the Farewell Discourses (John 13–17)? What do these themes tell us about the Johannine community?

REVIEW QUESTIONS

1. What claims about the authorship of the Fourth Gospel are made by the gospel itself and church tradition? Why do most scholars doubt that John the apostle wrote it?

2. For what two reasons do scholars think that the Fourth Gospel arose among a community of Jewish Christians?

3. What is the major literary problem of the Fourth Gospel? How do scholars generally account for it?

4. Compare and contrast John and the Synoptics with respect to Jesus' ministry, miracles, and message.

5. What distinctive ideas about Jesus distinguish John's portrait of Jesus from that in the Synoptics? How might John's unique portrait of Jesus have arisen?

6. Describe the relations between the Johannine community and other religious groups, as these relations can be inferred from the Fourth Gospel.

7. Describe the main beliefs and practices of the Johannine community, as these can be inferred from the Fourth Gospel.

8. Briefly describe the five major sections of the Fourth Gospel.

9. Identify: Beloved Disciple, aporias, signs source, Paraclete.

SUGGESTIONS FOR FURTHER STUDY

Bennema, Cornelis. *Encountering Jesus: Character Studies in the Gospel of John* (2nd ed.; Fortress, 2014). Presents a theory of character and uses it to analyze the characters in the Gospel of John.

Brown, Raymond E. *The Community of the Beloved Disciple: The Life, Loves, and Hates of an Individual Church in New Testament Times* (Paulist, 1979). Reconstructs the social history of the Johannine community reflected in the gospel and letters of John.

Brown, Raymond E. *The Gospel According to John* (Anchor Bible; 2 vols.; Doubleday; Yale University Press, 1966, 1970). A standard commentary on the English text of the Gospel of John.

Culpepper, R. Alan. *Anatomy of the Fourth Gospel: A Study in Literary Design* (Fortress, 1983). Illuminating analysis of the Fourth Gospel from a literary-critical perspective.

Kysar, Robert. *John, the Maverick Gospel* (3rd ed.; Westminster John Knox, 2007). Accessible introduction to the themes of the Fourth Gospel.

Martyn, J. Louis. *History and Theology in the Fourth Gospel* (3rd ed.; Westminster John Knox, 2003). Groundbreaking work on the social setting of the gospel among Jews being expelled from the synagogue.

Sloyan, Gerald S. *What Are They Saying about John?* (rev. ed.; Paulist, 2006). Surveys scholarly research on the Gospel of John.

Smith, D. Moody. *John among the Gospels* (2nd rev. ed.; University of South Carolina Press, 2001). Surveys scholarly opinion on the relation between John and the Synoptics.

15   The Apocryphal Jesus

During the early centuries of Christianity, numerous works about Jesus circulated besides the four gospels that the church eventually canonized. These apocryphal (non-canonical) works developed particular aspects of the Jesus portrayed in the canonical gospels, such as his birth or death. The Infancy Gospel of James, the Infancy Gospel of Thomas, and the Gospel of Peter will serve here as examples of this literature.

INFANCY GOSPELS

Infancy gospels focus on the birth or childhood of Jesus. Since the canonical gospels say little about Jesus as a child, these works satisfied the curiosity that Christians had about that part of Jesus' life.

The Infancy Gospel of James

The Infancy Gospel (or Protevangelium) of James was written under the pseudonym of "James," probably referring to the brother of Jesus. Some scholars date it as early as the second century. It takes elements from the birth narratives of Matthew and Luke and combines them with other traditions not found in these gospels, especially stories about the birth and childhood of Mary.

In this gospel, Jesus is not the only one with a miraculous birth: Mary too is born from a virgin. Her mother Anna conceives without the assistance of Joachim, Anna's husband. Between the ages of three and twelve, Mary lives in the temple at Jerusalem, supernaturally fed by an angel. When the priests seek a husband for her, Joseph, an old widower with sons, is miraculously designated as her guardian when a dove comes out of his staff and settles on his head.

As Mary spins thread for the temple veil, the angel Gabriel appears and announces that she will give birth to Jesus. An angel also assures Joseph that the child is from the Holy Spirit. When Annas the scribe sees Mary, he reports to the priest that Joseph has unlawfully gotten her pregnant. However, a test with holy water (cf. Numbers 5:11–31) shows that neither has sinned.

As Joseph and Mary travel to Bethlehem, Mary goes into labor and takes refuge in a cave. Joseph finds a Hebrew midwife named Salome, but her help is apparently not needed. God appears in the cave, first as a dark cloud and then as a blinding light, after which the baby appears and takes Mary's breast. When Salome uses her finger to see if Mary is still a virgin, her hand "falls away in fire." She is healed by touching Jesus.

After wise men arrive seeking the new king of the Jews, Herod has the infants of Bethlehem killed, but Mary hides Jesus in a cow stable. The story concludes by relating how Herod also sought the death of the infant John (the Baptist) and killed his father, Zechariah.

As this summary indicates, the Infancy Gospel of James defends Jesus against the accusation that he was illegitimate by introducing a test with holy water. It also heightens the miraculous element in the story of Jesus' birth by having Jesus appear in a blinding light.

Furthermore, this gospel shows the developing interest that Christians had in Mary as a sacred figure in her own right. The account of Mary's supernatural birth from a virgin provides the earliest witness to the Catholic doctrine of Mary's "immaculate conception," the doctrine that she was conceived without the taint of original sin. Salome's examination provides the earliest witness to the Catholic doctrine of Mary's "perpetual virginity," the doctrine that she remained a virgin even after the birth of Jesus.

The Infancy Gospel of Thomas

Another infancy gospel is attributed to "Thomas the Israelite," presumably the apostle of that name. It should be distinguished from the collection of sayings known as the Gospel of Thomas. Two main versions of this infancy gospel exist in Greek, one longer (A) and one shorter (B). The date of the work as a whole is uncertain, but at least one story in it was known already in the second century.

This infancy gospel says nothing about Jesus' birth but relates his "magnificent childhood deeds" between the ages of five and eight (or twelve). It consists of two main types of stories: miracle stories and curse stories.

(1) This gospel takes the miracle tradition represented in other gospels and retrojects it into the childhood of Jesus. The young Jesus gives life to clay sparrows, raises another child from the dead, heals a cut foot, carries water in his mantle, and miraculously evens out two boards of different lengths. This boy needs no instruction: when a tutor tries to teach him the alphabet, Jesus astounds him with his knowledge. (2) Curse stories are a type of negative miracle story, in which the miracle worker uses his or her power for destructive rather than beneficial purposes. Twice in this gospel Jesus curses a young boy who offends him, and the boy drops dead. Clearly this young Jesus did not put up with any nonsense.

Figure 15.1
A twelfth-century mosaic of Jesus Christ. Though no one knows what Jesus looked like, artists throughout history have exercised their imagination in depicting him. Hagia Sophia, Istanbul, Turkey (Santi Rodriguez/ Alamy Stock Photo).

THE GOSPEL OF PETER

At the end of the second century, Serapion, bishop of Antioch, wrote a book entitled *Concerning the So-Called Gospel According to Peter*. Serapion's book no longer exists except for a passage quoted by Eusebius of Caesarea (*Ecclesiastical History* 6.12). According to that passage, Serapion found the church at Rhossus using a gospel written in the name of Peter. At first he allowed them to read it, but when he examined it more closely he found that "most things were from the correct teaching of the Savior, but some things were further expanded." Serapion attributed this gospel to Docetists, Christians who denied that Christ had a real, physical body or who distinguished between the purely spiritual Christ and the human Jesus.

Until 1886, nothing more was known about the Gospel of Peter. In that year, however, a grave uncovered in Egypt yielded a manuscript fragment from the eighth or ninth century that probably came from this lost gospel. The fragment begins in the middle of Jesus' trial and breaks off in the middle of what is apparently a resurrection appearance. Peter speaks in it in the first person as the author.

Many of the events in the story correspond to those in the canonical gospels: Pilate washes his hands as in Matthew, Jesus appears before Herod Antipas as in Luke, soldiers guard the tomb as in Matthew, the women find only a young man in the tomb as in Mark, and certain disciples fish in Galilee after the crucifixion as in John.

Other elements of the story have no parallel in the canonical gospels. Some of the more interesting features of the fragment are the following.

- Pilate and the Roman soldiers, though present, play no role in the crucifixion of Jesus. It is Herod Antipas who turns Jesus over to be crucified, and the Jews carry out the crucifixion. This gospel thus represents a growing tendency in early Christianity to shift the responsibility for Jesus' death away from the Romans onto the Jews.
- On the cross, Jesus "remained silent as if (or since) he had no pain." Some interpreters see this statement as evidence for a docetic view of Christ.
- At his death, Jesus cried, "My Power, Power, you have abandoned me," and was then "taken up." One could interpret this to mean that the divine Christ abandoned the human Jesus, as in certain docetic views. Perhaps, however, "my Power" refers to God, and what was taken up was Jesus' soul.
- Those who guard the tomb include not only Roman soldiers, but also the Jewish elders and scribes, and all witness the resurrection of Jesus.
- The story heightens the miraculous in the resurrection narrative with fabulous elements: three men whose heads reach to the sky, or beyond, and a talking cross.
- The story incorporates the tradition that Jesus preached to the dead in Hades during the time his body was in the tomb (cf. 1 Peter 3:18–20).
- The fragment apparently places the resurrection appearances in Galilee rather than Jerusalem.

Figure 15.2
Jesus frees souls
imprisoned in
Hades. Both 1
Peter 3:18–20
and the Gospel
of Peter 41–42
mention this
story, and it is
further developed
in the apocryphal
Gospel of
Nicodemus.
Painting by
Duccio di
Buoninsegna
(c. 1260–1318).
Museo dell'Opera
Metropolitana,
Siena, Italy
(Scala/Art
Resource, NY).

Several questions concerning this fragment remain. Did it originally
include stories about Jesus before his death, like the canonical gospels, or
only a passion and resurrection narrative? Does it present a docetic view
of Christ? Most importantly, what relation does it have to the canonical
gospels? It seems most likely that the author of this gospel knew and used
the canonical gospels, imaginatively expanding their traditions.

DISCUSSION QUESTIONS

1. Read the Infancy Gospel of Thomas in Appendix 7 (pp. 575–578). Read
   also these curse stories from Jewish and Christian scriptures: Leviticus
   10:1–7 and 2 Samuel 6:1–7 (Yahweh); 2 Kings 2:23–24 (the prophet
   Elisha); Matthew 21:18–22 (Jesus); Acts 5:1–11 (Peter); Acts 13:4–12
   (Paul). Describe the portrait of Jesus presented in the Infancy Gospel
   of Thomas, comparing it with those found in the canonical gospels.
   What purpose or function do curse stories serve in this portrait, and

how does this function compare with that of the other curse stories assigned? Why would this portrait of Jesus be appealing to those among whom this gospel circulated?

2. Read the Gospel of Peter in Appendix 8 (pp. 579–582). Read also the accounts of Jesus' resurrection in the New Testament: Paul (1 Corinthians 15:1–8; Acts 9:3–9); Matthew 27:62–28:20; Mark 16:1–8, 9–20; Luke 24; John 20–21. Compare and contrast these different accounts of Jesus' resurrection with respect to the nature of Jesus' resurrection body, the location of the appearances, and the individuals to whom he appeared. What developments do you see in these traditions?

SUGGESTIONS FOR FURTHER STUDY

Ehrman, Bart D. *Lost Scriptures: Books That Did Not Make It into the New Testament* (Oxford University Press, 2003). A collection of early Christian gospels, acts, epistles, and apocalypses outside of the New Testament with brief introductions.

Ehrman, Bart D., and Zlatko Pleše, eds. *The Other Gospels: Accounts of Jesus from Outside the New Testament* (Oxford University Press, 2014). Includes a selection of non-canonical gospels in English translation with brief introductions.

Elliott, J. K., ed. *The Apocryphal Jesus: Legends of the Early Church* (Oxford University Press, 1996). Takes stories about Jesus from apocryphal works and arranges them in the order of Jesus' life.

Elliott, J. K., ed. *The Apocryphal New Testament: A Collection of Apocryphal Christian Literature in an English Translation* (Clarendon, 1993). One-volume collection of apocryphal writings in English translation, with brief introductions.

Foster, Paul, ed. *The Non-Canonical Gospels* (Bloomsbury T&T Clark, 2008). A collection of introductory essays by various authors on early Christian gospels outside the canon.

Koester, Helmut. *Ancient Christian Gospels: Their History and Development* (Trinity Press International, 1990). Introduction to early Christian gospels, both canonical and non-canonical.

Schneemelcher, Wilhelm, ed. *New Testament Apocrypha* (rev. ed.; 2 vols.; Westminster John Knox, 1991, 1992). Substantial collection of apocryphal writings in English translation, with extended introductions.

16   The Quest for the Historical Jesus

The gospels portray Jesus from the perspective of various authors and communities in the early church. They tell us what the early church believed about Jesus. But to what extent do these portrayals tell us about Jesus as he actually was? Clearly not everything in the gospels can be taken as historical fact, since the gospels themselves do not always agree. How can we distinguish between what is historically accurate and what is not? How can we distinguish between the Christ presented by the gospels and the actual Jesus of history? These are questions that modern scholars have sought to answer as they have engaged in a quest for "the historical Jesus."

EVALUATING THE SOURCES

Any inquiry into the past is limited by the extent and quality of the historical sources available. The quest for the historical Jesus therefore must begin by considering what sources give us information about Jesus and how reliable these sources are.

The Relevant Sources

Sources that potentially give information about Jesus include ancient non-Christian writings, non-canonical gospels and sayings, and the New Testament.

Ancient non-Christian writings have little to say about Jesus. While Roman literature contains a few references to him, these tell us little more than that he existed (Tacitus, *Annals* 15.44; Suetonius, *Claudius* 25.4). Jesus also gets mentioned in the work of the Jewish historian Josephus (*Antiquities* 18.63–64), but since this passage describes Jesus in glowing terms as the Messiah, Josephus the Jew probably did not write it. It was apparently inserted, or at least revised, by a Christian scribe who copied the manuscript. Josephus does make reference to John the Baptist and James the brother of Jesus (*Antiquities* 18.116–19; 20.197–203).

Non-canonical gospels and sayings that circulated in some parts of the early church also have little value for reconstructing the historical Jesus. One exception may be the Gospel of Thomas, a collection of sayings attributed to Jesus. Many scholars think that some of the sayings in this collection are closer to the original than similar sayings in the canonical gospels. Other scholars, however, believe that Thomas is dependent on the canonical gospels and offers no independent evidence for the historical Jesus.

The few references to Jesus' life and teachings in other New Testament books besides the gospels add little to our knowledge. The four canonical gospels, therefore, by default remain our primary sources for information about Jesus.

Problems with Using the Gospels

The four canonical gospels present their own kinds of difficulties for reconstructing an accurate picture of Jesus. They cannot be taken at face value as historical reports. Scholars recognized this first about the Gospel of John. Since John's portrait of Jesus differs radically from that of the Synoptics, a choice had to be made between the two. It could not be true, for instance, that Jesus both concealed his identity and went around proclaiming it. The choice for most scholarship was the Synoptics. It was recognized that while John may preserve elements of historical information, its account in general reflects an idealized portrait of Jesus drawn in light of the resurrection and the experience of the Johannine community. Few scholars today would use the Gospel of John to reconstruct the historical Jesus.

Eventually scholarship came to realize that the Synoptics presented the same sorts of problems. The material in the Synoptics does not come directly from eyewitnesses but has been passed down in the church in a chain of oral and written tradition. This tradition has taken shape in light of the beliefs and concerns of the Christian community. Much of it does not give us accurate information about the historical Jesus. Early Christians attributed sayings to Jesus that he did not actually speak; they embellished or even created stories about him; they took ideas that first

Figure 16.1
A fishing boat returning to Capernaum on the shore of the Sea of Galilee. The gospels locate much of Jesus' activity in this area. Erich Lessing/Art Resource, NY.

arose in the church and retrojected them into the story of Jesus. Scholars now recognize that the gospels are very much books of the church. They often tell us more about the faith and practices of the early church than about Jesus himself. To get to the actual historical person, therefore, scholars have tried to get "behind" the gospels as we now have them.

STAGES OF THE QUEST

The quest for the historical Jesus has proceeded in three stages: the first quest, the new quest, and the third quest.

The **first quest** occurred mainly in the nineteenth century as numerous authors wrote biographies or "lives" of Jesus. Albert Schweitzer reviewed these lives in *The Quest of the Historical Jesus* (1906), showing that the authors tended to interpret the gospels in light of their own presuppositions and to create a Jesus in their own image. He maintained that most failed to interpret Jesus against the proper background – Jewish eschatology. This stage of the quest came to an end with the advent of form criticism, which showed that no biography of Jesus in the modern sense is possible. Since the gospels were composed from unconnected units of tradition, arranged by the evangelists, we have no way of knowing the actual order of events in Jesus' life. Furthermore, some of the traditions arose in the church and tell us nothing about Jesus as he actually was.

Jesus and the Kingdom

Central to the quest has been the issue of what Jesus taught about the kingdom of God. Did he proclaim that God was about to establish the kingdom in the very near future, or did he speak of the kingdom as something already present in his own ministry?

Albert Schweitzer (1906), following Johannes Weiss (*Jesus' Proclamation of the Kingdom of God*, 1892), emphasized that Jesus understood the kingdom of God in a future eschatological or apocalyptic sense. The apocalyptic kingdom of God was a kingdom that God would establish by intervening dramatically in human history. It would bring to an end all human governments, which were thought to be controlled by Satan, and mark the beginning of a new age in which God and/or his Messiah would directly rule the earth. The establishment of the kingdom would be accompanied by a cosmic cataclysm: the sun would cease to shine, and the stars would fall from the sky. According to Weiss and Schweitzer, Jesus mistakenly thought that God would establish this kingdom in the very near future.

In reaction to Schweitzer, C. H. Dodd (*The Parables of the Kingdom*, 1935) argued that Jesus conceived of the kingdom as already completely present in his own ministry. To support his view, Dodd translated Jesus' message in Mark 1:15 ("the kingdom of God is at hand") as "the kingdom of God has arrived." According to this "realized eschatology," Jesus did not expect a future, apocalyptic kingdom, though the early church attributed this view to him.

After Dodd, most scholars argued that Jesus considered the kingdom in some sense both present and future: Jesus expected God to establish the kingdom in the future but saw it as already present in some sense in his own ministry. The kingdom was an eschatological concept, but somehow it was already anticipated in Jesus.

In the third quest, a number of scholars have rejected the view that Jesus expected the kingdom of God in the future, or at least in the near future. For these scholars, as for Dodd, Jesus understood the kingdom exclusively or primarily as something already present in his ministry. Jesus was not content to wait for God to intervene dramatically and create a new world order in the future: he wished to reform the society in which he lived in the present. The kingdom was a way of living in the present and the community that lived in that way.

Other scholars, however, continue to set Jesus' thought about the kingdom in an eschatological context. For example, E. P. Sanders (1993), like Schweitzer, believes that Jesus expected God to act dramatically in the very near future to establish the kingdom of God. Sanders points out that both John the Baptist and the early church expected God to establish an apocalyptic kingdom in the near future. Jesus provides the link between John, whose baptism he accepted, and the early church, which arose from his followers. One could logically infer, therefore, that the early church received their apocalyptic expectation from Jesus, who received it from John the Baptist.

Form criticism gave rise to a deep skepticism concerning our ability to know anything about the historical Jesus, especially details of a biographical nature. Rudolf Bultmann, one of the pioneers of New Testament form criticism, wrote in 1926, "I do indeed think that we can now know almost nothing concerning the life and personality of Jesus, since the early Christian sources show no interest in either, are moreover fragmentary and often legendary; and other sources about Jesus do not exist" (*Jesus and the Word*, p. 8). Despite these difficulties, some of Bultmann's students initiated a **"new quest"** for the historical Jesus. This began in 1954 with the publication of Ernst Käsemann's essay, "The Problem of the Historical Jesus." The second stage of the quest differed from the first, in that it came after form criticism and took that discipline seriously. Scholars therefore began to develop criteria for distinguishing between authentic and inauthentic traditions about Jesus. The second quest was also largely theologically oriented, seeking to preserve the historical Jesus for Christian theology.

Outside of Bultmann's tradition, a revival of interest in the historical Jesus began in the 1980s and even earlier. This **third quest** was in part a reaction against the skepticism enunciated by Bultmann. Scholars of the third quest believe that we can know quite a bit about the historical Jesus. This stage has also gone hand in hand with a new interest in the social world of first-century Palestine. By reconstructing the social environment in which Jesus lived, scholars hope to gain new insights about Jesus himself. Questers draw on a variety of disciplines, such as sociology, anthropology, and the history of religions, to reconstruct that social world.

CRITERIA OF AUTHENTICITY

The problematic nature of our sources poses the greatest difficulty for knowing the historical Jesus. The question is, how do we distinguish what Jesus actually said and did from what the church attributed to him? How do we distinguish the authentic tradition in the gospels from traditions that originated in the church? Unfortunately, no simple answer to this question has been found. Scholars have tried using various criteria for distinguishing between authentic tradition and later developments, but none gives foolproof results. Such criteria include the criteria of multiple attestation, embarrassment, dissimilarity, and coherence.

According to the **criterion of multiple attestation**, if a saying, idea, or deed attributed to Jesus occurs in several independent gospel sources, it is more likely to be authentic than one that appears in only a single gospel source. Note that a tradition that occurs in the triple tradition (material occurring in all three Synoptics) is not counted as having three independent attestations but only one, since here all three gospels depended

Figure 16.2　Inscription from ancient Caesarea, headquarters of the Roman governors of Judea. The first line (TIBERIEUM) refers to Tiberius, emperor at the time of Jesus' death. The second (-IUS PILATUS) mentions Pontius Pilate, the Roman governor under whom Jesus was crucified. Israel Museum, Jerusalem (Erich Lessing/Art Resource, NY).

on the same source. An example of a tradition with three independent attestations would be the accusation that Jesus cast out demons by the power of Beelzebul, a tradition that occurs in the Markan material (Mark 3:22; Matt 12:24), in Q (Luke 11:15; Matt 12:24), and in Matthew's special material (Matt 9:34). The criterion of multiple attestation helps to identify the earliest tradition, since the tradition must be earlier than any of the independent sources in which it is found. The fact that a tradition is early, however, does not prove that it gives accurate information about Jesus.

The **criterion of embarrassment** states that material that tended to embarrass the church or contradict its viewpoint would probably not have been created by the church and may therefore preserve historical information. If we accept this criterion, the tradition that John the Baptist baptized Jesus is probably true. The church, in competition with disciples of John, tended to exalt Jesus over John and would not have created a tradition that subordinated Jesus to John. This criterion might be a useful tool, except that no gospel contains a great deal that would embarrass the church.

The **criterion of dissimilarity** affirms that if a tradition reflects a concern that was typical of the early church (or first-century Judaism), then such material may have originated in that context. If, however, the tradition is dissimilar from the concerns of both Judaism and the early church, then it has not come from these sources and may well be authentic tradition about Jesus. For instance, the tradition that Jesus preached about the kingdom of God may be accurate, since neither Judaism nor the New Testament outside of the gospels frequently referred to the kingdom of God. Thus if a tradition has no parallels in Judaism or the early church (and therefore could not come from those sources), this criterion supports the conclusion that it came from Jesus. But what if a tradition *does* have parallels in Judaism or the early church? Does this mean that it could not have come from Jesus? No, since much of Jesus' teaching would naturally have parallels among other Jewish teachers of his day and would have passed on into the teaching of the church. This criterion therefore can support the authenticity of certain traditions but cannot prove the inauthenticity of the remaining traditions.

The **criterion of coherence** (or consistency) affirms that a tradition about Jesus may be authentic if it is consistent with (coheres with) other traditions accepted as authentic. This criterion can be helpful, but one can use it only after identifying a certain amount of authentic material on the basis of other criteria.

DIFFERING PICTURES OF THE HISTORICAL JESUS

While these criteria for authenticity may be helpful guidelines, they do not ensure purely "objective" results. Scholars must still exercise judgment, and decisions concerning what is authentic continue to vary. Unfortunately, therefore, the quest for the historical Jesus, even in its latest stage, has produced no consensus on what we can know about Jesus. Portraits of Jesus continue to vary. Some scholars see him as a revolutionary who sought political power; others see him as a deluded apocalyptic visionary, proclaiming the end of the world. For some he was a rabbi, teaching a new interpretation of the Law; or a sage, spouting Zen-like maxims that overturned proverbial wisdom. For others he was a prophet, calling Israel to repentance and warning of impending judgment; or a social reformer, seeking to implement a new vision of society. The following examples represent a sample of the different reconstructions of the historical Jesus that scholars have proposed over the past three centuries.

Jesus the Revolutionary

Hermann Samuel Reimarus may have been the first to make a critical evaluation of the traditions about Jesus. He kept his work unpublished during his lifetime. After his death, sections of it were published in 1774–78 as *Fragmente eines Ungennanten* (Fragments of an Unknown Author). Reimarus interpreted Jesus as a revolutionary, seeking to overthrow the government and to make himself ruler. Jesus, like John the Baptist, preached that the kingdom of God would soon come. It would be a political kingdom on earth in which Jesus himself would reign as king. He preached that people should repent in order to prepare for its coming. They should be converted to true righteousness, a righteousness stricter than the superficial holiness of the Pharisees. When he believed the people were ready to accept him, Jesus went to Jerusalem, resorted to violence in the temple, told the people publicly that he was the Messiah, and advocated the overthrow of the Jewish leaders. He counted on the people to support his claim to kingship, but in vain.

He was arrested and crucified, and his hope of gaining power came to nothing.

Jesus the Eschatological Prophet

The greatest number of reconstructions have pictured Jesus as an eschatological prophet. An eschatological prophet proclaims that God is about to end the present world order and establish a new age and a new order. The new order might be a kingdom on the present earth, ruled by a messianic king and replacing the kingdoms of the old age. Or it might be a kingdom on a totally new earth, ruled over by God after he raised the dead and executed the final judgment. In any case, the eschatological prophet would proclaim that the kingdom was imminent – just around the corner. But while a revolutionary would try to bring about the kingdom by force, an eschatological prophet would wait for God to do it. Numerous scholars have portrayed Jesus as such a prophet, announcing the imminent arrival of the kingdom and perhaps seeing himself as the king in that kingdom. In these reconstructions, Jesus did not escape the problem that besets all prophets who predict that the end is near: so far all have been wrong.

Albert Schweitzer (1906), for example, saw Jesus as a deluded apocalyptic visionary. Jesus knew from the time of his baptism that he would be the Messiah, the king in the transcendent kingdom of God. He began to proclaim that the kingdom of God was near. When the kingdom failed to appear, he conceived the new idea that he must suffer for the sins of the people before God would establish the kingdom. He therefore went to Jerusalem and deliberately provoked the Jewish leaders into killing him by making a disturbance in the temple. On the cross, he realized that he had been mistaken and died in disillusionment, with the cry "My God, my God, why have you forsaken me?"

Rudolf Bultmann (1926) portrayed Jesus as both a rabbi (see below) and an eschatological prophet. As a prophet, Jesus proclaimed the imminent coming of the kingdom of God: Satan's rule had expired, the end of the present age was near, now was the time of decision. Jesus did not think of himself as the Messiah, but pointed ahead to the coming of "the Son of Man," an eschatological figure other than himself. He entered Jerusalem with a crowd of followers and cleansed the temple in preparation for the imminent coming of the kingdom. The kingdom did not come, however; instead the authorities had him executed.

E. P. Sanders (1993), among others, has maintained the eschatological perspective in the third quest. Jesus was an eschatological prophet like John the Baptist. In the synagogues of Galilee he proclaimed that God was about to establish his kingdom on earth. Jesus expected that he himself would rule as God's viceroy in the coming kingdom. At that time, God would restore the twelve tribes of Israel, and peace and justice would prevail. Jesus also had a reputation as a healer and exorcist. He saw his miracles as signs that God's final victory over evil was beginning. Instead of preaching repentance and judgment like John, Jesus emphasized God's love for even the most sinful. About the year 30 CE, Jesus and his followers went to Jerusalem for the Passover. His action in the temple was a symbolic prediction that God would destroy the temple and build a new one in the new age. The high priest, fearing a disturbance, arrested him for this act and because his followers had hailed him as king. Pilate had him crucified as the king of the Jews, considering him a religious fanatic who posed a threat to law and order.

Jesus the Jewish Rabbi

For Rudolf Bultmann (1926), Jesus was not only an eschatological prophet (see above), but also a rabbi, an interpreter and teacher of the Jewish Law. As a rabbi, Jesus received scribal training and passed the tests necessary for becoming a scribe. Much of his teaching resembled that of other rabbis. Like other rabbis, Jesus demanded obedience to the will of God, but he radicalized this demand as something that a person does not obey simply because it is commanded, but understands and affirms within oneself. The most important element of his message was his concept of God. While Judaism emphasized the remoteness of God, Jesus emphasized his nearness.

Jesus the Social Reformer

A number of scholars in the third quest have pictured Jesus as a social reformer. Unlike the eschatological prophet, the social reformer does not expect God to sweep away the current society but wishes to improve it by persuasion or political and social action.

Marcus Borg (1987) found that Jesus had characteristics of four religious personality types: charismatic healer, sage, founder of a revitalization movement, and prophet. In all of these roles, Jesus' central concern was to transform the existing social order of his day. The conventional wisdom of his day emphasized God's holiness. To be holy, one had to remain separate from those who were not, the sinful and socially unacceptable. Jesus emphasized God's grace and compassion rather than his holiness. His table fellowship with outcasts was an enacted parable of this grace and compassion. His twelve followers, representing the twelve tribes of Israel, were to be the nucleus of a new society, patterned on compassion rather than holiness. He warned that Jerusalem and the temple would be destroyed by military conquest unless the culture actually changed its direction from holiness to compassion. Jesus went to Jerusalem to make an appeal to his people at the center of their national and religious life. He expelled the sellers of sacrificial animals from the temple, because they represented the politics of holiness. The Jewish leaders perceived him as a threat to the established order and as a false teacher in league with Beelzebul. They arrested him and turned him over to Pilate for trial as one who claimed to be a king. Jesus thus died for a crime of which he was innocent.

John Dominic Crossan (1994) pictured Jesus as a Jewish peasant Cynic who criticized the hierarchical and oppressive structure of his society and as an alternative advocated equality for all. Jesus' alternative society, the kingdom of God, was not a hope for the future, but a way of life in the present. It was the way one would live if God were in charge. The kingdom meant the peasant dream of a just and equal world. Its central ideal was "radical egalitarianism." In the kingdom all people were equal, regardless of social or economic class or gender. Jesus not only discussed the kingdom, but also enacted it by associating with all classes of people. Jesus was like a Cynic in that he appealed to ordinary people, acted out his message, and used dress and equipment to symbolize his message. Jesus went to Jerusalem only once. There he became indignant at the temple as the seat and symbol of all that was non-egalitarian and oppressive in his society. He symbolically destroyed the temple by putting a stop to the financial and sacrificial activity going on there. The soldiers arrested him and crucified him immediately. His followers fled for their own safety and never learned what became of his body.

Jesus the Feminist

Elisabeth Schüssler Fiorenza (1983), like Crossan, emphasized Jesus' egalitarianism, but with special focus on his attitude toward patriarchy. Jesus established a renewal movement within Judaism that presented an alternative to the dominant patriarchal structures of the day.

While Jesus hoped for God's future kingdom, he believed that the kingdom was already experientially present in his own ministry and movement. The kingdom meant the wholeness of each individual and the wholeness of Israel, the inclusion of all members of Israel. In particular, Jesus included in the kingdom the destitute poor, the sick and crippled, tax collectors, sinners, and prostitutes – and many of these were women.

Jesus saw himself as the prophet and child of Sophia (Wisdom), a feminine image for God in Judaism. This God accepted everyone with all-inclusive love. This Sophia-God did not demand Jesus' death; that was brought about by the Romans. His death, like that of all other prophets, resulted from violence against Sophia's messengers, who proclaimed the equality of all her children.

Jesus spoke against patriarchal structures, even if indirectly. He taught that patriarchal marriage did not exist in the world of God. He also called people out of their patriarchal families into his "discipleship of equals." This new family included brothers, sisters, and mothers, but no fathers. He thus abolished patriarchal power in the new community. Jesus challenged those in power to relinquish domination and become equal with the powerless. Jesus did call God "father," not, however, to legitimate patriarchy, but to exclude it from the community: neither the "brothers" nor the "sisters" could claim the father's authority that was reserved for God alone. Thus liberation from patriarchal structures was at the heart of Jesus' proclamation of the kingdom of God.

Jesus the Sage

For Burton Mack (*A Myth of Innocence*, 1988), Jesus was a popular sage (wise man), specifically a Cynic. He criticized the social world of Galilee, but, unlike a social reformer, he did not suggest an alternative program. He spoke in aphorisms and parables which overturned conventional wisdom and cultural conventions. The kingdom that he invited others to enter was not a future apocalyptic entity, but a way of looking at things: a "stance of confidence in the midst of confused and contrary social circumstances."

Jesus of the Jesus Seminar

The Jesus Seminar represents a collective effort by a group of scholars to pursue the quest for the historical Jesus. Founded in 1985 by Robert

Funk, the twice-yearly meetings of the Seminar generally have drawn together thirty to forty scholars, whose initial purpose was to determine the actual words of the historical Jesus. Members voted on each saying in the four canonical gospels and the Gospel of Thomas by casting one of four color-coded beads into a ballot box. A red bead indicated a strong positive vote for authenticity, while a black bead indicated a strong negative vote. Intermediate positions were indicated by pink, on the positive side, and gray, on the negative side. The colors were given a numerical value, and the values of the votes were averaged to arrive at the consensus of the members. The Seminar published the results of its work in *The Five Gospels* (Funk and Hoover 1993), which printed the words of Jesus in the four colors used in voting. Relatively few sayings appear in red, the color of authenticity. Most of those that do come from Q or Thomas. Subsequently the Seminar proceeded in the same manner to produce a book on the authentic deeds of Jesus.

REACTION AGAINST THE QUEST

Despite the diversity in these portraits of the historical Jesus, they have one thing in common: all depict a purely human Jesus, not the

Figure 16.3
An ancient ossuary, a container for holding the bones of a deceased person. This one, discovered in 1990, bears the name in Aramaic of Joseph Caiaphas, the high priest at the time of Jesus' death. www.BibleLandPictures.com/Alamy Stock Photo.

supernatural and theological Jesus of traditional Christianity. The Jesus in these portraits does not come down from heaven, is not born of a virgin, does not claim to be God, does not perform supernatural deeds, does not die for the sins of the world, is not raised from the dead, does not ascend back to heaven, and is not expected to return. This purely human look results from one or more assumptions held by the interpreters: (1) that theological claims about God's activity in the world fall outside the realm of history, which deals only with the human world; (2) that the theological and supernatural claims in the gospels do not pass the criteria of authenticity; (3) that supernatural events do not happen.

This reconstruction of Jesus as purely human leaves a gap between the historical Jesus and the Christ of faith, the Christ worshipped by the church. Traditionally, the church has valued most highly precisely those supernatural or theological elements of the story omitted by the historical approach. This reconstruction also leaves a gap between the message of Jesus and the message of the church. Whereas Jesus preached the kingdom, the church preached Jesus.

Not surprisingly, this type of reconstruction has not received a warm welcome in all quarters. Accordingly, some have taken a different approach to the matter. One example is N. T. Wright, an Anglican priest. In *Jesus and the Victory of God* (1996), Wright has the explicit goal of eliminating the gap between the Jesus of history and the Christ of faith. He wants to reconcile history with theology. Wright compares historical scholarship on Jesus to the prodigal son in Luke's parable (Luke 15:11–32). This son has left the father (God) and the older brother (theology) to waste his substance on "riotous but ruinous historicism." This bad brother, historical scholarship, should be welcomed home, but only if it "comes to its senses" and abandons "the dissolute methodologies that have made it appear so bankrupt." By abandoning these methodologies, Wright finds historical value in many aspects of the gospels that more critical scholars have attributed to the theology of the early church.

The portrait of Jesus that emerges bears an obvious resemblance to the Christ of faith. Though Jesus appeared to the public as a prophet proclaiming the imminent kingdom of God, he secretly thought of himself as the Messiah, without advocating revolution, and as in some sense God, though not in the later Trinitarian sense. As Messiah, he believed it was his task to go to Jerusalem and die a redemptive death.

Contemporary Significance of the Historical Jesus

The Jesus of traditional Christianity offers forgiveness of sins and hope of eternal life. By comparison, the critical scholar's Jesus may seem to offer very little to people today. This is not to say, however, that these scholars find no contemporary significance in Jesus at all. Most who have quested for the historical Jesus have been at least partially motivated by an interest in Jesus' significance for the present and have addressed themselves to the question. We give here four examples.

For Albert Schweitzer,

> it is not Jesus as historically known, but Jesus as spiritually arisen within people, who is significant for our time and can help it … The abiding and eternal in Jesus is absolutely independent of historical knowledge and can only be understood by contact with his spirit which is still at work in the world. In proportion as we have the spirit of Jesus we have the true knowledge of Jesus.

For Schweitzer personally, having "the spirit of Jesus" meant living a life of service as a medical missionary in West Africa.

For Rudolf Bultmann, too, it is not the historical Jesus who has contemporary significance. Rather, it is the Jesus proclaimed in the kerygma, the message preached by the church about the crucifixion and resurrection of Jesus. This message, however, cannot be taken literally. It must be "demythologized," that is, stripped of its mythological content, and reinterpreted in terms of existentialist philosophy. This means that one must apply the idea of death and resurrection symbolically to oneself, die to the past and be reborn. In this way, a person can achieve "authentic existence" – a life that is free from the past and open to the future.

Unlike Schweitzer and Bultmann, Marcus Borg does find contemporary significance in the historical Jesus. As a Spirit-filled charismatic, Jesus witnesses to the reality of the Spirit, to the fact that "another world" exists beyond that apparent to the senses. At the same time, Jesus provides a picture of what life in the Spirit is like: free from fear and anxiety and characterized by love, courage, insight, joy, and compassion. Borg sees Jesus as both an "epiphany of God" and a "model for human life." As an epiphany of God, Jesus disclosed what God is like. He did so in both his teaching and his manner of being. As a model for human life, Jesus provides a pattern for being reborn of the Spirit, living a life of compassion, and seeking to transform culture by the power of the Spirit.

According to John Dominic Crossan,

> Jesus incarnates a dream, a profound and ancient dream, deeply embedded in the human spirit, for a world of radical justice, radical equality; for a world not of domination but of empowerment; and above all for the announcement that that is what God, that is what the holy and the sacred, is concerned about – not about domination but about empowerment, about a world of justice. That is the permanent, abiding legacy of Jesus, and as long as that dream is alive, Jesus is alive. (from an interview for "Jesus: His Life," A&E Television Network, 1995)

He believed that after death he would be vindicated and exalted to share the throne of God. Wright suggests that Jesus' resurrection would show that he had succeeded in his task, but Wright leaves that study for a later book.

FINAL THOUGHTS ON JESUS

If we keep in view the whole 2,000-year history of Jesus, one conclusion emerges as inescapable: no period of history has been able to pin Jesus down to a single image. Even during his lifetime, people had different ideas about Jesus. Was he John the Baptist come back to life? Was he the long-awaited Elijah? Was he like one of the prophets of old? Or could he be the Messiah (Mark 6:14–15; 8:27–29)? After his death, his followers continued to paint his portrait in differing hues. Mark thought of him as a human Messiah, intent on keeping his identity a secret. John portrayed him as an incarnation of God striding over the earth, proclaiming his identity at every opportunity. Matthew favored a Judaic Jesus, reinterpreting the Law, but still insisting that his followers keep it. Luke preferred a compassionate Jesus, friend of the outcast and the sinner. For Paul and his tradition, Jesus was the sacrifice who died for the sins of the world. For the Gnostics, he was the Revealer, who helped the soul find its way home. For the Docetists, he was a purely spiritual being, never joined to defiling flesh. Constantine and succeeding emperors tried to establish one official image of Jesus and partially succeeded, but people still had their own ideas. In every generation, new images of Jesus have appeared, not only among Christians, but also among Jews, Muslims, Hindus, and devotees of the New Age. It should come as no surprise, therefore, that modern scholarship has not settled on a single image of Jesus. Jesus is a hard fellow to pin down. He continues to be all things to all people.

DISCUSSION QUESTIONS

1. Choose one of the reconstructions of the historical Jesus summarized in the present chapter. Discuss how the material in the gospels either supports or does not support this reconstruction.
2. When the gospels include two different versions of a saying, scholars engaged in the quest for the historical Jesus try to determine which is

the earlier or more original, assuming that, if Jesus spoke this saying, he could have spoken only the more original form. Compare and contrast the beatitudes in Matthew (Matt 5:3–12) with the beatitudes in Luke (Luke 6:20–23). What form of this pericope seems most original? Justify your answer. What does the original form of this pericope imply about Jesus, if he spoke it?

REVIEW QUESTIONS

1. What are the primary sources for our knowledge about the historical Jesus? What difficulties are involved in using these sources?

   [handwritten: M, M, L, J / 4 canonical gospels]

2. Describe the three stages of the quest for the historical Jesus. *[handwritten: 3 quests]*

3. What different views have scholars held about what Jesus meant by the kingdom of God? *[handwritten: gods messianic kingdom]*

4. Describe the criteria that scholars have used to determine the authenticity of the gospel traditions. *[handwritten: multiple attestation, dissimillitary, embarassment, coherence / the cross section adding up]*

5. Describe some of the different portraits of Jesus that scholars have proposed in the quest for the historical Jesus.

6. What contemporary significance have scholars such as Schweitzer, Bultmann, Borg, and Crossan found in Jesus?

SUGGESTIONS FOR FURTHER STUDY

Bond, Helen K. *The Historical Jesus: A Guide for the Perplexed* (Bloomsbury T&T Clark, 2012). Introduction to the scholarship and key themes of historical Jesus research.

Borg, Marcus J. *Jesus: A New Vision* (HarperSanFrancisco, 1987). An accessible presentation of Jesus as a non-eschatological figure.

Bultmann, Rudolf. *Jesus and the Word* (German 1926; English: Scribner's, 1934). A pioneer of form criticism sees Jesus as a rabbi and eschatological prophet.

Crossan, John Dominic. *Jesus: A Revolutionary Biography* (HarperSanFrancisco, 1994). Pictures Jesus as a Jewish peasant looking for equality.

Funk, Robert W., and Roy W. Hoover. *The Five Gospels: The Search for the Authentic Words of Jesus* (Macmillan, 1993). A committee of scholars, the Jesus Seminar, seeks to determine what Jesus actually said.

Sanders, E. P. *The Historical Figure of Jesus* (Penguin, 1993). A clear presentation of Jesus as an eschatological prophet.

Schüssler Fiorenza, Elisabeth. *In Memory of Her: A Feminist Theological Reconstruction of Christian Origins* (Crossroad, 1983). Argues that Jesus' original movement had a non-patriarchal character, which gave way over time to the patriarchal perspective that characterized the later church.

Schweitzer, Albert. *The Quest of the Historical Jesus* (German 1906; English: Dover, 1968). A renowned scholar and humanitarian reviews the first quest and portrays Jesus as a prophet looking for an imminent apocalyptic kingdom.

Wright, N. T. *Jesus and the Victory of God* (Fortress, 1996). Wants to eliminate the gap between the Jesus of history and the Christ of faith.

PART III

Acts

17   The Book of Acts

The book of Acts or "Acts of the Apostles" supplies a sequel to the Third Gospel. Both were written by the same person, traditionally identified as "Luke." For a discussion of the author, date, and setting of Luke–Acts, see Chapter 13.

With respect to genre, Luke's second volume falls into the category of sacred history as defined in Chapter 9 (see "The Genre of a Gospel"). It provides the earliest history of the Christian church. While it differs in many respects from modern works of history, it has affinities with the works of ancient Greek and Roman historians. Even more closely, it resembles the sacred history found in certain books of the Old Testament, such as Genesis, Exodus, Joshua, Judges, Samuel, and Kings. Like them, it relates history from a theological perspective, in which the God of Israel has a role to play. It presents the origin of Christianity as the result of divine providence.

The book of Acts recounts the founding of the church and the spread of its message to the Roman Empire. According to this account, some of Jesus' students gathered in Jerusalem after his death and began to proclaim that God had raised him from the dead and made him the Messiah. They formed a Jewish community known as "the sect of the Nazoreans." Certain members of this group began to preach to Gentiles and took on the name "Christians." A Jew named Paul then took up the Christian message and preached it from one end of the Roman Empire to the other.

CENTRAL THEME: FROM JEW TO GENTILE

The central theme of Luke–Acts is that the message of salvation was sent to the Gentiles because the Jews rejected it. We can infer the centrality of

267

this theme not only because it appears so frequently in Luke–Acts, but also because it appears at all the high points of the story.

In emphasizing this theme, the author of Luke–Acts sought to justify a situation that existed in his day: the church consisted primarily of Gentiles rather than Jews. Though the message about Jesus began among Jews, most Jews had rejected it, while many Gentiles had accepted it. This situation raised a theological problem: how did a Jewish Messiah wind up with a Gentile church? God had promised the Messiah to the Jews. How then could the church be the people of the Messiah when most were not Jews? To defend the church as the legitimate people of the Messiah, the author of Luke–Acts had to explain how it came to consist primarily of Gentiles. Repeatedly, we see him giving the same explanation: because the Jews rejected Christian preaching about the Messiah, God sent the message to the Gentiles. Gentile Christians were therefore the legitimate heirs of God's promises to the Jews. This theme is developed in both Luke and Acts.

The Theme in Luke's Gospel

In the Gospel of Luke, this theme appears at the beginning, middle, and end of Jesus' ministry. Luke introduces the theme in his first story about Jesus' ministry (Luke 4:16–30). When the people of his home town do not accept him as Messiah, Jesus declares that "No prophet is acceptable in his own country" (Luke 4:24). He then gives examples of Israelite prophets who were accepted by Gentiles but not by Israelites. This episode foreshadows what would happen later as Christian missionaries preached about Jesus. With this story, Luke justifies preaching to the Gentiles: since the Jews reject the message, God sends it to those who will hear.

Other passages in the gospel also foreshadow Jewish rejection and Gentile acceptance of Jesus. In Luke 7:9, Jesus praises a Gentile's faith, contrasting it with the lack of faith among Israelites. In Luke 8:19–21, Jesus identifies his true family not as those who are physically related to him (i.e. the Jews), but as all who hear and do his word. Other sayings predict that Gentiles will enter the kingdom while Jews are excluded (Luke 13:22–30; cf. 11:27–28). Not the invited guests, but others, will partake of the banquet of the kingdom (Luke 14:15–24).

The theme recurs at the conclusion of Luke's gospel. The risen Jesus commissions his disciples to preach the gospel "to all the nations

(Gentiles), beginning from Jerusalem" (Luke 24:47). They will preach first to Jews in Jerusalem, but then take the message to Gentiles.

The Theme in Acts

The same theme occurs throughout the book of Acts. Jesus repeats his mission charge at the beginning of Acts, telling the disciples to preach "in Jerusalem, in all Judea and Samaria, and to the end of the earth" (1:8). The rest of Acts chronicles the fulfillment of this three-fold program: (1) the mission in Jerusalem fails as Jewish leaders reject the message and persecute the Christians; (2) the mission to Samaria and Judea serves as a transition to the Gentile mission; (3) the Gentile mission succeeds with the conversion of Cornelius, the establishment of a Gentile church in Antioch, the Jerusalem Conference that frees Gentile converts from the Law, and the missionary journeys of Paul among Gentiles.

The first part of Acts relates the **failure of the mission to Jews**. After Jesus ascends to heaven, his disciples begin to proclaim his resurrection in Jerusalem. At first they preach only to Jews. As Peter says, since Jews inherited God's promises to Abraham, it was necessary to speak to them first (3:25–26). Many of the Jewish people accept the message.

As Acts proceeds, however, Jewish leaders increasingly oppose the message. The priests and Sadducees arrest Peter and John, and later all of the apostles. Both times, the apostles are released with a warning not to continue preaching. Luke gives three reasons for the opposition: (1) the apostles were preaching to the people about resurrection, an idea that the Sadducees rejected (4:2); (2) the priests and Sadducees were jealous of the apostles' healing ministry (5:17); (3) the apostles were blaming the Jewish leaders for Jesus' death (6:28).

This opposition comes to a head over the teaching of Stephen, an out-spoken defender of the new faith. Stephen's opponents bring him to trial before the Sanhedrin, charging him with speaking against the temple and the Law. Stephen lashes out, charging the Jews with always resisting the Spirit of God (7:51–53). The Jewish leadership responds by putting Stephen to death. They start a severe persecution of the Jesus movement in Jerusalem, causing many disciples to flee the city. Stephen's death thus marks a major turning point in Luke's story: since the Jews in Jerusalem have rejected the message, it will be taken to the Gentiles outside of Jerusalem.

The next part of Acts relates the **transition to the Gentile mission**. Luke relates two steps that prepare for the spread of the gospel to Gentiles. The first is missionary activity among the Samaritans. When the disciples flee Jerusalem, some go to Samaria and preach there (8:4–25). Though the Samaritans practiced a form of the same religion as the Jews, they were not Jews. Preaching to these non-Jews thus paved the way for preaching to Gentiles.

The second step is the conversion of Saul of Tarsus, who would become the chief missionary to the Gentiles. Saul first appears in the story as a zealous persecutor of the new sect of Nazoreans. On a trip to Damascus, however, he has a vision of the risen Jesus. This experience turns him around completely, so that he becomes as zealous in spreading the Christian message as he had been formerly in persecuting it. He later takes the Roman name "Paul" and becomes active in preaching to Gentiles. Luke regards the conversion of Saul/Paul as such a significant event that he relates it three different times (chs. 9, 22, 26).

The final part of Acts relates the **mission to Gentiles**. In telling this story, Luke focuses on four central events: the conversion of Cornelius, the establishment of a Gentile church, the Jerusalem Conference, and the missionary journeys of Paul.

First, Peter inaugurates the Gentile mission. Directed by a series of revelations from God, he preaches to Cornelius and his household, who are Gentile God-fearers, that is, Gentiles who worshipped Israel's God but did not become circumcised or keep the Jewish food laws. While Peter is still preaching, the Holy Spirit falls on his audience. God thus confirms that the message of eternal life in Christ is for all nations. For Luke, this conversion is significant enough to relate twice (chs. 10, 11).

Second, a Gentile church is established in Antioch of Syria. When believers in Antioch begin to preach to Gentiles, the apostles at Jerusalem send a man named Barnabas to oversee the church there. Barnabas asks Saul/Paul to join him, and together they teach and strengthen the believers at Antioch. It is here that the believers are first called Christians.

Third, the Jerusalem Conference decides that Gentile converts do not have to keep the Jewish Law. In Antioch, certain Jewish Christians maintained that Gentile converts had to be circumcised and keep the Law of Moses in order to be saved. Paul and Barnabas dispute this, and the argument is carried to the apostles and elders in Jerusalem (ch. 15). This meeting, the Jerusalem Conference, upholds the teaching of Paul and Barnabas that Gentiles are saved through faith in Jesus, not by becoming Jews and keeping the Law. This decision makes it easier

Figure 17.1
A view of modern Antioch. Acts locates the first mixed church of Jews and Gentiles here. G. Eric Matson Collection, Library of Congress, Washington, D.C.

for Gentiles to become Christians. It also shows that Christianity can no longer be considered merely a sect of Judaism: it is now a separate religion, in which Gentiles have equal access to God with Jews on the same basis.

Fourth and finally, Paul's missionary journeys illustrate the transition from Jew to Gentile. The account of Paul's missionary activity takes up the entire second half of Acts (chs. 13–28). In Paul's preaching, a pattern develops: he first preaches to Jews, who reject the message; he then turns to Gentiles, who accept it. Luke introduces this pattern in the first story about Paul's missionary preaching. When the Jews at Antioch in Pisidia speak against Paul's message, he replies, "The word of God had to be spoken to you first. But since you reject it and judge yourselves unworthy of eternal life, we are turning to the Gentiles" (13:46). Acts' story comes to a climax with the apostle Paul preaching to a group of Jews in Rome. When they reject the message, Paul says, "Then let it be known to you that this salvation of God has been sent to the Gentiles. They will listen" (28:28). This concluding statement of Paul in Luke–Acts summarizes its central message: because Israel has rejected God's salvation, that salvation has been sent to the Gentiles. The Gentiles are now the legitimate heirs of God's promises to Israel.

OTHER MAJOR THEMES OF ACTS

In addition to its central theme, other major themes run through Acts: (1) the coming of the Holy Spirit; (2) the preaching of the apostles; (3) the establishment of the church; and (4) the innocence of Christians.

The Coming of the Holy Spirit

Throughout his two-volume work, Luke places a special emphasis on the role of the Holy Spirit in the events of salvation. In his gospel, he stresses the role of the Spirit more than any other evangelist. In all the Synoptics, John the Baptist promises that Jesus will baptize people in the Holy Spirit, but only Luke repeats this promise at the end of his Gospel (Luke 24:48), pointing forward to its fulfillment in Acts.

The first chapter of Acts picks up where the gospel left off by reminding the reader that Jesus instructed his disciples to wait in Jerusalem for the promised Holy Spirit (1:1–5, 8). Chapter 2 of Acts describes the coming of the Spirit like a mighty, rushing wind. The disciples are filled with the Holy Spirit and begin to testify to the resurrection of Jesus. Peter speaks to a crowd that has gathered and explains that the Holy Spirit can be received by all who repent and are baptized in the name of Jesus Christ (2:38–39). Luke interprets the coming of the Spirit as a sign that "the last days" before the day of the Lord have arrived (2:17–20).

From Chapter 2 on, the "Acts of the Apostles" might be better named "Acts of the Holy Spirit," for the Spirit becomes the driving force in spreading the gospel and establishing churches. Luke not only refers to the Spirit frequently, but also relates how it was poured out on three further groups of believers: the first Samaritan believers (8:14–17), the first

Gentile believers (10:44–48), and some disciples who knew only John's baptism (19:1–7). Luke uses the first two cases to show that God approves the spread of the gospel to non-Jews. The third demonstrates the superiority of Jesus' baptism to that of John.

The Preaching of the Apostles

In Acts 1:8, Jesus promises his disciples that the Spirit will empower them to testify about him effectively. This is precisely what happens in Acts 2. When the disciples receive the Spirit, Peter preaches about Jesus, and around 3,000 people join the disciples. Peter's sermon shows Luke's concern to give examples of Christian preaching. Luke gives five such examples, three of Peter and two of Paul: (1) Peter's sermon on the day of Pentecost (2:14–42); (2) Peter's sermon in the temple (3:12–26); (3) Peter's sermon to Cornelius (10:34–43); (4) Paul's sermon in the synagogue at Antioch of Pisidia (13:16–41); (5) Paul's sermon to the Greek philosophers in Athens (17:22–31).

These sermons are directed to different audiences. The first two are directed solely to Jews. The third addresses Gentile God-fearers. The fourth sermon is given in a synagogue, where both Jews and God-fearers would be in the audience. The fifth sermon alone addresses a Gentile audience unfamiliar with Jewish religion. In each sermon, the speaker adapts his message to the audience and situation, yet all five sermons agree in focusing on Jesus' resurrection and the need for repentance.

Other speeches in Acts show the disciples defending themselves and their faith against attack. These include Stephen's speech at his trial (ch. 7) and various speeches of Paul (chs. 20, 22, 24, 26).

The Establishment of the Church

After the coming of the Spirit, Peter's preaching on Pentecost results in the establishment of the church. On the day of Pentecost itself, around 3,000 people join the disciples in Jerusalem (2:41). After Peter's sermon in the temple, Luke puts the number at about 5,000 men (4:4), not counting women and children. In Acts 5:11, Luke refers to this community of believers as the "church" (Greek *ekklesia*, "assembly"), the translation of a term used in the Hebrew Scriptures to designate the "congregation" or "assembly" of God's people. Three aspects of Luke's description of the church call for comment.

Figure 17.2 The acropolis in Athens seen from the Areopagus (Mars' Hill). Luke situates Paul's sermon to Epicurean and Stoic philosophers on Mars' Hill (Acts 17:22–31). Erich Lessing/Art Resource, NY.

The first is the church's practice of **sharing possessions**. Luke describes this early community as devoting themselves to the apostles' teaching, fellowship, communal meals, prayer, and attendance at the temple (2:42, 46). He especially emphasizes that the believers share their possessions with one another so that no one lacks (2:45; 4:32–37). He thus carries over the theme of Jesus' concern for the poor, so prominent in his gospel. He describes the church as a place where this concern continues among Jesus' disciples.

The second is the **leadership** of the church. The leaders of the Jerusalem church consist of the twelve apostles and a body of elders (15:2, etc.). Of the twelve, only Peter receives particular notice. In the later chapters, James the brother of Jesus seems to occupy the leading place in the church (12:17; 15:13; 21:18). As missionaries establish churches outside of Jerusalem, they appoint elders as leaders (14:23; 20:17).

The third is the **transition from Nazoreans to Christians**. At first all of the members of the community are Jewish. They continue to practice Jewish customs and worship in the temple with other Jews. Hence the people regard them not as a new religion, but simply as a new "sect" of Judaism, comparable to the sects of the Pharisees and Sadducees. The Jews call it "the sect of the Nazoreans" (24:5; cf. 24:14, 28:22), while the early believers call it "the Way" (9:2; 19:9, 23; 22:4; 24:14, 22), meaning "the way of the Lord" (18:25), "the way of God" (18:26), or "the way of salvation" (16:17). Only after the gospel spreads to the Gentiles in Antioch are the believers called "Christians" (11:26).

The Innocence of Christians

In Luke–Acts, various Christians are tried before Jewish and Roman courts. One of Luke's concerns is to show that such Christians are innocent of all wrongdoing. In Luke's account of Jesus' trial, he emphasizes that the Roman governor Pilate found no guilt in him (Luke 23:4, 14–15, 22). Later a Roman centurion also proclaims him innocent (Luke 23:47). In Acts, when witnesses testify that Stephen has spoken against the temple and the Law, Luke labels them "false witnesses" (Acts 6:13). Stephen is thus an innocent victim. Likewise, when Jews accuse Paul before Gallio, a Roman official, Gallio dismisses the case (Acts 18:12–17). After Paul's arrest in Jerusalem, King Herod Agrippa II says to the Roman procurator Festus, "This man could have been released if he had not appealed to Caesar" (Acts 26:32).

This emphasis on the innocence of accused Christians probably has an apologetic purpose. Luke may have wished to defend the Christian movement against charges that it was subversive to the Roman government. He therefore portrays Roman officials acting favorably toward Christian preachers in order to show that other Roman authorities likewise should not persecute Christianity.

ACTS AS HISTORY

Without the book of Acts, we would know very little about the origin of the Christian church. In this respect, its value can hardly be overstated. Three factors, however, limit its value as history.

First, it is a "slanted" history. Luke is not writing from a desire to chronicle history objectively. He wants to make a point. As we have seen, his primary concern is to portray Gentile Christians as the legitimate people of the Jewish Messiah. He is therefore prone to favor the Christian perspective at the expense of Judaism.

Second, Acts is a selective history. It focuses on a few individuals, primarily Peter and Paul, and on a few events that represent the general course of events. Much significant information is omitted, such as the ministries of the other apostles. The author may have omitted information not relevant to his purpose. He was also undoubtedly limited by his sources. Scholars have found at least two possible indications of written sources in Acts. First, in the early chapters of Acts the language contains Semitic idioms, suggesting that Luke may have used a written Aramaic source or sources. Second, in certain sections of Acts, the narration shifts from third-person "they" to first-person "we" (16:9–18; 20:5–21:18; 27:1–28:16). These "we" sections may indicate that the author himself participated in the events described. Some scholars, however, believe that in these places the author incorporated a journal or diary written by someone else.

A third factor that limits the historical value of Acts is the fact that it is only partially reliable. There is evidence of both accuracy and inaccuracy in the account. On the one hand, the author shows precise knowledge of geographical locations, political offices, legal procedures, and nautical terminology. On the other hand, certain factual and chronological errors appear in the account. Whether or not these invalidate the basic reliability of Acts is disputed. Several features of Acts raise questions about its reliability as history: its inconsistencies, its emphasis on the miraculous, its use of speeches, and its portrayal of Paul.

Figure 17.3
The ancient amphitheatre at Ephesus, site of an angry demonstration against Paul, according to Acts 19:23–41. Sonia Halliday Photo Library.

Inconsistencies in Acts

The traditions in Acts sometimes contradict other traditions in Luke, in Acts, or elsewhere.

1. In Luke's gospel, Jesus ascends to heaven on the same day he is resurrected (Luke 24:36–53), whereas in Acts he ascends forty days after the resurrection (Acts 1:1–9).

2. According to the gospel, Jesus commanded his disciples after his resurrection to preach to all the Gentile nations (Luke 24:46–47). In

Acts, however, the disciples show no knowledge of such a command. It is the Holy Spirit that directs Peter to preach to Gentiles, and this direction comes as a surprise to all involved. When some of the disciples object to the practice, no one justifies it by replying that Jesus commanded it (Acts 10:1–11:18). In this case, the tradition of Acts is superior to that in Luke. As Acts correctly depicts, the Gentile mission began as a new development in the early church. Only subsequently did someone assume that Jesus must have commanded it and create the tradition found in Luke.

3. According to one story in Acts, Peter was the first to preach the Christian message to Gentiles (Acts 10:1–11:18). According to another tradition, however, Christians preached to Gentiles after fleeing from persecution in Jerusalem (11:19–21), a persecution that Acts places before the story about Peter (8:1–4). It seems likely that the story about Peter arose to justify the Gentile mission by appealing to a leading apostle.

4. Minor inconsistencies appear in the three accounts of Paul's conversion (Acts 9:1–19; 22:1–16; 26:9–18). In one version, Paul's companions hear a voice but see no one (9:7); in another, they see a light but hear no voice (22:9). In one version, it is a man named Ananias who tells Paul that he will be an apostle to the Gentiles (22:10–16); in another, it is God (26:14–18).

5. Both Acts and Matthew speak of a field near Jerusalem known as the "Field of Blood," and both give an etiology (story of origin) that connects the name with Judas (Matt 27:3–10; Acts 1:18–19). Their etiologies differ, however. In Matthew, Judas returns the thirty pieces of silver which the priest paid him to betray Jesus, then hangs himself. The priests then buy a field with this "blood money" – hence the name "Field of Blood." In Acts, Judas buys the field. He then for some reason bursts open and spills his intestines in the field – hence the name of the field. Apparently, there was a field near Jerusalem with the intriguing name "Field of Blood." Christian popular imagination connected it with Judas in at least two different ways. Neither story can be accepted as reliable history.

The Miraculous in Acts

A second feature that raises questions about the reliability of Acts is its emphasis on the miraculous. In Acts miracles occur with regularity. The apostles perform numerous healings and exorcisms like those of Jesus in the gospels. They also invoke curses: Peter speaks a word and two people drop dead (5:1–11); Paul speaks a word and a man goes blind (13:6–12). Other miracles occur as well: the disciples speak in languages they have never learned and people understand them (2:1–12); the Spirit instantly transports Philip from one place to another (8:39–40); Paul suffers no harm from the bite of a poisonous snake (28:3–6). Luke seems to have a special fondness for miraculous prison breaks: three times apostles imprisoned for their testimony are inexplicably sprung from locked cells (5:17–26; 12:1–11; 16:25–34). Constant communication comes down from the heavenly world through angels, visions, dreams, and prophecies.

Clearly Luke belonged to a culture where people believed in the miraculous to a greater degree than most people in our own. Such a culture would give a supernatural explanation to events that our culture would explain from a non-supernatural perspective. Furthermore, in that culture people would be inclined to give credence to stories that our culture would consider incredible. We must recognize these differences in cultural perspective in evaluating the historicity of Acts.

The Speeches in Acts

The author's method of telling the story in Acts involves having the characters give speeches at significant points in the narrative. To what extent does this reflect reliable history? We can be sure that the author was not present on all of these occasions, nor were there verbatim transcripts of the speeches. The speeches, therefore, were probably composed by Luke himself. Composing such speeches was a standard practice for ancient historians. The Greek historian Thucydides, for example, describes his own method of composing speeches:

> I have found it difficult to remember the precise words used in the speeches which I listened to myself, and my various informants have experienced the same difficulty; so my method has been, while keeping as closely as possible to the general sense of the words that were actually used, to make the speaker say what, in my opinion, was called for by each occasion. (*Peloponnesian War* 1.22)

Luke too must have composed the speeches in Acts on the basis of what he felt was appropriate to the occasion. In certain instances, however, he has made the speaker say something that could not have been said at the time. For example, in Acts 5:36, the rabbi Gamaliel mentions the revolt of a man named Theudas, although Theudas' revolt did not occur until about ten years after the time Gamaliel was supposedly speaking.

Paul in Acts

A fourth problem in regarding Acts as reliable history concerns its portrayal of Paul. The last part of Acts features the apostle Paul as the main character (chs. 9, 13–28). If the "we" sections in Acts indicate the author's own participation, then he knew Paul and traveled with him on occasion. In this case, we would expect Acts' information about Paul to be fairly accurate. In many instances it is, as Paul's letters confirm. In other cases, however, the information in Acts is difficult to reconcile with the information in Paul's letters. For example, Acts describes a conference in Jerusalem as a general meeting of the entire church (Acts 15). When Paul describes what is apparently the same event, he pictures it as a private meeting between himself and a few leaders in Jerusalem (Gal 2:1–10). In Acts, the conference produces a significant decree; Paul never mentions such a decree, even where we would expect him to. Because of difficulties such as this, we must exercise caution in using Acts' account where it is not corroborated by Paul's letters.

Outline of Acts

Acts 1:8 gives a summary outline of the book of Acts. There the risen Jesus gives instructions to his disciples before his ascension:

> But you shall receive power when the Holy Spirit has come upon you; and you shall be my witnesses in Jerusalem and in all Judea and Samaria and to the end of the earth.

Through the power of the Holy Spirit, the disciples will testify about Jesus in three successively wider arenas: Jerusalem, Judea and Samaria, the ends of the earth. These three stages of testifying constitute the three major divisions of the story of Acts:

Preliminaries: waiting for the Spirit (ch. 1)
1. Testifying in Jerusalem (2:1–8:3)
2. Testifying in Judea and Samaria (8:4–12:25)
3. Testifying to the end of the earth (chs. 13–28)

READING GUIDE: ACTS

Read the book of Acts with the help of the following guide.

Waiting for the Spirit (ch. 1)

As in his gospel, Luke begins with an address to "Theophilus" (1:1). He then picks up where the gospel left off, with Jesus ascending to heaven.

Afterward, as the disciples wait in Jerusalem for the coming of the Holy Spirit, they choose a successor for Judas, the apostle who betrayed Jesus. The chief requirement laid down for Judas' successor is that he be a witness of Jesus' ministry and resurrection, so that he can testify to the fact (1:21–22).

Testifying in Jerusalem (2:1–8:3)

In Luke's account, the church begins on **the day of Pentecost (ch. 2)**. At the festival of Pentecost, fifty days after the Passover at which Jesus was crucified, the Holy Spirit falls on the disciples waiting in Jerusalem. Through the inspiration of the Spirit, they prophesy and speak in languages they have not learned. This activity attracts a crowd, providing an audience for Peter's preaching about Jesus.

Peter's sermon has four basic parts: (1) an explanation of the Spirit's arrival as fulfillment of a scripture, Joel 2:28–32, in which God promises to pour out his Spirit on all humanity "in the last days" (2:14–21); (2) a recital of the basic events of Jesus' career (2:22–24); (3) arguments from scripture to show that Jesus' resurrection and exaltation were planned by God, making him "both Lord and Christ" (2:25–36); (4) an exhortation to repent and be baptized (2:37–40).

The **healing of a lame man (3:1–4:31)** at the temple attracts another crowd, providing a second opportunity for Peter to preach about Jesus. This time the disturbance leads to the arrest of Peter and John by the priests and Sadducees. They are released with a warning not to preach any more, but they ignore the warning.

Luke gives an example of how the church's **sharing of possessions (4:32–5:11)** could lead to abuses of the system. Apparently, those who chose to participate in the communal program would fully share in the benefits only if they fully contributed their goods. Ananias and Sapphira seek to reap the benefits while secretly retaining part of their goods. The subsequent fatal judgment on them sounds a warning to others who would try the same. This curse story was apparently told in the community to discourage such abuses.

The **opposition increases (5:12–42)** as further miracles performed by the apostles lead to a second arrest, an arrest of the apostles as a group. The counsel of Gamaliel, a respected rabbi on the Sanhedrin, saves their lives, but they are beaten and again warned not to preach about Jesus.

A conflict arises between **the Hebrews and the Hellenists (6:1–7)** over distribution of community goods to the widows. The Hebrews were Aramaic-speaking Jews of Palestine, while the Hellenists were Greek-speaking Jews from the Diaspora. The seven Hellenists chosen to serve their widows probably did more than serve tables: they were probably the leaders of the Hellenists, just as the twelve were leaders of the Hebrews. Stephen and Philip, who are introduced here, will play a greater role later in the story.

The **martyrdom of Stephen (6:8–8:3)** marks a transition point in the story. The Jewish authorities arrest Stephen for speaking against the temple and the Law, two of the central pillars of Second-Temple Judaism. In Stephen's speech at his trial, he responds to the first charge (7:44–50), but for the most part his speech is less of a defense than an attack on his accusers.

The Jewish court is enraged at Stephen, but it is not until he confesses Jesus as the exalted Son of Man that they kill him. Stephen's death thus parallels the deaths of other early Christians who were martyred for confessing their faith in Jesus.

Stephen's death unleashes a wave of persecution against the church, which scatters from Jerusalem. Since the apostles, representing the Hebrews, remain, the persecution was apparently directed against the Hellenists, perhaps because their attitudes to the temple and the Law were less traditional than those of the Hebrews. It is at this point that the story introduces Saul, who will later become the central character in Acts.

Testifying in Judea and Samaria (8:4–12:25)

As believers disperse to the country around Jerusalem, the second stage of witnessing (to Judea and Samaria) begins.

Luke relates two episodes from the **ministry of Philip (8:4–40)**, one of the seven leaders of the Hellenists. When Philip initiates a ministry to the Samaritans, his action is validated by the apostles, who come down to impart the Holy Spirit to the new believers. Luke relates here an encounter between Peter and Simon the Sorcerer, an individual who figures in later history as the founder of a Gnostic sect. The second episode involving Philip describes the conversion of an Ethiopian eunuch.

The **conversion of Saul (9:1–31)** prepares for the Gentile mission. While on the way to Damascus to further persecute Christians, Saul encounters the risen Jesus in a vision. Since Saul has been blinded by the appearance, God sends Ananias to restore his sight, saying of Saul, "he is a vessel of mine chosen to carry my name before Gentiles and kings and sons of Israel" (9:15). This prophetic word describes the role that Saul will play in the remainder of Acts.

The **conversion of Cornelius (9:32–11:18)** opens the door to Gentiles. Luke, after relating some miracles performed by Peter (9:32–43), describes his role in converting Cornelius, a Roman centurion and a God-fearer. According to this story, Cornelius and his household are the first Gentile converts to Christianity. Numerous times in this story God intervenes directly, through an angel, a vision, a voice, or some other act of God. The story thus functions to defend the Gentile mission against its opponents by presenting it as the result of God's direct intervention.

The Gentile mission gets another boost from **the church at Antioch (11:19–30)**. According to Acts 10:1–11:18, Peter was the first to preach to Gentiles. In Acts 11:19–21, Luke preserves a different tradition: that Hellenists who fled from Jerusalem after Stephen's death were the first. This leads to the establishment of the first Gentile church, at Antioch in Syria. The apostles at Jerusalem appoint Barnabas to oversee the church, and he gets Saul to help. It is in this Gentile setting that the believers receive the name that will stick with them: "Christians."

Further persecution (12:1–25) arises from Herod Agrippa I, a grandson of Herod the Great, who ruled all of Palestine from 41 CE until his death in 44 CE. To please the Jewish opponents of Christianity, he puts to death James the brother of John, one of the twelve, and imprisons Peter for a time.

Testifying to the End of the Earth (chs. 13–28)

From chapter 13 on, Acts focuses on the ministry of the apostle Paul and the spread of the gospel into the Gentile world.

The Gentile mission begins in earnest with the **first missionary journey of Barnabas and Saul (13:1–14:28)**. The church at Antioch

Figure 17.4
Missionary
journey of
Barnabas
and Paul.

commissions Barnabas and Saul to undertake a missionary journey to the Gentiles. At their first stop, the island of Cyprus (13:1–12), Luke shifts from using the name "Saul" (a Hebrew name) to "Paul" (a Roman name), indicating Paul's desire to identify more fully with his Gentile audience.

Upon leaving Cyprus, they establish churches in the Roman province of Galatia. Luke gives an example of Paul's missionary preaching to Jews and God-fearers in the synagogue in Antioch of Pisidia (13:13–52). Paul and Barnabas then preach in Iconium (14:1–7), Lystra (14:8–20), and Derbe (14:20–21), before returning to Antioch in Syria (14:21–28).

The accounts of Paul's ministry in these cities follow a repeated pattern: he goes to the Jews first, and when they reject the message he turns to the Gentiles. This pattern reflects Luke's central theme.

After Barnabas and Paul return, the **Jerusalem conference (15:1–35)** takes place. A controversy arises in the church at Antioch. Judaic Christians

Figure 17.5
Paul's second missionary journey, beginning at Antioch in Syria.

who are Pharisees, while accepting the conversion of Gentiles, demand that Gentiles be circumcised and taught to keep the Law of Moses. In effect they argue that Gentiles must become Jews in order to share in the promises to Israel. Paul and Barnabas resist this perspective. When the strife becomes severe, the matter is taken before the apostles and elders at Jerusalem for resolution. According to Luke, the church decided that Gentiles need not be circumcised or keep the Law, except for a few regulations that seemed to apply to Gentiles as well as Jews (15:20). For instance, the rule against eating blood or a strangled animal (one whose blood had not been drained) comes from the legal code in Leviticus 17, which forbade blood both for Israelites and for Gentiles who lived among them.

The conference is followed by the **second missionary journey of Paul (15:36–18:22)**. Paul and Barnabas start to make another trip together but quarrel over whether or not to take John Mark, who is elsewhere identified as Barnabas' cousin (Col 4:10). After separating from Barnabas, Paul takes Silas and goes through Asia Minor strengthening the churches previously established (15:36–16:10). There they pick up Timothy to accompany them (16:1–3). The first "we" section occurs in 16:9–18.

Paul spends most of this trip in the two provinces of Greece: Macedonia (to the north) and Achaia (to the south). In Macedonia he establishes churches in the cities of Philippi (16:11–40), Thessalonica (17:1–9), and Beroea (17:10–15). In Achaia, he establishes churches in the cities of Athens (17:16–34) and Corinth (18:1–17) before returning for a time to Antioch (18:18–22).

The **third missionary journey of Paul (18:23–21:16)** begins as Paul leaves Antioch for the last time. This time he makes his headquarters in Ephesus, where he spends two years (18:23–19:41). He then resolves to make a final visit to Macedonia and Achaia, then to return to Jerusalem and from there to go to Rome. On the way to Jerusalem (20:1–21:16), he receives prophetic warnings that he will be imprisoned there (20:22–25; 21:4, 9–14). The second "we" section begins in 20:5 and continues to 21:18.

Paul's return to Jerusalem results in **Paul's imprisonment (21:17–28:16)**. In Jerusalem, when Jews from Asia stir up a crowd against Paul, he is rescued by a Roman tribune and brought before the Jewish Sanhedrin (21:17–23:11). When a plot against his life is discovered, he is sent to Caesarea where he stands trial before Felix, the governor of Judea. Felix leaves Paul in prison when he is replaced as governor by Porcius Festus (23:12–24:27). When Festus seeks to favor the Jews by sending Paul back to Jerusalem, Paul appeals the case to Caesar's court. Before leaving for Rome, Paul has the opportunity to speak before King Agrippa (Herod Agrippa II) and his wife Bernice (chs. 25–26). On the voyage to Rome, a storm leads to shipwreck on the island of Malta, but after three months another ship arrives to take them to Rome. The story of the voyage is told in the final "we" section (27:1–28:16). This section of Acts fulfills the prophecy about Paul in Acts 9:15–16, that he would carry the Christian message before kings.

As the **conclusion (28:17–30)**, Luke ends his story with an episode in which Paul tries unsuccessfully to convert the Jews in Rome. This episode concludes with Paul stating Luke's central theme: "Let it be known to you, then, that this salvation of God has been sent to the Gentiles; they will listen" (28:28). With this conclusion, Luke's purpose is completed: he has chronicled the spread of the gospel to "the end of the earth" and vindicated the transition from Jewish to Gentile Christianity. Perhaps for this reason, Luke does not tell us the result of Paul's trial before Caesar. According to tradition, however, Paul was beheaded in Rome during the reign of the emperor Nero (c. 64 CE).

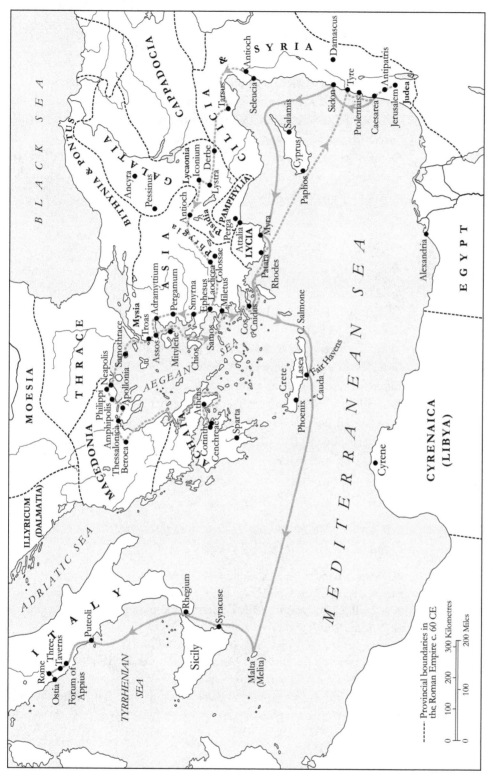

Figure 17.6 Paul's third missionary journey (broken line) and journey to Rome (solid line).

287

DISCUSSION QUESTIONS

1. *Jewish Christianity in Jerusalem.* Describe the beliefs and practices of early Jewish Christianity in Jerusalem, according to Acts 1:1–8:3.
2. *Christianity in the Greco-Roman World.* As the message about Jesus spread out of its Jewish context into the wider Gentile world, it encountered other religions and philosophies already established. Describe the encounters related in Acts 14:8–18, 17:16–34, and 19:23–41, including both the attitudes of the Christian missionaries and the attitudes of non-Christians toward them.

REVIEW QUESTIONS

1. What is the central theme of Luke–Acts? What theological problem does this theme address? How is this theme developed in Acts?
2. What other major themes run through Acts? How are these themes developed in Acts?
3. What is the significance of Acts for the study of early Christianity? What factors limit the value of Acts as history? What features of Acts raise questions about its historical reliability?
4. Identify the following and indicate what significance they have in Acts: James the brother of Jesus, the sect of the Nazoreans, the Way, Stephen, Saul/Paul, Cornelius, Antioch of Syria, Barnabas, the Jerusalem Conference.
5. How is the summary outline in Acts 1:8 reflected in the major divisions of Acts?

SUGGESTIONS FOR FURTHER STUDY

See also the bibliography at the end of Chapter 13.

Barrett, C. K. *A Critical and Exegetical Commentary on the Acts of the Apostles* (2 vols.; ICC; Bloomsbury T&T Clark, 1994, 1998). A standard commentary on the Greek text of Acts.

Fitzmyer, Joseph A. *The Acts of the Apostles: A New Translation with Introduction and Commentary* (Anchor Bible; Doubleday; Yale University Press, 1998). A useful commentary on Acts.

Holladay, Carl R. *Acts: A Commentary* (Westminster John Knox, 2016). A useful commentary on Acts.

Jervell, Jacob. *The Theology of the Acts of the Apostles* (Cambridge University Press, 1996). Discusses the sources, purpose, historical setting, major themes, and significance of Acts.

Marguerat, Daniel. *The First Christian Historian: Writing the 'Acts of the Apostles'* (Cambridge University Press, 2002). Essays on various aspects of Acts and Luke–Acts, including the genre, unity, and narrative purpose of Luke–Acts, its view of God and the Holy Spirit, its attitude to Judaism, and the theme of travel.

Pervo, Richard I. *Acts: A Commentary* (Hermeneia; Fortress, 2008). A major commentary on Acts.

Pervo, Richard I. *Dating Acts: Between the Evangelists and the Apologists* (Polebridge, 2006). Argues that the book of Acts was written in the second century.

Winter, Bruce W. et al., eds. *The Book of Acts in its First Century Setting* (6 vols.; Eerdmans, 1993–97). Essays on all aspects of Acts.

PART IV
Pauline Christianity

18   Paul, His Letters, and His Churches

After Jesus, the apostle Paul ranks as the most significant figure in early Christian history. Paul became a Christian less than a decade after Jesus died in 30 or 33 CE. He knew some of the earliest Christian leaders, such as Peter and James the brother of Jesus. He even claimed to have had a vision of the resurrected Jesus. Much of the book of Acts focuses on Paul, and his name also appears on the thirteen letters that follow Acts. Here we take a look at the man, his letters, and the religion practiced by him and his churches.

THE SIGNIFICANCE OF PAUL

Paul is significant for Christian history as an apostle, an author, and a theologian.

Paul is called an **apostle** by Luke and by Paul himself (Acts 14:4, 14; Gal 1:1; Rom 1:1). The Greek term *apostolos*, meaning "one sent," is linguistically equivalent to the Latin term "emissary" or "missionary" (from *missus*, "sent"). In the New Testament, however, the term sometimes has the further connotation of eyewitness to the resurrection of Jesus (Acts 1:21–26; 1 Cor 9:1). Since Paul had a vision of the risen Jesus, he classed himself as an apostle along with those in Jerusalem who had been apostles before him (1 Cor 15:7–9; Gal 1:17). As an apostle primarily to the Gentiles (Rom 1:5; Gal 2:7–8), Paul helped spread the Christian religion to the limits of the Roman Empire in the first century. He played a key role in transforming Christianity from a Jewish sect into a world religion.

As an **author**, Paul wrote letters that make up almost a fourth of the New Testament. Only Luke contributed a greater portion. More important than their quantity, however, is the date of Paul's letters: they are the earliest Christian documents that have been preserved. They date

Figure 18.1 Imaginative portrait of the apostle Paul. Painting by Rembrandt (c. 1657). Widener Collection, National Gallery of Art, Washington, D.C.

from the 50s and 60s of the first century, well before the gospels, all of which appeared after 70 CE. Paul's letters thus give us glimpses of a type of Christianity that had developed by the middle of the first century.

As a **theologian**, Paul formulated several doctrines that became important in the Proto-Orthodox tradition of Christianity. He was one of the first Christians we know about to clearly enunciate that salvation came through faith in Jesus rather than following the Jewish Law. He was also one of the first we know about to interpret Jesus' death in sacrificial terms as an atonement for sins.

THE LIFE OF PAUL

Sources for our knowledge of Paul include his own letters and the book of Acts, though the latter must be used with caution.

Acts gives several details about Paul's background that Paul does not mention in his letters. The apostle's original name was "Saul." Only after he became a missionary to the Gentiles did he trade this Jewish name for the Roman name "Paul" (Acts 13:9). Saul or Paul was born in Tarsus, a city of Cilicia (Acts 21:39; 22:3). Though a Jew, he possessed Roman citizenship (Acts 16:37–38; 22:25–29). He was brought up in Jerusalem as a student of the rabbi Gamaliel (Acts 22:3). Paul himself supplies the further information that he belonged to the Jewish tribe of Benjamin (Phil 3:5). Paul was a Pharisee, extremely zealous for the traditions of Judaism, an attitude that led him to seek out Christians to imprison (Phil 3:4–6; Gal 1:13–14; 1 Cor 15:9; Acts 23:6; 26:5, 9–11). According to Acts, he took part in the stoning of Stephen (Acts 7:58–8:3).

While going to Damascus, Paul had an experience that he considered a revelation or vision of the risen Jesus (Gal 1:15–17; 1 Cor 9:1; 15:8; Acts 9:1–19; 22:4–16; 26:9–18). This experience had a profound effect on Paul, transforming him from a persecutor to a preacher of Christianity. He traveled throughout the Roman world, preaching "to the Jew first and also to the Greek" (Rom 1:16; Acts 13:46).

Paul may have adopted several different tactics for getting his message to potential converts. Acts portrays him preaching in local synagogues (Acts 17:1–2 etc.), the city marketplace (Acts 17:17), an outdoor arena (Acts 17:19), a private home (Acts 18:7), and a public hall (Acts 19:9). He may have supported himself by making tents (Acts 18:3), a picture consistent with the fact that all Jewish boys were required to learn a trade. Paul speaks of laboring night and day, apparently preaching to those who visited his place of work (1 Thes 2:9). After establishing Christian congregations in various towns, he moved on but continued to strengthen the churches through visits and letters.

Paul wound up in prison on more than one occasion (2 Cor 11:23). Near the end of his ministry, he was arrested in Jerusalem. After a period of imprisonment in Judea, he appealed his case to Caesar and was taken to Rome for trial. Neither Acts nor Paul's letters tell us how Paul died. According to a later tradition, he met his death as a martyr in Rome under the emperor Nero (c. 64 CE).

Chronology of Paul's ministry	
Only approximate dates can be given for the events of Paul's ministry.	
Crucifixion of Jesus	30–33
Paul's conversion	34
Paul leaves Damascus	36
The Jerusalem Conference	49
1 Thessalonians written from Corinth	50–51
Paul before Gallio in Corinth	51–52
1 and 2 Corinthians	55–56
Letter to the Romans	57
Death of Paul	64

THE LETTERS OF PAUL

When Paul wrote a letter to a church, that church read it and made copies for other churches (Col 4:16). Churches made collections of Paul's letters, and eventually a collection consisting of thirteen letters came to be included in the New Testament. According to one theory, the letters of Paul as we have them now were published as an edited collection. This theory would account for evidence that several of the letters have undergone editing or interpolation (e.g. Romans, 1 Corinthians, 2 Corinthians, 1 Thessalonians, Philippians). Though all thirteen of these letters bear the name of Paul, most scholars accept only seven to ten as authentic, i.e. actually written by Paul.

Paul directed most of his letters to specific situations or problems that he knew about in the churches. Sometimes he explained what these situations were; at other times he did not, since the people to whom he wrote already knew the situation. For us, therefore, who are not familiar with the situation, it can be difficult to understand Paul's letters. Reading one is often like listening to one end of a telephone conversation: we know what Paul was saying on his end of the line, but we can only infer what the people on the other end were saying or doing.

How many letters did Paul write?

The New Testament includes thirteen letters ascribed to Paul. At least seven of these are authentic. The Pastoral Epistles (1 and 2 Timothy and Titus) were probably written by some other author using Paul's name as a pseudonym. The authenticity of the three remaining letters (2 Thessalonians, Colossians, Ephesians) is disputed: some scholars consider them authentic, while others consider them pseudonymous.

AUTHENTIC	DISPUTED	PSEUDONYMOUS
Romans	2 Thessalonians	1 Timothy
Galatians	Colossians	2 Timothy
1 Corinthians	Ephesians	Titus
2 Corinthians		
1 Thessalonians		
Philippians		
Philemon		

THE RELIGION OF PAUL AND HIS CHURCHES

Paul's letters do not present his teaching in a systematic way. He addressed them to specific situations in his churches, providing instruction, exhortation, advice, warning, and encouragement for particular needs. Yet, despite the unsystematic nature of the letters, they do give us an idea of the religion practiced by Paul and his churches. The nature of that religion can be observed by looking at some of its dimensions: the conceptual, social, ritual, and ethical.

The Conceptual Dimension

The conceptual dimension of Paul's religion included three main aspects: an eschatological orientation, a non-Judaic perspective on the Jewish Law, and a belief in justification through faith in Jesus.

First, like the Jesus movement before him, Paul's brand of Christianity had an **eschatological or apocalyptic orientation**, a view that the present world order was evil and that God would soon replace it with a new order. Early Christianity shared many values with the surrounding culture. For example, some of its ethical teachings resembled those of popular Greek philosophy. Yet, like apocalyptic groups in general, it viewed the larger culture as hopelessly corrupt. Paul and his followers distinguished themselves from "the world" (the larger surrounding culture). In their view, the world was under the control of Satan. It was a place of moral and spiritual "darkness."

Paul taught that God would bring the old social order to an end and replace it with a new order in which righteousness would prevail. He looked forward to the imminent dawning of a new age inaugurated by the return of Jesus. At that time, the dead would be resurrected and brought before God for judgment. Creation would be redeemed from bondage, and death would be eliminated. Christ would reign, and believers would share his glory. For Paul, blessings already present in Christ were merely a "down payment" of the blessings that were to come. Paul believed that the day of judgment was near. He warned the Romans to stay alert because "the day has drawn near" (Rom 13:11–12). He wrote the Philippians that "the Lord is at hand" (Phil 4:5).

In the meantime, the Christians were to shine as "lights" that anticipated the light that would dawn with the new age (Phil 2:15). Paul taught that Christians should maintain a detached attitude toward the normal concerns of society: sexuality and marriage, family ties, and business affairs.

Second, unlike Judaic Christianity, Paul and his churches held a **non-Judaic perspective on the Jewish Law**. Both Paul and Judaic Christianity expected a judgment in which God (or Jesus) would mete out punishment for sin. Where Paul differed was in his understanding of how one could be saved from that punishment. Judaic Christianity saw keeping the Jewish Law as the path to life with God. Paul's view of the Law, while somewhat unclear, differed radically from this perspective. For Paul, the Law brought not life but death. No one was justified (made righteous) in God's sight through the Law. The basic problem, as Paul saw it, was not the Law itself, but the weakness of human nature. Human nature is "flesh," while God is "spirit." Flesh and spirit oppose each other, because an evil power called "sin" dwells in the flesh, causing it to act against the will of God. Though the Law is good in itself, it has an unfortunate effect on human beings who are "in the flesh." It sets up a standard of conduct that the flesh cannot meet, thereby exposing sin and bringing people under a curse. As a result, human beings are at enmity with God, enslaved to the evil powers of the universe, headed for "wrath" or punishment on the day of God's judgment, and subject to death.

Third, central to Paul's view of salvation was his belief in **justification through faith in Jesus**. While Judaic Christianity regarded the Law as the means of salvation, Paul replaced the Law with the death of Jesus, interpreted as a sacrifice. The sacrificial rites at the Jewish temple included sacrifices for individuals who transgressed the Law inadvertently, a sacrifice for the sins of the community on the Day of Atonement, and the sacrifice of a lamb at Passover. Such sacrifices involved the shedding of an animal's blood. Paul rarely discussed what he thought of these sacrifices, but for him the death of Jesus was the ultimate sacrifice. In some way that he does not fully explain, Paul believed that the shedding of Jesus' blood appeased God's wrath so that he forgave the transgressions of human beings. One merely had to have "faith in Jesus" to receive the benefits of this sacrifice (Rom 3:21–26). Through faith in Jesus, combined with baptism, the believer was "justified" (no longer subject to God's wrath on the day of judgment), "reconciled" (no longer at enmity with God), and "redeemed" (no longer subject to the evil powers of the flesh).

The radical difference between Paul and the Judaic Christianity that preceded him has led some scholars to regard Paul as the real founder of Christianity as we know it today. There may be a good deal of truth to this claim. Though Paul clearly drew many of his ideas from earlier tradition, he was one of the first major, influential figures to deny that the Jewish Law provided the path to salvation.

What caused Paul to make such a decisive break with his Jewish heritage? There were probably several **reasons for Paul's perspective**. Perhaps he felt that the path to life through keeping the Law was too narrow for most people to walk successfully. Such a concern is expressed by another Jew close to Paul's time, the author of 4 Ezra (7:46 [116]–8:3). Or perhaps he felt, as he states in Galatians 2:21, that "if justification were through the Law, then Christ died for no reason." Thus his attitude toward the Law may have developed from his need to find a reason for Jesus' death. Or perhaps, as apostle to the Gentiles, he saw circumcision as an obstacle to the conversion of Gentiles and dietary regulations as an obstacle to full fellowship between Jews and Gentiles. By making the Law unnecessary and placing the salvation of Jew and Gentile on the same basis, he made it easier for Gentiles to accept the message and removed the barrier that kept Jew and Gentile apart.

Whatever reasons Paul may have had, he took a step that decisively affected the future of the Jesus movement. It was Paul's perspective that was adopted by the Gentile Proto-Orthodox tradition and that subsequently became the orthodox teaching of Christianity. Apart from the Jewish Law, Christianity could no longer be considered a sect of Judaism. It became a distinct religion in its own right.

The Social Dimension

In examining the social dimension of Paul's religion, we will consider places of meeting, social classes of members, social cohesion, church leadership, and the roles of women.

With respect to **places of meeting**, Paul's converts met in private homes, just as the church in Jerusalem did. Often an entire household might be converted together, which would then constitute the nucleus of a **house church**. These households were extended families, consisting of the male head of the household, family members, slaves, hired workers, and others. To this nucleus, other converts would be added to make up the complete house church. Several of these house churches would normally exist in a single city. The whole church in a city might also meet together on occasion.

Members of Paul's churches came from all **social classes**: the rich and the poor, the old and the young, women, children, and slaves. Some of Paul's letters deal with problems that arose in the churches as a result of this wide variety in church membership. He seeks to settle conflicts between different social groups.

Despite conflicts between members, certain features of the church promoted **social cohesion**. Upon being baptized, converts became part of the Christian family with Christian "brothers" and "sisters." Members of these congregations had a sense of belonging not only to the local church but to the world-wide church as well. Paul pictured the church as the body of Christ, a united whole which yet had many individual parts or members (Rom 12:4–5; 1 Cor 12:12–31; cf. Col 1:24; Eph 5:23). He further described it as the bride of Christ (2 Cor 11:2; cf. Eph 5:24–32) and as God's temple, inhabited by the Holy Spirit (1 Cor 3:16–17; 2 Cor 6:16; cf. Eph 2:19–22).

We do not get a completely clear picture of **church leadership** from Paul's letters. These refer primarily to itinerant ministers, Paul and his co-workers, who would visit a church for a period of time. Presumably resident leaders included the wealthier members of the churches who owned the houses in which the churches met. In 1 Thessalonians 5:12–14, Paul writes the church to recognize "those who labor among you and lead you in the Lord and admonish you." These leaders are in turn encouraged

Figure 18.2
Old road between
Israel and
Damascus. It was
probably this road
that Paul was
traveling when he
had his conversion
experience. Erich
Lessing/Art
Resource, NY.

to "admonish the disorderly, comfort the discouraged, care for the sick, and be patient toward all." In Philippians 1:1, Paul mentions "overseers" or "bishops" (Greek *episcopoi*). Once he refers to Phoebe, a "deacon" ("server" or "minister") of the church at Cenchreae (Rom 16:1–2).

With respect to the **role of women in ministry**, women seem to have played a prominent part in Paul's churches, to judge by the list of greetings that Paul sends in Romans 16. In addition to Phoebe the deacon just mentioned, Paul refers to Prisca and Aquila, a wife and husband team who were Paul's co-workers and hosted a church in their home (Rom 16:3–5). It may be significant that Paul names Prisca first, as though she played the leading role. Acts calls her "Priscilla" and portrays her and her husband instructing a man about baptism (Acts 18:24–26). Paul may refer to another

Figure 18.3
Street in ancient
Ephesus, the city
of Asia where
Paul had his
headquarters
during the last
years before
his arrest in
Jerusalem. Erich
Lessing/Art
Resource, NY.

husband and wife team when he greets Andronicus and Junia, who were "outstanding among the apostles" (Rom 16:7). Paul also sends greetings to a number of other women, including Mary, Tryphaena, Tryphosis, and Persis, all of whom he says have worked hard in the Lord (Rom 16:6, 12). In writing to the church at Philippi, Paul refers to Euodia and Syntyche, two women who worked with Paul in spreading the gospel (Phil 4:2–3).

With respect to the **role of women in worship services**, the letters of Paul give a conflicting impression. In 1 Corinthians 11:3–16 women are allowed to pray or prophesy as long as their heads are covered. In 1 Corinthians 14:33b–36, however, women are not permitted to speak in church. It is likely that women did pray and prophesy in Paul's churches, since we have reference to women prophets elsewhere (Acts 21:9). In Galatians 3:28, Paul makes the well-known statement that in Christ "there is neither male nor female." However, the egalitarian impact of this statement may be somewhat mitigated by the one that immediately precedes: "in Christ Jesus you are all sons of God" (Gal 3:26).

The Ritual Dimension

Members of Paul's church participated in various ritual events. Converts became members through the ritual of baptism, immersion in water. As members, they met together to worship and to take a communal meal, the Lord's Supper.

In Paul's churches, **baptism** made one a "son" of God, whether one was male or female, and was also the occasion on which one received the Holy Spirit (Gal 3:26–28; 4:6–7; cf. Mark 1:9–11). The centrality of Jesus' death in Paul's thought carried over into his understanding of baptism. He saw it as a participation in the death and resurrection of Jesus: entering the water symbolized being buried with Christ, while coming up out of the water symbolized being resurrected with him (Rom 6:1–11). Before being baptized, the candidate for baptism probably made a confession of faith such as the one Paul refers to in Romans 10:9: "if you confess with your lips that Jesus is Lord and believe in your heart that God raised him from the dead, you will be saved."

Meetings in Paul's churches apparently took place on "the Lord's Day" (1 Cor 16:2), the first day of the week, in honor of Christ's resurrection on that day. Various members participated in meetings by exercising "spiritual gifts" bestowed by the Holy Spirit. They believed that the power of the Spirit enabled them to prophesy (to speak words given directly by God), to teach or exhort, to speak in tongues (to speak in a language unknown to the speaker), to interpret the unknown language, and to heal sickness and disease (1 Cor 12–14; Rom 12:3–8). Singing or chanting and making music also formed part of the worship (1 Cor 14:26; cf. Col 3:16; Eph 5:19).

Paul refers to a communal meal that he calls the **Lord's Supper**, which consisted of bread and wine (1 Cor 11:20–34; cf. 10:14–22). Paul interprets the consumption of these elements as a commemoration of the death of Jesus: the bread represents the body of Jesus, while the wine represents his blood. The sharing of this meal represented the unity of the church as the body of Christ.

The Ethical Dimension

Paul's rejection of the Law as a means to justification did not mean that he rejected its moral demands. Like earlier Christian tradition, however, he considered the moral demands of the Law summed up in the commandment "Love your neighbor as yourself" (Rom 13:8–10). One who does this, he says, has fulfilled the Law.

With the Greco-Roman tradition, Paul shared a negative attitude toward the passions of the body, or in Paul's language "the flesh." His solution to the flesh was to crucify it, by symbolically participating in the death of Christ in baptism. Dying to the flesh allowed one to live for

Sources of Paul's Ideas

A variety of influences shaped Paul's ideas. Some of his distinctive perspectives probably owed a good deal to his Damascus-road experience and his experience with the Gentile mission. Other aspects of his thought, however, show a debt to his Jewish heritage, the Hellenistic culture of the world in which he lived, and prior Christian tradition.

Paul derived many of his ideas from his **Jewish heritage**. As a Pharisee, he already believed in resurrection of the dead. He retained the Jewish hope of a coming new age, with the difference that now he expected Jesus to be the one to inaugurate it. He also continued to regard the Jewish scriptures as authoritative. From his new perspective, he searched the scriptures to find support for his new faith in Jesus. In arguing from the scriptures, he often used methods of argument and interpretation that were typical of Jewish rabbis.

Hellenistic culture also helped to shape Paul's thinking. Paul's ethical instructions may reflect the influence of Hellenistic moral exhortation. In many respects, Paul's ethical teachings resemble those of Greek and Roman philosophers in content, form, and terminology. Hellenistic influence also appears in Paul's use of the rhetorical device called a "diatribe." In the diatribe, the writer argues with an imaginary opponent, answering questions supposedly raised by the opponent. Paul uses this style in his letter to the Romans. Some scholars have suggested that Paul's teaching on baptism and the Lord's Supper owes much to Hellenistic mystery religions. Since the rituals of these religions were kept secret, however, we do not know much about them.

Some of Paul's ideas came from **prior Christian tradition**. While Paul's vision of Jesus convinced him that Jesus had risen from the dead, he also knew traditions about the resurrection from those who were Christians before him (1 Cor 15:3; cf. 15:1). Paul also apparently had knowledge of Christian teaching attributed to Jesus. For example, he cites several commands of Jesus: that a woman should not leave her husband (1 Cor 7:10; cf. Mark 10:12) and that those who preach the gospel should make their living from it (1 Cor 9:14; cf. Matt 10:10, Luke 10:7). Numerous other aspects of his teaching show similarities to that found in the gospels, such as the idea that the greatest commandment is to love others (Rom 13:8–10; cf. Mark 12:28–34). Paul also passes on traditions that he received about the Lord's Supper (1 Cor 11:23–26; cf. Mark 14:22–25).

God. As a new creation, the believer would no longer live in the flesh but "walk" in the Spirit, thus able to live a life pleasing to God (Rom 6:1–14; 8:1–16). The Holy Spirit, which one received at baptism, would dwell in the believer and produce a good character in the same way that a good tree produces good fruit. The "fruits" of the Spirit include such traits as love, joy, and peace (Gal 5:16–26).

Paul's letters contain a great deal of **moral exhortation** or "parenesis," that is, encouragement to behave properly. This parenesis may be an extended exhortation on a single theme, such as the ode to love in 1 Corinthians 13, or it may be a series of imperatives and exhortations on diverse themes, such as the following.

> Let love be genuine; hate what is evil, hold fast to what is good; love one another with brotherly affection; outdo one another in showing honor. Never flag in zeal, be aglow with the Spirit, serve the Lord. Rejoice in your hope, be patient in tribulation, be constant in prayer. Contribute to the needs of the saints, practice hospitality. Bless those who persecute you; bless and do not curse them. (Rom 12:9–14)

STUDYING PAUL'S LETTERS

In the next several chapters, we will examine Paul's acknowledged letters and the three disputed letters. Thematically, these fall into four major groups:

- Gentiles and the Law: Galatians, Romans
- Problems of church life: 1 and 2 Corinthians
- The imminent parousia: 1 and 2 Thessalonians
- Letters from prison: Philippians, Philemon, Colossians, Ephesians

We will discuss the Pastoral Epistles later with other literature of Proto-Orthodoxy.

REVIEW QUESTIONS

1. In what three respects is Paul significant for Christian history?
2. Summarize the central features of Paul's life.
3. Which letters attributed to Paul do scholars generally accept as authentic? Which are disputed? Which are generally considered pseudonymous?

4. Describe three main aspects of the conceptual dimension of Paul's religion. How did Paul's ideas about the Law and the death of Jesus differ from those of Judaic Christianity before him? What were some possible reasons for Paul's perspective?

5. Describe the social dimension of religion in Paul's churches with respect to places of meeting, social classes of members, social cohesion, church leadership, and the roles of women.

6. Describe the main rituals in Paul's churches.

7. Describe the ethical dimension of Paul's religion.

8. How were Paul's ideas shaped by his Jewish heritage, Hellenistic culture, and prior Christian tradition?

SUGGESTIONS FOR FURTHER STUDY

Cousar, Charles B. *The Letters of Paul* (Abingdon, 1996). Introduction to Paul's letters, rhetoric, sources of thought, churches, and theology.

Jewett, Robert. *Dating Paul's Life* (SCM, 2012). Attempts to establish a chronology of Paul's life and letters.

Meeks, Wayne A. *The First Urban Christians: The Social World of the Apostle Paul* (2nd ed.; Yale University Press, 2003). Significant work on the social and ritual dimensions of Paul's churches.

Sanders, E. P. *Paul and Palestinian Judaism* (Fortress, 1977). Classic work, which argues that ancient Judaism was not a legalistic religion of works but was characterized by "covenantal nomism."

Thurston, Bonnie. *Women in the New Testament: Questions and Commentary* (Crossroad, 1998; reprinted, Wipf & Stock, 2004). Outlines the position of women in the Greco-Roman world and examines the role of women in New Testament texts, beginning with Paul's letters.

Zetterholm, Magnus. *Approaches to Paul: A Student's Guide to Recent Scholarship* (Fortress, 2009). Surveys the history of scholarship on Paul's relation to Judaism, including "the new perspective on Paul" and beyond.

19 Gentiles and the Law (1)
Galatians

The book of Acts relates the transformation of Christianity from a Jewish sect into a world religion composed primarily of Gentiles. This transformation did not come easily. In the early days, many Jewish believers insisted that salvation belonged to the Jews. After all, God's promises in the scriptures were directed to Jews. Jesus himself was a Jew. As long as the gospel was confined to Jerusalem, no major challenge to this view arose. Once the message began to spread beyond Jerusalem, however, some of the Hellenists preached to Gentiles in Antioch (Acts 11:19–20). Apparently, the more conservative Judaic Christians had a hard time accepting this development. The story of Peter preaching to Cornelius in Acts 10–11 seeks to justify the Gentile mission to the more doubtful members of the community.

This problem, however, was not easily resolved. Some conservative Judaic Christians insisted that Gentiles had to become Jews in order to be saved: they had to keep the Law of Moses, and the males among them had to be circumcised (Acts 15:1, 5). This requirement was the same as the requirement for Gentile converts to Judaism. In Judaism, individual Gentiles could enter the community of Israel by becoming "proselytes," converts to Judaism. For Gentile males this involved being circumcised, and for all Gentile proselytes it involved keeping the Jewish Law. According to the Judaic Christians, this process of becoming a proselyte was still the way for Gentiles to become part of the people of God. In their view, the Jesus movement represented the true Israel, but this community was still a Jewish institution. Gentiles therefore had to become Jewish proselytes in order to join the community.

The apostle Paul had a different view. Paul opposed requiring Gentile converts to keep the Jewish Law, specifically circumcision, dietary regulations, and observation of special Jewish days. All these practices set the Jews apart from the Gentiles as a separate social group. Requiring them of Gentiles also made Gentiles less willing to become Christians. Paul justified his position by arguing that salvation came through faith in Jesus, not through keeping the Jewish Law. Gentiles therefore did not have to keep the Law in order to be saved.

This view of Paul and others came into conflict with the conservative view. The question of whether Gentile converts had to keep the Law thus became a central issue in the early church. This issue occupies the central place in two of Paul's letters: Galatians and Romans. These letters, probably written in this order, show different degrees of conflict. Paul wrote Galatians in the heat of the battle to churches that were being persuaded to accept the teaching of the conservatives. He uses strong and passionate language to warn the Galatian churches against relying on the Law of Moses instead of faith in Christ. Paul's letter to the Romans shows Paul in a calmer mood, as he carefully composes a letter which sets out in an orderly way his teaching that Jews and Gentiles come to God on the same basis: all are justified by faith in Christ, not by works of the Law. We will examine Galatians in the present chapter and Romans in the next.

THE RECIPIENTS OF GALATIANS

Paul addresses the Galatian letter to "the churches in Galatia" (Gal 1:2). Later in the letter, he calls his readers "Galatians" (or "Gauls") (Gal 3:1). Where was Galatia and who were these Galatian Christians? Originally the term "Galatia" referred to a geographical region in central Asia Minor (modern Turkey). This region received its name from the Galatians (Celts or Gauls), an ethnic group who lived there. In 25 BCE the Romans took control of this area and created a province called Galatia. It included not only Galatia proper in the north, but also other districts in the south, including Pisidia and parts of Lycaonia. Did Paul write then to Galatia in the narrow sense (the geographical region in the north) or in the broader sense (the Roman province, including territories to the south of Galatia proper)? These two possibilities have given rise to two different theories.

According to the **South Galatian (province) theory**, Paul used the term "Galatia" in the broader sense, referring to the Roman province. He was writing not to churches of Galatia proper in the north, but to

Figure 19.1
The Roman province of Galatia in Asia Minor. Scholars debate whether Paul wrote Galatians to churches in the northern or the southern part of the province.

churches in the southern part of the province. These would include the churches of Antioch, Iconium, Lystra, and Derbe, which Paul and Barnabas established in the first phase of their missionary activity (Acts 13:13–14:28) and which Paul visited again later (Acts 16:1–5).

According to the **North Galatian (region) theory**, Paul used the term "Galatia" in the narrow sense, referring to Galatia proper in the northern part of the province. The book of Acts indicates that Paul visited this "Galatian region" in the second period of his missionary activity (Acts 16:6) and again in the third (Acts 18:23). The strongest reason for believing that Paul was writing to this region comes from Galatians 3:1, where Paul calls his readers "Galatians" ("Gauls"). While literature of the period uses the term "Galatia" in two senses, the term "Gauls" occurs only in reference to the ethnic group that lived in the northern part of the province. For this and other reasons, the majority of scholars incline toward the North Galatian theory.

ACTS AND GALATIANS

Acts and Galatians both relate that Paul conferred with the leading apostles in Jerusalem over the question of whether Gentile converts had to be circumcised. However, there are three discrepancies between their accounts.

1. According to Acts, the Jerusalem Conference took place on Paul's third trip to Jerusalem. According to Paul, it took place on his second visit:

Paul visits Jerusalem after leaving Damascus.	Acts 9:26–30	Gal 1:18–24
Paul visits Jerusalem with contribution from Antioch.	Acts 11:27–30; 12:25	–
Jerusalem Conference: Paul confers with Jerusalem apostles about circumcising Gentile converts.	Acts 15:1–35	Gal 2:1–10

Some scholars would eliminate this discrepancy by identifying Galatians 2:1–10 with the second visit in Acts rather than the third, and assuming that Paul wrote Galatians before the third visit had occurred. It appears, however, that Galatians 2:1–10 describes the same event as Acts 15, since in both cases the point at issue is the same: whether or not Gentile converts had to undergo circumcision and keep the Jewish Law.

2. Acts describes the conference as attended by the whole council of apostles and elders, whereas Paul describes it as a private meeting with the three leading apostles or "pillars."

3. Acts describes a written decree that issued from the conference, instructing Gentile converts to abstain from sacrifices offered to idols, blood, animals killed by strangling, and unchastity (Acts 15:19–29). Paul never mentions this decree.

More important than these discrepancies is the point on which both accounts agree: Paul, Barnabas, and the leading apostles in Jerusalem agreed that Gentile converts did not have to be circumcised.

DATE AND PROVENANCE OF GALATIANS

The question of when and where Galatians was written has several possible answers, depending on our reconstruction of its historical setting.

If the North Galatian theory is correct, the letter would have been written sometime after Paul first visited the region of Galatia in his second phase of missionary activity (Acts 16:6). Galatians 1:6 suggests that Paul wrote Galatians "soon" after his missionary work there. Possibly, then, Paul wrote the letter from Macedonia or Achaia in the early 50s (Acts 16:6–18:17). The letter might even be Paul's earliest if he wrote it before 1 Thessalonians.

A later date is favored by some proponents of the North Galatian theory. Since Paul refers to his "former" visit to Galatia (Gal 4:13), some scholars infer that Paul had already visited Galatia twice at the time of writing. This would put the date of the letter sometime after Acts 18:23 in Paul's third phase of missionary activity. Paul may have written it from Ephesus (Acts 19:1–20) or Macedonia or Achaia (Acts 20:1–3) in the mid to late 50s.

PAUL'S OPPONENTS IN GALATIA

Paul writes to the churches in Galatia because certain people there were teaching things that he strenuously opposed. Since we have no written records from his opponents themselves, we must infer their identity and views from what Paul says.

1. Traditionally, scholars have identified Paul's opponents as **conservative Judaic Christians** like the Pharisaic Christians in Acts 15:1–5. These conservatives maintained the importance of keeping the Law, even for Gentiles.

2. The view that Paul's opponents were **Gentile Christians** is based primarily on Gal 6:13, where the present participle ("those who are being circumcised") implies that they were Gentiles receiving circumcision. A textual variant however, has a perfect participle ("those who have been circumcised").

3. The view that Paul's opponents were **Gnostic or syncretistic Jewish Christians** (i.e. Jewish Christians who mixed Hellenistic religious ideas and practices with their Judaism) depends primarily on a particular interpretation of Galatians 4:8–11. Here Paul laments that the Galatians are observing "days and months and seasons and years," implying that this practice marks a return to slavery under the "elemental spirits" of the world. Some scholars interpret these calendrical observations as aspects of Hellenistic astrology, linked by Paul to demonic spirits. They conclude that his opponents had been influenced by such Hellenistic

practices. Given the context of the letter as a whole, however, it is likely that Paul is referring not to astrology but to Jewish holy days and special times required by the Law. Since Paul believed that Jews under the Law as well as Gentiles were enslaved to "the elemental spirits of the world" (Gal 4:3), observance of the Law would mark a return to bondage under these spirits.

HISTORICAL SETTING OF GALATIANS

Assuming the North Galatian theory, we can give the following reconstruction of the situation that gave rise to Paul's letter. Other reconstructions are also possible.

After Paul's mission trip with Barnabas, events led to the **Jerusalem Conference**. Conservative Judaic Christians from Judea came to Antioch and argued that Gentile converts had to be circumcised. Paul, Barnabas, and others, including the Gentile Titus, went to Jerusalem to confer with the Jerusalem apostles over the matter (Acts 15:1–5; Gal 2:4–5). The Jerusalem apostles, represented by the "pillars" (Peter, James, and John), agreed with Paul and Barnabas that Gentiles did not have to be circumcised or keep the rest of the Jewish Law (Gal 2:1–10 = Acts 15). They did not require Titus to be circumcised. The pillars made their decision known to the church, and Paul and Barnabas returned to Antioch.

Subsequently a **dispute over eating** arose at Antioch. The Jerusalem Conference did not solve all the problems. Specifically, the question remained of whether Jewish Christians could share meals with Gentiles who did not keep the Jewish food laws. Paul came into conflict with Peter and Barnabas over this matter in Antioch (Gal 2:11–14).

Following the Antioch incident, Paul made his **second missionary journey**. Paul and Barnabas split up – either over this dispute or over the matter of John Mark as Acts relates (Acts 15:36–41). Paul revisited the churches in southern Galatia and then did his first missionary work in Galatia proper to the north (Acts 16:1–2, 6). When Paul evangelized Galatia, he referred to the Jerusalem agreement to support his teaching on circumcision (Acts 16:4). This left him open to the charge that he was dependent on the Jerusalem apostles.

After Paul left Galatia, a **conflict over the Law** arose there. Someone began to teach that Gentile converts had to be circumcised and keep the Jewish Law in order to be saved. They disagreed with the Jerusalem

Galatians as Rhetoric

Rhetorical criticism studies how early Christian literature used the techniques of ancient rhetoric, the art of persuading through speech. The commentary of Hans Dieter Betz on Galatians exemplifies this type of interpretation. Betz analyzes Galatians as an "apologetic letter," a letter that substituted for an "apologetic speech" when the author could not be present with the audience. In such a speech, the speaker presented a defense before a real or fictitious court of law. In the case of Galatians, Paul himself was the defendant, his opponents were his accusers, and the Galatians formed the jury. In defending himself and his message, Paul used the apologetic speech, which in ancient rhetoric followed a traditional structure. The following outline of Galatians as an apologetic speech/letter is based on Betz with a few modifications. Other critics analyze the rhetoric differently.

The *epistolary prescript* (1:1–5) or salutation, typical of a letter, precedes the elements of the speech itself.

The first element of the speech was the *exordium* (1:6–12) or introduction. Here Paul states the problem (the Galatians have departed from his gospel), the accusation (Paul's gospel came from men, not God), and a denial of the accusation (Paul received his gospel directly from Jesus).

Following the exordium was the *narratio* (1:13–24) or narrative, a summary of events that had occurred relative to the case under consideration. Here Paul relates his previous encounters with the Jerusalem apostles to show that he did not receive his gospel from them.

In the *propositio* (2:15–21), the statement of the subject or theme, Paul sets out the two contentions that he will subsequently argue more fully: that justification comes not by the Law but by faith in Jesus (2:15–16), and that such freedom from the Law should not lead to sinful behavior (2:17–21).

In the *probatio* (3:1–5:12) or proof, Paul sets out the arguments or proofs for his first contention, that justification comes not by the Law but by faith in Jesus.

In the *exhortatio* (5:13–6:10) or exhortation, Paul presents his second contention, exhorting his audience not to allow freedom from the Law to lead to sinful behavior.

The final section, the *conclusio* or epistolary postscript (6:11–18), serves as a conclusion to both the speech and the letter.

This analysis of Galatians serves as the outline for the reading guide below.

decision and rejected the authority of the Jerusalem pillars in this matter. This contradicted what Paul had previously taught there. Paul's opponents charged that Paul taught what he did merely to please the apostles at Jerusalem (cf. Gal 1:10). The gospel that Paul had taught in Galatia was thus not from God (like the Law) but from human beings. They further argued that this teaching, freedom from the Law, would lead the Gentile converts into sin (cf. Gal 2:17). Paul's opponents pressured the Gentile converts in Galatia to be circumcised, and some of them were (Gal 6:12–13). Some Gentile converts also began to observe the Jewish holy days and special times (Gal 4:10). The whole question produced strife between the various parties in the Galatian churches (Gal 5:13–15).

In response to this development, Paul wrote the **letter to the Galatians**. Paul heard about the situation soon after he left Galatia (Gal 1:6). He may have been in Macedonia or Achaia (Acts 16:6–18:17). Since he says that his body was carrying "the marks of Jesus" (Gal 6:17), it may have been soon after his beating in Philippi (Acts 16:22–23).

READING GUIDE: GALATIANS

Read the letter to the Galatians with the help of the following guide.

Epistolary Prescript or Salutation (1:1–5)

Already in the salutation, Paul anticipates one of his central arguments in the letter: that his message as an apostle did not come to him through human channels (1:1). Significantly, Paul omits the thanksgiving for the church that he adds in most letters after the salutation, an omission that indicates his displeasure with the church.

Exordium or Introduction (1:6–12)

Paul describes the problem in Galatia as a conflict between two "gospels": one that he preached to the Galatians and one that he considered a perversion of the true gospel. As the rest of the letter makes clear, these two gospels propose two different ways by which a person is "justified." The term "justification," from the sphere of the law court, could also be translated "acquittal." The term implies that there will be a day of judgment when God will sit to judge the lives of human beings. A person who is "justified" is one who is acquitted, that is, judged "not guilty" and therefore not punished. According to Paul's gospel, a person is justified through believing in Christ. The other "gospel," that of Paul's opponents, insisted that in order to be justified one must be circumcised and keep the Law of Moses. Paul utters a curse on anyone who preaches a different gospel than his own.

At this point Paul begins to defend his gospel against the charges of his opponents (1:10). Apparently they accused Paul of persuading people "by men" rather than "by God." That is, he got his message from the Jerusalem apostles and used their authority to convince the Galatians that Gentile converts did not have to be circumcised. Paul denies the accusation, maintaining that he received his gospel directly from Jesus.

Narratio: Paul Defends His Gospel (1:13–2:14)

Paul recounts his previous **relations with the Jerusalem apostles (1:13–2:10)** to show that he did not receive his gospel from them. He makes two main points: that he originally received his gospel not from the Jerusalem apostles, but from God (1:13–24); and that when he recounted his gospel to the Jerusalem apostles, they added nothing to it (2:1–10).

In the **Antioch incident (2:11–14)**, a further question concerning the Gentiles arose: could Jewish Christians eat with Gentiles? The problem for a Jewish Christian was twofold: (1) Jews who followed the Law could not eat the same kinds of foods as Gentiles; (2) Gentiles who did not follow the Law were ritually "unclean" and would render Jews who associated with them unclean as well. Nevertheless, some Jewish Christians at Antioch had started eating with Gentiles, and even Peter joined in when he visited there. When more conservative Jewish Christians came from James in Jerusalem, however, Peter, Barnabas, and other Jewish Christians stopped the practice out of consideration for these visitors. Paul disagreed with Peter's decision and apparently told him so in no uncertain terms.

Propositio: Statement of the Issues (2:15–21)

In the next part of the letter, Paul states the issues that are involved in the dispute, expressing his own point of view in two contentions: that justification came not by works of the Law but by faith in Jesus

(2:15–16), and that such freedom from the Law should not lead to sinful behavior (2:17–21).

Probatio: Arguments for the First Contention (3:1–5:12)

Paul then takes up his first contention, giving arguments to support his view that justification came through faith in Christ, not by works of the Law.

He begins by giving **four arguments (3:1–18)** to show that justification comes through faith in Christ, not through keeping the Law. (1) The Galatians experienced the power of the Spirit when they accepted Paul's gospel. Thus God validated Paul's message of justification by faith (3:1–5). (2) Scriptures about the Hebrew patriarch Abraham show that Abraham was justified by faith and that Gentiles would be justified in the same way (3:6–9). (3) Everyone who relies on the Law for justification is under a curse (Paul does not say why), but Christ redeemed believers from the curse (3:10–14). (4) God promised justification to Abraham and his offspring (which Paul interprets to mean Christians) on the basis of faith. The Law, which came later, could not invalidate the earlier promise (3:15–18).

Next Paul raises the question of the **purpose of the Law (3:19–4:11)**. If the Law did not bring justification, then what was its purpose? Paul's answer is not completely clear, but it has to do with shutting up all things "under sin" (3:19–22). Perhaps he means that the Law made everyone aware of their sin, so that they would be ready to accept justification by faith. He also compares the Law to a "custodian," the attendant (usually a slave) who accompanied a child to and from school and oversaw the child's conduct. He compares becoming a Christian with growing up, so that one no longer needs an attendant (3:23–29).

Paul also speaks of other guardians, the elemental spirits of the world, without clarifying their relation to the Law. Perhaps some of them were the "angels" through whom the Law was given (3:19). In any case, both Jews and Gentiles were once like children under these guardians. But when humanity came of age and received its inheritance, adoption as sons of God, the guardians became unnecessary (4:1–7). Paul affirms that the Galatians, by observing special times, are returning to bondage under these cosmic spirits (4:8–10).

Taking a more personal approach, Paul next makes a **personal appeal (4:11–20)**. He reminds the Galatians of their former devotion to him in order to turn them back to their previous attitude.

Paul then gives an **allegorical interpretation of scripture (4:21–5:1)**. He uses a story from the Torah (Gen 21:1–14) to make the point that being under the Law is slavery, while being under Christ through faith is freedom. Abraham, the ancestor of the Jewish people, had two wives: Sarah (a free woman) and Hagar (a slave). In Paul's interpretation, these represent two covenants. Hagar represents the Law of Judaism, which "gives birth" to slaves, while Sarah represents the Christian religion, which produces free sons and heirs of God.

Paul concludes this section with a **warning against circumcision (5:2–12)**. In contrast to his opponents, who want Gentiles to be circumcised, Paul finds no advantage in being either circumcised or uncircumcised. The important thing is "faith working through love" (5:6).

Exhortatio: the Second Contention (5:13–6:10)

Paul then turns to his second contention, that freedom from the Law should not lead to sinful behavior. He warns the Galatians not to use their freedom as an excuse to get in "the flesh," that part of human nature that is subject to sin. He may be responding to an accusation of his opponents that his teaching about freedom from the Law leads to sin. He is clearly concerned, however, with the actual conduct of the Galatians. He warns them against various "works of the flesh," but especially strife and pride. He may have felt that the controversy in Galatia had brought out these characteristics in some of the Christians there. Paul emphasizes the Holy Spirit as a new principle that replaces the Law and the flesh. One who lives by the Spirit will fulfill the spirit of the Law, which is summed up in the commandment, "Love your neighbor as yourself."

Conclusio/Epistolary Postscript (6:11–18)

Paul concludes with some parting shots against his opponents. A final blessing on those who agreed with him (6:16) balances the introductory curse on those who did not (1:8–9).

DISCUSSION QUESTION

The spread of Christianity from Jews to Gentiles raised a number of issues pertaining to the Law (e.g. the necessity of circumcision) and the relations between Jewish and Gentile Christians (e.g. eating together).

Not every early Christian had the same perspective on these issues. Compare and contrast the perspectives of Paul, Barnabas, Peter, James, Paul's opponents in Galatia, and the Galatians on these issues.

REVIEW QUESTIONS

1. What two letters of Paul focus on the controversy over whether Gentile converts had to keep the Law? How does Paul's mood differ in these letters?
2. What are two different theories about the identity of the Galatians?
3. Identify three discrepancies between Acts' account of the Jerusalem Conference (Acts 15) and Paul's account (Galatians 2:1–10). On what significant point do they agree?
4. What are three different views about the identity of Paul's opponents in Galatia?
5. Describe the conflict in Galatia that prompted Paul to write the letter of Galatians.

SUGGESTIONS FOR FURTHER STUDY

Betz, Hans Dieter. *Galatians: A Commentary on Paul's Letter to the Churches in Galatia* (Hermeneia; Fortress, 1979). A standard commentary on Galatians.

Dunn, James D. G. *The Theology of Paul's Letter to the Galatians* (Cambridge University Press, 1993). Elucidates the major themes of the letter.

Esler, Philip F. *Galatians* (Routledge, 1998). Treats significant issues in Galatians from the perspective of social-scientific criticism.

Howard, George. *Paul: Crisis in Galatia* (2nd ed.; Cambridge University Press, 1990). Discusses Paul's opponents in Galatia and Paul's response.

Martyn, J. Louis. *Galatians: A New Translation with Introduction and Commentary* (Anchor Bible; Doubleday [Yale University Press], 1997). A standard commentary on Galatians.

Nanos, Mark D., ed. *The Galatians Debate: Contemporary Issues in Rhetorical and Historical Interpretation* (Hendrickson, 2002). A collection of essays by various scholars exploring rhetorical, epistolary, and socio-historical approaches to Galatians.

20 Gentiles and the Law (2)
Romans

Paul's letter to the Romans is the most important expression of his thought. Like Galatians, it centers on the question of whether justification comes by faith or by works of the Law.

This contrast between faith and works became a central tenet of the theology of Martin Luther during the Protestant Reformation. Luther passed down to subsequent Protestant scholarship an influential perspective on Paul's teaching in Romans and Galatians. According to this perspective, ancient Judaism was a religion of legalism in which one was justified by "works" or deeds, while Paul advocated a religion of grace in which one was justified by faith. Paul's purpose was to contrast justification by faith with legalistic works righteousness.

During the twentieth century, this perspective came into question. Krister Stendahl (1963) argued that Luther, concerned with the individual's consciousness of sin, misinterpreted Paul, who was concerned with the relation between Jews and Gentiles in the church. While Paul was concerned with aspects of the Jewish Law that separated Jews from Gentiles (i.e. circumcision and dietary restrictions), Luther read into Paul's teaching a concern for legalism in general. E. P. Sanders (1977) further argued that ancient Judaism was not a legalistic religion of works but was characterized by "covenantal nomism," the view that in Judaism one's relation to God was established by the covenant, while obedience to the Law was a response to membership in the covenant. James D. G. Dunn (1983) adopted Sanders' perspective and christened it "the new perspective on Paul."

Thus while Luther and many subsequent interpreters have used the letter to the Romans as a standard against basing salvation on any type of legalism, Paul was concerned with other issues relevant for his own day. His opposition to the Jewish Law stemmed from the fact that it separated

Figure 20.1
Scale model of
ancient Rome
at the time of
Constantine.
Museo della
Civiltà Romana,
Rome (Alinari/Art
Resource, NY).

Jews from Gentiles, while as apostle to the Gentiles he advocated a religion in which salvation came to Jews and Gentiles on the same basis.

CHRISTIANITY IN ROME

Geographically, the city of Rome sat on seven hills to the east of the Tiber River in Italy. Politically, it stood at the heart of the Roman Empire as the home of its central government, the Roman emperor and Senate. The population of Rome, estimated at from 1.5 to 4 million, included extremes of rich and poor. Correspondingly, its buildings reflected extremes of magnificence and squalor. The thriving religious life of the city encompassed an eclectic mixture. Temples and altars devoted to the Roman gods competed with cults brought by foreigners from all parts of the empire. Among the foreigners were Jews, who, like other foreign groups, lived together in certain quarters of Rome. In the first century, numerous Jewish synagogues met in the city.

It was probably in the synagogues of the Jews that Christianity was first preached in Rome. Jewish Christians from Palestine or Syria took the message of Jesus the Messiah to Jews there before Paul ever reached the city. Apparently, this preaching produced a tumult among the Jews in Rome. The Roman historian Suetonius records that the emperor Claudius (41–54 CE) "expelled the Jews from Rome because they were constantly causing disturbances at the instigation of Chrestus" (*Claudius* 25.4). Many scholars believe that Suetonius mistook the Latin term "Christus" (Christ) for a proper name "Chrestus," which would have had the same pronunciation. If so, Claudius expelled the Jews for arguing about Christ. This expulsion probably occurred about 49 CE, since when Paul came to Corinth about that time he met two Jewish Christians, Prisca and Aquila, who had recently left Rome because of Claudius' edict (Acts 18:1–2). If this reconstruction is correct, then, by 49 CE at the latest, Jewish Christians had taken Christianity to Rome, where it produced noticeable disturbances among the Jews there.

A few years later, when Paul wrote to the church in Rome, he wrote as if the Christian community there consisted predominantly of Gentiles (Rom 1:5–6, 13; 6:17–22; 11:13; 15:15–16), but also of Jews (1:16; 2:9, 17–24; 15:7–9). Apparently, though Jewish Christians began the Roman church, Gentile converts soon joined them. When Claudius expelled the Jews in 49, the Gentile Christians would have been left in charge of the church. When Claudius died in 54, many of the Jewish Christians would have returned to Rome, finding the situation changed and perhaps finding themselves in a minority. Quite possibly, therefore, when Paul wrote to the Romans about three years later, he was addressing a church community that was having to grapple with the reintegration of Jews among Gentiles.

DATE AND PROVENANCE OF ROMANS

Paul wrote his letter to the Romans at the end of his third phase of missionary activity, shortly before his final, fateful trip to Jerusalem (Rom 16:25). At the time, about 57 CE, he was apparently spending the winter in Greece, probably at Corinth (Acts 20:2–3). There he was staying in the house where the church met, the home of Gaius (Rom 16:23), a leading member of the Corinthian church (1 Cor 1:14). He planned to go from there to Jerusalem, taking a contribution for the poor that had been collected among his churches. He would then move on to Rome (Acts 19:21–22; 20:2–3). To prepare for his arrival in Rome, Paul wrote the church there a letter. In it he expressed his desire to preach the gospel among them and to receive their support for further missionary work in Spain (Rom 1:8–15; 15:22–33). In writing to this church that he had never visited, Paul set forth his "gospel," the gospel of justification by faith which he preached.

Order of Romans in select manuscripts

PAPYRUS 46	ℵ, B, C	D
text (1–14)	text (1–14)	text (1–14)
text (15:1–33a)	text (15:1–33a)	text (15:1–33a)
doxology	amen (15:33b)	amen (15:33b)
text (16:1–20a)	text (16:1–20a)	text (16:1–20a)
benediction (16:20b)	benediction (16:20b)	
greeting (16:21–23)	greeting (16:21–23)	greeting (16:21–23)
		benediction (16:24)
	doxology (16:25–27)	doxology (16:25–27)

A	BYZANTINE	G
text (1–14)	text (1–14)	text (1–14)
doxology	doxology	blank space
text (15:1–33a)	text (15:1–33a)	text (15:1–33a)
	amen (15:33b)	
text (16:1–20a)	text (16:1–20a)	text (16:1–20a)
benediction (16:20b)	benediction (16:20b)	
greeting (16:21–23)	greeting (16:21–23)	greeting (16:21–23)
	benediction (16:24)	benediction (16:24)
doxology (16:25–27)		

DIFFERENT VERSIONS OF ROMANS

Two features of Romans suggest that different versions of this letter were sent to different locations: significant textual variants and evidence that Romans 16:1–20 was meant for Ephesus instead of Rome.

   1. The manuscripts of Romans preserve significant textual variations at the beginning and end of the letter. At the beginning, a few manuscripts omit "in Rome" (1:7, 1:15), leaving the letter without any specific address. At the end, after chapter 14, the different manuscripts show three different conclusions with numerous variations in the order of the material. (a) A concluding doxology (16:25–27) occurs in some manuscripts at the end of chapter 14, in others at the end of chapter 15, in others at the end of chapter 16, and in still others at more than one of these places. (b) A concluding benediction occurs in some manuscripts at 16:20a before the greeting from Paul's co-workers (16:21–23), in others at 16:24 after the greeting, and in others at both places. (c) A concluding "amen" occurs in some manuscripts at the end of 15:33, and is absent in others.

2. Related to the textual problem is the nature of Romans 16:1–20. In this section Paul sends greetings to twenty-eight specific friends and co-workers, twenty-six by name. None of Paul's other letters have such a lengthy list of greetings. On the one hand, such a list would make sense in a letter to the Roman church, which Paul did not found, since Paul would have wanted to establish a bridge between himself and this church. On the other hand, if Paul is writing this chapter to the church in Rome, which he had never visited, it is strange that he would know so many people there. Furthermore, at least three names belong to people that Paul knew in Ephesus: Prisca and Aquila, whom Paul met in Corinth and took with him to Ephesus (Rom 16:3–5a; Acts 18:1–3, 18–19), and Epaenetus, whom Paul calls the first convert of Asia, the province in which Ephesus was located (Rom 16:5 b). Many scholars therefore believe that Romans 16:1–20 was actually meant for Ephesus, where Paul worked for two years and knew many people.

The textual variations and the possibility that Romans 16:1–20 was directed to Ephesus instead of Rome suggest that different forms of the letter once existed and were sent to different locations. All of the variations can be explained by assuming that three distinct forms of the letter existed: one addressed to Rome, a longer version (still with Roman address) sent to Ephesus, and a shorter version with no specific address.

Reconstructed versions of Romans		
TO ROME	**TO EPHESUS**	**GENERAL**
Romans 1–14	Romans 1–14	Romans 1–14
Romans 15:1–33a	Romans 15:1–33a	
amen (15:33b)	amen (15:33b)	
greeting (16:21–23)	Romans 16:1–20a	
benediction (16:24)	benediction (16:20b)	doxology (16:25–27)

Since Paul seems to have a specific location in mind from the beginning (1:8–15), he probably wrote the Roman version of the letter first. He then took a copy of this letter and sent it to Ephesus with a revised ending (16:1–20), in which he substituted specific greetings (16:3–16) for the general greeting sent to Rome (16:21–23). He ended both letters with a similar benediction, both forms of which have been preserved in the textual tradition (16:24; 16:20b). Later an editor took one version of the letter and made it more general by shortening it, adding a doxology, and changing the address: the original address "to those in Rome" (1:7) became "to those in the love of God" (1:7 variant). Paul himself probably did not create this shortened form, since whoever abbreviated it broke it off in the middle of Paul's discussion of the weak and the strong.

Apparently all three forms of the letter were copied and circulated in the early church. When later scribes found three different versions of the letter, they combined them in various ways. Hence different manuscripts have the various elements of the letters in different orders.

PURPOSE OF ROMANS

Scholars have given considerable thought to the question of why Paul wrote the letter of Romans. Some of the answers given include the following (Donfried 1991).

1. *To introduce himself and his gospel to a church from which he hoped to receive financial support.* Paul says that he had long wanted to visit the church in Rome but had so far been prevented (1:13). He plans to visit them soon and hopes that they will assist him (financially) as he goes on to Spain to preach there (15:22–24). Perhaps, then, he wrote the letter to introduce himself, to explain his gospel, and to defend himself against any negative reports they may have had about him or his message.

2. *To resolve a conflict between the "weak" and the "strong" in the Roman church.* In Romans 14:1–15:13, Paul speaks of those who are weak in faith and those who are strong in faith. The weak hold certain beliefs that the strong do not share, such as the beliefs that they should not eat food considered unclean (14:2, 14–15) and should observe certain days (14:5). Scholars usually identify the strong as Gentile Christians and the weak as Jewish Christians. Some suggest that Paul had found out about a specific conflict in the Roman church between the weak and the strong. Paul wrote to resolve the conflict between the two groups, exhorting the strong not to despise the weak, and the weak not to condemn the strong.

3. *To promote acceptance of the contribution for Jerusalem.* When Paul wrote Romans, he was about to visit Jerusalem. He was taking a contribution that Gentile Christians had collected for the poor in the church there (15:25–29). He was worried that the Jerusalem church

might not find the offering acceptable, perhaps because some there did not approve of Paul or the Gentile mission (15:30–32). Some scholars believe that Paul had Jerusalem primarily in mind when he wrote Romans. He sent a copy of the letter there to explain his gospel so that the Jerusalem church would not reject the Gentiles or their contribution.

4. *To serve as a last will and testament.* According to this theory, Paul had a strong feeling that his trip to Jerusalem might lead to his death (Rom 15:31). He therefore wrote the letter of Romans to leave behind as a sort of final summary of his main ideas about his life's work. He drew on his previous experiences rather than having a specific situation in Rome in mind.

5. *To serve as a circular letter to various churches.* As we have seen, the letter to the Romans probably also existed in a form with no specific address. Paul, or a later editor, may have sent this letter to various churches, perhaps as a general summary of his teaching.

Outline of Romans

English translations of Romans generally follow the order of the Alexandrian textual tradition, represented by the manuscripts ℵ, B, and C.

1. Introduction (1:1–15)
2. Body
   a. The gospel preached by Paul (1:16–8:39)
   b. The place of Israel in God's plan (chs. 9–11)
   c. Instructions for the new life in Christ (12:1–15:13)
3. Conclusion (15:14–16:27)

CENTRAL THEME OF ROMANS

Throughout Romans, Paul has in view the relation between Jews and Gentiles, both in salvation and in the concrete circumstances of the church. This central theme comes to expression in the three main divisions of the body of the letter.

1. In Romans 1:16–8:39, Paul argues that both Jew and Gentile obtain salvation on the same basis: faith in Jesus. Jews do not have an advantage

in the Law, since "no flesh will be justified before [God] by works of the Law" (4:20). In taking this position, Paul distinguishes his own perspective from that of Judaic Christianity. Judaic Christians disagreed with each other on whether or not Gentiles had to keep the Law, but they all agreed that it was necessary for Jews. By contrast, Paul's argument in Romans would lead to the logical conclusion that not even Jews had to keep the Law to be saved. Paul had no objection if Jewish Christians continued to practice the Law, though he regarded such Christians as "weak" in faith. But he emphasized that such observance of the Law had no effect on salvation. For both Jew and Gentile there was one God, "who will justify the circumcised by faith and the uncircumcised through the same faith" (3:30). The Law did not bring salvation, but the knowledge of sin: "I would not have known sin, except through the Law" (7:7).

2. In Romans 9–11, the theme of Jew and Gentile continues. Paul grapples with the question of why Gentiles had accepted the Jewish Messiah while most Jews had not. Paul concluded that this situation was part of God's plan of salvation for both Jews and Gentiles. God had caused the Jews to reject the gospel so that the Gentiles would receive it, but somehow "all Israel" would eventually be saved. In the meantime, Paul warns the Gentile Christians not to exalt themselves over the Jews.

3. The theme of Jew and Gentile recurs in Romans 14–15. There Paul encourages harmonious relations between the "weak" and the "strong" in faith. The weak were apparently Jewish Christians who abstained from meat and wine and observed special days. Though Judaism did not prohibit eating meat, many Jews in the Diaspora abstained from fear that the meat was "unclean" or had been offered to idols. Many also abstained from wine. The strong, then, would include both Gentile Christians and any Jewish Christians who did not share the scruples of their fellows. It is uncertain whether Paul knew of such differing perspectives in the Roman church or wrote out of his previous experience in other churches with a mixture of Jews and Gentiles. In any case, he urges all concerned to accept each other, just as Christ ministered for the sake of both Jews and Gentiles (15:7–9).

READING GUIDE: ROMANS

Read Paul's letter to the Romans with the help of the following guide.

Introduction (1:1–15)

Paul begins his letter with a salutation (1:1–7) and mentions his personal concern for the Roman Christians (1:8–15).

The Gospel Preached by Paul (1:16–8:39)

In the first main division of Romans, Paul gives a detailed explanation of the gospel that he preaches. He does not merely repeat the bare facts of the gospel (the death, burial, and resurrection of Jesus), but explains how these facts are important for the salvation of the believer. Paul wants to show that salvation does not come through the Jewish Law but through faith in Christ. Having the Law therefore does not give the Jews an advantage. Both Jew and Gentile have equal access to God through faith in Jesus.

Paul begins this section by stating **the theme of the letter (1:16–17)**. In his gospel, Paul preaches that salvation or "God's righteousness" comes through faith to everyone who believes, whether Jew or Greek. The Greek word translated "righteousness" could also be translated as "justification." As in Galatians, it is a term from the law court, referring to a person's acquittal or vindication on the day of judgment.

Paul presents his gospel by first describing **the human predicament (1:18–3:20)** that makes salvation necessary. According to Paul, God's wrath is directed against all impiety and unrighteousness of human beings (1:18–32). Because they did not worship God, their hearts were darkened, and God turned them over to impurity, so that their bodies were dishonored, and to an unfit mind, to do the things that are not appropriate.

Paul then addresses an imaginary Gentile who disapproves of the people who do such things (2:1–5). Paul accuses this person of doing the same things and says that he will not escape the judgment of God. Because of his unrepentant heart, he is storing up wrath for himself on the day of God's wrath and judgment. At the end of this accusation, a passage presents a more traditional Jewish view of God's judgment, in which both Jews and Gentiles could be justified by keeping the ethical standards of the Law (2:6–16).

Paul then addresses an imaginary Jew, who relies on the Law and boasts in God (2:17–24). Paul accuses him of teaching others to follow the Law but breaking the Law himself. At the end of this accusation, a passage presents the idea that not those who are literally circumcised, but those who are spiritually circumcised in heart would receive praise from God (2:25–29). Jews have one advantage: they were entrusted with the scriptures (3:1–8).

Paul concludes that Jews and Greeks are all under sin (3:9–20). Not even a single person is righteous. The whole world stands under God's judgment. Therefore no flesh will be justified by works of the Law, for through the Law came recognition of sin (3:20).

Paul's solution to the human predicament has two parts. First, people need **the righteousness (or justification) of God (3:21–5:11)**. This they can receive through faith in Jesus Christ. All have sinned and fail to attain God's glory, but they can be justified freely by God's grace through the redemption provided in Christ. God has set Jesus in front of himself, and the blood of Jesus appeases the wrath of God for those who have faith (3:21–26). Both Jews and Gentiles are justified by faith apart from works of the Law (3:27–31).

Paul argues that justification by faith is taught in the Law, especially in the story about Abraham in Genesis 15:1–6. Abraham believed God, and his faith was credited to him as righteousness (4:1–8). This happened before he was circumcised, so that he became the spiritual father of all who believe, whether they are uncircumcised or circumcised (4:9–12). It was through faith, not the Law, that Abraham received the promise that he would be the father of many (Gentile) nations (4:13–25).

Those who have been justified by faith have peace with God and hope to share the glory of God. God's love is shown in his son's death, which reconciled sinners to God (5:1–11).

In the second part of Paul's solution to the human predicament, he explains how believers can also have **deliverance from the power of sin (5:12–8:39)**. God is not content simply to forgive sinners and leave them in their corrupt state, in which they will continue to sin as before. God also wants to transform them so that they are delivered from the compulsion to sin.

He begins by describing how sin and death entered the world through the transgression of Adam, as related in Genesis 3 (5:12–21). These two powers ruled over all of Adam's descendants; and because all sinned, all died. Before Moses gave the Law, sin was not counted. However, after the Law came, the numerous transgressions of the Law were counted. Consequently the grace of God and the justification given freely by Jesus had to cover not just the one transgression of Adam, but all the transgressions committed since the giving of the Law.

Paul warns against continuing to sin so that God's grace may abound. The power of sin is broken by baptism, through which the believer participates in the death and resurrection of Jesus. Through baptism one dies to the old life of sin and rises to a new life without sin (6:1–14). Those who have been baptized have been freed from slavery to sin in order to become slaves of obedience and righteousness (6:15–23). Paul uses an analogy from marriage to help make his point: when a woman's husband dies, he no longer rules over her. So too, when one puts to death the flesh in baptism, the Law of the flesh no longer rules over one (7:1–6).

The Law itself is not sin, but it brings the knowledge of sin, and this knowledge brings death (7:7–13). Sin dwells in the flesh, the physical body, and takes the mind captive. With the mind a person wants to do right, but sin in the flesh overrules the mind and makes a person incapable of doing right (7:14–25). Here Paul draws on ideas popularized in the ancient world by Plato. In Plato's body/soul dualism, the soul was divine, and the mind, the rational part of the soul, was the most divine. When a soul was joined to a body, the body had a negative effect on the soul, enslaving it to various appetites and passions. Paul's picture of the flesh at war with the mind reflects this widespread idea from his culture. His own contribution was to use the term "sin" to name the various passions and appetites of the body and to say that this power entered the world through the transgression of Adam.

Paul has already stated that through baptism one could put the flesh to death and live a new life no longer subject to the power of sin. He now adds that if one receives the Holy Spirit, the mind can be ruled by the Spirit rather than by the flesh (8:1–17). The present salvation will be completed only in the future; in the meantime, nothing can separate the believer from the love of God (8:18–39).

Place of Israel in God's Plan (chs. 9–11)

In the second major division of the letter, Paul confronts the same problem seen already in Luke–Acts: the fact that most Jews had rejected the gospel. If Jesus was the Messiah promised to Israel, then why did most Israelites reject the gospel? Paul wrestles with this problem, concluding that God had "hardened" the hearts of the Jews so that they would not accept the gospel. He recognizes that this may seem unfair, but he defends God's justice. He argues that God had a reason for hardening their hearts and would ultimately restore all Israel.

First Paul addresses the **hardening of Israel (chs. 9–10)**. He is grieved that his fellow Israelites have rejected the gospel (9:1–5). Even so, he argues, God's promises to Abraham and Israel have not failed, because the real "Israel" consists of all who are children of Abraham through faith in Jesus (9:6–13). This spiritual Israel has received the promises instead of the physical Israel.

In that case, is God unjust in his dealings with physical Israel? Paul answers no, because God has the right to show mercy to whom he wishes and to harden whom he wishes (9:14–18). God is a potter who has the right to make his vessels the way he chooses (9:19–29).

Somewhat inconsistently, Paul then seeks to shift the blame from God to the Jews. The Jews, he says, have stumbled by seeking justification through works of the Law rather than through faith in Christ (9:30–10:21).

Paul then describes the **restoration of Israel (ch. 11)**. Despite the fact that God has hardened the hearts of Israel, he has not rejected his people (11:1a). In the first place, a "remnant" chosen by grace has accepted the gospel, even though the rest were hardened (11:1b–10). In the second place, Israel did not stumble that they might fall, but so that salvation might come to the Gentiles (11:11–16). In the third place, all Israel will be restored. They are like the branches of an olive tree that have been cut out, leaving room for other branches, the Gentiles, to be grafted in. Gentile Christians should therefore not boast over the natural branches, because they can be grafted back in (11:17–24). In fact, God's ultimate plan for Israel is a "secret" revealed to Paul: "there has been a hardening in part to Israel until the full number of the Gentiles comes in, and thereupon all Israel will be saved" (11:25–32). In all of this, Paul claims, God's plan shows his unfathomable wisdom (11:33–36).

Instructions for the New Life in Christ (12:1–15:13)

In the third major division, Paul describes the new life that should characterize a person who has died to sin and risen to live for God.

The believer should have **a sacrificed body and a renewed mind (12:1–2)**. Paul begins by referring back to the first major division, summarizing his gospel in terms of salvation for the body and the mind. The body is to be "a sacrifice come to life," that is crucified to sin and raised to new life with Christ. The mind is to be renewed by setting it on the Spirit, not on the flesh.

Paul then gives **various instructions (12:3–13:14)** concerning the new life in Christ. He admonishes his readers to serve humbly in their allotted functions as members of the body of Christ (12:3–8); to follow various admonitions (12:9–21); to submit to the appointed authorities (13:1–7); to love one another (13:8–10); and to live as children of the day (13:11–14).

Paul pays particular attention to the problem of **the weak and the strong (14:1–15:13)**. The person who is "weak in faith" believes that certain foods are unclean and that certain days should be observed as special. The "strong," on the other hand, know better. Some scholars have argued that this difference of perspective arose between different social classes at Rome: the poor (weak) and the wealthy (strong). However, the reference to food considered "unclean" (14:14–15) and the example of how Jesus served both Jew and Gentile (15:7–9) may indicate that the difference existed between Jews and Gentiles. Paul instructs the weak and the strong on how to get along with each other. They should not judge a fellow believer (14:1–12) or cause a fellow believer to stumble (14:13–15:6), but accept one another as Christ accepted them, both Jews and Gentiles (15:7–13).

Conclusion (15:14–16:27)

Paul ends on a more personal note, describing his **plans for the future (15:14–33)** and requesting the prayers of the church in Rome.

The next section may be an **addendum for Ephesus (16:1–20)**. In it, Paul introduces Phoebe, a deacon of the church in Cenchreae (16:1–2). She was probably the woman who carried the letter to Ephesus. Cenchreae was a city near Corinth. Paul was apparently spending the winter in this area when he wrote the letter. He then greets numerous friends and co-workers, presumably at Ephesus (16:3–16), warns against teaching that went beyond what he had taught (16:17–20a), and concludes with a benediction (16:20b).

A more general **greeting from Paul's co-workers (16:21–23)** probably belonged to the original letter sent to Rome rather than the Ephesian version. Like the more specific greeting sent to Ephesus, it concluded with a benediction (16:24, similar to 16:20b), which most English translations omit.

The concluding **doxology (16:25–27)** probably belonged to the abbreviated version of the letter that ended after chapter 14.

DISCUSSION QUESTIONS

1. In *Romans 1:18–3:31*, review those statements in which Paul asserts that no one is made righteous by keeping the Law. Compare and contrast this view with Mark 2:15–17, Mark 10:17–21, and Luke 15:1–7. What reasons might Paul have had for taking this view?

2. In *Romans 7:7–25*, Paul explains the compulsion to sin as the result of a power called "sin" dwelling in the flesh and taking the mind captive.

He says that this power prevents people from doing the good that they want to do. Explain what you think he means in this passage. From your own experience, does his description seem meaningful or not? Explain.

3. In *Romans 9–11*, Paul argues that God has hardened the hearts of most Jews as part of his plan to bring salvation to the Gentiles. What problem arises with the idea that God has hardened the hearts of the Jews, or of some Jews and not others? If Paul is right, why was it necessary? Does the ultimate restoration of Israel alleviate the problem? What other reasons might account for the fact that most Jews did not accept the Christian message?

REVIEW QUESTIONS

1. What group probably first took Christianity to Rome? Later in Romans, Paul assumed that the church consisted of what group or groups?
2. When and where did Paul write the letter of Romans?
3. What features of Romans suggest that different versions of the letter were sent to different locations?
4. What are some of the theories concerning the purpose of Romans?
5. What is the central theme of Romans? How does it come to expression in the three main divisions of the body of the letter?

SUGGESTIONS FOR FURTHER STUDY

Cranfield, C. E. B. *A Critical and Exegetical Commentary on the Epistle to the Romans* (2 vols.; ICC; Bloomsbury T&T Clark, 1975, 1979). A standard commentary on the Greek text of Romans.

Donfried, K. P., ed. *The Romans Debate* (rev. ed.; Hendrickson, 1991). A collection of essays by various scholars discussing Paul's purpose for writing Romans.

Fitzmyer, Joseph A. *Romans: A New Translation with Introduction and Commentary* (Anchor Bible; Doubleday; Yale University Press, 1993). One of several good commentaries on Romans; includes extensive bibliography.

Jewett, Robert. *Romans: A Commentary* (Hermeneia; Fortress, 2007). A major commentary on Paul's letter to the Romans.

Lampe, Peter. *From Paul to Valentinus: Christians at Rome in the First Two Centuries* (Fortress, 2003). Uses history, archaeology, theology, and social analysis to delineate the rise and development of the earliest churches in Rome.

Sanders, E. P. *Paul and Palestinian Judaism* (Fortress, 1977). Argues that ancient Judaism was not a legalistic religion of works but was characterized by "covenantal nomism."

21 Problems of Church Life (1)
1 Corinthians

The city of Corinth became prosperous as a center of trade and banking. It stood on a narrow isthmus between two harbors. The eastern port of Cenchreae traded with Asia Minor, the western port of Lechaeum with Italy. The Romans destroyed the original Greek city in 146 BCE, but Julius Caesar refounded it as a Roman colony in 44 BCE. In Paul's day, Corinth was the capital of the Roman province Achaia (Greece). There the proconsul of the province resided, along with a population of about half a million people.

The earlier Greek city had acquired a reputation not only for wealth but also for sexual license. The geographer Strabo claimed that a thousand temple prostitutes had plied their trade in the temple of Aphrodite. The expression "a Corinthian girl" came to mean a prostitute, and "to corinthianize" meant to practice fornication. Scholars today tend to doubt Strabo's claim, since Greek religion did not generally include sacred prostitution, and the reputation of the city may owe more to Athenian slander than to reality. Nevertheless, it is interesting that in the later Roman city, consorting with prostitutes did become a problem among the members of Paul's church (1 Cor 6:12–20).

Every other year, the stadium at Corinth hosted athletic contests, the Isthmian games, second in fame only to the Olympic games. Paul may have been in Corinth when the games were held in 49 and 51 CE. He and his audience would certainly have had these in mind when he compared the Christian life to a race (1 Cor 9:24–27).

Two letters of Paul addressed to the church at Corinth have been preserved. These give us an insight into the types of problems that could arise in Paul's churches. Besides prostitution, First Corinthians deals with a number of moral and social problems experienced by the church at Corinth. Both First and Second Corinthians also deal with a conflict between Paul and the Corinthian Christians.

HISTORICAL SETTING OF 1 CORINTHIANS

Paul Evangelizes Corinth

According to Acts, Paul first visited Corinth after leaving Athens (Acts 18:1–17). His co-workers Timothy and Silvanus joined him there (2 Cor 1:19; Acts 18:5). There he also met Prisca and Aquila, a Jewish couple who had just come from Italy when the emperor Claudius expelled all Jews from Rome. Either Prisca and Aquila were already Christians or Paul converted them, since they are mentioned elsewhere as Christian ministers (1 Cor 16:19; Rom 16:3; Acts 18:18, 26). They and Paul shared the same trade of tentmaking and went into business together. Paul took pride in the fact that he worked to support his ministry without relying on financial support from the Corinthians (1 Cor 9:3–19). Archaeologists have uncovered a number of small shops at Corinth that give us an idea of Paul's working conditions. Shops were generally 4 meters high, 4 meters deep, and 2.8 to 4 meters wide. The doorway provided the only source of light, and the room would have been cold in winter.

In his shop, opening onto a busy street or crowded marketplace, Paul had the opportunity to meet all classes of people, and we can imagine that he took this opportunity to share his message. He also preached in the local Jewish synagogue, and, after leaving the synagogue, at a private home (Acts 18:4–7). Financial support from churches in Macedonia enabled him to quit work and devote himself to his ministry (Acts 18:5; 2 Cor 11:8–9). After Paul had ministered in Corinth a year and six months, some Jews of the city accused him before the proconsul Gallio, who refused to hear the case (Acts 18:11–17). This encounter with Gallio gives us the one fairly certain date in Paul's chronology, since Gallio was probably proconsul in 51–52 CE. Shortly afterward, Paul left Corinth.

Paul at Ephesus

According to Acts, when Paul left Corinth, he passed through Ephesus, leaving Prisca and Aquila there. Paul himself returned to Antioch in Syria. While he was gone, a preacher named Apollos went to Corinth and ministered, apparently quite effectively (Acts 18:24–19:1). Meanwhile Paul returned to Ephesus and established his headquarters there for over two years (Acts 19:1–20). From there he wrote letters and took trips to churches he had previously established, including the one at Corinth.

Figure 21.1
The bema (raised platform) in the forum at Corinth, where the proconsul Gallio dismissed charges brought against Paul, according to Acts 18:12–17. Erich Lessing/Art Resource, NY.

In Ephesus, Paul received a visit from some Corinthian Christians, members of the household of a woman named Chloe (1 Cor 1:11). They brought news concerning divisions in the church: the Corinthians had divided into factions, some supporting Paul, others favoring Apollos or some other leader. Some who supported the other apostles apparently held Paul in low regard. Chloe's people may have reported other problems as well. Some members of the church were using the principle "All things are lawful for me" to justify consorting with prostitutes and other practices (1 Cor 6:12; 10:23). Paul also received a letter from the Corinthians, asking for instruction on certain issues (1 Cor 7:1). It may have been Chloe's people or members of the household of Stephanas who brought this letter (1 Cor 16:15–18).

Paul replied to the reports and the letter by writing what is now known as the letter of First Corinthians. He organized it topically, introducing some of the topics with the words "Now concerning ...":

- Now concerning the things about which you wrote (7:1)
- Now concerning virgins (7:25)
- Now concerning food offered to idols (8:1)

- Now concerning spiritual gifts (12:1)
- Now concerning the contribution (16:1)
- Now concerning brother Apollos (16:12)

This introductory formula first occurs at the point where Paul begins to respond to the Corinthians' letter. However, other topics, after this point as well as before, lack this formula. These include factions in the church (1:10–4:21); fornication and other improper behavior (5:1–6:20); resisting evil desires (9:24–10:13); worship of idols (10:14–22); abuses at the Lord's Supper (11:2, 17–34); and denying the resurrection (15:1–58). The letter also includes two passages that put restrictions on the ministry of women in the church (1 Cor 11:3–16; 14:33b–38).

THE SOCIAL SETTING AT CORINTH

Paul speaks of evangelizing both Jews and non-Jews at Corinth (1 Cor 9:19–23), yet in addressing the church he seems to refer to them as primarily Gentiles (1 Cor 12:2). Acts refers to one member as a "God-fearer" (Acts 18:7), a Gentile who worshipped the Jewish God without making a full conversion to Judaism.

Paul indicates that most members of the church came from the lower classes: "not many of you are wise, not many powerful, not many well born" (1 Cor 1:26). The phrase "not many" would leave room for at least a few from the upper classes: the educated, the wealthy and powerful, those born into leading families. These few would probably have been the dominant members of the congregation. Paul and Acts mention some of the Corinthian Christians by name, and Gerd Theissen (1982) has inferred that most of these belonged to the upper class, noting that they held offices, had households, provided assistance to the congregation, and traveled. These included Crispus, a Jewish synagogue ruler converted by Paul (Acts 18:8; 1 Cor 1:14); Erastus, "treasurer of the city" (Rom 16:23, written from Corinth); Stephanas (1 Cor 1:16; 16:15–18); Phoebe from the nearby port city of Cenchreae (Rom 16:1); Gaius, in whose home the whole church met (Rom 16:23); Prisca and Aquila, with whom Paul initially stayed at Corinth (Acts 18:2–3); and Titius Justus, with whom Paul subsequently stayed (Acts 18:7). Some of the problems at Corinth may have resulted from differences between the members in social and economic standing.

Paul speaks of "the whole church" meeting in the home of Gaius (Rom 16:23). This specification of the whole may imply that smaller groups within the church met in other homes. These would have been the homes of the wealthier members, who had houses large enough to accommodate meetings. Archaeologists have uncovered one of the nicer homes at Corinth, which, according to one estimate, would have accommodated no more than forty people. If the church grew much larger than this, it would have been difficult for the whole group to meet together. Probably, therefore, they usually met in the smaller groups. Such separation could easily foster differences between the groups and may partially account for the factions that developed in the church.

READING GUIDE: I CORINTHIANS

Read the letter of First Corinthians with the help of the following guide.

Introduction (1:1–9)

Paul associates "Sosthenes" with himself in writing the letter. This is probably the Sosthenes mentioned in Acts 18:17 as the ruler of the synagogue at Corinth. He was apparently with Paul in Ephesus when Paul wrote the letter.

Factions in the Church (1:10–4:21)

The church at Corinth had split into factions. Paul's initial comments on this problem indicate the **nature of the factions (1:10–16)**. Each group associated itself with a different leader: Paul, Apollos, Cephas (Peter), or Christ (1:12). These factions may have associated themselves with the minister who baptized them (1:13–17). As the sequel shows, the primary split involved the followers of Paul and Apollos.

In addressing this problem, Paul gives a **critique of eloquent wisdom (1:17–3:4)**. He spends a great deal of time criticizing "eloquent wisdom" (1:17; 2:1), perhaps because Apollos was an eloquent speaker, well versed in the scriptures (Acts 18:24). We can infer that Apollos' faction praised Apollos' eloquence and wisdom while criticizing Paul for his lack of the same. Paul defends himself by claiming that he came not with human wisdom, which the world esteems, but with the wisdom of God, which seems foolish to the world. He came not with human eloquence, but with the demonstration of God's power. He could have imparted deeper wisdom, he says, but the Corinthians were not mature enough to receive it.

The next part of this section distinguishes the **functions of Paul and Apollos (3:5–4:6)**. Paul urges the Corinthians not to compare Apollos and himself, because each performed a different function for the church. If the church is like a field, Paul planted while Apollos watered. If the church is like a building, Paul laid the foundation while Apollos built on it. In other words, Paul had the initial task of presenting the simple, more fundamental gospel, while Apollos' role was to present more advanced teaching that would lead the church to maturity. Paul is arguing that he should not be compared unfavorably to Apollos with respect to the depth of his teaching, since his role called for a more basic approach than that of Apollos.

Paul concludes this topic by criticizing the **Corinthians' arrogance (4:7–21)**. Some of the Corinthians who were not in Paul's camp apparently adopted a superior attitude toward him. Paul describes their attitude: Paul is foolish, but they are wise; Paul is weak, but they are strong; Paul is disreputable, but they are worthy of honor (4:10). They have become "inflated" (4:6, 18), but Paul threatens to deflate them when he comes.

Improper Behavior (5:1–6:20)

Turning from the problem of factions, Paul addresses several types of improper behavior: a man living with his father's wife (5:1–8), other types of immorality (5:9–13), Christians suing other Christians in the secular courts (6:1–8), and sexual immorality, specifically consorting with prostitutes (6:9–20). Paul accuses the Corinthians of taking pride in the man living with his father's wife (5:2, 6). Those who consort with prostitutes invoke the principle "All things are lawful for me" (6:12) and recite the proverb "Food for the belly and the belly for food" (6:13).

In 1 Corinthians 5:9, Paul says, "I have written [or "I wrote"] to you in the letter not to associate with fornicators." To what letter was he referring? Possibly he referred to what he had just written in First Corinthians, since he has just warned them not to associate with a fornicator (1 Cor 5:1–8). A similar use of "I have written" (an epistolary aorist) occurs in 1 John 2:14. In that case, Paul is clarifying what he just said, to head off any potential misunderstanding by the Corinthians. Most scholars, however, think that Paul's statement refers to a previous letter, written before First Corinthians. In that case, either the letter has been lost, or a fragment of it is preserved in 2 Corinthians 6:14–7:1.

The Married and the Single (7:1–40)

At this point, Paul begins to answer the questions asked by the Corinthians in their letter to him (1 Cor 7:1, 25). Taking up the first two issues, he gives various instructions on the subject of marriage. Paul's teaching on this subject has two sources. (1) In forbidding divorce, he refers to a command of the Lord (1 Cor 7:10). He may be referring to a traditional saying of Jesus (Mark 10:11–12; Matt 5:32). (2) In other instances, he expresses his own opinion or judgment (1 Cor 7:12, 17, 25, 40).

Food Offered to Idols (8:1–11:1)

The next problem addressed by Paul involved eating meat that had been sacrificed to non-Christian deities. Paul addresses two situations in which the problem arose: eating a sacrificial meal in the deity's temple and buying sacrificial meat from the market to eat in a private home.

Paul first addresses the issue of **eating in an idol's temple (8:1–13)**. In sacrificing an animal to a deity, the worshipper ate part of the sacrifice in the deity's temple. Most of the Corinthian Christians would have grown up participating in these sacrificial meals, and some apparently continued to do so after they became Christians. Here Paul grants that a person who knew that an idol had no significance would be doing no wrong by eating such a meal. Nevertheless, he argues against participating. A Christian who had this knowledge and could eat with a clear conscience might influence a "weaker" Christian to eat and so violate their conscience. Rather than cause a weaker Christian to sin, Paul advises those with knowledge to forgo their right to eat.

From a sociological perspective, the "weak" may have been the poorer and less educated Christians of the lower classes. The normal diet for these people consisted of bread. They normally ate meat only when it was offered free at public celebrations, where the meat was dedicated to the presiding gods. They would therefore have associated meat exclusively with the worship of non-Christian deities. Those Christians with "knowledge" would have been the more highly educated and wealthier members of the upper classes. Able to afford meat more routinely, they would not have associated it exclusively with worship of the gods. More fully integrated into the public life of the city, they would also have found it more difficult to avoid public functions where meat dedicated to the gods was served.

The next part of this section presents **Paul as a role model (9:1–23)**. Paul offers himself as a model of giving up one's rights for the sake of others: he gives up his right to be paid for preaching the gospel and his right to take a wife as a companion on his travels. Philosophers in the ancient world had long discussed the best means of supporting themselves: begging, charging fees, entering a household as a resident guest, or working. Paul knew the tradition that Jesus had his messengers receive support from the people they were evangelizing (9:14). Yet he himself followed a different course, either working or receiving support from churches he had previously established.

Paul emphasizes that his audience needs effort and discipline in order to **resist evil desires (9:24–10:13)**, such as fornication and idol worship. He uses illustrations from athletics and a scripture from the Old Testament to make his point.

In 8:1–13, Paul saw eating in an idol's temple as wrong only if it offended some other Christian's conscience. In contrast, he later treats it as wrong in itself, as **worship of idols (10:14–22)**. Eating such a meal represented having fellowship with the deity. Though granting that an idol in itself is nothing, Paul claims that the deities represented by idols are demons. Christians, he says, cannot have fellowship with God in the Christian meals and still eat meals with demons.

Paul concludes this section by addressing the issue of **eating meat from the market (10:23–11:1)**. Extra meat that was not consumed in the sacrificial meal might be sold in the public market. Some of the Corinthians justified eating this meat on the principle "All things are lawful" (10:23). Paul's advice was to eat meat from the market without worrying about it, unless someone else pointed out that it was offered to an idol. In that case, one should not eat, out of consideration for the other person's conscience.

Covering the Head (11:3–16)

In some earlier form of the letter, 11:2 was followed directly by 11:17. Paul wrote that he commended the Corinthians in some things (11:2) but could not commend their practice of the Lord's Supper (11:17). In the present form of the letter, 11:3–16 interrupts this thought. According to this passage, women (or wives) who pray or prophesy in church should have their heads covered. The background to this idea may be Jewish. Among Jews of that time, a married woman customarily wore a covering on her head. If she went outside without such a covering, her husband could divorce her. Unmarried women did not have to observe this custom.

Figure 21.2
Third-century
fresco depicting
the Christian
communal
meal. Catacomb
of S. Callisto,
Rome (Scala/Art
Resource, NY).

The Lord's Supper (11:2, 17–34)

With respect to the Lord's Supper, the exact nature of the problem remains obscure. Apparently the Corinthian Christians did not arrive at the meeting at the same time. Instead of waiting to share their food in a communal meal, different groups, as they arrived, began their own private meals, presumably with food that they had brought. This practice would have accentuated the differences in social and economic status in the congregation. The wealthy had enough to make merry and get drunk, while the poor went hungry. Those who had nothing would be put to shame. Paul tells the Corinthians to wait for one another so that they can eat together. If they are too hungry to wait or not satisfied by the communal meal, they should eat at home before they come. The purpose of the Lord's Supper was not simply to eat, but to eat together.

Paul believed that this abuse at the Lord's Supper had resulted in the sickness and death of some of those celebrating it. He thus drew a spiritual connection between the meal, representing the body and blood of Jesus, and the church, also conceived as the body of Christ. Abuse of the former led to sickness in the latter.

Spiritual Gifts (12:1–14:40)

The theme of the church as the body of Christ continues in Paul's discussion of spiritual gifts. Just as the physical body has various members with different functions, so the body of Christ has various members with different spiritual gifts (ch. 12). While Paul encourages use of the gifts, he offers two correctives to their misuse. First, priority should be given to love (ch. 13). Second, the gifts should be used in an orderly manner and only when they constructively benefit the church (ch. 14).

A passage near the end of Paul's discussion of spiritual gifts forbids women to speak in church (14:33b–38). In the context, speaking in church would have to refer to prophesying and speaking in tongues. This could be another interpolation, since it can be removed without affecting the flow of thought. Verses 39–40 would be a natural conclusion to verse 33a.

The Resurrection (ch. 15)

Apparently some people at Corinth denied a future resurrection from the dead (15:12). Paul assumes that they did believe in the resurrection of Jesus, since he uses this as an argument against them: if there is no resurrection of the dead, then neither was Jesus raised (15:12–19). Paul does not state whether they believed in immortality of the soul or no afterlife at all. He seems to assume the latter, since he argues that his opponents' viewpoint eliminated any incentive for living well in the present (15:32–33), an argument that would not be applicable to belief in immortality of the soul. His opponents may have found one obstacle to belief in bodily resurrection in the question of what kind of body might be involved (15:35). Paul says that it would not be flesh and blood (15:50). Instead it would be a "heavenly" body (15:49), the same term that he uses when discussing the glory of the "heavenly bodies," the sun, moon, and stars (15:40–41). Here he probably draws on earlier conceptions, both Greek and Jewish, of the stars as living beings with bodies consisting of a fiery substance.

Concluding Matters (ch. 16)

Paul concludes with instructions about the collection he is making for the church in Jerusalem (16:1–4), a word about his travel plans (16:5–12), and some final exhortations and greetings (16:13–24).

DISCUSSION QUESTIONS

1. *Celibacy and marriage.* In 1 Corinthians 7, what reasons does Paul give for staying single? What reasons for getting married? Are all of these reasons valid? Why or why not? Compare and contrast his views with

those in Psalms 127 and 128. What reasons might you have for staying single or getting married other than the ones given in these passages?

2. *Women in the church.* In 1 Corinthians 11:3–16, what arguments does the author give to show that a woman should cover her head when she prays or prophesies? What difficulties do you encounter when trying to understand the logic of these arguments? Compare and contrast this passage with Gal 3:27–28, 1 Cor 14:33b–38, and 1 Timothy 2:8–15. What difficulties do you encounter when trying to relate these passages to each other? What relevance do these passages have for today?

REVIEW QUESTIONS

1. Describe Paul's first visit to Corinth.
2. Describe the events that led up to Paul's writing of First Corinthians.
3. Describe the organization of First Corinthians.
4. Describe the social setting of the church at Corinth.
5. Describe the problems in the church that Paul addresses in First Corinthians.

SUGGESTIONS FOR FURTHER STUDY

Conzelmann, Hans. *1 Corinthians* (Hermeneia; Fortress, 1975). A standard commentary on First Corinthians.

Dunn, James D. G. *1 Corinthians* (Sheffield Academic Press [Bloomsbury T&T Clark], 1995). A brief survey of scholarship on the various problems that Paul addresses in First Corinthians.

Fitzmyer, Joseph A. *First Corinthians: A New Translation with Introduction and Commentary* (Anchor Yale Bible; Yale University Press, 2008). A major commentary on First Corinthians.

Furnish, Victor P. *The Theology of the First Letter to the Corinthians* (Cambridge University Press, 1999). Analyzes Paul's thought and beliefs in First Corinthians.

Martin, Dale B. *The Corinthian Body* (Yale University Press, 1995). Explores Paul's "body" language in First Corinthians in light of Greco-Roman ideas about the body.

Murphy-O'Connor, J. *St. Paul's Corinth: Texts and Archaeology* (3rd ed.; Liturgical Press, 2002). A collection of ancient texts relating to Corinth and descriptions of it based on texts and archaeology.

Theissen, Gerd. *The Social Setting of Pauline Christianity: Essays on Corinth* (Fortress, 1982). Explains the conflicts at Corinth by reconstructing the social conditions of the community.

22 Problems of Church Life (2)
2 Corinthians

If we gave a prize to Paul's most incomprehensible letter, Second Corinthians would probably win it. Even seasoned readers of Paul's letters come away from this one with little enlightenment. Part of the problem lies in the fact that we have little idea of the letter's historical context. Paul is responding to one or more conflicts between himself and other parties at Corinth, but, other than what we can infer from the letter, we have no idea who those parties were or precisely what the fuss was about. The other part of the problem lies in the fact that the letter seems to be composite. An editor apparently put it together from several distinct components. These can be recognized from the abrupt changes of tone, interruptions in the flow of thought, and inconsistencies between different parts of the letter.

COMPONENTS OF 2 CORINTHIANS

How many different documents went to make up Second Corinthians? Opinions differ, but the letter has at least three components: a conciliatory letter, a letter fragment, and part of a severe letter.

Much of chapters 1–9 belongs to a **conciliatory letter (1:1–2:13; 7:5–16)**. In these chapters, Paul rejoices that a conflict between himself and the Corinthian church has been resolved. He speaks of a painful visit that he had made to Corinth (2:1) and a letter that he had written with tears (2:1–4; 7:8–12). He has just had good news from Titus that the letter produced repentance in the Corinthian church and that they have reaffirmed their love for Paul.

A **long digression (2:14–6:13; 7:2–4)** interrupts the conciliatory letter. This may have belonged to the severe letter, since it interrupts Paul's account of his journey from Ephesus to Macedonia (2:13 continued at 7:5). In the digression, Paul defends his ministry.

Two chapters give **instructions for the collection (chs. 8–9).** These may have come from different letters. Though chapter 8 discusses a contribution that Paul is collecting from Corinth, chapter 9 introduces this topic as though for the first time.

An unrelated **letter fragment (6:14–7:1)** interrupts the long digression. Since it contains terms and ideas that are not typical of Paul, he may not have written it.

Chapters 10–13 are part of **the severe letter (chs. 10–13).** These chapters present an abrupt change of tone from the conciliatory letter. In that, Paul rejoiced that the situation had been resolved, while in chapters 10–13 he writes severely, as if the problem still existed. In these chapters, Paul defends his ministry as an apostle. Apparently, the Corinthians were showing less appreciation for Paul than for some other apostles, whom he sarcastically dubs the "super-apostles." These chapters may be part of the tearful letter that Paul mentions in the conciliatory letter (2 Cor 2:1–4; 7:8–12). If so, Paul wrote chapters 10–13 before the conciliatory letter in 1–7.

PAUL'S LETTERS AND VISITS TO CORINTH

While Paul stayed at Ephesus, he had numerous contacts with the church at Corinth that he had established previously. We have already seen that he wrote First Corinthians from there. From the letter of Second Corinthians we can deduce something of his later contacts with the church.

First came the **painful visit**. Sometime after writing First Corinthians, Paul visited Corinth for the second time. He did not find things to his satisfaction. His views apparently met resistance from some in the church. The situation proved painful for both him and the Corinthians (2 Cor 2:1). Apparently, he found some Corinthians favoring other apostles over himself and continuing to practice immorality (2 Cor 13:2). After warning them, Paul returned to Ephesus.

Paul then wrote the **severe letter (2 Cor 10–13)**. When Paul was about to leave Ephesus, he planned to visit Corinth again. He wrote a letter to prepare for his coming, hoping to move the Corinthians to repent and to accept his authority. If 2 Corinthians 10–13 was part of this letter, then Paul listed his qualifications as an apostle, pointing out that he was in no way inferior to the "super-apostles" favored by the Corinthians. He felt

Figure 22.1
A page from
Papyrus 46
(about 200 CE)
containing 2
Corinthians
13:5–13. This is the
oldest manuscript
of Paul's
letters that has
survived. Special
Collections
Library, University
of Michigan.

that he was becoming a fool by boasting but also felt that the Corinthians had driven him to it. He tells the Corinthians to mend their ways and warns that he is coming for the third time.

Before going to Corinth, Paul wrote the **conciliatory letter (2 Cor 1:1–2:13; 7:5–16)**. Paul had sent the severe letter by Titus, saying that he was about to come to Corinth. However, he changed his mind and went to Macedonia first (2 Cor 1:15–16; 1:23–2:1, 12–13). He was joined there by Titus, who reported that the situation at Corinth had improved in response to Paul's letter (2 Cor 7:5–16). Paul then wrote a conciliatory letter, rejoicing at the Corinthians' repentance. He sent the letter by Titus and two others with instructions to complete their contribution for the poor Christians in Judea (2 Cor 8–9).

Finally Paul made his **last visit to Corinth**. After leaving Macedonia, Paul spent the three months of winter in Achaia (Greece), apparently at Corinth (Acts 20: 1–3). From there he wrote the letter to the Romans before his final visit to Jerusalem.

READING GUIDE: 2 CORINTHIANS

Read the letter of Second Corinthians with the help of the following guide.

2 Corinthians 10–13

We will first examine 2 Corinthians 10–13, since if these chapters belonged to the severe letter, Paul wrote them before 2 Corinthians 1–9. Paul addresses several problems at Corinth: criticism of himself (10:9–11); high regard for other apostles, whom Paul labels "super-apostles" or "false apostles" (11:1–6, 13–15); and continuing immorality (12:21).

Paul begins with a **defense of his ministry (10:1–12:13)**. He defends his own ministry by comparing himself with the "super-apostles" in the areas of apostolic authority (10:1–18), knowledge (11:1–6), self-support (11:7–15), Jewishness (11:16–22), labors and afflictions (11:23–33), revelations (12:1–10) and miracles (12:11–13). Paul finds himself in no way inferior to these other apostles.

Paul concludes with a **warning (12:14–13:14)**. He warns the Corinthians to repent and mend their ways before he visits them for the third time.

2 Corinthians 1–7

Paul wrote this final letter to the Corinthians after receiving news through Titus that his previous letter (perhaps partially preserved in 2 Cor 10–13) produced the desired repentance among them.

In the **introduction (1:1–11)**, Paul indicates that he has suffered some major affliction in Asia Minor (at Ephesus). He feels that God has comforted him in such afflictions so that he will be able to comfort others in similar situations.

Paul then begins a **review of previous events (1:12–2:13)**. He summarizes what has happened between himself and the Corinthians. In his severe letter, he told them that he was about to visit them, but to spare them another painful visit he changed his mind (1:15–2:2). His severe letter caused the Corinthians to discipline someone in the congregation (2:3–11). Before he knew about these results, he left Ephesus and went to Troas. But because he did not find Titus there, who would tell him the results of the severe letter, he went on to Macedonia.

Paul's review of the situation is interrupted by a **long digression (2:14–6:13; 7:2–4)**. This may originally have been part of the severe letter. In it, he further describes and defends his ministry. He pictures himself as a sincere minister of the new covenant, which is superior to the old (2:14–4:6). This ministry is physically crushing, but Paul is encouraged by the hope of resurrection (4:7–5:10). Paul is motivated by the love of Christ in a ministry of reconciliation (5:11–21). He exhorts the Corinthians to open their hearts to him (6:1–13; 7:2–4).

A **letter fragment (6:14–7:1)** interrupts the digression. It contains terms and ideas similar to those at Qumran: "Belial" as a name for the spirit of evil; light and darkness as symbols of good and evil; separation from those outside the community. Since Paul does not elsewhere use the term "Belial" or advocate separation from "unbelievers," he may not have written this passage. If he did write it, it may be part of a letter that Paul wrote before First Corinthians (cf. 1 Cor 5:9).

The letter then returns to the **review of previous events (7:5–16)**, which was interrupted after 2:13. Paul reports that Titus has joined him in Macedonia, bringing news of the Corinthians' repentance.

2 Corinthians 8–9

Chapters 8 and 9 both deal with Paul's collection for the poor in Jerusalem, though they may have been written at different times. Paul encourages the Corinthians to complete the collection they had begun earlier (1 Cor 16:1–4). He and others later took this collection to poor Christians in Judea on Paul's last visit to Jerusalem.

DISCUSSION QUESTION

Summarize what we can know about the "super-apostles" from what Paul says about them in 2 Corinthians 10–13.

REVIEW QUESTIONS

1. Identify the main components of Second Corinthians.
2. Summarize Paul's contacts with the church at Corinth after he wrote First Corinthians.

SUGGESTIONS FOR FURTHER STUDY

Betz, Hans Dieter. *2 Corinthians 8 and 9: A Commentary on Two Administrative Letters of the Apostle Paul* (Hermeneia; Fortress, 1985). Interprets 2 Corinthians 8 as a letter to Corinth, and 2 Corinthians 9 as a separate letter to Achaia.

Furnish, Victor P. *II Corinthians* (Anchor Bible; Doubleday [Yale University Press], 1984). A standard commentary on Second Corinthians.

Kreitzer, Larry. *2 Corinthians* (Sheffield Academic Press, 1996). A student's guide to the major issues raised in the study of Second Corinthians.

Murphy-O'Connor, Jerome. *The Theology of the Second Letter to the Corinthians* (Cambridge University Press, 1991). Discusses the background, major themes, and significance of Second Corinthians.

Roetzel, Calvin J. *2 Corinthians* (Abingdon, 2007). Short commentary proposing that Second Corinthians is a composite of five letters.

23 The Imminent Parousia
1 and 2 Thessalonians

Paul taught his churches to expect the "parousia," the coming of Jesus on the "day of the Lord." When Jesus did not appear, problems arose. Such problems are the focus of two letters attributed to Paul: First and Second Thessalonians. The first letter deals with the problem of Christians who had died without seeing the expected return of Christ. The second corrects the view that the day of the Lord had already arrived.

HISTORICAL CONTEXT OF 1 THESSALONIANS

Acts 17:1–15 relates how Paul and Silas brought the gospel to Thessalonica, the capital of the Roman province of Macedonia. Preaching in the Jewish synagogue, Paul converted "some" of the Jews and "a great many" of the Greeks. When the Jews of the city opposed the message and stirred up a crowd against them, Paul and Silas fled to the neighboring town of Beroea. When the Jews of Thessalonica heard that Paul was preaching in Beroea, they came there and again forced Paul to leave.

Paul subsequently traveled to Athens (Acts 17:16–33), from where he sent Timothy to check up on the church he had established in Thessalonica (1 Thes 3:1–3). When Timothy returned, Paul either was still in Athens (cf. 1 Thes 3:6) or had moved on to Corinth (Acts 18:1, 5). Hearing from Timothy that the Thessalonian Christians were standing firm in their faith, Paul wrote the letter of First Thessalonians to them. Written about 50–51 CE, this letter is the earliest writing in the New Testament, with the possible exceptions of Galatians and James, and hence the earliest preserved document of Christianity.

Paul's reasons for writing this letter can be inferred from the letter itself: (1) to encourage the Thessalonians in the midst of their persecution and affliction; (2) to defend himself against certain accusations; (3) to encourage the Thessalonians to live in a manner worthy of the gospel; and (4) to assure the Thessalonian Christians that those of their number who died before the day of the Lord would still get to be with Christ.

READING GUIDE: I THESSALONIANS

Read the letter of First Thessalonians with the help of the following guide.

Paul and the Thessalonians (1:1–3:13)

In the first section of the letter, Paul reviews his previous relationship with the Thessalonians from the time he first established their church. Paul founded the church in the midst of great opposition, which was continuing. He feared that this opposition might have caused the Thessalonians to abandon their allegiance to Christ. He encourages them by mentioning his own suffering in Philippi (2:2; cf. Acts 16:11–40) and his concern for the affliction being experienced by the Thessalonians (1:6–7; 2:14–16; 3:1–5).

In the **introduction (1:1–10)**, as in many of his letters, Paul begins with a salutation (1:1) followed by a thanksgiving (1:2–10). He gives thanks to God because the Thessalonians accepted his message. The Thessalonian converts were primarily Gentiles, since they "turned to God from idols to serve a living and true God" (1:9). The new faith that Paul taught them was "to wait for his Son from heaven, whom he raised from the dead, Jesus, the one who delivers us from the wrath to come" (1:10).

A section of **self-defense (2:1–12)** follows. Paul seems to be defending his conduct (cf. 1:5), perhaps responding to accusations made by his opponents in Thessalonica.

Paul then adds a **second thanksgiving (2:13–16)**. He compares the affliction of the Thessalonians to that of the churches in Judea: "you too suffered the same things from your fellow-countrymen as they did from the Jews" (2:14). Some interpreters take "fellow-countrymen" here to refer to Gentiles rather than Jews. However, Paul's bitterness toward the Jews in the rest of this passage would be more explicable if the opposition were coming from them, as Acts states (Acts 17:5–9, 11, 13). In 2:16, the sentence "But God's wrath has come upon them at last" seems to refer to the destruction of Jerusalem by the Romans in 70 CE. If so, this sentence was interpolated by a copyist or editor after Paul's death.

Paul next expresses his **concern for the church (2:17–3:13)**. He describes his anxiety about the church and his relief at Timothy's report that the Thessalonians were standing firm in their faith. He concludes this section with a prayer on their behalf (3:11–13).

Exhortation to Live a Christian Life (4:1–12)

In the second section, Paul presents various exhortations on living the Christian life. He urges the Thessalonians to abstain from sexual sins (4:1–8), to love one another (4:9–10), and to work for a living (4:11–12). Some interpreters believe that certain members of the congregation had stopped working because they believed that Jesus was about to return. Paul, however, gives no explanation for their conduct. Later in the letter he refers to them as "idlers" (5:14).

The Day of the Lord (4:13–5:11)

The third section of the letter deals with issues relating to the expected return of Jesus on "the day of the Lord."

Paul first addresses the issue of what happens to **the dead in Christ (4:13–18)**. When Paul preached to the Thessalonians, he told them to wait for the coming of Jesus, who would return soon to establish the kingdom of God. Paul himself apparently expected to be alive at Jesus' return (4:15, 17). Yet as time continued, Jesus did not come, and some of the Christians at Thessalonica died. (In 4:13 Paul speaks euphemistically of the dead as those who have "fallen asleep.") These deaths apparently raised a question for those who remained alive: would those who died miss out on the kingdom when Jesus returned? Paul wrote to reassure them that the dead in Christ would not miss out. When Christ returned, the dead would be raised first, and then those who remained alive would be "caught up" with them to meet Christ in the air. Paul does not say what would happen then. This passage provides the basis for the doctrine generally called "the rapture," a term taken from Latin *rapturus* ("going to be caught up").

Paul next addresses the question of the **time of Jesus' return (5:1–11)**. The Thessalonians apparently began to wonder when, in fact, Jesus would come. Paul reminds them of what he had previously taught them: the day of the Lord would come unexpectedly "like a thief in the night" for those who were unprepared. He urges the Thessalonians to stay alert so that they would not be surprised.

Exhortations and Conclusion (5:12–28)

After a series of short exhortations (5:12–22), Paul concludes with a prayer (5:23–24), a request for prayer (5:25), a holy kiss (5:26), an adjuration to have the letter read (5:27), and a benediction (5:28).

AUTHORSHIP OF 2 THESSALONIANS

No one doubts that Paul wrote First Thessalonians. Many scholars, however, have questioned the authenticity of Second Thessalonians. We will consider the arguments for and against Paul's authorship.

Arguments against Paul's Authorship

Some scholars ascribe the letter to an admirer of Paul who wrote after Paul's death. In this theory, the author of the letter consciously imitated 1 Thessalonians, a genuine letter of Paul. Several arguments are used to support this position.

First, the second letter to the Thessalonians has many **similarities to First Thessalonians**. The second letter has about 146 words that also occur in the first. The two letters also share a number of phrases, such as the following:

> For remember brothers our *labor and toil. Working night and day so as not to burden any of you*, we preached to you the gospel of God. (1 Thes 2:9)

> Nor did we eat food from anyone for free but with *labor and toil were working night and day so as not to burden any of you*. (2 Thes 3:8)

Other shared phrases include "work of faith" (1 Thes 1:3; 2 Thes 1:11), "for even when we were with you" (1 Thes 3:4; 2 Thes 3:10), "who do not know God" (1 Thes 4:5; 2 Thes 1:8), "for obtaining salvation through our Lord Jesus Christ" (1 Thes 5:9) or "for obtaining the glory of our Lord Jesus Christ" (2 Thes 2:14). For some scholars, the similarities between the two letters support the view that a later Paulinist modeled the second letter on the first. For others, the similarities suggest that the same person, Paul, wrote both letters.

Second, the second letter to the Thessalonians exhibits some **non-Pauline vocabulary**. It has a number of words and phrases that do not occur in the acknowledged letters of Paul: e.g. "we are bound to give thanks" (1:3; 2:13), "shaken in mind" (2:2), "believe the truth" (2:12), "speed on" (3:1). To some scholars, these indicate that Paul did not write the letter. However, every other letter of Paul also contains some vocabulary that does not occur in the other letters. Second Thessalonians has about the same percentage of such vocabulary as First Thessalonians.

Third, the second letter appears to some scholars to have **different eschatology** than the first letter.

1. In the first letter, the day of the Lord comes without warning "like a thief in the night" (1 Thes 5:1–3). In 2 Thessalonians, on the other hand, there is plenty of warning, since certain events must occur before that day: an apostasy and the coming of a "man of sin" (2 Thes 2:1–12). This apparent discrepancy can perhaps be resolved by recognizing that in 1 Thessalonians the day comes without warning only for unbelievers. For believers there would be no surprise (1 Thes 5:4). That perspective is compatible with the view that certain events would alert believers to the day's arrival.

2. In the first letter, Paul expects the day of the Lord soon, in his own lifetime (1 Thes 4:15, 17). In the second letter, Paul recounts events that must take place first, thus putting the day further in the future. Some scholars see this as an indication that this author no longer expected the day to come soon. However, the author does still expect that the events preceding that day will happen soon; in fact, "the mystery of lawlessness is already at work" (2 Thes 2:7). He is merely arguing against people who said that the day had already arrived (2 Thes 2:1–2).

3. The ideas about "the man of sin" in 2 Thessalonians do not occur in the acknowledged letters of Paul. This absence, however, could be explained by the fact that Paul nearly always wrote to address issues of concern on specific occasions. If the occasion did not call for it, he did not write about it.

A fourth argument is that the second letter has **more advanced christology** than the first. Second Thessalonians gives priority to Jesus in a few places where First Thessalonians gives priority to God. For instance, the first letter speaks of "brothers beloved by God" (1 Thes 1:4), while the second has "brothers beloved by the Lord" (2 Thes 2:13). Where 1 Thessalonians 3:11 puts God before Jesus ("May our God and Father himself and our Lord Jesus ..."), 2 Thessalonians 2:16 puts Jesus before God ("May our Lord Jesus Christ himself and God our Father ...").

Some scholars see this difference as an indication that 2 Thessalonians was written after Paul's time, when the church placed a greater emphasis on the importance of Jesus. This argument is nullified, however, by the fact that Paul sometimes put Jesus before God in his acknowledged letters (Gal 1:1).

Arguments for Paul's Authorship

A few features of Second Thessalonians suggest that Paul did write this letter.

1. Scholars who believe that Paul did not write this letter generally attribute it to a member of a Pauline school writing about 70–90 CE. However, one reference in the letter suggests that the Jerusalem temple still stood at the time of writing (2 Thes 2:4). If so, the letter was written before 70 CE, very possibly in Paul's lifetime.

2. The letter of Second Thessalonians presupposes the same situation as First Thessalonians. Both letters share three central themes. The theme of affliction and persecution appears in both letters (1 Thes 1:6; 2:14–16; 3:1–8; 2 Thes 1:3–10). Likewise both letters address the theme of the parousia or day of the Lord (1 Thes 4:13–18; 5:1–11; cf. 1:9–10; 3:11–13; 5:23–24; 2 Thes 1:4–10; 2:1–12). Likewise both letters include the theme of church members who are not working (1 Thes 4:10b–12; 5:14; 2 Thes 3:6–13). The letter of Second Thessalonians thus fits well in the chronology of Paul's life at a time close to that when he wrote First Thessalonians.

3. Both letters base their eschatological teaching on an interpretation of the Old Testament book of Daniel. In 1 Thessalonians 4:17, the idea that the church would be caught up in the clouds to meet the Lord probably arose by identifying the church with the "one like a son of man" who is brought before God with the clouds of heaven in Daniel 7:13. Similarly, in 2 Thessalonians 2:1–12, the idea that a "man of lawlessness" would precede the day of the Lord arose from interpreting the king of the north in Daniel 11:21–45 as a figure yet to come. This common reliance of both letters on Daniel suggests that the same author wrote both.

At present, neither the arguments against Paul's authorship nor the arguments for it have convinced all scholars. The authorship of this letter therefore remains in dispute.

DATE AND PURPOSE
OF 2 THESSALONIANS

If Paul wrote Second Thessalonians, he may have written it soon after the first letter, which was written about 50–51 CE from Corinth. Some scholars, however, believe that Paul wrote it before First Thessalonians.

If Paul wrote the letter, it had three main purposes: (1) to encourage the Thessalonians in the midst of their persecution; (2) to correct the view that the day of the Lord had already arrived; (3) to deal further with the problem of church members not working. If Paul did not write the letter, the author's primary purpose was to correct the view that the day of the Lord had already arrived, using Paul's name to give authority to the letter. The other themes of the letter were simply copied from 1 Thessalonians to give the letter a sense of authenticity.

READING GUIDE: 2 THESSALONIANS

Read the letter of Second Thessalonians with the help of the following guide.

Salutation and Thanksgiving (1:1–12)

If this is Paul's second letter, the Thessalonians are still experiencing persecution and affliction. Paul sees this as evidence that the Thessalonians are being made worthy of the kingdom of God. He encourages them by declaring that their oppressors will be punished on the day of the Lord.

The Day of the Lord (2:1–12)

The author wished to refute the idea that the day of the Lord had already arrived. His readers may have gotten this mistaken notion "through spirit or through word or through letter, as if through us" (2:2). The author mentions a letter but does not specify what it was. The grammar may mean either that the letter was a forgery that falsely claimed to be from Paul or that it was an actual letter of Paul that the readers misinterpreted.

The author corrects this misunderstanding by describing certain events that had to occur before the day of the Lord, including the coming of a "man of lawlessness" who would lead many people astray. The author's picture of this "son of perdition" is apparently derived from the book of Daniel (Dan 7:8, 19–27; 8:9–14, 22–26; 11:29–45). Daniel's description of an evil king who persecuted God's people originally referred to Antiochus Epiphanes in the second century BCE. The author, however, interprets these passages as if they referred to an Antichrist figure who was still to come and who would be destroyed by Christ on the day of the Lord.

Further Matters (2:13–3:15)

The remainder of the letter includes a second thanksgiving (2:13), a prayer for the Thessalonians (2:16–17) and a request for prayer (3:1). In 3:6–15 the author warns against members of the church who were not working for a living, developing in more detail a theme found also in First Thessalonians.

Conclusion (3:16–18)

After a concluding prayer and benediction (3:16), "Paul" gives a greeting in his own handwriting (3:17) and adds another benediction (3:18). Paul's personal greeting implies that he dictated the rest of the letter to a scribe. Scholars who believe that a later Paulinist wrote the letter interpret the personal greeting as an attempt to make the letter seem genuine. However, Paul himself sometimes added such notices in his acknowledged letters (Gal 6:11; 1 Cor 16:21).

DISCUSSION QUESTION

Much of the early church's teaching about the end-time came from interpretation of Old Testament writings such as Daniel. Read Daniel 7 and the description of the "king of the north" in Daniel 11:21–45. Both of these texts originally referred to Antiochus Epiphanes, the Seleucid ruler who tried to Hellenize the Jews in the second century BCE. How did Paul (and the author of Second Thessalonians if not Paul) reinterpret these passages in order to arrive at the eschatological teaching in 1 Thessalonians 4:13–18 and 2 Thessalonians 2:1–12?

REVIEW QUESTIONS

1. Which of Paul's letters focus especially on problems associated with the parousia?

2. Where and when did Paul write 1 Thessalonians?

3. What were Paul's reasons for writing 1 Thessalonians?

4. Discuss the arguments for and against Paul's authorship of 2 Thessalonians.

5. What three central themes do the Thessalonian letters have in common?

6. What was the purpose of 2 Thessalonians if Paul wrote it? If Paul did not write it?

SUGGESTIONS FOR FURTHER STUDY

Donfried, Karl P. *Paul, Thessalonica, and Early Christianity* (Bloomsbury T&T Clark, 2002). A collection of essays relating primarily to the Thessalonian letters.

Donfried, Karl P., and I. Howard Marshall. *The Theology of the Shorter Pauline Letters* (Cambridge University Press, 1993). A brief discussion of the setting, themes, and significance of the Thessalonian letters, among others.

Furnish, Victor Paul. *1 Thessalonians, 2 Thessalonians* (Abingdon, 2007). A non-technical commentary. Treats 2 Thessalonians as deutero-Pauline.

Jewett, Robert. *The Thessalonian Correspondence: Pauline Rhetoric and Millenarian Piety* (Fortress, 1986). Discusses the critical issues and suggests that the Thessalonians' attitude could be described as "millenarian radicalism."

Malherbe, Abraham J. *The Letters to the Thessalonians: A New Translation with Introduction and Commentary* (Anchor Bible; Doubleday; Yale University Press, 2000). A standard commentary on 1 and 2 Thessalonians. Treats 2 Thessalonians as Pauline.

Malherbe, Abraham J. *Paul and the Thessalonians: The Philosophic Tradition of Pastoral Care* (Fortress, 1987). Shows how Paul followed a Greco-Roman philosophical tradition of pastoral care to establish, shape, and nurture the Thessalonian community.

24 Prison Epistles (1)
Philippians and Philemon

The four letters of Philippians, Philemon, Colossians, and Ephesians have traditionally been called the **Prison Epistles** because they imply that Paul wrote them while in prison (Phil 1:7, 12–18; Philem 1, 9, 10, 13, 23; Col 4:3; Eph 3:1, 4:1, 6:20). Scholars agree that Paul actually wrote Philippians and Philemon. Most doubt, however, that he wrote Colossians, and even more doubt that he wrote Ephesians. We will examine the acknowledged Prison Epistles in the present chapter, the disputed ones in the next.

COMPOSITION OF PHILIPPIANS

While some scholars argue that Philippians constitutes a single, unified letter, others think that it has been compiled from two or three letters or letter fragments. This conclusion is based on both internal and external evidence.

Internal Evidence

Philippians seems to presuppose at least two different historical situations. In 4:10–19 Paul informs the Philippians, as if for the first time, that their messenger **Epaphroditus** had arrived with the gift that they sent. Philippians 2:25–30, however, seems to refer to a later time: the Philippians already know not only that Epaphroditus had reached Paul, but also that he had fallen sick and nearly died and that he had subsequently recovered.

Philippians also contains abrupt transitions and more than one conclusion. The letter proceeds smoothly down to 3:1, where it begins to conclude: "Finally, my brothers ..." Instead of concluding, however, it shifts subjects abruptly and continues for another chapter down to 4:7. Then it begins to conclude again: "Finally, brothers …" (4:8–9). Again, instead of concluding, it continues with Paul's thanks for the gift sent through Epaphroditus (4:10–19).

These features of Philippians suggest that it consists of at least two separate letters that have been combined: a letter warning against Judaic Christians and thanking the Philippians for their gift (3:2–4:19), and a letter of encouragement written later after Epaphroditus recovered from his sickness (1:1–3:1). Some scholars distinguish Paul's note of thanks in 4:10–19 as yet a third letter.

External Evidence

External evidence also suggests that Paul wrote more than one letter to the Philippians. Polycarp, bishop of Smyrna, writing to the Philippians in the early second century, mentioned "letters" that Paul had written to their church (Polycarp to the Philippians 3:2). Apparently an editor combined these letters, perhaps to make a single letter that could be read in church.

HISTORICAL SETTING OF PHILIPPIANS

Assuming that Philippians consists of at least two letters, we can deduce the following historical setting for them.

Paul first wrote a **polemical letter with a note of thanks (3:2–4:19)**. On his second missionary journey, Paul established a church in Philippi, the chief city in the province of Macedonia (Acts 16:11–40). Later, as Paul was ministering in some other city, the Philippians sent Epaphroditus with a gift to support Paul financially. They had sent him such gifts before to support his ministry (Phil 4:15–16; cf. 2 Cor 11:9). Whether Paul was imprisoned before or after Epaphroditus arrived is unclear. In any case, after Epaphroditus delivered the gift, he fell sick. Paul sent a letter back to the Philippians, in which he warned against Judaic Christians and sought to resolve a disagreement between two women in the church (Phil 3:2–4:9). He also thanked the Philippians for their gift (4:10–19). The messenger who took the letter informed the Philippians of Epaphroditus' sickness, and they expressed their concern.

The messenger then returned to Paul and Epaphroditus. When Epaphroditus heard that the Philippians were concerned about his sickness, he became distressed (2:26). After he recovered, Paul sent him

Figure 24.1 St. Paul in Prison. Painting by Rembrandt (1606–69). The sword alludes to the tradition that Paul was beheaded in Rome. Staatsgalerie, Stuttgart (gettyimages).

back to the Philippians with a **letter of encouragement (1:1–3:1)**. In it Paul sent news about his situation in prison. He told them he would send Timothy when he learned the outcome of his approaching trial. He expressed confidence that he would be released and come to them soon.

PLACE AND DATE OF PAUL'S IMPRISONMENT

In the letter of encouragement, Paul speaks of being in "bonds" for the sake of the gospel (1:7, 13, 17). He awaits a trial that could result in his execution (1:20; 2:17–18), but he expects instead to be released (1:19, 25–26). As soon as he finds out what will happen, he will send news to the Philippians through Timothy, and he trusts that he himself will come shortly after (2:19–24).

Where was Paul imprisoned when he wrote this? Scholars are divided between three possible answers: Rome, Caesarea, or Ephesus. Acts relates only that Paul was imprisoned at Caesarea and Rome, but Paul himself mentions other imprisonments before these (2 Cor 6:5; 11:23). Hints in Paul's letters suggest that he may have been imprisoned in Ephesus, either near the beginning of his stay there (1 Cor 15:32) or near the end (2 Cor 1:8–11).

Two terms in Philippians have associations with the emperor of Rome, but do not narrow the place of imprisonment to Rome. (1) In 1:13 Paul refers either to "the praetorium" or to "the Praetorian [Guard]." The Praetorian Guard consisted of soldiers in the service of the Roman emperor. The guard had its headquarters just outside of Rome, but soldiers of the guard also served in provincial capitals such as Ephesus. The term "praetorium" could refer to the residence of a Roman official, such as "Herod's praetorium" in Caesarea (Acts 23:35). The term, therefore, does not help identify the site of Paul's imprisonment. (2) The same is true for "the household of Caesar," which Paul mentions in 4:22. Caesar's household consisted of slaves and freedmen who served the emperor as government staff. They resided not only at Rome, but also in many other places, including Ephesus.

Two considerations favor Ephesus over Rome or Caesarea as the place of imprisonment. First, Paul plans to go to Philippi once he is released (Phil 1:25–26; 2:24). We know that Paul did go on more than one occasion from Ephesus to Philippi (1 Cor 16:5–9; 2 Cor 2:12–13). When he left for Jerusalem and Caesarea, however, he did not intend to return to Philippi.

His intention was to go to Rome, and from Rome he intended to go to Spain (Rom 15:22–29; Acts 19:21).

Second, a great deal of traveling took place between Philippi and Paul's place of imprisonment: Epaphroditus went from Philippi to Paul, another messenger went from Paul to Philippi and back, Epaphroditus went to Philippi, Paul planned to send Timothy to Philippi, and Paul himself planned to come to Philippi. All of this traveling suggests that Paul's place of imprisonment lay not too far from Philippi. That would be true of Ephesus, but not Rome or Caesarea.

If Paul's imprisonment took place in Ephesus near the beginning of Paul's stay there (1 Cor 15:32), it occurred in the early 50s before the Corinthian correspondence. If it took place near the end of his stay in Ephesus (2 Cor 1:8–11), the date would have been sometime in the mid 50s, after 1 Corinthians, but before 2 Corinthians.

CENTRAL THEMES OF PHILIPPIANS

Five central themes find expression in the letter to the Philippians.

First is the theme of **partnership in the gospel** (1:3–6; 4:14–18). Paul thanks the Philippians for their continued financial support as partners in his missionary activity.

Second is **polemic against Judaic Christians** (3:2–4:1). Paul roundly denounces Judaic Christians, who teach that Christians must be circumcised.

Third is **exhortation to be of one mind** (2:1–11; 4:2–3). Paul encourages two women in the church to settle their differences and to be of one mind. In a famous passage, Paul uses Christ as an example of the proper attitude of humility and selflessness.

Fourth is **exhortation to rejoice** (3:1; 4:4; etc.). Paul emphasizes Christian joy in this letter, using the terms "joy" or "rejoice" fourteen times.

Fifth is **Paul's view of life and death** (1:19–26). Paul's imprisonment brings with it the possibility that he may be executed. His reflections on this possibility give us an insight into how Christian faith shaped his attitude toward life and death.

READING GUIDE: PHILIPPIANS

Read Paul's letter to the Philippians with the help of the following guide.

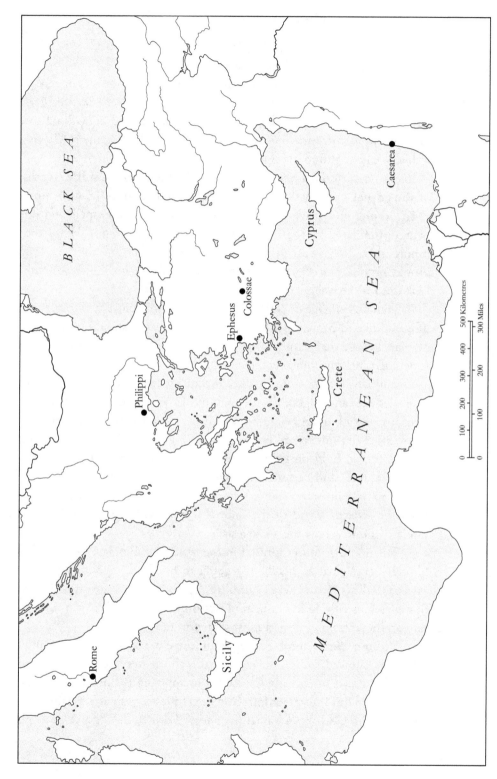

Figure 24.2 The possible sites of Paul's imprisonment at the time he wrote Philippians and Philemon: Rome, Caesarea, or Ephesus.

Letter of Encouragement (1:1–3:1)

In the **introduction (1:1–11)** Paul, with joy and thankfulness, remembers the Philippians' "partnership in the gospel" (1:4–5).

He then writes **concerning his imprisonment (1:12–26)**. Paul expects to be released from prison for the sake of those to whom he ministers. For his own sake, his preference would be to depart and be with Christ. He sums up his attitude toward life and death in the statement "To me, to live is Christ and to die is gain" (1:21).

In the heart of the letter, he exhorts his audience to live **a life worthy of the gospel (1:27–2:18)**. Such conduct would entail standing "in one spirit, in one soul striving together for the faith of the gospel" and not being intimidated by those opposed to the gospel (1:27–30). He further exhorts them to have an attitude of unity and love for one another. They should not act out of strife or self-glorification but in humility should look out for the welfare of others (2:1–4).

In a famous passage (2:5–11), Paul uses Christ to exemplify the attitudes of humility and concern for others that his audience should have. Some scholars believe that Paul quoted this passage from a pre-Pauline hymn. It depicts Christ in four successive stages.

1. Initially, Christ was "in the form of a god (or God)." Here Paul expresses the same high christology found in the Gospel of John: before Jesus became a human being, he existed as a preexistent divine being.

2. Christ did not regard being equal to a god (or God) as something that he should hold on to but instead "he emptied himself, taking the form of a slave" and became like a human. This self-emptying, whatever it may mean, illustrates Christ's humility. He willingly abased himself from the state of a god to the state of a human, not to serve his own interests but to serve others like a slave.

3. When Christ found himself in the form of a human, "he humbled himself" even further, obediently going to his death, specifically death on a cross. This second act of humility shows the degree to which Christ humbles himself. He leaves behind not only his divine life, but also his human life, forsaking it for a most shameful form of death.

4. Because Christ humbled himself in these ways, "God super-exalted him and bestowed on him the name that is above every name." Here Paul probably follows other early Christians in applying Psalm 110:1 to Jesus. According to this interpretation, God exalted Jesus to sit at his right hand and gave him God's own name, the name "Lord" (cf. Acts 2:32–36; Eph

1:19–23; Heb 1:3–4). Paul goes on to say that God did this so that every being in heaven, on earth, and in the underworld should bow the knee and acknowledge that Jesus Christ is "Lord" to the glory of God the Father (cf. Isa 45:23). In describing Jesus as one who emptied himself and humbled himself, Paul gives his audience an example to follow and implies that those who humble themselves will be exalted by God.

In the conclusion to this passage of exhortation (2:12–18), Paul exhorts his audience to work out their salvation with fear and trembling, to do everything without grumbling and arguments, and to rejoice with him.

Paul then writes **concerning Timothy and Epaphroditus (2:19–30)**. Paul will send Timothy when he learns the outcome of his trial. In the meantime, he sends Epaphroditus with the letter of encouragement.

In the **first conclusion (3:1)** of the present letter to the Philippians, Paul begins to conclude the letter of encouragement with the words "Finally, my brothers." He exhorts his audience to rejoice in the Lord, repeating what he said in 2:18 or possibly what he had said in a previous letter (4:4).

Polemical Letter (3:2–4:19)

Instead of concluding, the letter abruptly shifts to what may have originally been a different letter, which Paul wrote before the letter of encouragement.

No salutation or introduction has been preserved for this letter. It begins abruptly with a passage of **polemic (3:2–4:1)**. Paul warns against "the dogs," that is, Judaic Christians who preach the need for circumcision and keeping the Law (3:2–16). He directs a further warning against the "enemies of the cross," that is, people who glory in shameful conduct and have an earthly instead of a heavenly perspective (3:17–4:1).

Next comes a **series of exhortations (4:2–7)** emphasizing the need for unity and joy. Paul urges two women to come into agreement (4:2–3). Some scholars would assign 4:4–7 to the letter of encouragement.

The exhortations are followed by the **second conclusion (4:8–9)** of the present letter. The words "Finally, brothers …" introduce the second conclusion as they did the first (3:1).

Next comes a **note of thanks (4:10–19)**. Paul thanks the Philippians for the gift they sent through Epaphroditus. Some scholars regard this as a distinct letter.

The letter's **conclusion (4:20–23)** includes a doxology (4:20), three sentences of greeting (4:21–22), and a benediction (4:23). It is uncertain to which of the component letters these belonged.

HISTORICAL SETTING OF PHILEMON

Paul wrote the short letter of Philemon as a prisoner (1, 9, 10, 13, 23), addressing it primarily to **Philemon**, one of his converts (1, 19). He wrote concerning **Onesimus**, a slave who belonged to Philemon. Apparently, Onesimus had run away from Philemon and joined Paul while Paul was in prison. Paul sent Onesimus back to Philemon, asking Philemon to allow the slave to return and serve Paul on Philemon's behalf. Paul makes a play on the name "Onesimus" ("beneficial" or "useful"), when he says he would like to "benefit" from Philemon (20), as well as when he says that Onesimus was formerly "useless" to Philemon but is now "useful" to Paul (11).

Links to Philippians

The letter itself does not specify the location of either Paul or Philemon. Two clues, however, suggest that Paul may have written Philemon from the same place where he wrote Philippians, which, as we have seen, was probably Ephesus during the early or mid 50s. Philemon would have been nearby in Colossae.

1. In Philemon 23, Paul mentions "Epaphras, my fellow captive in Christ Jesus." The name "Epaphras" is a shortened form of "Epaphroditus." This Epaphras, then, may have been the same person as Epaphroditus, who ran errands between Paul and the Philippians (Phil 2:25; 4:18).

2. In the letter to Philemon, Paul expects to be released from prison (Philem 22), just as he does in Philippians (Phil 1:24–26, 2:24). He asks Philemon to prepare a guest room for him (Philem 22). These plans are consistent with his plans in Philippians: after his release, Paul will spend some time with Philemon, apparently nearby, then go on to Philippi in Macedonia.

Other Clues

Two other clues likewise suggest that Paul wrote the letters to Philemon and the Philippians from Ephesus.

1. Around the year 108 CE, Ignatius, the bishop of Antioch in Syria, wrote to the church in Ephesus, mentioning "Onesimus, a man of inexpressible love and your bishop" (Eph 1:3). This, of course, could have been a different Onesimus. If he was the same Onesimus, he would have been around eighty years old when Ignatius wrote. If he was the same man, we can infer that Philemon complied with Paul's request. Onesimus returned to Paul (apparently in Ephesus), at some point gained his freedom, and eventually became bishop of the Ephesian church.

2. If Paul wrote the letter of Colossians (which is disputed), it sheds light on Onesimus' background. Colossians is addressed to the church at Colossae in Asia Minor near Ephesus. According to this letter, Onesimus came from Colossae (Col 4:9). Assuming that Onesimus fled from Philemon in Colossae, many scholars find it more likely that he encountered Paul imprisoned nearby in Ephesus rather than in distant Rome or Caesarea.

DISCUSSION QUESTION

Read Philemon along with the following passages relating to slavery: those in other acknowledged letters of Paul (Gal 3:27–28; 1 Cor 7:17–24) and those in letters whose authorship is disputed (Col 3:9–11; 3:22–4:1; Eph 6:5–9). What attitudes toward slavery do these passages reflect? How do they differ from modern attitudes?

REVIEW QUESTIONS

1. Identify: Prison Epistles, Epaphroditus, Philemon, Onesimus.
2. What evidence suggests that Philippians was compiled from more than one letter or letter fragment?
3. Describe the historical setting of Philippians.
4. What considerations favor Ephesus over Caesarea and Rome as Paul's place of imprisonment when he wrote Philippians?
5. What are the central themes of Philippians?
6. Why did Paul write the letter to Philemon?
7. What clues suggest that Paul wrote Philemon from the same place where he wrote Philippians? What clues suggests that this place was Ephesus?

SUGGESTIONS FOR FURTHER STUDY

Donfried, Karl P., and I. Howard Marshall. *The Theology of the Shorter Pauline Letters* (Cambridge University Press, 1993). A brief discussion of the setting, themes, and significance of Philippians and Philemon, among others.

Fitzmyer, Joseph A. *The Letter to Philemon: A New Translation with Introduction and Commentary* (Anchor Bible; Doubleday; Yale University Press, 2000. A standard commentary on Philemon.

Martin, Ralph P. *A Hymn of Christ: Philippians 2:5–11 in Recent Interpretation and in the Setting of Early Christian Worship* (3rd ed.; InterVarsity, 1997). Interprets Philippians 2:5–11 as a pre-Pauline hymn used in early Christian worship.

Reumann, John. *Philippians: A New Translation with Introduction and Commentary* (Anchor Yale Bible; Yale University Press, 2008). A standard commentary on Philippians. Treats Philippians as a composite of three letters.

25   Prison Epistles (2)
Colossians and Ephesians

The letters of Colossians and Ephesians show striking similarities in content and wording. Though both claim to be written from prison by Paul, scholars debate whether Paul wrote both of them, one of them, or neither.

MYTH AND RITUAL IN COLOSSIANS

Before we discuss the authorship of Colossians, it will help to examine its main religious ideas. To analyze these, we will use two categories from the comparative study of religion: myth and ritual. "Myth," as scholars of religion use the term, refers to a story that has special significance for a religion or culture. Often the story relates the actions of supernatural beings or heroes. Myths of origin tell how things got to be the way they are. For example, numerous cultures have creation myths, which tell how the world began. Other myths of origin include myths concerning the origin of death and myths of alienation, which tell how humans became alienated from their creator. Some religions also have redeemer myths, which tell how a divine being or hero rescued the world in some way. We also find eschatological myths, which relate the end or culmination of history. Related to myths are rituals, sacred actions or ceremonies, which enable the practitioner to participate in the events of the myth.

Using these categories to analyze Colossians, we find that the author knew a creation myth, an alienation myth, a redeemer myth, and an eschatological myth. He also knew a ritual, baptism, which allowed his readers to participate in the mythic drama of redemption. Though the author did not relate these myths in sequence, we can reconstruct much of them from what he did say.

Creation Myth

According to the author's creation myth, in the beginning "the invisible God" dwelt "above" in a realm of "light" (1:15; 3:1; 1:12). God brought forth a "Son," who was "the image" of his father. He was "the firstborn of all creation." He existed "before all other things" (1:13, 15, 17). God also brought forth the "pleroma," "the fullness" of divinity (1:19; 2:9). Among Gnostics, this term referred to the totality of spiritual powers or beings that emanated from God in the realm of light. It probably has a personal sense here as well, since the pleroma has the ability to decide on a course of action: it "consented to dwell" in the Son (1:19).

The Son created everything else. Through him were created "all things in the heavens and upon the earth, both the visible and the invisible, whether thrones or lordships or rulers or authorities." Not only were these created "through him," they were created "in him." He was not only the creator but also the realm in which creation existed. He contained all things and "all things were held together in him" (1:16–17). Such a conception resembles the Stoic universe, which was both creator and cosmos.

Alienation Myth

Something went wrong with the world that the Son created. Colossians does not tell us how this happened, only the consequences. The things on the earth and the things in the heavens fell out of the light into the darkness. They came under "the authority of the darkness" (1:13). They became "alienated" from the light, "hostile in mind," performing "evil deeds" (1:21).

This evil state of affairs exists for humans as long as they are in "the body of the flesh" (2:11). In this state they are subject to "the elemental spirits of the world" (2:8, 20), the spiritual "rulers and authorities" (2:15). They are "dead" in their "transgressions" (2:13), and there is a "hand-written set of decrees" (the Jewish Law) that is against them (2:14).

Redeemer Myth

God devised a plan to restore the fallen creation, to "reconcile" it back into his Son (1:20). Leaving the realm of light, the Son took on a "body of flesh" on the earth (1:22), in the way that a person puts on clothing. The "whole pleroma" agreed to dwell in him "in bodily form" (1:19; 2:9), perhaps when the Spirit descended on Jesus at his baptism.

Christ's body of flesh was then taken to the cross and nailed there. In taking off the clothing of the flesh through death, Christ stripped off the rulers and authorities who ruled over the flesh, thus triumphing over them (2:15). The blood of his cross made peace between creation and the divine realm (1:20).

God then raised Christ from the dead (2:12). He was "the firstborn from the dead" (1:18). In what sense God raised Christ never becomes clear. Did he raise the physical body in some transformed state, or did he raise Christ's inner person and abandon the troublesome body of flesh? In any case, Christ returned to God and now sits above at his right hand (3:1).

Ritual of Redemption

Believers participate in the Redeemer's triumph through the ritual of baptism. In baptism the believer participates in the death of Christ (2:20; 3:3). Since death removes the body of flesh, baptism is analogous to circumcision, which also removes the flesh (2:11). It also resembles taking off clothing: the believer puts to death or takes off the old person (3:5, 9). Stripping off the body of flesh frees the believer from the elemental spirits that rule the world (2:15, 20). It rescues one from the authority of the darkness (1:13). The believer receives forgiveness for transgressions committed in the flesh, and the handwritten set of decrees against him or her is canceled (1:14; 2:13–14).

In baptism the believer is also symbolically buried and raised with Christ (2:12). The resurrection resembles putting on new clothing, putting on a new person (3:10, 12). For the author of Colossians, this resurrection has in some sense already taken place: "he brought you to life with him" (2:13), "you have been raised with Christ" (3:1; cf. 2:12).

The believer who unites with Christ moves from one realm to another. The old realm, characterized as the authority of the darkness, gives way to the new, characterized as the body of Christ, the church, the kingdom of God's Son, and the allotment of the saints in the light (1:12–13, 18).

This redemption extends not merely to humans, but to all things, whether on earth or in the heavens (1:20). Thus God reconciles the entire cosmos, restores it to its previous state in the Son within the realm of light.

Eschatological Myth

Presently the new life that believers have is "hidden" with Christ in God. At some time in the future, Christ will be "revealed," and believers will be revealed with him in glory (3:3–4). The "wrath of God" will come against "the sons of disobedience" (3:6). Believers will receive what is reserved for them in the heavens, which at present they only hope for (1:5).

DID PAUL WRITE COLOSSIANS?

Could Paul have written this letter, or must we regard it as a "deutero-Pauline" work, written by someone in a Pauline school after Paul's death?

We can pursue this question first by comparing the myth and ritual of Colossians with what we find in the acknowledged letters of Paul. Since Paul's acknowledged letters do not provide enough information to reconstruct his creation myth, we have no basis for comparison there. In other respects, most of the concepts in Colossians have fairly close parallels in Paul's acknowledged letters. Paul, however, does not speak of the "pleroma" consenting to dwell in Jesus or of Jesus "stripping off" the rulers and authorities through death. Paul's conception of resurrection clearly involves the physical body, while that in Colossians is less clear. Generally Paul speaks of the believer's resurrection as still in the future (Rom 6:4, 8), while Colossians speaks of it as already having happened. Yet Paul, too, can speak of the resurrection as in some sense already present. Believers are to consider themselves already alive in Christ (Rom 6:11), as people who have come alive from the dead (Rom 6:13), their bodies as a sacrifice that has come to life (Rom 12:1).

A second way of pursuing the question involves comparing the vocabulary and style of Colossians with Paul's acknowledged letters. Though Paul's key term, "justification," does not occur in Colossians, neither does it appear in Philemon, 1 Thessalonians, or 2 Thessalonians, and it occurs only once in 1 Corinthians. Colossians does employ longer, more complex sentences than Paul normally writes. For example, the lengthy passages Colossians 1:3–8 and 1:9–16a both consist of single sentences. However, long complex sentences can also be found in Paul's acknowledged letters (Rom 1:1–7; 1 Cor 1:4–8).

A third approach compares Colossians with Christian writings from a later time than Paul. Some aspects of the letter may fit better in a period after Paul's death. For example, Colossians 3:18–4:1 gives instructions to members of the household: wives, husbands, children, slaves, and masters (cf. Eph 5:21–6:9). Wives are to submit to husbands, children to parents, and slaves to masters. Such "household codes" typically appear in Christian writings of the late first and early second century (1 Pet 2:18–3:7; Titus 2:1–10; 1 Clement 21:6–9; Polycarp to the Philippians

4:2; Ignatius to Polycarp 4:3–5:2; Didache 4:9–11; Barnabas 19:5–7). The question is whether or not Paul shared the patriarchal attitude of these codes. If he did, Colossians may have expressed Paul's own attitude and served as a model for later writers.

From examining this evidence, scholars come to different conclusions about the authorship of Colossians. On the one hand, certain features of the letter suggest non-Pauline authorship; on the other hand, nothing in the letter seems to absolutely require it. It is probably safe to say that the majority of scholars today do not accept it as a letter of Paul.

HISTORICAL SETTING OF COLOSSIANS

Assuming Paul as Author

If Paul himself wrote the letter of Colossians, he wrote it about the same time as Philemon, from the same prison, since both letters presuppose the same situation. In both letters, Paul has words for Archippus, a leader of the church (Philem 2; Col 4:17). In both letters Epaphras, an associate of Paul from Colossae, is with Paul (Philem 23; Col 1:7, 4:12–13). Also with Paul in both are Aristarchus, Mark, Luke, and Demas (Philem 24; Col 4:10, 14, 24). Both letters mention Onesimus. In Colossians, he accompanies Tychicus, who delivered the letter to the Colossian church (Col 4:7–9). Perhaps Onesimus was at this time delivering the letter of Philemon to his master (Philem 10–12).

In Colossians, Paul writes to a church that he has never visited (Col 2:1). He has heard about the church in Colossae from Epaphras, who was apparently the first to preach the gospel there and in the neighboring cities of Laodicea and Hierapolis (Col 1:7–8; 4:12–13). Epaphras apparently informed Paul that a divergent teaching was being promoted in the church at Colossae, and Paul writes to counter this teaching. As an associate of Paul, Epaphras apparently worked under his direction. This would explain the fact that Paul feels a sense of responsibility for the congregations in the cities where Epaphras has ministered (Col 1:9, 24; 2:1, 5).

Assuming Non-Pauline Authorship

If Paul did not write Colossians, we do not know who wrote it or when or where. Possibly the author belonged to a Pauline school and wrote in the late first or early second century. We can infer the purpose of the letter from its central concern: to combat a type of teaching with which the author disagreed. The author used the name of Paul to give the letter authority and drew on details from the letter of Philemon to create a plausible setting for the Colossian letter in Paul's lifetime. Certain features of the letter, such as the reference to the pleroma, the emphasis on salvation as removal of the flesh, and the possibility of understanding its references to resurrection in a non-physical sense, could mean that the author represented some type of Gnostic Christianity.

READING GUIDE: COLOSSIANS

Read the letter to the Colossians with the help of the following guide.

Introduction (1:1–11)

The author begins in typical Pauline fashion with a salutation (1:1–2) and a thanksgiving (1:3–8). These are followed by a prayer for the Colossians' spiritual growth (1:9–11).

Cosmic Reconciliation (1:12–2:7)

The prayer leads into a description of God's redemptive work in Christ. Colossians visualizes the reconciliation of the entire cosmos or universe to God. This reconciliation takes place through Christ, who occupies the position of "firstborn" in both creation and redemption.

The author describes the redeemed individual as going **from darkness to light (1:12–14)**. He speaks of two realms: "the authority of the darkness" and "the kingdom" of God's Son, which is a realm of "light." The saints (Christians) have been delivered or redeemed out of the former into the latter through having their sins forgiven.

Both creation and redemption involve the **preeminence of the Son (1:15–20)** over all other spiritual powers. The Son is preeminent in both the universe and the church. First, he was "the firstborn of all creation" (1:15). The whole universe was created not only through him but in him. The entire creation exists in him and is therefore held together by him (1:15–17). Second, the Son was also the head of the church, "the firstborn from the dead" (1:18). All the "fullness" (pleroma), the totality of divine being or beings, dwelt in him and reconciled all things to God through his blood (1:18–20). Some scholars have theorized that this passage derives from a pre-Christian hymn adapted by the author of Colossians.

The redemption just described has significance for the **Colossians' experience (1:21–23)**. Though formerly alienated from God, they have now been reconciled.

Supplementing the work of Christ is **Paul's ministry to the church (1:24–2:7)**. "Paul" describes his message as a "mystery" or secret, previously hidden but now revealed by God. He presents himself as a minister of the church, striving to bring the church to a full understanding of this mystery. He expresses concern that the Colossians may be "deluded" by some other teaching (2:4).

A Divergent Philosophy (2:8–23)

The author apparently wrote to combat a specific teaching that was being promoted in the church. In warning against it, he describes it as "philosophy and empty deceit." He regards this teaching as stemming from human tradition or the elemental spirits of the world and not from Christ (2:8).

In criticizing this divergent philosophy, the author first gives two **arguments against following the "elemental spirits" (2:9–15)**, on which it was based. First (2:9–10), the elemental spirits or "principalities and powers" are inferior to Christ, since he is their head and thus provides Christians with the full measure of divinity. Second (2:11–15), Christians are no longer subject to the principalities and powers or their regulations. The author metaphorically depicts Christian baptism as a sort of circumcision, a removal of flesh. The "flesh" is that part of human nature subject to the "principalities and powers" (the ruling spirits of the world) and their written regulations (probably referring to the Jewish Law). Baptism, as a type of circumcision, strips off the flesh and hence the authority of the ruling spirits and their Law.

The author goes on to warn against three specific **features of the divergent philosophy (2:16–23)**. (1) One should not have to keep regulations concerning food ("questions of food and drink," 2:16), or observe religious days and seasons ("festival … new moon … Sabbath," 2:16). The mention of "Sabbath" shows that the philosophy had a Jewish background, although it probably incorporated Hellenistic ideas as well. (2) Nor should one have to practice "self-abasement" (2:18). By self-abasement, the author seems to mean asceticism or self-denial, submitting to regulations such as "don't handle, don't taste, don't touch" (2:21). He further describes it as severe treatment of the body, the exercise of will-power in an attempt to subdue the natural desires of the body (2:23).

(3) The author also condemns "worship of the angels" (2:18) whatever this may mean. Possibly the phrase should be translated as "ritual of the angels," in which case it would refer to observances prescribed by the Jewish Law, which, according to a common belief, was given through angels (Gal 3:19; Heb 2:2).

A Life Worthy of the Lord (3:1–4:6)

In the introduction to the letter, the author says that he prays for the Colossians "to walk worthily of the Lord" (1:10). Here he describes what such a "walk" or life involves.

First, the author contrasts **the new life and the old (3:1–17)**. He uses several baptismal images to contrast the new Christian life with the old life of sin. The believer shares the death, resurrection, and ascension of Christ, thus putting to death the old life "on the earth" and rising again to the new life "above" (3:1–7). As in the dressing and undressing of the baptismal ritual, the believer "takes off" the old life of sin and "puts on" the new life of virtue (3:8–17).

Next the author gives some further **moral exhortation (3:15–4:6)**. This includes a household code (3:18–4:1) and various other exhortations (4:2–6).

Conclusion (4:7–18)

The author concludes with greetings from various co-workers.

ORIGIN OF EPHESIANS

To understand the origin of the letter to the Ephesians we need answers to three questions. Did the same person write both Ephesians and Colossians? Did Paul write Ephesians? And what literary relationship exists between Ephesians and Colossians?

First, did the same person write both Ephesians and Colossians? Both claim the same author (Paul), and they do resemble each other in content and language. About a third of the words in Colossians appear also in Ephesians. At the same time, however, the two letters sometimes appear to use one and the same word with a different meaning. For example, in Colossians, the "mystery" or "secret" revealed by God is Christ (1:27), while in Ephesians it is the union of Gentiles with Jews in the body of Christ

(3:4–6). From such differences, many scholars have inferred that the two letters had different authors, one of which borrowed from the other.

Colossians and Ephesians compared

COLOSSIANS	EPHESIANS
Salutation (1:1–2)	Salutation (1:1–2)
	Extended blessing of God (1:3–14)
	a. Spiritual blessings in Christ (1:3–8)
	b. Secret of unity in Christ (1:9–14)
Thanksgiving (1:3–4)	Thanksgiving (1:15–16a)
Ministry of Epaphras (1:5–8)	
Prayer for understanding (1:9–14)	Prayer for understanding (1:16b–19)
Ode to Christ (1:15–20)	Ode to Christ (1:20–23)
Reconciliation of the alienated (1:21–22)	Reconciliation of the alienated (2:1–10)
Proviso (1:23a)	
	Unity of Gentiles with Jews (2:11–22)
Ministry of Paul (1:23b–29)	Ministry of Paul (3:1–13)
Word to Colossae and Laodicea (2:1–5)	
Rooted and established (2:6–7)	Rooted and established (3:14–19)
	Doxology (3:20–21)
Warning against Jewish teaching (2:8–18)	
	Plea for unity of the body (4:1–14)
Growth from the head (2:19)	Growth from the head (4:15–16)
Warning continued (2:20–23)	
Seek things above (3:1–4)	
The old life and the new (3:5–15)	The old life and the new (4:17–5:17)
Song and music (3:16–17)	Song and music (5:18–20)
Household code (3:18–4:1)	Household code (5:21–6:9)
	Spiritual warfare (6:10–17)
Pray for Paul (4:2–4)	Pray for Paul (6:18–20)
Wise conduct and speech (4:5–6)	See 5:15–16, 4:29
About Tychicus and Onesimus (4:7–9)	About Tychicus (6:21–22)
Greetings from co-workers (4:10–17)	
Paul's signature (4:18a)	Peace, love, faith (6:23)
Best wishes (4:18b)	Best wishes (6:24)

Second, did Paul write Ephesians? The author of Ephesians identifies himself as Paul, yet certain ideas in the letter appear to differ from Paul's normal usage. For example, in Ephesians 2:16 Christ is the agent of reconciliation, while God performs this function in Paul's acknowledged letters. In Ephesians 2:20, the church is built on the foundation of the apostles and prophets, Christ being the cornerstone, while in 1 Corinthians 3:11 Christ is the exclusive foundation. Furthermore certain features of the letter seem to stand closer to the thought of a later time than to the thought of Paul, such as the reference to "the holy apostles and prophets" (Eph 3:5) and the household code in Ephesians 5:21–6:9. Finally, Ephesians consistently employs longer, more complex sentences than Paul normally writes. For instance, after the salutation (1:1–2), the rest of the first chapter consists of only three sentences (1:3–14, 1:15–21, 1:22–23). According to one estimate, such features of Ephesians have convinced about 80 percent of critical scholars that Paul did not write it.

Third, what literary relationship exists between Ephesians and Colossians? A comparison of the letters (see the box above) shows that the letters follow the same basic order with some differences in the material included. What relationship would explain these features? Most scholars think that Ephesians depends on Colossians. Let us assume therefore that an unknown editor revised the letter of Colossians to produce Ephesians. How would this explain the similarities and differences?

1. For the most part, the two letters take up the same topics in the same order. This indicates that the editor retained most of the topics in Colossians in the same order they occurred there. Hence his revision, Ephesians, has the same basic structure as Colossians.

2. A few passages occur only in Colossians. With one exception (Col 3:1–4), these are on topics that relate specifically to the situation at Colossae or Laodicea and would not be relevant to any other situation (Col 1:5–8; 2:1–5; 2:8–18, 20–23; 4:10–17). We can infer that the editor wished to revise the letter so that it would be relevant to a different, more general audience than the church at Colossae. He therefore omitted any material that would be relevant only to the specific situation at Colossae, and therefore irrelevant for his readers.

3. A few passages occur only in Ephesians. Several of these address the same topic: the unity of Gentiles with Jews in the one body of Christ (Eph 1:9–14; 2:11–22; cf. 4:1–14). Other topics appear as well (Eph 1:3–8; 3:20–21; 6:10–17). Whoever wrote this letter seems especially concerned to promote the unity of Jews and Gentiles.

Figure 25.1
Greek inscription on a stone from the outer wall of Herod's temple, warning Gentiles not to enter the inner court on pain of death. Ephesians speaks of Christ breaking down this wall that kept Gentiles from the house of God (2:11–22). Archaeological Museum, Istanbul, Turkey (Erich Lessing/Art Resource, NY).

4. When the two letters discuss the same topic, generally Ephesians is longer and uses more "flowery" language. This indicates that the editor did not simply copy the letter of Colossians, but rewrote it in his own words, expanding on its ideas.

5. Colossians ends with Paul's signature (Col 4:18a), where Ephesians has merely a wish for peace and love (Eph 6:23). The absence of Paul's signature in Ephesians suggests that the editor was not Paul. If Paul had been revising one of his own letters, he would not have hesitated to retain his own signature. The actual editor, however, while feeling the freedom to revise a letter that he probably thought Paul wrote, did not wish to fake Paul's signature. He therefore substituted a sentence wishing his readers peace and love.

6. The editor does retain from Colossians one reference to a specific situation: the passage identifying Tychicus as the one carrying the letter from Paul to the readers (6:21–22). Why would the editor retain this when he so carefully omitted every other reference to a specific situation? Could it be that this is the one piece of specific information that continued to be relevant for the revised letter of Ephesians? Or did the editor retain it simply to create a sense of authenticity for his letter?

These features of Ephesians are consistent with the view that it originated when an editor revised the letter of Colossians. This editor was not Paul but probably believed that Paul had written Colossians. He took a letter written to a specific audience and revised it to make it applicable to a more general audience.

RECIPIENTS OF EPHESIANS

Though this letter bears the traditional name "Ephesians," scholars agree that it was not written exclusively to the church in Ephesus. The traditional name comes from 1:1, where many manuscripts have the reading, "to the saints who are at Ephesus and believers in Christ Jesus." Other important manuscripts, however, omit the words "at Ephesus," thus reading "to the saints who are also believers in Christ Jesus." An examination of the letter confirms that it could not have been written exclusively to Ephesus. The author, speaking as Paul, writes to a church with which he had no personal contact. He had only heard of their faith and could only assume that they had heard of him (Eph 1:15; 3:1–3). Since Paul spent two years with the church at Ephesus (Acts 19:10), he could hardly have written that he did not know them.

If not the Ephesians, then who received the letter? According to one theory, Paul or one of his disciples wrote this letter as a circular letter to the churches of Asia. Since it went to more than one church, the author left a blank space in the address, which was filled in by Tychicus as he delivered copies of the letter to the various churches. The copies that survived came partly from the version that left a blank and partly from the version of the letter addressed to Ephesus.

A variation of this theory avoids the need to attribute the letter to Paul or one of his disciples. A later author wrote it as a circular letter with no specific address, but a scribe at Ephesus found the letter there and added Ephesus as the address. Later scribes made copies from both the version with no address and the version addressed to Ephesus.

HISTORICAL SETTING OF EPHESIANS

If Ephesians represents a revision of Colossians, then our judgments about its historical setting depend in part on our prior decisions about Colossians.

If Paul wrote Colossians, then Ephesians could have been written during his lifetime, even with his approval. We could imagine Paul somewhere in prison, unable to write, entrusting an associate with the task of revising his letter to Colossae for a different audience, perhaps the churches of Asia Minor. We could even imagine that this associate was Tychicus, who then carried the letter to its destination.

If Colossians came not from Paul, but from a semi-Gnostic author in the late first or early second century, then Ephesians would have to be dated still later. The letter's lack of reference to any specific situation prevents us from identifying its place of origin or destination.

READING GUIDE: EPHESIANS

Read the letter of Ephesians with the help of the following guide.

Introduction (1:1–14)

After the salutation (1:1–2) the author introduces the two central themes of the first part of the letter: (1) God has blessed the believer with "every spiritual blessing in the heavenly places in Christ" (1:3–7, esp. 1:3); and (2) he has made known "the secret of his will," which is to unite all things in Christ (1:8–14, esp. 1:9–10).

Theological Instruction (1:15–3:21)

In the first part of the letter, the author develops the two themes presented in the introduction.

He first addresses the theme of **spiritual blessings in the heavenly places (1:15–2:10)**. According to the author, Christ has been seated at the right hand of God in the heavenly places (1:15–23). As members of his body through faith, believers have participated in his exaltation and have been seated with him there (2:1–10).

Next he addresses the **secret of God's will (2:11–3:21)**. God has revealed his hidden purpose to unite everything in Christ. In particular, Jew and Gentile have been reconciled to God in one body in Christ (2:11–22). Paul has been appointed to make the secret known (3:1–13).

The first section concludes with a **prayer and a doxology (3:14–21)**: a prayer for the readers (3:14–19) and a doxology giving honor to God (3:20–21).

A Life Worthy of the Christian Calling (4:1–6:20)

The second part of the letter gives ethical instruction so that the readers may lead a life worthy of their calling (Eph 4:1; cf. Col 1:10).

The author depicts the **church as one body (4:1–16)**. As in 1 Corinthians 12, the author emphasizes the unity of the body of Christ while describing the different functions of its members. Like a human body, the church must grow to maturity through the proper functioning of each member.

The author contrasts the **old person and the new (4:17–5:20)**. As in Paul's acknowledged letters, he bases moral conduct on participation in the death and resurrection of Christ. The believer must put off the old human nature and put on the new.

The author also gives **instructions to household members (5:21–6:9)**. This "household code" is more detailed than that in Colossians 3:18–4:1.

Finally, the author depicts the Christian life as **spiritual warfare (6:10–20)**. He compares the Christian life to a war in which the attacking forces are not humans, but evil spirits.

Conclusion (6:21–24)

In conclusion, the author identifies the messenger as Tychicus and wishes his audience peace and love.

DISCUSSION QUESTIONS

1. *Creation and redemption.* Describe the creation myth and the redemption myth that are expressed in Colossians 1:15–20. Respond to one or more of the following questions. What does it mean for Christ to be "the image of the invisible God"? In what two different senses is he the "firstborn"? What is his relation to the rest of creation both before and after reconciliation? You may use other passages from Colossians to clarify your answer.

2. *Roles of husband and wife.* In Ephesians 5:22–33, the author compares husband and wife with Christ and the church and with head and body. Do you think these analogies for marriage are helpful for today? Why or why not?

REVIEW QUESTIONS

1. What different types of myths occur in Colossians? Briefly summarize each. How does the ritual of baptism enable the Christian believer to participate in the events of the myth?

2. What are three ways of pursuing the question of whether Paul wrote Colossians?

3. Describe the historical setting of the Colossian letter, first assuming that Paul wrote it, then assuming that he did not.

4. What similarities and differences exist between Colossians and Ephesians? How are these features explained by the theory that an editor revised Colossians to produce Ephesians?

5. What evidence shows that Ephesians was not written exclusively to the church in Ephesus? What are two theories about the audience to whom the letter was actually written?

SUGGESTIONS FOR FURTHER STUDY

Best, Ernest. *Ephesians* (New Testament Guides; Sheffield Academic Press, 1993). A brief discussion of critical issues, contents, leading themes, occasion and purpose.

Best, Ernest. *Ephesians* (ICC; Bloomsbury T&T Clark, 1998). A standard commentary on Ephesians.

DeMaris, Richard E. *The Colossian Controversy: Wisdom in Dispute at Colossae* (Sheffield Academic Press, 1994). Surveys theories concerning the teaching opposed in Colossians, arguing that it consisted of a combination of Judaism and Middle Platonism.

Kiley, Mark. *Colossians as Pseudepigraphy* (JSOT, 1986). Marshals the arguments against Paul's authorship, discusses ancient attitudes toward pseudepigraphy, and argues that Colossians was modeled on Philippians and Philemon by someone other than Paul.

Lincoln, Andrew T., and A. J. M. Wedderburn. *The Theology of the Later Pauline Letters* (Cambridge University Press, 1993). Discusses the background, theology, and significance of Colossians and Ephesians.

Lohse, Eduard. *Colossians and Philemon* (Hermeneia; Fortress, 1971). Still the standard commentary on Colossians.

PART V
Judaic Christianity

26   Judaic Christianity

As explained in Chapter 7, the term "Jewish Christian" in a broad sense refers to any Jew who believed in Jesus as some sort of savior figure. In this sense, Paul was a Jewish Christian, as were any number of other people who disagreed with him and with each other. While Jewish Christianity was diverse, this chapter focuses on one particular type: Jews who acknowledged Jesus as the Messiah but continued to practice the religion of Judaism as the way to God. We have been referring to these people as "Judaic Christians." Here we will look at their history, literature, and religion.

HISTORY OF JUDAIC CHRISTIANITY

Judaic Christians in Acts and Paul

According to Acts, different attitudes toward the Law already existed in the community at Jerusalem. Jews charged the Hellenist Stephen with having a lenient attitude toward the Law, and in the aftermath the Hellenists got run out of town. The apostles, representing the Hebrews, stayed on, presumably because they had a more traditional view of the Law. In this account, then, different attitudes toward the Law existed in Christianity from the beginning, with the Hebrews being the more conservative. While we might suspect that not all Hebrews were conservative and not all Hellenists liberal, this picture of differing attitudes toward the Law is historically plausible. It is likely therefore that those who remained in Jerusalem at the death of Stephen were predominantly Judaic Christians.

The issue of the Law came to a head once more when Gentiles joined the movement. In Acts, Judaic Christians teach that Gentile converts must keep the Law in order to be saved (Acts 15:1, 5). James and the apostles at Jerusalem convene a council, rule against them, and that is the end of the matter. The letters of Paul give a somewhat different picture, since Paul seems to run into these Judaic Christians with regularity. The emissaries of James who come to Antioch seem to represent this perspective (Gal 2:11–14). Paul, who taught freedom from the Law, wasted no kind words on Judaic Christians who taught the need to keep the Law. He characterized them as dogs (Phil 3:2), cursed them (Gal 1:8), and wished they would not simply circumcise, but castrate themselves (Gal 5:12).

Judaic Christians after 70 ce

We have only sketchy knowledge concerning Judaic Christianity after the destruction of Jerusalem in 70 CE. According to one tradition, the church at Jerusalem fled shortly before the war to Pella, a Gentile city east of the Jordan River (Eusebius, *Ecclesiastical History* 3.5.3). Earlier traditions speak of a flight from Jerusalem without specifying Pella as the destination (Mark 13:14; Rev 12:6, 13–14). Another tradition assumes that Jewish Christians remained in Jerusalem following the war and that a cousin of Jesus named Simeon took the place of leadership vacated when James the brother of Jesus was killed (Eusebius, *Ecclesiastical History* 4.22.4). Whatever may be the case, after the destruction of Jerusalem the Jewish church never regained a position of preeminence there.

As we have seen, the author of Acts says that the Judaic Christians in Jerusalem were called "the sect of the **Nazoreans**" (Acts 24:5). The Nazoreans were ultimately repudiated by the larger Jewish community. At some time between 80 and 95 CE, certain Jewish synagogues in the East revised the daily prayer to include the curse "May the Nazoreans and heretics perish in a moment."

Proto-Orthodox Christianity also repudiated Judaic Christians. For example, Ignatius, the Proto-Orthodox bishop of Antioch in the early second century, knew of Judaic Christians, whom he condemned: "It is wrong to speak of Jesus Christ and practice Judaism." Ignatius justifies this attitude with the surprising, and inaccurate, claim that "Christianity did not base its faith on Judaism, but Judaism on Christianity" (Magnesians 10:3).

Judaic Christians according to Justin

About the middle of the second century, the Christian apologist Justin mentions Judaic Christians (*Dialogue* 46–47). They continued to observe the Jewish Law, practicing circumcision, keeping the Sabbath and other

Figure 26.1
A detail from the Arch of Titus, built to celebrate Titus' conquest of Jerusalem in 70 CE. The scene shows the Romans carrying away loot, including the sacred seven-branched lampstand from the temple. Alinari/Art Resource, NY.

Jewish holy days, and observing the rules of ritual purity. Some of these taught Gentile Christians that they too must observe the Law in order to be saved and apparently persuaded some Gentile Christians to do so. Justin, who had lived in Palestine, had a certain amount of tolerance for Christians who continued to practice Judaism. He believed that Judaic Christians who observed the Law would be saved if they did not try to persuade Gentiles that they must do the same. He also believed that even the Gentile Christians who were persuaded to keep the Law would be saved. However, he knew of other people who disagreed and who refused to associate with those Christians who kept the Law.

Judaic Christians according to Irenaeus

At the end of the second century (c. 182–88 CE), Irenaeus described the beliefs and practices of Judaic Christians whom he called "**Ebionites.**" This term, a Hebrew word meaning "the poor," first appears in Irenaeus as the name of a distinct sect, but more general references to Jewish Christians as "the poor" occur already in the New Testament (Matt 5:3; Rom 15:26; Gal 2:10; James 2:5). According to Irenaeus,

> Those who are called Ebionites agree that the world was made by God; but their opinions with respect to the Lord are similar to those

of Cerinthus and Carpocrates. They use the Gospel according to Matthew only, and repudiate the Apostle Paul, maintaining that he was an apostate from the Law. As to the prophetic writings, they endeavor to expound them in a somewhat singular manner. They practice circumcision, persevere in the observance of those customs which are enjoined by the Law, and are so Judaic in their style of life that they even adore Jerusalem as if it were the house of God. (*Against Heresies* 1.26.2, ANF)

According to this description, Ebionites continued to observe the Jewish Law and opposed the teaching of Paul that one could be justified by faith in Jesus apart from the Law. Like Cerinthus (cf. Irenaeus, *Against Heresies* 1.26.1), they believed that Jesus was a normal human being, born in a normal manner to Joseph and Mary, and that his power came from the Spirit that descended on him after his baptism. Presumably they regarded Jesus as the Messiah, though Irenaeus leaves this unsaid. Irenaeus' statement that they used the Gospel of Matthew is probably mistaken, since Matthew includes the story of Jesus' birth from a virgin. Later authors such as Jerome suggest that they used one or more gospels written in Hebrew or Aramaic similar to the Gospel of Matthew. Unlike Justin, Irenaeus did not regard such Judaic Christianity as a viable way of salvation. He included the Ebionites along with Gnostics and other groups that he considered heretical.

Other References to Judaic Christians

Several other Christian writers also mention Jewish Christians who lived east of the Jordan after the war. They generally refer to these as either Ebionites or Nazoreans. Sometimes the writers use these names interchangeably; at other times, in reference to different groups with distinctive perspectives. Such references occur down to the beginning of the fifth century, most of them probably based on Irenaeus. After that time we hear little more about Judaic Christians. A type of Christianity that had existed from the beginning of the movement thus faded into obscurity.

LITERATURE OF JUDAIC CHRISTIANITY

Fortunately for our knowledge of early Christianity, some Judaic-Christian literature survived the demise of its authors. Some of this material we have already encountered in our study of the gospels.

The **Markan material**, the material that Mark shares with Matthew and/or Luke, has a Judaic-Christian cast. The controversy stories in particular presuppose a group of Judaic Christians who kept the Law while disputing its interpretation with other Jewish groups. Keeping the commandments of the Law led to eternal life (Mark 10:17–19). Those who kept the Law were "righteous" (Mark 2:17).

The **source known as Q** reflects a Judaic-Christian community engaged in missionary activity among other Jews and waiting for the coming Son of Man. For this community, the Law would remain in force as long as heaven and earth endured (Matt 5:18/Luke 16:17).

Much of **Matthew's special material** came from a similar type of community. Jesus did not abolish the Law, which meant that even the least of its commandments remained in force (Matt 5:17, 19).

The **letter of James**, which we will discuss in Chapter 27, reveals a type of Judaic-Christian community that emphasized the need to perform the good deeds required by the Law.

The **Didache**, which we will discuss in Chapter 28, preserves instructions for the rituals and leadership of a Judaic-Christian community. It instructs members to keep as much of the Law as they can (Didache 6:2–3).

The **Pseudo-Clementine Recognitions 1.27–71**, a fictional debate between the disciples of Jesus and other Jewish groups, has a Judaic-Christian character.

Early Christian authors also give isolated quotations from one or more lost **Jewish-Christian gospels**. They attribute the quotations variously to the Gospel of the Nazoreans, the Gospel of the Ebionites, or the Gospel of the Hebrews, but whether these were the same or different gospels remains uncertain.

THE RELIGION OF JUDAIC CHRISTIANITY

An examination of the sources that have survived allows us to gain a modest understanding of the main beliefs and practices of Judaic Christianity. As we did in discussing the religion of Pauline Christianity (Chapter 18), we will examine its conceptual, social, ritual, and ethical dimensions.

Conceptual Dimension

Judaic Christians differed from other varieties of early Christianity primarily in their **view of the Law**. They continued to rely on the Jewish Law as the way to God. We have already seen this, for example, in the

Synoptic controversy stories, in Q, and in Matthew's special material (e.g. Matt 5:17–19). The same is true of Justin's Judaic Christians and Irenaeus' Ebionites. After the destruction of the temple, Judaic Christians could no longer offer sacrifices, but would have continued other aspects of Judaism.

Judaic Christians also differed in their **view of Jesus' nature and function**. With respect to his nature, Irenaeus' Ebionites thought of him as a normal human being, though empowered by the Spirit of God, a perspective that is also reflected in the triple tradition.

With respect to Jesus' function, Judaic Christianity identified him as the Messiah, the son of God, and the Son of Man. However, just as Judaism in general had different conceptions of the Messiah, so did Judaic Christianity. One strand thought of him as the Davidic Messiah, the son of David (Matt 1:1; Didache 9:2). Another argued that the Messiah was not the son of David but superior to David (Mark 12:35–37). Both strands thought of the Messiah primarily as an eschatological figure. Jesus' primary function as Messiah still lay in the future when he would return to execute judgment.

Unlike Paul, Judaic Christianity placed little emphasis on the death of Jesus as a saving event. For Paul, faith in the atoning power of Jesus' death had replaced the Jewish Law as the means of salvation. Judaic Christians, however, rejected this view. The triple tradition views Jesus' death primarily as an embarrassment to the claim that he was the Messiah. It seeks to defend Jesus' messianic status against this embarrassment by emphasizing the necessity of his death (Mark 8:31; 9:30–31; 10:32–34). In the triple tradition and in Q, Jesus dies as a prophet whose message was rejected (Mark 12:1–9; Matt 5:11–12/ Luke 6:22–23; Matt 23:34/Luke 11:49; Matt 23:37–39/Luke 13:34–35; cf. Luke 13:31–33). In most of the surviving Judaic-Christian literature, including Matthew's special material, James, and the Didache, the death of Jesus receives little or no attention.

Social Dimension

Judaic Christians held religious **meetings** like those of other Jews. They met in local synagogues with other Jews until they were expelled or left to form their own synagogues. The book of James reflects a situation in which Judaic Christians met in their own synagogues or churches (James 2:2; 5:14). The community of Matthew's special material had its own churches (Matt 16:18; 18:17). Presumably they continued to observe the Jewish Sabbath on the seventh day. At least some also met on the first day of the week in honor of Christ's resurrection on that day (Didache 14:1; Eusebius, *Ecclesiastical History* 3.27.5).

In Judaic-Christian groups, **leadership** was provided by two types of ministers: itinerant and resident. The itinerant ministers included apostles and prophets who ministered to various communities for a period of time or stopped off on the way to some other place. Such travelers might take undue advantage of the community's hospitality or bring a message that conflicted with what it had been taught. Some groups therefore drew up guidelines to distinguish those they considered true apostles and prophets from those they considered false (Matt 7:15–20; Didache 11:1–12).

The resident ministers included prophets and teachers who decided to take up residence with a particular community (Acts 13:1; Didache 13:1–7). The community esteemed such persons and supported them, generally with goods rather than money. Other resident leaders were elders ("presbyters" in Greek). In Jewish communities, the elders were a group of eminent older men who served as a sort of advisory council to the community. Acts mentions elders in the churches of Judea (Acts 11:29–30; 15:2). James also mentions "the elders of the church" (James 5:14). Instead of elders, the Didache refers to *episcopoi*, i.e. "overseers" or "bishops" (Didache 15:1–2; cf. Phil 1:1).

Ritual Dimension

Judaic Christians continued to observe the **rites and practices of Judaism**. Justin and Irenaeus refer to Judaic Christians who practiced circumcision. The Didache shows that Judaic Christians continued to observe the food laws, although it does not condemn non-observance: "Concerning food, bear what you can" (Didache 6:3). The surviving Judaic-Christian literature emphasizes the importance of three pillars of Jewish piety: charitable giving, prayer, and fasting (e.g. Matt 6:1–18; James 2:14–17; Didache 1:5–6; 4:5–8; 8:1–3). The prayer known as "the Lord's Prayer" became a part of the ritual prayer of Judaic Christians (Matt 6:9–13; cf. Luke 11:1–4), which they prayed three times a day (Didache 8:1–3).

Judaic Christians also practiced **baptism**. The Didache gives the earliest example of instruction given to the convert before baptism (Didache

1:1–7:1). This community either immersed the convert in water or poured water on his or her head (Didache 7:1–3).

The significance of baptism varied among different groups. While Paul interpreted baptism as a participation in the death, burial, and resurrection of Jesus (Rom 6:1–11), no Judaic-Christian text makes this connection. Two different perspectives do appear. (1) Some Judaic Christians did not distinguish their baptism from that of John (Acts 19:1–7). It imparted forgiveness of sins in preparation for the coming kingdom of God. Such a perspective may be reflected in the pre-baptismal instruction given in the Didache (1:1–7:1), which makes no mention of Jesus' death and resurrection or the Spirit, but does give extensive moral instruction. (2) Other Judaic Christians may have distinguished their baptism from that of John as the ritual through which one received the Holy Spirit and became a "son" of God (Mark 1:9–11; cf. Gal 4:6; Acts 19:1–7).

Judaic Christians also shared **community meals** that had religious as well as social significance. In the early Jewish community at Jerusalem, the believers ate together daily (Acts 2:46). In other places, believers shared a weekly meal when they came together on the first day of the week (Didache 14:1).

Christian community meals resembled regular Jewish family meals. Among Jews, the staple diet was bread. At a Jewish meal, the male head of the household took the bread, gave thanks to God, broke the bread in pieces with his hands, and distributed it (cf. Acts 27:35). This practice characterized the meals of Christians, who met to "break bread." The nature of the community meal differed from place to place and at different periods of history.

1. Mark 6:32–44 (cf. 8:1–9) describes a complete meal that consisted of bread and fish. Though the story is about Jesus, the person who composed it probably modeled it on Judaic-Christian meal practices that were familiar to the author. Murals painted by Christians in the catacombs at Rome give a prominent place to fish in the common meals.

2. Didache 9–10 describes a complete meal that consisted of wine and bread. The author calls the meal the "Eucharist" ("thanksgiving"), a name transferred from the prayers of thanksgiving offered to God with the meal. The meal in the Didache had the same significance as the community meal at Qumran: it foreshadowed the gathering of the community into the messianic kingdom of the new age (Didache 9:4; 10:5). Unlike Paul, the author does not connect the meal with the death of Jesus.

Ethical Dimension

In the Judaic-Christian literature that survives, we see a tendency to identify the heart of the Law with two commandments: to love God and to love your neighbor (Mark 12:28–34; Q/Luke 10:25–28; James 2:8; Didache 1:2; cf. Rom 13:8–10). James exhorts his readers to show love of neighbor in practical ways, such as providing necessities for the poor (1:27; 2:14–17). Going beyond love of neighbor, Q and the Didache call for love of one's enemies (Matt 5:45–48/Luke 6:27–28, 32–36; Didache 1:3) and nonresistance to evil (Matt 5:39b–42/Luke 6:29–30; Didache 1:4). The Didache gives a detailed description of good and bad conduct in terms of two paths one might take: the path of life and the path of death (Didache 1–6; cf. Matt 7:13–14/Luke 13:23–24).

REVIEW QUESTIONS

1. Identify: Nazoreans, Ebionites.
2. Describe the attitudes expressed toward Judaic Christians by Paul, Ignatius, Justin, and Irenaeus.
3. What literature from Judaic Christianity has survived?
4. What was the primary difference between Judaic Christianity and other forms of early Christianity?
5. What views did Judaic Christians have about Jesus' nature and function?
6. Describe the meetings and leadership of Judaic Christianity.
7. What Jewish practices and customs did Judaic Christians continue to observe?
6. How did Judaic-Christian views of baptism and community meals differ from those of Paul?
7. Describe the ethical dimension of Judaic Christianity.

SUGGESTIONS FOR FURTHER STUDY

Jackson-McCabe, Matt, ed. *Jewish Christianity Reconsidered: Rethinking Ancient Groups and Texts* (Fortress, 2007). A collection of essays by various scholars on Jewish-Christian groups and texts.

Klijn, A. F. J. *Jewish-Christian Gospel Tradition* (Brill, 1992). Examines the lost gospels of Jewish Christianity based on quotations from them in Proto-Orthodox authors.

Klijn, A. F. J., and G. J. Reinink. *Patristic Evidence for Jewish-Christian Sects* (Brill, 1973). A study of references to Jewish Christianity in early Christian writers.

Luedemann, Gerd. *Opposition to Paul in Jewish Christianity* (Fortress, 1989). Reviews the history of scholarship on Jewish Christianity and examines the ancient sources that mention opposition to Paul by Jewish Christians.

Vielhauer, Philipp, and Georg Strecker. "Jewish-Christian Gospels," in *New Testament Apocrypha*, ed. W. Schneemelcher, 1.134–78 (rev. ed.; Westminster John Knox, 1991). Discusses and translates early Christian quotations from Jewish-Christian gospels.

27   The Letter of James

The Protestant reformer Martin Luther had a definite dislike for the letter of James. He called it "an epistle of straw" and tried to exclude it from the canon. He thought that James contradicted Paul's teaching on justification by faith and preached the Law rather than Christ. Luther was right that James has a different perspective than Paul, but before we remove it from the canon, we should understand why it differs. Unlike Paul, this letter represents the tradition of Judaic Christianity, a perspective found among Jewish Christians who continued to keep the Law. It consists primarily of instruction and encouragement to live a good life, emphasizing the need to "do" or to keep the ethical aspects of the Law. Like other literature of Judaic Christianity, it places little emphasis on faith in Jesus or his death but regards Jesus primarily as the future Messiah.

JAMES WHO?

The author of the letter identifies himself simply as "James, a servant of God and Lord Jesus Christ" (1:1). Tradition identifies him as James the brother of Jesus, the leader of the early church in Jerusalem. The Jewish historian Josephus and the second-century church historian Hegesippus mention this James. According to these accounts, he was called "James the Just" because of his reputation for righteousness. The Jewish leaders in Jerusalem put him to death shortly before the Romans destroyed the city.

While the letter probably claims this James as its author, we cannot automatically assume that James actually wrote it. The name of "James" also appears on several clearly pseudonymous works from the early

Parallels between James and Matthew

James has literary affinities with Greco-Roman moralists, Jewish literature, and other early Christian literature. Note the following parallels to the sayings tradition in Matthew. James, unlike Matthew, does not attribute this tradition to Jesus.

MATTHEW	JAMES
Blessed are the poor in spirit, for theirs is the kingdom of heaven. (Matt 5:3)	Did God not choose the poor in the world as rich in faith and heirs of the kingdom ...? (James 2:5)
But I tell you not to swear at all, neither by heaven ... nor by earth ... nor by Jerusalem ... nor by your head ... But let your word be "yes, yes, no, no." What is more than these is of the evil one. (Matt 5:34–37)	But above all, my brothers, do not swear, neither by heaven nor by earth nor by any other oath. But let your "yes" be "yes" and your "no" be "no" lest you fall under judgment. (James 5:12)
Whoever exalts himself will be humbled, and whoever humbles himself will be exalted. (Matt 23:12)	Humble yourself before God, and he will exalt you. (James 4:10)

centuries of Christianity, including the Infancy Gospel of James, the Apocryphon of James, and the Acts of James. Many scholars consider this letter pseudonymous also, raising several objections against the view that James the brother of Jesus wrote it.

1. The author's use of Greek seems too fluent for a peasant who spoke Aramaic as his native language. He writes good grammatical Greek and employs literary rhetorical devices. These features of language suggest that the author was not a Palestinian, but a Hellenistic Jew. But do we really know enough about James to judge what type of Greek he would have written? Growing up in bilingual Galilee, James may have spoken Greek as a second language from birth and increased his fluency through education. Perhaps he even used a scribe to write the letter.

2. The author never claims to be the brother of Jesus. Some scholars assume that, if he were the brother of Jesus, he would mention that

relationship. However, if he were someone pretending to be the brother of Jesus, it would be even more likely that he would mention that relationship. If he were the brother of Jesus, that relationship might be so well known to his audience that he felt no need to mention it.

3. In James 2:18–26 the author seems to be arguing against Paul's teaching on justification by faith, but if so, he misunderstood Paul's position (see below). Would James, who knew Paul, have made such a mistake? Perhaps not, yet misunderstandings of Paul arose even during his lifetime (Rom 3:8). Whether or not James could have made such a mistake depends on how well he knew Paul's teaching.

If the letter is pseudonymous, it may have come from a Jewish-Christian writer of the late first century. Some scholars, however, argue that James the brother of Jesus may well have written it. The details of the letter fit well within the context of a Jewish-Christian community in Palestine. Furthermore, it came from a time when the hope that Jesus would return soon had not yet faded (5:7–9). Such a perspective would be more likely in the period before 70 CE, during the lifetime of James, than in the period after 70 CE. If the letter does come from James the brother of Jesus, then it must have been written before his death, dated by Josephus as 62 CE and by Hegesippus as 66 CE. The place of writing would be Jerusalem.

THE JUDAIC CHRISTIANITY OF JAMES

Several features of James show that it originated among Judaic Christians: its Jewish conception of the community, its Jewish conception of faith, its view of salvation by the Law, and the limited role it gives to Jesus.

Jewish Conception of the Community

The author of James uses Jewish terminology to refer to the community to which he writes. First, though he does refer to the congregation as a church (5:14), he also terms it a synagogue (2:2). Second, in writing to Jews outside of Palestine, he addresses them as "the twelve tribes in the Diaspora" (1:1). The "Diaspora" or "dispersion" refers to the nations outside of Palestine to which the Israelites had been scattered by exile and other social forces. The term "twelve tribes" here probably refers not to Jews in general but to Jewish Christians seen as a new Israel. Judaic Christians believed that they represented the regathering of the tribes into a new Israel, each tribe headed by an apostle of Jesus (cf. Matt 19:28/ Luke 22:28–30).

Jewish Conception of Faith

James defines "faith" in a typically Jewish way: "you believe that God is one" (2:19). He refers here to the Jewish confession of faith expressed in the shema: "Hear, O Israel, the Lord (is) our God, the Lord is one" (Deut 6:4). For this author, then, faith means the Jewish confession of faith in one God.

Salvation by the Law

James makes no references to the cultic aspects of the Law, such as circumcision and dietary regulations. Whether or not the community observed these remains unstated. The ethical aspects of the Law, however, have a central place in the teaching of James. The community regarded one commandment of the Law as central: "Love your neighbor as yourself" (2:8; cf. Lev 19:18). James calls this "the royal law" (2:8). It fulfills the commandments "Do not commit adultery" and "Do not commit murder" and prohibits showing partiality (2:8–11). It is "the law of freedom" by which the community will be judged (2:12). It is "the perfect law of freedom" (1:25) which one must not simply hear but do (1:22–25). Doing it involves performing good deeds, such as visiting orphans and widows (1:27) and providing clothes and food for those in need (2:14–17). It is the heart of the Law, which is "the word of truth" given by God (1:17–18), "the implanted word" which is able to save the souls of those who receive it (1:21) and do it (1:22–25).

The letter of James is most famous for the passage in 2:14–26, which argues that a person is justified by works and not by faith alone. This claim seems to contradict Paul's perspective, that a person is justified by faith without works (Rom 3:28). Perhaps the author did want to argue with the Pauline slogan "faith without works." However, to understand James, we must realize that Paul and James represent two different kinds of Christianity and that they use the terms "faith" and "works" in different senses.

On the one hand, Paul wrote for a mixed community of Jews and Gentiles. By "faith" he meant faith in Jesus, and by "works" he meant regulations of the Law such as circumcision. In preaching justification by faith apart from works of the Law, he meant that Jews and Gentiles were justified before God on the same basis, faith in Jesus, without keeping regulations of the Law such as circumcision and dietary restrictions.

On the other hand, James wrote for a community that consisted solely of Jews who continued to follow the Jewish Law as the way to eternal life. By "faith" he meant the Jewish belief in one God (2:19), and by "works" he meant good deeds, such as helping those in need of food and clothing (2:15–16), which fulfilled the command to love one's neighbor. In arguing that faith without works is useless, he meant that in order for his Jewish-Christian community to be justified, they needed not only to believe in one God, but also to perform the good deeds that fulfilled the Law's most important commandment, to "love your neighbor as yourself."

Thus while both Paul and James use the terms "faith" and "works," they use these in different senses to make two different points to two different kinds of early Christian communities.

Limited Role for Jesus

James places little emphasis on Jesus, mentioning him only three times (1:1; 2:1; 5:7–9). Unlike Paul, he bases no teaching on the death or resurrection of Christ. As we have just seen, salvation for James does not come from the death of Jesus but from keeping the ethics of the Law, which saves the souls of those who do it, particularly the "royal law" by which the community will be judged. Nor does James refer to the life of Jesus or use Jesus as an example. Instead, his examples are Abraham, Rahab, Job, and Elijah, characters in the Jewish scriptures (2:23–25; 5:10–11, 17–18). Even when James gives teaching parallel to that in Matthew, he does not attribute it to Jesus.

For James, the important thing about Jesus is not his life, his teaching, or his death, but his future coming as Lord and Christ to execute judgment. He mentions "the faith of our Lord Jesus Christ of glory," apparently meaning the belief that Jesus is Lord and Christ and has been glorified in heaven (2:1). He exhorts his readers to be patient until "the parousia of the Lord" (5:7). This event is imminent: "the parousia of the Lord is at hand" (5:8). When it occurs, Jesus will execute judgment: "behold, the judge stands at the doors" (5:9). This view of Jesus as the future Messiah, with no significance attached to his death, links James to the perspective of other works of Judaic Christianity but distinguishes it from the Christian tradition represented by Paul.

SOCIAL SETTING OF JAMES

The letter of James reveals a few things about the social setting of the author and his community. We can infer that it was written to Judaic Christians in the Diaspora who worshipped in their own synagogues (2:2) or churches (5:14). They had their own elders (5:14), who prayed for the sick, anointing them with oil in the name of the Lord (5:14).

We can also infer that conflict existed between rich and poor in these communities. The congregation included both rich and poor, though the author identifies his readers primarily with the poor (1:9–10). He warns them against a tendency to give preferential treatment to the rich (2:1–4) and encourages them to show special concern for their orphans and widows (2:27). In certain passages, the author condemns the rich, probably meaning those outside the Christian congregation.

He makes two accusations against the rich. First, he accuses them of **economic oppression**. The economy was based on agriculture and trade. Wealthy landowners used hired labor to work their fields (5:4). Merchants traveled to various cities to buy and sell (4:13). The author accuses the landowners of growing wealthy by depriving the workers of their wages (5:4).

Second, he accuses them of **religious persecution**. It was also the wealthy, probably as leaders of the Jewish community, who persecuted Judaic Christians because of their faith in Jesus. They brought them before courts, probably Jewish courts, and denounced the name of Jesus (2:6–7). Apparently they put some of them to death (5:5–6).

The author encourages his readers to regard these difficulties as tests of faith that produce character (1:2–4; 1:12). He comforts them with the hope that the parousia of Jesus is imminent, though he acknowledges the need for patience and endurance (5:7–11).

Outline of James

Scholars have sought to discern a logical structure in James, without notable success. The letter strings together a series of exhortations and admonitions in no discernible order. Notice the following topics:

1:1	Salutation
1:2–4	Trials that test faith
1:5–8	Ask for wisdom with faith
1:9–11	The poor and the rich
1:12–15	Temptation to sin
1:16–18	Good gifts from the Father
1:19–20	Be slow to anger
1:21–25	Hear and do the word
1:26–27	True religion
2:1–13	Do not favor the rich
2:14–26	Faith without works is dead
3:1–12	The untamable tongue
3:13–18	True wisdom
4:1–10	Wars and fights
4:11–12	Do not slander one another
4:13–17	Do not boast about the future
5:1–6	Condemnation of the unjust rich
5:7–11	Have patience and endurance
5:12	Avoid oaths
5:13–18	Pray for healing with faith
5:19–20	Bring back a straying sinner

DISCUSSION QUESTIONS

1. Several themes in James appear more than once. Identify these recurring themes and discuss what they reveal about the author and his community.
2. Compare Paul's teaching in Romans 3:21–4:25 with that of James in James 2:8–26. Compare and contrast their views with respect to the Law, faith, works, and the example of Abraham. How would you explain the differences?

REVIEW QUESTIONS

1. According to tradition, who wrote the letter of James? What objections have been raised against this view? What features of the letter support this view?

2. What features of James show that it originated among Judaic Christians?
3. How do Paul and James differ in their use of the terms "faith" and "works"?
4. What can we know about the social setting of the author and his community?

SUGGESTIONS FOR FURTHER STUDY

Allison, Dale C., Jr. *James: A Critical and Exegetical Commentary* (ICC; Bloomsbury T&T Clark, 2013). A commentary on the Greek text of the letter of James.

Batten, Alicia J. *What Are They Saying about the Letter of James?* (Paulist, 2009). A survey of scholarship on the letter of James.

Batten, Alicia J., and John S. Kloppenborg, eds. *James, 1 and 2 Peter, and Early Jesus Traditions* (Bloomsbury T&T Clark, 2014). Explores the connection between early traditions about Jesus and the letters of James, First Peter, and Second Peter.

Chester, Andrew, and Ralph P. Martin. *The Theology of the Letters of James, Peter, and Jude* (Cambridge University Press, 1994). Discusses the background, central themes, and theological significance of James.

Chilton, Bruce, and Craig A. Evans, eds. *James the Just and Christian Origins* (Brill, 1999). A collection of essays focusing on a central figure in early Jewish Christianity.

Johnson, Luke Timothy. *The Letter of James: A New Translation with Introduction and Commentary* (Anchor Bible; Doubleday; Yale University Press, 1995). A commentary on the letter of James with an extensive introduction.

Maynard-Reid, Pedrito U. *Poverty and Wealth in James* (Orbis, 1987). Examines the social setting of James, focusing on the theme of poverty and wealth.

28   The Didache

In 1873, Philotheos Bryennios, a metropolitan in the Byzantine Church, discovered a Greek manuscript in the library of the Monastery of the Holy Sepulchre in Constantinople. Among other writings in the manuscript, he found one entitled "Teaching [*Didache* in Greek] of the Twelve Apostles." A previously unattested writing from ancient Christianity, it is now included in the Apostolic Fathers. It is the earliest known manual of church order, giving instructions for various aspects of Christian practice, such as baptism, the Eucharist, and support of church leaders. It reflects the practices of a group of Judaic Christians in the late first or early second century.

SOURCES

The author of the Didache, sometimes called "the Didachist," drew on an earlier source, a Jewish tractate. He also refers to a gospel known to the community.

Most of the material in chapters 1–6 originally existed independently as part of a **Jewish tractate on the two ways**. This described "two ways" or "two paths," the path to life and the path to death, a common theme in Jewish moral exhortation. In pre-Christian Judaism, different versions of this tractate circulated, which various Christian writers incorporated into their works. One version was adopted into the Didache, another version into the Epistle of Barnabas 18–21. The Didachist revised this document in several places. He added a section that has sayings from Christian tradition, such as the saying about loving one's enemy (1:3b–2:1). He also added a conclusion about keeping the ritual requirements of the Law (6:2–3). The Didachist's community used the two ways material as instruction for Christian converts who were about to be baptized (7:1).

Figure 28.1
Third-century
depiction of
Christian baptism.
Museo Nazionale
Romano, Rome
(Erich Lessing/Art
Resource, NY).

Four times the Didachist also refers to a **gospel** that the community knew (8:2; 11:3; 15:3; 15:4). In each case, the topic of instruction parallels Matthew's distinctive material.

TOPIC	DIDACHE	MATTHEW
Lord's Prayer	8:2	6:9–13 (cf. Luke 11:2–4)
False prophets	11:3	7:15, 17, 19–20
Correcting another	15:3	5:21–22; 18:15–17
Alms, prayers, fasting	15:4 (cf. 8:1)	6:1–6, 16–18

Without referring to the community's gospel, the Didache also quotes or alludes to other special material in Matthew. It also quotes or alludes to other sayings in Matthew that have parallels in Luke. The Didachist's gospel was probably not the Gospel of Matthew itself, since in these sayings the Didache sometimes stands closer in wording to Matthew, but other times closer to Luke.

Outline of the Didache

The Didache comprises five distinct sections:

1. *The two paths* (chs. 1–6): a section of moral exhortation describing the "two paths" or ways that lead either to life or to death. The Didachist has taken a traditional Jewish document and added some Christian sayings. The result was read to converts who were about to be baptized (7:1).

2. *Rituals* (chs. 7–10): instructions for performing the rituals of the community. These consisted of traditional Jewish practices (almsgiving, ritual prayer, fasting) with the addition of baptism and the Eucharist.

3. *Itinerant and resident ministers* (chs. 11–13): instructions for receiving itinerant Christians, especially ministers. Here the author gives guidelines for evaluating apostles and prophets, traveling Christians, and prophets and teachers.

4. *Further instructions* (chs. 14–15): another set of instructions for the Eucharist, church leaders (bishops and deacons), prayers and charitable giving.

5. *Eschatological hope* (ch. 16): a section of teaching about eschatological events.

THE JUDAIC CHRISTIANITY
OF THE DIDACHE

The Didachist's community consisted not of a single congregation, but a group of related congregations. This conclusion can be inferred from 13:3–4, where the author assumes that some congregations will have prophets and others will not. These congregations practiced a type of Christianity that has a distinctively Judaic character in several respects.

1. The members of the community continued to keep the Jewish Law. The moral law is summed up in the double command to love God and one's neighbor (1:2), a summary typical of Judaic Christianity (Mark

12:28–34; Q/Luke 10:25–28; James 2:8; cf. Rom 13:8–10). The "two paths" material expands on that summary with specific commands and prohibitions. The community members also kept the ritual aspects of the Law, as indicated in 6:2–3:

> 2 For if you can bear the whole yoke of the Lord, you will be perfect. But if you cannot, do what you can. 3 Concerning food, bear what you can. But keep strictly away from what has been sacrificed to an idol, for it is the worship of dead gods.

The "yoke of the Lord" is a common metaphor in Judaism for the Jewish Law, a meaning it probably has here. The Didachist distinguishes between two levels of observance: those who are "perfect" keep the whole Law, including its ritual aspects, while others are to keep as much of it as they can. The Didachist calls special attention to the dietary regulations: as with other aspects of the Law, community members should keep what they can, but all are to avoid eating what was sacrificed to an idol. This distinction between the perfect who keep the whole Law and other community members who do not appears also in Matthew's special material (Matt 5:19, 48).

2. The community adapted certain Jewish practices that could not be kept after the destruction of the temple and its priesthood. (a) While the temple stood, Jewish Law required that Jews bring the "first fruits" of their animals and crops to support the priests in Jerusalem. It was probably when this became impossible that the Didachist's community adapted the Law by transferring both the function and support of the priests to their own prophets: "So you shall take the first fruits of the produce of the winepress and the threshing-floor, of cattle and of sheep, and you shall give the first fruits to the prophets. For they are your high priests" (13:3). (b) After sacrifice at Jerusalem became impossible, the community apparently found a new understanding of sacrifice in scriptures where Yahweh called for a sacrifice consisting of praise or thanksgiving (e.g. Psalm 50:12–14). They adapted the Law by regarding their own Eucharist (literally "thanksgiving") as a sacrifice of thanksgiving to God (14:1–3). Both adaptations show a concern to maintain the Law, even under altered circumstances.

3. The religiosity of the community continued to be Jewish, emphasizing three pillars of Jewish piety: charitable giving, prayer, and fasting (1:5–6; 4:5–8; 8:1–3; cf. Matt 6:1–18; James 2:14–17). While the community continued these practices, they distinguished their own practices

from those of other Jews. Whereas other Jews fasted on Mondays and Thursdays, community members fasted on Wednesdays and Fridays (8:1). Whereas other Jews prayed traditional Jewish prayers three times a day, community members prayed the Lord's Prayer three times a day (8:2–3). Whereas other Jews met on the Sabbath, the seventh day of the week, community members met on the Lord's Day, the first day of the week (14:1). These differences indicate that the Didachist's community, while Judaic, had separated from the larger Jewish community, establishing its own times and forms of worship.

4. The Didachist assumes that keeping the Law is the way to God and makes no mention of Jesus' death as a saving event. As we might expect among Judaic Christians who kept the Law, we find no references to Paul's letters or teaching. Particularly noteworthy by its absence is Paul's view that faith in Jesus' death had replaced the Jewish Law as the means of salvation. Such a teaching finds no place in this community. Even the prayers of the Eucharist do not identify the bread and wine as the body and blood of Jesus (9:2–4; 10:2–6). The role assigned to Jesus is typical of what we find in other Judaic-Christian literature: he is the future Messiah whose coming is expected (16:1, 6–8).

DATE AND PROVENANCE OF THE DIDACHE

We have seen that the Didachist's congregations no longer supported the high priests or offered sacrifice at Jerusalem, probably because the temple no longer stood. The Didachist probably wrote, therefore, sometime after 70 CE. How much after is hard to say. A reasonable estimate of its date would be the late first or early second century. Probable locations for these Judaic-Christian congregations would be Palestine, Transjordan, or Syria.

COMMUNITY CONCERNS IN THE DIDACHE

The Didache shows three central themes or concerns: community rituals, ministers, and eschatology.

Rituals

The Didachist sets out procedures for practicing the rituals of the community: baptism, fasting and prayer, and the Eucharist. The baptizer read the ethical instruction in Didache 1–6 to the convert, and both fasted before the event (7:1, 4). Community members prayed the Lord's Prayer three times daily (8:3). Baptized members partook of the Eucharist, a full meal of wine and bread (9:1–5; 10:1).

Itinerant and Resident Ministers

The Didache mentions three different sets of Christian ministers: itinerant apostles and prophets, resident prophets and teachers, and resident bishops and deacons.

1. The Didache presupposes a situation in which **itinerant ministers** and other traveling Christians sometimes passed through the community. Such visits posed two problems: distinguishing true prophets from false, and abuse of hospitality.

The problem of recognizing false prophets arose as itinerant visitors claimed to be apostles or prophets who spoke in the name of God. Such a claim, if believed, would give the individual great authority. The Didachist warns against testing or judging such prophetic individuals who spoke "in spirit." They did not have to pray the standardized prayers at the Eucharist but could give thanks however they wished (10:7). If they performed symbolic actions like the prophets of ancient Israel, they were not to be judged (11:11). The Didachist recognized, however, that not everyone who spoke in the name of God was a true prophet. Prophets could be distinguished by their behavior: the true prophet should have "the ways of the Lord" (11:8). They could also be distinguished by their teaching. The Didache itself served as a standard of judgment. One could bring a different teaching as long as it was consistent with those set out in the Didache; but if it invalidated those teachings, the teacher should not be accepted (11:1–2).

The problem of abusing hospitality arose as some of these visitors used the name of Christian as an excuse to live off the community. The Didachist calls such persons "Christ-merchants" (12:5) and gives guidelines for recognizing them. A visitor claiming to be an apostle or prophet was a false prophet if he stayed three days or asked for money (11:5–6, 12). A traveling Christian should stay no more than two or three

Figure 28.2
Third-century fresco of a Christian praying. As this scene shows, early Christians raised their eyes and hands to the sky as they prayed. The practice of bowing the head and closing the eyes developed later. Catacomb of the Giordani, Rome (Scala/Art Resource, NY).

days, and one who wished to settle with the community should support himself (12:2–3).

2. The community also had **resident prophets and teachers**, who had decided to settle with the community. The community supported such individuals with the "first fruits" of their produce (13:1–7).

3. The Didachist also instructs the community to appoint **bishops (overseers) and deacons**, who are to be honored along with the prophets and teachers (15:1–2). In this respect, the Didache may represent a transition from one form of leadership to another. In Proto-Orthodox

Christianity, at least, the more "charismatic" or Spirit-directed offices of prophet and teacher (cf. Acts 13:1) eventually gave way to those of bishop and deacon. The Didachist gives no information about the function of these officials.

Eschatology

The final chapter of the Didache describes events that the Didachist expected before the coming of Jesus: false prophets, loss of love, lawlessness, persecution, a false Christ, and various signs (16:1–8). Most of this material has parallels in Matthew and/or Luke.

DISCUSSION QUESTION

Read the selection from the Didache in Appendix 9 (pp. 583–590). Indicate the chief differences between this type of Christianity and Paul's type, as summarized in Chapter 18.

REVIEW QUESTIONS

1. What sources did the Didachist use in compiling his work?
2. Identify the five main sections of the Didache.
3. In what respects does the Christianity represented in the Didache have a Judaic character?
4. What are the probable date and provenance of the Didache?
5. What are the central concerns of the Didache? What different types of Christian ministers does it mention? What problems did the itinerant ministers pose for the community?

SUGGESTIONS FOR FURTHER STUDY

Draper, Jonathan A., ed. *The Didache in Modern Research* (Leiden: Brill, 1996). A collection of essays by various authors on various aspects of the Didache.

Draper, Jonathan A., and Clayton N. Jefford. *The Didache: A Missing Piece of the Puzzle in Early Christianity* (Society of Biblical Literature, 2015). A collection of seminar papers by various scholars on various aspects of the Didache.

Jefford, Clayton, ed. *The Didache in Context: Essays on its Text, History, and Transmission* (Brill, 1995). A collection of essays on the Didache by various scholars.

Jefford, Clayton. *The Sayings of Jesus in the Teaching of the Twelve Apostles* (Brill, 1989). Argues that the Didache originated in the same Judaic-Christian community that produced the Gospel of Matthew.

Niederwimmer, Kurt. *The Didache: A Commentary* (Hermeneia; Fortress, 1998). An excellent commentary on the Didache.

Van de Sandt, Huub, and David Flusser. *The Didache: Its Jewish Sources and its Place in Early Judaism and Christianity* (Royal Van Gorcum; Fortress, 2002). Focuses on the Jewish roots of the Didache.

PART VI
Gnostic Christianity

29   Gnostic Christianity

Most scholars use the term "Gnosticism" to refer to a variety of religious movements, both Christian and non-Christian, that flourished in the Greco-Roman world from the second to the fifth century. Other scholars use the term in a more restricted sense to refer to one of these movements, a specific group of Christians who called themselves "Gnostics." Still others argue that the term "Gnosticism" is so vague that it should not be used at all. While the term eludes precise definition, it is hard to avoid it. Here we use the term in the first sense and focus on what can be called "Gnostic Christianity." By this we mean a variety of religious groups that fused Christian elements with a Greek (primarily Platonic) world-view.

SOURCES OF OUR KNOWLEDGE

Our knowledge of Gnosticism comes from two sources: the writings of early Christian opponents of the Gnostics and texts written by the Gnostics themselves.

Writings of Opponents

Until the middle of the twentieth century, our knowledge of Gnostic Christianity came primarily from its opponents, various Proto-Orthodox Christian writers such as Irenaeus, Hippolytus, and Epiphanius. These authors regarded Gnostics as "heretics" and summarized their views in order to refute them. From the amount of attention that these writers gave to the matter, it is clear that Gnostic Christianity was widespread in the early Christian centuries. Some scholars have argued that the Gnostic Christians outnumbered the Proto-Orthodox Christians in some areas.

419

This state of affairs began to change when Constantine became emperor. Constantine and other emperors after him made Christianity the religion of the state and sought to unify it as a means of unifying the empire. In 381 the emperor Theodosius I recognized the Proto-Orthodox tradition as normative Christianity and outlawed all other perspectives, including that of Gnostic Christianity. After that time, Gnostic Christianity faded from the scene in the Roman Empire. To the east of the empire, Gnostic ideas have survived down to the present in the religion of the Mandaeans in Iraq and Iran.

The Nag Hammadi Library

Most Gnostic writings have not survived. In 1945, however, a significant discovery brought to light a collection of Gnostic texts that had been hidden for centuries. At Nag Hammadi, a town near Cairo, Egypt, an Egyptian peasant digging for nitrates to fertilize his crops found a large, red, earthenware jar buried in the ground. It contained ancient papyrus manuscripts in the form of codices or books. Thirteen manuscripts were eventually acquired by scholars and now reside at the Coptic Museum in Cairo.

These thirteen papyrus codices contain forty-five distinct works, some complete and some fragmentary. These are written in Coptic, a language derived from ancient Egyptian. The Coptic texts date from about 350 CE. Most are translations of Greek works, some of which probably date from the first half of the second century. Since most of the texts have a Gnostic flavor, they probably comprised the library of a Gnostic sect. They were placed in the jar and buried, probably to save them from being destroyed by authorities of official Christianity.

These works belong to various literary genres. Several are revelatory discourses, narratives in which Christ appears to the disciples and reveals secret teachings. Others are treatises, sermons, meditations, collections of sayings, and otherworld journeys. Several bear the title "gospel," but belong to different genres than the canonical passion gospels. The Gospel of Truth and the Gospel of the Egyptians both relate myths concerning the origin of the world. The Gospel of Thomas is a collection of sayings attributed to Jesus. The Gospel of Philip is a series of meditations. The Gospel of Mary is a revelatory discourse. Many of the works are pseudonymous, written under an assumed name.

Figure 29.1 Manuscript covers of the Nag Hammadi Coptic library. These covers enclosed papyrus manuscripts containing Gnostic texts, found in a jar unearthed near Nag Hammadi, Egypt. Coptic Museum, Old Cairo (Nag Hammadi Archive, Claremont Colleges Digital Library).

THE RELIGION OF GNOSTIC CHRISTIANITY

We know more about the ideas of Gnosticism than about other aspects of their religion. No two Gnostic groups held exactly the same beliefs. Some ideas, however, appear to be central to most Gnostic systems of thought.

The Universe and Its Deities

Plato distinguished between a realm of perfect, unchanging "being" and the physical world of change and decay. Similarly, the Gnostic universe consists of two realms, a spiritual world and the material world. The spiritual world is a higher realm of unchanging perfection and light. The material world is considered a lower realm of darkness and ignorance. Each of the two realms, spiritual and material, has its own set of ruling deities.

In the spiritual realm dwells the **ultimate deity**, conceived in terms drawn from Greek philosophy. This deity is eternal, perfect, unknowable, and beyond description. In some Gnostic systems, subordinate deities or **aeons** emanate from the supreme deity. These aeons ("eternities") are both beings and spheres in the spiritual world. They often have abstract names, such as "Truth" or "Life." Male and female aeons are often paired. The full number of aeons is called the "pleroma" ("fullness").

Some Gnostic systems distinguish between the supreme deity and the ruler of the material world. This ruler is a **Demiurge** (craftsman) who fashions the material world and gives it order. He is sometimes identified with Yahweh, the God of Judaism. He is depicted as arrogant and ignorant. Unaware of the spiritual world, he thinks that there is no other god above him. The Demiurge gives birth to various **rulers, powers, and authorities** (angels or demons) to assist him in ruling the material world. These include the rulers of the planetary spheres and the rulers of the underworld.

Origin and Fate of the Soul

Gnostic ideas about the origin and fate of the soul closely resemble those of Plato in most respects.

Like Plato, Gnostics believed in the **preexistence of the soul**. It existed before the body. It is an emanation from the supreme deity, part of the light of the spiritual world.

Gnostics also thought that birth involved the **fall of the soul**. Though souls belong to the spiritual world, they have come to dwell in mortal bodies in the material world. Gnostics give various explanations of how this came about. The Apocryphon of John, for example, gives the explanation in the form of a myth about Sophia ("Wisdom"), one of the female aeons. Sophia wanted to bring forth an aeon or emanation, but she did so without the consent of her male consort. Her offspring was therefore imperfect, taking the form of a lion-faced serpent. She named him "Ialtabaoth," a corrupt form of "Yah Sabaoth," one of the names of the God of Judaism. She threw this misconception outside of the pleroma into the darkness, where he became ruler of the material world. But since he emanated from her, part of her power remained in him, a part of the light that the pleroma now lacked. The aeons of the pleroma devised a plan to get the light back. First they had to get the light or power out of Ialtabaoth. They tricked him into creating Adam and breathing the power into him to give him life. Thus the light came to reside as soul in the mortal bodies of Adam and Eve and their descendants. Now whenever a human being dies, there is a chance for that soul to ascend to the spiritual world and restore its light to the pleroma.

Gnostics conceived of the **body as a tomb**. The body, since it belongs to the material world, has a negative effect on the soul, enslaving it to various passions and making it forget its true origin and divine nature. It is as though the soul were trapped in a tomb.

Salvation for the soul comes when it knows (remembers) its own divine nature and origin. Hence the term *gnosis* ("knowledge") from which comes "Gnosticism." This knowledge is not primarily knowing facts, but knowing oneself: identifying with one's true self, the soul, and recognizing one's unity with the divine light of the spiritual world. In some Gnostic systems, a redeemer descends from the upper world to bring this knowledge to the trapped souls. The salvation that results from this knowing consists of immortality of the soul apart from the body. At death the soul leaves the body and ascends to the spiritual world to remain forever.

Reincarnation awaits the souls that lack self-knowledge. At the death of the body, these cannot ascend to the spiritual world. They are stopped by the powers of the material world and forced to reincarnate in another body.

Nature and Function of Christ

An aeon called "Jesus" or "Christ" generally played a role in Gnostic Christian systems of thought. This conception of Christ, however, differed significantly from the conceptions of Judaic and Proto-Orthodox Christians, with respect to both his nature and his function.

Gnostics had various ideas about the **nature of Christ**. Often, however, since the Gnostics took a negative view of the body, the Gnostic Christ had no human body but existed as a purely spiritual being. As a spiritual being he neither became trapped in a material body nor suffered death. He merely "seemed" to be human and only "seemed" to suffer and die. Such a view is called **docetism** (from Greek *dokein*, "to seem"). One form of this view made no distinction between Jesus and Christ: there was one purely spiritual being called Jesus or Christ, who merely appeared to be human and to suffer. In some accounts, he escaped death by having Judas Iscariot or Simon of Cyrene change places with him before the crucifixion. Another form of this view distinguished between Jesus and Christ: Jesus was a normal human being, while Christ was a divine spirit who descended upon Jesus at his baptism. Before the crucifixion, Christ left Jesus, so that Jesus suffered but Christ did not. Irenaeus attributed this latter perspective to Cerinthus, one of the earliest known Gnostic Christians.

The Docetic Christ of Cerinthus

Irenaeus, bishop of Lyons, wrote a lengthy refutation of Gnostic views from the perspective of Proto-Orthodoxy. Here he describes the docetic views of Cerinthus, an early Gnostic:

> Cerinthus, again, a man who was educated in the wisdom of the Egyptians, taught that the world was not made by the primary God, but by a certain Power far separated from him, and at a distance from that Principality who is supreme over the universe, and ignorant of him who is above all. He represented Jesus as having not been born of a virgin, but as being the son of Joseph and Mary according to the ordinary course of human generation, while he nevertheless was more righteous, prudent, and wise than other men. Moreover, after his baptism, Christ descended upon him in the form of a dove from the Supreme Ruler, and he then proclaimed the unknown Father and performed miracles. But at last Christ departed from Jesus, and then Jesus suffered and rose again, while Christ remained impassible [incapable of suffering], inasmuch as he was a spiritual being. (*Against Heresies* 1.26.1, ANF)

Gnostics also had distinctive ideas about the **function of Christ**. In Judaic Christianity, Jesus' primary function was to return as the eschatological messianic judge. He had this function in Proto-Orthodoxy as well but had the further purpose of shedding his blood for the atonement of sins. The Gnostic Christ usually played neither of these roles but functioned primarily as a revealer. He descended from the spiritual world to remind forgetful souls of their true nature and origin. He imparted this knowledge in secret teaching to chosen disciples then returned to the spiritual world.

The Ethical Dimension

The Gnostics believed that the divine souls within them, their true selves, did not belong to the evil, created world. This belief led some groups to practice asceticism or self-denial, such as refraining from sex and certain foods. They reasoned that since Gnostics did not belong to the world, they must abstain from ordinary human life in the world.

Some of the Gnostic writings discovered at Nag Hammadi reflect this point of view. Other groups of Gnostics were charged by their opponents with taking the opposite perspective: teaching and practicing freedom from moral restraint. Though their opponents probably exaggerated, it is possible that some Gnostic groups did have a more libertine ethic.

Social and Ritual Dimensions

We know very little about the social and ritual dimensions of Gnostic Christianity. We do know that in many cases Gnostic Christians worshipped in the same churches as Proto-Orthodox Christians, at least until they were driven out or left. They could recite the same scriptures and participate in the same rituals as the Proto-Orthodox, all the while interpreting them in a different sense that they considered more profound.

With respect to distinctively Gnostic **rituals**, the Gospel of Philip 67:27 mentions baptism, chrism, eucharist, ransom, and bridal chamber, the last two of which have no counterpart in Proto-Orthodox ritual. Philip gives no explanation of any of these. The Acts of John 94–96 describes a scene in which the disciples join hands in a circle and dance around Jesus, a scene probably based on the actual practice of some Gnostic group.

The **role of the feminine** in Gnosticism is somewhat ambiguous. Unlike monotheistic Christians who worshipped a single male God, Gnostic Christians saw both feminine and masculine aspects in the divine nature. The ultimate deity itself contained masculine and feminine features, and its offspring were pairs of male and female aeons. On the human level, Gnostics gave a prominent role to certain female disciples of Jesus, particularly Mary Magdalene. In the Gospel of Mary she receives special secret revelation from Jesus and teaches the male disciples.

While female figures had a place in the literature of the Gnostics, we do not know to what extent this fact affected the roles of actual women in Gnostic groups. The ascetic tradition within Gnosticism rejected sexuality and saw the woman as an impediment to male self-restraint. The Gospel of Thomas concludes with the assertion that a woman can enter the kingdom of heaven only if she "makes herself male" (Thomas 114).

Jesus and Mary

Female disciples of Jesus play an important role in Gnostic texts. The Gospel of Philip, for example, contains an intriguing reference to Mary Magdalene, where unfortunately the poor condition of the manuscript makes it impossible to read all the words:

> The Savior loved Mary Magdalene more than all the other disciples, and he used to kiss her often on her […] (Gospel of Philip 63:34–35)

REVIEW QUESTIONS

1. What are our two sources of knowledge about Gnosticism?
2. Describe the two realms of the Gnostic universe and the deities that rule them.
3. Describe the origin and fate of the soul in Gnostic thought.
4. Describe the nature and function of Christ in Gnostic Christian thought. Identify: docetism.
5. Describe what we know about the ethical, social, and ritual dimensions of Gnostic Christianity.
6. Describe the role of the feminine in Gnostic thought and practice.

SUGGESTIONS FOR FURTHER STUDY

Primary Sources in English Translation

Foerster, Werner. *Gnosis: A Selection of Gnostic Texts*. English translation edited by R. McL. Wilson (2 vols.; Clarendon, 1972, 1974). Volume 1 contains selections from opponents of Gnosticism. Volume 2 contains selected Gnostic and Mandaean texts.

Layton, Bentley. *The Gnostic Scriptures: A New Translation with Annotations and Introductions* (Doubleday; Yale University Press, 1987). Selected Gnostic texts and selections from Proto-Orthodox opponents of Gnosticism with introductions and bibliography.

Meyer, Marvin, ed. *The Nag Hammadi Scriptures: The International Edition* (HarperOne, 2007). Standard English translation of the writings discovered at Nag Hammadi.

Studies

Franzmann, Majella. *Jesus in the Nag Hammadi Writings* (T&T Clark, 1996). Surveys the various portrayals of Jesus in the Nag Hammadi writings.

King, Karen L., ed. *Images of the Feminine in Gnosticism* (Fortress, 1988). A collection of essays that explore the use of gender imagery in Gnostic texts.

Pagels, Elaine. *The Gnostic Gospels* (Random House, 1979). Examines various aspects of the conflict between Gnostic and Proto-Orthodox Christianity.

Pearson, Birger. *Ancient Gnosticism: Traditions and Literature* (Fortress, 2007). Discusses the various Gnostic schools and the literature associated with each.

Perkins, Pheme. *Gnosticism and the New Testament* (Fortress, 1993). Explores the significance of Gnosticism for the New Testament and early Christianity.

30   The Gospel of Thomas

In the movie *Stigmata* (1999), the plot revolves around an ancient Aramaic gospel supposedly written with the very words of Jesus himself. In this gospel Jesus says,

> The kingdom of God is inside you and all around you, not in buildings of wood and stone. Split a piece of wood and I am there; lift a stone and you will find me.

While the gospel described in the film does not actually exist, the film gives a sense of authenticity to it by adapting words from a gospel that does exist, the Gospel of Thomas. The saying from the *Stigmata* gospel combines two sayings found in Thomas:

> Jesus said, "… the kingdom is inside of you and outside of you." (Thomas 3A)

> Jesus said, "… Split a piece of wood; I am there. Lift up the stone and you will find me there." (Thomas 77)

While Hollywood has discovered the Gospel of Thomas, most of the world remains unaware of it. It was originally written in Greek, but until recent years only three fragmentary manuscripts of the Greek were known to survive. Fortunately the Nag Hammadi library discovered in 1945 contained a complete manuscript in Coptic translation.

AUTHOR AND DATE

The Gospel of Thomas consists of about 114 sayings attributed to "the living Jesus." According to the Preface, these sayings were written down by "Didymus Judas Thomas." The names "Didymus" and "Thomas" are

428

equivalents: both mean "twin," the former in Greek and the latter in Aramaic. In the Synoptic tradition, Thomas is one of the apostles of Jesus (Mark 3:18). Judas or Jude is one of the brothers of Jesus (Mark 6:3). Certain early Christians identified Thomas (twin) with Judas (brother of Jesus) and concluded that Judas/Thomas was the twin brother of Jesus. The Gospel of Thomas presents Thomas as the disciple most in tune with Jesus himself.

Several writings from early Christianity are associated with this Judas/Thomas. He is credited with writing not only the Gospel of Thomas, a collection of Jesus' sayings, but also the Infancy Gospel of Thomas, a collection of stories about Jesus' childhood (Appendix 7). Both works are pseudonymous: the actual author uses Thomas' name to lend authority to the traditions. Two other works, The Book of Thomas the Contender and The Acts of Thomas, relate traditions about Thomas himself. Scholars generally believe that this Thomas literature originated in northern Mesopotamia, perhaps in the city of Edessa.

The Gospel of Thomas must be earlier than 200 CE, the date of the earliest Greek manuscript. How much earlier is uncertain, with estimates ranging from 50 to 150 CE.

THOMAS AND THE CANONICAL GOSPELS

Some of the sayings in Thomas resemble those found in the canonical gospels: for example, "Blessed are the poor, for yours is the kingdom of heaven" (Thomas 54; cf. Luke 6:20; Matt 5:3). Other sayings are completely different: for instance, "Blessed is the lion that the man eats so that the lion becomes man; and abominable is the man that the lion eats so that the man becomes lion" (Thomas 7).

Scholars have reached no consensus on the relation between Thomas and the canonical gospels. Some think that Thomas was dependent on the canonical gospels, that the author adapted sayings from the canonical gospels in light of Gnostic ideas. Other scholars regard Thomas as independent of the canonical gospels. On this view, the sayings in Thomas came not from these gospels but from an independent line of tradition. If that is the case, some of the sayings in Thomas could preserve wording that is more original than the parallels in the canonical gospels.

CENTRAL IDEAS

According to the opening lines of Thomas, its contents are "secret sayings" which require special wisdom or knowledge to interpret. Even a

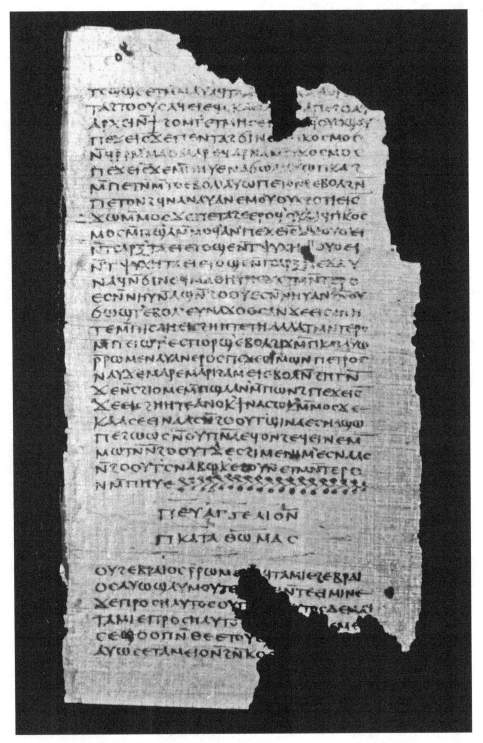

Figure 30.1 Last page of the Gospel of Thomas in the Coptic manuscript found at Nag Hammadi. The title, "The Gospel According to Thomas," comes at the end before the next selection. www.BibleLandPictures.com (Zev Radovan).

saying that is familiar from another gospel may not be easy to interpret in Thomas, since it may have a different meaning in this context. The key to understanding the sayings in Thomas lies in knowing the worldview of the author and his community. This can be reconstructed from the sayings by noticing the similarity of their ideas to the ideas of other Gnostic Christian groups. Some of the central ideas in Thomas relate to cosmology (the nature of the universe), the journey of the soul, the community of the elect, and the role of Jesus.

Cosmology

The universe of Thomas consists of the divine realm and the material world. Infusing the world is a world-soul.

In the **divine realm** resides a pantheon of three divine beings: the Father, the Son, and the Holy Spirit (44). The Spirit may be the one Jesus calls "my true mother" (101). These exist above in a timeless realm of light (50, 77, 83), also called "the place of life" (4). A primary characteristic of the timeless realm is "repose" or rest (50, 51, 60, 86, 90), a state of unchanging existence (19c, 61bc, 76).

Outside of the divine realm is the **material world**. Whether or not Thomas presupposes a separate creator-god who shaped the material world is uncertain. In any case, Thomas takes a negative view toward the material world. Compared with the divine realm of light, this world, including the physical body, is a place of "poverty" (3b, 29) or a "corpse" (56, 80).

Both Plato and the Stoics thought that the world had a soul. The Stoics called this **world-soul** the "Logos" and conceived of it as a fiery essence that pervaded all things, especially the rational part of the human soul, but also non-rational matter such as wood and stone. Thomas identified this world-soul with Jesus, the Son. Like the Stoic "Logos," he is a rational fire or light (10, 82) that dwells in all matter just as a soul dwells in a body (77). Thomas refers to this world-soul as "the All" (2, 67, 77). Other Greek writers used this term to refer to the entire universe, but Thomas seems to use it only of the divine soul of the universe. The All is found above all in the human self or soul (67).

Journey of the Soul

Thomas presupposes the **preexistence of the soul**. Souls existed before they were born on earth (19a). They originated as emanations from the ultimate divine being, "the Father." They are thus "sons of the Father" and originally dwelt in the Father's heavenly realm of light (50).

The **plight of the soul** involves its union with the body. At birth, a soul comes from the divine realm (50) and becomes trapped in the material world, in a body of flesh. The body affects the soul negatively, inducing it to forget where it came from and to enter the world "empty," without knowledge or memory of its previous existence (28, 97). The soul in the body is like a treasure hidden in a field (109), leaven hidden in dough (96), a single pearl in a cargo (76). It is the light within a man of light (24), a thing of wealth within the poverty of the physical body (29).

The **salvation of the soul** consists of leaving the body behind (21a, 37) and returning to the heavenly realm of light (18, 49). The soul can return to the heavenly realm only if it knows itself, which is to know the Father: that is, if it knows that it is a part of the divine light of the Father (3 b, 59, 111 b).

Thomas does not mention **reincarnation of the soul** but may presuppose it. In Gnostic thought, spiritual powers held sway over the material world and acted in a hostile manner toward the soul. In some systems, the chief ruler had the form of a snake, or a snake with a lion's face. When unprepared (ignorant) souls died, he consumed them and returned them to the material world to be reincarnated. Some such idea may be reflected in Thomas (59, 60).

The Community of the Elect

In Thomas, the **kingdom of God** is not, as in Jewish apocalyptic thought, a political system in which God would rule on earth at the end of the age sometime in the future. Nor is it associated with resurrection of the body or a final judgment. The "kingdom of the Father" is either the divine realm of light (49) or a state of being that exists invisibly already in the present within individuals (3a, 51, 113). It is the community of souls who recognize themselves as the light of God and exist in a state of repose.

Those who know themselves are the **elect** (chosen by God). As parts of the divine light, the elect are one with each other as well as with the light (4, 23, 48, 106). In parables, Thomas expresses their superiority to others in terms of size: they are the large fish (8), the large sheep (107). The elect are called to renounce the affairs of this world (27, 42), including sexuality (87, 112), family ties (55, 99, 101), power (81), and wealth (36, 54, 63,

64, 69b, 78, 95, 110). They live as celibate males or monks (16, 49, 75). The community does include women disciples (61b), but women must make themselves like males (114).

Thomas expresses a **rejection of Judaism or Judaic Christianity**. The ideas in Thomas for the most part have their home in the thought-world of Hellenism. Its sayings reflect a conflict with some form of Judaism or Judaic Christianity. It rejects specifically Jewish religious practices as unnecessary, even harmful (6a/14, 53, 104), and castigates the Pharisees and other Jews (39, 43, 102).

The Role of Jesus

The traditions of Jesus' incarnation, miracles, death, and resurrection have little or no significance in Thomas. Instead, Jesus comes into the world in order to remind souls of their true origin and nature (5, 28). For souls like Thomas, who know themselves as sons of the Father, Jesus is not a superior but an equal (13, 108).

DISCUSSION QUESTION

Read the selections from the Gospel of Thomas in Appendix 10 (pp. 591–598). (The whole gospel can be found on the Internet at http://gnosis.org/naghamm/nhl_thomas.htm.) Indicate what the following sayings would mean in the context of Thomas: 1, 3, 7, 9, 18, 19a, 37, 49, 50, 76, 77, 90, 97, 108.

REVIEW QUESTIONS

1. Discuss the authorship and date of the Gospel of Thomas.
2. What different views do scholars take on the relationship between the sayings in Thomas and those in the canonical gospels?
3. Explain the central ideas of Thomas, including cosmology, the journey of the soul, the community of the elect, and the role of Jesus.

SUGGESTIONS FOR FURTHER STUDY

Goodacre, Mark. *Thomas and the Gospels: The Case for Thomas's Familiarity with the Synoptics* (Eerdmans, 2012). Argues that Thomas used the Synoptic Gospels as a source.

Meyer, Marvin. *The Gospel of Thomas: The Hidden Sayings of Jesus* (HarperSanFrancisco, 1992). Includes the Coptic text with English translation, an introduction, and explanatory notes.

Patterson, Stephen J. *The Gospel of Thomas and Jesus* (Polebridge, 1993). Argues that the sayings in Thomas are not dependent on the canonical gospels, that Thomas's community consisted of itinerant beggars, and that Thomas can contribute to the quest for the historical Jesus.

Patterson, Stephen J., Hans-Gebhard Bethge, and James M. Robinson. *The Fifth Gospel: The Gospel of Thomas Comes of Age* (new edition; Bloomsbury T&T Clark, 2011). Includes the Coptic text with English translation and two essays: a general introduction and an account of the discovery, publication, and impact of the Nag Hammadi texts.

Plisch, Uwe Karsten. *The Gospel of Thomas: Original Text with Commentary* (Deutsche Bibelgesellschaft, 2008). The Coptic text and Greek fragments of Thomas with English translation and commentary.

Uro, Risto. *Thomas: Seeking the Historical Context of the Gospel of Thomas* (Bloomsbury T&T Clark, 2003). Essays on various issues relating to the Gospel of Thomas.

PART VII

Proto-Orthodox Christianity

31   Proto-Orthodox Christianity

The type of Christianity that ultimately became predominant was neither Judaic nor Gnostic. It developed out of Pauline, Johannine, and related forms of Christianity and consisted primarily of Gentiles. Christians of this type regarded their own perspective as orthodoxy (correct belief), while rejecting other perspectives as heresy (false doctrine). They also called their church "catholic," meaning "universal." Scholars call this type of early Christianity "Proto-Orthodoxy" or "early Catholicism," because it was the forerunner of the types of Christianity that developed later, known as Orthodoxy and Catholicism. The Proto-Orthodox considered both Judaic Christianity and Gnostic Christianity as heresy and ultimately prevailed against both.

As we use the term here, Proto-Orthodoxy developed after Paul and extended down to the first church council at Nicaea in 325, when the state church began to officially define orthodoxy and heresy. Here we will be concerned only with the emergence of Proto-Orthodoxy in the first part of this period, the end of the first and beginning of the second century.

In the period we are considering, Proto-Orthodox Christianity had not yet developed a formal creed or statement of beliefs. Yet certain authors already equated Christian faith with a body of beliefs that had been handed down. Jude speaks of "the faith once and for all delivered to the saints" (Jude 3). The Pastoral Epistles also frequently speak of "the faith" as if it were a body of doctrine (e.g. 1 Tim 1:19; 2 Tim 3:8; Titus 1:13).

Likewise Proto-Orthodoxy had not yet developed a standardized canon of either the Old Testament or the New Testament. The churches in different locations still used different collections of writings for reading in the church. Yet already some authors refer to "the scriptures" as an inspired body of literature (2 Timothy 3:14–17; 2 Peter 1:20–21). Paul's letters had begun to be considered a part of scripture (2 Peter 3:15–16).

Some of the typical features of Proto-Orthodox religion can be seen in an examination of its conceptual, social, and ritual dimensions.

CONCEPTUAL DIMENSION

The distinctive character of Proto-Orthodoxy can best be understood by comparing it with Judaic Christianity on the one hand and Gnostic Christianity on the other. While Proto-Orthodoxy separated itself from Judaism, it stayed much closer to its Jewish roots than did Gnostic Christianity. In fact, the conflict between Proto-Orthodoxy and Gnosticism can be viewed as a conflict between two world-views, one primarily Hebraic, the other primarily Greek (see box below). In most of their concepts, the Proto-Orthodox stayed closer to the Hebraic perspective, while Gnosticism took the Greek view.

Hebraic and Greek world-views

HEBRAIC WORLDVIEW	GREEK (PLATONIC) WORLDVIEW
Belief in one god	Belief in many gods
God and creator identical	Supreme god and Demiurge distinct
God is personal	Supreme god is impersonal
Positive view of material world	Negative view of material world
Positive view of body	Negative view of body
No preexistence of soul	Preexistence of soul
No reincarnation of soul	Reincarnation of soul
Sin separates from God	Ignorance separates from God
Sacrificial blood atones for sin	Self-knowledge cures ignorance
Salvation as resurrection of body	Salvation as escape of soul from body
Salvation as life on perfected earth	Salvation as life in heavenly world

Concept of God

The Proto-Orthodox combined Jewish and Greek views in their concept of God.

1. They viewed God as one, yet more than one. They inherited from Judaism a belief in one god. In their own minds, they adhered to this perspective, yet they modified the strict monotheism of Judaism by also identifying Jesus as God. While allowing a place for Jesus alongside the deity, they rejected the multiplicity of gods inherent in the Gnostic concept of aeons.

2. They viewed God as personal, yet impersonal. The god of Judaism was a personal god with human characteristics, quite different from the remote, impersonal, and impassible deity of Greek philosophy. Whereas the Gnostic tradition often distinguished these as separate gods, the Proto-Orthodox tradition maintained monotheism by trying to combine these two conceptions into one.

3. They viewed God as creator. The god of Judaism created the world and when he finished, he pronounced it good (Gen 1:31). Gnostics agreed that the god of Judaism created the world but denied that it was good or that the god who created it was good. The good god was the remote god of Greek philosophy, to whom they attributed no role in the creation of the world. Proto-Orthodoxy maintained the Jewish conception.

Concept of Salvation

Both Proto-Orthodox and Gnostic Christianity were religions of salvation, but they differed with respect to the plight from which one needed salvation, the means of salvation, the nature of salvation, and the place of salvation.

1. The Proto-Orthodox tradition identified the plight as sin. They inherited from Judaism the idea of sin as transgression of God's law, as that which separated one from God and made one liable to condemnation at a future judgment. For the Gnostics, what separated from God was not sin but ignorance, a failure to remember or realize the unity of one's own soul with the divine. This ignorance was caused by the entrapment of the soul in the material world, specifically in the body.

2. With respect to the means of salvation, Proto-Orthodoxy followed the sacrificial cult in Judaism and supposed that atonement for sins required the shedding of blood. Like Paul, they believed that salvation was accomplished by the death of Jesus, interpreted as a sacrifice for sins. The blood of Jesus thus receives their attention, as in this exhortation from 1 Clement:

> Let us gaze at the blood of Christ and realize how precious it is to his Father, because when poured out for our salvation it brought the gift of repentance to the whole world. (1 Clement 7:4)

This adaptation of the Hebraic perspective found little acceptance among Gnostics, who saw themselves liberated by self-knowledge, a realization of their soul's unity with the divine.

3. As to the nature of salvation, the Proto-Orthodox looked for resurrection of the body. Such a view held little attraction for Gnostics. Like Plato they saw no intimate connection between the soul and a single body. The soul might put on and take off numerous bodies, like changes of clothing, in the course of numerous reincarnations. They wanted the soul to be freed from the body not rejoined to it. In contrast, the Proto-Orthodox followed the Hebraic tradition that saw an intimate connection between soul and body. According to this Hebraic view, each soul had only one body. Though the soul after death might exist without a body, such a state was hardly satisfactory. Ultimately, at least for Pharisees and Judaic Christians, body and soul would be rejoined at the resurrection of the dead. While the Proto-Orthodox tradition maintained this Jewish perspective on body and soul, they did accept the Greek view that bodily passions had a negative effect on the soul. This idea led to an ascetic tradition within Proto-Orthodoxy, an attempt to suppress the desires of the body. It did not, however, lead them to abandon the idea of resurrection, since they believed the resurrection body would not be subject to such passions.

4. As for the place of salvation, the Platonic tradition expected liberated souls to dwell in the heavenly world. In Plato's conception, such souls dwelt among the stars, while Gnostics sent them to the spiritual realm beyond the stars. In contrast, hope for the future in the Hebraic tradition was a this-worldly hope, a hope for life in the body on a renewed earth. The Proto-Orthodox tradition for the most part took this perspective. The book of Revelation, for example, depicts a period of a thousand years (a millennium), in which resurrected Christians reign with Christ on earth. Subsequently, Christians do not ascend to heaven, but heaven comes down to earth. Later Proto-Orthodox writers such as Justin and Irenaeus continued to hold this view.

Concept of Christ

With respect to the nature of Christ, the Proto-Orthodox regarded him as both human and divine. In contrast to docetic Christians, who regarded Christ as a purely spiritual divine being without a physical body, the Proto-Orthodox regarded him as not only divine but also truly human. Since their conception of salvation included salvation of the body, it was thought necessary that their savior have a human body and human blood to shed. However, in contrast to certain Judaic Christians, who regarded Jesus as purely human, the Proto-Orthodox regarded him as not only human but also divine. He was a demigod, born of a virgin, as well as an incarnation who could in fact be called "God." Such a conception begins the sermon preserved as 2 Clement: "Brothers, we must think about Jesus Christ as we do about God" (2 Clement 1:1). The attempt to emphasize both human and divine elements in one being led to some rather strange conceptions, as when Ignatius speaks of "the blood of God" (Ignatius, Eph 1:1).

With respect to the work of Christ, the Proto-Orthodox emphasized two primary functions. The first of these was to die as a sacrificial atonement for sins. Neither Judaic nor Gnostic Christians shared this perspective. For Judaic Christians, keeping the Law, not the death of Christ, was the path to eternal life, and Gnostic Christians generally regarded Christ as a revealer of self-knowledge rather than as a sacrifice.

The second function was to return as judge of the living and the dead. This perspective was shared by Judaic Christians, who looked for the return of Jesus as the future Messiah. The first generation of Christians had expected Jesus to return in their own lifetime. When that did not happen, succeeding generations had to grapple with the delay of the parousia. Some Christians continued to maintain that the end was near (Heb 10:25; 1 John 2:18; Rev 1:1). Others apparently began to doubt that Jesus would return, since we find several Proto-Orthodox writers combating this perspective (1 Clement 23:3–5; 2 Pet 3:1–13; 2 Clement 11–12). As hope for the immediate return of Jesus began to fade, the church found it necessary to deal with the prospect of continued existence in the world.

SOCIAL DIMENSION

Under the social dimension of Proto-Orthodox religion, we will consider leadership and the household code.

Leadership

The responsibility for opposing divergent teaching fell primarily on the leadership of the church. In the second century and after, the form of leadership developed in ways that made it easier to exclude such teaching.

First, a professional ministry or **clergy** developed. Full-time professionals took over leadership positions that had previously been occupied by church members who worked at other occupations. This shift brought with it an increased distinction between the leaders and the rest of the congregation – between the clergy and the laity.

Second, the leadership developed into a hierarchy. Originally the leadership of a church consisted of several elders (presbyters) or several *episcopoi*, i.e. overseers or "bishops" (Phil 1:1; Didache 15:1–2). Later a single bishop with a council of elders ruled the church in a city or region. This system, sometimes called the **monarchic episcopate**, gave the individual bishop greater power to suppress divergent perspectives. The letters of Ignatius show this system in operation in Antioch and Asia Minor at the beginning of the second century. Ignatius himself was the bishop of Antioch, and even calls himself the bishop of Syria, the province of which Antioch was the capital (Ignatius, Romans 1:2). In his letters, he also names the bishops of various cities in Asia Minor. Along with the bishop and the elders, Proto-Orthodox writers frequently refer to "deacons" ("servers"). These three offices became typical in Proto-Orthodox churches.

Third, a theory of **apostolic succession** developed. The Proto-Orthodox bishops claimed that they were the legitimate successors of the apostles. According to this theory, the apostles appointed a bishop for each church, this bishop appointed another after him, and so on, down to the present bishop, who was thus the legitimate leader of the church. To bolster this theory, some of the bishops began to claim that an apostle established the church in their city. They also drew up lists of succession, which gave the names of the bishops who had supposedly ruled in unbroken succession since that apostle. Scholars have shown that many such claims and lists were simply created by the bishops. They functioned to legitimate the bishop over his competitors, primarily the Gnostic leaders. The theory of apostolic succession made the bishops appear to be guardians of a tradition that had been passed down from the apostles to succeeding bishops of a church. The bishops thus possessed the true doctrine, the standard by which other teachings were judged unorthodox. This idea can be seen at the end of the first century in the Pastoral Epistles and 1 Clement, and comes to full expression at the end of the second century in the writing of Irenaeus.

Household Code

Proto-Orthodox authors appear particularly interested in maintaining the hereditary patriarchal order of the Roman household. "Household codes" instruct wives to submit to husbands, children to parents, and slaves to masters. Such instructions appear repeatedly in the literature: 1

Tim 6:1–2; Titus 2:1–10; 1 Pet 2:18–3:7; 1 Clement 21:6–9; Ignatius to Polycarp 4:3–5:2; Polycarp to the Philippians 4:2; Didache 4:9–11; Barnabas 19:5–7 (cf. Col 3:18–4:1; Eph 5:21–6:9).

RITUAL DIMENSION

The two main Proto-Orthodox rituals were baptism and community meals.

At the end of our period, Justin describes **baptism** as it was practiced in Rome about the middle of the second century (*Apology* 61). Prior to the baptism, the candidate and other members of the church spent time fasting and praying. The candidate was then led to the water and baptized "in the name of God, the Father and Lord of the universe, and of our Savior Jesus Christ, and of the Holy Spirit." Justin identifies three benefits imparted by baptism: remission of past sins, regeneration or rebirth, and illumination of the understanding.

Early Christian **community meals** varied. As the Proto-Orthodox church developed, there existed a tendency toward standardization. The Judaic-Christian perspective, which made no connection between the meal and Jesus' death, gave place to that of Paul, which did. The term **Eucharist** thus came to apply to a meal in which the bread and wine

Figure 31.1
Sixth-century mosaic of a basket of bread between two fish, reminiscent of the story of Jesus feeding the crowds and of early Christian communal meals. Church of the Multiplication, Tabgah, Israel (Erich Lessing/Art Resource, NY).

represented the body and blood of Jesus (Ignatius, Phil 4; Smyr 7:1; 8:1; Justin, *Apology* 65–66). Later, in Roman Catholicism, this became "the Mass." The term **agape** ("love"), meaning "love feast," was used to refer to a fellowship meal shared by the church (Jude 12; 2 Pet 2:13 v.l.; Ignatius, Smyr 8:1).

PROTO-ORTHODOX LITERATURE

In this introductory study, we cannot discuss the full range of Proto-Orthodox literature, but will limit ourselves to writings that appeared before about 150 CE. These are found in the New Testament or the Apostolic Fathers. They focus on three central concerns: conflict between different groups within the church, the relation between Christianity and Judaism, and conflict between Christianity and the Roman world.

Concerns of Proto-Orthodox literature

CONFLICT IN THE CHURCH	RELATION TO JUDAISM	CONFLICT WITH THE ROMAN WORLD
Pastoral Epistles	Hebrews	1 Peter
Jude and 2 Peter	Epistle of Barnabas	Revelation
Johannine Epistles		Ignatius to the Romans
Letters of Ignatius		
1 Clement		

The Shepherd of Hermas also falls into the period we are studying, but since it does not deal with any of these concerns we will not discuss it.

REVIEW QUESTIONS

1. Compare and contrast Proto-Orthodox, Judaic, and Gnostic Christianity with respect to their concepts of God, salvation, and Christ.
2. Describe three developments in Proto-Orthodox church leadership in the second century.
3. What was the purpose of the household code?
4. Describe the two main rituals of Proto-Orthodox Christianity. Identify: Eucharist, agape.
5. What three central concerns surface in early Proto-Orthodox literature? What writings focus on these concerns?

SUGGESTIONS FOR FURTHER STUDY

Bauer, Walter. *Orthodoxy and Heresy in Earliest Christianity* (2nd ed.; Fortress, 1971). Discusses the diversity of early Christianity and the attempt to define a normative position within that diversity.

Campenhausen, Hans von. *Ecclesiastical Authority and Spiritual Power in the Church of the First Three Centuries* (A&C Black, 1969; reprinted, Baker Academic, 1995). Discusses the development of church authority in the first three centuries of Christianity.

Kelly, J. N. D. *Early Christian Creeds* (3rd ed.; Taylor and Francis, 1972). Traces the development of "orthodox" creedal statements and creeds from the New Testament to the Middle Ages.

32   Conflict in the Church (1)
Pastoral Epistles

The next several chapters illustrate one of the most common concerns of Proto-Orthodox literature: conflict between different groups within the church. Conflicts generally arose over questions of doctrine and leadership: what should be taught and who had the right to decide. Generally the conflict in the church involved two groups, one with a Proto-Orthodox perspective and one with a different perspective. The literature that we are examining gives the Proto-Orthodox point of view, attacking the other perspective. It does not always clearly explain the other point of view. The divergent perspective may not have been the same in every case, but when we do get information about it, it often looks like some early form of Gnostic Christianity.

The letters of First Timothy, Second Timothy, and Titus promote a Proto-Orthodox perspective against several divergent teachings. These three letters have been called the **Pastoral Epistles** because they deal with matters of concern to church leaders, who exercised pastoral care for the church. The author is concerned to invest authority in church leaders who can combat divergent perspectives within the church.

Unlike most of Paul's letters, which are addressed to churches, these letters are addressed to two of Paul's younger co-workers. **Timothy** was recruited by Paul at Lystra on his second missionary journey (Acts 16:1–3) and accompanied him thereafter (Acts 17:14–15; 18:5; 19:22; 20:4). He is mentioned frequently in Paul's letters (Rom 16:21; 1 Cor 4:17; 16:10; 2 Cor 1:9; Phil 2:19; 1 Thes 3:2, 6) and is named as co-author in several of these (2 Cor 1:1; Phil 1:1; 1 Thes 1:1; 2 Thes 1:1; Phlm 1; cf. Col 1:1). The letter of Hebrews also mentions him (Heb 13:23). **Titus** accompanied Paul to Jerusalem (Gal 2:1, 3) and carried messages between Paul and the church at Corinth (2 Cor 2:13; 7:6, 13, 14; 8:6, 16, 23; 12:18). Acts does not mention him unless he is to be identified with Titius (or Titus) Justus, a God-fearer from Corinth (Acts 18:7).

AUTHOR

Though the author of the Pastorals writes as Paul, most scholars today doubt that Paul wrote them. Three aspects of the letters have raised doubts about Paul's authorship: their style and vocabulary, setting in Paul's life, and references to features of Proto-Orthodoxy.

Style and Vocabulary

The Pastorals share a common literary style and a common vocabulary, which differ significantly from the other letters attributed to Paul. In a classic study, P. N. Harrison (1921) compared the vocabulary of the Pastorals with the vocabulary of the ten other Pauline letters (the seven acknowledged and the three disputed). The Pastorals differ from these other Pauline letters in having a significantly greater number of *hapax legomena* (words used only once in the New Testament) and a significantly greater number of words not found elsewhere in the Pauline letters. They also differ in lacking many of the words that occur regularly in the ten other Pauline letters, including the particles, enclitics, prepositions, pronouns, and connecting words. Each of the ten Pauline letters varies from the others to a certain degree, but those variations fall within the same limits. The variations of the Pastorals, however, fall well outside those limits. While the vocabulary of the Pastorals does not match that of the ten other Pauline letters, it does match that of second-century Christian authors: the Apostolic Fathers (95–145 CE) and the apologists (140–70 CE). On the basis of this evidence, Harrison concluded that the Pastorals were written not by Paul but by an early Christian author from the first half of the second century.

Many of the stylistic features and central concepts of the Pastoral Epistles appear only infrequently or not at all in the acknowledged letters of Paul. For example, the sentence "The saying is sure" occurs in all three letters a total of five times (1 Tim 1:15; 3:1; 4:9; 2 Tim 2:11; Titus 3:8) but is never used elsewhere by Paul. The Pastorals also have an emphasis on adhering to true belief or teaching that Paul's acknowledged letters lack. For instance, the term "teaching" (or "doctrine"), used fifteen times in the Pastorals (1 Tim 1:10; 4:1, 6, 13, 16; 5:17; 6:1, 3; 2 Tim 3:10, 16; 4:3; Titus 1:9; 2:1, 7, 10), occurs only twice in Paul's acknowledged letters (Rom 12:7; 15:4) and twice in the disputed letters (Eph 4:14; Col 2:22). The Pastorals frequently use the term "the faith" in the sense of a body of beliefs or teachings (1 Tim 1:19; 3:9; 4:1, 6; 6:10, 12, 21; 2 Tim 3:8;

4:7; Titus 1:13; 2:2), a sense alien to Paul. The concept of "soundness" – "sound teaching" (1 Tim 1:10; 2 Tim 4:3; Titus 1:9; 2:1), "sound words" (1 Tim 6:3; 2 Tim 1:13; Titus 2:8), or being "sound in the faith" (Titus 1:13; 2:2) – occurs nine times in the Pastorals but nowhere else in Paul. The concept of knowing the truth, frequent in the Pastorals (1 Tim 2:4; 4:3; 2 Tim 2:25; 3:7; Titus 1:1), is likewise absent from Paul. Most strikingly, the concept of "piety" (or "godliness"), so central to the Pastorals (1 Tim 2:2; 3:16; 4:7, 8; 5:4; 6:3, 5, 6, 11; 2 Tim 3:5, 12; Titus 1:1; 2:12), appears nowhere else in Paul. Numerous other examples could be given.

Setting in Paul's Life

Furthermore, the Pastorals do not appear to fit into the framework of Paul's life as described by Acts and by Paul's acknowledged letters. On first view, it might seem possible to fit First Timothy and Titus into Paul's period of activity at Ephesus during his second missionary journey. In First Timothy, Paul writes from Macedonia to Timothy in Ephesus (1 Tim 1:3). In Titus, he writes to Timothy in Crete (1:5), perhaps from nearby Ephesus or Macedonia. However, all three letters must have been written at the same period, since they manifest the same distinctive style and deal with the same concerns. Since Second Timothy purports to be from Paul's imprisonment in Rome, the other two letters could not be from an earlier time.

According to a tradition cited by the church historian Eusebius, Paul was released from prison in Rome, did further missionary activity, then suffered martyrdom in a second Roman imprisonment (*Ecclesiastical History* 2.22.2). Some scholars, accepting this tradition, believe that Paul wrote First Timothy and Titus after his first imprisonment while engaged in further missionary activity in the East, then wrote Second Timothy during his second imprisonment. They account for the Pastorals' peculiarities in vocabulary and style by arguing that Paul wrote these letters as an old man, after his ideas and style had developed. This view, however, which assumes further missionary activity in the East, is contradicted by both Romans 15:23, where Paul says he has no room for further work in those regions, and Acts 20:25 (cf. 20:38), which indicates that Paul would not return to that area.

Features of Proto-Orthodoxy

The Pastorals reflect several features of Proto-Orthodox Christianity, which developed after Paul's death: the monarchic episcopate, the theory of apostolic succession, and a body of inspired scripture.

Church organization in the Pastorals appears to be more developed than in Paul's day. The Proto-Orthodox church developed the **monarchic episcopate**, in which one bishop (overseer) held pre-eminence over a number of lesser elders. This system may be implied in the Pastorals, since the term "bishop" appears only in the singular, while "elders" appears in the plural as well. One argument against this view is that the term "bishop" in Titus 1:7 is singular because it follows the singular "anyone" in 1:5, which refers to a single elder. If so, then the terms "elder" and "bishop" could be interchangeable designations for the same official. In this case, the Pastorals know only two offices, that of the elders (bishops) and that of the deacons, the same offices known in the churches of Paul (Phil 1:1; Rom 16:1; Acts 14:23; 20:17, 28).

The Pastorals also present the theory of **apostolic succession**, an idea first found elsewhere at the end of the first century. According to this theory, the true teaching of the church was passed down in an unbroken chain of tradition from the apostles to local church leaders. This chain of tradition served to establish the authority of the "orthodox" bishop over his rivals, such as Gnostic church leaders. The Pastorals support this claim: the true tradition passes from God to Paul (1 Tim 1:11; 2 Tim 1:11–12), from Paul to his younger co-workers (1 Tim 1:18; 2 Tim 1:13–14), and from them to other responsible leaders who can teach yet others (2 Tim 2:1–2; Titus 1:5–9).

The Pastorals also emphasize the importance of **inspired scripture** (2 Tim 3:15–17). The "sacred writings" that Timothy knew from childhood would consist primarily of the Jewish scriptures. However, in referring to "every scripture," the author may have in mind later Christian texts as well. His view that these are "God-breathed" suggests that he has in mind a developed canon of scripture that is regarded as inspired. This perspective seems to fit best into a time after Paul.

Conclusion

These aspects of the letters have convinced most scholars that some unknown church leader wrote them using Paul's name to give them greater authority. Since the author traces a line of tradition from Paul to Timothy and Titus, then on to other "faithful men" with the ability to teach yet others (2 Tim 2:1), he himself may have been one of the "faithful men" in the third or fourth generation of leaders in a Pauline church. Most likely he was a bishop in one of the churches that Paul established. Since he writes in Paul's name to Timothy in Ephesus (1 Tim 1:3) and Titus in Crete (Titus 1:5), some scholars have inferred that he was located in the area of the Aegean Sea. The perspective of his letters probably fits best in the second century. This author wanted to invoke Paul's authority to support his own vision of proper church order and "sound teaching."

Early Christian pseudepigraphy

The practice of pseudepigraphy, writing under an assumed name, flourished in early Christianity among all varieties of Christian groups, whether Judaic-Christian, Gnostic-Christian, or Proto-Orthodox. The New Testament Apocrypha and the Nag Hammadi Library abound with gospels, books of acts, and apocalypses written in the name of famous apostles.

Even the New Testament probably includes several pseudepigraphal works: the Pastoral Epistles, Jude, First Peter, and Second Peter. We have seen that many scholars also regard Second Thessalonians, Colossians, and Ephesians as pseudepigraphal works written in the name of Paul. Likewise many scholars believe that the letter of James was written under an assumed name.

What motivated early Christians to write under an assumed name? Generally the authors used the names of apostles or significant figures from the apostolic period, such as Peter or Paul. Such a practice had two functions. First, the use of such a name lent the authority of the apostle to the author's writing. Some authors apparently felt that their writings would be more readily accepted if people thought they came from an apostle. Second, the use of a name from the past gave the author's ideas the impression of antiquity. In a culture that valued tradition, authors wanted to present their own views as rooted in the past, specifically the apostolic period.

How could early Christians justify what appears to us as a deceptive practice? Apparently they felt that the ends justified the means. Scholars have shown that Plato's theory of "the good lie" influenced early Christian writers. According to Plato, a lie was permissible if it was for the good of the person lied to. We can assume, then, that some early Christian authors felt that they were writing for the good of the church and that this purpose justified the deception. Those who were deceived, however, took a different view of the matter. For instance, about 170 CE a Proto-Orthodox church leader wrote the Acts of Paul under the name of Paul. When his associates discovered the forgery, they deposed him from office. The value of the pseudepigraphy therefore depended on its remaining undiscovered.

SOCIAL CONTROL IN THE PASTORALS

All three Pastorals share the same basic concern: social control. The Pastoralist vests control of the social order in a male hierarchy: in the family a male head of the household, and in the church a male council of elders led by a bishop. Those occupying a lower rung on the social ladder are to be subordinate to this hierarchy. The Pastoralist wishes to see church members conform to this social order in both the household and the church. He designates conformity with this order as *eusebeia*. This Greek term corresponds to the Latin *pietas* ("**piety**" or "dutiful conduct"), a key virtue in Roman culture. Piety demanded that a Roman be dutiful to his family, friends, nation, and gods. In the Pastorals, this key term functions as an all-purpose word to describe what the author considers right, including both right belief and right conduct. The Pastoralist's concern with piety or proper social order comes to expression in three main themes in the Pastoral Epistles: order in the household; order in the house of God (the church); and control of teaching in the church.

Order in the Household

The Pastoralist exhorts members of the family to take their place in the approved social order of the Roman household (1 Tim 5:1–6:2; Titus 2:1–10). One's standing in that order depended on gender (male/female), age (old/young), marital status (married/widowed), and social class (master/slave). Appropriate conduct in the family consisted of piety or duty. The father's duty was to look out for the interests of his family, while it was their duty to give him respect and obedience. While the father pursued a career, the wife's duty was to devote herself to her family. Children were to be dutiful toward their parents. In the Pastorals, the author exhorts Timothy and Titus to instruct family members in "what befits sound teaching" (Titus 2:1) or "the teaching which accords with piety" (1 Tim 6:3) so that they will live "pious lives" (Titus 2:12). Piety for children included taking care of a widowed mother (1 Tim 5:4).

Order in the House of God

Romans thought of the state as an extended family. Just as the family had a father at its head, so the heads of state were called "fathers." Just as

relationships in the family were governed by piety or duty, so too were relationships in the state, at least ideally. The aristocrats in charge were supposed to look out for the interests of the masses, while the masses owed them obedience and respect. In a similar way, the Pastoralist conceives of the larger social body, the church, as an extended family. He gives instructions in "how one must behave in God's house, which is the church of the living God" (1 Tim 3:15). Like the family household, the household of God has its proper order.

At the top stand the bishop and the elders. The elders constitute a council that transmits authority by "laying hands" on those appointed to an office (1 Tim 4:14; 5:22). The bishop is apparently one of the elders who occupies a place of pre-eminence. The Pastoralist sets out specific qualifications for elders and the bishop (1 Tim 3; Titus 1:5–9). Elders, especially those who teach, may receive payment (1 Tim 5:17–18). Church members are supposed to be subordinate to the elders, and the Pastoralist denounces those who are not (Titus 1:10).

The author also gives qualifications for deacons ("servers") but does not specify their function (1 Tim 3:8–13). It is unclear whether the "women" mentioned in this passage are themselves deacons or wives of deacons. The church also supports a special class of "widows" (1 Tim 5:3–16). The Pastoralist permits men of the congregation to participate in communal prayer, but enjoins silence on the women (1 Tim 2:1–15).

Control of Teaching in the Church

The Pastoralist recognizes that control of the church will reside in the hands of those who control the church's teaching. The Pastoralist vests that control in the bishop and the elders. They have the responsibility to exhort with the "sound teaching" and to refute those who disagree (Titus 1:9). The Pastoralist never specifies the content of the true teaching, merely designating it as "sound teaching," "the faith," the "gospel," or "piety." He doubtless has in mind what it is but is more concerned with who has it. He locates the true teaching in a chain of tradition: it passed from God to Paul, from Paul to Timothy and Titus, and from Timothy and Titus to other faithful men, among whom the Pastoralist no doubt numbered himself and those in his camp.

What concerns the Pastoralist is that not everyone accepts the claim of the bishop and elders to control the church's teaching. There are "many" who teach things that contradict the "sound teaching." Since these do not submit to the Pastoralist's point of view, they are "insubordinate" (Titus 1:10). He has nothing good to say about them, impugning their motivation as a desire for financial gain (1 Tim 6:3–10; Titus 1:11) and charging that their minds and consciences have been corrupted (1 Tim 1:19; 4:2; Titus 1:15; 2 Tim 3:8).

It is unclear whether the Pastoralist had in mind a single group of opponents or more than one. We can infer that some of his opponents were Jewish since he singles out "those of the circumcision" as the worst offenders (Titus 1:10). We can distinguish at least four different aspects of the teaching that he opposed.

1. First Timothy 4:1–4 refers to people who forbid marriage and abstain from certain foods. The Pastoralist presents this perspective as not present during the time of Paul but arising "in later times." He refers here to practices that were common in the second century and later: abstinence from marriage and meat. People who practiced such abstinence were

known as **Encratites**, from the Greek word *enkrateia* ("restraint" or "self-control"). Irenaeus (c. 180) associated such practices with Saturninus and Marcion, both of whom flourished around 140 CE, and with Tatian several decades later (*Against Heresies* 1.28).

2. Both letters to Timothy polemicize against "myths" (1 Tim 1:4; 4:7; 2 Tim 4:4), and the letter to Titus calls these "Jewish myths" (Titus 1:14). The Pastoralist may be referring to Gnostic mythology based on the Jewish book of Genesis, such as that found in the Apocryphon of John.

3. The Pastoralist also inveighs against "genealogies" (Titus 3:9) or "endless genealogies" (1 Tim 1:4). He may be referring to Gnostic accounts of the emanation of the aeons. In such accounts, one aeon or pair of aeons emanated from the original light, a second aeon or pair of aeons emanated from the first, a third emanated from the second, and so forth.

4. The Pastoralist attributes to Hymenaeus and Philetus, persons who are otherwise unknown, the view that the resurrection had already occurred (2 Tim 2:17–18; cf. 1 Tim 1:20). These may have held a view similar to that which Tertullian (c. 150–229) ascribed to some unnamed adversaries. In this view, people who are ignorant of God are dead, just as if they were buried in a grave. But when they come to know God, they are reanimated and resurrected. They burst forth from the sepulcher of the old man and are with the Lord after they put on Christ in baptism (Tertullian, *On the Resurrection of the Flesh* 19). A similar non-literal understanding of resurrection appears in the Gnostic Christian work *Treatise on the Resurrection*. In both cases, one could say that those who have acquired knowledge of the truth have experienced resurrection from the dead already in the present life.

The teaching opposed by the Pastoralist probably included not only Encratism, but also some form of Gnostic Christianity. If so, it may be significant that the Pastoralist calls this perspective "knowledge (*gnosis*) falsely co called" (1 Tim 6:20).

READING GUIDE: I TIMOTHY

Read the letter of First Timothy with the help of the following guide.

The letter's **introduction (1:1–2)** includes the name of Paul as the sender (1:1), the name of Timothy as the recipient (1:2a), and a salutation (1:2b).

The author first condemns **false teaching (1:3–20)**. "Paul" recalls that he left Timothy in Ephesus when he went to Macedonia. Paul did in fact travel from Ephesus to Macedonia near the end of his second missionary journey (2 Cor 2:12–13; Acts 20:1), but, according to Acts, Timothy had already left Ephesus for Macedonia at that time (Acts 19:22).

According to the present letter, Paul left Timothy in Ephesus to stop certain persons from promoting a divergent teaching (1:3–7). The nature of this teaching is unclear. It was based on the Hebrew Scriptures: those who presented it wished to be "teachers of the Law" (1:7). They occupied themselves with "myths and endless genealogies" (1:4). Paul asserts that, rightly understood, the Law applies not to the righteous but to the lawless (1:8–11).

In contrast to these, Paul has been entrusted by God with the gospel (1:11). Mention of this fact leads him to thank God for showing him this mercy (1:12–17). In 1:18–20, he then commits to Timothy a charge to maintain a good conscience, unlike Hymenaeus and Alexander (cf. 2 Tim 2:17–18; 4:14–15). Paul says that he delivered them to Satan, i.e. expelled them from the church.

Next the author gives **instructions for the assembly (2:1–15)**. Prayers are to be made for all people, especially kings and those in authority (2:1–7). Men are to pray with uplifted hands (2:1–8), while women are to learn in silence and bear children (2:9–15). Paul bases the subordination of women on the creation myth in Genesis 2 and the alienation myth in Genesis 3 (2:13–14).

The author then gives qualifications for a **bishop and deacons (3:1–13)**. An essential qualification for the holder of each office is that he exercise control over his own wife and children.

Paul characterizes his letter so far as instruction on "how one must behave in God's house" (3:14–15). He summarizes "**the mystery of piety**" in a brief creedal statement about Jesus (3:16).

The next section gives a **prediction of apostasy (4:1–5)**. "Paul" predicts that in later times some will depart from the faith by adopting the teaching that one should abstain from marriage and certain kinds of food. Here the Pastoralist refers to the teaching of the Encratites, who abstained from marriage and meat. This prediction is a *vaticinium ex eventu*, a prophecy after the fact. The Pastoralist was familiar with the Encratites in his own day, probably sometime in the second century. By pretending to be Paul, he could "predict" something that he knew would happen in the time after Paul lived. He uses the authority of Paul to condemn this teaching. He attributes his opponents' perspective to "deceitful spirits" and "demons," but his own perspective to "the Spirit" (of God).

In a **charge to Timothy (4:6–16)**, Paul urges Timothy to be "a good minister of Christ Jesus" by avoiding the false teaching, training himself in piety, setting an example for others, and devoting himself to his duties toward the church.

Paul then gives Timothy **instructions for various groups (5:1–6:2)** in the household and the church: older men and women (5:1–2), widows (5:3–16), elders (5:17–20), Timothy himself (5:21–25), and slaves (6:1–2).

In a section on **godliness and gain (6:3–19)**, Paul accuses the false teachers of using piety as a means of gain. But the love of money is the root of all evils (6:3–10). Timothy is to shun this type of behavior and aim for righteousness (6:11–16). He is to teach the wealthy to set their hopes on God, not riches (6:17–19).

In the **conclusion (6:20–21)**, the author gives a final warning against what is falsely called "knowledge" (*gnosis*) and a brief benediction.

READING GUIDE: TITUS

Read the letter to Titus with the help of the following guide.

The letter's **introduction (1:1–4)** includes the name and description of Paul as the sender (1:1–3), the name of Titus as the recipient (1:4a), and a salutation (1:4b). Paul's lengthy description of his role as an apostle resembles that in Romans (Rom 1:1–6). However, the Pastoralist uses several expressions that Paul does not use in his acknowledged letters: "slave of God," "piety," "our savior God," and the idea that Paul was made an apostle "by the command" of God.

Writing as Paul, the author then gives qualifications for **elders and a bishop (1:5–9)**. Paul's instructions to Titus presuppose that he himself had previously been in Crete. He left Titus there to complete the work and to appoint elders in every town. The main qualification of elders is that they be good family men. The author's transition from plural (elders) to singular (bishop) may indicate that a single bishop came from among the elders and presided over them. Qualifications of the bishop include the ability to exhort with "the sound teaching" and to refute those who disagree.

This qualification serves as a transition to the following topic of **false teachers (1:10–16)**. Paul complains of "many" who are "insubordinate," that is, who do not submit to his perspective. These may have been professional teachers since Paul alleges that they teach for the sake of "base gain." Their teaching must be religious since "they profess to know God." They have apparently been successful with a number of families so that "they pervert whole houses." Paul showers these people with invective: they are "empty in their talk and deceived in their thinking." He characterizes them as "detestable and disobedient and unfit for any good deed." Against these teachers, or those who accept their teaching, Paul cites with approval an ethnic slur leveled against Cretans by Epimenides of Cnossus (sixth century BCE): "Cretans are always liars, evil beasts, idle gluttons." As the worst offenders, Paul singles out "those of the circumcision." This expression elsewhere refers to Judaic Christians (Gal 2:11; Col 4:11; Acts 10:45; 11:2). Aspects of their teaching include "Jewish myths" and "commandments of humans." These commandments may be the prohibitions against marriage and meat mentioned in 1 Timothy (4:1–5). If these teachers considered marriage and meat impure, it would explain why Paul asserts to the contrary that "All things are pure to the pure." Paul informs Titus that these teachers must be "silenced." He must "correct sharply" the Cretans so that "they may be sound in the faith" and not give heed to such teaching.

Titus, in contrast to the false teachers, is to speak **sound teaching (2:1–3:11)**. He is to instruct various groups in the church in proper behavior: the older men, the older women, the younger women, the younger men, and the slaves (2:2–10). Such behavior is to be a response to the grace of God (2:11–15). Titus is to remind his audience of their salvation from their former lives (3:1–8) and to admonish divisive persons (3:9–11).

In the **conclusion (3:12–15)**, Paul shares his future plans and gives instruction concerning some of his co-workers. He ends with greetings and a benediction.

READING GUIDE: 2 TIMOTHY

Read the letter of Second Timothy with the help of the following guide.

In First Timothy and Titus, Paul is at liberty. In Second Timothy, by contrast, he is imprisoned in Rome (1:16–17), expecting his death to come soon (4:6–8). He writes a final letter to Timothy, who is apparently still in Ephesus (1 Tim 1:3) with Onesiphorus and Prisca and Aquila (1:16–18; 4:19). Tychicus apparently carried Paul's letter to Timothy in Ephesus (4:12).

The letter's **introduction (1:1–2)** includes the name of Paul as the sender (1:1); the name of Timothy, Paul's "beloved child," as the recipient (1:2a); and a salutation (1:2b).

In the following **thanksgiving (1:3–5)**, Paul tells Timothy that he thanks God whenever he remembers him.

The first main part of the letter consists of an **exhortation to Timothy (1:6–2:13)**. Paul reminds Timothy to rekindle the gift of God that he received when Paul laid hands on him (1:6–7), presumably the ministry of an evangelist (cf. 4:5). Timothy should not be ashamed of testifying about Jesus or ashamed of Paul, but should share in suffering for the gospel, the message of salvation through Jesus (1:8–10). Paul himself suffers for the gospel but is not ashamed. He exhorts Timothy to follow and guard the "pattern of sound words" that God entrusted to Paul and which he passed on to Timothy (1:11–14). Of the Christians from the Roman province of Asia, only Onesiphorus from Ephesus was not ashamed of Paul's chains and visited him in Rome (1:15–18). Timothy should take what he has heard from Paul and entrust it to other faithful men who can teach it to others (2:1–2). He should share in suffering like a soldier of Christ, compete like an athlete, and share in the crops like a farmer (2:3–7). He should remember Paul's gospel, for which Paul endures suffering so that the elect may obtain salvation (2:8–10). Those who die and endure with Christ will live and reign with him, but those who deny him he will deny (2:11–13).

The second part of the letter focuses on **sound teaching and false teaching (2:14–4:5)**. Paul contrasts the type of minister Timothy should be with other teachers who have swerved from the truth. Timothy should avoid disputes over words and empty chatter, such as the words of Hymenaeus (cf. 1 Tim 1:20) and Philetus, who teach that the resurrection has already occurred (2:14–19).

Just as a large house contains vessels for reputable and disreputable purposes, so in the church one who purifies himself from the disreputable will be a vessel for reputable purposes, such as righteousness, faith, love, and peace. Timothy should avoid foolish, uninformed disputes but correct his opponents with gentleness in the hope that they will come to know the truth and escape from the devil's trap (2:20–26).

In a *vaticinium ex eventu* Paul warns that in the last days there will be men characterized by every sort of vice, whom Timothy should avoid. Among these are those who insinuate themselves into households and captivate gullible women. They are like Jannes and Jambres, the names that Jewish tradition gave to the magicians who opposed Moses (Ex 7:11,

22; 9:11; cf. *Damascus Document* 5:18–19 in the Dead Sea Scrolls). But their folly will become apparent (3:1–9).

Timothy has followed Paul's teaching, behavior, and sufferings. All who wish to live piously in Christ will be persecuted, while evil impostors continue to deceive and be deceived. But Timothy should continue in what he has learned from Paul and the scriptures (3:10–17).

Paul solemnly charges Timothy to proclaim the message. He warns that a time will come when people will not put up with sound teaching but turn away to the myths (4:1–5).

The third part of the letter focuses on **Paul's approaching death (4:6–18)**. Paul knows that the time has come for him to depart and receive a crown of righteousness (4:6–8). He wants Timothy to come to him quickly since most of his co-workers are absent (4:9–15). At his first defense no one stood by him, but the Lord rescued him from the fate of being eaten by lions in the arena (4:16–18).

In the **conclusion (4:19–22)**, Paul greets people in Ephesus, relays greetings from people in Rome, and concludes with a benediction.

DISCUSSION QUESTION

How do the Pastoral Epistles illustrate the typical features of Proto-Orthodox Christianity that are discussed in Chapter 31?

REVIEW QUESTIONS

1. What is one of the most common concerns of Proto-Orthodox literature, one that is reflected in the Pastoral Epistles?
2. Identify or define: Pastoral Epistles, Timothy, Titus.
3. What three aspects of the Pastoral Epistles have convinced most scholars that Paul did not write them?
4. How do the vocabulary and style of the Pastoral Epistles indicate that Paul did not write them?
5. How do the Pastoral Epistles relate to the framework of Paul's life as described by Acts and Paul's acknowledged letters?
6. The Pastoral Epistles refer to what features of Proto-Orthodox Christianity? Identify or define: monarchic episcopate, apostolic succession.
7. What motivated early Christians to write under an assumed name? How did they justify this practice?

8. What is the basic concern of the Pastoral Epistles? What three themes express this concern? Identify or define: piety.
9. Summarize the Pastoralist's view of order in the household and order in the church.
10. Distinguish four different aspects of the teaching that the Pastoralist opposed. Identify: Encratites.

SUGGESTIONS FOR FURTHER STUDY

Dibelius, Martin. *The Pastoral Epistles: A Commentary on the Pastoral Epistles* (rev. by Hans Conzelmann; Hermeneia; Fortress, 1972). A standard commentary on the Pastoral Epistles.

Donelson, Lewis R. *Pseudepigraphy and Ethical Argument in the Pastoral Epistles* (Mohr, 1986). Examines ancient pseudepigraphal writings and Greco-Roman ethics to illuminate the theology and ethics of the Pastorals.

Harrison, P. N. *The Problem of the Pastoral Epistles* (Milford, 1921; reprinted, Forgotten Books, 2012). A classic study that shows the differences in style between the Pastorals and Paul's letters.

Levine, Amy-Jill, with Marianne Blickenstaff, eds. *A Feminist Companion to the Deutero-Pauline Epistles* (Bloomsbury T&T Clark, 2003). Includes four essays on the place of women in the Pastoral Epistles.

MacDonald, Margaret Y. *The Pauline Churches: A Socio-Historical Study of Institutionalization in the Pauline and Deutero-Pauline Writings* (Cambridge University Press, 1989). Traces developments in attitudes toward the world, ethics, ministry, ritual, and belief from Paul to the Pastoral Epistles.

Verner, David C. *The Household of God: The Social World of the Pastoral Epistles* (Scholars, 1983). Uses the concept "the household of God" as a key to the social structure, social status, and social tensions in the church of the Pastorals.

Young, Frances. *The Theology of the Pastoral Letters* (Cambridge University Press, 1994). Delineates the major themes and concerns of the Pastorals.

33   Conflict in the Church (2)
Jude and 2 Peter

Like the other letters in this section, the letters of Jude and Second Peter oppose some form of divergent teaching from a Proto-Orthodox perspective. The two letters stand in close relationship to one another, opposing the same form of teaching in wording that is often identical. Both address Christians in general rather than a specific church or individual.

AUTHOR OF JUDE

The author of the letter of Jude identifies himself as "Jude ... the brother of James" (Jude 1). The name Jude, also translated as "Judas," belongs to several men in the New Testament. We know of only one, however, who had a brother named James. This Judas was brother of the James who led the church in Jerusalem, both men being brothers of Jesus (Mark 6:3; Matt 13:55). It is probably this Jude to which the letter refers.

Jude the brother of Jesus probably did not write this letter, since the author writes as if the apostles belonged to an earlier time (Jude 17–18) and speaks of "the faith" as a deposit of tradition passed down from former times (Jude 3), in a way reminiscent of second-century writings such as the Pastoral Epistles. Some later Jude may have written the letter, but it is more likely that a later writer merely used the name of Jude, the brother of James and Jesus, in order to lend authority to the letter.

AUTHOR OF 2 PETER

Though the author of the letter of Second Peter identifies himself as the apostle "Symeon Peter," nearly all scholars doubt this claim. These doubts are raised by several considerations. First, Christian writers do not mention this letter until the third century, when Origen states that

461

its authenticity was disputed (about 240 CE). Second, the author's Greek style and language are quite ornate and literary, not what one would expect from a Galilean fisherman. Third, the author refers to Paul's letters as "scriptures" (2 Pet 3:16), a status that Paul's letters probably did not have in Peter's lifetime. Fourth, the letter appears to come from a time later than the first century, since the hope for the imminent return of Jesus has faded and some are wondering whether Jesus will return at all (2 Pet 3:3–10). Fifth, the author of Second Peter may have borrowed from Jude, a practice that seems unlikely for an apostle. Sixth, the style of the letter differs from that of First Peter (a significant factor only if Peter wrote First Peter). These considerations suggest that a second-century author wrote the letter, using the authority of Peter's name.

Shared wording in Jude and 2 Peter

The following comparison shows the similarities between the two letters by underlining the words that they have in common. Four different theories could account for this common wording. (1) The author of Second Peter borrowed from Jude. (2) The author of Jude borrowed from Second Peter. (3) Both authors borrowed from a common source. (4) One author wrote both letters under two different assumed names.

JUDE 4–18	2 PETER 2:1–3:4
… impious people, changing the grace of our God into <u>licentiousness</u> and <u>denying</u> our only <u>master</u> and Lord, Jesus Christ (4)	… false teachers, who will bring in heresies of destruction, even <u>denying the master</u> who bought them … And many will follow their <u>licentious acts</u> … (2:1–2)
<u>angels</u> who did not keep their own principality but left their own habitation he has <u>kept</u> under <u>gloom</u> in everlasting bonds <u>for</u> the <u>judgment</u> of a great day (6)	For if God did not spare <u>angels</u> who sinned, but committed them to pits of <u>gloom</u>, sending them to Tartarus, where they are being <u>kept for judgment</u> … (2:4)
just as <u>Sodom and Gomorrah</u> and the cities around them, who in the same way as these committed fornication and went after different flesh, lie before us as an <u>example</u> of eternal fire (7)	… and condemned the cities of <u>Sodom and Gomorrah</u>, reducing them to ashes, having provided an <u>example</u> of things to come for the ungodly … (2:6)
… they defile the <u>flesh</u> and set aside <u>lordship</u> and <u>revile glories</u>. But Michael the <u>archangel</u>, when in disputing with the Devil he argued about the body of Moses, <u>did not dare to bring a judgment of reviling</u>, but said, "<u>The Lord</u> rebuke you." (8–9)	… those who go after <u>flesh</u> in desire of pollution <u>and</u> despise <u>lordship</u>. <u>Daring</u>, audacious, they do not fear <u>glories</u>, <u>reviling</u> where <u>angels</u> greater in strength and power <u>do not bring a reviling judgment</u> against them from <u>the Lord</u> (2:10–11)

But these people revile whatever they do not understand, and by those things which they do know by instinct like the irrational animals, they are destroyed. (10)	But these people, like irrational animals, creatures of instinct born for capture and destruction, reviling in matters in which they are ignorant, with their destruction will also be destroyed. (2:12)
they went in the path of Cain, and abandoned themselves to the error of Balaam for payment, and perished in the rebellion of Korah (11)	leaving a straight path, they erred, following the path of Balaam the son of Bosor, who loved the payment of unrighteousness … (2:15)
These are the blemishes in your love feasts, feasting with you fearlessly, shepherding themselves; waterless clouds carried along by winds; trees of autumn without fruit, which twice having died have been uprooted; stormy waves of the sea, washing up their own shameful deeds like foam; wandering stars, for whom the gloom of the darkness has been reserved for ever. (12–13)	… blemishes and spots, revelling in their deceptions, feasting with you … (2:13) These are waterless springs and mists driven by storm, for whom the gloom of the darkness has been reserved (2:17)
… their mouth speaks bombastic words (16)	… uttering bombastic words (2:18)
… remember the words spoken formerly by the apostles of our Lord Jesus Christ, that they said to you that in the last time there will be scoffers going according to their desires for ungodly things … (17–18)	… to remember the words spoken formerly by the holy prophets and the command of the Lord and Savior spoken by your apostles, knowing this first, that in the last days scoffers will come with scoffing, going according to their own desires and saying, "Where is the promise of his coming?" (3:2–4)

THE OPPONENTS OF JUDE AND 2 PETER

Both letters denounce a group of persons in the same terms. This group consists of "impious people" according to Jude 4 or "false teachers" according to 2 Peter 2:1. These persons are not outsiders but belong to the Christian community (Jude 4) and participate in the Christian love feasts (Jude 12; 2 Pet 2:13). The letters make two primary charges against these people. The first is christological: they are "denying our only master and Lord, Jesus Christ" (Jude 4) or "denying the master who bought them" (2 Pet 2:1). "Peter" makes a more specific statement: they deny that Jesus will come again (2 Pet 3:3). The second charge is ethical: they are "changing the grace of our God into licentiousness" (Jude 4), and "many will follow their licentious acts" (2 Pet 2:2). The term "licentiousness" in this context

Figure 33.1
A sixth- or seventh-century icon portraying Peter. Early Christians wrote a number of works in Peter's name, including Second Peter. Monastery of St. Catherine at Sinai (Art Collection 3/Alamy Stock Photo).

means giving free reign to the desires of the body, but the letters give no specific details about this alleged licentious behavior.

The group opposed in these letters may represent some type of Gnostic Christianity. Gnostic Christians often attended the same churches as the Proto-Orthodox. They often distinguished between Christ and Jesus, which might lead to the charge that they denied "our only master and Lord." They had no use for the return of Christ or the new heaven and earth that would accompany it (2 Pet 3:13), since they looked for translation to the heavenly realm above. And Proto-Orthodox opponents often charged them with licentious behavior, although the Gnostic sources themselves do not support such a charge.

Use of non-canonical texts

Both Jude and Second Peter refer to two Jewish writings other than the Hebrew Scriptures: the apocalyptic book of 1 Enoch, included in the Old Testament Pseudepigrapha, and the Assumption of Moses, a lost work mentioned by early Christian writers. Both Jude and Second Peter allude to 1 Enoch 6–16, which recounts a story, based on Genesis 6:1–4, about angels who mated with human women and were punished by God (Jude 6, 13; 2 Pet 2:4, 17). Jude also includes another reference to 1 Enoch (Jude 14–15 = 1 Enoch 1:9). Both Jude and Second Peter also refer to a story in the Assumption of Moses about a dispute between the archangel Michael and the Devil (Jude 8–10; 2 Pet 2:10–11).

The authors use these non-canonical texts as authorities in the same way they use the Hebrew Scriptures. Apparently, then, at the time and place in which these letters were written, Christians had not adopted the fixed canon of the Old Testament that later prevailed. In Judaism, the canon of the Hebrew Scriptures had become relatively fixed by the late first century, yet for many Jews too the Pseudepigrapha still had value as scripture.

READING GUIDE: JUDE

Read the letter of Jude with the help of the following guide.

The letter's **introduction (1–2)** includes the name and identification of Jude as the sender, a general address to those "called" to be Christians, and a salutation.

The body of the letter begins with a **warning against impious persons (3–19)**. Jude exhorts his readers to contend for "the faith," which has been challenged by certain "impious" persons who have sneaked in. He makes two charges against them: they practice licentiousness and deny Jesus Christ (3–4). In condemning these people, he cites examples of disobedient parties whom God punished (5–7). These consist of people saved from Egypt who did not believe (Num 14), angels who mated with human women (1 Enoch 6–16), and the cities of Sodom and Gomorrah (Gen 19).

Jude then details the faults of these people. Unlike Michael the archangel in his dispute with Satan (Assumption of Moses), they reject lordship and blaspheme glories (8–10). They went in the way of Cain, who killed his brother (Gen 4); they abandoned themselves to the error of Balaam, who cursed the Israelites for money (Num 22–25; 31:13–16); and they perished in the rebellion of Korah, who unlawfully sought to be a priest (Num 16). They carouse at the love feasts of the church (12–13). Enoch prophesied that the Lord would come to execute judgment on them (14–15; 1 Enoch 1:9). They are despicable in various ways (16).

The letter continues with a **warning against scoffers (17–19)**. Jude reminds his audience that the apostles predicted the coming of scoffers in the last time (17–19).

In a **final exhortation (17–23)**, Jude exhorts his audience, in contrast to these, to build themselves up, pray, keep themselves in the love of God, and wait for Jesus to return. They should convince, save, and have mercy on those whom they can.

As a **conclusion (24–25)**, Jude gives a lengthy doxology, to which he adds "Amen."

READING GUIDE: 2 PETER

Read the letter of Second Peter with the help of the following guide.

The letter's **introduction (1:1–2)** includes the name and identification of "Symeon Peter" as the sender, a general address to those who have a faith like his, and a salutation.

The body of the letter begins with a section on **sharing the divine nature (1:3–15)**. Peter exhorts his audience that, since God's divine power has bestowed on them everything necessary to share in the divine nature, they should supplement their faith with various other virtues, which are aspects of the divine nature, in order to make sure that they will enter Christ's kingdom. He writes so that they will have a reminder of this exhortation after his death, knowing that he will soon die as Jesus showed him (cf. John 21:18–19).

The next section defends the view of **Jesus as God's son (1:16–21)**. Peter contrasts his view of Jesus with "cleverly devised myths" that others have followed. As we learn later, he has in mind people who deny Jesus (2:1). In refutation of their view, he emphasizes in two ways that Jesus was the son of God. First, he recalls the gospel story of Jesus' transfiguration (Mark 9:2–8). Peter claims that he was an eyewitness of this event and heard God address Jesus as his son. Second, this testimony confirms "the prophetic word," i.e. the Jewish scriptures, which Peter interprets as predictions which also affirm that Jesus was God's son. Apparently Peter's opponents would not agree with his interpretation of the scriptures, so he denies that private individuals have the ability or authority to interpret scripture. Presumably he vests that authority with the orthodox representatives of the church, among whom he counts himself.

The next section parallels the letter of Jude with a **warning against false teachers (2:1–22)**. Peter's prediction of the coming of "false teachers" is a *vaticinium ex eventu*, a prophecy after the fact. The author of the letter was familiar with such teachers in his own day. By pretending to be Peter, he could "predict" something that he knew would happen in the time after Peter lived. He uses the authority of Peter to condemn this teaching. Like the author of Jude, he accuses them of denying Jesus and practicing licentiousness (2:1–2). He affirms that God will bring judgment on them, just as he did on the fallen angels (2:4; cf. 1 Enoch 6–16), the people destroyed by the flood (2:5; cf. Gen 6–9), and the cities of Sodom and Gomorrah (2:6–8; cf. Gen 19).

In 2:10b–22, Peter heaps abuse on these teachers. Unlike Michael in his dispute with the devil (Assumption of Moses), they revile lordship (2:10b–13a). They revel and carouse (2:13b–14a). Out of greed, they forsake the right way like Balaam (2:14b–16; cf. Num 22–25; 31:13–16). They lure weak Christians into committing licentious deeds by appealing to the desires of their flesh and promising freedom (2:17–22).

The parallel to Jude continues with a **warning against scoffers (3:1–10)**. The author assumes that Peter wrote the letter of First Peter and so identifies his own letter as Peter's second (3:1–2). He makes another prophecy after the fact, predicting the coming of "scoffers." The author of Jude characterized his opponents as "scoffers" without elaborating (Jude 18). The present author goes further in describing these scoffers: they scoff at the idea that Jesus will return. From its beginning, the church taught that Jesus would return within a generation. When he did not, some Christians, such as those condemned in this letter, began to doubt that he would return at all. The author of Second Peter seeks to justify Jesus' delay by distinguishing divine time and human time: with God "a thousand years are like a single day"

(Psalm 90:4). Eventually, he says, Jesus will return and the earth will be destroyed by fire. No other author in the New Testament associates Jesus' return with destruction of the earth by fire. This author may have gotten the idea from the Stoics, who did expect the earth to be consumed by fire.

In a **final exhortation (3:11–18a)**, Peter exhorts his audience to live holy and pious lives as they wait for a new heaven and earth (3:11–13). He cites the letters of Paul to support his position, referring to them as "scriptures," but he warns that unlearned people misinterpret them (3:14–16). He exhorts his audience not to be carried away with their error (3:17–18a).

As a **conclusion (3:18b)** Peter gives a brief doxology.

DISCUSSION QUESTION

What rhetorical strategies do the authors of Jude and Second Peter employ to support their own position and undermine the position of their opponents?

REVIEW QUESTIONS

1. What aspects of the letter of Jude indicate that Jude the brother of Jesus did not write it?
2. Why do most scholars believe that Peter did not write Second Peter?
3. What are four possible explanations for the common wording in Jude and Second Peter?
4. What two primary charges do these authors make against their opponents? Who might these opponents have been?
5. To what two non-canonical works do these letters refer?

SUGGESTIONS FOR FURTHER STUDY

Bauckham, Richard. *Jude and the Relatives of Jesus in the Early Church* (Bloomsbury T&T Clark, 1990). Examines the role of Jesus' relatives in early Jewish Christianity, arguing that the letter of Jude was written by Jesus' brother.

Charles, J. Daryl. *Literary Strategy in the Epistle of Jude* (University of Scranton Press, 1993). Examines the literary devices used by the author of Jude to persuade his audience.

Chester, Andrew, and Ralph P. Martin. *The Theology of the Letters of James, Peter, and Jude* (Cambridge University Press, 1994). Brief discussion of the setting and themes of Jude and Second Peter.

Davids, Peter H. *The Letters of 2 Peter and Jude* (Eerdmans, 2006). A commentary on Second Peter and Jude.

Kelly, J. N. D. *The Epistles of Peter and of Jude* (Black, 1969; reprinted, Hendrickson, 1999). A standard commentary on Jude and Second Peter along with First Peter.

Watson, Duane Frederick. *Invention, Arrangement, and Style: Rhetorical Criticism of Jude and 2 Peter* (Scholars, 1988). Outlines the method of rhetorical criticism and uses this method to analyze Jude and Second Peter.

34 Conflict in the Church (3)
Johannine Epistles

The Johannine Epistles, like the letters of Ignatius discussed in the next chapter, reflect a conflict between two groups within the church, one Proto-Orthodox and one docetic. In these letters, we hear only one side of the dispute, the Proto-Orthodox perspective.

AUTHOR AND DATE

The three letters designated First, Second, and Third John have such similar style and content that they must come from the same author. Tradition attributes them, along with the Fourth Gospel, to John the apostle, the son of Zebedee. In the letters themselves, however, the author does not identify himself, calling himself simply **the Elder** (2 John 1; 3 John 1). Because the second-century bishop Papias speaks of a leader at Ephesus called "the Elder John," whom he distinguished from John the apostle, some scholars think that the Elder John wrote the letters.

Whoever the author may have been, the letters are clearly related to the Fourth Gospel in both style and content. Many of the same themes occur in both. These similarities show that, at the very least, "the Elder" of the letters must have belonged to the same community from which the Fourth Gospel came. His mind was saturated with the ideas expressed in that gospel. He may even have played a role in its composition.

It is likely that the Gospel of John came first, followed by the letters of John. Whereas the gospel reflects a situation in which Jewish Christians were being expelled from the synagogue, the letters show no evidence of that conflict, probably because they belong to a later stage of the community after this separation had already occurred. If the Gospel of John appeared sometime between 80 and 110 CE, then the letters were written after the gospel in the late first or early second century.

Themes common to John and 1 John

These examples, while not exhaustive, illustrate themes shared by the Gospel of John and the letter of First John.

THEME	GOSPEL OF JOHN	1 JOHN
Christ as "the Word" (Logos)	1:1, 14	1:1
Christ or God as light	1:9; 8:12; 9:5; etc.	1:5; 2:8
Walking or abiding in the light or the darkness	8:12; 11:9–10; 12:35, 46	1:6–7; 2:10–11
The new commandment: love one another	13:34; 15:12	2:7–8; 3:11, 23; 4:12, 21
To be of the world or not of the world	8:23; 15:19; 17:14, 16; 18:36	2:16; 4:5
Children of God and children of the Devil	8:44	3:10
Hated by the world	7:7; 15:18–19, 23–25; 17:14	3:13
Eternal life as a present possession	3:36; 5:24; 6:47, 54	3:14; 5:11–13
Christ as the only (*monogenes*) Son	1:14, 18; 3:16, 18	4:9
God sent the Son into the world	3:16–17; 10:36; 17:18	4:9, 14

THE ELDER'S OPPONENTS

The Elder finds himself in conflict with a group of people who formerly belonged to his own church, or group of churches, but have now broken away:

> Children, the hour is late, and just as you heard that an antichrist is coming, even now many antichrists have come, from which we know that the hour is late. They went out from us, but they were not part of us. For if they had been part of us, they would have remained with us. (1 John 2:18–19)

The Elder gives few details about his opponents, but by noticing what he condemns we can reconstruct several characteristics of their viewpoint. These include a docetic christology, a docetic concept of salvation, a claim of prophetic inspiration, rejection of the Elder's authority, and a claim of fellowship with God.

Docetic Christology

The Elder's opponents held a docetic view of Jesus or Christ. The Elder calls them **antichrists**, meaning people who hold what he regards as an anti-Christian perspective. A little later he identifies this perspective: "Who is the liar if not he who denies that Jesus is the Christ? This is the antichrist" (2:22). Thus he labels his opponents as antichrists because they deny that Jesus is the Christ. Still later, the Elder explains more fully:

> Every spirit that confesses Jesus Christ having come in flesh is from God. And every spirit that does not confess Jesus is not from God. And this (spirit) is that of the antichrist. (1 John 4:2–3; cf. 2 John 7)

The Elder's opponents deny that Jesus is "Christ having come in flesh." This perspective seems to be a form of **docetism**, which denied the physical nature of Christ. In the early second century, Ignatius of Antioch polemicized against a group of docetists who believed that Christ only seemed to have a human body (see Chapter 35). The Elder's opponents may have held a view similar to theirs. Or like Cerinthus, they may have taught a distinction between Jesus and the Christ. In this perspective, Jesus was a normal human, while Christ was a purely spiritual being (Irenaeus, *Against Heresies* 1.26.1).

To oppose some such docetic teaching, the Elder stresses in various ways that Christ actually became flesh and blood as Jesus. At the beginning of the letter, he writes that an unidentified "we" actually saw and touched the preexistent Christ, the word of truth that existed from the beginning (1:1). He wants to make the point that the preexistent Christ took on a visible and tangible human body. Near the end of the letter, the Elder also emphasizes that Jesus the Christ had blood: "This is he who came with water and blood, Jesus Christ; not with the water only, but with the water and with the blood" (5:6). Here he is probably referring to a story that occurs only in the Gospel of John. When Jesus is on the cross, a soldier pierces his side with a spear and out comes both water and blood (John 19:34–35). The evangelist calls attention to this as if it had special significance. Given the conflict over docetism in the community, we can infer that the water probably represents spiritual life while the blood represents physical life. The Elder wants to stress that Jesus was not purely spiritual ("not with the water only") but both spiritual and physical ("with the water and with the blood").

Docetic Concept of Salvation

To match their docetic christology, the Elder's opponents also must have had a docetic or Gnostic concept of salvation. This conflicted with the Elder's perspective. The Elder, like the rest of the Proto-Orthodox tradition, had a sacrificial concept of salvation: "the blood of Jesus his son cleanses us from every sin" (1:7; cf. 2:1–2). For him, blood was necessary to atone for sin. From his opponents' perspective, however, Christ had neither flesh nor blood. How then did they deal with sin? The Elder gives us a hint. Twice he explicitly rejects someone's claim not to have any sin:

> If we say that we have no sin, we deceive ourselves and the truth is not in us. (1 John 1:8)

> If we say that we have not sinned, we make him a liar and his word is not in us. (1 John 1:10)

Who was claiming not to have any sin? Probably the Elder's opponents. From a Gnostic perspective, the soul needed salvation not from sin but from ignorance: ignorance of the soul's divine nature and origin, ignorance that kept the soul bound in the body. If the Elder's opponents had such a perspective, they may have claimed that they had realized the divine nature of their soul, which did not sin, and therefore had no need for a concept of salvation based on atonement for sins by blood.

Claim of Prophetic Inspiration

Both sides in the dispute claimed to have prophets who spoke under the inspiration of the spirit of God. But what happens when the spirit of God in one group contradicts the spirit of God in the other group? Each group would no doubt claim that its own revelations came from the true spirit, while the revelations of the other group were false. Such in fact is what the Elder does claim for his group. According to the Elder, his opponents are "false prophets" who have gone out into the world (1 John 4:1). Those who have stayed with him, however, have been anointed with the real spirit of God, which teaches them the truth (1 John 2:20, 27). His own group has "the spirit of truth," while his opponents have "the spirit of deception" (1 John 4:6). How can one tell the difference? According to the Elder, "This is how you know the spirit of God: every spirit that confesses Jesus Christ having come in flesh is of God, and every spirit that does not confess Jesus is not of God" (1 John 4:2–3). In other words, those who agree with the Proto-Orthodox view of Jesus have the true spirit, while those who disagree have a false spirit.

Rejection of the Elder's Authority

In leaving the Elder's community, his opponents showed their rejection of his authority. The Elder, considering himself a representative of God, saw this rejection of himself as a rejection of God:

> We are of God. One who knows God listens to us; one who is not of God does not listen to us. This is how we know the spirit of truth and the spirit of deception. (1 John 4:6)

In other words, those who listen to the Elder know God, while those who do not are following a spirit of deception.

The Elder is apparently unhappy that his opponents are no longer listening to him. The letter of Third John gives an example of a church leader who did not listen to the Elder. The Elder wrote a letter to some church in his group. Certain Christian men carried the letter to the church, but Diotrephes, the leader of the church, would not allow them to read it. Those who wanted to receive the messengers he kicked out of the church. Clearly this man had no interest in listening to the Elder.

Claim of Fellowship with God

The Elder's opponents believed that they were on good terms with God. We can infer this fact from the numerous times the Elder argues against those who claimed to have such a relationship:

> If we say we have fellowship with him and walk in the dark, we are lying and not doing the truth. (1 John 1:6)

> He who says "I know him" and does not keep his commandments is a liar, and the truth is not in him. (1 John 2:4)

> He who claims to remain in him ought himself to walk just as he [Jesus] walked. (1 John 2:6)

> He who claims to be in the light and hates his brother is still in the darkness. (1 John 2:9)

If someone says "I love God" and hates his brother, he is a liar. (1 John 4:20)

The Elder felt that his opponents could not be in communion with God because, in his view, they had violated the commandment to believe that Jesus was the son of God and the commandment to love one another.

THE ELDER'S PURPOSE AND STRATEGIES

Why did the Elder write such a letter as First John? According to his own statement, he wished to warn his audience against the divergent teaching: "I have written this to you about those trying to deceive you" (2:26; cf. 2:21). He writes not to his opponents, but to a group that he expects to share his own perspective. His primary purpose is to reinforce their allegiance to this perspective. He employs several rhetorical strategies to accomplish this purpose.

1. One strategy that he uses is to emphasize that as long as they remain with him they are on the right track. Hence the numerous uses of the word "remain," sometimes translated "abide." The opponents did not remain: "for if they had been part of us they would have remained with us" (1 John 2:19). "Everyone who moves onward and does not remain in the teaching of Christ does not have God" (2 John 9). Those to whom the Elder writes, however, are urged to remain: "remain in him" (1 John 2:27, 28). "If what you heard from the beginning remains in you, you will remain in the son and the Father" (1 John 2:24).

2. Another way of reinforcing their allegiance is by emphasizing that as long as they continue with the Elder they can know that they are right. Hence the numerous uses of the phrase "we know":

- we know that we know him (1 John 2:3)
- we know that we are in him (1 John 2:5)
- we know love (1 John 3:16)
- we will know that we are of the truth (1 John 3:19)
- we know that he remains in us (1 John 3:24)
- we know the spirit of truth (1 John 4:6)
- we know that we remain in him (1 John 4:13)
- we know that we love the children of God (1 John 5:2)
- we know the True One (1 John 5:20)

3. A third strategy he employs is to paint the conflict in contrasting terms, positive for his own perspective and negative for that of his opponents.

THE ELDER'S GROUP	HIS OPPONENTS
light	darkness
of God	of the world
the true God	idols
spirit of truth	spirit of deception
Christ	antichrist
children of God	children of the Devil
righteousness	lawlessness
love	hate
life	death

Apparently the Elder felt that he and his opponents shared no common ground.

READING GUIDE: I JOHN

Read the letter of First John with the help of the following guide.

Though numerous attempts have been made to recognize a logical structure in First John, none have been completely successful. The author seems to go in circles, returning to the same themes again and again in no apparent order. In several instances, the last sentence or clause of a section introduces the theme of the next section (1:7b; 3:10b, 18, 24).

The letter has an **introduction (1:1–4)**, but, unlike a regular letter, it does not identify the sender or recipient and lacks a salutation. It begins by referring to the preexistent Christ as "the word of life" that existed from the beginning, thus recalling the prologue of the Fourth Gospel (John 1:1–5). The author claims that some unspecified "we" saw and touched this word, as manifested in the visible and tangible human nature of Jesus. The Elder emphasizes seeing and feeling the word bodily, probably to oppose the docetic teaching that Christ was a spiritual being without a physical body.

Throughout the letter, the Elder gives a series of contrasts between the true and the false. He identified his own community with the true, and those who had left it with the false. He begins with **four contrasts (1:5–2:11)**. The first three are the contrast between light and darkness

(1:5–7), between confessing one's sin or claiming to have no sin (1:8–2:2), and between keeping God's commandments or not (2:3–6). The fourth contrast is between loving one's brother or hating one's brother (2:7–11). With respect to love, the Elder refers to a new commandment, which is no longer new to his audience. According to the Gospel of John, at the Last Supper Jesus gave his disciples a "new commandment": that they should love one another (John 13:34; 15:12). This apparently became the primary ethical principle of the Johannine community. The Elder comes back to it repeatedly (1 John 2:7; 3:11, 23; 4:12, 21).

The Elder next states his **reasons for writing (2:12–14)** in three sentences beginning with "I write" and three beginning with "I have written." Their translation is uncertain. The Elder may state either the purpose of his letter ("I write because") or its content ("I write that").

The contrasts return with **three more contrasts (2:15–3:10)**. First is the contrast between love of God and love of the world (2:15–17). Second is the contrast between confessing or denying the Son (2:18–28), which is at the heart of the Elder's concern. He warns against the many "antichrists" who have gone out from his community. He defines an antichrist as someone who denies that Jesus is the Christ. Those who deny the Son are liars, while those who confess the Son have an "anointing" (i.e. the Holy Spirit) which teaches them to know the true from the false. The antichrists who denied the Son did not remain in the community, but those to whom the Elder writes will remain in the Son if what they were taught remains in them. The third contrast is between children of God and children of the Devil (2:29–3:10). Here the Elder wants to brand his opponents as sinners and his own group as righteous, but in so doing he entangles himself in an inconsistency. On the one hand, he says that true children of God do not sin, indeed cannot sin (3:6–9; cf. 5:18). On the other hand, he has previously affirmed that everyone (even a child of God) does sin and should admit it (1:8–10).

The Elder now returns to **contrasts previously made (3:11–5:5)**. The first section returns to the contrast between loving one's brother and hating one's brother (3:11–18). The second repeats the theme of keeping God's commandments (3:19–24). These commandments are not the commandments of the Jewish Law but the commandments to believe in the name of God's son Jesus Christ and to love one another. The third section renews the contrast between the Spirit of God and the spirit of the antichrist (4:1–6). The Spirit of God confesses "Jesus Christ having come in flesh," while the spirit of antichrist does not confess this. The fourth section (4:7–21) focuses primarily on the theme of loving one's brother. The fifth section once again focuses on the theme of keeping God's commandments (5:1–5). The first commandment is to believe that Jesus is the Christ or the son of God. The second is to love one another.

The Elder next names **three witnesses to the Son (5:6–13)**: the spirit, the water, and the blood. The reference to water and blood may allude to John 19:34–35, which relates that water and blood flowed from Jesus' pierced side. In some manner not specified, these witnesses constitute God's testimony that Jesus is his son. Those who have the Son have eternal life, while those who do not have the Son do not have eternal life.

A final theme is that of **asking and receiving (5:14–17)**. Those who know that they have eternal life have confidence that God will give them what they ask for (cf. 3:22). If they ask God to give life to a brother who has sinned, God will give it as long as that person has not committed a sin that results in death.

The **conclusion (5:18–21)** consists of three sentences that begin with the verb "we know." What is known is that no child of God sins; that the Elder and his group are from God, while the world lies in the evil one; and that the son of God has come to bring knowledge of the true God. The Elder identifies Jesus Christ as the true God and warns his audience to keep away from idols, i.e. false gods.

READING GUIDE: 2 JOHN

Read the letter of Second John with the help of the following guide.

The key words in Second and Third John are **truth** and **love**, which occur in these letters eleven times and six times, respectively. The term "truth" refers to the first commandment of the community: to believe in the name of God's Son Jesus Christ. The term "love" refers to the second commandment: to love one another. These two terms summarize the central concerns of the author, which are to oppose deception with the "truth" and to encourage "love" for other members of the community.

The letter's **introduction (1–3)** includes an identification of the sender, an address, and a salutation. The sender identifies himself simply as "the Elder," expecting his audience to know who he is. The address to "**the elect lady** and her children" probably refers to a church and its members, over which the Elder exercises authority.

The body of the letter consists of an **exhortation (4–11)**. The Elder exhorts his audience to keep the commandments of God. One of these is to love one another. The other is to believe in the name of God's Son Jesus Christ (cf. 1 John 3:23). The Elder warns against deceivers who break the latter commandment by "not confessing Jesus Christ coming in flesh." Such a person is "the deceiver and the antichrist" and should not be received into one's house or even greeted.

In the **conclusion (12–13)**, the Elder indicates that he hopes to come soon in person and sends greetings from "the children of your elect sister," i.e. a sister church from which the elder is writing.

READING GUIDE: 3 JOHN

Read the letter of Third John with the help of the following guide.

The brief **introduction (1)** includes an identification of the sender as "the Elder" and an address to **Gaius**, presumably a leading member of a church in a nearby city.

The first main part of the letter concerns the relation between **Gaius and some brothers (2–8)**. The Elder expresses his joy because some "brothers" have come from visiting Gaius and have testified that Gaius "walks in truth." These brothers were apparently traveling in order to promote the gospel, so the Elder exhorts Gaius to provide financial support to them in order to send them on their way.

The second main part of the letter concerns **news of Diotrephes (9–12)**. The Elder reports events at another church in his group. To this church he wrote a letter, possibly First or Second John. Certain Christian men carried the letter to the church, but one of its leading members, **Diotrephes**, did not receive these messengers into his home. He also prohibited other members from receiving them and expelled them from the church if they did. The Elder exhorts Gaius not to imitate Diotrephes but to receive **Demetrius**, who is apparently the man carrying the Elder's letter to Gaius.

In the **conclusion (13–15)**, the Elder indicates that he hopes to come soon in person and ends with greetings.

DISCUSSION QUESTION

Discuss the contrasts that the Elder makes between his own community and the former members who have not remained with him.

REVIEW QUESTIONS

1. What can we infer about the author and date of the Johannine Epistles? Identify: the Elder.
2. What distinctive themes are shared by the Gospel of John and the Johannine Epistles?
3. What characteristics of the Elder's opponents can be reconstructed from the Johannine Epistles? Identify: antichrists, docetism.
4. What is the Elder's primary purpose in writing First John? What rhetorical strategies does he employ to achieve it?
5. What two words summarize the central concerns of Second and Third John? Identify: the elect lady, Gaius, Diotrephes, Demetrius.

SUGGESTIONS FOR FURTHER STUDY

Brown, Raymond E. *The Community of the Beloved Disciple: The Life, Loves, and Hates of an Individual Church in New Testament Times* (Paulist, 1979). Reconstructs the history of the Johannine community reflected in the gospel and letters of John.

Brown, Raymond E. *The Epistles of John* (Anchor Bible; Doubleday; Yale University Press, 1982). A standard commentary on the letters of John.

Culpepper, R. Alan, and Paul N. Anderson, eds. *Communities in Dispute: Current Scholarship on the Johannine Epistles* (Society of Biblical Literature, 2014). A collection of essays by various scholars on issues relating to the Johannine Epistles.

Edwards, Ruth B. *The Johannine Epistles* (Sheffield Academic Press, 1996). A student's guide to the critical issues and leading theological ideas of the letters.

Lieu, Judith M. *The Theology of the Johannine Epistles* (Cambridge University Press, 1991). A brief treatment of the historical setting, main ideas, and significance of the letters.

Strecker, Georg. *The Johannine Letters* (Hermeneia; Fortress, 1996). A standard commentary on the Johannine Epistles.

35 Conflict in the Church (4)
Letters of Ignatius

Sometime in the early second century, Ignatius, the bishop of Antioch in Syria, was arrested and sent to Rome for execution as a Christian. On the way, he wrote at least seven letters to various churches and individuals. These letters reflect an ongoing polemic of Ignatius against other forms of Christianity, specifically Judaic and docetic. Ignatius emphasizes submission to the Proto-Orthodox bishop as the key to church unity.

HISTORICAL SETTING AND DATE

As Roman soldiers escorted Ignatius from Antioch through Asia Minor, he had the opportunity to speak to the church at Philadelphia. He then arrived in Smyrna, where he apparently remained for some time. There he was visited by bishops and other church leaders from Ephesus, Magnesia, and Tralles; and from there he wrote a letter to each of those churches. He also wrote a fourth letter to the church in Rome, his destination. From Smyrna, the soldiers took him to Troas, where he had time to write three more letters: to the churches at Philadelphia and Smyrna, and to Polycarp, bishop of the church at Smyrna. Thus his seven letters appeared in the following order: Ephesians, Magnesians, Trallians, Romans, Philadelphians, Smyrnaeans, Polycarp.

From Troas Ignatius sailed to Neapolis, the seaport of Philippi. There we lose track of him. Presumably he continued on to Rome and was executed there.

Eusebius, in his church history, placed Ignatius' martyrdom during the reign of Trajan, i.e. 98–117 (*Ecclesiastical History* 3.36). In another work, he dated it more specifically to 107 or 108. Scholars cannot confirm either date, but most accept a date around 110.

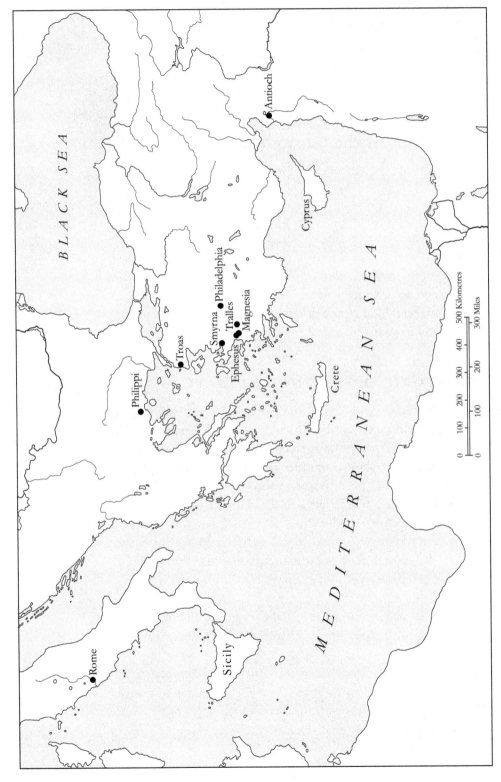

Figure 35.1 Sites on Ignatius' journey from Antioch to Rome.

Figure 35.2
The Via Egnatia near Philippi. Ignatius probably traveled on this major Roman road from Philippi to Rome. Erich Lessing/Art Resource, NY.

PRIMARY CONCERNS

Ignatius shows three primary concerns in his letters: to repudiate other forms of Christianity, to urge his readers to submit to the authority of the bishop and elders, and to inform his readers that he looks forward to his martyrdom.

1. Ignatius had little use for other Christians besides the Proto-Orthodox. These others, to be sure, "carry about the name" (Christ or Christian), but only "with evil guile." Actually they are "wild beasts" or "mad dogs, stealthily biting" (Eph 7:1). Ignatius condemns two specific forms of Christianity: Judaic and docetic.

Figure 35.3
A tenth-century
illustration of the
martyrdom of
Ignatius. Madeline
Grimoldi Archives,
© Biblioteca
Apostolica
Vaticana.

In two letters he warns against some Judaic form of Christianity (Mag 8–11; Phil 6–9). "It is wrong," he says, "to speak of Jesus Christ and to practice Judaism" (Mag 10:3). Those who live according to Judaism confess that they have not received grace (Mag 8:1). Christianity is not based on Judaism, but Judaism on Christianity (Mag 10:3), since the Hebrew prophets lived not according to Judaism but according to Christ (Mag 8:2). Ignatius may have had in mind Gentile Christians who advocated Judaism, since in one place he says, "it is better to hear Christianity from a man who has circumcision, than Judaism from an uncircumcised man" (Phil 6:1).

In other letters, Ignatius condemns some form of docetic Christianity. These Christians taught that Jesus only seemed to suffer, that in fact he had no physical body, no flesh (Tral 10:1; Smyr 2:1; cf. 6:1; 7:1). In response, Ignatius emphasizes the physical reality of Jesus: his birth, flesh and blood, suffering, death, and bodily resurrection (Eph 7:2; 20:2; Tral 8:1; 9–11; Rom 7:3; Smyr 1–7; 12:2).

Presumably Ignatius perceived these other forms of Christianity as an actual threat, either in his home church at Antioch or in the churches of Asia Minor. It is likely that he knew of divergent groups who disagreed with the Proto-Orthodox leaders and went their own way. Perhaps his own authority as bishop had been challenged at Antioch.

2. In responding to these divergent perspectives, Ignatius emphasized submission to the Proto-Orthodox authorities as the key to unity. He hammers again and again on the need to accept the established hierarchy: the bishop, the elders, and the deacons (Rom 2–6; 20:2; Mag 2–7; 13; Tral 2–3; 7; 12:2; 13:2; Phil salutation, 1–4; 7:1–8:1; Smyr 8:1–9:1; 13:2; Pol 4:1; 5:2; 6:1). For Ignatius, no church activity was legitimate apart from the supervision of the bishop.

3. A third concern of Ignatius emerges especially in his letter to the Romans. Here he writes ahead to the place of his coming execution, urging the Roman Christians not to try to save him. He expresses no dread of martyrdom but welcomes it as a way of going to be with Jesus.

Polycarp to the Philippians

Soon after Ignatius passed through Philippi, the church there wrote to Polycarp, bishop of Smyrna, where Ignatius had spent some time. They asked for copies of the letters that Ignatius had written to Polycarp and to the church at Smyrna. They also invited Polycarp to write them a letter of exhortation (Polycarp, Philippians 3:1; 13:2). We do not have the letter that the Philippians wrote, but we do have the letter that Polycarp wrote back. At the end of it, he writes that he is sending the letters they requested as well as other letters of Ignatius that he had (13:2). This exchange of letters shows us how the collection of Ignatius' letters began. Other collections, such as that of Paul's letters, must have begun in a similar way. Such letters from leading Christian figures were read in the churches on a periodic basis.

The rest of Polycarp's letter consists primarily of general exhortation to do the will of God. It is not particularly noteworthy except for the fact that Polycarp repeatedly alludes to various Christian writings with which he is familiar. He alludes to most of the books of the New Testament as well as 1 Clement, showing that most of these works were written by about 110.

DISCUSSION QUESTION

Read Ignatius' letter to the Smyrnaeans in Appendix 11 (pp. 599–601). Compare and contrast the rhetorical strategies that Ignatius and the author of the Johannine Epistles employ to combat docetism.

REVIEW QUESTIONS

1. Identify Ignatius. How many letters did he write? When did he write them?
2. What are the primary concerns of Ignatius' letters?
3. What is the significance of Polycarp's letter to the Philippians?

SUGGESTIONS FOR FURTHER STUDY

Jefford, Clayton. "The Letters of Ignatius" and "The Letter of Polycarp to the Philippians," in *Reading the Apostolic Fathers: A Student's Introduction*, 43–62, 73–86 (2nd ed.; Baker Academic, 2012). Brief introduction to Ignatius' letters and Polycarp's letter with further bibliography.

Foster, Paul, and Michael Holmes. "The Epistles of Ignatius of Antioch" and "Polycarp of Smyrna, *Epistle to the Philippians*," in Paul Foster, ed., *The Writings of the Apostolic Fathers*, 81–107, 108–25 (Bloomsbury T&T Clark, 2007). Brief introduction to Ignatius' letters and Polycarp's letter.

Robinson, Thomas A. *Ignatius of Antioch and the Parting of the Ways: Early Jewish-Christian Relations* (Hendrickson, 2009). Examines the letters of Ignatius to better understand how Christianity parted from Judaism to become a primarily Gentile movement.

Schoedel, William R. *Ignatius of Antioch: A Commentary on the Letters of Ignatius of Antioch* (Hermeneia; Fortress, 1985). A full-scale commentary on the letters of Ignatius.

36 Conflict in the Church (5)
1 Clement

The first letter of Clement addresses a conflict in the church at Corinth. Though it is lengthy, it gives few details concerning the nature of the conflict.

HISTORICAL SETTING OF 1 CLEMENT

The letter entitled First Clement belongs to the collection of writings known as the Apostolic Fathers. The opening words tell us that it was written from "the church of God that sojourns at Rome to the church of God that sojourns at Corinth." The author writes from Rome to protest against a conflict that has divided the church at Corinth. He refers to this conflict as a "filthy and unholy sedition that a few rash and self-willed persons have caused to flame up" (1:1). Later we learn that one faction in the church has deposed the previous leaders, the elders (44:1–6; 47:6). The author takes the side of the deposed leaders, urging those who put them out of office to repent and submit to them (57:1–2). Several notable members of the church at Rome carried this letter to Corinth (63:3–4; 65:1).

Beyond this general understanding of the situation, we have no details concerning the nature of the conflict, the issues involved, or the positions taken by either side in the dispute. We do not know if the conflict revolved around differences in doctrine or some other issue. If the author of First Clement knew, he does not reveal it. He does not address any of the issues in dispute but simply argues that the status quo should not be changed.

Apparently the letter accomplished its purpose, since Dionysius, bishop of the church at Corinth around 170 CE, says that it was read in the Corinthian church from time to time on the Lord's Day (Eusebius,

487

Ecclesiastical History 4.23.11). If the group that the letter attacked had won, they probably would not have preserved it.

Summary of 1 Clement

The letter of First Clement falls into three main sections.

1. Chapters 1–20 consist of examples, primarily from the Old Testament, that the author feels are relevant to the situation at Corinth. He begins by praising the past reputation of the church at Corinth (1:2–2:8) and contrasting it with their current strife (3). He then gives examples of people destroyed through jealousy (4–6); examples of God allowing repentance (7–8); examples of obedience to God (9–12); an exhortation to humility, with examples (13–18); and examples of nature's obedience to God (19–20). This section concludes with a doxology (20:12).

2. Chapters 21–39 consist of a variety of exhortations that seem to have only a loose connection to the situation at Corinth. The author touches on such themes as proper order in the family (21:6–9), the delay of the parousia (23), and the future resurrection (24–26). The rest can best be described as general exhortation to fear God and do right.

3. Chapters 40–65 address the conflict at Corinth more specifically. The author argues that the leadership of the church must follow a certain order, in a succession instituted by the apostles (40–44). For the rest, he condemns the schism and exhorts those who began it to repent and submit to the elders.

AUTHOR AND DATE

The letter does not give the name of its author; it states only that he is writing on behalf of the church at Rome. Later authors, however, beginning with Dionysius about 170 CE, attribute the letter to Clement. This Clement is listed by Irenaeus, writing about 180, as the third bishop of Rome (*Against Heresies* 3.3.3).

We have no further information about Clement, except for a possible reference to him by Hermas, another author from the church at Rome. According to Hermas, an angel told him to send a copy of his book to Clement:

> So you shall write two little books and send one to Clement and one to Grapte. Clement will then send it to the cities abroad, for that task has been entrusted to him, and Grapte will admonish the widows and

Figure 36.1
Fourth-century bas-relief of the apostles Peter and Paul, symbols of authority for the Proto-Orthodox church. Museo Archeologico Nazionale, Aquileia, Italy (Erich Lessing/Art Resource, NY).

the orphans. You, though, will read it in this city with the elders in charge of the church. (Shepherd of Hermas, Vision 2.4.3)

Here we find a Clement at Rome who has the same function as the author of First Clement: to send instruction from the church at Rome to churches in other cities. Whether this is the same Clement who wrote First Clement or whether a Clement wrote the letter at all is uncertain. In any case, for the sake of convenience we will refer to the author as Clement.

According to Eusebius (*Ecclesiastical History* 3.15; 3.34), Clement served as bishop of Rome from the twelfth year of Domitian to the third year of Trajan, i.e. 92–100. If this information is correct, and if Clement authored the letter, he wrote it near the end of the first century. This general date fits other indications from the letter itself. The author mentions the deaths of Peter and Paul as having occurred in "our generation" (5:1–7). Thus the apostolic age was in the past, but not too far in the past.

CHURCH LEADERSHIP IN I CLEMENT

The most widely discussed aspect of First Clement has been its view of church leadership. Chapters 40–44 of the letter show an important stage in the development of church offices. Here Clement justifies a hierarchy of offices in the church and seeks to legitimate the current holders of those offices by appeal to the idea of apostolic succession.

To justify a hierarchy of offices, Clement appeals to the priestly hierarchy in Israel. In this hierarchy three ranks of officials stood above the laity or common people: in descending order, the high priest, the other priests, and the Levites (40:5). Clement sees such ranks in the church as well (41:1). Though he does not explicitly identify the ranks here, one can infer that he has in mind the bishop, the presbyters (elders), and the deacons. Just as in Israel offerings could be made only in Jerusalem at appointed times under the supervision of the priestly hierarchy, so, argues Clement, Christian worship should be conducted only at the set time and place and under the supervision of the church hierarchy (40–41).

To legitimate the current office holders, First Clement provides one of the earliest instances of the idea of apostolic succession. According to this idea, the apostles appointed the first leaders (42:4), and after these leaders died other approved men took their place (44:2). Therefore since the current church leaders stood in the line of the apostles, Clement argues, they should not be removed from office (44:3).

DISCUSSION QUESTION

Read the selections from First Clement in Appendix 12 (pp. 602–605). How do these selections illustrate the typical features of Proto-Orthodox Christianity that we discussed in Chapter 31?

REVIEW QUESTIONS

1. Why was the letter of First Clement written?
2. What do we know about the author and date of First Clement?
3. What significance does First Clement have for the development of church leadership?

SUGGESTIONS FOR FURTHER STUDY

Bowe, Barbara Ellen. *A Church in Crisis: Ecclesiology and Paraenesis in Clement of Rome* (Fortress, 1988). Examines the rhetoric, genre, and understanding of the church in First Clement.

Brown, Raymond E. "The Roman Church at the Beginning of the Third Christian Generation (A.D. 96 – I Clement)," in Raymond E. Brown and John P. Meier, *Antioch and Rome: New Testament Cradles of Catholic Christianity*, 159–83 (Paulist, 1983). Examines First Clement in arguing that Christianity at Rome had a more Judaic character than Pauline Christianity.

Hagner, Donald. *The Use of the Old and New Testaments in Clement of Rome* (Brill, 1973). Examines what New Testament writings were known to Clement and how he regarded their authority and inspiration in comparison with those of the Old Testament.

Jeffers, James S. *Conflict at Rome: Social Order and Hierarchy in Early Christianity* (Fortress, 1991). Argues that Clement, belonging to a socially elite group in the Roman church, embraced a traditional Roman ideology of hierarchy that laid the basis for Roman Catholic theology and practice.

Jefford, Clayton. "The First Letter of Clement of Rome to the Corinthians (1 Clement)," in *Reading the Apostolic Fathers: A Student's Introduction*, 103–22 (2nd ed.; Baker Academic, 2012). Brief introduction to First Clement with further bibliography.

37 Relation of Christianity to Judaism (1)
Hebrews

The letters that we have examined in the last five chapters all reflect a conflict between Proto-Orthodoxy and some other perspective within the church. At this point we turn to another central concern of Proto-Orthodox literature: the relation of Christianity to Judaism.

First-century Judaism gave birth to several different movements: not only Rabbinic Judaism and Judaic Christianity, but also the Gentile Christian church. This Gentile movement inherited the Jewish scriptures, but since it did not follow the Jewish Law, it ultimately could not consider itself a form of Judaism. How did a Jewish mother give birth to this Gentile child? And how would this child now define its relationship to its mother?

We have already seen Paul and Luke grappling with these questions. Paul gave more than one answer. Sometimes he emphasized the discontinuity between the two groups, speaking of two distinct covenants: God had made an old covenant of slavery with the Jewish people, but a new covenant of freedom with Christians (Gal 4:24; 1 Cor 11:25; 2 Cor 3:6, 14). At other times he emphasized the continuity, picturing both groups as part of a single tree: both Jews and Gentiles were branches of the one tree, and even though some Jewish branches had been broken off to make room for the Gentiles, they would someday be grafted back in (Rom 11:13–24). Luke thought primarily in terms of succession: God had offered the gospel to the Jews, but they rejected it, so it went to the Gentiles.

Proto-Orthodox authors also considered this question. Two works in particular focus on the relation of Christianity to Judaism, though they do not use these terms. The author of Hebrews, sharing Paul's first perspective, thought in terms of two covenants, an old covenant that God made with Israel and a new covenant that God made with Christians. The new, he believed, had made the old obsolete. The author of Barnabas, somewhat like Luke, thought in terms of a single covenant that went to Christians when Israel lost it. Unlike Luke, however, Barnabas argued that Israel had lost the covenant in the distant past, in fact immediately after God gave it to them on Mount Sinai. Despite their differences, both Hebrews and Barnabas in effect maintained that Christianity had superseded or replaced Judaism. We will examine Hebrews in the present chapter and Barnabas in the next.

AUTHOR AND DATE OF HEBREWS

The state of our knowledge does not permit certainty concerning who wrote the letter of Hebrews. Origen, an early Christian scholar, came to the same conclusion, remarking, "God knows." Writers in the early church held various opinions about who wrote it. They suggested Clement of Rome, Luke, and Barnabas, but eventually Paul got credit for it. Partly on the basis of Pauline authorship, it found a place in the canon of the New Testament. The letter itself, however, makes no claim concerning authorship, and several indications show that Paul did not write it. For one thing, it lacks the opening salutation and thanksgiving that is typical of Paul's letters. For another, the author identifies himself with those who had received the gospel from earlier eyewitnesses (2:3), whereas Paul claimed a direct revelation from Christ as the source of his faith.

The author of Hebrews mentions Timothy, one of Paul's closest associates (Heb 13:23). This reference suggests that the author too may have belonged to the circle of Paul's associates. Scholars have therefore tried to link the letter to various known associates of Paul, including Barnabas, Apollos, Priscilla, Aquila, and Clement of Rome.

Some relationship does exist between Hebrews and First Clement, traditionally attributed to Clement of Rome. Both show a similar style of exhortation and use of Old Testament characters as examples. More significantly, both letters use some of the same phrases and ideas (cf. Heb 11; 1 Clem 4; 9–10; 12; 17:1–2). Either Clement knew the letter of Hebrews and referred to it from memory, or else he wrote both letters and used some of the same ideas in each.

If Clement of Rome did not write Hebrews, but merely alludes to it, then Hebrews must have been written before First Clement (c. 96 CE). If Clement wrote both letters, Hebrews may have been written about the same time as First Clement at the end of the first century.

RECIPIENTS

We know little about the people to whom the author wrote. The traditional view identifies this audience as Jewish Christians in danger of relapsing into Judaism. Hence the title "to the Hebrews." However, nothing in the letter specifically requires a Jewish audience. The author never states that they were in danger of relapsing into Judaism. They do receive warnings not to fall away from Christianity, but none against reverting to Judaism or adopting circumcision or practicing Jewish customs, such as we find in Galatians. The author does refer frequently to the Jewish scriptures, but since the Gentile church adopted these as its own, such references do not necessarily imply a Jewish audience. At one point, the author lists the foundational teachings that he assumed his audience had received: "a foundation of repentance from dead works and faith toward God; of teaching about baptisms, laying on of hands, resurrection of the dead, and eternal judgment" (6:1–2). The need to teach about "faith toward God" would suggest an audience of Gentiles rather than Jews.

Several passages in the letter suggest that the members of his audience were under pressure to renounce their Christian faith. The author speaks of an earlier period in the life of the community when they experienced persecution: some were publicly exposed to ridicule and affliction, some were imprisoned, others had their property seized (Heb 10:32–34). No one in the community, however, had yet been killed (12:4). The author counsels that they need continued endurance in the face of suffering.

A further clue comes from the closing greeting: "Those from Italy greet you" (Heb 13:24). On the one hand, this wording might imply that the letter was written *to* Italy, presumably Rome: believers who had left Italy and hence were "from Italy" were sending greetings back to Italy. If so, the letter must have been written before 64 CE when Nero put numerous Christians in Rome to death. Otherwise the author could not write that no one there had yet been killed (12:4). On the other hand, the closing greeting might imply that the letter was written *from* Italy: the author was perhaps writing from Rome and sending greetings from other churches in Italy as well. In this case, we have no way of knowing who the recipients were.

GENRE OF HEBREWS

The work called "to the Hebrews" has features of both a sermon and a letter. The author calls it "a word of exhortation" (Heb 13:22), something like a written sermon. It has a conclusion like a letter but lacks the salutation that normally begins a letter (cf. 1 John).

MESSAGE OF HEBREWS

Throughout his sermon-letter, the author alternates between two types of discourse: teaching and exhortation (urging a course of action). His teaching presents the view that the new covenant of salvation in Christ is superior to the old covenant, the religion of Israel, and has in fact replaced or superseded it. His exhortation warns his audience not to fall away from such a superior salvation.

1. In his teaching, the author expresses his understanding of the relationship between Christianity and the religion of Israel. He believed that Christianity had superseded the religion of ancient Israel, as this is described in the Hebrew Scriptures. By implication, therefore, Christianity had superseded the religion of Judaism. To make his point, he develops an idea found earlier in Paul's letters: Israel had an "old" covenant, while Christians had a "new" one (Gal 4:24; 1 Cor 11:25; 2 Cor 3:6, 14). The author supports this idea by appealing to the Hebrew Scriptures themselves. He quotes the prophet Jeremiah, who envisioned a new covenant: "Behold the days are coming, says the Lord, when I will establish a new covenant with the house of Israel and with the house of Judah" (Jeremiah 31:31–34). The last words of this quotation indicate that Jeremiah had in mind a covenant between God on the one hand and the nations of Israel and Judah on the other. The author of Hebrews, however, took this to refer to a new covenant between God and Christians. From this passage he drew a conclusion that has offended the Jewish people ever since: "When it says 'new,' it makes the first [covenant] obsolete" (8:13).

In comparing the new covenant with the old, the author constantly emphasizes the superiority of the new. The new covenant has a better source of revelation: while God spoke to Israel through prophets, angels, and Moses, he has spoken to Christians through his own preexistent son.

The new covenant also has a superior sacrificial cult. First, it has a superior high priest. This high priest is Jesus, whose priesthood is not from the line of Aaron, but from Melchizedek, another priest mentioned in the Hebrew Scriptures. Jesus' priesthood is better, because he never dies and never needs to be replaced.

Second, the new covenant has a superior sacrifice. This sacrifice is also Jesus, whose blood is better than that of bulls and goats and only had to be offered once.

And third, it has a superior sanctuary, not earthly but heavenly. The first covenant had an earthly "tabernacle" or "sanctuary," a tent in which God dwelt among the Israelites on earth. The author saw this tent as merely a copy of the true sanctuary in heaven where God lived. It was into this superior sanctuary that Christ entered as high priest to present his offering. This idea of heavenly patterns goes back ultimately to the Greek philosopher Plato, who thought that all physical objects and even mental concepts were patterned after immaterial "forms" or archetypes. Later writers, such as the Jewish philosopher Philo of Alexandria, developed this idea. The author of Hebrews stands in this tradition of Platonic thought.

2. Throughout his teaching, the author intersperses exhortations, urging his audience to hold fast to their Christian confession of faith. Such exhortations suggest that he knew of circumstances, perhaps persecution, that might move them to renounce their confession.

READING GUIDE: HEBREWS

Read the letter to the Hebrews with the help of the following guide.

A Superior Source of Revelation (1:1–4:13)

In the first section, the author wants to show that the source of revelation for the Christian faith is superior to that offered to Israel in the past. Whereas God spoke to Israel through prophets, angels, and Moses, he spoke to Christians through his son.

First, Christ is **superior to the prophets (1:1–3)**. God spoke to Israel through prophets but to Christians through his preexistent son.

Second, Christ is **superior to the angels (1:1–2:18)**. The Jewish scripture relates that after God led the people of Israel out of Egypt, he gave them the Law on Mount Sinai. According to later Jewish tradition, the Law was delivered to Israel by God's angels. In this understanding, the present world is under the authority of these angels. The author of Hebrews wants to say that Christ, as the son of God, is superior to these angels who gave the Law and rule the present world. Christ has been enthroned above the angels (1:1–14).

HIGH PRIEST OF ISRAEL.

Figure 37.1 A Jewish high priest in ceremonial garb. Hebrews portrays Jesus as the high priest of a new covenant. Chronicle/Alamy Stock Photo.

Here the author inserts an exhortation: one should not neglect such a great salvation, because, if transgressing the inferior revelation brought punishment, the punishment would be much worse for those who neglected the superior revelation (2:1–4).

He then returns to the teaching: Christ was briefly made lower than angels when he became human but has now been exalted to heaven where he serves as high priest on behalf of his followers. In the age to come, all things will be subjected to him, not to the angels (2:5–18).

Third, Christ is **superior to Moses** (3:1–6). Moses was the leader of Israel who brought the people out of Egypt and received the Law from God. The author stresses that while Moses was a servant of God, Jesus was a son.

This comparison between Jesus and Moses leads to an **exhortation to enter God's rest** (3:7–4:13). According to the Jewish scriptures, Moses tried to lead the people into the promised land, his promised place of "rest," but the people did not believe God's promise that he would help them conquer the inhabitants of the land. Because of their unbelief, God swore that they would not enter the land but wander in the wilderness for forty years. After Moses and that generation died, Joshua led the people into the promised land. The author uses this story as an analogy. Jesus, whose name in Greek is the same as "Joshua," is leading his people into the promised rest. Christians should therefore not fall into unbelief like the Israelites, lest they too fail to enter it.

A Superior Priesthood (4:14–7:28)

In the second section, the author wants to show that Christianity has a high priest and a priesthood that are superior to those of Israel.

He begins by presenting Jesus as a **superior high priest** (4:14–5:10). While the temple stood in Jerusalem, a high priest served as the highest religious leader in Judaism. The high priest was a mediator between the people and God, offering sacrifices to atone for the sins of the people. According to a tradition found in the Jewish scriptures, the first high priest was Aaron, the brother of Moses. The law associated with this tradition prohibited anyone except Aaron's descendants from becoming high priest.

The author of Hebrews wants to show that Jesus too is a high priest, not of the old order of Aaron, but of the order of Melchizedek ("king of righteousness"). This person is mentioned twice in the Hebrew Scriptures. Genesis 14:17–20 relates a story in which Melchizedek met Abraham, the father of the Jewish race, as he was returning victorious from a battle. There Melchizedek is called the king of "Salem" ("peace," referring to

Jerusalem) and "priest of God Most High." He was thus a priest of God who was not of Aaron's order. His name occurs again in Psalm 110:4, in which Yahweh says to the Davidic king, "You are a priest forever after the order of Melchizedek." The author of Hebrews finds this declaration fulfilled in Christ. As a high priest of Melchizedek's order, Christ acts before God on behalf of human beings.

Before explaining further, the author digresses from his subject to give an **exhortation (5:11–6:20)**. He criticizes his audience's lack of progress in understanding difficult teachings such as he is presenting. He warns that those who fall away after they have accepted Christ cannot be renewed to repentance.

Returning to his subject, the author expounds on how Jesus has a **superior priesthood (7:1–28)**. Since Abraham paid a tithe to Melchizedek, the author concludes that Melchizedek was greater than Abraham, and hence greater than Abraham's descendant Levi, the ancestor of Aaron and the subsequent Jewish high priests. Thus the priesthood of Jesus, who is of the order of Melchizedek, is superior to the Jewish priesthood. Unlike the Aaronic priests, who had to be replaced when they died, Christ continues as priest forever. Unlike those priests, who had to offer sacrifice for their own sins, Jesus is a sinless high priest.

Christological exegesis in Hebrews

The author of Hebrews believed that the Hebrew Scriptures spoke about Christ. His letter illustrates how early Christian preachers interpreted the Hebrew Scriptures christologically. That is, they took passages of scripture that originally referred to other matters and interpreted them as references to Jesus the Christ. This type of exegesis (interpretation) enabled them to develop new ideas about Jesus. In the case of Hebrews, the author focuses primarily on two scriptures about a mysterious figure named "Melchizedek," who was a priest of God (Genesis 14:17–20; Psalm 110:4). The author uses this figure to develop the idea that Jesus is a great high priest who serves in a heavenly sanctuary. No other writing in the New Testament contains this idea.

A Superior Sanctuary, Covenant, and Sacrifice (8:1–10:18)

In the third section, the author wants to show that as a superior high priest, Christ serves in a new sanctuary, mediates a new covenant, and has offered a new sacrifice, all of which are superior to those of Israel.

As a high priest, Christ serves in a **superior sanctuary (8:1–5)**, the true temple of God in heaven. The priests of Israel offered gifts and sacrifices in an earthly sanctuary, the temple at Jerusalem. But Jewish scripture also spoke of them serving in the time of Moses and Aaron in the tabernacle, a tent sanctuary resembling the temple. According to the author, the tabernacle on earth was merely a copy of the true temple in heaven, where Christ serves as high priest.

Christ is also the mediator of a **superior covenant (8:6–13)**, based on better promises, the new covenant predicted in scripture by Jeremiah (Jer 31:31–34).

The first covenant had an **earthly sacrificial cult (9:1–10)**. It had an earthly sanctuary, the tabernacle, which had two rooms. Priests went regularly into the outer room, the Holy Place; but into the inner room, the Most Holy Place, only the high priest entered once a year, taking animal blood to atone for sins. According to the author, the inner room symbolizes the heavenly sanctuary, while the outer room symbolizes the earthly sanctuary of the present age. In the first covenant, access is granted to the earthly sanctuary, but the way is not yet opened into the heavenly sanctuary.

In contrast, the new covenant has a **heavenly sacrificial cult (9:11–14)**. Christ has entered the true sanctuary in heaven, not with the blood of bulls and goats, but with his own blood. According to the author, the blood of animals could purify only the flesh, while the blood of Christ purifies the conscience.

The second covenant, like the first, is a **covenant established by death (9:15–24)**. The death of Jesus inaugurates the new covenant, since a covenant (i.e. a will) takes effect only at the death of the one who makes it. Similarly, even the first covenant was ratified with blood. In the same way, the earthly sanctuary was purified with blood, but the heavenly sanctuary into which Christ entered had to be purified with better sacrifices.

The superiority of the new covenant is shown by the fact that it required only a **single sacrifice (9:25–10:18)**. In the sacrificial rite of the new covenant, Christ does not offer a sacrifice yearly, like the earthly high priest, but offers himself once and for all. According to the author, the yearly sacrifices in the first covenant did not remove the consciousness of sin because the blood of bulls and goats could not take away sins. In contrast, Christ offered his body as a single sacrifice that brought forgiveness of sins.

Exhortation: Hold Fast the Confession of Faith (10:19–13:19)

At this point the author switches from a primary emphasis on teaching to an emphasis on exhortation, exhorting his audience to hold fast to their confession of faith in Jesus. He exhorts them to draw near to God, to hold fast the confession of their hope, and to endure until the coming of Jesus (10:19–39). He points to the heroes of the past as models of persevering in faith (11:1–40), also reminding his audience of how Jesus endured suffering (12:1–4; cf. 2:10; 5:7–9; 13:12–14). He interprets their suffering as discipline from God meant to correct them, a discipline that indicates they are God's children (12:5–17). He warns them of the seriousness of rejecting the new covenant (12:18–29) and gives various other exhortations (13:1–19).

Conclusion (13:20–25)

The author concludes with a benediction and doxology (13:20–21), an appeal to bear with his "word of exhortation" (13:22), a note that he plans to see them with Timothy (13:23), greetings (13:24), and a benediction (13:25).

DISCUSSION QUESTION

The author of Hebrews conceives of "the new covenant" as essentially a new sacrificial cult, analogous to the temple ritual of ancient Judaism. Consider his conception of sacrifice and atonement. In this conception, how does the blood of a sacrifice atone for sin? What makes the blood of Jesus more acceptable to God than the blood of animals? What conception of God does this sacrificial rite presuppose?

REVIEW QUESTIONS

1. How did Paul, Luke, the author of Hebrews, and the author of Barnabas explain the relation between Christianity and Judaism?
2. What features of the letter to the Hebrews show that Paul did not write it? What is the relation between Hebrews and First Clement?
3. What can we infer about the date of Hebrews?
4. What can we infer about the recipients of Hebrews?

5. What is the genre of Hebrews?
6. What two types of discourse does the author employ? What is the message of each?
7. In what ways does the author find the religion of Christianity superior to that of Israel?
8. Identify: Melchizedek.

SUGGESTIONS FOR FURTHER STUDY

Attridge, Harold W. *The Epistle to the Hebrews* (Hermeneia; Fortress, 1989). A standard commentary on Hebrews.

Horton, Fred L., Jr. *The Melchizedek Tradition: A Critical Examination of the Sources to the Fifth Century A.D. and in the Epistle to the Hebrews* (Cambridge University Press, 1976). Examines the development of traditions about Melchizedek in early Jewish and Christian sources.

Hurst, L. D. *The Epistle to the Hebrews: Its Background of Thought* (Cambridge University Press, 1990). Surveys the Christian and non-Christian backgrounds against which the letter has been read.

Koester, Craig R. *Hebrews: A New Translation with Introduction and Commentary* (Anchor Bible; Doubleday; Yale University Press, 2001). A standard commentary on Hebrews.

Lincoln, Andrew T. *Hebrews: A Guide* (Bloomsbury T&T Clark, 2006). An introduction to Hebrews.

Lindars, Barnabas. *The Theology of the Letter to the Hebrews* (Cambridge University Press, 1991). Discusses the historical setting, central ideas, and significance of the letter.

Schenck, Kenneth. *Understanding the Book of Hebrews: The Story Behind the Sermon* (Westminster John Knox, 2003). A helpful introduction, which reconstructs the "story world" implicit in Hebrews as an entryway into the overall thought of the document.

38 Relation of Christianity to Judaism (2)
Epistle of Barnabas

Like Hebrews, the Epistle of Barnabas illustrates the Proto-Orthodox concern for defining the relation between Christianity and Judaism. It argues that Christianity has superseded or replaced Judaism.

AUTHOR AND DATE

In the manuscripts of this letter, the designation "Epistle of Barnabas" appears at the end. Thus someone attributed the letter to Barnabas, the colleague and traveling companion of Paul. Most scholars, however, doubt that this postscript gives accurate information about the author. In the text of the letter, the author never identifies himself. While the author therefore remains anonymous, it is convenient to refer to him as "Barnabas."

The date of the letter can be determined from two passages in it. In the first passage, the author interprets the vision of Daniel 7 as a reference to his own time. The fourth beast in Daniel's vision, which the author of Barnabas undoubtedly interprets as Rome, has ten horns, representing ten kings. An eleventh king comes after: "And after them a small king will arise, who will subdue three of the kings under one" (Barnabas 4:4). We cannot be certain how the author counted the emperors of Rome: whether he began with Julius Caesar or Augustus and whether or not he counted the three who briefly held power during the year of civil war (Galba, Otho, Vitellius). However, any method of counting the first eleven emperors would bring us no further than the reign of Hadrian (117–38). Therefore, the letter must have been written sometime before 138 CE.

The second passage shows that it was written after the destruction of the Jewish temple in 70 CE, perhaps after the second Jewish war:

Furthermore, he says again, "Behold, those who destroyed this temple will themselves build it." It is happening. For since they [the Jews] fought, it was destroyed by the enemies [the Romans]. Now the servants of the enemies will themselves rebuild it. (Barnabas 16:3–4)

This mention of rebuilding the temple may refer to Hadrian's building of a Roman shrine on the site of the Jewish temple after the second Jewish war. If so, the letter was written about 132 CE.

CENTRAL THEMES OF BARNABAS

The Epistle of Barnabas falls into two major divisions: chapters 1–17 and chapters 18–21. Each part has a different theme.

The first part of Barnabas focuses primarily on the relation between Christianity and Judaism. It addresses the covenant, the Law, and the Jewish scriptures. The author argues (1) that God's covenant belongs only to Christians, not to both Jews and Christians; (2) that Christians have a new law, superior to the old law of the Jews, which was never valid anyway; and (3) that the Jewish scriptures are actually a Christian book.

The Covenant

In Jewish understanding, Yahweh made a covenant or agreement between himself and Israel: Yahweh would be Israel's God, while Israel would be Yahweh's people. According to Barnabas, God took this covenant away from the Jews. God offered the covenant to Israel at Mount Sinai, but they lost it immediately by committing idolatry. It was then kept for Christians. The covenant therefore does not belong to both Jews and Christians; it belongs only to Christians (4:6–8; 13:1–14:9).

The Law

As their part of the covenant, Israel agreed to keep Yahweh's law. According to Barnabas, however, Judaism followed an old law, while Christianity followed a new law. He contrasts "their law" (3:6) with "the new law of our Lord Jesus Christ" (2:6). These two laws enjoined different practices. For example, the old law required animal sacrifices, while the new required the sacrifice of a heart that glorified God (2:4–10). The old required literal circumcision of the flesh, while the new required circumcision of the heart (9:1–9). Barnabas claims that the law of the Jews, the religion that they practiced, was never valid. Even before Christianity, God abolished such practices as animal sacrifice and circumcision (2:6; 9:4). In adopting these practices, the Jews sought God in error (2:9); "they went astray because an evil angel was instructing them" (9:4).

Thus in his understanding of the covenant and the Law, Barnabas takes an even more negative view of Judaism than the author of Hebrews. According to Hebrews, God made two covenants, one with Israel and one with Christians. The Jewish Law, as part of the covenant with Israel, had been valid in its time, even though it was now obsolete, superseded by Christianity. Barnabas takes the more negative view that the Jews had lost their covenant from the beginning and had never had a valid Law.

The Jewish Scriptures

While Barnabas repudiates the religion of Judaism, he does not wish to repudiate their scriptures, in which that religion is expressed. He wants to maintain that the Jewish scriptures actually teach Christianity rather than Judaism. To make this somewhat surprising claim, Barnabas has to engage in some interpretive gymnastics. He uses several strategies to turn the Jewish scriptures into a Christian book.

1. He uses passages from the Hebrew prophets, who often criticized aspects of their own religion, to argue that God rejected Jewish practices. For instance, he quotes passages that are critical of the Jewish institutions of sacrifice (2:5, 7–8), fasting (3:1–5), and the temple (16:2). What Barnabas does not seem to consider is that these criticisms were spoken by Jews to Jews and preserved among Jews. Jews regarded these passages as a part of their own tradition, not as an invalidation of it.

2. Barnabas interprets many of the Jewish laws metaphorically rather than literally, so that they support Christian rather than Jewish practice. For example, he argues that the laws concerning circumcision (9:1–9), dietary regulations (10:1–12), and the Sabbath (15:1–9) should not be taken literally. The command to circumcise the flesh actually means to circumcise the heart. The command not to eat pork actually means not to associate with people who are like pigs. The Sabbath is not literally the seventh day of the week, but the seventh millennium at the end of history. The Jews simply never understood their own scriptures, but the true meaning has now been revealed to Barnabas.

3. Barnabas interprets certain passages typologically; that is, he finds that they prefigure or foreshadow Christian institutions. For instance, the passages about the Day of Atonement and the ritual of the red heifer both prefigure Jesus' atoning death (7:1–8:7). In other passages, he finds references to Christian baptism, the cross, and Jesus (11:1–12:11). Through such strategies, Barnabas attempts to retain the Jewish scriptures while rejecting the religion taught within them.

The Two Ways

The second part of Barnabas (chs. 18–21) contains the teaching on the "two paths" or "two ways" that also occurs in the Didache (Didache 1–6). It consists of moral exhortation, describing both the path one should take and the path one should not. This teaching probably came from a Jewish document that was adopted into Christianity. As it circulated, it underwent various revisions. The version that occurs in Barnabas differs in several respects, therefore, from the version that appears in the Didache. Still other versions appear in other writings of early Christianity.

DISCUSSION QUESTION

Read the selections from the Epistle of Barnabas in Appendix 13 (pp. 606–610). Imagine that you are the leader of a Judaic-Christian community in the early second century, one of the communities represented by Matthew, James, or the Didache. Someone in your community has just brought you copies of Hebrews and Barnabas. Write a response to these letters indicating how you, as a Judaic Christian, agree or disagree with them.

REVIEW QUESTIONS

1. What can we infer about the author and date of the Epistle of Barnabas?
2. What is the theme of the first part of Barnabas (chs. 1–17)? What three arguments does the author make?
3. How does Barnabas' view of the covenant and the Law differ from that of Hebrews?

4. What three strategies does Barnabas employ to interpret the Jewish scriptures as a Christian book?
5. What is included in the second part of Barnabas (chs. 18–21)?

SUGGESTIONS FOR FURTHER STUDY

Hvalvik, Reidar. *The Struggle for Scripture and Covenant: The Purpose of the Epistle of Barnabas and Jewish-Christian Competition in the Second Century* (Mohr Siebeck, 1996). Aims to identify the purpose of the writing and to describe the relationship between Christianity and Judaism in the second century.

Jefford, Clayton. "The Letter of Barnabas," in *Reading the Apostolic Fathers: A Student's Introduction*, 1–22 (2nd ed.; Baker Academic, 2012). A brief introduction to Barnabas with further bibliography.

Paget, James Carleton. *The Epistle of Barnabas: Outlook and Background* (Mohr Siebeck, 1994). Argues that the author made use of a variety of traditions that he adapted to form a fairly coherent perspective.

Paget, James Carleton. "The Letter of Barnabas," in Paul Foster, ed., *The Writings of the Apostolic Fathers*, 72–80 (Bloomsbury T&T Clark, 2007). A brief discussion of the letter of Barnabas.

39   Conflict with the Roman World (1)
1 Peter

We have examined two central concerns of Proto-Orthodox literature: the problem of conflict within the Christian community and the relation of Christianity to Judaism. At this point we turn to a third major concern of this literature: the conflict between Christianity and the Roman world.

ASPECTS OF THE CONFLICT

This conflict involved Christian withdrawal from society, Roman antagonism toward Christianity, and the Christian response to this antagonism.

Christian Withdrawal from Society

In the Roman world, religion played an integral role in society and the state. There was no "separation of church and state," such as developed in the United States. Rather, the Roman government supported a religion of the state. Being a citizen of Rome meant participating in the state religion, offering sacrifices to the Roman gods and to the emperor as a divine human. In addition to the state religion, cults dedicated to various deities existed. Worship involved both individual offerings and festivals in which the whole community might participate. Inhabitants of the Greco-Roman world saw these rites as a way of keeping the gods in a good mood so that they would bless the community. Participation in them also had a social dimension: it showed that one belonged to and supported the community.

It was precisely these religious and social aspects of community life from which Christian converts withdrew. As they became Christians, they adopted the Jewish code of monotheism, worship of one God. They could no longer participate in the polytheistic worship of their society. Consequently, they developed what sociologists would call a "sectarian" consciousness. They adopted a perspective that excluded all others as wrong, thus erecting boundaries between themselves and the larger society. Seeing themselves as outside society and superior to it, they developed a sense of alienation from that society.

Roman Antagonism to Christianity

The Roman government and society responded to the Christians' separatist attitude with antagonism. They accused Christians above all of "hatred of the human race" (Tacitus, *Annals* 15.44). Like other new religious groups throughout history, Christians faced accusations of engaging in various abominable practices. The Roman historian Tacitus shows knowledge of such accusations when he refers to Christians as a group of people hated for their shameful deeds (*Annals* 15.44). Rumors spread that Christians engaged in secret incestuous and cannibalistic orgies. After all, did they not they call each other "brother" and "sister," and yet greet each other with a kiss (Rom 16:16; 1 Cor 16:20; 2 Cor 13:12; 1 Thes 5:26)? Did they not share a meal in which they ate the body and drank the blood of a dead man? Why would they meet secretly in private homes unless they were trying to hide such shameful deeds?

The greatest hostility was directed toward the Christians' unwillingness to worship the non-Christian gods. The general populace took this as a sign of atheism. They held Christians responsible for natural disasters, which they attributed to the displeasure of the gods to whom Christians no longer sacrificed. Such atheism was also bad for business, since donations to temples and income from the sale of sacrificial animals and images of the gods all dropped off as Christianity grew. On an official level, such atheism was interpreted as disloyalty to the state. Why would Christians not pay respect to the emperor and other gods of the state unless they were seditious and lacked patriotism?

Sporadically, antagonism toward Christians turned to persecution. In 64 CE, Nero executed a large number of Christians in Rome, accusing them of starting a fire that burned much of Rome (Tacitus, *Annals* 15.44). Officially at least, they died not because they were Christians, but because of this specific criminal charge against them. Later persecution, however, arose primarily because Christians refused to worship the emperor and other gods of the state. The book of Revelation testifies that for this reason Roman officials executed Christians in the province of Asia. Traditionally this book has been dated to the reign of the Roman emperor Domitian (81–96 CE), though the role of Domitian as a persecutor remains uncertain. Definitely by the reign of his successor Trajan (98–117 CE), the Roman governor Pliny persecuted Christians in Bithynia-Pontus, one of the provinces to which the letter of First Peter is addressed. Pliny interrogated Christians, ordering them to offer incense to the gods and the emperor. Those who refused were put to death. Trajan approved this procedure but declined to establish any sort of general rule for dealing with Christians. This lack of a definite law or policy meant that local officials would adopt different procedures in different times and places. Many Christians lost their lives in Roman arenas where the authorities put on shows for the people. At these times Christians were thrown to wild animals in the arena or served as victims in staged combats.

The Christian Response

Roman antagonism reinforced the Christians' sense of alienation and increased their internal solidarity with each other. Christian authors wrote letters, such as Revelation and First Peter, to encourage persecuted Christians. Knowing that they were not alone gave them a sense of unity with other Christians throughout the world.

Making a virtue out of necessity, the Christians found their heroes in those who confessed or witnessed to their faith in the face of persecution. The term "martyr," originally meaning "witness," came to refer to those who died for their faith. Martyrdom, in the period before Constantine, became a Christian ideal, so that martyrs were exalted to the highest rank in the heavenly kingdom. Certain martyrs became famous as accounts of their trials and deaths were preserved in writing. The earliest of these, the Martyrdom of Polycarp, now included in the Apostolic Fathers, relates a martyrdom that occurred in about 156.

Also beginning about the middle of the second century, Christian intellectuals began writing "apologies" or defenses of the Christian faith. The apologists, generally addressing the reigning emperor, defended Christian beliefs and practices, arguing that Rome had no reason to persecute Christians.

In the period that we are considering, prior to 150, conflict between Christians and the Roman world is the central concern of First Peter, Revelation, and Ignatius' letter to the Romans. Revelation shows an apocalyptic response to persecution in the province of Asia. Ignatius' letter

Figure 39.1 The Christian Martyrs' Last Prayer. Painting by Jean-Léon Gérôme (1824–1904). The Walters Art Museum, Baltimore, MD.

to the Romans (a selection from which is given in Appendix 14) shows Ignatius' apparent enthusiasm for martyrdom. First Peter, examined in the present chapter, depicts the alienation of early Christianity from Greco-Roman society and the corresponding antagonism of Greco-Roman society toward Christianity.

AUTHORSHIP OF FIRST PETER

The author of First Peter identifies himself as "Peter, an apostle of Jesus Christ" (1:1). Most scholars doubt this claim for several reasons: his fluent Greek, familiarity with Pauline tradition, Gentile audience, and historical setting.

Fluent Greek

First, the author writes fluently in Greek, a skill that seems unusual for an uneducated fisherman who spoke Aramaic as his native language. Some scholars do not find this objection compelling, arguing that Peter's Greek may have been polished by Silvanus, the scribe to whom the letter was dictated (1 Pet 5:12).

Familiarity with Pauline Tradition

Second, the letter contains many phrases and ideas found in the Pauline letters. For instance, one of Paul's favorite expressions, "in Christ," appears several times (1 Pet 3:16; 5:10, 14). Like the Pauline letters, First Peter speaks of sharing Christ's sufferings in order to share his glory (Rom 8:17; 1 Pet 4:13). Both command obedience to the secular government (Rom 13:1–7; 1 Pet 2:13–16). Both put forth household codes (Col 3:17–4:1; Eph 5:21–6:9; 1 Pet 2:18–3:7). These similarities suggest that the author knew the letters of Paul and may have been familiar with them as a collection. If so, he must have written after the time of both Paul and Peter.

Proponents of Peter's authorship point out that while First Peter also has affinities with the letter of James, these show not that one depended on the other, but that both drew on a common fund of tradition. Similarly, they claim, the affinities of First Peter with the Pauline letters merely show that the ideas in Paul's letters were not unique to him but were part of the general teaching of the early church. Peter drew not on Paul's letters, but on a fund of tradition that he shared with Paul and his disciples.

There is unquestionably some truth to this argument. However, the affinities between First Peter and Paul seem to go beyond mere reliance on a common tradition. The author of First Peter also seems to take over Paul's associates. He dictates the letter to "Silvanus," who was a co-worker of Paul (1 Pet 5:12; 1 Thes 1:1; 2:1), and he associates himself with "Mark," another of Paul's co-workers (Philem 24; Col 4:10). He begins the letter by identifying himself as "an apostle of Jesus Christ" (1 Pet 1:1), just as Paul does in his salutations (2 Cor 1:1; Col 1:1; Eph 1:1), and he ends the letter by sending "a holy kiss," as Paul occasionally does (1 Pet 5:14; Rom 16:16; 1 Cor 16:20). It thus appears that the author modeled even the details of his letter on the letters of Paul.

Gentile Audience

Third, several passages in First Peter make clear that the author wrote to Gentile Christians (1:14, 18; 4:3). This raises the question of why Peter would be taking pastoral responsibility for Gentiles. At the Jerusalem Conference, the leading figures agreed that Paul and Barnabas would go to the Gentiles, while Peter would be an apostle to the Jews (Gal 2:7–9). The author of First Peter seems unaware of this fact.

Historical Setting

Finally, the historical setting presupposed in the letter suggests that Peter did not write it, since it reflects a situation that probably did not exist in Peter's lifetime: antagonism toward Christians throughout the entire Roman Empire (5:9). In Peter's day, Christianity still appeared to be a sect of Judaism, and most opposition to it came from other Jews. Only later, as Christianity became distinguished from Judaism, did the general populace of the Roman Empire come to oppose it. This is the situation presupposed in First Peter. Such empire-wide hostility to Christianity fits better in the late first or early second century than in the time of Peter.

Peter as a Pseudonym

If Peter did not write the letter, then it is pseudonymous, written by a later church leader using Peter's name. Early Christian authors not uncommonly attributed their writings to Peter. Other known instances of such works include the Gospel of Peter, the Preaching of Peter, two different Apocalypses of Peter, the Letter of Peter to Philip, and the letter of Second Peter.

The author of First Peter writes from the church in "Babylon" (5:13). In the book of Revelation, the term "Babylon" stands as a symbolic name for Rome, and in First Peter it no doubt has the same sense. The connection of Peter with Rome became one of central significance in the development of Western Christianity. The tradition arose that Peter founded the church of Rome, and the bishops of Rome claimed to be the heirs of his authority. We have no certain information about how early this perspective arose, but it may well be that it is already present in First Peter. The author is an "elder" in Rome who identifies himself with Peter (1 Pet 5:1; 5:13; 1:1). Possibly he belonged to the council of elders in Rome, perhaps occupying a place of preeminence among them, and as such felt himself to be the heir of Peter. Such a possibility would explain his choice of the pseudonym "Peter."

Figure 39.2
Provinces of Asia Minor to which First Peter is addressed.

RECIPIENTS AND DATE

The author of First Peter writes to Christians in five areas of Asia Minor: "Pontus, Galatia, Cappadocia, Asia, and Bithynia" (1:1). He had in mind Gentiles converted to Christianity from their previous lifestyle (1:14, 18; 4:3). The Gentile converts in such a large geographical area probably came from all walks of life and all social classes, as they did in other parts of the Roman Empire. Pliny, governor of Bithynia (about 111–15 CE), confirms this supposition when he states that Christians there included "many of every age, of every class, and of both sexes." Christianity had penetrated "not only the cities, but also the villages and farms" (Pliny,

Figure 39.3
Marble bust of the Roman emperor Trajan (98–117 CE). Correspondence between Trajan and Pliny has been preserved that shows official Roman policy toward Christians at the time. Louvre (Erich Lessing/Art Resource, NY).

Letters 10.96). Though diverse in social standing, these Christians had in common an allegiance to a new way of life that separated them from their former associates. Consequently, they were experiencing an ordeal of suffering that was shared by Christians throughout the world (4:12; 5:9).

The letter of First Peter can be dated after 70 CE, since the author refers to Rome as "Babylon" (5:13). Babylon was the ancient empire that destroyed the Jewish temple when it took the Jewish nation into exile in the sixth century BCE. Early Christians adopted the name "Babylon" as a symbolic name for Rome, the contemporary manifestation of Babylon as the persecutor of Christians (e.g. Rev 18). Such a usage would not have developed until Rome began to persecute Christians in 64 CE and probably not until Rome destroyed the second Jewish temple in 70 CE.

The letter can be dated before about 110 CE, when Polycarp quotes from it in his letter to the Philippians (e.g. Phil 1:3//1 Pet 1:8). Within the period 70–110 CE, a plausible date would be the reign of Trajan (98–117 CE), when we have evidence of Roman persecution of Christians in Bithynia-Pontus. The years 98–110 thus emerge as the most probable date of the letter.

SOCIAL SETTING OF I PETER

In the letter of First Peter, we glimpse the Christian sense of alienation from the world and Roman society's antagonism toward this separatist attitude.

As Gentile converts became Christians, they withdrew from participation in the religious and social events of their community. They looked back on these practices as "idol worship" and saw the sometimes exuberant celebrations associated with it as debauchery. A key passage in First Peter expresses this viewpoint:

> For you spent enough time in the past doing what the Gentiles like, engaging in debaucheries, lusts, wine celebrations, sexual revels, drinking bouts, and illicit acts of idol worship. They think it strange that you are not joining them in the same wild profligacy, and they verbally abuse you. (1 Pet 4:3–4)

As the Christians stopped participating in the religion and other aspects of their society, they came to see themselves as outsiders in that society. The author of First Peter expresses this perspective by addressing his audience as "resident aliens" and "visiting strangers" of the "Diaspora" (1:1;

1:17; 2:11). Here the term "Diaspora," literally meaning territory outside the Jewish homeland, is used in a metaphorical sense. For the author of First Peter, the true homeland of Christians currently exists in heaven (1:4) and will only be revealed on earth at the parousia (1:13). In the meantime, Christians live outside their true homeland, just as Jews in the Diaspora live outside theirs. In the world, therefore, Christians are living as "resident aliens," that is as residents in a foreign country without the rights and privileges of full citizens. All of these terms express a sense of alienation from society. The author of First Peter and probably the Christians to whom he wrote no longer felt at home in their social environment.

The Gentile community responded to the Christians' withdrawal with antagonism. The letter of First Peter pictures various levels of antagonism toward the Christians. Their fellow citizens speak against them as "evildoers" (2:12; 3:16; 4:4; 4:14). The letter may or may not presuppose official interrogations. In either case, the Christians must be prepared to give a "defense" (*apologia*) of their faith to those who ask them (3:14–15). Though the author never mentions whether the hostility directed against Christians might lead to their deaths, he may well have such an outcome in mind. The letter throughout keeps in view the possibility of sharing the sufferings of Christ, who did die. The author describes the situation as a "trial by fire" (4:12) that was being experienced by Christians throughout the whole world (5:9).

MESSAGE OF I PETER

The author of First Peter addresses two primary exhortations to his audience: to have hope and joy in their sufferings and to maintain good conduct in their current situation.

The first exhortation appears in the frequent use of the terms "suffer" (2:19, 20, 21, 23; 3:14, 17, 18; 4:1, 1, 15, 19; 5:10) and "suffering" (1:11; 4:13; 5:1, 9). No writing in the New Testament uses these terms as often as First Peter. The author encourages his readers in their sufferings, explaining them as both the will of God (1:7; 4:17–19) and the work of the Devil (5:8–11). He emphasizes that Christ suffered too, leaving an example (2:21–23). He also gives Christ as an example of how belief in God provides an alternative sense of status. Though Christ was rejected by humans, the author affirms that he was chosen by God as a precious cornerstone in God's spiritual house. Similarly Christians, though rejected by their society, find their sense of belonging and status as stones in the same house or household (2:4–10). This status exists to some degree as a present possession within the alternative society experienced within the Christian community. Even more so, it exists as a future hope. At Christ's return, those who share his sufferings will also share his glory (1:3–13; 3:14; 4:12–14; 5:1). On this basis the author urges his audience to rejoice and consider their sufferings as a blessing (4:13–14). Furthermore, he says, if they suffer, they should suffer as Christians, not as wrongdoers, since it is better to suffer for doing right than for doing wrong (2:20; 3:17; 4:15–16).

The second primary exhortation appears in the frequent use of the term "conduct" or "behavior" and related words (1:15, 17, 18; 2:12; 3:1, 2, 16). The author exhorts his audience to maintain "good conduct" as foreigners living away from their heavenly home. This exhortation is related to the first, since the author hopes that the Christians' good conduct will silence those who speak against them as evildoers (2:15; 3:16). The author exhorts his audience to be holy in all their conduct (1:15), to conduct themselves with reverence during the time they live as foreigners (1:17), to remember that they have been ransomed from their former manner of conduct (1:18), and to maintain good conduct among the Gentiles (2:12). Maintaining good conduct apparently includes following the standard patriarchal order in the household, since the author includes a "household code" similar to those in Colossians, Ephesians, and the Pastorals (1 Pet 2:18–3:7). Good conduct for slaves consists of submitting to their masters, even those that abuse them (2:18–25). Reverent and chaste conduct for wives consists of submitting to their husbands and holds the possibility of converting those who are non-Christians (3:1–6).

READING GUIDE: I PETER

Read the letter of First Peter with the help of the following guide.

In the **introduction (1:1–2)**, the author, writing as "Peter," addresses his audience in Asia Minor as "visiting strangers," people living away from their true homeland as foreigners.

From the beginning of the letter, the author tries to provide his audience with **hope in suffering (1:3–13)**. He speaks to Christians who currently suffer "various trials" (1:6) and explains these as necessary to test their faith (1:7). He encourages them by stressing their hope for the future: an inheritance kept for them in heaven (1:3–4) and the salvation of their souls (1:9), which prophets spoke about (1:10–12), and which would be revealed when Christ returned (1:5, 7, 13).

In the meantime, the author exhorts his audience to maintain **holy conduct (1:14–2:10)**. He urges them to "be holy in all your conduct" (1:15). The word "holy" and related terms occur frequently in this section of the letter (1:15–16, 22; 2:5, 9). In 1:16, the author bases this call to holiness on Yahweh's word to Israel in Leviticus: "You shall be holy, because I am holy" (Lev 11:44, 45; 19:2; 20:7). As an incentive to holy conduct, the author reminds them of certain Christian conceptions about salvation. They were ransomed from their former conduct by the blood of Jesus (1:18–21). They were reborn into a new life by accepting the message proclaimed to them (1:22–25). As the goal of their salvation, they are becoming stones in a spiritual temple of God, or a holy priesthood offering spiritual sacrifices (2:1–10).

The theme of "conduct" continues as the author exhorts his audience to maintain **good conduct among the Gentiles (2:11–3:12)** while living as foreigners among them. He hoped that such good conduct would convince their opponents that they were not evildoers (2:11–12). In the author's view, good conduct meant submitting to every human institution (2:13): submitting to government (2:13–17), household slaves submitting to masters (2:18–25), wives submitting to husbands (3:1–6), and husbands being considerate of their wives (3:7).

At this point, the author returns to the theme of **suffering as a Christian (3:13–4:19)**. If Christians suffer, they should suffer for doing right, not wrong (3:13–17). Christ also suffered, after which he preached to "the spirits in prison," apparently the spirits of those who died in Noah's flood (3:18–22). In some way not specified, the author sees suffering in the flesh as a prerequisite for ceasing from sin (4:1–6). After various exhortations (4:7–11), the author encourages Christians who share the sufferings of Christ to rejoice, since they will also share his glory when he returns (4:12–19).

The author gives some final exhortations to **elders and younger men (5:1–11)**. Here he attributes Christian suffering to the Devil (5:8–11).

In the **conclusion (5:12–14)**, the author identifies Silvanus as his scribe, then ends with greetings and a benediction.

DISCUSSION QUESTION

Read the selections in Appendix 14 on Roman persecution of Christianity (pp. 611–614). What light do these texts shed on the letter of First Peter?

REVIEW QUESTIONS

1. In what ways did early Christians adopt a separatist attitude toward their society? In what ways did Roman society respond with antagonism? How did Christians respond to this antagonism?

2. Why do most scholars doubt that Peter wrote the letter of First Peter? If Peter did not write the letter, what can we infer about the author?

3. To whom was First Peter written? From where was it written? At what date might it have been written? Identify: Babylon.

4. Explain how First Peter reflects alienation of Christians from their society. What types of antagonism toward Christians are reflected in the letter?

5. What are the two primary exhortations that the author of First Peter addresses to his audience? How are they related?

SUGGESTIONS FOR FURTHER STUDY

Achtemeier, Paul J. *1 Peter: A Commentary on First Peter* (Hermeneia; Fortress, 1996). A standard commentary on First Peter.

Bird, Jennifer G. *Abuse, Power and Fearful Obedience: Reconsidering 1 Peter's Commands to Wives* (Bloomsbury T&T Clark, 2011). Gives a critique of the household code in First Peter 3:1–6, using feminist, postcolonial, and materialist methods.

Chester, Andrew, and Ralph P. Martin. *The Theology of the Letters of James, Peter, and Jude* (Cambridge University Press, 1994). Includes a brief discussion of the setting and themes of First Peter.

Elliott, John H. *1 Peter: A New Translation with Introduction and Commentary* (Anchor Bible; Doubleday; Yale University Press, 2000). A standard commentary on First Peter.

Horrell, David G. *1 Peter* (Bloomsbury T&T Clark, 2008). An introduction to scholarship on First Peter.

Talbert, Charles H., ed. *Perspectives on First Peter* (Mercer University Press, 1986; reprinted, Wipf & Stock, 2010). Essays by various scholars.

40 Conflict with the Roman World (2)
Revelation

Reading the book of Revelation for the first time can be a mind-boggling experience. Visions of strange beasts with multiple heads and eyes alternate with scenes of fearful destruction and vengeful glee. Here a woman in celestial apparel bears a child that is snatched from the jaws of a great red dragon. There a beast with two horns makes everyone worship another beast with seven heads and ten horns. There is war in heaven and war on earth, punctuated with terrible plagues and judgments. Angels come on stage periodically, sealing foreheads, blowing trumpets, wielding sickles, and throwing bowls of wrath onto the earth. These scenes may attract or repulse us, fill us with confusion or fear. We may share what the narrator himself felt after describing one particularly strange vision: "I was amazed with great amazement" (17:6).

This book with its exotic imagery has had a perennial appeal for certain groups throughout Christian history. That appeal lies in the fact that it purports to describe the events leading up to the return of Jesus. At the end of the story, Jesus returns from heaven on a white horse to establish a kingdom on earth for a thousand years (a "millennium"), after which comes the final judgment. Prior to his return, a Satanic beast whose number is 666 heads up a ten-nation confederacy and mounts a persecution against Christians. Though the term "Antichrist" never appears in Revelation, interpreters have traditionally applied that term to this figure or some other in the book. Through much of Christian history, interpreters of Revelation have found the Antichrist in their own time, using the book of Revelation as a blueprint for deciphering current events. Europeans in the Middle Ages saw the forces of Antichrist in the armies of Islam, which Christian Europe fought for control of the Holy Land. Protestant Reformers identified the Antichrist with the institution against which they protested, the Roman Catholic papacy. More recent interpreters have found the ten-nation confederacy of the Antichrist in the European Common Market (now the European Union). That interpretation reached its peak in 1981 when the tenth member joined the Market, but subsequently suffered a setback as membership grew well beyond that number.

Television evangelists and others in the same tradition continue to read Revelation with a Bible in one hand and a newspaper in the other. This popular type of interpretation, however, has few followers among critical biblical scholars. The historical-critical method that developed in the modern period has taught us to interpret this book not in the context of our own day, but in the historical context of the author and his audience. When we do that, we see that the author was concerned not with events in the far distant future, but with events that either occurred or were expected to occur in his own day. Written in the late first or early second century, the book dealt with the problem of Roman persecution of Christianity. The author, like other early Christians, expected Jesus to return soon. He used this hope to encourage churches experiencing persecution, by depicting in a vision the overthrow of Rome and the return of Jesus to establish the kingdom of God.

The historical-critical method has also taught us to interpret the book in its literary context. As unique as it may seem, Revelation actually belongs to a genre of literature that was not uncommon at the time, a type of literature called "apocalyptic." In order to understand Revelation in its literary context, we must see how it embodies typical features of apocalyptic literature.

APOCALYPTIC LITERATURE

We previously described apocalyptic literature in Chapter 5 and gave examples of it in Appendixes 3.2–4 (1 Enoch and 4 Ezra). Here we give a more detailed discussion.

Definitions

The book of Revelation gets its name from the first word in it, the Greek term **"apocalypse,"** meaning a "revelation" or "uncovering." An apocalypse can be defined as a literary genre in which an individual receives a revelation or "unveiling" of the normally invisible spiritual world. This definition implies two orders of reality: a physical realm which can be perceived by the normal senses and a spiritual realm which cannot (i.e. God, angels, demons, heaven, hell, etc.). In an apocalypse, God reveals some aspect of the spiritual realm or some truth that can only be learned in that realm, such as knowledge about heaven or hell or the future.

The term **"apocalyptic literature"** refers to writings which contain one or more apocalypses. In addition to the book of Revelation, from which this literature gets its name, apocalyptic literature includes the books of Daniel and Zechariah 1–8 in the Hebrew Bible. Most of the extant apocalyptic literature, however, is found in the Pseudepigrapha.

Many apocalypses claim to give revelation about eschatology, what would happen at the "end," either the end of an individual life or the end of the present world age. Here we are concerned only with the latter. Cosmic **apocalyptic eschatology** is a view of the future that looks for the end of the present world order and the establishment of a new and better world order brought about by divine intervention in the near future.

Types of Apocalypses

There are two primary types of apocalypses. The first is the **otherworld journey**. Sometimes the seer (the character in the apocalypse) receives a vision of the spiritual world, usually by taking a journey out of the normal world. In First Enoch, for example, Enoch is caught up to heaven and receives a guided tour, in which he sees the hidden realities behind the scenes: God, angels, the places of reward and punishment, and various other aspects of the heavenly world.

The second type is the **historical apocalypse**. In this, the seer receives a review of the course of history, culminating in the end of the present age. In Daniel 9–11, for example, angels reveal to Daniel the course of history from Daniel's time to the end of the age. In 1 Enoch 85–90, Enoch has a dream in which he sees the course of history from creation to the final judgment. Though no two of these historical reviews describe the end-time in exactly the same way, they express broad agreement concerning the overall picture. Generally, they see the present time as an age in which evil prevails and the righteous suffer. Evil will continue to grow worse until it comes to a head. God will then intervene, bringing the old order to an end and establishing a new age of peace and righteousness.

The book of Revelation incorporates both the otherworld journey and the historical review. The seer takes an otherworld journey when he is caught up to heaven (4:1) and sees the throne of God (chs. 4–5). Later an angel gives him a guided tour of the heavenly Jerusalem (21:9–22:9). The seer also receives two historical reviews, two series of visions that portray the course of eschatological history from his own day to the final judgment (6:1–11:19 and 12:1–21:8).

Features of Apocalyptic Literature

We can understand the book of Revelation better by seeing how it incorporates some of the chief features of apocalyptic literature.

An apocalypse gets its name from the fact that the seer receives a **revelation**. The seer may receive the revelation by various means, and the book of Revelation includes most of these: a vision or dream (Rev 1:10, 12), an otherworld journey (Rev 4:1), and instruction from a heavenly being (Rev 17:1; cf. 5:5, 7:13).

The visions given to the seer often appear in **symbolism**. For example, in Revelation 12, John sees a great red dragon, later identified as the Devil. If one knows what the symbols represent, the meaning of the vision is clear. If not, the vision may seem mysterious and esoteric.

Another feature of apocalyptic literature is **determinism**. The future has already been strictly determined, so that it can be known through revelation. The seer of Revelation adopts this perspective in predicting what he believes "must take place" (1:1).

All historical apocalypses exhibit the **expectation of an imminent end**. The author believes that the end of the age will come very soon. The author of Revelation is no exception. He expects Jesus to return soon. Four times he quotes Jesus as saying, "I am coming soon" (3:11; 22:7, 12, 20). Twice he emphasizes that "the time is near" (1:3; 22:10). Twice he states that the revelation concerns "what must soon take place" (1:1; 22:6). In this respect, Revelation shares the major drawback of all attempts to predict the end of the world: so far all have been wrong.

Most apocalyptic works are characterized by **pseudonymity**. They are pseudonymous ("written under a false name"); that is, they are attributed to famous persons of the past who did not actually write them. Apocalyptic writings in the Pseudepigrapha are attributed, for example, to Adam, Enoch, Abraham, Baruch, and Ezra. In identifying himself as "John," the author of Revelation may be writing pseudonymously as John the son of Zebedee, an apostle of Jesus.

If an author in the first or second century wrote as if he were Adam, he could narrate the history of the world from Adam to his own time as if Adam were predicting it. Such fictional prediction, called *vaticinium ex eventu* ("prophecy after the fact"), occurs frequently in historical apocalypses. Generally the author gives a review of history down to his own time by *vaticinium ex eventu*. He then begins to predict the events of the end-time that he believes will soon happen. Since his "predictions" of the past are always more accurate than his predictions of the future, we can determine the time that he wrote by noticing the point at which his

Figure 40.1
The seven churches of the Roman province of Asia to which the book of Revelation is addressed.

predictions cease to be accurate descriptions of actual historical events. The author of Revelation incorporates *vaticinium ex eventu* to some degree, as we shall see in the reading guide.

Social Setting of Apocalyptic Eschatology

Apocalyptic eschatology, as a hope for the future, generally appears among people who are dissatisfied with the present world. They look to divine intervention to bring about a more satisfactory world. The sources of their dissatisfaction with the present may not always be apparent. In some instances, however, it is clear that the dissatisfaction arose during a time of persecution. For example, the book of Daniel, which expresses an apocalyptic hope for the future, took shape among Jews at a time when they were being persecuted by Antiochus Epiphanes. Similarly, the book of Revelation reflects a time when Christians were persecuted by the Roman Empire. These writings therefore focused on the future not merely to satisfy curiosity, but to encourage people suffering unjustly in their present. They gave hope by predicting that good would ultimately triumph over evil, that God would reward the righteous and judge their persecutors. The lasting appeal of such literature rests on the continued perception that the world as we know it could stand a good deal of improvement.

GENRE OF REVELATION

The book of Revelation, while usually classified as an apocalypse, actually has features of more than one genre and more than one type of discourse.

First, it combines two literary genres: the letter and the apocalypse. Following a preface (1:1–3), the letter begins with a salutation: the author, John, writes to seven churches in the Roman province of Asia (1:4–8). The letter ends with a closing benediction (22:21). While the work as a whole takes the form of a letter, an apocalypse forms one part of the letter (chs. 4–21).

Secondly, within the letter, the author employs two primary forms of discourse: prophecy and apocalyptic prediction of the future. "Prophecy" in the biblical sense is not primarily prediction, but speaking a message in the name of God: it may include exhortation, encouragement, or threat of judgment. This type of discourse occurs in the letters to the seven churches (chs. 2–3), as the author exhorts and encourages the churches in the name of Christ. Most of the rest of the letter (chs. 4–21) constitutes an apocalypse that purports to reveal heavenly secrets.

AUTHOR AND DATE

The author of Revelation identifies himself simply as "John" (1:1, 4, 9; 22:8). He writes to seven churches in the Roman province of Asia, describing a vision he received while on Patmos, a small island off the coast of Asia.

Early Christian writers such as Justin (about 160 CE) and Clement of Alexandria identified this John with John the Apostle, the son of Zebedee, to whom also the Fourth Gospel has traditionally been assigned. As early as the third century, however, Dionysius of Alexandria pointed to the difference in style between the Gospel of John and Revelation as evidence of different authors. The language of the gospel, though simple, is grammatically correct, whereas the language of Revelation is often ungrammatical. The two works also differ significantly in their eschatology. The

Gospel of John emphasizes that one can have salvation (eternal life) in the present and has few references to a future consummation. Revelation, in contrast, focuses on a future salvation at the end of the present age.

Most scholars today therefore attribute the Revelation and the gospel to different authors, neither of which was the apostle John. The author of Revelation may have written pseudonymously in the name of the apostle John, or he may have been an early Christian prophet named John.

According to Irenaeus, bishop of Lyons (about 190 CE), the book appeared near the end of the reign of Domitian, the Roman emperor who reigned from 81 to 96 CE. Most scholars accept this date. However, the widespread persecution that the book presupposes may correspond better to events in the reign of Trajan (98–117 CE).

SETTING AND PURPOSE OF REVELATION

Revelation has its historical and social setting in the conflict between Rome and Christianity. As we saw in discussing First Peter, ancient Rome made no separation between religion and the state. The Roman state promoted a religion of the state, which it expected all people in the empire to practice. This state religion included the emperor cult: burning incense to the statue of the emperor as a divine human. While the Romans excused Jews from this requirement, since they belonged to an ancient monotheistic religion, the more recent Christian religion received no such exemption. Conflict between Roman and Christian perspectives became inevitable. While the Christians felt that worshipping the Roman gods violated their sole allegiance to Christ, Romans saw their refusal to honor the gods as atheism, lack of patriotism, and pure stubbornness. It is in the context of such conflict that the author of Revelation writes. He warns of a great persecution, in which an agent of the emperor cult requires Christians to worship the statue of the emperor or be killed. The author expects this conflict to be resolved by the return of Christ and the destruction of the Roman Empire.

The author develops this theme in a symbolic vision by depicting the events leading up to Christ's return: persecution of Christians by the Roman Empire, various judgments on the earth, and the destruction of the empire. Immediately after the destruction of Rome, Christ returns and establishes the kingdom of God on earth for a thousand years. Afterward comes the final judgment, the creation of a new heaven and earth, and the descent of God to dwell with his people on the new earth.

The purpose of the vision was to correct the churches, encourage them, and exhort them. It corrected what was lacking in their devotion in order to prepare them for the return of Jesus. It encouraged them with the hope that the persecution they endured would soon be ended and bring a reward. It exhorted them to stand fast despite the pressure to renounce their faith.

Outline of Revelation

Jesus' instructions to John in 1:19 define the three major sections of the book. Jesus tells John to write down

1. "what you have seen" (the vision of Christ in 1:9–20);
2. "what is" (the letters to the seven churches in 2:1–3:22);
3. "what is going to happen after this" (the preview of the future in 4:1–22:9).

Scholars disagree about the structure of the apocalyptic portion of the book (4:1–22:9). Some interpret the visions in chronological order. Others believe that some visions "recapitulate" earlier visions, i.e. they describe the same events from a different perspective. For example, the seven bowls of judgment in chapter 16 seem to be simply a different version of the seven trumpets of judgment in chapters 8–11. Unfortunately, no two theories of recapitulation agree exactly. In the reading guide, we will assume that the apocalypse contains two distinct series of visions: the first in chapters 4–11, the second in chapters 12–22. The visions of the second series do not follow the first chronologically but start over again and provide a different view of events leading up to the end.

READING GUIDE: REVELATION

Read the book of Revelation with the help of the following guide.

What Was and Is (chs. 1–3)

John's letter is preceded by a **preface (1:1–3)**. It was probably added by another hand, since it speaks of John in the third person.

The letter itself begins with a **salutation (1:4–5a)**. John writes to seven churches, which correspond to the seven spirits of God (see Isaiah 11:1–2). The number seven thus plays a significant role in Revelation from the beginning. The salutation is followed by a doxology (1:5b-6), an apocalyptic prediction (1:7), and a prophetic utterance in which John speaks as a prophet in the name of Jesus (1:8).

John then recounts a **vision of Jesus (1:9–20)** that he had while "in the Spirit." A vision of "one like a son of man," the glorified Jesus, overwhelms him. Jesus tells him to write what will become the three sections of Revelation (1:19).

John then writes **letters to seven churches (2:1–3:22)**. The seven churches to which John writes were seven literal churches in the Roman province of Asia. In these letters, John, as a Christian prophet speaking in the name of Jesus, gives both praise and rebuke to the churches. His purpose is to prepare them for the imminent parousia.

Prelude to What Is to Come (chs. 4–5)

In 1:19, Jesus told John to write "what is going to happen after this." This preview of the future begins in 4:1, where a voice summons John to heaven with a similar phrase: "I will show you what must happen after this."

When John is caught up to heaven, he sees the **heavenly worship (ch. 4)**. God is on his throne, being worshipped by various heavenly beings (cf. Isaiah 6; Ezekiel 1).

The vision then focuses on two objects: **the scroll and the lamb (ch. 5)**. John sees a scroll in the right hand of God and a lamb that has recovered from being slain. The lamb represents Jesus, who died and rose from the dead. The scroll has writing on both sides and is sealed with seven seals. That is, a sheet of papyrus has been rolled up and seven lumps of melted wax have been applied to the outside edge of the sheet and allowed to harden. These wax seals must be broken in order to unroll the scroll. This scroll has been variously interpreted. Whatever its precise significance, it must be opened in order for the events of the end-time to occur, the events that will lead to the establishment of God's rule over the earth. Only Jesus, because of his death on behalf of others, has been found worthy to open the scroll and establish the kingdom of God.

Figure 40.2 John and his vision of one like a son of man surrounded by seven golden lampstands (Rev 1:12–20). Woodcut by Albrecht Dürer, *Apocalipsis in figuris*, 1511 (Heritage Image Partnership Ltd/Alamy Stock Photo).

The Scroll with Seven Seals (6:1–8:6)

As the Lamb breaks each of the scroll's seven seals, the events of the end-time begin to occur: God's people are persecuted, God sends judgments on the earth, and God establishes his rule on earth.

When the Lamb breaks each of the **first four seals (6:1–8)**, a horseman rides forth. These four horsemen represent the beginning of eschatological woes: conquest (6:1–2), war (6:3–4), famine (6:5–6), and pestilence (6:7–8).

Breaking the **fifth seal (6:9–11)** reveals martyrs who have died for their faith and indicates that others will also be killed. It is probable that the first five seals are *vaticinia ex eventu*. That is, the author believed that they had already occurred. As he looked out on the world, he could see conquest, war, famine, and pestilence. He could see Christians suffering martyrdom for their faith. What he saw convinced him that he stood at the end of history. Five of the seven seals had already been opened; only two remained. These would bring the day of the Lord and the kingdom of God.

When the Lamb opens the **sixth seal (6:12–17)**, an earthquake and celestial signs announce the arrival of the day of the Lord, the day when Yahweh would afflict the earth with severe judgments at the end of the age.

After the sixth seal, there is an **interlude (7:1–17)**. Before the seventh seal is opened and the judgments fall, John sees two groups of people, representing the two major groups in the Christian church of his day: 144,000 Jewish Christians on earth who receive God's seal of protection, and a great multitude of Gentile Christians who have experienced "great tribulation" in the world but are now comforted in heaven before the throne of God. Jewish Christians appear on earth because, as Jews, they would be exempt from the requirement to participate in the Roman state religion and therefore would not be killed. Gentile Christians, however, appear in heaven because, with no such exemption, they would be compelled to either participate or suffer martyrdom. This vision reassures Jewish Christians that they would receive protection from the judgments that God was about to unleash on the earth (cf. 9:4). It reassures Gentile Christians who would die for their faith that they would be rewarded in heaven.

When the Lamb opens the **seventh seal (8:1–6)**, seven angels with trumpets prepare to bring the judgments of the day of the Lord upon the earth, judgments that preface the arrival of God's kingdom.

The Seven Trumpets (8:7–11:19)

The seven angels blowing trumpets release seven plagues.

The **first four trumpets (8:7–12)** bring plagues on the earth (8:7), the sea (8:8–9), the fresh water (8:10–11), and the heavenly bodies (8:12). These plagues resemble those inflicted on Egypt in the story of the exodus (Exodus 7:8–11:10).

A **flying eagle (8:13)** warns that the remaining three trumpets will bring severe "woes" on the earth.

The **fifth trumpet (9:1–12)** releases the first woe, demonic locusts from the abyss, which torment but do not kill.

The **sixth trumpet (9:13–21)** releases the second woe, armies at the Euphrates River that kill a third of humanity.

After the sixth trumpet there is another **interlude (10:1–11:14)**. Before the seventh trumpet sounds, an angel from heaven swears that God's plan will be complete at the blast of the seventh trumpet (10:1–7). From this angel John takes a little scroll to eat (10:8–11). The act is symbolic. By eating the scroll, John takes within himself the words written on the scroll in order to speak them forth as prophecy. The prophecy is about two witnesses, two prophets of God who preach for a period of three and a half years before the end (11:1–14). These represent Moses and Elijah, two Israelite prophets that Jewish tradition expected to return before the day of the Lord (Mal 3:1–5; 4:4–6). They have the power of Elijah to hold back the rain (1 Kings 17:1) and the power of Moses to turn the waters to blood and to smite the earth with plagues (Exod 7:14–24 etc.). They minister during a period when Jerusalem and the temple precinct are "trampled" by Gentiles. This period of 1,260 days or forty-two months or three and a half years comes from the book of Daniel (Dan 7:25; 12:7). The beast who kills these prophets is explained later in Revelation (13:1–10).

Unexpectedly, the **seventh trumpet (11:15–19)** brings no third woe. Instead, voices announce that the Messiah has begun his reign. The kingdom of God has arrived. The time has come for the final judgment of the dead, with rewards for Christians and destruction for their persecutors. The goal of history has arrived as the new age begins.

The Great Persecution (chs. 12–14)

With chapter 12, a new series of visions begins that does not chronologically follow the previous series, but backs up to an earlier time in the author's past. These visions begin with a *vaticinium ex eventu* of events (as the author interprets them) from the time of Jesus down to the time of the author (12:1–13:12). John then begins to predict the events of the end-time.

The first vision concerns the **birth of a male child (12:1–6)**. John sees a glorious woman about to give birth. This woman probably represents the heavenly Jerusalem, embodied on earth in the Jewish-Christian church in Jerusalem, the mother church of all Christians. Metaphorically she gives birth to the Messiah, Jesus, who is to rule over the nations with a rod of iron (cf. Psalm 2; Rev 2:26–27). The great dragon with seven heads, an image passed down from ancient Canaanite combat myths, seeks to devour the child, but the child is caught up to heaven. The dragon represents Satan embodied on earth in the Roman Empire. Pontius Pilate, the Roman governor of Judea, sought to destroy Jesus, but, according to Christian tradition, Jesus rose from the dead and ascended to heaven.

The next vision concerns **Satan's expulsion from heaven (12:7–12)**. In ancient Jewish thought, Satan dwelt in heaven, not in hell. Once Jesus receives the authority over nations that Satan formerly exercised, no place remains for Satan in the heavenly world. He and his angels are therefore cast out of heaven to the earth (cf. Luke 10:18). Like the author of First Peter, John explained the persecution of Christians in his day as the work of the Devil. Satan was on the earth seeking someone to devour (1 Pet 5:8).

On earth, Satan launches a **Satanic persecution (12:13–17)**. He tries unsuccessfully to persecute the woman, who flees to the wilderness. This vision probably describes events connected with the siege of Jerusalem by Roman armies under Vespasian and Titus. According to Christian tradition, before the Romans destroyed Jerusalem in 70 CE, the Jewish-Christian community in Jerusalem fled to Pella, a city on the other side of the Jordan River (Eusebius, *Ecclesiastical History*, 3.5.3). The dragon then turns his anger against the woman's other children, Christians who keep the commandments of God and testify about Jesus.

Satan raises up two beastly henchmen to help him persecute Christians. The first is a **beast from the sea (13:1–10)**, with a fatal wound that has been healed. This beast represents a Roman emperor who has been brought back from the dead. In John's day, a rumor existed that the Roman emperor Nero, who committed suicide in 68 CE, had not died but fled to Parthia, from where he would return and reconquer the Roman Empire (Sibylline Oracles 4.119–24, 137–39; 5.361–85). The beast from the sea is thus a revived Nero, the first Roman emperor to persecute

Christians. Like Nero, the beast has authority to imprison and kill "the saints," i.e. Christians. Depending upon when John wrote, he regarded either Domitian or Trajan as such a persecutor.

The second beast is a **beast from the land (13:11–18)**. This beast exercises authority on behalf of the first beast, the Roman emperor. The second beast is therefore probably a Roman governor, perhaps the governor of Asia, the Roman province to which John wrote. The second beast requires everyone to receive the mark "666." This number represents the name of the first beast. In Hebrew and Greek, the letters also represented numbers. By adding the numerical values of the letters in a name, one would arrive at the "number" of that name. The Greek name "Nero Caesar" written in Hebrew characters would have the number 666. It thus indicates cryptically that the first beast, a Roman emperor, is the reincarnation of Nero and that the second beast, perhaps the governor of Asia, requires people to worship him. The second beast promotes worship of the Roman emperor by making everyone worship his statue. This corresponds to the practice described by Pliny, Roman governor of Bithynia-Pontus during the reign of Trajan (see Appendix 14.2–3). Pliny required Christians to reverence the emperor as a divine man by burning incense and pouring wine out to his statue. Those who refused he put to death.

The next vision shows **144,000 on Mount Zion (14:1–5)**. The 144,000 seen here parallel the 144,000 Jewish Christians seen in 7:1–8. They are now identified as male virgins who are given a place of honor in the kingdom (14:4). If taken literally, this part of the vision illustrates a significant trend in early Christianity: the glorification of celibacy. A significant part of the church came to regard those who remained celibate (i.e. monks) as more "spiritual" than those who married. If the virginity is metaphorical, the 144,000 may be virgins because they have no relations with the beast.

Next comes a series of **proclamations (14:6–13)**. Three angels and a voice from heaven warn against worshipping the beast and pronounce a blessing on those who die for their faith.

The persecution is pictured as a **great harvest (14:14–20)**, symbolic of death. As the martyrs are cut down like wheat or like grapes, great quantities of blood are shed. At what point the author shifts from describing the past (by *vaticinium ex eventu*) to predicting the future is unclear. Had the Christians of Asia experienced a bloodbath such as that described, or was this part of John's expectation for the future? Since we have scant knowledge concerning the experience of Christians in Asia during the relevant time period, we cannot say for certain.

Figure 40.3 Twelfth-century illustration of visions from Revelation 12–13. In the center is the woman clothed with the sun and standing on the moon. At the upper left, her male child is caught up to heaven. At the lower right, the dragon with seven heads sends a flood after her that is swallowed by the earth. At the lower left, the beast from the sea with seven heads wages war against the rest of her children. Herrad of Landsberg, *Hortus deliciarum* (Art Collection 3/Alamy Stock Photo).

The Seven Bowls of God's Wrath (chs. 15–16)

The next vision reveals a **scene in heaven (ch. 15)**. The Christian martyrs who have just died in the persecution are now seen in heaven with God (15:2–4). Seven angels prepare to pour out seven plagues of judgment on the people who are left on earth. Clearly by this point, John has shifted from describing the past to describing the judgment on the persecutors that he envisioned for the near future.

The seven plagues are pictured as seven **bowls of wrath (ch. 16)**. These seven plagues parallel those of the seven trumpets of judgment (8:7–11:19). The bowls of wrath bring severe plagues on those people who have worshipped the beast and are part of its kingdom. The seventh bowl (16:17–21) brings about the destruction of the city at the source of the persecution: namely "Babylon," a symbolic name for Rome.

Judgment of Babylon Described (17:1–19:10)

The seventh bowl of wrath brought God's judgment on "the great city" Babylon. The next section presents a more detailed picture of the city's overthrow.

One of the angels shows John a vision of the **great whore Babylon (17:1–6)**. The vision represents Babylon as a woman seated on a beast with seven heads. Later we learn that the seven heads represent seven hills on which the woman is seated (17:9) and the woman represents "the great city that holds kingship over the kings of the earth" (17:18). No one in John's day could mistake the allusion to Rome, situated on seven hills. The symbolic name "Babylon" links Rome with the ancient enemy of the Jewish people, the world empire that destroyed the Jewish temple and took the Jewish people into exile. Like its ancient namesake, the Rome of John's day had also destroyed the Jewish temple and now persecuted Christians. John sees the city as a great whore, drunk with the blood of God's people. She represents the antithesis of the city of God, Jerusalem, represented in Revelation 12 as a beautiful woman clothed in glory.

The angel then gives an **interpretation of the vision (17:7–14)**. According to the angel, the heads also represent seven Roman emperors. Five belonged to the author's past, the sixth was contemporary with the author ("the one who is"), and the seventh would come next and reign only a short while. The beast itself represented an eighth emperor, who would be a reincarnation of one of the seven (i.e. Nero). Opinions differ as to which emperors John had in mind. According to one possibility,

Vespasian (69–79 CE) was "the one who is," Titus (79–81 CE) was "he who must remain a short time," and Domitian (81–96 CE) was the revived Nero. If so, then John employed *vaticinium ex eventu*, actually writing in the time of Domitian but implying that he wrote in the time of Vespasian so that his comments about the last two emperors would appear to be predictions. Another possibility is that Domitian (81–96 CE) was "the one who is," Nerva (96–98 CE) was "he who must remain a short time," and Trajan (98–117 CE) was the revived Nero. In this case as well, John employed *vaticinium ex eventu*, actually writing in the time of Trajan. The latter possibility has one advantage over the former: while we do not know whether Domitian persecuted Christians, we do know that Trajan did (see Appendix 14.2–3).

In a **further explanation (17:15–18)**, the angel says that the beast, along with ten kings allied with him (represented as ten horns), would hate the whore and destroy her. Apparently John thought that the revived Nero would destroy the city of Rome and thus unwittingly carry out the purpose of God (17:17). However, John's predictions did not come to pass. Rome continued on under other emperors. It was eventually sacked by barbarians in 410, and Roman rule in the western empire came to an end in 476 or 480.

After John's vision of the great whore, a series of **seven episodes (18:1–19:10)** expounds on the anticipated destruction of Rome. First, an angel announces the fall of Babylon (18:1–3), describing her as ruling a vast world empire. She holds ultimate political power, so that the kings of the earth curry her favor – committing "fornication" with her, as John sees it. She also holds ultimate economic power: the merchants of the earth sell their cargoes of luxury goods in her ports. Second, a voice from heaven calls God's people to come out of her (18:4–8). Third, the kings and merchants of earth lament the fall of this political and economic system, while heaven is encouraged to rejoice (18:9–20). Fourth, an angel symbolically foretells her destruction by casting a great stone into the sea (18:21–24). Fifth, heaven rejoices over the fall of the whore (19:1–5). Sixth, the souls of Christians in heaven rejoice that the time has come for the Lamb (Christ) to marry his bride (the church). Seventh and finally, an angel instructs John to write that those who are invited to the marriage celebration of the Lamb are blessed (19:9–10).

God's Rule Established (19:11–22:5)

According to the vision, the overthrow of Roman rule would mark the time for God to establish his own rule over the earth. This occurs in two stages: first a messianic kingdom is established on earth for a thousand years, and then a final judgment is conducted. This sequence matches that found in Fourth Ezra 7:26–44, a Jewish apocalypse, though in this apocalypse the Messiah would reign for four hundred years and then die.

The first step in this sequence is the **return of Jesus (19:11–21)**. John sees Jesus return on a white horse accompanied by heavenly armies, also on white horses (19:11–16). His description of Jesus is largely based on Old Testament passages. Like the Davidic king, Jesus judges and wages war with righteousness (cf. Isa 11:4), and he will rule the nations with a rod of iron (cf. Psa 2:7–9). Like the divine warrior Yahweh, his garments are stained with the blood of the enemies that he tramples, just as the garments of workers who tread grapes in a winepress are stained with the juice (cf. Isa 63:1–6). A sword, symbolizing the word of God, goes forth from his mouth.

Jesus and his army defeat the beast and his army, thus ending the beast's rule over the earth (19:17–21). With the sword of his mouth, Jesus slays the armies of the beast (cf. Isa 11:4), thus providing a great feast of flesh for the carrion birds (cf. Ezek 38:17–20). The beast and the false prophet are captured and thrown alive into "the lake of fire that burns with sulfur." This lake of fire represents a development of the Jewish concept of Gehenna, originally a valley south of Jerusalem, but which tradition developed into a place of punishment in unquenchable fire.

After Jesus prevails over the beast, a **messianic kingdom (20:1–6)** is established on earth for a thousand years, i.e. for a "millennium." John may have drawn this specific period of time from the idea that a thousand years in God's sight are like a day (Psa 90:4; 2 Peter 3:8). At the beginning of this period, an angel chains Satan in "the abyss," a place of imprisonment in the underworld. Those who had a place in the messianic kingdom would thus be free from the persecution to which Satan had previously subjected them. John then sees "those to whom judgment was committed," i.e. the rulers of the kingdom, seated on thrones. These would include Jesus himself and perhaps his apostles (cf. Matt 19:27–28; Luke 22:28–30). The souls of those killed by the beast also come to life and reign with Jesus. John distinguishes this "first resurrection" from the general resurrection of all the dead that will occur later.

At the conclusion of the messianic kingdom comes **Satan's final attack (20:7–10)**. Satan is released for a short time, and he assembles

"Gog and Magog" to fight against "the camp of the saints and the beloved city," i.e. the messianic kingdom established in Jerusalem and ruled by Jesus. But fire from heaven consumes his armies, and Satan is thrown into the lake of fire permanently. It seems strange that Satan would be released after once being captured. Apparently John knew Ezekiel's prediction, which never came to pass, that an invading army led by Gog, ruler of the land of Magog, would attack Jerusalem and be destroyed (Ezek 38–39). In John's interpretation, this prediction would be fulfilled in the future, so he assumed that Satan had to be released in order to direct it.

After Satan's defeat comes the **final judgment (20:11–15)**. It is not clear whether God or Jesus sits on the great white throne to conduct this judgment, and it is not clear whether the judgment occurs in heaven or on earth. All the dead are resurrected and judged by their deeds, which have been recorded on scrolls. Another scroll lists the names of all those people whose deeds make them worthy of eternal life. Since this judgment is based on deeds, not on faith in Jesus, it has nothing exclusively Christian about it. Those whose deeds do not merit life are thrown into the lake of fire.

John then sees a **new heaven and earth (21:1–8)**, created to replace the old (cf. Isa 65:17–25; 66:22). The city of "new Jerusalem" comes down out of heaven to the new earth. This is the city of God's people, in which God himself dwells, and it comes down to earth so that God dwells on earth with his people. It is metaphorically depicted as God's bride. It is a place free from death and sorrow (cf. Isa 65:19–23). It is the place of new life, in contrast to the lake of fire, which is a "second death."

An angel then gives John a **guided tour of the new Jerusalem (21:9–22:5)**. It has "pearly gates" and streets of gold. Precious jewels adorn its foundations. A river of water of life runs through it, and trees of life give different kinds of fruit (cf. Ezek 47:1–12).

Epilogue (22:6–21)

After John finishes his guided tour, he gets some final words from the angelic guide and from Jesus. This epilogue affirms that the words of the book are "faithful and true" (22:6), given by Jesus through an angel. Five times it guarantees that the events described would happen soon (22:6, 7, 10, 12, 20).

Figure 40.4
Michael the archangel thrusting down Satan in chains. This altarpiece by Guido Reni (c. 1630) combines visions from Revelation 12:7–9 and 20:1–3. S. Maria della Concezione, Rome (Bridgeman-Giraudon/Art Resource, NY).

DISCUSSION QUESTIONS

1. *Revelation 1–11*. Discuss the characteristics of apocalyptic literature that appear in Revelation 1–11.
2. *Revelation 12–22*. Discuss the apocalyptic eschatology in Revelation 12–22.

REVIEW QUESTIONS

1. How does the historical-critical method of interpreting Revelation differ from the popular type of interpretation?
2. Define: apocalypse, apocalyptic literature, apocalyptic eschatology.
3. Identify and describe the two primary types of apocalypses that occur in Revelation.
4. In what ways does the book of Revelation incorporate features of apocalyptic literature?
5. What type of dissatisfaction is reflected in apocalyptic eschatology?
6. What different genres and types of discourse appear in Revelation?
7. What evidence suggests that the "John" who wrote Revelation is different than the author of the Fourth Gospel?
8. Describe the setting and purpose of Revelation.
9. What are the three major sections of Revelation?

SUGGESTIONS FOR FURTHER STUDY

See also the bibliography on apocalyptic literature in Chapter 5.

Bauckham, Richard. *The Theology of the Book of Revelation* (Cambridge University Press, 1993). A brief discussion of the main images and ideas of Revelation.

Boxall, Ian. *The Revelation of Saint John* (Hendrickson, 2009). A commentary on the book of Revelation.

Collins, Adela Yarbro. *The Apocalypse* (Glazier, 1979). A good brief commentary on Revelation.

Friesen, S. J. *Imperial Cults and the Apocalypse of John: Revelation in the Ruins* (Oxford University Press, 2006). Gives a detailed analysis of imperial cults in Asia Minor in the first century CE and shows how John's message resisted the values promoted by the cults.

Himmelfarb, Martha. *The Apocalypse: A Brief History* (Wiley-Blackwell, 2010). A history of the apocalypse genre, focused on selected examples from ancient Judaism to the present.

Levine, Amy-Jill, with Maria Mayo Robbins, eds. *A Feminist Companion to the Apocalypse of John* (Bloomsbury T&T Clark, 2009). Critiques of Revelation from feminist and other perspectives.

Wainwright, A. W. *Mysterious Apocalypse: Interpreting the Book of Revelation* (Abingdon, 1993). A history of the ways in which Revelation has been interpreted from ancient times to the present.

Appendixes

Appendix 1
Lucian on Sacrifices

Lucian of Samosata (125–180 CE) wrote a number of satirical works, poking fun at the beliefs and customs of his day. In *On Sacrifices* 12–13 he gives this description of a sacrifice.

When [people] have established altars and prescriptions and implements for sprinkling holy water, they bring the sacrifices: the farmer an ox from the plough, the shepherd a lamb, the goatherd a goat, someone else frankincense or a cake. The poor man, though, appeases the god merely by kissing his own right hand. The sacrificers, however, for I return to them, after decking the animal with garlands and finding out long before whether it is unblemished, lest they slaughter something of no use, bring it to the altar and kill it in the sight of the god, as the animal lows something mournful – probably avoiding inauspicious language and already piping a halftone for the sacrifice. Who would not suppose that the gods enjoy seeing all this? And though the placard says that anyone without pure hands should not enter the area sprinkled with holy water, there stands the priest himself stained with blood and, just like the Cyclops, cutting it up and removing the entrails and extracting the heart and pouring the blood around the altar – for what is not pious when sacrificing? On top of all this, after kindling a fire, he places on it the goat, carrying it in the skin itself, and the sheep, carrying it in the wool itself. And the smell of burnt fat, divinely sweet and suitably sacred, wafts upward and is gradually dispersed into heaven itself.

Appendix 2
The Essenes

The Jewish historian Josephus, writing in the first century CE, left several important works, including *The Jewish War* and *The Antiquities of the Jews*. In both he describes the three main branches of Judaism in the first century CE, calling them "philosophies" with an eye to the Greek culture of his day. Josephus claims that, as a youth, he became personally acquainted with all three groups. Though he eventually adopted the rules of the Pharisees, he devotes most of his description to the Essenes. The following passage on the Essenes is from *Jewish War* 2.119–61.

Three types of philosophy are taught among Jews. Adherents of the first are called Pharisees; those of the second, Sadducees.

In the third, which has a reputation for practicing solemnity, they are called Essenes. Jews by birth, they have more affection for one another than the others. They avoid the pleasures as a vice and regard self-control and not surrendering to the passions as a virtue. They hold marriage in contempt, but, accepting the children of others while they are still easy to teach, they regard them as their kin and indoctrinate them with their customs. They do so not to abolish marriage and the reproduction that results from it, but to keep themselves from the wantonness of women, convinced that no woman keeps her pledge to one man.

They despise wealth. The sharing among them is amazing, and you will not find anyone among them who possesses more than another. For they have a law that those entering the sect must surrender their property to the order, so that neither inferiority of poverty nor superiority of wealth is seen among any of them, but they all, like brothers, have a single fund in which the possessions of each are combined.

They regard oil as a defilement, and if anyone is involuntarily anointed, he washes his body. For they consider it good to have a dry skin and to always dress in white.

The caretakers of the common goods are elected and are selected by all for their respective functions.

They have no single city, but many of them reside in each. And when members come from elsewhere, all that they have is spread out for them as if it were their own, and they enter the homes of people they have never seen before like old acquaintances. Therefore when making their journeys, they take nothing at all with them, except arms because of the bandits. A caretaker in each city of the order is appointed expressly for strangers, to dispense clothes and provisions … They neither buy nor sell anything among themselves, but each gives what he has to anyone who needs it and in return receives something useful from him. And they are permitted to take from whomever they wish without giving anything in return.

Toward the deity they are particularly pious. Before the sun comes up, they speak nothing mundane, but offer certain traditional prayers to him, as though entreating him to rise. After this, those in charge dismiss them to their respective occupations. After working intently until the fifth hour,[1] they again assemble in one place. Binding linen coverings around their waists, they bathe their bodies in cold water. After this purification, they come together in a private room, which none of the heterodox is allowed to enter. Pure now themselves, they come to the dining room as if to some sacred precinct. When they have taken their seats with silence, the baker sets the loaves of bread before them in order, and the cook sets before each a single dish of a single meat. The priest prays before the meal, and no one may taste the food before the prayer. When he has finished breakfast, he prays again. Thus as they begin and as they end, they honor God as the provider of life. Then laying down their clothes as sacred, they again turn to work until evening. Upon returning, they dine in the same way, joined by any guests who happen to be present among them …

Every word spoken by them is more binding than an oath, while they avoid swearing, considering it worse than perjury. For they say that a person who is not believed without swearing by God is already found guilty.

---

[1] 11:00 a.m.

They show an extraordinary interest in the instructions of the ancients, selecting especially those meant to benefit soul and body. From these they seek out for themselves medicinal roots and properties of stones for the cure of symptoms.

Those who desire to join their sect do not gain entrance immediately, but, while he remains outside for a year, they prescribe for him the same lifestyle, giving him a small axe, the loincloth mentioned above, and white clothing. If during this time he gives proof of self-control, he comes nearer to the lifestyle and shares the purer water for purification but is not yet accepted into the societies. For after the demonstration of perseverance, his character is tested for two more years, and then, if found worthy, he is admitted into the group. But before he touches the common meal, he swears fearful oaths to them: first, to reverence the deity; then to practice justice toward others and not to hurt anyone, either on his own initiative or under orders; always to hate the unjust and fight alongside the just; always to keep his word to everyone, especially to those in control, since ruling is not left to anyone apart from God; and, if he himself should rule, never to abuse his authority nor to outshine his subjects in clothing or in any greater adornment; always to love the truth and to expose liars; to keep his hands from theft and his soul pure from unholy gain; and neither to conceal anything from the members nor to reveal any secret of theirs to others, even if someone should torture him to death …

Those convicted of serious sins they cast out of the order, and the expelled person often perishes by a most pitiable fate. For, bound by their oaths and customs, he cannot partake of other people's food but perishes as he eats grass and his body wastes away with hunger. For this reason, out of pity they have taken back many near their last breath, regarding this punishment almost to death as sufficient for their sins …

They guard against … working on the seventh day in very different ways than all other Jews. For they not only prepare their meals one day before, to avoid lighting a fire on that day, but they also do not dare to move any utensil or to relieve themselves. On the other days, after digging a hole a foot deep with the mattock – for such is the little axe given by them to the neophytes – and covering themselves with their garment so as not to offend the rays of God, they sit over it. Then they drag the excavated dirt into the hole. And when they do this, they choose the most isolated places.[2] And though the elimination of wastes is natural, they wash after it, as is customary for those defiled.

---

[2] In all of this procedure, the Essenes followed the instructions in Deuteronomy 23:12–14.

They are divided according to the length of their training into four grades, and the junior members are so inferior to the seniors that the seniors bathe if they touch the juniors, just as if they had come into contact with a Gentile ...

For they are also firmly convinced of this opinion: that the bodies are perishable and the matter composing them impermanent, whereas the souls remain immortal forever. Constantly coming in from the finest ether, the souls are entangled in the bodies as if in prisons, drawn down by a sort of natural spell. But when they are released from the bonds of the flesh, then, as if liberated from a long enslavement, they rejoice and are borne aloft. And holding the same opinion as the sons of the Greeks, they declare that for the good souls a life beyond Oceanus[3] is reserved, a place not oppressed by thunderstorms or snowstorms or heat waves, but which is always refreshed by a gentle west wind blowing in from Oceanus; while for the bad souls they set aside a gloomy, wintry cavern, full of unending punishments ...

There are some among them who even profess to foretell the future, being educated in sacred books and various purifications and pronouncements of prophets. And seldom if ever do they miss the mark in their predictions.

There is also another order of Essenes, agreeing with the others in lifestyle, customs, and regulations, but distinguished by their opinion about marriage. For they think that those who do not marry cut off the greatest part of life, reproduction, and furthermore that, if everyone held the same view, the race would very quickly die out. However, they marry their wives only after testing them for three months,[4] when they have menstruated three times as proof of their ability to bear children. They have no intercourse with them when they are pregnant, showing that they marry not for the sake of pleasure but from need of children. The women take baths clothed in garments, the men in a loincloth. Such are the customs of this order.

---

[3] The river that ancient people thought encircled the inhabited earth.
[4] Literally "years," which appears to be a mistake.

Appendix 3
Jewish Messianic Hopes

3.1 The Messiah in Psalms of Solomon

Psalm of Solomon 17:21–46

The Psalms of Solomon, an anonymous collection of Jewish psalms, probably date from the middle of the first century BCE. The seventeenth psalm expresses a prayer for the coming of the royal Messiah of David's line.

21 Behold, Lord, and raise up for them their king, the son of David, in the time which you have chosen, to reign over Israel your servant. 22 And undergird him with strength to crush unjust rulers, to cleanse Jerusalem from Gentiles who trample it down with destruction, 23 and with the wisdom of righteousness to expel sinners from any inheritance, to smash the sinner's arrogance like clay pots …

26 He will gather a holy people, which he will lead with righteousness, and he will judge the tribes of a people sanctified by the Lord its God. 27 He will not allow injustice any longer to be lodged in their midst, and no person who knows evil will dwell with them. For he will know that all of them are sons of God, 28 and he will distribute them by their tribes upon the land …

30 He will have nations of peoples serve him under his yoke, and he will glorify the Lord with a banner over all the earth …

32 He himself will be king, righteous, taught by God, over them. There is no injustice in their midst in his days, because all are holy, and their king is the Lord's Anointed …

36 He will be pure from sin so as to rule a great people, to convict rulers and remove sinners by the power of a word. 37 He will not weaken in his days concerning his God, because God made him mighty in Holy Spirit and wise in perceptive counsel with strength and righteousness …

41 With equality he will lead them all, and there will be no arrogance among them such that some of them are oppressed ...

44 Blessed are those born in those days to see the good things of Israel in the assembly of tribes, things which God will do. 45 May God hasten his mercy upon Israel; may he rescue us from the uncleanness of profane enemies. 46 The Lord himself is our king forever and ever.

3.2 The Messiah in 1 Enoch

1 Enoch 48:1–7; 69:26–29

The Similitudes (or Parables) of Enoch form one part of the book of 1 Enoch (1 Enoch 37–71). A Jewish work, this part of 1 Enoch is generally dated to sometime during the first century CE. In the following selection, Enoch, the seventh from Adam in the genealogy of Genesis (Gen 5:21–24), has been caught up to heaven and describes what he sees. One of the things he sees is "that son of man," a reference to the "one like a son of man" mentioned in Daniel 7:13. Like most Jewish exegetes of the time, the author of the Similitudes interpreted this manlike figure as the Messiah. In his conception, there is no indication that the Messiah is a descendant of David. Rather, the Messiah is an angel-like being who was hidden by God before the creation of the world. The function of the Messiah here is to sit on a glorious throne and conduct the final judgment. The translation has been adapted from R. H. Charles, *The Apocrypha and Pseudepigrapha of the Old Testament* (Clarendon, 1913), 2.216–17, 235.

48:1 In that place I saw the fountain of righteousness which was inexhaustible, and around it were many fountains of wisdom. And all the thirsty drank from them and were filled with wisdom; and their dwellings were with the righteous and holy and elect. 2 At that hour that son of man was named in the presence of the Lord of Spirits, and his name before the Head of Days. 3 Even before the sun and the signs were created, before the stars of the heaven were made, his name was named before the Lord of Spirits. 4 He shall be a staff to the righteous, on which they may lean and not fall, and he shall be the light of the Gentiles and the hope of those whose hearts are troubled. 5 All who dwell on earth shall fall down and worship him and will praise and bless and celebrate with song the Lord of Spirits. 6 For this reason he has been chosen and hidden before him, before the creation of the world and for evermore. 7 And the wisdom of the Lord of Spirits has revealed him to the holy and righteous; for he has preserved the lot of the righteous, because they have hated and despised this world of unrighteousness, and have hated all its works and ways in the name of the Lord of Spirits; for in his name they are saved and their life has been according to his good pleasure …

69:26 There was great joy among them, and they blessed and glorified and extolled, because the name of that son of man had been revealed to them. 27 And he sat on his throne of glory, and the totality of judgment was given to the son of man, and he caused the sinners to pass away and be destroyed from off the face of the earth. 28 Those who have led the world astray shall be bound with chains and imprisoned in their assembly-place of destruction, and all their works shall vanish from the face of the earth. 29 And from henceforth there shall be nothing corruptible; for that son of man has appeared and has seated himself on his throne of glory, and all evil shall pass away before his face, and the word of that son of man shall go forth and be strong before the Lord of Spirits.

3.3 The Messiah in 4 Ezra

4 Ezra 7:26–44

The Jewish apocalypse of 4 Ezra is generally dated to around 100 CE. Two passages from it are included here. In the first selection God is speaking to Ezra the scribe, revealing the events of the end-time. This depiction of eschatological events combines two distinct conceptions: a messianic kingdom and a final judgment by God. Here the messianic kingdom comes first, lasting 400 years. Afterwards comes the final judgment, conducted by God.

26 "For behold the time will come when the signs that I have foretold to you will come and the bride will appear; and as the state begins to appear, the land that is now withdrawn will also be revealed. 27 And everyone who is delivered from the predicted ills will see my wonders. 28 For my son the Messiah will be revealed with those who are with him, and those who are left will rejoice four hundred years. 29 After those years my son the Messiah will die along with all who have human breath. 30 The age will be changed into the silence of antiquity for seven days, as in previous beginnings, so that no one is abandoned. 31 After seven days, the age which is not yet awake will be roused and the corrupt age will die. 32 The earth will restore those who sleep in it, the dust those who silently dwell in it, and the chambers will restore the souls that have been committed to them. 33 The Most High will be revealed upon the seat of

judgment, mercies will pass away, and patience will be gathered up. 34 Judgment alone will remain, and truth will stand, and faithfulness will recover. 35 Work will follow and its recompense will be shown; just deeds will awaken and unjust deeds will not sleep. 36 The lake of torment will appear, and opposite it will be the place of rest; the oven of Gehenna will be shown, and opposite it the paradise of joy.

37 "Then the Most High will say to the raised nations, 'See and understand whom you have denied or whom you did not serve or whose attentions you rejected. 38 Look over here and over there: here joy and rest, there fire and torments.' You will say this to them on the day of judgment. 39 This is the kind of day which has no sun nor moon nor stars 40 nor cloud nor thunder nor lightning nor wind nor water nor air nor darkness nor evening nor morning 41 nor summer nor spring nor heat nor winter nor frost nor cold nor hail nor rain nor dew 42 nor noon nor night nor dawn nor daylight nor brightness nor light, but only the splendor of the brightness of the Most High, from which all may begin to see the things that are placed before them. 43 For it will have the length of a week of years. 44 This is my judgment and its order, and to you alone have I shown these things."

3.4 The Messiah in 4 Ezra

4 Ezra 13

In this second selection from 4 Ezra, Ezra relates a dream that he had. It is a vision of a man (the Messiah) defeating the enemies of Israel and regathering the scattered tribes of Israel.

13:1 After seven days, I dreamed a dream at night. 2 I saw a wind rising from the sea and stirring up all its waves. 3 I saw this wind make something like the figure of a man ascend from the heart of the sea, and I saw that man fly with the clouds of the sky.[1] Wherever he turned his face to look, everything that was seen under him trembled; 4 and wherever his voice went out from his mouth, all who heard his voice burned, just as wax melts when it feels fire. 5 After this I saw an innumerable multitude of men gather from the four winds of the sky to wage war against the man who had ascended from the sea. 6 I saw him carve out for himself a large mountain and fly up onto it. 7 I tried to see the region or place from which the mountain had been carved, but could not. 8 After this I saw that all those who had gathered against him to defeat him were very

---

[1] Daniel 7:13.

much afraid, but they dared to fight. 9 When he saw the attack of the approaching multitude, he neither raised his hand nor held a spear nor any weapon of war. 10 I saw how he merely sent forth something like a stream of fire from his mouth, and a flaming breath from his lips, and sent forth the sparks of a tempest from his tongue. 11 All these were mixed together – the stream of fire and the flaming breath and the sparks of the tempest – and fell on the attack of the multitude that was prepared to fight and burned them all up, so that suddenly nothing remained of the innumerable multitude except the dust of ashes and the smell of smoke. I was amazed when I saw it. 12 After this I saw the same man descending from the mountain and summoning to himself another multitude that was peaceful. 13 The faces of many men came to him, some glad and some sad. Some in fact were bound; others were bringing some of those that were being offered.

Appendix 4
Divine Humans and their Births

4.1 Humans Honored as Gods

Diodorus Siculus, *The Library of History* 4.1.4; 6.1.2

Diodorus Siculus, a Greek historian of the first century BCE, explains how some men came to be considered gods because of their benefactions to humanity.

For very great and numerous deeds were performed by the heroes and demigods and many other good men. Since succeeding generations shared the benefits conferred by these men, they honored them, some with sacrifices appropriate for gods, others with sacrifices appropriate for heroes …

Concerning gods, then, the men of ancient times have passed down to later generations two conceptions. For some, they say, are eternal and imperishable, such as sun and moon and the other stars in the sky, and in addition to these, winds and the other things that happen to be of the same nature as these. For each of these has eternal origin and duration. Other gods, they say, were originally earthly humans but through their benefactions to humanity gained immortal honor and glory, such as Heracles, Dionysus, Aristaeus, and the others like them.

4.2 Divine Natures Sent from Heaven

Eusebius, *Treatise against Hierocles* 6

The Christian bishop Eusebius of Caesarea (264–349 CE) wrote a treatise against a book in which the Roman governor Hierocles had compared Jesus unfavorably with the divine man Apollonius of Tyana. In the course of his work, Eusebius expresses his version of an idea widely held in his day: that a "divine nature" from heaven from time to time comes to earth to become human.

[A person] might pray, though, for some helper to come from somewhere above, from those who reside in heaven, and to appear to him as a teacher of the salvation that is there ... Hence there would be no reason why a divine nature, being a benefactor and savior and taking forethought for the things to come, should not come into association with human beings ... [God] will ungrudgingly bestow rays, as it were, of the light that comes from him. From those about him, he now and then sends forth those that are especially close for the salvation and assistance of those down here. The one of these who, if he should happen to be fortunate, has been cleansed in mind and has dispersed the mist of mortality, will be recorded as truly divine, bearing the image of some great god in his soul ... And in this way human nature might share in that which is more than human.

4.3 The Divine Emperor Augustus

The Provincial Assembly of Asia Minor passed the following resolution concerning Caesar Augustus near the middle of his reign (c. 9 BCE). From Frederick C. Grant, *Ancient Roman Religion* (Liberal Arts Press, 1957), 174.

Whereas the Providence which has regulated our whole existence, and which has shown such care and liberality, has brought our life to the climax of perfection in giving to us [the emperor] Augustus, whom it [Providence] filled with virtue for the welfare of humanity, and who, being sent to us and our descendants as a Savior, has put an end to war and has set all things in order; and [whereas,] having become manifest, Caesar has fulfilled all the hopes of earlier times ... not only in surpassing all the benefactors who preceded him but also in leaving to his successors no hope of surpassing him; and whereas, finally, the birthday of the god [Augustus] has been for the whole world the beginning of good news [*evangelion*] concerning him, [therefore, let a new era begin from his birth, and let his birthday mark the beginning of the new year].

4.4 The Birth of Heracles

Diodorus Siculus, *The Library of History* 4.9.1–10.1

9.1 Perseus, they say, was the son of Zeus and Danae, the daughter of Acrisius. Perseus slept with Andromeda, the daughter of Kepheus, and she bore Electryon. Then Electryon cohabited with Euridike, the daughter of Pelops, and she gave birth to Alkmene. And Zeus, sleeping with Alkmene through deceit, fathered Heracles. 2 So the whole root of Heracles' heritage from both parents is said to lead back to the greatest of the gods [Zeus], in the way described.

The valor that was about him was seen not only in his actions, but also known before his birth. For when Zeus was sleeping with Alkmene, he made the night three times its normal length, and by the magnitude of the time spent for the child's conception he foreshadowed the superior might of the one who would be born.

3 On the whole, he did not consummate this union because of erotic desire, as with other women, but mainly for the sake of procreation. For that reason, and because he wanted to make the intercourse legitimate, he did not want to force Alkmene, though he had no hope of seducing her because of her virtue. So he decided to use deception, and through this he tricked Alkmene by making himself like Amphitryon [her husband] in every respect.

4 When the natural time of pregnancy had passed, Zeus, with the birth of Heracles in mind, announced in advance with all the gods present that he would make the one of Perseus' descendants born on that day king. But Hera, filled with jealousy and having her daughter Eileithyia as a helper, delayed the labor pains of Alkmene and brought Eurystheus to light before the normal time.

5 Zeus, who had been outmaneuvered, wanted to fulfill his promise and still take forethought for the manifestation of Heracles. Therefore, they say, he persuaded Hera to agree that Eurystheus would be king, as he had promised, but that Heracles, set under Eurystheus, would complete whatever twelve labors Eurystheus should assign, and having done this, would obtain immortality.

6 When Alkmene gave birth, fearing the jealousy of Hera, she set the infant out at the place that is now called after him the Heraclean Plain. At this very time, Athena passed by with Hera. Amazed at the nature of the child, she persuaded Hera to offer it her breast. But when the child sucked at the breast more forcefully than normal for his age, Hera, in great pain, tore the infant away. Athena, taking it to its mother, urged her to nurse it …

10.1 After this Hera sent two serpents to destroy the infant. But the boy, undismayed, grabbed the neck of a serpent in each of his hands and strangled them. Consequently, the inhabitants of Argos, on learning what had happened, gave him the name "Heracles" because he had gained glory (*kleos*) because of Hera, though he was previously called Alcaeus.

4.5 The Birth of Alexander the Great

Plutarch, *Parallel Lives*, Alexander 2.1–3.2

With respect to Alexander's lineage, it is universally believed that he was a descendant of Heracles through Karanos on his father's side, and a descendant of Aikos through Neoptolemos on his mother's side. It is said that Philip [Alexander's father] was initiated into the mysteries at Samothrace with Olympias [Alexander's mother] when he was still a youth, and that he was attracted to her, a child bereft of parents, and arranged the marriage by persuading her brother Arymbas.

The bride, before the night on which they were united in the bedroom, imagined that a lightning bolt fell into her womb with a peal of thunder. From the blow much fire was kindled; then, breaking into flames that were carried everywhere, it was extinguished ...

Once a dragon [or serpent] was seen stretched out beside the body of Olympias as she slept.[1] And they say that this especially dimmed the ardor and affections of Philip, so that he no longer came often to sleep beside her, either fearing some spells and enchantments of the woman against himself or piously avoiding the intercourse as that of a woman joined to a higher being ...

However, they say that after the vision Philip sent Chaeron of Megalopolis to Delphi. An oracle was conveyed to Philip from the god [Apollo], who commanded him to sacrifice to Ammon and worship that god especially and to remove the other eye, which he had placed against the crack of the door when he observed the god in the form of a dragon lying with his wife.[2]

4.6 The Birth and Childhood of Augustus

Suetonius, *The Lives of the Caesars* 2.94.3–9

In 120 CE the Roman historian Suetonius published *The Lives of the Caesars*, a work which included the biographies of twelve emperors from Julius to Domitian. The life of Augustus contains stories about his divine birth and various omens that foreshadowed his greatness.

---

[1] The ancient world associated serpents with immortality because they periodically renewed their bodies by shedding their old skins. Hence Greco-Roman stories sometimes portray the immortal gods in the form of serpents.

[2] Apollo tells Philip, who lost his right eye during the siege of Methone, to remove his other eye because he committed sacrilege by watching his wife have intercourse with the god Zeus-Ammon in the form of a serpent.

3 According to Julius Marathus, a few months before Augustus was born a prodigy occurred in public at Rome, by which it was announced that nature was pregnant with a king for the Roman people. The frightened Senate resolved that no one born in that year should be trained (for public office). Those who had pregnant wives saw to it that the Senate's decree was not filed in the archives, since each took hope for himself.

4 In the book *Theologumenon* by Asclepias Mendetis, I read that when Atia [mother of Augustus] came in the middle of the night to the sacred rite of Apollo, her litter was set down in the temple, and while the other matrons slept, she also fell asleep. A serpent unexpectedly slithered up to her and after a short while departed. When she awoke, she purified herself as if from copulation with her husband. And immediately a mark appeared on her body that looked like a painted serpent. And it could never be removed, so that she soon perpetually avoided the public baths. Augustus was born in the tenth month after that and for this reason was considered the son of Apollo.

Atia too, before she gave birth, dreamed that her intestines were carried to the stars and spread over the whole extent of the lands and the sky. The father, Octavius, also dreamed that the radiance of the sun rose from Atia's womb.

5 On the day he was born, the conspiracy of Catiline was being dealt with in the Senate-house, and Octavius arrived late because of his wife's childbirth. And as is commonly known, Publius Nigidius, after the cause of delay was discovered, when he found out the hour of birth too, declared that the ruler of the world had been born.

Afterwards when Octavius was leading an army through remote parts of Thrace, in the sacred grove of Father Liber he consulted the deity about his son with barbarian ceremonies, and the same thing was declared to him by the priests. For when wine was poured over the altar, such a flame sprang up that it rose above the temple roof and was carried all the way to the sky. And such an omen had appeared for only one other man, Alexander the Great, when he was sacrificing at the same altar.

6 And furthermore, on the very next night he seemed to see his son greater than mortal in form, with the thunderbolt and scepter and apparel of Jove Optimus Maximus, and with a radiant crown, upon a laurel-wreathed chariot drawn by twelve horses of exceptional whiteness.

While still an infant, as it stands written by C. Drusus, Augustus was placed by the nurse at evening in his cradle on the ground floor. By the next morning he had disappeared. After a long search he was finally found in a lofty tower, lying with his face toward the rising sun.

7 When he first began to talk, at his grandfather's suburban estate some frogs were making a great racket. He ordered them to be quiet, and since then they deny that frogs croak there.

As he was having lunch in the woods at the fourth milestone on the Campanian road, an eagle unexpectedly snatched the bread from his hand, and when it had flown to a great height, unexpectedly glided gently back down and returned it.

8 After Quintus Catulus had dedicated the Capitol, he dreamed on two successive nights. On the first, he dreamed that Jove Optimus Maximus called aside one of several freeborn boys playing around his altar and deposited in the lap of his toga an image of the republic that he was carrying in his hand. On the following night, he dreamed that he noticed the same boy in the lap of Jove Capitolinus and that when he ordered him to be removed he was prohibited by a warning of the god, because the boy was being trained as protector of the republic. And on the next day, when Catulus met Augustus, whom he otherwise did not know, he looked at him closely, not without astonishment, and said that he was very similar to the boy about whom he had dreamed.

Some report the first dream of Catulus differently, as if when several freeborn boys requested a guardian, Jupiter pointed out one of them to whom they were to refer all their wishes. And after touching his little mouth with his fingers he brought them back to his own mouth.

9 As Marcus Cicero was following Gaius Caesar to the temple, by chance he was relating to his friends a dream of the previous night: a boy of noble appearance, sent down from heaven on a golden chain, stood at the doors of the Capitol, and to him Jove handed a whip. Then suddenly catching sight of Augustus, who was still unknown to most of them and who had been invited to the sacrifice by his uncle Caesar, he declared that he was the very one whose image had appeared to him during his dream.

4.7 The Birth of Plato

Origen, *Contra Celsum* 1.37

In his book *Contra Celsum* (c. 248 CE), Origen, an early Christian teacher, responded to criticisms of Christianity made by the non-Christian Celsus. In the process of defending the virgin birth of Jesus, Origen mentions a Greek story about the birth of the philosopher Plato.

But to Greeks who disbelieve in the virgin birth of Jesus it must be said that the Creator showed in the birth of various animals that what he did with one animal, he could do with others, if he wished, and even with humans. Among the animals, certain females are found that have no intercourse with a male, as those who have written about animals say about vultures. And without copulation this animal sees to it that the generations continue. So why is it incredible if God, deciding to send a certain divine teacher to the human race, made the nature of the one to be born in a different way than the spermatic nature that results from the copulation of males with women? And according to the Greeks themselves, not all humans came into being from a man and woman. For if the world had a beginning, as even many of the Greeks thought, it was necessary for the first people to come into being not as a result of intercourse, but from earth, after spermatic natures had formed in the earth – which I think is more incredible than Jesus coming into being in one half like the rest of humanity.

And in speaking to Greeks it is not out of place to use Greek stories, so that we may not seem to be the only ones who have made use of this incredible story. For some have thought fit – writing not about some ancient stories and heroics but even about things that happened yesterday and the day before – to record, as though it were possible, that Plato was born from Amphictione after Ariston [her husband] had been prevented from sleeping with her until she gave birth to the child conceived from Apollo. But these are really myths that have moved people to make up such a thing about a man whom they believed to have greater wisdom and power than most. They believed that the formation of his body took its beginning from better and more divine sperms, since this is fitting for men who are greater than normal.

Appendix 5
Apotheoses

5.1 The Apotheosis of Heracles

Diodorus Siculus, *The Library of History* 4.38.3–39.2

Through treachery, Heracles puts on a shirt that has been soaked in poison. Because of his suffering, he sends his servants to Delphi to ask the god Apollo what he must do to be healed.

38.3 The god replied that they should take Heracles with his war gear to Oite and prepare a huge pyre near him. The rest, he said, would be up to Zeus.

4 When the men with Iolaus had done what had been commanded and were watching from a distance to see what would happen, Heracles, despairing of his situation, got on the pyre and began to urge each one who approached to light it. When no one dared, Philoctetes alone was persuaded to comply. Accepting the gift of Heracles' bow and arrows for his service, he lit the pyre. Immediately lightning bolts also fell from the air and the whole pyre was consumed. 5. After this, when the men with Iolaus came to collect the bones and found no bone at all, they assumed that Heracles, in accordance with the oracles, had passed over from men to gods.

39.1 Therefore they made offerings to the dead as to a hero and threw up burial mounds, after which they departed to Trachis ... The Athenians were the first to honor Heracles with sacrifices as a god. And pointing to their own piety to the god as an example for others, they induced all the Greeks first, and after this all people throughout the world, to honor Heracles as a god.

2 We should add to what has been said that after the apotheosis of Heracles, Zeus persuaded Hera to adopt him and thenceforth for all time to show a mother's favor.

5.2 The Apotheosis of Romulus

Ovid, *Metamorphoses* 14.805–28

The *Metamorphoses*, completed in 7 CE by the Roman poet Ovid, includes an account of the apotheosis of Romulus, the founder of Rome.

Tatius[1] had fallen, and you, Romulus, were giving just laws to the two peoples, when Mars, his helmet laid aside, addressed the father of gods and men thus: "Since the Roman state is strong with a firm foundation and does not depend on one man for protection, the time has come, Father, to grant the reward promised to me and your worthy grandson: to carry him away from earth and set him in heaven. You once said to me with the council of gods present – for I noted your kind words with an attentive mind and recall them now – 'There will be one man whom you will lift up into the blue sky.' Let the sum of your words be reckoned and paid."

The omnipotent one nodded, and with dark clouds covered the skies and with thunder and lightning frightened the world. Gradivus[2] perceived sure signs of the abduction that had been promised to him. Leaning on his spear, dauntless, he mounted the chariot, with horses subdued by the bloody yoke-beam, and cracked the whip. Leaning forward, he glided down through the skies and came to a stop on the topmost crest of the wooded Palatine.[3]

As Ilia's son[4] was administering laws without tyranny, Mars carried him away. His mortal body dissolved into thin air, just as a lead bullet shot from a wide sling fades away gradually in midair. A shape came up, beautiful and more worthy of the high couches of the gods: such is the form of the tabea-clad[5] Quirinus.[6]

5.3 Deification of Antinous

Dio Cassius, *Roman History* 69.11.2–4

Antinous, a slave and lover of the emperor Hadrian, died in 130 CE. Hadrian had him deified as the god Osiris, instituting his worship by building temples, setting up sacred images, and appointing prophets.

[1] Joint ruler of the Sabines and Romans with Romulus
[2] A title of Mars
[3] A hill in Rome
[4] Romulus
[5] A tabea was a white robe with scarlet stripes and purple seams
[6] A title of Romulus

In Egypt also Hadrian rebuilt the city henceforth named for Antinous. Antinous was from Bithynium, a city of Bithynia, which we also call Claudiopolis. He had been a favorite of the emperor and had died in Egypt, either by falling into the Nile, as Hadrian writes, or as the truth is, by being offered in sacrifice. For Hadrian, as I have stated, was always very curious and employed divinations and incantations of all kinds. Accordingly, he honored Antinous, either because of his love for him or because the youth had voluntarily undertaken to die (it being necessary that a life should be surrendered freely for the accomplishment of the ends Hadrian had in view), by building a city on the spot where he had suffered this fate and naming it after him; and he also set up statues, or rather sacred images of him, practically all over the world. Finally he declared that he had seen a star which he took to be that of Antinous, and gladly lent an ear to the fictitious tales woven by his associates to the effect that the star had really come into being from the spirit of Antinous and had then appeared for the first time.

Appendix 6
Miracle Stories in the Ancient World

Here we look at miracle stories from three traditions: Jewish, Greco-Roman, and Christian. For miracle stories in the Bible, only the references are given.

JEWISH MIRACLE STORIES

6.1 Miracle Stories in the Hebrew Bible

The Hebrew Bible relates a number of miracle stories that have gathered around the figure of a famous prophet. Read the following:
- Miracles of Moses: Exodus 16:1–21; 17:1–7
- Miracles of Elijah: 1 Kings 17
- Miracles of Elisha: 2 Kings 4:1–5:14

6.2 Hanina ben Dosa

b Berakoth 33a, 34b

Hanina ben Dosa, a Jewish rabbi in Palestine in the first century CE, had a reputation for total righteousness. The following stories about him appear in the Babylonian Talmud, compiled in the fifth century CE. The first story was apparently created as a historicization of Genesis 3:15, Yahweh's curse on the serpent.

Our rabbis taught: In a certain place a serpent was injuring the wives. They went and told Rabbi Hanina ben Dosa. He said to them, "Show me its hole." They showed him its hole; he put his heel over the mouth of the hole. It came out and bit him, and the serpent died. He put it on his shoulder and brought it to the house of study. He said to them, "See, my sons, it is not the serpent that kills, but sin that kills." At that time they said, "Woe to the man that a serpent meets, but woe to the serpent that Rabbi Hanina ben Dosa meets!"

Our rabbis taught: It so happened that Rabbi Gamaliel's son got sick. He sent two scholars to ask Rabbi Hanina ben Dosa to seek mercy for him. When he saw them, he went to a room upstairs and sought mercy for him. When he came back down, he said to them, "Go, the fever has left him." They said to him, "Are you a prophet then?" He said to them, "I am not a prophet nor am I the son of a prophet,[1] but this is from my experience. If my prayer flows in my mouth, I know that it is accepted, and if not, I know that it is rejected." They sat and wrote down the exact time. When they came to Rabbi Gamaliel he said to them, "By the Temple service! You did not miss it by too little or too much, but it happened just so. At that very moment the fever left him and he asked us for a drink of water!"

6.3 A Jewish Exorcist

Josephus, *Antiquities* 8.45–49

Twice the New Testament mentions Jewish exorcists (Matt 12:27/Luke 11:19; Acts 19:13–17). According to Josephus, these exorcists used traditional techniques that were attributed to the famous King Solomon. Jewish tradition associated Solomon with great wisdom, including knowledge about controlling demons. Here Josephus praises Solomon's wisdom and describes the use made of it by a Jewish exorcist.

God enabled [Solomon] to learn the techniques useful against demons for the benefit and healing of people. Having composed incantations with which afflictions are comforted, he also left behind methods of exorcisms with which those who are bound by demons drive them out so that they never return. And even to the present day, among us this therapy is most prevalent. For I observed a certain Eleazar, one of my countrymen, in the presence of Vespasian and his sons and tribunes and a number of other soldiers, releasing from the demons people who were being seized by them. The method of therapy was like this: to the nose of the possessed person he applied a ring that had under its seal one of the roots that Solomon prescribed. Then, as the person smelled it, he drew

---

[1] Amos 7:14.

out the demon through the nostrils,[2] and once the person fell down, spoke an adjuration of Solomon never to return to him and recited the incantations that Solomon composed.

Wishing to persuade and demonstrate to the bystanders that he had this ability, Eleazar would set either a cup or a foot-tub full of water a little way in front and order the demon as he went out of the person to turn these over and provide evidence to those who saw it that it had left the person. When this happened, it made clear Solomon's understanding and wisdom, for the sake of which we were led to speak about these things, so that all may know the greatness of his nature and the love that God had for him, and that no one under the sun might be unaware of the king's excellence in every kind of virtue.

GRECO-ROMAN MIRACLE STORIES

6.4 The Cult of Asclepius

Among the Greeks and Romans, the sick often consulted Asclepius, one of a number of local healing gods. Asclepius was not one of the eternal gods, but had been a human physician before his deification. His primary shrine was at Epidaurus near Corinth in Greece, but his cult spread in the Hellenistic period to include more than three hundred known sanctuaries. His popularity rested on his role as the "savior" or healer of human beings, a role in which he displayed sympathy and compassion for humanity.

Upon entering the sanctuary, the patient made a vow to Asclepius, which would be fulfilled if the patient was cured. The patient slept in a special room called the "Abaton" in order to receive a healing dream, in which the god would appear to heal the affliction. At some sanctuaries, the patient also received medical treatment from the sanctuary staff. Numerous stories of successful healings have been preserved on marble plaques found at the sanctuary in Epidaurus. Most of the following inscriptions date from the fourth century BCE.

W1 Cleo was pregnant for five years. After being pregnant for five years, she came to the god as a suppliant and slept in the Abaton. As

---

[2] People in the ancient world conceived of a demon as a "spirit," a term that literally means "breath." Hence it was appropriate for the alien "breath" to depart through the nostrils.

soon as she left it and the temple precincts, she bore a son. Immediately after birth, he washed himself in the fountain and walked around with his mother.

W3 A man with all the fingers of his hand crippled except one came to the god as a supplicant. When he saw the tablets in the temple, he doubted the healings and sneered at the inscriptions. While he slept, he dreamed that he was divining with bones under the temple. As he was about to cast the bones, the god appeared, seized his hand, and stretched out the fingers. He seemed to bend the hand to stretch out the fingers one by one. When he had straightened all of them, the god asked him if he still doubted the inscriptions on the tablets in the temple. "No," he said. Asclepius replied, "Since before you did not believe things that are not incredible, from now on your name will be 'Skeptic.'" When it was day, he came out healed.

W4 Ambrosia of Athens had one good eye. She came to the god as a supplicant. As she read about the healings in the temple, she mocked some things as incredible and impossible, such as the lame and blind being healed by merely having a dream. While sleeping there, she dreamed that the god stood over her. He told her that he would make her healthy, but she would have to place a silver pig in the temple as a reminder of her stupidity. While speaking to her, he cut into the place where her other eye was diseased and poured in some medicine. When it was day, she went out healed.

W17 A man who suffered terribly from a malignant sore on his toe was healed by a serpent.[3] During the daytime, he was taken outside by the temple assistants and set on a seat, where he fell asleep. Meanwhile, a snake came out of the Abaton, healed his toe with its tongue, and went back inside. When the patient woke up healed, he said he had dreamed that a beautiful young man put medicine on his toe.

W37 Cleimenes of Argus was paralyzed in body. He came to the Abaton, slept there, and had a dream. In it the god wound a red woolen fillet around his body and led him a short distance from the temple for a bath in a lake with very cold water. When he acted cowardly, Asclepius said he would not heal people who were too cowardly for it, but if they came to him in his temple full of hope and confident that he would do no harm to them, he would send them away well. When he woke up, he took a bath and walked out healed.

---

[3] Asclepius in the form of a serpent

6.5 Two Healings by Vespasian

Tacitus, *Histories* 4.81

Tacitus, a Roman historian, relates two healings supposed to have been performed by the Roman general Vespasian in 69 CE, shortly before he became emperor. The same story in a shorter form is told by Suetonius (*de vita Vesp.* 7).

During those months in which Vespasian was waiting at Alexandria for the season of summer winds and a calm sea, many miracles occurred, which showed the favor of heaven and a certain inclination of the deities toward Vespasian. One of the common people of Alexandria, known to have decay of the eyes, threw himself at the feet of Vespasian, imploring him with a groan to cure his blindness. He had been directed by the god Serapis, whom this nation, devoted to superstitions, honors before all others. And he begged that the emperor would deign to daub his eye sockets and eyeballs with his spit. Another man with an impaired hand, on the advice of the same god, pleaded that Caesar would step on it with his foot.

At first Vespasian treated the requests with ridicule and scorn. Then when they persisted, he wavered, at one moment fearing the notoriety of failure, at the next induced to hope by the entreaty of the men and the voices of flatterers. Finally he ordered the physicians to evaluate whether such blindness or debility could be overcome by human means. The physicians discussed each respectively. With respect to the former, the power of sight had not been destroyed and would return if the obstructions were dislodged. With respect to the latter, the joints that had slipped out of position and become crooked could be restored if healing force were applied. Perhaps it was the will of the god, and the emperor had been selected for the divine ministry. Furthermore, a successful cure would bring glory to Caesar, while a failure would bring derision only to the wretches.

Consequently, since Vespasian was certain that all things were open to his fortune and that nothing was any longer incredible, while the crowd that stood by watched attentively, he carried out the prescriptions with a cheerful face. Immediately the hand was restored to use, and daylight shone again for the blind man. People who were there relate both incidents even now when there is no longer anything to be gained by lying.

6.6 Apollonius Performs an Exorcism

Philostratus, *The Life of Apollonius of Tyana* 4.20

In the third century CE, Philostratus wrote a biography of Apollonius of Tyana, who lived in the first and second centuries CE. He claimed that one of his sources was a work by a disciple of Apollonius named Damis, though many scholars doubt this claim. In Philostratus' account, Apollonius has a miraculous birth, great wisdom, ability to perform miracles, and an ascent to heaven at the end of his life. The following selection recounts an exorcism that he performed.

As he was lecturing about pouring libations, there happened to be at the talk a fancy young man with such a reputation for licentiousness that at length he even became the subject of a dirty song ... The young man drowned out the lecture with loud and unrestrained laughter. Apollonius looked at him and said, "It is not you who act so rudely, but the demon who compels you without your knowledge." And in fact the young man had become demon-possessed without it being recognized. For he laughed at things no one else did, and he would start crying for no reason, and he talked and sang to himself. Most thought that it was unruly youth that made him get so carried away, but he was then responding to the demon and only seemed to act drunk, insofar as he acted drunk then.

As Apollonius looked at him, the phantom, in fear and anger, let out cries such as come from people being burned or tortured, and he swore that he would stay away from the young man and never attack anyone again. But Apollonius, angrily saying such things as a master might to a slave who was wily and cunning and shameless and the like, commanded him to show proof of his departure. "I will knock down that statue over there," he said, indicating one of those around the royal court, in front of which these things were taking place. And when the statue moved then fell, what could one write about the hubbub over this and the way they clapped their hands in amazement?

But the youth, as if he had just awakened, rubbed his eyes and looked at the rays of the sun. And he drew the awe of all, who had now turned toward him. He no longer appeared licentious or looked unruly, but had returned to his own nature no less than if he had taken medicine. And turning away from the fancy mantles and dresses and the other luxury, he came to a love of austerity and the threadbare cloak, and reclothed himself in the ways of Apollonius.

6.7 Pythagoras Performs Wonders

Iamblichus, *On the Pythagorean Way of Life* 36, 134–36

Iamblichus, living in the third century CE, drew on earlier sources to write about the Greek philosopher Pythagoras, who lived in the sixth century BCE. Though Iamblichus rejected the story that the god Apollo was Pythagoras' actual father, he believed that Pythagoras' soul had been especially close to Apollo in heaven before Apollo sent it down to earth. That soul had gone through several reincarnations before being born as Pythagoras. The following selection recounts some of the miracle stories that Iamblichus told about him.

At that time, as Pythagoras was going from Sybaris to Croton, he stopped near some men fishing with a net along the shore. While the laden net was still being dragged in from the sea, he determined the quantity of fish they were pulling in and told them the number. The men promised to do whatever he said if he was right. When the count turned out to be accurate, he told them to throw the fish back in alive. And what was more amazing, during the time the fish were out of water being counted, not one of them died while he stood by. After paying the fishermen the price of the fish, he left for Croton. The fishermen spread the news of what had happened, and when they found out his name from the servants, they told everyone. Those who heard wanted to see the stranger, which was readily arranged. And since anyone who saw him was struck by his appearance, one received an impression of him that corresponded to what he truly was …

Once when crossing the Nessus River with many of his disciples, he spoke aloud to it, and the river said loud and clear, "Hello, Pythagoras."

Almost all authorities affirm that on one and the same day he was present in both Metapontium of Italy and Tauromenium of Sicily and that he lectured in public to his disciples in both places, though there are very many miles between them both by land and by sea which would take many days to cross …

And ten thousand other things more divine and amazing than these are related about the man consistently and uniformly: infallibly predicting earthquakes, swiftly averting plagues, quieting forceful winds and hailstorms instantly, calming the waves of rivers and seas so that his disciples could cross easily.

Such abilities were shared by Empedocles the Agrigentine, Epimenides the Cretan, and Abaris the Hyperborean, and in many places they too performed such deeds. The poems about them make this clear. In particular, the nickname of Empedocles was "wind-stopper," that of Epimenides "purifier," and that of Abaris "sky-walker," apparently because, riding on the arrow given to him by Apollo of the Hyperboreans he crossed rivers and seas and impassible places by walking on air somehow.

Some have suspected that Pythagoras experienced this too the time when in both Metapontium and Tauromenium he spoke to the disciples in both places on the same day. And it is said that, on the basis of a well that he drank from, he announced beforehand that there would be an earthquake; and, concerning a ship running with a fair wind, that it would sink. Let these things, then, be proofs of his piety.

6.8 Wine Miracle of Dionysus

Pausanias, *Description of Greece* 6.26.1–2

Pausanias, a Greek geographer who lived in the second century CE, relates this story about a miracle that occurred regularly at a festival of Dionysus (the god of wine) in the province of Elis.

Of the gods, the Eleans worship Dionysus especially, and they say the god visits them at the festival of Thyia. The place where they hold the festival that they call Thyia is about eight stadia from the city. The priests carry pots, three in number, into the building and set them down empty, in the presence of the citizens and strangers, if any should be visiting. The priests, and any others who are so inclined, put seals on the doors of the building. The next day they are allowed to observe the identifying marks on the seals, and going into the building they find the pots filled with wine. The most respected men of the Eleans, and strangers with them, swore these things happened as I have said, though I myself did not arrive at the time of the festival. Andrians too say that every other year at their festival of Dionysus wine flows of its own accord from the temple.

6.9 Lucian's View of Miracles

Lucian of Samosata, *The Lover of Lies* 11–13, 16

Lucian of Samosata (125–80 CE) took a satirical attitude to many of the beliefs and customs of his day. This selection is taken from a fictional conversation between Tychiades, representing Lucian's own perspective, and a group of men at the house of Eucrates.

Lucian satirizes the willingness of people to believe in supernatural manifestations.

"Never mind him," said Ion, "and I will tell you something amazing. I was still a lad, about fourteen years old, more or less. Someone came to tell my father that Midas the vinedresser, ordinarily a healthy and hard-working house-slave, had been bitten by a viper around noon and was lying down, with his leg already putrid …

"As this was being reported, we saw Midas himself being brought up on a hammock by his fellow slaves. He was all swollen, livid, clammy to the touch, barely still breathing. My father was distressed of course, but one of his friends who was present said to him, 'Cheer up. I'm going right away to fetch you a Babylonian man, one of the Chaldeans as they call them, who will heal this fellow.' And, to make a long story short, the Babylonian came and raised Midas, driving the poison out of his body with some spell and also attaching to his foot a stone that he had chipped from the gravestone of a dead maiden.

"Maybe this is nothing out of the ordinary, though Midas himself did pick up the hammock on which he had been carried and went off to the field, so potent were the spell and that gravestone. But the Babylonian did other things truly divine. For instance, he went to the field early in the morning and recited some priestly words over it, seven names out of an old book, and went around the place three times purifying it with sulfur and a torch. Then he called out all the reptiles that were inside the boundaries. They came then as if being drawn to the spell – a lot of snakes, asps, vipers, horned serpents, darters, and toads, as well as puff-toads. One old serpent was missing, though, which from old age, I suppose, was not able to crawl out or misunderstood the command. The magician said they were not all there, but he appointed one of the snakes, the youngest, and sent him as an ambassador to the serpent, and after a while he came too. When they were assembled, the Babylonian blew on them and they were all instantly burned up by the blast. We were amazed."

"Tell me, Ion," I said, "did the snake, the young ambassador I mean, let the serpent lean on his arm, since he was, as you say, already aged; or did the serpent have a cane and support himself?"

"You mock," said Cleodemus. "I myself was once more skeptical of such things than you. For I thought that on no account was it possible for them to happen. However, when I first saw the foreign stranger flying – he was from the Hyperboreans, so he claimed – I believed and was conquered after long resistance. For what was I to do when I saw him moving through the air in broad daylight and walking on water and passing through fire step by step in a leisurely manner?"

"You saw this?" I asked, "The Hyperborean man flying or standing on the water?"

"Why certainly," he said, "wearing hide sandals such as those people usually wear. As for the minor things, what need is there even to speak of all these that he performed – sending out Cupids, bringing up demons, calling back the day-old dead, rendering Hecate herself visible, and drawing down the Moon?" …

"You act absurdly," said Ion, "doubting everything. So for my part I would like to ask you what you say about those who deliver the demon-possessed from terrors, so clearly exorcising the phantoms. And I don't have to say this, but everyone knows about the Syrian from Palestine, who is adept at this. He takes all those who fall down at the sight of the moon and roll their eyes and foam at the mouth, and nevertheless he raises them up and sends them away sound in mind, delivering them from the horrible things for a large fee. For when he stands over them as they lie there and asks from where they have come into the body, the sick person himself is silent, but the demon answers, speaking Greek or some foreign language depending on where he is from, telling how and from where he came into the man. The Syrian puts him under oaths – and if he does not obey, threatens him – and so drives out the demon. I actually even saw one coming out, black and smoky in color."

"It's not a big deal," I said, "for you to see such things, Ion, since even the (invisible) forms that Plato the father of your school points to are clear to you – a difficult thing to see for those of us who are near-sighted."

CHRISTIAN MIRACLE STORIES

Numerous stories in the Christian tradition relate miracles performed by Jesus or his followers. Read the following from the New Testament:

- Nature miracles: Matt 14:13–27; Mark 4:35–41; John 2:1–11; Acts 8:34–40; 28:1–6
- Miracles of knowledge: John 21:1–14
- Healings: Matt 8:1–4; Luke 5:17–26; John 4:46–54; John 9:1–7
- Exorcisms: Luke 8:26–39; 9:37–43; Acts 19:11–17
- Resuscitations: Luke 7:11–17

Appendix 7
The Infancy Gospel of Thomas

For an introduction to this gospel see Chapter 15. The shorter version of the gospel (Version B) is given here.

1:1 I, Thomas the Israelite, thought it necessary to inform all the brothers from the Gentiles about all the magnificent childhood deeds that our Lord Jesus Christ performed as he lived bodily in the city of Nazareth.

Jesus Curses a Child

2:1 When he came to the fifth year of his life, one day when there had been a rain, having left the house where his mother was, he was playing in the dirt, where water was flowing down. Where he made pools, the water came down, and the pools were filled with water. Then he said, "I want you to become pure and excellent water." And immediately it became so. 2 A certain child of Annas the scribe came through. Picking up a willow branch, he messed up the pools with the branch, and the water poured out. Jesus turned and said to him, "Impious transgressor, how did the pools hurt you that you should empty them? You will not proceed on your way, but will wither away like the branch that you hold." 3 Going on, after a little while he fell down and expired. When the children who were playing with him saw it, they were amazed and went and told the father of the dead child. He came running and found the child dead, and he went to Joseph complaining.

Jesus Makes Sparrows

3:1 Out of that clay, Jesus made twelve sparrows. Since it was a Sabbath, a child ran and told Joseph, "Your child is playing around the stream, making sparrows out of the clay, which is not permitted." 2 When he heard, he went and said to the child, "Why are you doing this, profaning the Sabbath?" Jesus did not answer him, but looking at the sparrows he said, "Go, fly away, and remember me while you live." Taking flight at his command, they went into the air. When Joseph saw it, he was amazed.

Jesus Curses Another Child

4:1 Some days later, as Jesus was going through the city, a certain child threw a stone at him and hit his shoulder. Jesus said to him, "You will not proceed on your way," and immediately, he too fell down and died. Those who were present were shocked and said, "Where does this child come from, that every word he speaks becomes an actual fact?" 2 But they too went and complained to Joseph, saying, "You cannot live with us in this city. If you want to, teach your child to bless and not to curse. For he is killing our children, and everything he says becomes an actual fact." 5:1 As Joseph sat on his chair, the child stood before him. Taking hold of his ear, he squeezed it severely. Jesus glared at him and said, "That is enough for you."

Jesus and His Teacher

6:1 The next day, taking him by the hand, he led him to a certain tutor by the name of Zacchaeus. He said to him, "Take this child, tutor, and teach him letters." He replied, "Turn him over to me, brother, and I will teach the writing, and I will persuade him to bless everyone and not to curse." 2 When Jesus heard this, he laughed and said to them, "You tell what you know, but I know more than you, because I existed before the ages. I know when the fathers of your fathers were born, and I know how many the years of your life are." Someone who heard this was astonished. 3 Again Jesus said to them, "You are amazed because I told you that I know how many the years of your life are. Truly I know when the world was created. You do not believe me now, but when you see my cross, then you will believe that I speak the truth." They were astonished when they heard these things.

7:1 Zacchaeus wrote the alphabet in Hebrew and said to him, "aleph"; and the child said, "aleph." Again the teacher said, "aleph," and the child likewise. Then again the teacher said "aleph" for the third time. Then Jesus, looking at the tutor, said, "Since you do not know the aleph, how can you teach someone else the beth?" And beginning from the aleph, the child by himself recited the twenty-two letters. 2 Then he said further, "Listen, teacher, to the order of the first letter and learn how many strokes and bars it has and how many marks common, crossing over, brought together." When Zacchaeus heard such terms for the first letter, he was astonished and had no reply for him. Turning, he said to Joseph, "Brother, this child is truly not earthborn. So take him away from me."

Jesus Resurrects a Child

8:1 After this, one day Jesus was playing with other children on a two-story house. One child was pushed down by another, and being thrown down to the ground, he died. When the children playing with him saw it, they fled, and Jesus alone was left standing on the roof from which the child had been thrown down. 2 When the parents of the dead child found out, they ran there with weeping. Finding the child lying dead on the ground and Jesus standing above, they supposed that the child had been thrown down by him, and glaring at him, they heaped abuse on him. 3 When Jesus saw this, he immediately jumped down from the two-story house and stood at the head of the dead child and said to him, "Zenon," for this is what the child was called, "if I threw you down, get up and say so." At his command, the child got up, and bowing down before Jesus he said, "Lord, you did not throw me down, but when I was dead you brought me to life."

Jesus Heals a Foot

9:1 A few days later, one of the neighbors who was chopping wood cut off the bottom of his foot with the axe, and, losing blood, he was about to die. 2 Many people ran there together and Jesus came with them. 3 Touching the struck foot of the young man, he immediately healed it and said to him, "Get up, chop your wood." Getting up, he bowed down to him, and giving thanks he chopped the wood. Likewise everyone who was there, in amazement, thanked him.

A Water Miracle

10:1 When he was six years old, his mother, Mary, sent him to get water from the spring. As he went, his water jar broke. Going into the spring, he folded his outer garment, and drawing water from the spring, he filled it. He took it and brought away the water to his mother. When she saw this, she was astonished and hugged and kissed him.

Jesus Helps Joseph

11:1 When Jesus reached the eighth year of his life, Joseph was commissioned by a certain rich man to build him a bed, for he was a carpenter. When he went out in the field to a grove of trees, Jesus went with him. Cutting down two trees and shaping them with an axe, he put one beside the other. Measuring it, he found it shorter. When he saw this, he was upset and sought to find another. 2 When Jesus saw this, he said to him, "Put these two together so that the cut ends of both are even." Joseph, perplexed about what the child wanted, did as he was told. He said to him further, "Hold the short tree firmly." Wondering, Joseph held it. Then Jesus, taking hold of the other end, pulled its other cut end. He made this end, too, even with the other tree. And he said to Joseph, "Do not be upset any longer, but do your work without hindrance." When he saw that, he was highly amazed and said to himself, "I am blessed that God gave me such a child." 3 When they returned to the city, Joseph told Mary. When she heard and saw the magnificent, incredible deeds of her son, she rejoiced, glorifying him with the Father and the Holy Spirit now and forever and for the ages of the ages. Amen.

Appendix 8
The Gospel of Peter

For an introduction to the Gospel of Peter, see Chapter 15.

Jesus' Trial

1 But of the Jews, no one washed his hands, neither Herod nor any of his judges. And since they did not want to wash, Pilate stood up. 2 Then Herod the king commanded that the Lord should be escorted out, saying to them, "Do what I commanded you to do to him."

3 Joseph, a friend of both Pilate and the Lord, was standing there, and, knowing that they were going to crucify him, requested the body of the Lord for burial. 4 Pilate sent to Herod and requested the body from him. 5 Herod said, "Brother Pilate, even if no one had requested him, we would have buried him, since a Sabbath is dawning. For it is written in the Law that the sun should not set on a slain person."

He turned him over to the people one day before Unleavened Bread, their festival. 6 Those who took the Lord pushed him along as they ran and said, "Let us drag along the son of God, now that we have power over him." 7 They dressed him in a purple robe and sat him on a seat of judgment, saying, "Judge justly, king of Israel." 8 One of them brought a crown of thorns and put it on the Lord's head. 9 Others standing there spit in his face; others slapped his cheeks; others poked him with a reed; and some flogged him, saying, "Let us honor the son of God with this honor."

Jesus' Crucifixion

10 They brought two criminals and crucified the Lord between them. But he remained silent, as though having no pain. 11 And when they had

raised the cross, they inscribed on it, "This is the king of Israel." 12 Setting his garments in front of him, they divided them and cast lots over them. 13 One of those criminals reproached them, saying, "We have suffered in this way because of the evils that we did, but how did this man harm you by becoming the savior of human beings?" 14 Becoming irritated at him, they gave orders not to break his legs, so that he would die in torment.

15 It was midday and darkness covered all of Judea. They were disturbed and anxious that the sun should not set, since he was still alive. For it is written for them that the sun should not set on a slain person. 16 One of them said, "Give him gall to drink with cheap wine." So they mixed it and gave it to him to drink. 17 They fulfilled all and completed the sins on their heads. 18 Many went about with lamps, thinking that it was night, and fell down. 19 And the Lord cried out, saying, "My Power, Power, you have abandoned me!" And having said this, he [or it] was taken up. 20 At the same time, the veil of the Temple of Jerusalem was torn in two.

21 Then they pulled the nails out of the Lord's hands and put him on the ground. The whole ground trembled and there was great fear. 22 Then the sun shone, and it was found to be the ninth hour. 23 The Jews rejoiced and gave his body to Joseph to bury, since he had seen all the good he had done. 24 Taking the Lord, he washed him, wrapped him in a linen sheet, and took him to his own tomb, called the garden of Joseph.

25 Then the Jews and the elders and the priests, realizing what harm they had done to themselves, began to lament and say, "Woe for our sins! The judgment and the end of Jerusalem is at hand."

26 I and the companions were grieved, and we hid, wounded in heart. For we were being sought by them as criminals who wanted to set the temple on fire. 27 Over all of these things we were fasting and sat mourning and weeping night and day until the Sabbath.

28 When the scribes and Pharisees and elders gathered together, they heard that all the people were grumbling and beating their breasts, saying, "If these great signs happened at his death, see how righteous he was." 29 The elders became afraid and went to Pilate, begging him and saying, 30 "Give us soldiers so that we may guard his tomb for three days, lest his disciples come and steal him and the people suppose that he was raised from the dead and do us harm." 31 So Pilate gave them Petronius the centurion with soldiers to guard the grave. Elders and scribes came with them to the tomb. 32 And all who were there, together with the centurion and the soldiers, rolled a great stone and put it over the entrance of the tomb. 33 They plastered seven seals over it and, pitching a tent,

they kept guard. 34 Early in the morning, as the Sabbath was dawning, a crowd came from Jerusalem and the surrounding countryside to see the sealed tomb.

Jesus' Resurrection

35 In the night when the Lord's Day was dawning, as the soldiers were keeping guard, two per watch, there was a loud voice in the sky. 36 They saw the skies opened and two men coming down from there, glowing brightly and approaching the grave. 37 That stone set over the entrance, rolling by itself, partially withdrew, and the grave was opened, and both the young men entered.

38 When those soldiers saw this, they woke up the centurion and the elders, for they too were there keeping guard. 39 As they were relating to them what they had seen, they saw three men coming out of the grave, the two supporting the other, and a cross following them. 40 They saw the heads of the two reaching to the sky and the head of the one led by them extending above the skies.[1] 41 They heard a voice from the skies ask, "Did you preach to those who sleep?"[2] 42 And from the cross was heard a reply: "Yes."

43 So they were planning with each other to go and make these things known to Pilate. 44 While they still had this in mind, again there appeared opened skies and a man coming down and entering the tomb. 45 When they saw this, those about the centurion hurried at night to Pilate, leaving the grave that they were guarding, and related all that they had seen, greatly agitated and saying, "Truly he was a son of God!" 46 Pilate replied, "I am unstained by the blood of the son of God, but this seemed good to you." 47 Then all came begging and imploring him to order the centurion and the soldiers not to tell anyone what they had seen. 48 "For it is better," they said, "for us to incur a great sin before God than to fall into the hands of the Jewish people and be stoned." 49 So Pilate ordered the centurion and the soldiers not to say anything.

50 Early on the Lord's Day, Mary Magdalene, a disciple of the Lord (from fear of the Jews, since they were inflamed by anger, she had not

---

[1] In Greco-Roman literature, when gods or goddesses reveal themselves in their true form, they are often portrayed as extremely tall. In the present case, the height of the two men (angels) and Jesus shows that they are divine beings.

[2] The tradition that Jesus preached to the dead in Hades during the time that his body was in the tomb appears also in 1 Peter 3:18–20.

done at the tomb of the Lord what women customarily did for their dead loved ones), 51 taking her friends with her, went to the tomb where he had been placed. 52 They were afraid that the Jews might see them and said, "Even if we were not able to weep and mourn on the day he was crucified, let us do this now at his tomb. 53 But who will roll away for us the stone placed over the entrance of the tomb, so that we may enter and sit beside him and do what we ought? 54 For the stone was large, and we are afraid that someone may see us. But if we are not able, and if we must leave what we are taking at the entrance in memory of him, let us weep and mourn until we go home."

55 When they went, they found the tomb opened. Approaching, they stooped down and saw sitting there in the middle of the tomb a man, youthful and clothed in a most radiant robe. He said to them, 56 "Why have you come? Whom do you seek? Not that crucified one? He has risen and gone. If you do not believe, stoop down and see the place where he lay, that he is not there. For he has risen and gone to the place from where he was sent." 57 Then the women fled in fear.

58 It was the last day of Unleavened Bread, and many were leaving, returning to their homes as the festival ended. 59 We, the twelve disciples of the Lord, were weeping and grieving, and each, grieving over what had happened, departed to his home. 60 I, Simon Peter, and my brother Andrew, taking our nets, went out onto the sea. With us was Levi the son of Alphaeus, whom the Lord ... [Here the manuscript breaks off.]

Appendix 9
The Didache

For an introduction to the Didache, see Chapter 28.

THE TWO PATHS

1:1 There are two paths (or ways), one of life and one of death, and there is a great difference between the two paths.[1]

The Path of Life

2 The path of life is this: First you shall love the God who made you; second, your neighbor as yourself.[2] And do not do to another anything that you do not want to happen to you.[3]

3 The teaching of these words is this:

Bless those who curse you and pray for your enemies. Fast for those who persecute you. For what credit is it if you love those who love you? Don't the Gentiles do the same? For your part, however, love those who hate you and you will never have an enemy.[4]

4 Abstain from fleshly and bodily desires.[5]

If anyone gives you a blow on the right cheek, turn the other one to him as well, and you will be perfect. If anyone drafts you to go a mile, go with him two. If anyone takes your cloak, give him your tunic too.

---

[1] Matt 7:13–14
[2] Deuteronomy 6:5; Leviticus 19:18; Matt 22:34–40; Mark 12:28–34; Luke 10:25–28; Rom 13:8–10; James 2:8
[3] Matt 7:12; Luke 6:31
[4] Matt 5:43–48; Luke 6:27–28, 32–36
[5] 1 Pet 2:11

If anyone takes your property from you, don't ask to get it back, for you can't anyway.[6]

5 Give to everyone who asks you, and don't ask for it back.[7] For the Father wishes us to give to all from the gifts that he himself has given. Blessed is he who gives in accord with the commandment, for he is not guilty. Woe to the one who takes. For if anyone who has need takes, he will not be guilty; but he who has no need will be tried as to why he took and for what. And going to prison, he will be questioned about the things he did; and he will not get out of there until he has repaid the last penny.[8] 6 But about this it has also been said, "Let your donation sweat in your hands until you know to whom you are giving."

2:1 Now the second commandment of the teaching:

2 You shall not commit murder, you shall not commit adultery, you shall not sodomize a boy, you shall not commit fornication, you shall not steal, you shall not practice magic, you shall not use potions, you shall not kill a child by abortion nor kill it after it has been born, you shall not desire your neighbor's property, 3 you shall not swear falsely, you shall not testify falsely, you shall not malign, you shall not hold a grudge. 4 You shall not be double-minded nor double-tongued, for to speak with two tongues is a death trap. 5 Your speech shall not be false or empty, but completed by action. 6 You shall not be greedy nor rapacious nor hypocritical nor malicious nor arrogant. You shall make no evil plan against your neighbor. 7 You shall hate no one, but some you shall correct, for others you shall pray, and others you shall love more than your own life.

> [The Didache continues with further moral instruction, including exhortations prefaced by the address "My child" (3:1–4:4), instructions on giving (4:5–8), instructions on order in the household (4:9–11), and a final summary (4:12–14).]

4:14 … This is the path of life.

The Path of Death

5:1 But the path of death is this: First of all it is evil and full of cursing. Murders, adulteries, lusts, fornications, thefts, idolatries, magic spells, potions, robberies, false testimonies, hypocrisies. Double-mindedness,

[6] Matt 5:38–39, 48; Luke 6:29, 30b
[7] Matt 5:42; Luke 6:30a
[8] Matt 5:25–26; Luke 12:57–59

deceit, arrogance, malice, stubbornness, greed, foul language, jealousy, audacity, pride, boastfulness. 2 Persecutors of good people, hating truth, loving falsehood, not knowing the reward of righteousness, not adhering to good nor to righteous judgment, vigilant not for the good but for the bad, who are far from gentleness and patience, loving useless things, seeking reward, not pitying the poor, not working for one who is overworked, not knowing the one who made them, murderers of children, corrupters of the body fashioned by God, turning away the needy, overworking the afflicted, advocates of the rich, lawless judges of the poor, totally sinful. Save yourselves, children, from all of these.

Conclusion

6:1 See that no one leads you away from the teaching of this path, since he teaches you apart from God. 2 For if you can bear the whole yoke of the Lord, you will be perfect. But if you cannot, do what you can. 3 Concerning food, bear what you can. But keep strictly away from what has been sacrificed to an idol, for it is the worship of dead gods.

RITUALS

Baptism

7:1 Concerning baptism, baptize like this: After you have spoken all these things, baptize in the name of the Father and the Son and the Holy Spirit in running water.[9] 2 But if you do not have running water, baptize in other water; and if you can't in cold water, then in warm water. 3 But if you have neither, pour water onto the head three times in the name of Father, Son, and Holy Spirit. 4 And before the baptism, the baptizer and the one being baptized should fast, as well as any others who can. And tell the one being baptized to fast one or two days beforehand.

Fasting and Prayer

8:1 Do not let your fasts be with the hypocrites. For they fast on Mondays and Thursdays, but you should fast on Wednesdays and Fridays.[10] 2 Nor

---

[9] Matt 28:19
[10] Matt 6:16–18

should you pray like the hypocrites.[11] But as the Lord commanded in his gospel, pray like this:

> Our Father who is in heaven, may your name be held sacred. May your kingdom come; may your will be done on earth as in heaven. Give us today our bread for tomorrow. And release us from our debt, as we release our debtors. And do not lead us into testing, but deliver us from the evil one. For yours is the power and the glory forever.[12]

3 Pray like this three times a day.

The Eucharist

9:1 And concerning the Eucharist, give thanks like this. 2 First for the cup: "We thank you, our Father, for the holy vine of your servant David, which you made known to us through your servant Jesus. To you be the glory forever." 3 And for the bread: "We thank you, our Father, for the life and knowledge that you made known to us through your servant Jesus. To you be the glory forever. 4 For just as this bread was scattered on the mountains and when gathered became one, so let your church be gathered from the ends of the earth into your kingdom. For yours is the glory and the power through Jesus Christ forever." 5 Let no one eat or drink of your Eucharist except those who have been baptized in the name of the Lord. For concerning this, the Lord has said, "Do not give what is holy to the dogs."[13]

10:1 After you are full, give thanks like this. 2 "We give thanks to you, Holy Father, for your holy name, which you made to dwell in our hearts, and for the knowledge and faith and immortality that you made known to us through Jesus your child. To you be the glory forever. 3 You, almighty Master, created all things for the sake of your name and gave food and drink to humans for enjoyment so that they might thank you. And to us you granted spiritual food and drink and eternal life through your child. 4 Above all we thank you because you are powerful. To you be the glory forever. 5 Remember, Lord, your church, to deliver it from every evil and to perfect it in your love. And gather it, which has been sanctified, from the four winds into your kingdom that you have prepared for it.[14] For yours is the power and the glory forever. 6 Let grace come and let

---

[11] Matt 6:5–6
[12] Matt 6:9–13; cf. Luke 11:1–4
[13] Matt 7:6
[14] Mark 13:27; Matt 24:31

this world pass away. Hosanna to the God of David.[15] If anyone is holy, let him come. If anyone is not, let him repent. Maranatha.[16] Amen."

7 But let the prophets give thanks however they wish.

ITINERANT AND RESIDENT MINISTERS

11:1 If anyone comes and teaches you all these things mentioned above, accept him. 2 But if the one who teaches should turn and teach a different teaching that invalidates them, do not listen to him; but if it increases righteousness and knowledge of the Lord, accept him as the Lord.

Apostles and Prophets

3 And concerning the apostles and prophets, in accordance with the decree of the gospel do like this.

4 Let every apostle who comes to you be received as the Lord. 5 But he shall remain only one day and, if necessary, the next day too. If he remains three, he is a false prophet. 6 When the apostle leaves, let him receive nothing except enough bread to get him to his next lodging. If he asks for money, he is a false prophet.

7 You shall not test or judge any prophet speaking in spirit. For every other sin will be forgiven, but this sin will not be forgiven.[17] 8 Not everyone who speaks in spirit is a prophet, but only if he has the ways of the Lord. So the false prophet and the prophet will be known from their ways.[18] 9 Any prophet who ordains a meal in spirit shall not eat of it; otherwise he is a false prophet. 10 Any prophet who teaches the truth, if he does not do what he teaches, is a false prophet. 11 Any prophet recognized as true who acts in a cosmic mystery of the church, but does not teach others to do likewise, whatever he does, he shall not be judged by you. For he has his judgment with God. For the ancient prophets too did likewise. 12 If anyone says in spirit, "Give me money" or something else, you shall not listen to him. But if concerning others in need he says to give, let no one judge him.

---

[15] Matt 21:9, 15
[16] "Maranatha" is Aramaic for "Lord, come" (cf. 1 Cor 16:22)
[17] Mark 3:28–29; Matt 12:31–32; Luke 12:10
[18] Matt 7:16–20; 12:33–37; Luke 6:43–45

Traveling Christians

12:1 Let everyone who comes in the name of the Lord be received. Then when you have tested him, you will know him, for you will have understanding of right and left. 2 If the one who comes is a traveler, help him as much as you can. But he shall not stay with you more than two or three days, if necessary. 3 If he wishes to settle among you and is a craftsman, let him work and eat. 4 But if he has no craft, use your own judgment and take forethought for how no Christian shall live with you idle. 5 But if he is not willing to do so, he is a Christ-merchant. Keep away from such people.

Support for Prophets and Teachers

13:1 Every true prophet who wishes to settle among you is worthy of his food.[19] 2 Likewise the true teacher: like the worker, he too is worthy of his food. 3 So you shall take the first fruits of the produce of the winepress and the threshing-floor, of cattle and of sheep, and you shall give the first fruits to the prophets. For they are your high priests.[20] 4 But if you do not have a prophet, give to the poor. 5 If you make bread, take the first fruits and give it according to the commandment. 6 Likewise, when you open a jar of wine or oil, take the first fruits and give it to the prophets. 7 Also of money and clothing and every possession take the first fruits, as seems good to you, and give it according to the commandment.

FURTHER INSTRUCTIONS

The Eucharist

14:1 On the Lord's Day of the Lord, when you come together, break bread and give thanks, after confessing your transgressions beforehand so that your sacrifice may be pure. 2 But let no one who has a quarrel with his fellow come together with you until they are reconciled, so that your sacrifice may not be profaned.[21] 3 For this is what was said by the Lord: "In every place and time offer to me a pure sacrifice. Because I am a great king, says the Lord, and my name is admired among the Gentiles."[22]

[19] Matt 10:10; Luke 10:7; 1 Cor 9:13–14
[20] Exodus 22:29–30; 23:19; 34:26; Numbers 18:11–19; Deuteronomy 26:2–4
[21] Matt 5:23–24
[22] Malachi 1:11, 14

Overseers and Deacons

15:1 So appoint for yourselves overseers [*episcopoi*] and deacons worthy of the Lord, men who are humble, free from the love of money, true, and tested. For they too minister to you the ministry of the prophets and teachers. 2 So do not overlook them. For they are your honored men along with the prophets and teachers.

Reminder of the Gospel

3 Correct one another, not in anger but in peace, as you have it in the gospel.[23] Let no one speak to anyone who has transgressed against another person, nor let him hear anything from you, until he repents.[24] 4 Perform your prayers and your charitable giving and all your practices as you have it in the gospel of our Lord.[25]

ESCHATOLOGICAL HOPE

16:1 Watch over your life. Do not let your lamps go out or your loins be ungirded.[26] But be ready, for you do not know the hour in which your Lord is coming.[27] 2 Meet together frequently, seeking the things that concern your souls.[28] For the whole time of your faith will not profit you unless you are perfected in the last time.[29]

3 For in the last days, the false prophets and the seducers will multiply, and the sheep will be turned into wolves, and their love will be turned into hatred. 4 For as lawlessness increases, they will hate one another and persecute and betray one another.[30]

And then the world-deceiver shall appear as a son of God and perform signs and wonders,[31] and the earth shall be given over into his hands. And he shall do unlawful deeds which have never been done before. 5 Then the creation of humanity will come into the trial of fire, and many will

[23] Matt 18:15; Luke 17:3
[24] Matt 18:16–17
[25] Matt 6:1–18
[26] Luke 12:35; Matt 25:1–13
[27] Matt 24:44; Luke 12:40
[28] Heb 10:25
[29] Barnabas 4:9
[30] Matt 24:10–12
[31] Mark 13:22; Matt 24:24

stumble and perish. But those who remain in their faith will be saved by the curse itself.[32]

6 And then will appear the signs of the truth: first the sign of a spreading out in the sky; then the sign of a trumpet blast;[33] and third, resurrection of the dead – 7 not of all, though, but as it was said, "The Lord will come and all the holy ones with him." 8 Then the world will see the Lord coming upon the clouds of the sky.[34]

---

[32] Mark 13:13b; Matt 24:13
[33] Matt 24:30a, 31b
[34] Mark 13:26; Matt 24:30c; Luke 21:27

Appendix 10
Selections from the Gospel of Thomas

For an introduction to the Gospel of Thomas, see Chapter 30. The following selections from Thomas include some sayings with a canonical parallel and some without. References to canonical parallels are cited in brackets after the saying.

These are the secret sayings that the living Jesus uttered and that Didymus Judas Thomas wrote down.

1 And he said, "Whoever discovers the meaning of these sayings will not taste death."

2 Jesus said, "One who seeks should not stop seeking until he finds. And when he finds, he will be troubled. And if he is troubled, he will be amazed, and he will rule over the All."

3 Jesus said, "If your leaders say to you, 'Look, the kingdom is in the sky,' then the birds of the sky will precede you; if they say to you, 'It is in the sea,' then the fish will precede you. Instead the kingdom is inside of you and outside of you [Luke 17:20–21; cf. 113]. When you know yourselves, then you will be known, and you will realize that you are the sons of the living Father. But if you do not know yourselves, then you will be in poverty, and you are the poverty."

4 Jesus said, "The man old in days will not hesitate to ask a little child of seven days about the place of life, and he will live. For there are many of the first who will be last [Mark 10:31//Matt 19:30], and they will become a single one."

5 Jesus said, "Recognize him who is in front of your face, and he who is hidden from you will be revealed to you. For there is nothing hidden that will not become visible" [Mark 4:22//Luke 8:17; Matt 10:26].

6a His disciples asked him, they said to him, "Do you want us to fast? And how should we pray and give alms? And what diet should we observe?" 14 Jesus said to them, "If you fast, you will bring sin upon yourselves; and if you pray, you will be condemned; and if you give alms, you will do harm to your spirits. And if you go into any land and walk into the country, if they receive you, eat what they set before you; heal those who are sick among them [Luke 10:8–9a]. For what goes into your mouth will not defile you; but what will defile you is what comes out of your mouth" [Matt 15:11//Mark 7:15].[1]

7 Jesus said, "Blessed is the lion that the man eats so that the lion becomes man; and abominable is the man that the lion eats so that the man becomes lion."[2]

8 And he said, "The Man is like a wise fisherman who cast his net into the sea. He drew it up from the sea full of small fish. Among them the wise fisherman found a fine, large fish. He threw all of the small fish back into the sea. He chose the large fish without difficulty. He who has ears to hear should listen" [Matt 13:47–50; 13:43b].

9 Jesus said, "Look, the sower went out, filled his hand (with seed), and threw. Some fell on the road, and the birds came and gathered them. Others fell on the rock and did not take root under the ground and did not send grain up to the sky. Still others fell on the thorns, and they choked the seed, and the worm ate them. Still others fell on the good ground, and it bore fruit up to the good sky. It came to sixty per head and one hundred twenty per head" [Mark 4:3–8//Matt 13:3–8; Luke 8:5–8].

10 Jesus said, "I have thrown fire upon the world, and look, I am watching it until it blazes" [Luke 12:49].

13 Jesus said to his disciples, "Compare and tell me what I am like." Simon Peter said to him, "You are like a righteous angel." Matthew said to him, "You are like a wise philosopher." Thomas said to him, "Teacher, my mouth would be wholly unable to bear that I should say what you are like." Jesus said, "I am not your teacher. Since you have drunk, you have become intoxicated from the bubbling spring that I have measured out." And he took him, and withdrew, and spoke three sayings to him. When Thomas came back to his companions, they asked him, "What did Jesus say to you?" Thomas said to them, "If I tell you one of the sayings that he spoke to me, you will pick up rocks and throw them at me, and fire will come out of the rocks and burn you up."

---

[1] The question that the disciples ask in 6a is answered by Jesus in 14. At some point in the history of the gospel, the question and answer were separated. Here I have rejoined them.

[2] Both halves of the sentence read "so that the lion becomes man." In the second half, this clause is probably a copyist's error for "so that the man becomes lion."

16 Jesus said, "People may think that I came to put peace in the world and not know that I came to put divisions on the earth: fire, sword, and war. For there will be five in a household: there will be three against two and two against three, the father against the son and the son against the father [Matt 10:34–35//Luke 12:51–53]. And they will stand up and be made monks."

18 The disciples said to Jesus, "Tell us how our end will be." Jesus said, "Have you discovered the beginning so that you seek the end? For in the place where the beginning is, there will the end be. Blessed is he who will stand in the beginning. He will know the end and not taste death."

19a Jesus said, "Blessed is he who came into being before he came into being."

19c "For you have five trees there in paradise. They do not change in summer or winter, and their leaves do not fall. He who recognizes them will not taste death."

21a Mary asked Jesus, "What do your disciples resemble?" He said, "They resemble little children living in a field that is not theirs. When the owners of the field come, they will say, 'Give our field back to us.' They strip in front of them in order to give it back to them, and they give their field to them."

22 Jesus saw some babies nursing. He said to his disciples, "These nursing babies are like those who have entered the kingdom" [Mark 10:14//Matt 19:14//Luke 18:16]. They asked him, "Then shall we enter the kingdom by becoming babies?" Jesus said to them, "When you make the two one, and make the inside like the outside and the outside like the inside, and the skyward side like the groundward side; so that you make the male and the female into a single one, so that the male will not act male nor the female act female [Gal 3:28]; when you make eyes in place of an eye, and a hand in place of a hand, and a foot in place of a foot, an image in place of an image, then you will enter the kingdom."

23 Jesus said, "I will choose you, one from a thousand and two from ten thousand, and they will stand, made a single one."

24 His disciples said, "Show us the place where you are, since it is necessary for us to seek it." He said to them, "He who has ears should listen. There is light within a man of light, and it gives light to the whole world. If it does not give light, it is darkness" [Matt 6:22–23//Luke 11:34–35].

27 "If you do not fast with respect to the world, you will not find the kingdom. If you do not make the Sabbath into a Sabbath, you will not see the Father."

28 Jesus said, "I stood in the midst of the world and became visible to them in flesh. I found all of them drunk; I did not find any of them thirsty. And I felt pain in my soul for the sons of men, for they are blind in their hearts and they do not see. For they were empty when they came into the world, and they also seek to go out of the world empty. But now they are drunk. When they shake off their wine, then they will repent."

29 Jesus said, "If the flesh came into being because of spirit, the spirit is a marvel; if the spirit (came into being) on account of the body, the body is a marvel of marvels. But I marvel at this: how this great thing of wealth came to dwell in this poverty."

36 Jesus said, "Do not be concerned from morning until evening and from evening until morning about what you will wear" [Matt 6:25//Luke 12:22].

37 His disciples asked, "On what day will you become visible to us, and on what day will we see you?" Jesus said, "When you strip yourselves without being ashamed and take your garments and put them under your feet like little children and trample them, then you will see the Son of the Living One and not be afraid."

39 Jesus said, "The Pharisees and the scribes have taken the keys of knowledge and hidden them. They have neither entered nor allowed those who want to enter to do so [Matt 23:13//Luke 11:52]. But you be shrewd as snakes and innocent as doves" [Matt 10:16b].

42 Jesus said, "Be passing by."

43 His disciples asked him, "Who are you that you say these things to us?" "From the things I say to you, you do not know who I am, but you have become like the Jews. For they love the tree but hate its fruit, or they love the fruit but hate the tree" [Matt 12:33ab].

44 Jesus said, "He who has blasphemed against the Father will be forgiven, and he who has blasphemed against the Son will be forgiven, but he who has blasphemed against the Holy Spirit will not be forgiven, either on earth or in heaven" [Matt 12:32].

48 Jesus said, "If two make peace with each other in a single house [Matt 18:19], they will say to the mountain, 'Move away,' and it will move" [Mark 11:2 //Matt 21:21; Matt 17:20b//Luke 9:6; cf. 106].

49 Jesus said, "Blessed are those who are monks and chosen, for you will find the kingdom. For you are from it, (and) you will go back there."

50 Jesus said, "If they ask you, 'Where did you originate?' say to them, 'We came from the light, the place where the light came into being by itself. It stood and became visible in their image.' If they ask you, 'Is that

what you are?' say to them, 'We are its sons, and we are the chosen of the living Father.' If they ask you, 'What is the sign of your Father that is in you?' say to them, 'It is movement and rest.'"

51 His disciples asked him, "On what day will the rest for the dead take place, and on what day is the new world coming?" He said to them, "What you are looking forward to has come, but you do not recognize it."

53 His disciples asked him, "Is circumcision beneficial or not?" He said to them, "If it were beneficial, their father would beget them circumcised from their mother. But the true circumcision in spirit was useful in every respect."

54 Jesus said, "Blessed are the poor, for yours is the kingdom of the heavens" [Luke 6:20b//Matt 5:3].

55 Jesus said, "He who does not hate his father and mother cannot be my disciple, and he who does not hate his brothers and sisters and carry his cross like me will not be made worthy of me" [Luke 14:25–27//Matt 10:37–38].

56 Jesus said, "He who has come to know the world has found a corpse; and if he has found the corpse, the world is not worthy of him" [cf. 80].

59 Jesus said, "Look upon the Living One while you are alive, lest you die and seek to see him and not be able to see."

60 He saw a Samaritan carrying a lamb when he had gone to Judea. He said to his disciples, "He is around the lamb." They said to him, "So that he may kill it and eat it." He said to them, "While it is alive he will not eat it, but only after he kills it and it becomes a corpse." They said, "Otherwise he cannot do it." He said to them, "You also should seek after a place for yourselves within repose, lest you become a corpse and be eaten."

61b Salome asked, "Who are you, man? As if from (the) One, you have mounted my couch and eaten from my table." Jesus said to her, "I am he who came into existence from him who is the same. I was given some of the qualities of my Father." (She said) "I am your disciple." (He said) "For this reason I say, when it becomes the same, it will be full of light; but when it becomes divided, it will be full of darkness" [Matt 6:22b–23a// Luke 11:34b].

63 Jesus said, "There was a rich man who had a lot of money. He said, 'I will lend my money at interest so that I may sow, reap, plant, and fill my storehouses with produce so that I may lack nothing.' He had these thoughts in mind, and that night he died. He who has ears should listen" [Luke 12:16–21].

64 Jesus said, "A man was having guests. And when he had prepared the dinner, he sent his slave to invite the guests. He went to the first

and said to him, 'My master invites you.' He said, 'I have money for some merchants. They are coming to me this evening. I must go and place an order with them. I ask to be excused from the dinner.' He went to another and said to him, 'My master has invited you.' He said to him, 'My friend is getting married, and I am the one making dinner. I will not be able to come. I ask to be excused from the dinner.' He went to another and said to him, 'My master invites you.' He said to him, 'I have bought a village. I will be gone to collect rent. I will not be able to come. I ask to be excused.' The slave went and said to his master, 'Those whom you invited to the dinner have asked to be excused.' The master said to his slave, 'Go outside to the roads and bring those whom you find so that they may dine.' The buyers and the merchants will not enter the places of my Father" [Matt 22:1–10// Luke 14:16–24].

67 Jesus said, "He who knows the All but lacks himself, lacks the place (of) the All."

69b "Blessed are they who are hungry so that the stomach of the person in want may be satisfied" [Matt 5:6//Luke 6:21].

75 Jesus said, "There are many standing at the door, but those who will go into the wedding chamber are the monks."

76 Jesus said, "The kingdom of the Father is like a merchant who had a cargo when he found a pearl. That merchant was wise. He sold (or gave away) the cargo and bought himself that single pearl [Matt 13:45–46]. You, also, seek his treasure that does not give out, that remains, where neither moth gets in to eat nor worm destroys" [Matt 6:19–20//Luke 12:33b].

77 Jesus said, "I am that light which is over them all. I am the All. The All came from me, and the All split into me. Split a piece of wood; I am there. Lift up the stone and you will find me there."

78 Jesus said, "Why did you come out to the country? To see a reed moved by the wind? To see a man dressed in soft clothes like your kings and great men? It is they who are dressed in soft clothes, and they will not be able to understand the truth" [Matt 11:7–8//Luke 7:24–25].

80 Jesus said, "He who has come to know the world has found the body; and if he has found the body, the world is not worthy of him" [cf. 56].

81 Jesus said, "He who has become wealthy should become king, and he who has power should renounce (it)."

82 Jesus said, "He who is near me is near the fire, and he who is far from me is far from the kingdom."

83 Jesus said, "The images are visible to the Man, and the light that is in them is hidden in the image of the light of the Father. It [the light] will be revealed and its image hidden by its light."

86 Jesus said, "The foxes have a den and the birds have their nest, but the son of man has no place to lay his head and rest" [Matt 8:20// Luke 9:58].

87 Jesus said, "Wretched is the body that is captivated by a body; and wretched is the soul that is captivated by the two of these" [cf. 112].

90 Jesus said, "Come unto me, for my yoke is kind and my lordship gentle, and you will find rest for yourselves" [Matt 11:28–30].

95 Jesus said, "If you have money, do not lend it at interest, but give it to one from whom you will not get it back" [Luke 6:34, 35 b].

96 Jesus said, "The kingdom of the Father is like a woman. She took a little leaven, hid it in dough, made it into some large loaves of bread. He who has ears should listen" [Matt 13:33//Luke 13:20–21].

97 Jesus said, "The kingdom of the Father is like a woman carrying a jar full of meal. As she was walking on a distant road, the handle of the jar broke. The meal emptied out behind her on the road. She did not know it; she was not aware of a problem. When she arrived at her house, she put the jar down. She found it empty."

99 The disciples said to him, "Your brothers and your mother are standing outside." He said to them, "Those in this place who do the will of my Father are my brothers and my mother. It is they who will enter the kingdom of my Father" [Mark 3:31–35//Matt 12:46–50; Luke 8:19–21].

101 "He who does not hate his father and mother as I do cannot be my disciple [Luke 14:26; cf. Matt 10:37]. And he who does not love his father and mother as I do cannot be my disciple. For my mother [...], but my true mother gave me life."

102 Jesus said, "Woe to the Pharisees, for they are like a dog lying in the cattle manger. For it neither eats nor allows the cattle to eat" [cf. Matt 23:13//Luke 11:52].

104 They said to Jesus, "Come, let us pray today and fast." Jesus said, "What sin have I committed or how have I been overcome? But when the bridegroom leaves the bridal chamber, then let them fast and pray" [Mark 2:18–20//Matt 9:14–15//Luke 5:33–35].

106 Jesus said, "When you make the two one [Matt 18:19], you will become sons of the Man, and when you say, 'Mountain, move away,' it will move" [Mark 11:23//Matt 21:21; Matt 17:20b//Luke 9:6; cf. 48].

107 Jesus said, "The kingdom is like a shepherd who had a hundred sheep. One of them, the largest, went astray. He left the ninety-nine and

sought the one until he found it. After he had labored, he said to the sheep, 'I want you more than the ninety-nine'" [Matt 18:12–13//Luke 15:4–5].

108 Jesus said, "He who drinks from my mouth will become like me. I myself will become him, and the things that are hidden will become visible to him."

109 Jesus said, "The kingdom is like a man who had in his field a hidden treasure that he did not know about. When he died, he left it to his son, but his son did not know it. He took that field and sold it. The man who bought it went plowing and found the treasure. He began to lend money at interest to those whom he wished" [Matt 13:44].

110 Jesus said, "If someone has found the world and become wealthy, he should renounce the world."

111b Doesn't Jesus say, "If anyone has found himself, the world is not worthy of him?"

112 Jesus said, "Woe to that flesh which is captivated by the soul; woe to that soul which is captivated by the flesh" [cf. 87].

113 His disciples asked him, "On what day is the kingdom coming?" (He said) "It is not coming with observation. They will not say, 'Look, here' or 'Look, there.' But the kingdom of the Father is spread out on the earth, and people do not see it" [Luke 17:20–21; cf. 3a].

114 Simon Peter said to them, "Mary should leave us, for women are not worthy of the life." Jesus said, "Look, I will lead her in order to make her male so that she too may become a living spirit like you males. For every woman who makes herself male will enter the kingdom of the heavens."

Appendix 11
Ignatius to the Smyrnaeans 1–9

> For an introduction to Ignatius and his letters, see Chapter 35. In his letters Ignatius repeatedly warns against Christians who hold a docetic view of Christ. He directs his readers not to associate with these, but to follow the bishop. The following selection from his letter to the church in Smyrna illustrates these themes.

Ignatius, also called Theophoros, to the church of God the Father and the beloved Jesus Christ, which is blessed with every gift, filled with faith and love, deficient in no gift, most suited for divinity and clothed with holiness, to the church in Smyrna of Asia: may you rejoice most greatly in a blameless spirit and the word of God.

1:1 I glorify Jesus Christ, the God who has made you so wise. For I have observed that you are equipped with immovable faith, as if nailed to the cross of our Lord Jesus Christ in both flesh and spirit and established in love by the blood of Christ, fully convinced concerning our Lord that he was truly from the line of David with respect to the flesh, son of God with respect to the will and power of God, truly born from a virgin, baptized by John so that all righteousness might be fulfilled by him, 2 truly under Pontius Pilate and Herod the tetrarch nailed for us in the flesh (of whose divinely blessed passion we are some of the fruit), so that he might set up an ensign for all ages through the resurrection for his saints and believers, whether among Jews or among Gentiles, in the one body of his church.

2:1 For he suffered all this for us so that we might be saved. And he truly suffered, just as he truly raised himself. He did not, as some unbelievers say, suffer only in appearance [*dokein*] – it is they who only appear to be. And in accord with what they think, so it will happen to them: they will be disembodied and phantasmal.

3:1 For I know and believe that he was in flesh even after the resurrection. 2 And when he came to those around Peter, he said to them, "Take, handle me and see that I am not a disembodied phantom." And at once they touched him and believed, being joined to his flesh and his spirit. For this reason they despised death and were found to be beyond death. 3 And after the resurrection, he ate and drank with them as a being of flesh, though united spiritually with the Father.

4:1 Now I advise you of these things, beloved, knowing that you also hold the same view. But I guard you in advance from the beasts in human form, whom you must not only not receive but also if possible not even meet. You must only pray for them in case they may repent, which is difficult, but Jesus Christ our true life has authority over this. 2 For if these things were done by our Lord only in appearance, then I too am a prisoner only in appearance. And why have I too surrendered myself to death – to fire, to sword, to wild beasts? But near the sword is near to God; with the wild beasts is with God. Only in the name of Jesus Christ do I endure all things, so as to suffer with him, the perfect man himself enabling me.

5:1 Some ignorant people deny him, or rather were denied by him, being advocates of death instead of the truth. They were not persuaded by the prophecies nor the Law of Moses, nor even until now by the gospel nor our individual sufferings. 2 For they also have the same opinion about us. For what good does anyone do me if he praises me but blasphemes my Lord, by not confessing that he was clothed in flesh? But he who does not say this has denied him completely, being clothed with a corpse. 3 Their names, being unbelieving names, I did not think fit to write. But I wish that I might not even remember them until they repent concerning the passion, which is our resurrection.

6:1 Let no one be deceived. There is judgment even for the heavenly beings and the glory of the angels and the rulers, visible and invisible, if they do not believe in the blood of Christ. "He who has room let him receive."[1] Let not a high position puff up anyone. For faith and love are everything; nothing is more eminent than these. 2 But notice those who have a different opinion about the grace of Jesus Christ that has come to us, how contrary they are to the disposition of God. They do not care about love – not about the widow, nor about the orphan, nor about the afflicted, nor about the person imprisoned or released, nor about the hungry or thirsty.

7:1 They abstain from Eucharist and prayer, because they do not confess that the Eucharist is the flesh of our Savior Jesus Christ, the flesh

---

[1] Matt 19:12

that suffered for our sins, which the Father in his kindness raised. So those who speak against the gift of God die arguing. It would be better for them to love, so that they might also rise. 2 It is proper to keep away from such people and not to speak about them either in private or in public, but to pay attention to the prophets and especially to the gospel. In it, the passion has been made clear to us and the resurrection has been accomplished. But flee from divisions as the beginning of evils.

8:1 You should all follow the bishop, as Jesus Christ follows the Father, and the presbytery as the apostles. And respect the deacons as God's command. Without the bishop let no one do any of the things pertaining to the church. Let that be considered a valid Eucharist which is under the bishop or whoever he permits. 2 Wherever the bishop appears, there let the congregation be, just as wherever Jesus Christ is, there is the catholic church. Apart from the bishop it is not permissible either to baptize or to hold an agape (a love feast). But whatever he approves, this is also pleasing to God, so that everything that you do may be safe and valid.

9:1 It is reasonable, then, for us to return to soberness, while we still have time to repent towards God. It is good to know God and bishop. The person who honors a bishop has been honored by God. The person who does anything without the bishop's knowledge is serving the Devil. 2 So let all things abound to you in grace, for you are worthy. In everything you have refreshed me; and Jesus Christ, you. You have loved me in my absence and in my presence. God is your reward: if you endure all things for his sake you will obtain him.

Appendix 12
Selections from 1 Clement

For an introduction to 1 Clement, see Chapter 36. The letter is lengthy, often becoming tedious. The following selections represent some of the highlights. They illustrate typical features of Proto-Orthodox Christianity.

Peter and Paul (1 Clement 5)

5:1 But to cease from the examples of ancient men, let us come to those who became contenders more recently. Let us take the noble examples of our generation. 2 Because of jealousy and envy, the greatest and most righteous pillars were persecuted and contended unto death. 3 Let us set before our eyes the good apostles: 4 Peter, who because of unjust jealousy bore not one or two but many struggles and, having thus testified, went to the deserved place of glory. 5 Because of jealousy and strife, Paul showed the prize of endurance. 6 Seven times in bonds, exiled, stoned, having been a herald in both the East and the West, he gained the noble fame of his faith. 7 After teaching the whole world righteousness and coming to the limit of the West and testifying before the rulers, he was then released from the world and taken up into the holy place, becoming an exceedingly great model of endurance.

Social Code (1 Clement 21:6–8)

21:6 Let us reverence the Lord Jesus Christ, whose blood was given for us. Let us respect those who rule us; let us honor the elders; let us train the young with training in the fear of God. Let us direct our wives to what is good. 7 Let them exhibit the lovely character of purity, let them demonstrate the innocent will of their meekness, let them make clear the propriety of their tongue through their silence. Let them not offer their love preferentially but equally to all who fear God in holiness. 8 Let our children take part in the training in Christ. Let them learn how strong humility is with God, how powerful pure love is with God, how fear of him is good and great and saves all who live in it in a holy manner with a pure mind.

Delay of the Parousia (1 Clement 23:3–5)

23:3 Let this scripture be far from us, where it says, "Wretched are the double-minded, who doubt in their soul, who say, 'We heard these things even in the days of our fathers, and look, we have grown old and none of these things has happened to us.' 4 O fools, compare yourselves to a tree. Take a vine: first it sheds its leaves, then comes a bud, then a leaf, then a bloom, and after this an unripe grape, then a bunch of grapes alongside."[1] You see that in a short time the fruit of the tree comes to ripeness. 5 Truly his will shall be accomplished quickly and suddenly, the scripture also testifying that "he will come quickly and not delay," and "the Lord will come suddenly to his temple, even the Holy One for whom you wait."[2]

Arguments for Resurrection (1 Clement 24–26)

24:1 Let us consider, beloved, how the Master continuously indicates to us that the future resurrection is going to take place, of which he made the Lord Jesus Christ the first fruits by raising him from the dead. 2 Let us observe, beloved, the resurrection that takes place time and again. 3 Day and night show us resurrection: the night sleeps, the day rises; the day departs, the night comes on. 4 Let us take the crops: how and in what manner does the produce occur? 5 The sower went out and threw each of the seeds on the ground. These, falling on the ground, dry and bare, decompose. Then the greatness of the providence of the Master raises them up; and from the one, more grow and bring forth a crop.

25:1 Let us consider the marvelous sign that occurs in the regions of the East, that is, in the regions around Arabia. 2 For there is a bird which is called the Phoenix.[3] This bird, the only one of its kind, lives five hundred

---

[1] A quotation from an unknown work, also found in 2 Clement 11:2–4
[2] Isa 13:22; Mal 3:1
[3] The story of the Phoenix occurs in Herodotus (*Histories* 2.73) and Pliny (*Natural History* 10.2)

years. When it is about to depart in death, it makes itself a nest out of frankincense and myrrh and the other spices, and when the time is completed it goes in and dies. 3 From the rotting flesh, a sort of larva is born. Nourished on the moisture of the dead animal, it grows wings. When it has become like its parent, it picks up that nest, where the bones of its predecessor are, and carrying them, travels from the country of Arabia to Egypt, to the city called Heliopolis. 4 And in the daytime, as all are watching, it flies up to the altar of the Sun, puts them down, and starts back. 5 Then the priests examine the records of dates and find that it has come at the completion of the five-hundredth year.

26:1 Do we then regard it a great and surprising thing, if the Craftsman of all things will bring about the resurrection of those who have served him in holiness with the confidence of good faith, when even through a bird he shows us the greatness of his promise? 2 For it says somewhere, "And you will raise me up and I will acknowledge you," and "I lay down and slept, I got up, because you are with me." And further Job says, "And you will raise up my flesh, this which has gone through all these things."[4]

Church Order (1 Clement 40–42, 44)

40:1 ... we ought to do in order all that the Master commanded us to perform at appointed times. 2 He commanded the offerings and services to be performed and not to be at random or without order, but at designated times and hours. 3 Where and through whom he wishes them to be performed he himself designated by his supreme will, so that all things done in holiness with approval might be acceptable to his will. 4 So those who make their offerings at the appointed times are acceptable and blessed. For in following the laws of the Master they are not totally mistaken. 5 For the services proper for the high priest are given to him, and the place proper for the priests is appointed for them, and the ministries proper for the Levites are imposed on them. The lay person is bound by the ordinances for the laity.

41:1 Let each one of us, brothers, in his own rank, offer thanksgiving [Eucharist] to God, being in good conscience, not transgressing the designated measure of his service, with gravity. 2 Not everywhere, brothers, do they offer regular sacrifices or sacrifices of vows, or sacrifices for sin and transgression, but only in Jerusalem. And there it is not offered in every place, but in front of the temple at the altar, after the offering

---

4 Psalm 3:5; Job 19:26

has been inspected for defects by the high priest and the ministers previously mentioned. 3 Those therefore who do something contrary to what has come down of his will have death as the penalty. 4 You see, brothers, the more knowledge of which we have been deemed worthy, the greater the risk we run.

42:1 The apostles were given the good news for us from the Lord Jesus Christ; Jesus the Christ was sent from God. 2 So the Christ is from God and the apostles are from the Christ. So both things happened in an orderly manner from God's will. 3 So receiving orders, and being convinced by the resurrection of our Lord Jesus Christ, and being persuaded by the word of God, with conviction of the Holy Spirit, they went out proclaiming the good news that the kingdom of God is going to come. 4 As they preached, then, in regions and cities, they set up their first fruits, testing them in spirit, as overseers [bishops] and ministers deacons] of those who were going to believe. 5 And this was not something new. For overseers and ministers had been written about a long time ago. For somewhere the scripture says this: "I will establish their overseers with righteousness and their ministers with faith"[5] …

44:1 Our apostles also knew through our Lord Jesus Christ that there would be strife over the title of bishop. 2 So for this reason, since they had received perfect foreknowledge, they appointed those previously mentioned, and afterward gave an additional law that, if they should fall asleep, other approved men should succeed to their ministry. 3 Therefore we do not think it is right to expel from the ministry those who were appointed by them, or afterward by other reputable men with the consent of the whole church, and who have ministered irreproachably to the flock of Christ with humility, gently and without vulgarity, and who have been given a good report by all for a long time. 4 For our sin is not small if we expel from the episcopate those who have offered the gifts irreproachably and with holiness. 5 Blessed are the elders who have gone before, who obtained a fruitful and perfect release, for they have no concern that someone will remove them from the place established for them. 6 For we see that some of you have removed men governing well from the ministry awarded to them irreproachably.

[5] Isaiah 60:17

Appendix 13
Selections from the Epistle of Barnabas

For an introduction to the Epistle of Barnabas, see Chapter 38. The following selections illustrate highlights of the author's thought on the relation between Christianity and Judaism.

13.1 On Sacrifices (Barnabas 2:4–10a)

2:4 For he [the Lord] has made clear to us through all the prophets that he needs neither sacrifices nor whole burnt offerings nor other offerings, saying in one place, 5 "What is the abundance of your sacrifices to me, says the Lord? I am full of whole burnt offerings and I do not want the fat of lambs and the blood of bulls and goats, even if you should come to appear before me. For who sought these things from your hands? You shall not again walk in my courtyard. If you bring flour, it is vain. Incense is an abomination to me. I cannot stand your new moons and Sabbaths."[1] 6 He abolished these things, then, so that the new Law of our Lord Jesus Christ, being without a yoke of necessity, might not have an offering that is man-made. 7 Again he says to them [the Jews], "Did I command your fathers when they left the land of Egypt to offer me whole burnt offerings and sacrifices? 8 Instead I gave them this command:[2] Let none of you carry a grudge in his heart against his neighbor, and do not love a false oath."[3] 9 So we ought to perceive, since we are not stupid, the benevolence of our Father, because, not wanting us to seek in error like them, he tells us how we should approach him. 10 So to us he speaks thus: "Sacrifice to the Lord is a broken heart."[4] A sweet smell to the Lord is a heart that glorifies the one who made it.

[1] Isaiah 1:11–13
[2] Jeremiah 7:22–23
[3] Zechariah 8:17
[4] Psalm 51:17

13.2 On the Covenant (Barnabas 4:6–8)

4:6 And furthermore, since I am one of yourselves, and especially since I love all of you more than my own life, I ask you this also: to watch out for yourselves and not become like some, adding to your sins by saying that the covenant is theirs and ours. 7 It is ours. But they, in this way, lost it forever when Moses had just received it. For the scripture says, "And Moses was on the mountain fasting forty days and forty nights. And he received the covenant from the Lord, stone tablets, inscribed by the finger of the hand of the Lord."[5] 8 But when they turned to the idols, they lost it. For the Lord speaks thus: "Moses, Moses, go down quickly, because your people, those whom you led out of the land of Egypt, have broken the Law."[6] And Moses realized it and threw the two tablets out of his hands. And their covenant was broken, so that that of the beloved Jesus might be sealed in our hearts in hope of the faith in him.

13.3 On Circumcision (Barnabas 9:1–9)

9:1 For he speaks again concerning the ears, how he circumcised our hearts. For the Lord says in the prophet, "When they heard with the ear, they obeyed me."[7] And again he says, "Those far away will hear, they will know what I have done,"[8] and "Circumcise, says the Lord, your hearts."[9] … 3 So then he circumcised our hearing so that having heard the word we might believe. 4 But also the circumcision in which they [the Jews] have trusted has been abolished. For he has said that circumcision is not of the flesh. But they went astray because an evil angel was instructing them. 5 He says to them, "Thus says the Lord your God (here I find a command), Do not sow among thorns; be circumcised to the Lord."[10] What else does he say? "Circumcise the hardness of your heart and do not stiffen your neck."[11] Take this also: "Behold, says the Lord, all the Gentiles are uncircumcised in the foreskin, but this people is uncircumcised in heart."[12]

---

[5] Exodus 24:18; 31:18; cf. 34:28
[6] Exodus 32:7
[7] Psalm 18:44
[8] Isaiah 33:13
[9] Jeremiah 4:4
[10] Jeremiah 4:3–4
[11] Deuteronomy 10:16
[12] Jeremiah 9:25–26

6 But you will say, the people have been circumcised as a seal. But so have every Syrian and Arab and all the priests of the idols. Are they too then of their covenant? Even the Egyptians are circumcised. 7 Learn then, children of love, concerning all things abundantly: that Abraham, the first to give circumcision, circumcised as he looked forward in spirit to Jesus, having received doctrines from three letters. 8 For it says, "Abraham circumcised eighteen and three hundred men from his household."[13] What then was the knowledge given to him? Notice that he mentions the eighteen first and then, after an interval, three hundred. The eighteen is I (ten) H (eight); you have Jesus. And because the cross was going to have its form in the T, he mentions also the three hundred.[14] So he indicates Jesus in two letters, and the cross in one. 9 The one who put the implanted gift of his teaching in us knows. No one has learned from me a truer lesson, but I know that you are worthy.

13.4 On Dietary Regulations (Barnabas 10:1–12)

10:1 Now when Moses said, "You shall not eat the pig nor the eagle nor the hawk nor the crow nor any fish without scales on it,"[15] he had in mind three doctrines. 2 Furthermore, he says to them in Deuteronomy, "I will set forth my ordinances to this people."[16] So then God's commandment is not to refrain from eating, but Moses spoke in spirit. 3 So he spoke of the pig for this reason: you shall not associate, he means, with men of this sort, those who are like pigs. That is, when they live in luxury they forget the Lord, but when they are in need they recognize the Lord, just as the pig, when it is eating, does not know its master, but when it is hungry it squeals and once it has received is quiet again. 4 "Nor shall you eat the eagle nor the hawk nor the kite nor the crow." You shall not, he means, associate with or be like men of this sort, those who do not know how to obtain food for themselves by labor and sweat, but seize the property of others in their lawlessness and keep an eye out, walking as if in innocence, and look around to find someone they can strip because of their greed, just as these birds alone do not obtain food for themselves, but sitting idle seek how they may devour the flesh of others, becoming pestilent in their evil. 5 "And you shall not eat," he says, "eel or octopus or cuttlefish."

---

[13] Genesis 17:23, 27; 14:14

[14] Greek uses letters for numbers. Eighteen is IH, the first letters of the word IHΣΟΥΣ (Jesus). Three hundred is T (tau), a letter that looks like a cross

[15] Leviticus 11; Deuteronomy 14

[16] Deuteronomy 4:1, 5

You shall not, he means, be like or consort with men of this sort, those who are utterly impious and already condemned to death, just as these sea creatures alone swim accursed in the deep, not diving like the rest, but dwell in the ground under the deep. 6 "But the rabbit too you shall not eat." Why? You shall not be, he means, a molester of boys or be like men of this sort, because the hare every year has excessive defecation. For it has as many burrow-holes as it lives years. 7 "But neither shall you eat the hyena." You shall not, he means, be an adulterer or a pervert or be like men of this sort. Why? Because this animal in alternate years changes its nature and becomes now male, now female. 8 But he [Moses] also rightly hated the weasel. You shall not, he means, be a man of this sort, such as we hear of committing iniquity in their mouths because of uncleanness, nor shall you associate with the unclean women who commit the iniquity in their mouths. For this animal gives birth with its mouth.

9 Concerning foods, Moses received three doctrines and spoke thus in spirit. But they [the Jews] received them in accord with the desire of the flesh as being about food. 10 But David receives knowledge of the same three doctrines and says, "Blessed is the man who has not gone in the counsel of the impious," just as the fish go in darkness in the deep water, "and has not stood in the path of sinners," just as those who seem to fear the Lord sin like the pig, "and has not sat in the seat of pestilent men," like the birds sitting and waiting for prey.[17]

Grasp fully also the teaching concerning the food. 11 Again Moses says, "Eat every kind of animal that has a cloven hoof and chews a cud."[18] What does he mean? That receiving the food, he knows the one feeding him, and resting on him he seems to be glad. Well did he speak regarding the commandment. So what does he mean? Associate with those who fear the Lord, with those who meditate in their hearts on the command of the word that they received, with those who speak about the ordinances of the Lord and keep them, with those who know that meditation is an act of gladness and who ruminate on the word of the Lord. But what does the "cloven hoof" mean? That the righteous man both walks in this world and expects the holy age. See how well Moses legislated. 12 But where could they [the Jews] have gotten the ability to understand or comprehend these things? We speak, however, correctly understanding the commandments, as the Lord wished. That is why he circumcised our ears and hearts, so that we might comprehend these things.

---

[17] Psalm 1:1
[18] Leviticus 11:3; Deuteronomy 14:6

13.5 On the Sabbath (Barnabas 15:1–9)

15:1 Furthermore, then, also about the Sabbath it is written in the ten commandments, in which he [God] spoke on Mount Sinai to Moses face to face, "And sanctify the Sabbath of the Lord with pure hands and a pure heart."[19] 2 And in another place it says, "If my sons keep the Sabbath, then I will bestow my mercy on them."[20]

3 It mentions the Sabbath at the beginning of creation: "In six days God made the works of his hands, and he finished on the seventh day and rested on it and sanctified it."[21] 4 Notice, children, what it means that he finished in six days. This means that in six thousand years the Lord will finish all things. For the day with him signifies a thousand years. He himself corroborates me when he says, "Behold the day of the Lord will be like a thousand years."[22] Therefore, children, in six days, that is, in six thousand years, all things will be finished. 5 "And he rested on the seventh day." This means that when his Son comes and ends the time of the lawless one and judges the impious and changes the sun and the moon and the stars, then he will truly rest on the seventh day.

6 Furthermore, it says, "You shall sanctify it with pure hands and a pure heart." Now if anyone at present is pure in heart and able to sanctify the day that the Lord sanctified, then we have been totally deceived. 7 See then that we will sanctify it, resting truly, at that time, when we will be able to, when we ourselves have been made righteous and received the promise, when there is no longer any lawlessness, but all things have been made new by the Lord. At that time we will be able to sanctify it, when we ourselves have been sanctified first.

8 Furthermore he says to them, "I cannot stand your new moons and Sabbaths."[23] You see how he speaks? The present Sabbaths are not acceptable to me, but the one that I have made is, on which I will give rest to all things and make the beginning of an eighth day, that is, the beginning of another world. 9 That is why we also celebrate the eighth day with gladness, on which also Jesus rose from the dead and, after manifesting himself, ascended to the heavens.

---

[19] Exodus 20:8; Deuteronomy 5:12; Psalm 24:4
[20] Jeremiah 17:24–26
[21] Genesis 2:2–3
[22] Psalm 90:4
[23] Isaiah 1:13

Appendix 14
Conflict with Rome

14.1 Nero Blames the Christians

Tacitus, *Annals* 15.44

In 64 CE a great fire broke out in Rome, which burned down much of the city. Suspicions arose that the emperor, Nero, had given orders to burn the city so that he could build a new capital named after himself. To avert these suspicions, Nero made scapegoats out of the unpopular Christians. The Roman historian Tacitus gave the following account in his *Annals* (c. 116 CE).

But neither human work nor lavish grants of the emperor nor the means used to appease the gods caused the scandal to abate or dispelled the belief that the fire had been ordered. Therefore to end the rumor, Nero substituted defendants and punished with the most unusual penalties a group of people hated for their shameful deeds, whom the common people called Christians. The author of that name, Christus, had been punished with the death penalty by the procurator Pontius Pilate in the reign of Tiberius. Repressed temporarily, the deadly superstition broke out again not only in Judea, the source of that evil, but also in the City [Rome], where all things atrocious or shameful flow together from everywhere and are celebrated.

So first those who confessed were seized, then on their information vast numbers were convicted, not so much on the charge of arson as for hatred of the human race. Mockeries were added to their deaths. Some were covered with the skins of wild animals, so that they would be torn to death by dogs. Others were fastened to crosses to be burned, so that where daylight failed they might be lit and used for light at night. Nero had offered his gardens for that spectacle. He also provided a public show in the Circus, where he mixed with the common people in the garb of a chariot-racer or stood in his chariot. Hence, though these people were guilty and deserved the most extreme punishments, pity for them arose, from the feeling that they were being destroyed not for the public good, but for the savagery of one man.

14.2 Pliny to Trajan

Pliny, *Letters* 10.96

About 111 CE, the emperor Trajan sent C. Plinius Caecilius Secundus, or Pliny the Younger, as his legate to the province of Bithynia to quell political disturbances and reorganize the finances of the cities. Pliny died a few years later, sometime before 115. His official correspondence with Trajan during those years gives valuable insight into the workings of Roman provincial administration. The following letter to Trajan and Trajan's reply show Roman policy toward Christians during Trajan's reign.

It is my custom, Lord, to refer to you all matters about which I am in doubt. For who is better able to guide my uncertainty or instruct my ignorance? I never took part in judicial inquiries concerning Christians. For that reason I do not know what is customarily punished or investigated nor to what extent. I have had no small uncertainty whether there should be some distinction of ages, or whether children, no matter how young, should be treated no differently than the more mature; whether pardon may be given to someone who repents, or whether someone who was ever a Christian should gain no benefit from having ceased; whether the name itself [Christian], even apart from any crimes, should be punished, or only crimes connected with the name.

Meanwhile, I have followed this procedure towards those who were reported to me as Christians. I asked them whether they were Christians. Those who confessed I asked a second and a third time, threatening capital punishment. Those who persisted I ordered to be led away [to be executed]. For I did not doubt, whatever it may be that they confess, that certainly stubbornness and inflexible obstinacy ought to be punished. There were others of similar insanity whom, because they were Roman citizens, I recorded to be sent to the City [Rome].

Soon, as usually happens, accusation spread as a result of the procedure itself, so that several cases cropped up. An anonymous document was submitted containing the names of many. Some denied that they were Christians or ever had been. At my dictation they appealed to the gods and with incense and wine supplicated your statue (which for this purpose I had ordered to be brought in along with images of the deities), and furthermore they cursed Christ – none of which, it is said, can those who are truly Christians be compelled to do. So I judged that those who did so were to be released. Others named by the informer said that they were once Christians and soon denied it; that yes, they had been but had ceased to be, some three years ago, some several years ago, and a few as much as twenty-five years ago. All not only worshipped your statue and the images of the gods, but also cursed Christ.

They asserted, however, that the sum of their guilt or error had been this: that they were accustomed to meet on a set day before daylight, to sing responsively a song to Christ as to a god, and to bind themselves with an oath, not for some crime, but that they would not commit thefts, robberies, or adulteries, nor break their promise, nor refuse to return a deposit when asked for it; that, after going through these things they had had a custom of separating and of reassembling to partake of food, but ordinary and harmless food; that they had ceased doing even this after my edict, by which, according to your orders, I had forbidden the existence of societies. Consequently, I deemed it even more necessary to use torture to find out what the truth was from two slave women who were called assistants. But I found nothing other than an immoderate, perverse superstition.

For that reason, with the inquiry adjourned, I went straight to consult you. For the matter seemed to me worthy of consultation, especially on account of the number of those being tried. For many of every age, of every class, and of both sexes are and will be summoned to trial. For the contagion of this superstition has pervaded not only the cities, but also the villages and farms, a thing which it seems possible to stop and correct. It is certainly apparent enough that people have begun to frequent the temples, which just a short time ago were deserted, and to return to sacred rites that had been discontinued for a long time, and here and there to bring sacrificial animals, which until now rarely found a buyer. From this it is easy to imagine what a throng of people can be corrected if there be a place for repentance.

14.3 Trajan to Pliny

Pliny, *Letters* 10.97

You have taken the action that you should have, my Secundus, in sifting the cases of those who were reported to you as Christians. For no general rule can be laid down that would have some sort of fixed form. They are not to be sought out. If they are reported and convicted, they are to be punished, but on the condition that anyone who has denied that he is a Christian and made it clear in the matter itself, that is, by supplicating our gods, should obtain pardon on account of his repentance, however suspect he may have been in the past. In fact, anonymous documents that are submitted ought to have no place in any accusation. For it sets a bad precedent and does not belong to our age.

14.4 Ignatius to the Romans

Ignatius, *Romans* 4–5

Ignatius, bishop of Antioch in Syria, was arrested during the reign of Trajan (c. 108 CE) and sent to Rome for execution as a Christian (see Chapter 35 and Appendix 11). The following selection from his letter to the church of Rome, written on his way there, illustrates Ignatius' attitude toward his approaching martyrdom.

4:1 I am writing to all the churches, and I command all, that I willingly die for God, if you do not prevent it. I urge you not to do me an "untimely favor." Let me be food for wild beasts, through whom it is possible to reach God. I am God's grain, and by the teeth of wild beasts I am ground up so that I may be made pure bread of Christ. 2 Instead, coax the beasts, so that they may become my tomb and leave none of the parts of my body, so that when I fall asleep I may not be a burden to anyone. Then I will truly be a disciple of Jesus Christ, when the world no longer sees even my body. Entreat Christ on my behalf that through these instruments I might be made a sacrifice to God. 3 I do not command you like Peter and Paul. They were apostles, I am a condemned man; they were free men, while I until now have been a slave. But if I suffer, I will become a freedman of Jesus Christ, and I will rise in him a free man. Now bound I am learning to desire nothing.

5:1 From Syria to Rome I fight with wild beasts, over land and sea, night and day, bound to ten leopards (that is, a squad of soldiers), who become worse even when shown kindness. Through their injustices I am made more of a disciple, "but not by this am I justified." 2 May I benefit from the wild beasts prepared for me, and I pray they will be quick with me. I will even coax them to eat me quickly and not be afraid to touch me, as they have been with some. Even if they should be unwilling and not want to, I will force them to it. 3 Make allowance for me. I know what is best for me. Now I begin to be a disciple. Let nothing visible or invisible deny me that I should reach Jesus Christ. I will endure fire and cross and struggles with beasts, being cut up or torn apart, having my bones wrenched apart, my limbs cut off, my whole body ground up, all cruel tortures of the Devil, if I may only reach Jesus Christ.

Index

1 Clement: author and date, 488–89; church leadership in, 489–90; historical setting, 487–88; relation to letter of Hebrews, 493; selections from, 602–5; summary, 488

1 Corinthians: historical setting, 335–37; reading guide, 338–43; social setting, 337–38

1 Enoch, 35, 67, 83, 465, 466, 467, 522, 523, 551–52

1 Esdras, 109

1 John: reading guide, 476–78; themes common to John and 1 John, 476–77, *see also* Johannine Epistles

1 Maccabees, 19, 35, 109

1 Peter: authorship of, 512–14; message of, 517–18; reading guide, 518–19; recipients and date, 515–16; social setting, 516–17

1 Thessalonians: historical context, 351–52; reading guide, 352–54

1 Timothy: reading guide, 454–56, *see also* Pastoral Epistles

2 Clement, 7, 110, 441, 603 n. 1

2 Corinthians: components of, 345–46; reading guide, 348–49; setting in Paul's life, 346–48

2 Esdras, 109

2 John: reading guide, 478–79, *see also* Johannine Epistles

2 Maccabees, 19, 35, 109

2 Peter: author of, 114, 461–62; opponents of the author, 463–65; reading guide, 466–68; wording shared with Jude, 462–63

2 Thessalonians: authorship of, 354–56; date and purpose of, 357; reading guide, 357–58

2 Timothy: reading guide, 457–59, *see also* Pastoral Epistles

3 Esdras, 109

3 John: reading guide, 479, *see also* Johannine Epistles

3 Maccabees, 109

4 Ezra, 35, 66, 67–68, 70, 299, 522, 552–54

4 Maccabees, 109

Aaron: Messiah of, 66; priesthood of, 495, 498–99, 500

Abraham: as ancestor of Jesus, 179, 190, 211; in early Christianity, 269, 316, 317, 328, 329, 403, 498, 499, 608; in Judaism, 15, 127, 210, 524

abstinence from marriage and meat, 19, 453–54

Acropolis, 274

Acts, as a literary genre, 6

Acts of James, 400

Acts of John, 8, 425

Acts of Paul, 8, 112, 450

Acts of Peter and the Twelve Apostles, 111

Acts of the Apostles: central theme, 267; and Galatians, discrepancies between, 310; as history, 276–80; major themes, 272–76; outline of, 280; reading guide, 281–87

Acts of Thomas, 8, 429

Adam, 179, 211, 328–29, 422, 524, 551

aeon, 421, 422, 423, 425, 438, 454

afterlife, conceptions of, 56–57

agape (love feast), 444, 601

age to come, 43, 53, 59, 62, 65, 67, 71, 96, 250, 255, 297–98, 396, 498, 524, 532

agrarian society, 27

Alexander the Great, 16, 17, 26, 28; as demigod, 82, 558

Ananias and Sapphira, 281–82

Ananias of Damascus, 278, 283

Andrew, apostle, 233, 582

anointed one, 63

Antichrist, 358, 521–22

antichrists, 471, 472, 476, 477–78, 479

anti-Gentile bias, Matthew, 185–86, 188

anti-Jewish sentiment, 12–13, 189, 433, 495–96, 504–5

Antinous, 84, 563–64

Antioch in Pisidia, 272, 273, 284, 308

Antioch of Syria, 484; home of first church to include Gentiles, 99, 269, 270, 283; as place of origin of Matthew's gospel, 179; view of modern, 271

Antiochus IV Epiphanes, 19, 358, 525

aphorism, 139, 258

Aphrodite, 76, 334

apocalypse: defined, 6, 65, 523; types of, 523

Apocalypse of Peter, 8, 112

apocalyptic literature: book of Daniel as, 65–66, 523; book of Revelation as, 522–23; defined, 65, 522–23; features of, 524–25; the Shepherd of Hermas as, 7, *see also* eschatology apocalyptic

apocrypha: defined, 8; New Testament Apocrypha, 7–8, 35; Old Testament Apocrypha, 35, 108

Apocryphon of James, 400

Apocryphon of John, 8, 111, 422, 454

Apollo, 76, 80, 82, 558, 559, 561, 562, 571, 572

Apollonius of Tyana, 89, 555, 570

Apollos, 335–36, 337, 338–39, 493

apologetic, 140, 141, 156, 276, 313

apologists, 106, 447, 510

aporias in the Fourth Gospel, 220, 234, 237

apostle: in the apocryphal writings, 8; defined, 293; as itinerant missionaries, 395, 409, 412–13,

587; Paul as, 293; preaching by, in Acts, 273; super-apostles at Corinth, 346, 348; the twelve as, 96; writings attributed to, 111, 114, 157, 449–50, *see also individual apostles*

Apostolic Fathers, 3, 6–8, 28, 110, 407, 444, 447, 487, 510

apostolic period, 102, 115, 450

apostolic succession, 442, 449, 490

apotheosis, 83–84, 161, 562–63

Archelaus, 23

Areopagus, 274

ascension: of deified humans, 84, 161; of Jesus, 70, 132, 159, 163–64, 168, 171, 174, 201, 215–16, 223, 277, 280; of the soul, 56, 422–23

asceticism, 377, 424

Asclepius, 89, 567–68

Asia Minor, provinces, 514

Asia, seven churches of, 525

Assumption of Moses, 465, 466, 467

astrology, 81, 311–12

Athanasius, bishop of Alexandria, 113, 114

atheism of early Christians, 76, 509, 527

atonement: by Jesus' death, 98–99, 101, 295, 424, 439, 473, 506; by John's baptism, 57; in Judaism, 35–36, 38, 41, 43, 439, 441, 499–500

Augustine, bishop of Hippo, 113, 147

Augustus Caesar, 20, 22, 503; as divine human, 82, 556, 558–60

autograph, 115, 118

avatar, 82

Babylon: exile of Jews to, 16, 28, 29; as name for Rome, 514, 516, 536–37

baptism: in early Christianity, 303, 329, 373, 395–96, 408, 443; of Jesus, 55, 71, 93, 158–60, 229; as practiced by John, 55

Bar Cochba, 26

Barnabas, associate of Paul, 99–100, 270, 283–86, 309, 310, 312, 315

Baruch, 35, 109, 524

BCE, 13

Beatitudes, 181, 191–92

Belial, 53, 349

Beloved Disciple, 218–19, 230, 233, 238

Betz, Hans Dieter, 313

Bible, Christian: chapters and verses of, 6; defined, 4; English translations of, 118–21

birth narrative: defined, 138; in the Gospel of Luke, 200–1, 202, 205–6, 210–11; in the Gospel of Matthew, 183, 190–91

bishop: in the Didache, 395, 409, 413–14; in Paul's churches, 301; in Proto-Orthodox Christianity, 442, 449, 451, 452, 453, 455, 456, 485, 490, 599, 601

Book of Thomas the Contender, 429

Borg, Marcus, 256–57, 261

Bultmann, Rudolf, 250–51, 255, 256, 261

Caesar, title, 20

Caesarea, 252

Caiaphas, Joseph, 259

canon: defined, 108; of the Hebrew Scriptures (Old Testament), 108; of the New Testament, 108–15

CE, 13

celibacy: in early Christianity, 340, 433, 534; among Essenes, 48–49, 53

Cephas, 96, 338

Cerinthus, 338, 392, 423, 424, 472

charismatic: in early Christianity, 89–90, 414; Jesus as, 256, 261

charitable giving: in Judaic Christianity, 192, 395, 409, 410, 589; in Judaism, 35–36

Christ: Christ of faith, 260–62; composite Christ, 158; in Gnostic Christianity, 423–24; as messianic title, 43, 63, 68–69, 183, 200–1, 223; in Proto-Orthodox Christianity, 440–41, *see also* anointed one; Messiah; son of David

Christianity, relation of to Judaism, 317, 329–30, 492–93, 503

church, 95; as body of Christ, 300, 303, 342–43, 373, 380, 384; in Matthew, 184, 188, 194

Cicero, 90

circumcision: as analogy for baptism, 373, 377; in Barnabas, 504–5, 607–8; controversy over, 100–1, 270–71, 284–85, 307–8, 310, 312; in Judaic Christianity, 390, 392, 395, 402, 457; in Judaism, 19, 34; Paul's perspective on, 299–300, 307–8, 317, 319, 367, 402–3; in Thomas, 595

classes, socio-economic: in the Greco-Roman world, 27–28; in early Christianity, 300, 331, 337, 340, 515–16

Claudius, edict of, 320–21, 335

Clement of Alexandria, 115, 526

Clement of Rome, 488–89, 490, 493

clergy, 104, 441

Codex Vaticanus, 118

Colossae: church in, 375

Colossians, 5, 297, 305, 360, 371; authorship of, 374–76, 382–83; compared to Ephesians, 378–79, 380–82; historical setting of, 375–76; myth and ritual in, 371–74; Onesimus and, 369; reading guide, 376–78

Community Relations Discourse, 180, 194

confessional approach, 9, 10–12, 136–37

Constantine, 93, 105, 106, 262, 420, 510

controversy dialogue, 59, 138, 144, 157, 165–66, 169, 184, 193

Corinth, 334–35, 336

Cornelius, 269, 270, 273, 283, 307

cosmic reconciliation, 376–77

cosmology, 80–81, 431

Council of Florence, 113

covenant: in the Epistle of Barnabas, 504, 607; in Judaism, 4, 34; new covenant, 4, 53, 59, 349, 492, 495–96, 500

creed, 104, 437, 455

criteria of authenticity, 251–54, 260

criteria of canonicity, 114–15

criticism, types of, 133–37

Crossan, John Dominic, 257, 261

crucifixion of Jesus, 3, 23, 94

curse story, 243, 281–82

Cynics, 88, 257, 258

Daniel, book of, 33, 35, 65–66, 70, 109, 356, 357–58, 523, 525

David: as ancestor of Jesus, 158, 183, 190, 200–1, 210, 211, 394, 586, 599; as king of Israel, 15, *see also* son of David

Day of Atonement, 36, 38, 41, 506

day of Yahweh (or the Lord): in 1 and 2 Thessalonians, 351, 353, 355, 357–58; in Acts, 206, 272; in early Christianity, 71–72; in the Hebrew prophets, 62–63, 64–65; in Revelation, 531–32

deacon: in the Didache, 409, 412, 413–14, 589; in Pauline Christianity, 301, 331; in Proto-Orthodox Christianity, 442, 449, 453, 455, 485, 490, 601, 605

Dead Sea Scrolls, 49–52, 219

Decapolis, 25

deification, *see* apotheosis

deified human, 83–84, 161, 201, 216, 563–64

demigod, 82–83, 84, 555; Jesus as, 177, 183, 200, 201, 223, 440–41

Demiurge, 85, 422, 438

demon, 81–82, 88, 89, 159–60, 169, 341

determinism, 87, 524

deuterocanonical works, 35, 108

Deutero-Mark hypothesis, 152

Devil, *see* Satan

diaspora: Christians in, 97, 401–2, 404, 516–17; of Judaism, 29, 97, 98, 99, 282, 326

diatribe, 88, 304

Didache: as a manual of church order, 7, 407; community concerns in, 411–14; date and provenance, 411; Judaic Christianity of, 393, 409–11; outline of, 409; selections from, 583–90; sources of, 407–9

Didymus Judas Thomas, 428–29, 591

dietary regulations: in Barnabas, 505, 608–9; in Judaic Christianity, 395, 396, 402, 410; in Judaism, 36, 270; Paul's perspective on, 299, 307–8

Dionysius Exiguus, 23

Dionysius, bishop of Alexandria, 526

Dionysius, bishop of Corinth, 487, 488

Dionysus, 79, 555, 572

Diotrephes, 474, 479

discipleship in Luke, 206–7

divine human, 82–84, 89, 132, 508, 527, 555–61

divorce, 161, 165, 184, 340, 341

docetism: in 1 John, 473; in Gnostic Christianity, 423; in the letters of Ignatius, 484

Dodd, C. H., 250

Domitian, 84, 509–10, 527, 534, 537

double tradition, 147, 149

early Catholic Christianity, 102, 103, 111, 437, *see also* Proto-Orthodox Christianity

Ebionites, 391, 392–93

Ecclesiasticus, 34, 35, 109

Edict of Milan, 106

Elder John, 156, 470

elder, Christian, 275, 395, 442, 449, 452, 456, 485

elemental spirits, 81, 311–12, 316, 372, 373, 377

Elijah the prophet, 62, 64–65, 89, 90, 127, 171, 172, 210, 212, 216, 262, 403, 532, 565

Elisha the prophet, 89, 127, 212

Elizabeth, mother of John the Baptist, 210–11

emperor cult, 84, 509, 527, 534, 613

emperors, Roman, 21, 106, 536–37

Encratites, 453–54, 455

Enoch, 67, 216, 466, 523, 524, 551

Epaphras, 368, 375, 379

Epaphroditus, 360–63, 364, 367, 368, 375

Ephesians, letter of Ignatius, 7, 110, 219, 369, 481

Ephesians, letter of Paul: compared to Colossians, 378–79, 380–82; historical setting of, 383; origin/authorship of, 378–82; reading guide, 383–84; recipients of, 382

Ephesus, 27, 104; as destination of Ephesians, 382; as destination of Romans, 322–23, 331; as home of John the apostle or elder, 218–19; Paul in, 277, 286, 302, 311, 335–36, 338, 346–47, 349, 368, 450, 455, 457, 459; as site for Paul's imprisonment, 363–64, 365, 368–69

Epicureans, 57, 87

Epiphanius, 419

Epistle of Barnabas, 7, 110, 113, 407, 444; author and date, 503; central themes of, 504–6; selections from, 606–10

Epistle of the Apostles, 112

Epistle to Diognetus, 7

Epistle to the Laodiceans, 113

epistles, 6

Eschatological Discourse, 72, 166, 173, 180, 186, 193, 195, 214, 222

eschatology: apocalyptic, 65, 523, 525–26; of early Christianity, 71–72, 297–98, 414; of Judaism, 42–43, 62–65; realized, 250; of Samaritans, 55

Essenes, 46, 47, 48–49, 57, 58, 59, 66, 546–49

Esther, additions to, 109

eternal life, 261, 270, 272, 539, 586; from following the Law, 160–61, 165, 183, 187, 393, 403, 441; in Johannine Christianity, 72, 220, 222, 230–31, 234, 471, 478, 527

ethical perfectionism, 184, 188

Eucharist: in the Didache, 396, 407, 409, 410, 411, 412, 586–87, 588; in Gnostic Christianity, 425; in Proto-Orthodox Christianity, 443–44, 600–1, 604–5

Eusebius, bishop of Caesarea, 102, 104, 112–13, 156, 177–78, 243, 390, 395, 448, 481, 487, 489, 533, 555–56

evangelist: as a preacher, 193; defined, 125; as editor of a gospel, 130–32, 134–35, 144–45, 147, 157–58, 249

evil spirit, *see* demon

example story, 139

exorcism, 82, 89, 90, 138, 141, 160, 169, 170, 171, 256, 278, 566–67, 570, 574; absent from the Fourth Gospel, 222

Ezra, the scribe, 35, 37, 67, 552, 553

faith-building, 140, 141

Farrer's hypothesis, 148–49

fasting: before baptism, 412, 443, 585; in Barnabas, 505; in Judaic Christianity, 187, 192, 395, 408, 409, 410–11, 412, 585–86; in Second-Temple Judaism, 36, 39–41, 165; in Thomas, 591–92, 594, 597

Fate, 47, 48, 49, 81

Felix, governor of Judea, 286

feminist criticism, 137, 257–58

festivals, Jewish, 32, 34, 39–41, 43, 97, 222, 228

Festus, Porcius, governor of Judea, 275, 286

first fruits, 41, 588, 603, 605

flesh: of Jesus, 71, 82, 224, 225, 232, 262, 372–73, 472, 473–74, 477–78, 479; as seat of evil power, 85, 298–99, 303–5, 317, 326, 328–29, 330, 372, 376, 377, 432, 467

foot-washing, 230, 232, 237

forgiveness of sins, 261, 373, 396, 500

form criticism, 134, 137–40, 157, 249, 250–51

Fortune, 81

freedom fighters, Jewish, 53–55

fulfillment of scriptures in Mark, 162–63

fulfillment quotations in Matthew, 180–82

Funk, Robert, 258–59

Gabriel the archangel, 242

Gaius of Corinth, 321, 337

Gaius of the Johannine community, 479

Galatia: churches of, 284, 308; Roman province, 309

Galatians, letter to: and Acts, discrepancies between, 310; central issue in, 307–8; date and provenance, 310–11; historical setting, 312–14; male/female in, 302; Paul's opponents in Galatia, 311–12; reading guide, 314–17; recipients of, 308–9; as rhetoric, 313

Galilee, 23–25

Gallio, 275, 296, 335, 336

Gamaliel, 279–80, 282, 295, 566

Gentile Christianity, 58, 99–100, 492–93

Gentiles: dispute over eating with, 188–89, 312, 315; within the Second Temple complex, 38; as sinners, 36

glory of Jesus, 227, 403; shared by believers, 297–98, 354, 373–74, 512, 518, 519

gnosis (knowledge), 103, 423, 454, 456

Gnostic Christianity: compared to Proto-Orthodoxy, 438–41; defined, 419; in conflict with Proto-Orthodoxy, 453–54, 463–68; literature of, 8–9, 111–12, 126, 420, 428–33, 591–98; religion of, 57, 421–26; rise of, 103; sources of our knowledge of, 419–20

God-fearers, 101, 270, 273, 283, 284, 337, 446

gods, Greek and Roman, 75–80

golden rule, 59, 181, 192, 456

gospel (message): defined, 125; of Paul, 313, 314, 315, 321, 323–24, 325–30

gospel (writing), 5, 109–10; apocryphal or non-canonical, 8, 241–45, 575–78; canonical, formation of, 128–33; canonical, genre of, 126–28; defined, 6, 125; Gnostic-Christian, 111–12, 420, 428–33, 591–98; harmonistic approach to, 158–61; individual approach to, 158–61; infancy gospel, 125, 126, 241–45, 575–78; Jewish-Christian gospels, 393; passion gospel, 125; types of, 125–26

Gospel of John: aporias and sources, 220; author of, 218–19; the community and its relations, 227–30; community beliefs and practices, 230–32; compared with the Synoptics, 220–22; outline of, 233; portrait of Jesus, 222–27, 248; reading guide, 233–38; setting and date, 219–20

Gospel of Judas, 126

Gospel of Luke: author, 199–200; community concerns in, 202–8; outline of, 208; portrait of Jesus, 200–1; reading guide, 208–16; sources and settings, 200

Gospel of Mark: audience and date of, 157–58; as Christian apologetic, 156; community concerns in, 165–67; origin of, 156–57; portrait of Jesus, 158–61; purpose of, 161–65; reading guide, 167–75; as a story, 168

Gospel of Mary, 126, 420, 425

Gospel of Matthew: author of, 177–78; communities of Matthew's sources, 187–89; community of Matthew, 189; date, audience, and place of origin, 178–79; portrait of Jesus, 177, 182–87; reading guide, 189–97; redaction in, 180–82; sources of, 179, 187–89

Gospel of Nicodemus, 245

Gospel of Peter, 8, 126, 243–45, 579–82

Gospel of Philip, 111, 126, 420, 425, 426

Gospel of the Ebionites, 126, 392, 393

Gospel of the Egyptians, 420

Gospel of the Hebrews, 113, 126, 393

Gospel of the Nazoreans, 393

Gospel of Thomas, 8, 9, 111, 126, 248, 259, 420, 425, 428; author and date, 428–29; and the canonical gospels, 429; central ideas of, 429–33; selections from, 591–98

Gospel of Truth, 126, 420

Greco-Roman world: cosmology, 80–81; culture and society, 26–29; Fortune, Fate, astrology, and magic, 81–82; humans as divine, 82–84, 89, 132, 508, 527, 555; languages, 28; miracle stories, 88–90, 565–74; philosophies, 84–88; political history, 16–26; religion, 75–80

Greece, churches in, 284

Greek New Testament, 117–18

Griesbach hypothesis, 147

Hades, 56, 78, 244, 245

Hadrian, 20, 26, 84, 503, 563–64

Hanina ben Dosa, 89, 565–66

Hanukkah, 19, 41

Harrison, P. N., 447

Hasmoneans, 19, 22, 48

Hebrew (language), 28

Hebrew Scriptures, 33–34, 109

Hebrews in Jerusalem, 97–98, 282, 389

Hebrews, letter of: author and date, 493; christological exegesis in, 499; genre of, 494–95; message of, 495–96; reading guide, 496–501; recipients of, 494; relation of Christianity to Judaism, 492–93

Hegesippus, 399, 401

Hellenistic kingdoms, 17–19, 20, 84

Hellenistic period, 16, 29, 80, 84, 567

Hellenists, 97–99, 282

Hellenization, 16, 17–19, 28

Hera, 76, 83, 557, 562

Heracles, 82, 83, 84, 555, 556–57, 562

Hermas, 488

Herod Agrippa I, 23, 96, 283

Herod Agrippa II, 23, 275, 286

Herod Antipas, 23, 25, 36, 57, 93, 214, 244, 579, 599

Herod the Great, 22–23, 25, 26, 27, 38, 39, 54, 242

Herodian dynasty, 22–23

Herodians, 23, 169

Herodias, 57

Hestia, 75

high priest: Jesus as, 495, 497, 498–500; in Judaism, 33, 38–39, 42, 51, 63, 66, 102, 164, 173, 214, 238, 256, 259, 410, 411, 490, 495–96, 588, 604, 605

Hillel, 59

Hippolytus, 419

historical-critical method (historical criticism), 9–13, 135, 137, 158, 522

historical-theological criticism, 135–36, 137

Holy Spirit, 136, 396, 443, 550, 578, 585, 594, 605; at the baptism of Jesus, 71, 127, 158–159, 169, 206; at the birth of Jesus, 183, 190, 242; in the Johannine community, 230, 231, 477; in Luke-Acts, 130, 134, 202, 205–6, 212, 215, 272–73, 278, 280, 281, 283; in Judaic Christianity, 396, 585; upon the Messiah, 63, 71, 169; in Pauline Christianity, 300, 303, 305, 317; as power for miracles, 90; in Thomas, 431, 594

Honi the Circle-Drawer, 89

house churches, 94, 99, 101, 300, 337–38, 509

household codes, 374–75, 378, 380, 384, 442–43, 451, 518

household of Caesar, 363

Ialtabaoth, 422

ideological criticism, 136–37

Ignatius, bishop of Antioch, 179, 219, 369, 390, 441, 442, 481–85

Ignatius, letters of, 7, 110, 470, 472, 481; historical setting and date, 481; letter to the Romans, 510–12, 614; letter to the Smymaeans, 599–601; primary concerns, 483–85

images, prohibition against in Judaism, 36

Immanuel, 183, 191

immortality of the soul, 48, 49, 56–57, 103, 343, 423

incarnation: of divine humans, 82; of Jesus, 82, 223, 262, 433, 441

Infancy Gospel of James, 8, 126, 241–42, 400

Infancy Gospel of Thomas, 8, 126, 241, 242–43, 429, 575–78

inspiration: of prophets or oracles, 80, 206, 231, 281, 471, 473–74; of scriptures, 11, 33, 114–15, 130, 178, 449

Irenaeus, bishop of Lyons, 218–19, 391–92, 394, 395, 419, 423, 424, 440, 442, 454, 472, 488, 527

Isis, 78, 89

Israel, ancient, 15–16

James I of England and VI of Scotland, 119, 120

James the brother of Jesus, 101, 102, 241–42, 248, 293, 312, 389, 390, 399, 461

James the son of Zebedee, 96, 172

James, letter of, 95, 97, 112, 113, 351, 393, 394, 395, 397, 401, 512; authorship of, 399–401; Judaic Christianity of, 399, 401–4; outline of, 405; parallels with Matthew, 400–1; social setting, 404

Jamnia, 43

Jerome, 113, 392

Jerusalem: as capital of Judea, 16, 25; heavenly, 523, 533, 536; at the time of Jesus, 95

Jerusalem Conference, 269, 270–71, 284–85, 296, 310, 312, 513

Jesus movement, 58–60, 269, 297, 299, 307, 513

Jesus of Nazareth, 3, 93, 243; apocryphal Jesus, 8, 241–45; as Christian Messiah, 68–71, 161–65; date of birth, 23; in Gnostic Christianity, 423–24, 433; historical Jesus, 247–62; in Judaic Christianity, 394, 403–4, 411; John's portrait of, 223–27; language of, 28; Luke's portrait of, 200–1; Mark's portrait of, 158–61; Matthew's portrait of, 182–87; in Pauline Christianity, 299; in Proto-Orthodox Christianity, 440–41

Jesus Seminar, 258–59

Jewish Christianity, 58–60, 94–99, 102, 389–415; as audience for the Gospel of Matthew, 179; in controversies with other Jews, 59, 165–66; in the church in Rome, 320, 326, 330–31, *see also* Judaic Christianity

Jewish wars against the Romans, 25, 26, 36, 55, 102

Jews: origin of term, 16, *see also* Rabbinic Judaism; Second-Temple Judaism

Johannine Christianity: as non-Judaic, 97, 98–99, *see also* 1 John; 2 John; 3 John; Gospel of John; Johannine Epistles

Johannine Epistles: author and date, 470–71; opponents of the author, 471–75, 476; purposes and strategies of the author, 475–76, *see also* 1 John; 2 John; 3 John

John Hyrcanus, 46, 55

John Mark, 156–67, 285, 312

John the Baptist, 23, 55–57, 93, 127, 137, 167–69, 184, 190, 191, 193, 203, 206, 211, 220, 221, 231, 233, 234, 248, 250, 254, 256, 272; disciples of, 46, 55–57, 210–11, 228, 229, 234, 253; as Elijah, 65, 210; in Luke's birth narrative, 206, 210–11; as the Messiah, 57, 229

John the son of Zebedee, 96–97, 101, 218–19, 470, 524, 526–27

John, author of Revelation, 526–27

Joseph of Arimathaea, 174, 579, 580

Joseph, husband of Mary, 183, 190, 191, 211, 241–42, 392, 424, 578

Joseph, Israelite patriarch, 127

Josephus (historian), 19, 25, 46–49, 53, 56, 57, 58, 102, 247–48, 399, 401, 546

Judaic Christianity, 94–99, 102, 389; history of, 389–92, 484; literature of, 392–93; as opposed by Paul, 307–8, 311–12, 364, 367, 390; religion of, 393–97

Judaism, *see* Rabbinic Judaism; Second-Temple Judaism

Judas Iscariot, 173, 196, 214, 278, 281, 423

Judas Maccebeus (the Hammerer), 19, 41

Judas the Galilean, 53

Judas, apostle, not Iscariot, 237

Jude (Judas), brother of Jesus, 428–29, 461, 591

Jude, letter of: author of, 461; opponents of, 463–65; reading guide, 465–66; use of non-canonical texts, 465; wording shared with 2 Peter, 462–63

Judea, 15–16, 23; division of Palestine, 25; political history of, 15–26

Judith, 108

Julius Caesar, 20, 334, 503

justification: in James, 399, 401, 402–3; in Paul, 299, 303, 313, 314–16, 319–20, 321, 327, 328, 330, 374

Justin, 390–91, 392, 394, 395, 440, 443, 526

kerygma, 261

King James Version, 119

kingdom of God, 66, 72, 125, 160, 161, 208, 250, 432

L, hypothetical source, 149, 152

languages of Palestine, 28

Law, Jewish: as given through angels, 316, 378, 496; controversy over, 98, 100–1, 307–8, 312–14, 389–92; in the Epistle of Barnabas, 504–5; in Johannine Christianity, 98–99, 230–31; in Judaic Christianity, 94–95, 183–84, 187, 391–92, 393–94, 402–3, 409–11; in Judaism, 33, 34–38; in Pauline Christianity, 298–300, 317, 319–20, 325–26; primary commandments, 59, 303, 397

Lazarus, a beggar, 205, 214

Lazarus, friend of Jesus, 227, 235–36

letter collections, 110, 296, 485

Letter of Jeremiah, 109

Letter of Peter to Philip, 514

literary criticism, 136

Logos, 87, 223–24, 233, 431, 471

Lord, as title, 33, 69, 201, 227

Lord's Day, 303, 411, 487, 581, 588

Lord's Supper, 33, 214, 221, 230, 232, 237, 303, 304, 337, 342

Lucian of Samosata, 90, 545, 572–74

Luke, associate of Paul, 200, 493

Luther, Martin, 113, 319–20, 399

M, hypothetical source, 149, 152, 179

Maccabean Revolt, 19, 26

Mack, Burton, 258

magic, 81–82, 89, 458, 573, 584

Mandaeans, 420

manuscript: of 2 Corinthians, 347; of apocryphal works, 126, 244, 426, 582; of Dead Sea Scrolls, 49–52; of Didache, 407; of Ephesians, 382; of

Epistle of Barnabas, 503; of Josephus, 247–48; of Nag Hammadi library, 111, 420, 421, 430; of New Testament, 115–18, 151, 174, 177, 226, 235; of Romans, 322–23, 325

maranatha, 72, 587

Marcion, 111, 454

Mars, 76, 81, 82, 563

Mars' Hill, 274

martyrdom, 104–6, 510–12; of Ignatius, 481–84, 485, 512, 614; of John the apostle, 219; of Peter and Paul, 104–5, 238, 296, 448; in Revelation, 531, 534; of Stephen, 282

Martyrdom of Polycarp, 7, 510

Mary Magdalene, 175, 238, 426, 581–82

Mary, mother of Jesus, 96, 126, 183, 190, 191, 205, 210–11, 230, 241–42, 392, 424

Masada, 25, 54

master, as title, 201

Matthew, apostle, 177–78

maxim, 139, 254

meal, communal: of early Christianity, 80, 275, 303, 312, 342, 396–97, 412–13, 443–44, 509, 588; of Essenes, 49, 53, 547, 548, *see also* agape (love feast); Eucharist; Lord's Supper

meat offered to non-Christian deity, 310, 326, 340, 341, 410, 585

Melchizedek, 495, 498–99

Messiah: among Samaritans, 55; in early Christianity, 57, 58, 68–72; John the Baptist as, 57, 229; in Judaic Christianity, 94, 394; in Judaism, 43, 53, 63, 64, 65–68, 71, 550–54; in the Synoptic Gospels, 158–65, 182–83, 200–1, *see also* anointed one; Christ; son of David

messianic secret, 162, 169–71, 174, 182–83

methods of interpretation, 133–37

Michael the archangel, 462, 465, 467, 540

millennium, 440, 505, 521, 538

minor agreements of Michael and Luke against Mark, 150–52

miracle story: in Acts, 278–79; in the ancient world, 88–90, 565–74; collections of, 128–29, 137–38; explanations of, 90; as faith-building, 141; as a form, 138; in John, 222; in Mark, 159–60, 167, 170; in Infancy Gospel of Thomas, 242–43

miracle workers, 89–90

Mishnah, 43

mission, early Christian: to Gentiles, 99–102, 166, 186, 194, 202–3, 228–29, 267–72, 277–78, 283–87, 307; to Jews, 97, 166, 193–94; mission instructions, 97, 140, 186, 192–93, 214; to Samaritans, 99, 203, 228–29, 270

Missionary Discourse, 180, 192–93

monarchic episcopate, 442, 449

monk, 23, 433, 593, 594, 596

monotheism, 33, 438, 508

moral exhortation, 140–41, 184, 404, 407, 409, 467, 479, 485, 488, 506; in Paul, 304, 305, 313, 353, 354, 364, 367, 378

Moses, 15, 33, 63–64, 89, 127, 172, 226, 458, 462, 498, 500; Christ's superiority to, 495, 498; Law of, 33, 34, 55, 98, 231, 270, 285, 307, 308, 315

Mount Gerizim, 55

Mount Olympus, 75

Mount Sinai, 33, 34, 41, 64, 243, 464, 493, 496, 504, 610

Mount Zion, 55, 534

Muratorian Canon, 112

mystery religions, 78, 304

myth, 76–77, 90, 261, 371–74, 420, 422, 454, 455, 457, 459, 466, 533, 561; alienation myth, 371, 372, 455; creation myth, 371, 372, 374, 455; eschatological myth, 371, 373–74; redeemer myth, 371, 372–73

Nag Hammadi Library, 3, 8–9, 111, 420, 421, 425, 428, 430, 450

narrative criticism, 136, 137, 168

narratives in the gospels, 137–38

Nathaniel, 233

Nazoreans, 58, 94–95, 99, 102, 267, 270, 275, 390, 392

Nero, 20, 25, 104–5, 494, 509, 533–34, 536–37, 611–12

New American Bible, 121

new commandment, 237, 471, 477

New English Bible, 121

New International Version, 121

New Revised Standard Version, 121

New Testament: canon of, 108–15; as Christian scripture, 4; contents of, 5; English translations of, 118–21; Greek text of, 115–18; as testament, 4; types of literature in, 6

non-Judaic Christianity, 97–102

oath, 58, 59, 181, 184, 400, 405, 547–48, 574, 606, 613

Old Testament: canons of, 109; as Christian scripture, 4, *see also* Hebrew Scriptures

Olympias, 558

Onesimus, 368, 369, 375, 379

oracle, 69, 80, 177, 558, 562

oral gospel, 127

oral law, 46–47, 48

oral tradition, 48, 110, 128, 130–33, 156–57

Origen, 461–62, 493, 560

Orthodox Christianity, 3, 35, 103, 108, 121, 437

ossuary, 259

overseer, 301, 395, 413–14, 442, 449, 589, 605, *see also* bishop

pagan, 87, 102, 104, 105, 115

Palestine, 3, 10, 15; divisions of in the time of Jesus, 23; languages of, 28; political history of, 15–26

pantheism, 86

Papias, bishop of Hierapolis, 156–57, 177–78, 470

Papyrus Egerton 2, 126

parable, 139

Parable Discourse, 170, 180, 194

Paraclete, 231

parenesis, 140–41, 305

parousia, 71–72, 182, 222, 223, 305, 351, 356, 403–4, 517, 529; delay of, 72, 187, 441, 488, 603

passion narrative, 125, 138, 141, 163, 173–74, 196–97, 214–15, 221, 234, 237–38

passion predictions, 163, 171, 174

Passover, 39, 41, 43

Pastoral Epistles, 103, 437, 442, 444, 446; authorship of, 114, 297, 447–50; social control in, 451–54

patriarchy, 29, 137, 205, 257–58, 375, 442, 518

patron/client system, 28, 209

Paul the apostle, 94, 100, 294, 301, 362, 489; in Acts, 270, 271–72, 273, 274, 277, 283–87; as author of Hebrews, 493; as author of the Pastoral Epistles, 114, 447–50; death of, 102, 104–5, 602; letters of, 5, 6, 110, 293–95, 296, 305, 307–84; life of, 295–96; place and date of imprisonment, 363–65; significance of, 293–95; religion of, 300–6; sources of his ideas, 304–5

Pauline Christianity: religion of, 297–305

Pella, 390, 533

Pentecost, 41, 273, 281

Perea, 23, 25, 57, 93

pericope, 134, 138, 145, 151–52

persecution of early Christians, 104, 166–67, 351, 356, 357, 494; as eschatological event, 72, 414, 521, 531, 532–34; by Jewish opponents, 98, 269, 278, 282, 283, 404; by the Roman Empire, 104–6, 509–10, 516–18, 519, 521–22, 525–26, 527–28, 611–12

Persian Empire, 16

Peter the apostle, 464, 489; in Acts, 269, 270, 272, 273, 275, 276, 278, 279, 281, 283; as apostle to Jews, 188; in conflict with Paul, 188–89, 312, 315; death of, 102, 104–5, 602; as inferior to Beloved Disciple, 230; Peter's confession, 170, 183, 235; Peter's denial, 167, 174; as pseudonym, 461–62, 513–14; as source of Mark's gospel, 157

Petrine Christianity, 188, 230

Pharisees, 36, 46–48, 53, 57, 59–60; in Acts, 254, 275, 285; in the Synoptic Gospels, 131, 138, 161, 165, 169, 170, 184, 185, 188, 189, 192, 193, 195, 204; in Thomas, 433, 594, 597

Philemon, letter to, 5, 297, 305, 360, 368–69, 374, 375

Philip II of Macedon, 16, 558

Philip, apostle, 233, 237

Philip, evangelist, 89–90, 98, 279, 282–83

Philip, son of Herod, 23

Philippi, 302, 314, 352

Philippians, letter of Paul: central themes of, 364; composition of, 360–61; historical setting of, 361–63; reading guide, 364–68

Philippians, letter of Polycarp, 7, 485, 516

Philo of Alexandria, 29, 48, 224, 496

Philosophies, Greco-Roman, 84–88

Phoebe, 301, 331, 337

phoenix, 603–4

piety: Jewish, 34–38, 139, 187–88, 192, 395, 410–11; Roman, 28–29, 448, 451–52, 455–56, 562

Pilate, Pontius, 23, 36, 94, 174, 214, 238, 244, 252, 256, 257, 275, 533, 579, 580, 581, 599, 611

pillars of church in Jerusalem, 96–97, 101, 188, 310, 312, 314, 602

Plato: being and becoming, 85, 421; body/soul dualism, 56, 85, 86, 329, 422, 440; as divine human, 82, 560–61; forms, 85, 496, 574; theory of the good lie, 450; world-soul, 85, 87, 431

Platonism, 84–86, 419, 438

pleroma, 372, 374, 376, 421, 422

Pliny, governor of Bithynia, 510, 515–16, 534, 612–14

Pliny, Roman geographer, 49, 603 n. 3

Polycarp, bishop of Smyrna, 219, 361, 481, 485, 516

polytheism, Greco-Roman, 75–80, 101, 516

Pompey, 20

possessions, attitude towards: among Cynics, 88; among Essenes, 48–49, 53, 58, 59, 546–47; in Luke-Acts, 49, 204–5, 206–7, 214, 275, 281–82; in the Sermon on the Mount, 192

post-apostolic Christianity, 102–4

Praetorian Guard, 363

praetorium, 363

prayer: in Greco-Roman religion, 76; in Judaic Christianity, 187, 192, 395, 396, 408, 409, 410–11, 412, 585–86, 589; in Judaism, 35–36, 39, 41, 43, 47, 49, 192, 390, 547, 566; the Lord's Prayer, 134, 141, 148, 192, 395, 408, 411, 412; in Luke-Acts, 130, 134, 207, 214, 275; in Paul's letters, 305, 331, 354, 358, 376, 379, 383; in Proto-Orthodox Christianity, 413, 443, 453, 455, 600

Prayer of Manasseh, 108

Preaching of Peter, 513–14

predestination, 47, 48, 53

preexistence: of Jesus, 158, 223, 229, 576; of the soul, 85, 103, 422, 431–32, 438, 549

priest, Jewish: overview of, 38–39; Zadokite, 48, 49, *see also* high priest, Jewish

Prisca and Aquila, 301–2, 321, 323, 335, 337, 457

Priscilla, 301, 493

Prison Epistles, 360–70, 371–85

pronouncement story, 137–38

prophet: defined, 80; early Christian, 7, 231, 281, 302, 303, 341, 343, 395, 410, 412, 473, 526, 527, 529, 587, 588; Jesus as eschatological prophet, 159, 255–56; Jesus as prophet, 201; as miracle worker, 89, 565; prophet like Moses, 55, 62, 63–64, 177, 180, 532

Prophets, the, 33, 55, 601

proselyte, 307

prostitute, 27, 258, 334, 336, 339

Protestant Christianity, 3, 319, 399, 521; canon of, 108, 114; English translations of the Bible, 119–21

Protevangelium of James, 241

proto-gospels, 128, 133

Proto-Mark hypothesis, 152, 157, 175, 179

Proto-Orthodox Christianity, 103–4, 437–38; conceptual dimension, 438–41; literature of, 444, 446–539, 599–610, 614; opposition to Gnostic Christianity, 419–20; opposition to Judaic Christians, 390–92, 483–85; ritual dimension, 443–44; social dimension, 441–43

proverb, 139, 212, 234, 339

Psalm 151, 108

Psalms of Solomon, 35, 67, 550–51

pseudepigrapha: early Christian, 111–12, 450; Jewish, 35, 51, 465, 523, 524

Pseudo-Clementine Recognitions, 57, 229, 393

pseudonymity, 241, 297, 399, 400, 401, 429, 514, 524, 527

Ptolemaic dynasty, 17, 19

Ptolemy, 80–81

purity and impurity in Judaism, 36, 53, 57, 65, 391; clean and unclean, 19, 36, 47, 49, 165, 315, 324, 326, 330–31, 551

Pythagoras, 89, 90, 571–72

Q, hypothetical source, 149–51, 152, 179, 187, 200, 208, 393

Qumran community, 49–53, 59–60, 66, 96–97, 182, 349, 396

rabbi: Jesus as, 93–94, 160, 184, 254, 255, 256; in Judaism, 28, 32, 43, 59, 279–80, 282, 295, 304, 565–66

Rabbinic Judaism, 32, 43, 492

rapture, 353

realized eschatology, 250

redaction criticism, 133, 134, 137, 179, 180–82, 183, 185, 187, 189, 194

Reimarus, Hermann Samuel, 254–55

reincarnation, 423, 432, 438, 440, 534, 536, 571

repentance: in Luke-Acts, 203–4, 215, 272, 273, 281; as preached by Jesus, 159, 170, 185, 254, 256; as preached by John the Baptist, 55–57, 93

resurrection: in early Christianity, 59, 103, 298, 343, 438, 440, 454, 603–4; in Judaism, 47–49, 56, 65; in Zoroastrianism, 56; of Jesus, 70–71, 94

resurrection narrative, 117, 126, 149, 174–75, 187, 196–97, 212, 215–16, 233, 238, 244, 581–82

Revelation, book of, 5, 6, 521–22; as apocalyptic literature, 522–26; author and date, 526–27; genre of, 526; outline of, 528; reading guide, 528–40; setting and purpose of, 527–28

revelatory discourse, 8, 420

Revised English Bible, 121

Revised Standard Version, 121

rhetorical criticism, 136, 137, 313

righteousness: in Judaic Christianity, 138, 139, 184, 191–92, 204, 393; in Judaism, 35–36, 57, 63, 67; in Paul, 298, 327

ritual: in Colossians, 371, 373; in Gnostic Christianity, 425; in Greco-Roman religion, 75, 76–80, 545; in Judaic Christianity, 395–96, 412, 585–87, 588; in Pauline Christianity, 302–3; in Proto-Orthodox Christianity, 443–44; in Second Temple Judaism, 34–36, 36–39

Roman Catholic Christianity, 3, 103, 242, 437, 443–44, 521; canon of, 35, 108, 114; English translations of the Bible, 119, 121

Roman Empire: beginning of, 20; culture and society of, 26–29

Romans, letter of Ignatius, 7, 483–84, 485, 614

Romans, letter of Paul, 319–20; central theme of, 325–26; date and provenance, 321; different versions of, 321–24; outline of, 325; purpose of, 324–25; reading guide, 326–31

Rome: as possible site of Paul's imprisonment, 363–64; Christianity in, 320–21, 487–88, 513–14; rise of, 20; scale model of ancient Rome, 320

Romulus, apotheosis of, 563

rule of faith, 108, 114

Sabbath: in early Christianity, 94, 165, 234, 377, 390, 395, 505, 576, 610; in Judaism, 34, 42, 47, 49, 59

sacred history, 127–28, 267

sacrifice: among Samaritans, 55; body as, 330, 374, 614; in Greco-Roman religion, 19, 76, 79, 106, 545, 555, 558, 560, 562, 564; Jesus as, 98–99, 101, 231, 238, 262, 299, 439, 441, 496, 499–500; in Judaic Christianity, 94, 188, 394, 410, 411, 588; in Judaism, 34, 36–38, 39, 41, 43, 55, 57, 604–5; polemic against, 606

Sadducees, 46, 48, 57, 59, 87, 185, 269, 275, 281, 546

salvation: in Johannine Christianity, 230–31; in Judaic Christianity, 402–3; in Luke-Acts, 201, 202–5, 212, 213–14, 267–68, 272, 275, 286; in Pauline Christianity, 299; in Proto-Orthodox Christianity, 439–41; for the soul, 56, 103, 423, 432, 438, 473

Samaria, 24, 25

Samaritans, 55, 63; mission to, 99, 203, 228–29, 270

Sanders, E. P., 250, 256, 319

Sanhedrin, 38–39, 46, 98, 102, 162, 163, 174, 269, 282, 286

Satan/the Devil: as cause of suffering and persecution, 127, 517, 519, 533–34; children of, 471, 476, 477; defeat of, 538–39, 540; as dragon, 524; Michael's dispute with, 462, 465, 466, 467; as ruler of demons, 159–60, 193; as ruler of world, 159–60, 193, 250, 255, 298, 455, 521–22, 533

Saul of Tarsus, 99–100, 270, 283–84, 295, *see also* Paul the apostle

savior, 201, 556, 567

sayings in the gospels: incorrectly attributed to Jesus, 131–33, 134; types of, 138–40

sayings, collection of, 109–10, 144; Gospel of Thomas as, 8, 126, 248, 420, 428, 429

scholastic dialogue, 138

Schüssler Fiorenza, Elisabeth, 257–58

Schweitzer, Albert, 249, 250, 255, 261

scribe: Christian, 115–41, 151, 248, 324, 382; in composition of letters, 400, 512; Jewish, 47; Roman, 27

scriptorium, 115, 117

scripture: New Testament as, 4

Sea of Galilee, 25, 249

Second-Temple Judaism: hopes for the future, 62–72; political history of, 15–26; religion of, 32–43; varieties of, 46–59

Secret Gospel of Mark, 126

Seleucid dynasty, 17, 19, 20

Senate, Roman, 20, 26–27, 84, 320, 559

Septuagint, 34, 69, 108, 182

Serapion, bishop of Antioch, 243–44

Sermon on the Mount, 148, 156, 180, 184, 185, 191–92, 212

Sermon on the Plain, 180–81, 212

shema, 32–33, 402

Sheol, 56

Shepherd of Hermas, 7, 110, 112, 444

Sibylline Oracles, 80, 533

Sicarii (dagger men), 55

signs source, in the Fourth Gospel, 220, 231, 238

Silas, 285, 351

Silvanus, 335, 512, 513

Similitudes of Enoch, 66, 67, 68, 70, 551–52

Simon bar Coseba, 26

Simon of Cyrene, 423

Simon Peter, 582, 592, 598, *see also* Peter

Simon the Sorcerer, 283

sin: as power in flesh, 328–29; as transgression of Jewish law, 36–38, 439

Sitz im Leben, 134

slavery: in early Christianity, 300, 368, 442–43, 451, 456, 457, 518, 519, 595–96, 613; Roman, 25, 28, 29, 84, 237, 316, 363, 366, 563–64, 570, 573

Smyrnaeans, letter of Ignatius, 7, 481, 599–601

social-scientific criticism, 135

socio-historical criticism, 133, 134–35, 137, 165, 187

Solomon, 15–16, 38, 566–67

son of David, 171, 177, 183, 190, 394, 550

son of god: referring to angels, 82; referring to Christians, 302, 303, 316, 396, 432, 433, 595; referring to divine humans, 82–84, 183, 201; referring to false Christ, 589; referring to Jesus, 68, 70–71, 159, 162, 163, 164, 167, 168, 174, 183, 200, 201, 220, 223, 226, 228, 231, 233, 394, 467, 475, 478, 496, 579, 581, 599; referring to Jews, 550; referring to king or Messiah, 70–71, 159, 201

son of man: in Daniel, 65–66, 67, 70, 163–64, 356, 551; referring to Jesus, 68, 70, 132, 162, 163–64, 171, 173, 174, 183, 186, 200, 201, 223, 232, 255, 282, 393, 394, 529, 530, 597; in Similitudes of Enoch, 67, 551–52

Sophia, 258, 422

Sosthenes, 338

soul: dissolution of, 57, 87; enslaved by body, 56, 85, 103, 329, 422–23, 432, 439–40, 549; journey of in Thomas, 431–32, *see also* ascension of the soul; immortality of the soul; preexistence of the soul

source criticism, 133–34, 137, 144–55, 157, 179, 200, 220

speaking in tongues, 279, 281, 303, 343

special material, 147, 152, 179, 183–84, 187–89, 200, 393–94

spiritual gifts, 303, 337, 342–43

star, as living being, 85, 343, 440, 463, 555, 559, 564

Stendahl, Krister, 319

Stephen, 98, 99, 269, 273, 275, 282, 283, 295, 389

Stigmata (film), 428

Stoicism, 85–87, 224, 274, 372, 431, 468

Strabo, 334

Suetonius, 247, 320–21, 558–61, 569

synagogue: expulsion of Christians from, 98, 132, 219–20, 227–28, 394, 470; in Judaic Christianity, 94, 97, 189, 394–95, 401, 404; in Judaism, 28, 37, 41–42, 98, 390; as site of Christian evangelism, 42, 101, 295, 320, 335, 351

syncretism, 76

Synoptic Gospels: defined, 133–34, 144, *see also* Gospel of Luke; Gospel of Mark; Gospel of Matthew

Synoptic Problem: alternatives to Markan priority, 152; defined, 144–45; features of, 145–47; problem with Markan priority, 150–52; theories of Markan priority, 148–49; theories of Matthean priority, 147–48

Tacitus, 104, 247, 509, 569, 611–12

Talmud, 43, 565–66

Targum, 28

tax collectors: attitudes towards, 47, 131, 165, 203–4, 214, 258

taxation, Roman, 27, 53

teacher: in early Christianity, 110, 131, 395, 409, 412–14, 588, 589; Jesus as, 158–61, 184, 214, 253, 256, 257, 592; viewed as false by Proto-Orthodoxy, 455, 456–57, 458, 462, 463–65, 467

Teacher of Righteousness, 51

Teaching of the Twelve Apostles, 7, 113

temple: first Jewish, 15, 38; in Greco-Roman religion, 76, 84; renovated by Herod, 22–23, 38; second Jewish, 16, 19, 25, 26, 32, 38–39, 40; temple tax, Jewish, 194

Temple Scroll, 52

testament, defined, 4

Tetragrammaton, 33

textual criticism, 117–18, 174–75, 235, 322–23, 381–82

Theissen, Gerd, 337

Theodosius I, 420

Theophilus, 199, 209, 281

Thessalonica, 286, 351

Theudas, 280

Thomas, apostle, 237, 238, 242, 428–29

Thucydides, 279

Tiberius, 20, 23, 252, 611

Timothy: associate of Paul, 286, 335, 351, 353, 363, 364, 367, 493, 501; in the Pastoral Epistles, 446, 448

Titus: associate of Paul, 348, 349, 446; in the Pastoral Epistles, 446

Titus, Pastoral Epistle, 5, 297; reading guide, 456–57

Titus, Roman emperor, 20, 25, 391, 533, 537

Tobit, 108

Torah, 32, 33, 34, 37, 39–41, 46–47, 48, 55, 317

tradition of the elders, 47, 48, 165

traditions about Jesus, 128, 130–33

Trajan, 106, 218–19, 481, 489, 510, 515, 516, 527, 534, 537, 612–14

transfiguration of Jesus, 171, 172, 221, 467

Travel Narrative of Luke, 203, 208, 213–14

tribes of Israel: in Judaic Christianity, 96, 97, 203, 401–2; in Judaism, 15, 68, 295, 550, 553

Trinity, 205, 226

triple tradition, 145, 149, 150–52

twelve, the, 96–97, 275

two paths/two ways document, 407, 506, 583–85

two-document hypothesis, 149

two-gospel hypothesis, 147

Tychicus, 375, 379, 381, 382, 383, 384, 457

Tyndale, William, 119

variant readings, 115–17

vaticinium ex eventu, 455–56, 458–59, 467, 524–25, 533, 534, 537

Vespasian, 20, 25, 89, 533, 537, 566, 569

Via Egnatia, 483

Vulgate, 113, 119, 121

weak and strong in Paul, 324, 326, 330–31, 340
Wisdom of Solomon, 35, 108
Wisdom, personified, 224, *see also* Sophia
women: in Gnostic Christianity, 425, 433, 598; in
    Greco-Roman society, 29, 452; in Luke-Acts,
    205; in Pauline Christianity, 301–2, 341, 343; in
    Proto-Orthodox Christianity, 442–43, 451, 453,
    455; in Second-Temple Judaism, 38, 546, 549,
    see also household codes
Word, Jesus as, 223–25, 233, 471, 476, *see also* Logos
world-soul, 85, 87, 431
Wright, N. T., 260–62

Writings, the, 33, 55
Wyclif, John, 119

Yahweh, 15, 33, 34, 36–38, 55
Yohanan ben Zakkai, 43

Zealots, 55
Zechariah, father of John the Baptist, 206, 210,
    211, 242
Zeno of Citium, 85–86
Zeus, 19, 76, 77, 82, 83, 556–57, 562
Zoroastrianism, 56, 65